I0814654

Savannah in the New South

Savannah in the New South

From the Civil War to the Twenty-First Century

Walter J. Fraser, Jr.

The University of South Carolina Press

Published by the University of South Carolina Press
Columbia, South Carolina 29208

www.sc.edu/uscpress

Manufactured in the United States of America

27 26 25 24 23 22 21 20 19 18
10 9 8 7 6 5 4 3 2 1

Library of Congress Cataloging-in-Publication Data
can be found at http://catalog.loc.gov/.

ISBN: 978-1-61117-836-4 (cloth)
ISBN: 978-1-61117-837-1 (ebook)

This book was printed on a recycled paper
with 30 percent post consumer waste content.

For Lynn

This book is dedicated to Lynn Wolfe, my beloved wife, who has read, reread and offered welcomed advice on this manuscript and others over the past thirty-five years, in days both sunny and sometimes rainy.

Contents

Preface

Monuments in cities reveal much about the people and their country's past—Trafalgar Square in London; the larger-than-life statues that honor the Russians who died in defense of Stalingrad; the Lincoln memorial in Washington, D.C. And so it is with Savannah.

A bronze statue of General James Edward Oglethorpe in the uniform of an eighteenth-century British Army officer crafted by the renowned sculptor Daniel Chester French stands in Chippewa Square. He faces south in the direction of his enemies, ready to defend the city against attack by the Spaniards in Florida and their Native American allies. Atop a tall monument in Madison Square, Sergeant William Jasper rushes forward heroically. He holds aloft a flag he carried during the American assault against the British at the Spring Hill Redoubt in 1779 until a rain of bullets cut him down. During the same assault, a bullet severed the femoral artery of Count Casmir Pulaski, who fell from his horse and died for lack of a tourniquet; a statue in Monterey Square honors his heroism. In Johnson Square stands a monument to General Nathaniel Greene, whose forces swept the British from Georgia and oversaw their evacuation from Savannah. In Wright Square a cenotaph rises in honor of William Washington Gordon, Georgia's first graduate of West Point, who founded the Central of Georgia Railway, which revived Savannah's moribund economy in the 1840s. The city's tallest monument stands in Forsyth Park, where a Confederate soldier in battle dress faces north, symbolically defending the city from invasion by another Union Army.

Each monument is that of a white, trained military man who represents order, duty, and preservation of the city; together they give the city a somewhat martial atmosphere. White men like them, a civic-commercial elite, for over 250 years controlled Savannah's government, economy, politics, urban development, and its predominant culture even though the city's population was sometimes nearly evenly divided between black and white.

Dramatic change in the city's political leadership came only in the mid-1990s when the African American population had grown to 57 percent. Savannah elected two black men as mayor, Floyd Adams and then Dr. Otis Johnson. Each served two four-year terms, the maximum allowed. They were followed

Monuments to these men, like those who came after them, represent a white, civic-commercial elite who dominated Savannah's politics, culture, and economy for 250 years. Center, Confederate War Memorial. Top left, monument to Count Casimir Pulaski, killed in the Siege of Savannah in the Revolutionary War. Top right, monument to General James Oglethorpe, founder of Savannah and Georgia, 1733. Bottom left, monument to Georgia Revolutionary War hero Sergeant William Jasper, killed in the Siege of Savannah. Bottom right, cenotaph in honor of W. W. Gordon, founder of the Central of Georgia Railroad. Photographs courtesy of Bob Paddison.

The African American Family Monument, located on the John P. Rousakis Riverfront Plaza. The last line of the inscribed tribute, written by poet Maya Angelou, reads, "Today, we are standing up together with faith and even some joy." Photograph courtesy of Bob Paddison.

by Edna Jackson, the first African American female to serve as mayor; she took office in 2012. The City Council members elected with them were about evenly balanced between black and white.

With such profound change in the city's governmental leadership came new and very different monuments. Dr. Abigail Jordan, a University of Georgia graduate, initiated a petition drive in 1991 to erect a memorial to the city's African American community, some of whom were her forebearers. After eleven years of often acrimonious debate over the location, images, and inscription, a monument went up on River Street, where nearby shackled Africans once were herded ashore from slave ships.

A seven-foot bronze statue by local sculptor Dorothy Spradley depicts a standing father, mother, and two children dressed in twenty-first-century clothes, their broken chains at their feet. The original inscription on the base of the statue, written by Maya Angelou, read: "We were stolen, sold and bought together from the African continent. We got on the slave ships together. We lay back to belly in the holds of the slave ships in each others excrement and urine together, sometimes died together, and our lifeless bodies thrown overboard together." But the City Council objected to the wording, which they feared might offend some of the vast numbers of tourists who strolled nearby. Ms. Angelou proposed an additional line: "Today, we are standing up together, with faith and even some joy."[1]

Part of the inscription on the Haitian Monument in Franklin Square reads, "Their sacrifice reminds us that men of African descent were also present on many other battlefields during the Revolution." Photograph courtesy of Bob Paddison.

Another, smaller statue soon went up in Franklin Square memorializing the five hundred to seven hundred Haitian free men of color who assisted in the defense of Savannah during the American Revolution. The inscription on one panel reads: "The largest unit of soldiers of African descent who fought in the American Revolution was the brave 'Les Chasseurs Volontaires de Saint Domingue' from Haiti. This regiment consisted of free men who volunteered for a campaign to capture Savannah from the British in 1779. Their sacrifice reminds us that men of African descent were also present on many other battlefields during the Revolution."

The narrative that follows focuses on the lives of both blacks and whites and their interactions with one another. It suggests that apartheid has come at a profound cost to the city of Savannah since the end of slavery and the Civil War. It is history from the bottom up and the top down, with the consequence being collision—a story of heroes, heroines, and villains and their lives, labor, culture, and politics from Reconstruction to the present. Boosters, writers, and tour guides have long romanticized Savannah. This book is in many ways another side of the story.

Acknowledgments

This book and my life have moved through many cycles over the last few years, and I have learned again, as Thomas Jefferson said, that "writing is no harder than digging a ditch." But the process has been made easier and more meaningful because of the support of many, and though I risk overlooking some who should be mentioned, I would like to thank especially the following.

For photography used in the book, I am indebted to: Bob Paddison for photographing many Savannah monuments; Richard Burke for his photograph of a container vessel moving up the Savannah River to the port; Peter Bergeron and the staff of Worldwide Camera for their technical expertise and helpful suggestions on the use of digital images; and Steve Engerrand, deputy director of the Georgia Archives, who assisted me with photographs from the Vanishing Georgia collection. The Savannah Housing Authority's executive director, Earline Wesley Davis, graciously helped me locate and secure photographs that document urban renewal in Yamacraw, and Tammy Brawner, management analyst, helped in many stages of this process.

Even in today's digital age, I enjoy nothing more than being in a library, and I would like to thank all the librarians, archivists, and staff who made these forays so helpful, including the University of North Carolina, Chapel Hill, staff of the Wilson Library Special Collections for assistance with the resources of the Southern Historical Collection; Perkins Library, Duke University, staff of the Duke University Rare Book, Manuscript, and Special Collections Library; University of Georgia Special Collection Libraries staff of the Hargrett Rare Book and Manuscript Library and the Richard B. Russell Library for Political Research and Studies. I am very appreciative of the more than thirty years of assistance by the staff of the Zach S. Henderson Library at Georgia Southern University.

Closer to home I would also thank the staff of Armstrong State University: Lane Library especially; Judith S. Garrison, head of reference and instruction; Christian (Alec) Jarboc, peer reference assistant; Lauren McMillan, reference and instruction librarian; Melissa Jackson, interlibrary loan administrator; Aimee Reist, Learning Commons coordinator/librarian; and Caroline

Hopkinson, reference librarian for archives and special collections. I would also thank Ms. Barbara Mitchell and staff of the Asa H. Gordon Library at Savannah State University and Sharen Lee, Barry Stokes, Mark Darby, Mike Hill, Amanda Williams, Anne Butler, Nancy Tamarck, and Clemmie Little, who have assisted me in my research in the Kaye Kole Genealogy and Local History Room at the Bull Street Library, Savannah.

Luciana M. Spracher, director of the City of Savannah's Research Library & Municipal Archives, and Lacy Brooks, project archivist there, were both gracious with their time and helped me negotiate their many resources, including their images of the city of Savannah and especially the photographs and documents from the recently acquired W. W. Law Collection. Archivist Kelly Zacovic helped track down some especially elusive sources.

The staff of the Georgia Historical Society also aided me in locating many documents from their collection. I especially thank Katharine Rapkin, archivist, and Sauda Ganious, reference assistant, who with skill and patience helped me search out several elusive references. Also helpful was Ms. Lou Barnes, now retired from the *Savannah Morning News.*

My understanding of Savannah has been enhanced by the opportunity to interview, over the last thirty years, many who have shaped this city's history. Their names are listed in the bibliography. I would like to thank especially two who graciously agreed to more recent interviews, Mayor Edna Jackson, and former mayor Otis Johnson.

I would acknowledge the work of the Reverend Dr. Charles L. Hoskins, whose writing and chronology of African Americans in Savannah made important contributions to this book. I thank too Dr. Lisa Denmark, Georgia Southern University, whose comments and writing on the economic life of Savannah were especially helpful. Dr. Charles J. Elmore has written extensively about the intellectual, cultural, and social life of African Americans in Savannah. His views have enlightened not only this work but many others, as have the publications of Dr. Martha Keber, whose recent books describing community life on the east and west sides of Savannah served as invaluable resources. Dr. Paul Pressley has graciously given advice and encouragement.

I would also acknowledge the contributions of three colleagues who died as this book was being written: Marvin L. Goss, head of Special Collections, Zach S. Henderson Library; R. Frank Saunders Jr., professor emeritus, Department of History; and Mrs. Esther R. Mallard, research assistant, Department of History, all of Georgia Southern University.

Appreciation is extended also to the staff of the University of South Carolina Press, especially former director Jonathan Haupt for his interest in moving the project along from manuscript to book, and thank you also to the copy editor for her careful editing of the manuscript. Also at the Press, Managing Editor Bill Adams, Marketing Director Suzanne Axland, and Acting Director Linda Fogle have provided support and wise counsel.

Finally I would like to thank my wife, Lynn, for shepherding me and this manuscript over many bumps in the road. The book is better because of her, as am I. Where the book falls short, or where it contains errors of fact or judgment, these are mine and mine alone.

Introduction

In February 1733, after a long ocean voyage, English colonists struggled up forty-foot Yamacraw Bluff, located on the swift-flowing Savannah River, already a major commercial artery which snaked twenty-four miles to the open sea. The river's name became that of the first settlement in Georgia, the last of the original thirteen English colonies.

General James Edward Oglethorpe, an English soldier of fortune for King George II, led the expedition on behalf of the Trustees of Georgia. Unlike other English colonies, black slavery was banned from Georgia at its founding. Oglethorpe and the trustees opposed slavery for both pragmatic and principled reasons. They hoped to redeem poor English immigrants and build a colony of white yeoman farmers who would not have to compete with slaves, become idlers because of them, or worry about the threat of black "insurrections."

Even though Oglethorpe condemned enslavement as an "abominable and destructive custom," he did not hesitate to ask the officials in nearby Charles Town for hundreds of black slaves under white guards to fell trees, build fortifications, and lay out Savannah's streets and a grid-like pattern of squares; the Carolinians quickly responded to Oglethorpe. They had long wanted a settlement to serve as a military buffer to the Spanish in Florida as a means to protect their booming colony grown rich in the export of rice cultivated by black slaves.

Over time the Georgians repeatedly complained to the trustees and the London government that without slave labor they would never enjoy prosperity like that of their South Carolina neighbors. English officials came to embrace their view and on January 1, 1751, almost eight years after Oglethorpe departed the colony, the London government legalized slavery in Georgia.[1]

The population of Savannah was becoming diverse in its ethnicity, culture, language, and religion—the English Anglicans and the Native Americans soon were joined by Jews, Austrians, and Irish Catholics. The importation of black slaves added still more diversity. With slavery legalized in Georgia, rice planters from Carolina bought lands along the Georgia coast; settled them with their slaves; and planted, harvested, and exported rice through Savannah. A few hundred slaves arrived from the Caribbean in the 1750s.

Slave traders, sea captains, merchants, and plantation owners profited. By the mid-1750s, the population of Georgia, mainly in Savannah and south along the coast and on the sea islands, numbered 4,500 whites and nearly 2,000 slaves. With the growing numbers of blacks in the colony, the Georgia Assembly in 1755 enacted a slave code modeled on South Carolina's. Its stated purpose was to keep slaves "in due Subjection and Obedience."

Slaves who ran away from their owners and were recaptured could be whipped, and those resisting capture, "lawfully killed." Teaching slaves to read or write was forbidden; they were prohibited from blowing horns or beating drums as it might signal an insurrection; participation in an uprising, murder, destruction of exports, or striking a white person were crimes punishable by hanging or being burned to death.[2]

To confront the problem of runaways, the legislature passed a law in 1763 providing that a workhouse be constructed in Savannah for "the confinement of Negroes, and Punishment of such as are obstinate and disorderly." Captured runaways were held until claimed by the owner; if unclaimed after eighteen months, the warden sold the slaves and used the money to maintain the facility. While incarcerated, the slaves might be kept in shackles and administered a "moderate whipping." Upon request by an owner to the warden, incorrigible slaves were put to "hard labour."[3]

During the 1760s nearly 5,000 slaves arrived in Georgia from the West Indies and Africa, and fears of the white elite grew over the dramatic increase in the black population. Subsequently the legislature revised the slave code twice more, adding new and harsher measures such as those to prevent "the detestable Crime of Poisoning"; any black who committed or was privy to such an act or withheld information from authorities could be executed. Sexual anxieties of whites precipitated new codes that added the penalty of death for a slave who raped or attempted to assault a white woman sexually. Fearful of "insurrections," the legislature also enacted a law requiring white men to carry weapons into their church pews during services; the legislature also created a town watch, much like a police force, to closely observe the activities of the city's slaves.[4]

Savannah's ruling white elite also worried that the two dozen or more of the free mixed-race men, women, and children in the city—offspring of masters and their female slaves—might incite disorder. Indeed, it was no surprise that free persons of color who visited Savannah sometimes found their freedom threatened. One of these was Olaudah Equiano, a bright, literate free person of color of African descent.

After arriving in Savannah as a crewman on a vessel from the West Indies, Equiano was accosted by a local slave; they came to blows and Equiano "beat him soundly." The slave was the property of James Read, a prosperous Savannahian who ordered that Equiano be brought ashore "to be flogged all around the town for beating his slave." Equiano refused to leave his vessel "without judge or jury," went into hiding, and with the help of others escaped corporal punishment. On another occasion near Savannah, two white men seized Equiano, intent on "kidnapping" him and likely selling him as a runaway slave. Somehow Equiano managed to talk his way out of this predicament, but it and other experiences left him feeling the vulnerability of free persons of color in Savannah. As he wrote in his 1789 autobiography, "there was little or no law for a free negro."[5]

About 6,500 blacks arrived directly from Africa between the mid-1760s and the mid-1770s and were dispersed along the coast. Savannah's population swelled to over 4,000 whites and blacks. Slave dealers like the firm of Cowper and Telfair turned handsome profits, as did slave traders who sold the black cargoes either from the decks of ships or confined them in local "slave pens" until auctioned off. Slave owners in the city made money by "hiring out" skilled craftsmen, and white artisans came to resent the competition. Masters also permitted male and female slaves to hawk goods in the city market, a place where they traded gossip and news of pending events. By 1775, some 60 planters in the colony, 1 percent of the white population, owned half of the 18,000 slaves in Georgia. Savannah's economy was booming.[6]

Meanwhile, the English Parliament raised taxes and imposed more control over their American colonies. Savannah's elite, grown rich from the import of slaves and the export of rice, joined the other colonies in their revolution to declare independence from Great Britain.

Fear of invasion and the British promise of freedom to slaves led Savannah's government to dragoon black men and women to construct earthen fortifications around the city. In late 1778, a British invading force, guided by a local slave, Quash, struck the right flank of the unsuspecting Americans, routing them. With the exception of slaves who took refuge with the British and the Loyalists, much of the population fled. Planters in the countryside sustained heavy losses in crops, real estate, and slaves who rushed into British lines.[7]

Some runaways established a fortified community just north of Savannah and continued their fight for freedom. With war's end, angry white militias from Georgia and South Carolina raided the camp and seized Lewis, one of its leaders. He was tried quickly, hanged, decapitated and his head stuck on a pole planted on an island in the Savannah River. His skull was visible for some time, an example to other slaves who might be contemplating similar capital crimes. Savannahians and Charlestonians used this tactic on occasion for those committing the most egregious offenses.[8]

Because they lost thousands of slaves who died or escaped to the British during the American Revolution, Georgians led the way in reopening the slave trade after the War for Independence. From 1782 to 1820, at least 22,000 Africans, sometimes tightly packed and shackled in the fetid holds of sailing ships, arrived at Savannah's wharves after an average voyage of sixty-six days. In the 1790s, some 12,000 arrived. The export trade in rice and now large quantities of baled upland cotton revived rapidly. As in the past, Savannahians viewed the rapidly growing slave population with unease. The occasional rumors of white residents or visitors encouraging black servile insurrection sent armed men into the streets, searching for conspirators.[9]

With statehood declared, the capital of Georgia moved from Savannah—though never officially designated as the capital, it served as the seat of government—and the city established a mayor-and-council form of government to manage local affairs. The population approached 5,000 in the early 1800s, almost evenly divided between black and white. Savannah was now the twenty-first largest city in the United States. But with the outbreak of the War of 1812, the economy again collapsed and city growth stalled.[10]

Following the end of the conflict, river traffic revived once more until about 1820, when an economic panic and depression swept the country and a yellow-fever epidemic devastated Savannah, killing many more whites than blacks, who carried a genetic resistance to the disease. The city's economy again slipped into the doldrums and did not revive until William Washington Gordon, other entrepreneurs, and the city—which backed the project with a bond issue—united to create the Central of Georgia Railway (CGR).[11]

Together, slaves and Irish laborers sweated or nearly froze laying rails into the upper part of the state and building the railyards and offices in the city. By the 1840s the line dominated rail traffic in the Southeast, and engines pulled railcars loaded with cotton and lumber to Savannah's docks, where slaves and Irish migrants loaded the commodities onto oceangoing vessels. The CGR and burgeoning steamship lines created new jobs, and the new immigrants created a building boom. From 1840 to 1860, Savannah's population doubled to more than 22,000, making it the sixth largest city in the South.[12]

The population explosion exerted great pressure on Savannah's infrastructure, and the city financed a massive public-works program and created a professional police force to keep close watch on sailors, poor whites, and blacks.

To pay for civic improvements, the city raised taxes and issued more bonds. By the end of the 1850s, its bonded indebtedness was approximately the same as the city's annual budget.[13]

The surging economy concentrated more wealth into the hands of a few. Prominent Catholics and Jews embraced slavery and white supremacy and were welcomed into the civic and social clubs of the elite. By the late 1850s, the well-to-do, about 6 percent of the white population, owned 90 percent of Savannah's real estate; slaveholding was equally concentrated with 20 percent of the slaveholders owning 58 percent of the slaves in the city. New streets and squares were opened south of the city, where the civic-commercial elite erected costly mansions. By 1860, Forsyth Park marked the southern edge of the city. Here private militias organized for socializing, martial show, and intimidation with practiced military maneuvers designed to keep in line those who might threaten the status quo. Worshipers attended a new Catholic cathedral, two Jewish synagogues, and numerous Protestant churches. African Americans worshiped in four churches, which provided a homogeneous and supportive community, a temporary respite from control by their white masters.[14]

The poor crowded into the slums on the western and eastern edges of the city—Yamacraw and Old Fort—where in Savannah's subtropical climate diseases like cholera and typhoid fever flourished. Here in the mid-1850s mosquitoes bred and again carried yellow fever across the city. Hundreds of whites perished.[15]

In these slums occasional violence flared. But city life also offered opportunities for the development of close interracial relationships impossible in the countryside. Free people of color, non-slaveholding whites, and black slaves "hired out" by their owners lived close by each other; they worked cheek by jowl in the railyards of the CGR, the rice and lumber mills, and they drank to excess in local liquor shops where white proprietors sometimes acted as fences for stolen goods. Incarcerated together in the decaying local jail, poor whites and blacks served their time crammed into small cells. Such relationships may, in some cases, have softened the rough edges of racism.[16]

Poor blacks and whites frequented brothels where both black and white women offered their services. In the 1850s, Savannah bordellos outnumbered churches. The civic-commercial elite repeatedly and unsuccessfully tried to keep prostitutes off the streets and to shut down the "lewd houses." Nonslaveholding white men sometimes lived with black females, and some slave owners kept free or slave women and fathered offspring with them. The lowcountry's growing mixed-race population reflected this. Color mattered to the city's African Americans, and those of a lighter color usually married people like themselves. Several, like Anthony Odingsells, became remarkably successful. Odingsells owned more than a dozen slaves, along with property, livestock, and Little Wassaw Island.[17]

The white well-to-do remained suspicious, even fearful, of all forms of intimate interracial relationships except their own. To the civic-commercial elite, black-white fraternization violated social mores and decorum and fed fantasies that interracial relations might breed plots of arson or insurrection. The elite tried unsuccessfully to curtail such relationships with curfews, an intimidating police force, and volunteer militias.[18]

John Brown's raid on the federal arsenal in Virginia in 1859 to seize weapons and arm slaves rekindled long-held anxieties. Rumors swept Savannah of other slave plots, and the City Council enacted a law forbidding blacks to gather in crowds at public events. When some disregarded the law, police apprehended and flogged them. City leaders encouraged vigilantes, who roamed the streets harassing and occasionally seizing and bludgeoning people of color and poor or visiting whites on trumped-up charges of fomenting a slave rebellion.[19]

In the North, abolitionists intensified their calls for ending black servitude while Savannah's press condemned this "lawless crusade against slavery." Enthusiasm for disunion spread after Lincoln's election. With few exceptions, well-to-do slave owners supported secession from the Union. In early 1861 Georgia seceded and joined the Confederate States of America (CSA). The Georgian and now vice-president of the CSA, Alexander Stephens, spoke in the city. He denounced the Washington government's support of racial equality and then told Savannahians: "Our new government is founded upon exactly the opposite idea; . . . its cornerstone rests upon the great truth, that the negro is not equal to the white man; that slavery—subordination to the superior race—is his natural and normal condition."[20]

Heated rhetoric stirred white hostility toward blacks and fear among African Americans. Some seized the chaos of a war between white men as an opportunity to escape to freedom. As they fled to runaway camps in the swamps, they were often pursued by armed whites with "Negro dogs." The whites were determined to hunt down and return and punish or even kill those who dared to flee their masters.[21]

Enthusiasm for the war united Savannah's white population. Young militia members rushed to join up to preserve slavery and white supremacy. Men of the privileged class raised their own companies, and women crafted personal items and flags for the soldiers. Masters sent their black slaves to dig fortifications around the city.[22]

In November, Union troops seized Hilton Head Island; another thousand soldiers landed on Tybee Island and deployed heavy weapons. Panic swept Savannah. The wealthy sent their silver, women, children, and slaves into the interior of the state. The close proximity of Union soldiers encouraged more rebelliousness and flight among slaves. Black river pilots, free and slave, who knew how to navigate the maze of local rivers, helped dozens of slaves escape into Union lines, where they enlisted as soldiers and took up arms against their masters.[23]

In April 1862, Fort Pulaski fell, and now Union forces controlled the entrance to the Savannah River. More well-to-do citizens and war-related industries quickly moved inland, and a great hush fell over the city. Soldiers guarding the city went hungry and sickened and died of various diseases without medical attention. Morale declined and desertions soared. By mid-1863, corpses from the latest wave of disease lay unburied, debris cluttered the streets, and without gas for the streetlights, darkness shrouded Savannah.[24]

After the fall of Atlanta, Union General William Tecumseh Sherman and his more than sixty thousand battle-hardened soldiers headed south. Sherman believed he could shorten the war and bring about the capitulation of the Confederacy sooner by continuing to take the war to civilians and soldiers. During a three-hundred-mile march to the sea, Sherman faced little resistance and with impunity tore up the rails and rolling stock of the CGR.[25]

Confederate General William J. "Old Reliable" Hardee's nine thousand inadequately armed battle-weary troops guarded the approaches to Savannah. On December 12, 1864, Sherman's Army opened a heavy bombardment on Hardee's defenses and the day following overran a fort guarding the city's southeastern side. Facing encirclement and overwhelming odds, Hardee and his men escaped after dark on December 20 into South Carolina, across pontoon bridges built by slaves. To one Confederate soldier, the retreat resembled "an immense funeral procession stealing out of the city." General Hardee remembered it as his greatest military achievement.[26]

CHAPTER ONE

Reconstruction, Ruins, and Revival

1864–1872

A drenching rain fell as hacks carrying Mayor Richard Arnold and members of his City Council moved carefully through the darkness toward the lines of Union General William Tecumseh Sherman's sixty thousand battle-hardened soldiers encamped just beyond Savannah.[1] "Sherman's troops were so vast in number, and so filthy, that villagers in their path could allegedly smell them from miles away."[2] Arnold and the council agreed that the city must be surrendered to save it. Arnold, a Savannah-born graduate of Princeton and the University of Pennsylvania Medical School, hoped to get the best terms possible.

After briefly losing their way, the city officers encountered Yankee pickets around 4:00 A.M. and followed them to meet the divisional commander, General John W. Geary. At six-feet-five and fully bearded, Geary presented a dominating figure; he had served as territorial governor of Kansas and the first mayor of San Francisco. After Geary guaranteed Mayor Arnold that he would safeguard all citizens and private property and that anyone violating his orders would be shot, Arnold surrendered the city. When the war-weary troops heard the news, they broke into cheers. In the early morning of December 21, city leaders led Union soldiers into Savannah, where the Union flag was hoisted over the Exchange Building and the Customs House. Mayor Arnold and other white Savannahians looked on, no doubt with feelings of anger, loss, and resignation. Black onlookers were more sanguine, shouting, "Glory be to God, we are free!"[3]

Thousands of blue-clad soldiers remained on the outskirts of Savannah while thousands more overran its squares and erected tents, privies, and jerry-built wooden structures. Twenty-four-year-old Fanny Cohen, a Confederate sympathizer, was angered to see "what these wretches had done in the way of making themselves comfortable." The daughter of Octavus Cohen, a well-to-do merchant and cotton exporter, lived with her family in a fine home on Lafayette Square. On December 29, Fanny again complained that, during the unusually cold weather, "we have very little wood, the Yankees having robbed us of a great deal of it." The soldiers also seized foodstuffs from businesses in the city and ran roughshod over households while foraging in nearby Liberty County.[4]

"Uncle Billy's" Visit

Thousands of black men, women, and children trailing the army followed the soldiers into the city. One reporter described the African Americans as "weary, famished, sick, and almost naked." When civilian "mobs" began looting, Union soldiers quickly restored order in the streets. General Sherman arrived the day after the occupation force entered the city and wrote: "You would think it Sunday so quiet is everything . . . day and night." He telegraphed a message to President Lincoln: "I beg to present you as a Christmas gift the city of Savannah, with 150 heavy guns and plenty of ammunition, and also about 25,000 bales of cotton."[5]

General Sherman issued orders calling for accommodation with the citizens and respect for their prejudices. He also permitted Mayor Arnold and his council to continue their role as the governing body of the city; as such they were expected to cooperate with the occupying force to ensure the operation of the city's infrastructure and services.[6]

The army handed out rations to the destitute. Several weeks later, foodstuffs worth seventy thousand dollars shipped by charitable organizations in Boston and New York arrived at the wharves and were distributed at the city market. A *New York Times* reporter described the poor queuing up for the food as a "motley crowd [of] . . . both sexes, all ages, sizes, complexions, costumes, gray haired old men . . . well-dressed women wearing crepe for their husbands and sons . . . demi-white women wearing negro cloth, negro women dressed in gunny cloth; men with Confederate uniforms."[7] The writer summed up the scene: "Charity, like a kind angel, has suddenly stepped in to ward off the wolf which is howling at the door."[8] Still engaged in combat in the field, Confederate General Lafayette McLaws wrote his wife, who was living beyond the city as a refugee: "When I think of . . . your being in want and dependent on the kindness and even charity of the Yankee officials, I feel grateful that you are away."[9] At the request of the military authorities, the City Council confiscated rice stored in the city and traded it for food and fuel for the poor.[10]

Visitors found Savannah in a "most dilapidated and miserable condition," the effects of war "everywhere," the doors of homes and businesses shut tight, "sidewalks and wharves . . . going to ruin, and Sherman's dead horses . . . laying about the streets by the dozen," their stench mingling with the smells of privies and rotting garbage. One visitor wrote: "[T]his is a miserable hole and the sooner I get out of it the happier I shall be"; a "potent smell of poverty, idleness and . . . lethargy broods over everything."[11]

One of the first prominent Savannahians to greet General Sherman was Charles Green. Green, an Englishman and a wealthy cotton broker rumored to have increased his wealth during the war, offered Sherman rooms in his handsome mansion. General Sherman accepted; his staff officers found accommodations at the Pulaski Hotel, once a grand hostelry, now faded and frayed from four years of war. The proprietor welcomed the Yankees until they informed him that they did not intend to pay for their rooms. His business also suffered as Savannah's citizens now avoided the hotel's once-popular bar—they had little interest in dining with the occupiers. "They regard us just as the Romans did the Goths," Sherman quipped. One of his officers described Savannahians as wearing a mask of resigned acceptance; they remain "intensely rebel." The correspondent, William Reid, offered a slightly different view; he observed that some of the well-to-do Savannahians appeared to be "warm Union men" who trust the government to be "magnanimous."[12]

Indeed, some locals waited in lines to take the oath of loyalty to the United States. And when Sherman's army paraded in the city's broad streets, with flags flying and the troops marching to the music of "the best bands in the army," soldiers wrote of the experience that "the wildest enthusiasm" came from crowds, mainly of black people. Women of the privileged class and the clergy remained outwardly hostile to the Yankees.[13]

An ardent Confederate supporter, Savannah's Bishop Stephen Elliott of Christ Church Episcopal, fanned the anti-Yankee feelings. In one sermon, he told his congregation to remember that "such fury as Grant's, such cruelty as Butler's, such fanaticism as Sherman's . . . revive our courage and reanimate our efforts."[14]

Over the war years, as the white men of the South marched off to war with great bravado, the women at home prayed for them, cared for their families, celebrated their victories, and wept over the casualties. With some of their men yet fighting on many fronts in early 1865, these same Savannah women faced the enemy alone.

The Occupation

The well-read Fanny Cohen referred to the Yankee soldiers as "Vandals" and "Goths"; in public, she struggled to keep her emotions under control, and her father worried that she might endanger the family by her "open avowal of hatred" toward the occupiers. When military censors intercepted the correspondence of another local woman, they informed her that she had written "impudent letters" and faced expulsion from the city. Appearing before an officer, she declared there was nothing "treasonable or criminal" in the letters, she had only written the truth: "the South had been wronged; the North had been the aggressor." Officials permitted her to remain in Savannah.

Even before Sherman reached the city, he concluded that there was "no parallel to the deep and bitter enmity of the women of the South." Once in Savannah, he discovered that the local women, like those elsewhere, "talk as defiant as ever." A Confederate soldier in the trenches near Richmond celebrated the news that the Savannah women had confronted Union soldiers in both war and peace with "undying hostility."[15] It was the same across the South. An aide to General Ulysses S. Grant, who visited Charleston in 1865, noticed as they rode through the city, "several . . . ladies made faces at . . . us."[16]

But not all women were outwardly hostile; in fact some saw the arrival of the Union soldiers as a business opportunity. One young woman regularly entertained Union officers, "buttering them all well for her own ends"; an Indiana captain watched officers riding through the city's streets with local women and remarked, "Don't look like war now." Another soldier wrote his sister that he found "the sweetest girl here. . . . I was never so bewitched before." Frances Howard, the daughter of a well-to-do planter, baked pumpkin pies that her "servants" sold to Union soldiers for "fifteen dollars in greenbacks." Elizabeth Stiles, whose husband was killed on the eve of the evacuation of Savannah, made money by fashioning "ribbon bows and nets." One of Stile's family members sold jewelry, opened a flower business, and sent her "slave" into the streets to sell bouquets to the soldiers.[17]

Like New Orleans and Nashville, both having fallen to the Union Army early in the war, Savannah profited from the money spent by the soldiers; one author suggests that, during the occupation, the women of Nashville also succored the southern cause by turning their city into "the clap capital of the universe." In Robert Penn Warren's novel *Flood,* Bradwell Tolliver, the main character, suggests that the United Daughters of the Confederacy should build a monument inscribed "to those gallant girls . . . who gave their all to all."[18]

Savannah's privileged women who found the occupation soldiers so distasteful seethed with anger over "disloyal slaves." Carolina Lamar informed her husband, Charles, a former owner of the notorious slave ship *Wanderer,* that their slave William had "proved to be a traitor." As soon as the army arrived, that "wretch" informed the Yankees about the liquor stored in the Lamar home, and soldiers soon arrived to take away "every box of brandy, wine, ale and champagne." A week later, three house slaves—Harriett, Lucy, and Nella—departed without a word, leaving wash on the line, laundry in the tubs, and clothes in the washroom. Carolina called them "Poor deluded creatures."[19] But for the slaves the occupying army provided an easy, quick path to freedom.

Another Savannah woman who watched her slaves leave without saying goodbye became enraged at the dramatic change in the social order: "There is one thing I will not submit to that the negro is our equal." After her slaves left, Mrs. George J. Kollock, member of a Savannah family reported to treat their slaves humanely, told her son: "I . . . wash my hands of the race, and am obliged to the U.S. for taking off my hands the old & worthless negroes and children."[20]

Both southerners and northerners expected blacks to turn against their owners, but one Union occupier observed: "It is surprising to all of us to see how admirably the negroes of the city behave, in view of their knowledge that our coming sets them at liberty from the control of their masters." In the countryside, former slaves appeared to "delight" in seeing "task houses" where they had endured punishments burned to the ground and happily watched Union soldiers shoot plantation dogs previously employed to capture runaways.[21]

Now free, some ex-slaves held bitter feeling toward their owners, as one former house servant told a Union soldier: "All my life I've worked for them. I have given them houses and lands; they have rode in their fine carriages . . . taken voyages over waters." Scripture guided others in their new relationships with former masters. One black man, now free, said: "some of these masters have . . . whipped, and imprisoned, and sold us about. The Bible says that we must forgive our enemies . . . and we forgive them." A few taunted their former owners. A well-to-do Savannah woman reported that a "little negro amused herself by jumping up and down under my window, and singing at the top of her voice: 'All de rebel gone to h[ell] Now Par Sherman come.'" The black nursemaid of Mary Sharpe Jones's baby seemed determined to reveal to Yankee troops that the infant's father, Charles C. Jones Jr., was the former mayor of Savannah and a colonel in the Confederate Army.[22]

The attitude of Colonel Jones resembled that of many Savannahians. He believed that the "Negro" was childlike "in intellect—improvident . . . ignorant of the operation of any law . . . other than the will of his master . . . careless of the future, and without the most distant conception of the duty of life and labor now devolved upon him." But Jones's paternalistic views waned as his efforts to "use kindness" failed in negotiating work contracts with his former slaves on his plantations near Savannah. When they asked for higher wages than he offered, Jones resented their questioning his authority. Like other former slaveholders, Jones grew "perplexed and angered" by what he deemed ingratitude on the part of his former slaves.[23] Mrs. Sarah Gordon, a former slave owner and doyenne of a leading Savannah family, wrote her daughter-in-law, Nelly

Gordon: "It is dreadful to see the poor negroes now, just loafing around doing nothing, when before they were active, happy and always at work." She may have been deluding herself—slaves frequently hid their real feelings by "putting on old massa."[24]

Mayor Richard Arnold, more philosophical than most, wrote a northern friend: "Almost every house servant in the city has left his or her place. . . . Slavery is dead beyond the possibility of resuscitation. We inaugurated our revolution to save it because it was the corner stone of our Social institutions." Prophetically, Arnold concluded that the "sudden emancipation of the Blacks, the disruption of all labor on the plantations has reduced many families from affluence to literal poverty. . . . [I]t will be years and years before we recover."

While Arnold lamented the occupation and the new social order, he praised the "liberality" of northern citizens for sending foodstuffs to Savannah. He did resent, however, the *New York Tribune*'s assertion that southerners had "degenerated mentally and physically from a long continued diet of corn bread and bacon"[25]

Arnold, something of a bon vivant, recognized that it was in the best interest of the city to work closely with local Union commanders. He so ingratiated himself with them that they ignored the fact that his council and ward committees were headed by prominent Confederates— the civic-commercial elite. Less than a week after the occupiers arrived, Arnold held a public meeting where seven hundred citizens passed resolutions to bury "bygones in the grave of the past," to submit to the "national authority of the Constitution," and to ask Georgia's governor to end the war in the state. Arnold told his audience that such actions would restore peace. But across the South where combat continued and men died, some bitterly denounced Savannah's surrender and withdrawal from the war.[26]

While in the city, General Sherman made time to meet in an upstairs room of the Green mansion with some of the hundreds of blacks who looked on him as their great benefactor. He told his wife that both the "old and young" came to "pray and shout and mix up my name with that of Moses . . . as well as 'Abram Linkom,' the Great Messiah of 'Dis Jubilee." Revealing his own paternalism, he shook their hands and told them that now as freed people they must become "industrious and well-behaved."[27]

The army permitted many of these same blacks to gather with others to celebrate their freedom by parading through the streets and singing hymns. On New Year's Eve day, nearly 1,300 black and white firefighters marched in frayed uniforms alongside their decorated fire engines. Hundreds chanted "some unearthly song, not a word of which is intelligible to the uninitiated," a northern journalist wrote. The spectators—freedpeople, cotton speculators, public officials and northern missionaries—enjoyed the "spectacle." The next day, January 1, 1865, blacks came together in mass meetings, previously forbidden, to sing and march and celebrate emancipation.

On the eve of the war, the federal census of 1860 listed Savannah's population as 22,292; of these, 7,712 (35 percent) were slaves and 792 (less than 4 percent) were free African Americans, 70 percent of this group being biracial. By early 1865, estimates of the population reached 25,000, which included hundreds of blacks who entered the city with the Union Army. Ever the military officer, Sherman recognized that freedpeople had become an encumbrance to his command, writing, "my first duty will be to clear the [army] of surplus negroes, mules and horses."[28] The opportunity soon presented itself.

Edwin Stanton, the secretary of war, visited Sherman in Savannah and asked to meet with the city's black leaders. The general arranged a January 12 meeting at the mansion of Charles Green with twenty of the "most intelligent" persons, including newly freed slaves, those who had bought their freedom, and freeborn of mixed-race parentage. Across the South more than 95 percent of the slaves or former slaves were illiterate; but several in this group could read and write, including their "canny" spokesperson, the Reverend Garrison Frazier, who was well aware of national events. In their "Colloquy" or dialogue, Stanton asked how the federal government could assist the thousands of newly freed people of South Carolina and Georgia. Frazier presented a vision of freedom when he emphasized that former slaves needed land in order to be truly free. The elderly Frazier, a former Baptist minister, championed the advantages of "[p]lacing us where we could reap the fruit of our own labor [and] take care of ourselves."[29] The other black leaders present agreed.

Special Field Order No. 15

Stanton and Sherman agreed to launch a unique government resettlement program. Sherman soon issued "Special Field Order No. 15," whereby each freedman and his family might receive "forty acres" of coastal land between Charleston and the Florida border that had been "abandoned" by white planters. The plan, which embraced most of the South Carolina and Georgia lowcountry, passed into popular jargon as "forty acres and a mule." Special Field Order No. 15 also served Sherman's interests in relocating the freedpeople away from his army and beyond the crowded city of Savannah. Federal officials began carving up and assigning "possessory" title to acreage for qualified African Americans like Reverend Frazier, who would lead families to settle on the property.

Some of the able-bodied black males who were recruited as drivers and laborers for the Union Army were treated harshly; black men and women arrested for theft were shackled in ball and chain and worked under guard on the city streets. Black leaders angrily pointed out that such treatment reeked of slavery, especially since whites arrested for similar crimes only paid fines. In spite of the protests, Savannah city government soon adopted the army's policy of using chain gangs as a cheap source of labor, especially to keep the streets clean. No doubt black prisoners, shackled and put to work this way, served to remind all African Americans of the punishment they faced if they broke the law.[30]

The Reverend Ulysses L. Houston, pastor of what is today the Second Bryan Baptist Church, was present at the colloquy with Sherman and Stanton. Reverend Houston, an early, successful applicant for land under Special Field Order No. 15, led ninety-six families to settle five thousand acres on Skidaway Island a few miles southeast of the city. Once owned by the Joseph F. Waring family and other wealthy planters, by February 1865 it was home to approximately one thousand freedpeople. Houston hoped to establish a sawmill and to build a schoolhouse and a church. On nearby Ossabaw Island, the federal government gave "possessory title" of two thousand acres to seventy-eight freedpeople who settled there.[31]

Who Will Educate the Freedmen and Their Children?

Equal in their desire to have their own land to work, the freedpeople wanted an education for themselves and their children. In antebellum Savannah and across the South, teaching slaves to read or write was prohibited by law. Little wonder that they now wanted what had been denied them. One Mississippi freedman put it succinctly: education was "the next best thing to liberty." It offered a path to economic freedom, the ability to read the Bible, and individual and group uplift.[32] Upon the arrival of the Union Army, Savannah's black ministers moved quickly to provide education for the freedpeople.

On January 10, 1865, hundreds of young black children, many shoeless and shivering, marched from the Second African Baptist Church to the nearby Old Bryan Slave Mart at 418 West Bryan Street, where they sat on benches only recently vacated by slaves awaiting auction. Scattered about were the shackles and handcuffs used by the auctioneers. Another group of children entered a building on Fahm Street, formerly the Confederate Hospital, and awaited their teachers. The Reverend William T. Richardson, a representative of the northeastern-based American Missionary Association (AMA), watched the excitement among the people at such "a gathering of Freedmen's sons and daughters [this] proud city had never seen before."[33] The remarkable event was sponsored by the Savannah Education Association (SEA), founded by black ministers. Union General Geary helped them acquire school sites, and the SEA raised two thousand dollars locally to hire fifteen black male and female teachers. The classes began under Louis B. Toomer, one of the first principals, who formerly had taught in a clandestine school in antebellum Savannah.[34]

Another representative of the AMA, the Reverend S. W. Magill, also arrived in the city in early 1865, bringing books and white instructors for the SEA schools. Agents of the AMA and the Freedmen's Bureau continued to be astonished at the enthusiasm of the African Americans for education. John E. Hayes, once a reporter for the *New York Tribune* and now editor of the *Savannah Republican,* marveled at the "earnestness and avidity with which these liberated people seek information."[35] But the euphoria of northerners over the leadership of the SEA quickly faded.

The Reverend Magill soon complained about the inexperience of the "colored" leaders and teachers who "know nothing about educating." Since the AMA provided funding for the SEA, Magill was angered when its leaders refused to replace black teachers with white ones. But African Americans wanted sole control of the education for blacks, and Aaron A. Bradley encouraged them.

Born a South Carolina slave, Bradley fled the South, studied law and practiced for several decades in Boston. Now fifty, the light-skinned, freckled Bradley came to Savannah to organize blacks and to warn them against northern interlopers. AMA leaders found him a "very insolent and pestilent fellow"; the city's white leadership agreed. Bradley bedeviled them for the next several years.[36]

When the SEA overextended itself and appealed to the AMA for funds, the white leadership supplied the money only after the SEA agreed to employ white women as lead teachers and relegate black instructors to assistants. The AMA's tuition-free schools soon monopolized the instruction of African American children and adults in Savannah and ended the careers of educators like the young African American woman, Susie Baker King Taylor, who conducted fee-based private schools.[37]

AMA's Beach Institute won praise from a reporter for the Savannah *Daily Republican.* After attending an examination of the students at Beach Institute, he called the school "a laudable object for elevating the rising generation of colored people." Several years later, arsonists burned the institute, but it was soon rebuilt and reopened.[38]

Across Georgia whites objected to northerners—especially the white women of the AMA—teaching the freedpeople. The feelings were mutual as the AMA teachers had little regard for the white privileged class. One young music instructor in Savannah, Julia Marshall, a New York native, said, "it would be pleasant had I the power and *iron heel* strong enough to grind every one of these Secessionists deep in the earth."[39] Equally distasteful to Savannahians were white teachers like Cornelia Drake who wanted to turn her black pupils into little "Yankees."[40] Northern teachers in the South sometimes feared for their own lives. As one instructor in nearby Charleston described the situation, white teachers were so despised that "none of us would be surprised if they made a bonfire of us one dark night."[41]

Likely the main grievance of Georgians was fear that they might impart to black students "dangerous" ideas of social equality. They deemed it best to keep instruction in the hands of native Georgians who would perpetuate the social mores of the region. Such ideas persisted into the twentieth century among even the highly educated—an esteemed University of Georgia professor of history, E. Merton Coulter, referred to the northern teachers as "pious young females of the Puritan persuasion who . . . dangled before the Negroes the educational Utopia and innocently awakened in the African heart longings for what could not be."[42]

Whites worried that schooling might lead to integration. When the chief justice of the Supreme Court of the United States, Salmon P. Chase, visited Savannah in early 1865, the correspondent Whitelaw Reid watched "a fine-looking old gentleman . . . [with] silvery hair" approach Chase protesting "the admission of the negroes to the public schools." He told Chase: "we accept the death of slavery; but, sir, surely there are some things that are not tolerable. . . . Our people have not been brought up to associate with negroes. They don't think it decent; and the negroes will be none the better for being thrust thus into the places of white men's sons."[43] Apparently, some viewed social equality as the precursor to the mixing of the races.

When General Geary marched out of the city and into South Carolina with Sherman's main army in mid-January, blacks and whites alike regretted his leaving. Mayor Arnold and the City Council praised him as a "high toned gentleman and . . . chivalric Soldier."[44] He also had enforced strict order in the city, especially among the ex-slaves, and endorsed the policies of the civic-commercial elite.

Saxton, the Freedmen, and Disorder

Union General Rufus Saxton, who remained in the city, was attentive to the needs of the freedpeople—some white Savannahians thought too much so. Appointed by Sherman as the assistant commissioner of the federal Bureau of

Refugees, Freedmen, and Abandoned Lands (Freedman's Bureau), Saxton hoped to quickly relocate freedpeople to lands as specified in Sherman's Special Order No. 15. Within a short time he had settled forty thousand freedpeople on the sea islands of South Carolina and Georgia. Saxton named the Reverend Tunis G. Campbell, an African American agent of the Freedmen's Bureau, as "governor" of Burnside and Ossabaw islands near Savannah and others further south.

As the war neared a close, exploding ammunition depots rocked Charleston, Mobile, and Savannah. In Charleston, a cache of gunpowder detonated and burned across four city blocks, killing hundreds of poor whites and blacks.[45] A northern reporter described Charleston as "a city of ruins, of desolation, of vacant houses, of widowed women, of rotting wharves."[46] At Mobile, blacks hired by Union officials were removing an ammunition dump when it ignited; explosives and fires swept through twenty blocks of the city, mangling and incinerating about three hundred persons, including the blacks moving the cache.[47] Savannah experienced a like disaster on the evening of January 28.

The first witnesses reported flames shooting "high in the air" and smoke pouring from the windows of the Confederate Arsenal at the intersection of West Broad and Broughton streets. The closely packed munitions detonated. An eyewitness feared for his life as "explosions followed each other in quick succession . . . throwing bricks, mortar, and iron in every direction . . . pieces of shell fragments dropping all about us."

Fires spread rapidly through hovels along the riverfront and, as in Charleston and Mobile, the poor bore the brunt of the suffering. The conflagration displaced over one hundred black people, adding to the numbers of homeless and destitute in the city. Rumors spread that Confederates dressed in federal uniforms slipped into the city and set the arsenal ablaze. Federal patrols received orders to shoot to kill anyone abroad in Savannah after dark.[48] The patrols cooperated with the city police to curb lawlessness, but according to Savannah's military-controlled press, disorder, as in other southern cities, seemed to be rampant.

In Savannah, illicit grog shops flourished. An Irish woman distilled whiskey so strong it might kill if imbibed. Drunks and "unruly" freedmen brawled openly in the streets. When brothels were raided, the women simply relocated to other parts of the city. The press kept up a steady din about robberies, roaming dogs, the lack of sanitation and the filth in the city streets. Only following departure of the main body of Sherman's forces did the garrison troops begin clearing the city of the army's debris.[49]

Within two months the soldiers hauled away the carcasses of 568 rotting cows, horses, and mules; 7,219 loads of manure; and 8,311 carts of garbage. The garrison troops also whitewashed the buildings and warehouses overlooking the river and painted 6,200 trees up to a height of seven feet.[50]

Perhaps to take the minds of Savannahians off the Yankee occupation and as a gesture toward friendship, Union Army brass bands entertained the public in the theater built by the English architect William Jay, on Bull Street facing Chippewa Square. One of the stockholders in the building and the wealthiest man in the city before the war, Edward Padelford, served as a spokesman for the other owners. They leased the theater to variety shows which offered dramas and gymnastic events in January and the months thereafter. In late February, the Union newspaper, the *Savannah Daily Herald*, announced that an amateur performance of the play *Rent Day* would open for a city "starving-for-amusement." After the first performance, the paper reported that unfortunately the show was not a success as many cast members suffered "from stage fright." A few days later a "well organized troupe" of professionals from New York performed before a large and appreciative audience. But it soon became apparent that Savannah's theater-going population and the local economy could not support a sustained run of professional actors, and for some months the theater fell dark.[51] Furthermore, the gesture made to salve the feelings of Savannahians over the occupation of the city appeared to have little effect.

Black Soldiers, Lincoln's Assassination, and POWs

After twenty-three hundred black Union soldiers arrived in the city to relieve white troops on garrison duty, a unit guarding the roads into Savannah in March 1865 stopped a poor white farm woman to inspect the produce she planned to sell. She became enraged at the "nigger fur to stop a poor woman on the road . . . make me stand four hours in the hot sunshine, with the big, greasy corporal a settin' in a chair, and me a standin' up! O, them beasts."[52] Apparently race trumped class as the great divider.

Her attitude mirrored that of most whites across the South. A businessman in Charleston, who watched black militia parading during a celebration of Independence Day, observed that "few whites were moving about," as "[t]he day now belongs to the 'Nigger.'"[53] Northern correspondent Whitelaw Reid found similar attitudes in Mobile: "To be conquered by the Yankees was humiliating, but to have their own negroes armed and set over them they felt to be cruel and wanton insult." Reid thought that Mobilians' "combination of rage and helplessness would have been ludicrous, but for its dark suggestions for the future."[54]

In Savannah, one of the privileged class wrote: "My heart is filled with an intensity of hatred toward the authors of our misery. . . . If we go to our street doors to catch a breath of fresh air we are annoyed by the sight of armed Yankees (white and black). I cannot reconcile myself to this wretched state of servitude."[55] Feelings were the same in Charleston. A female member of a prominent family remarked: "We rarely go out, the streets are so niggery and Yankees so numerous."[56]

The bitterness toward the occupiers and former slaves persisted in Savannah. Many mourned families and friends. It has been projected that out of every 100 men who joined regiments in the city, 43 returned, 25 deserted, and 32 died of wounds or disease. The city's clergy continued to rail from their pulpits against the occupiers; city officials refused to raise the American flag over the City Exchange in celebration of Washington's Birthday. Widows in black witnessed a changed city and world—the sauciness of the freedpeople and the white beggars and males bathing nude in the river.

Despite the many disasters that befell the Confederacy over four years of war, some white Savannahians nurtured hope into the spring of 1865 that the war could be won. Others believed that Mayor Arnold surrendered the city too soon and circulated rumors that he drank heavily. But their hope turned to despair when news arrived in Savannah that General Robert E. Lee had surrendered his Army of Northern Virginia to General Ulysses S. Grant on April 9, 1865.[57]

President Lincoln desired a quick resolution of the relationship of the Confederate states to the Union. His assassination by a deranged Confederate sympathizer dramatically changed that prospect. Lincoln's assassination shocked Charleston's freedpeople, and they mourned his murder even as the white rector of the city's St. John's Episcopal Church refused to hold services for the dead president. Some white Savannahians in despair over Lee's surrender found "righteous retribution" in Lincoln's death. Former Confederate major William Basinger observed that Lincoln "committed a monstrous crime in making war upon us, and his tragic death was no more than just punishment for that crime." Mary Sharpe Jones's daughter-in-law, Caroline, believed that Lincoln's death was "one sweet drop in all that is painful."[58]

In spite of such attitudes, Mayor Arnold and city officials joined with Union military officers on April 22 to express public sorrow over the assassination of the president. Black cloth draped the classrooms of the freed children and hung from buildings and the trees in Johnson Square, where thousands gathered. Bells tolled and guns fired as black and white clergy prepared to take their assigned seats on the speaker's platform with local dignitaries. Suddenly, white men backed by soldiers herded the black clergymen to the rear. Outraged, James M. Simms, a former slave and now a spokesman for the freedpeople, told military officials that blacks had every right to mingle with whites for public events. The occupiers paid little heed.[59]

After the state of Georgia officially surrendered to Union officers in late April, Mayor Arnold traveled to Washington to meet with President Andrew Johnson and urged him to speedily restore the state to its original place in the Union. Arnold returned to Savannah, cheered by the meeting.[60]

During early May, a tug came down the river from Augusta carrying prisoners Jefferson Davis and Alexander Stephens, the president and vice-president of the Confederacy. At Savannah, under heavy guard, the prisoners transferred to a steamer bound for Hampton Roads, Virginia, where Davis was imprisoned and shackled at Fortress Monroe. Separated from her husband, Varina Davis, with their children, returned to Savannah emotionally distraught over the conditions of his imprisonment. They took lodgings at the Pulaski Hotel. While she remained under surveillance by military authorities, the Sisters of Mercy arranged for the youngsters to take classes at St. Vincent's Academy. The city's well-to-do extended Mrs. Davis every "generosity."[61] When former Confederate captain George A. Mercer heard rumors that Davis's jailers had "heaped indignities" upon him, Mercer lamented that such treatment would "affix a lasting stigma to the U.S. Government."[62]

Former Confederates and Former Slaves

As the weeks passed, soldiers from the disbanded Confederate armies drifted back to Savannah, some ill and in rags like the well-to-do George Washington Stiles whose family owned Green Island near Savannah. As ex-Confederates returned in their butternut-gray uniforms, Union officers in the city forbade wearing of the uniform. When they learned that their former adversaries owned no other clothes, they rescinded the order but specified that buttons on the Confederate uniform be removed or covered. A subsequent incident angered Confederate sympathizers in the city. In what one northern correspondent called a "brutal scene," a drunken Union sergeant insisted on slicing the buttons from the uniform of a white-haired Confederate brigadier general only recently arrived in Savannah.[63]

A depressed George A. Mercer returned to the city in May with his wife and child. He viewed the war as "a struggle for the rights of property [in slaves]" and thought the whole social order "subverted and Liberty . . . thrust upon an ignorant and inferior race." He wrote in his diary: "My present condition and future prospects cause me much mental distress."[64] He then waxed a bit romantic: The war "swelled the ranks of [the South's] enemies, and the slaves she nourished in her bosom were converted into her foes."[65]

It was around this time that black leaders organized Colored Union Leagues (CUL), which pledged support to the nascent Republican Party and promised to advocate for black voting rights. Whites watched suspiciously, perhaps unsettled by articles in the Savannah press promoting white supremacy. City Council members warned of violence as a parade formed on the morning of July 4, 1865. Even though many white Savannahians did not plan to celebrate Independence Day, the city's African American firemen with at least one of their fire engines joined a parade of black and white Union soldiers and members of the CUL. As the parade wound through the streets, white "toughs" suddenly seized the fire engine and knocked down and injured a fireman and soldier. In days following, members of the CUL continued to march, urged on by public speeches by James Simms, who called for citizenship rights for all. Lacking the right to vote or run for political office, blacks relied on speeches and parades as ways to participate in the larger political process and to express their manhood. White men sometimes used violent methods to control and suppress black activism.[66]

Racial violence did not surprise General Carl Schurz, who visited Savannah on a tour of the South to observe conditions for President Johnson. Schurz saw young men with "sullen faces" hanging around street corners bragging that they were "not conquered but only overpowered." Schurz eavesdropped on their plans to take "private vengeance" when the "Yankee bayonets" departed.[67] In Charleston, Union General Daniel E. Sickles detected a similar bitterness among southerners whose loyalty to the United States resembled only a "reluctant . . . sullen . . . allegiance."[68]

In late summer, when the federal government ended its distribution of rations to Savannah's destitute, Mayor Arnold predicted that the city's obligation to feed the poor would "complete the Bankruptcy of the city. The [interests] are unpaid on our bonds and are running up a fearful amount."[69]

Recognizing the threat of the city's indebtedness, the editor of the *Savannah Republican* urged citizens to forget the past and look forward to restoring the city to its rightful place as the "commercial emporium of Georgia." The editor, northern-born John Hayes, called on the "monied men of Savannah to rally to [your] own interests, and . . . seek to enrich our city" by attracting northern capital, enterprise, and "vim."[70] Perhaps Hayes's clarion call for material progress had some effect. "Much faith is placed in Northern Energy and Northern Capital," Mayor Arnold wrote. He noticed some economic stirrings, writing in the fall that every "decent" house in the city is rented.

No doubt the northern teachers moving to the city aided the improving economy. The AMA brought eleven new teachers to town as well as their superintendents and their wives and children. All needed housing; the sixteen teachers sponsored by the New England Freedmen's Aid Society also needed quarters, as did the ten teachers hired by the SEA, one of them being the outspoken James Simms.

Lawyers also found business. Blacks hired attorneys to bring suits against white property owners, who in turn hired lawyers to represent them. Union officers spent money in local bars and businesses, rented offices for the Freedmen's Bureau, and hired local artisans to renovate classrooms for black children. The city's "monied" leaders envisioned hope for a brighter economic future, especially as the rebuilt CGR promised delivery of bumper crops of cotton.[71] Despite the economic stirrings, the city's indebtedness remained a very serious problem, especially for Mayor Arnold.

In September, when the City Council assembled for the first meeting after the complete restoration of its powers, Savannah's funded debt stood at a staggering $2,000,000 with annual interest payments of more than $140,000. To put this in perspective, at the City Council meeting of August 23, 1865, Mayor Arnold told those assembled, "The resources of the city as to food are very limited and are fast diminishing. . . . literal starvation . . . [seems] the path of the future unless some relief be afforded." Attempting to meet the city's many financial obligations, Mayor Arnold and his council enacted a variety of money-raising measures that included shipping fees, drayage licenses, and property taxes.[72]

But with the cost of food, rents, and taxes rising, black longshoremen—physically strong African Americans who had the dangerous job of loading and unloading vessels—walked off their jobs. The workers wanted a raise in their daily wages from $2.00 to $2.50. Whites earned $3.00 for the same job. With knowledge of the city government, Union officers dispatched a squad of soldiers who intervened and arrested sixty black strikers. The *Savannah Republican* condemned the strikers as "a secret band of men" who wished "to extort by threats" money from their employers. The CUL announced that it would continue to organize for "mutual help and protection," asserting that the strikers were "some of our best. . . colored citizens."[73]

During the fall, three hundred white delegates from throughout the state assembled in Milledgeville, Georgia, to attend a constitutional convention. As prerequisites for readmission to the Union, Congress required the delegates to repeal the ordinance of secession, abolish slavery, and repudiate the Confederate war debt. The delegates complied.[74]

In mid-November, the white male voters across Georgia went to the polls and elected sixty-year-old Charles J. Jenkins, a member of the Georgia

Supreme Court during the war, as governor along with large numbers of ex-Confederates to the state legislature. The legislature in turn elected two senators to Congress—former vice-president of the CSA, Alexander H. Stephens, and former CSA senator, Herschel V. Johnson. Georgia voters also elected members to the U.S. House of Representatives, including high-ranking CSA military officers who were not yet eligible to take the oath of allegiance to the United States. The Georgia state legislators soon voted to permit African Americans the right to sign contracts, to own property, and to sue and be sued. But no action was taken that would allow them to run for office, to vote, serve on juries, or testify in court—except in cases directly affecting them. Joseph E. Brown, the former war governor of Georgia, spoke for most of the state's whites when he said: "unless madness rules . . . [blacks] will never be placed upon the basis of political equality with us. . . . [T]hey are not competent to the task of self-government."[75] The backgrounds, actions, and language of Georgia's political leaders angered northerners and their representatives in Congress.

On a Wednesday, early in December 1865, polls opened in Savannah for a mayoralty election, the first since the arrival of the occupying army. Union General Carl Schurz doubted if civil government could be restored in this once "hottest" of "rebel places," where the young believe they are yet "unconquered." Confirming his appraisal was the reappearance of the intimidating white, antebellum militias, previously outlawed by Union officers. In order to skirt the law, the militiamen insisted their units were but "social" organizations. The Oglethorpe Light Infantry now called itself the Oglethorpe Light Club; however, its members continued to carry arms and parade. So readily were the "clubs" accepted that city officials and Union officers together approved the turn out of the Oglethorpe Club in December to "monitor" events at the polls.[76]

The voters included the antebellum electorate, and they voted for one of their own for mayor, fifty-year-old former Confederate colonel Edward C. Anderson. Savannah-born, related to the prominent Clifford and Wayne families, and educated in the North, Anderson had served as a U.S. naval officer. He returned to the city before the Civil War and in the boom times of the 1850s became wealthy in business and was first elected mayor in 1854. During the war, Colonel Anderson, CSA, commanded the river batteries around the city and its prisoner-of-war stockade at the corner of Whitaker and Hall streets. Now, in 1865, Anderson, a former Confederate officer and member of the civic-commercial elite like many of the council members elected with him, again became Savannah's mayor.[77]

When Anderson took office, $2,000 remained in the city treasury, and Savannah owed in interest on bonds issued before the war the staggering sum of $371,570. He blamed the city's financial difficulties on the "vicissitudes" of four years of war and the loss of city revenues "appropriated by the military tax gatherers . . . domiciled in our midst." While blaming federal authorities for some of Savannah's financial problems, Anderson, like Arnold before him, agreed with the occupying Union officers on the issue of the racial hierarchy—blacks must remain subordinate to whites. By his actions, President Andrew Johnson agreed.[78]

Undoing Promissory Titles, and the Ubiquitous Aaron Bradley

President Johnson bowed to the demands of ex-Confederates for a return of their "abandoned" coastal properties and then revoked the rights to lands given the freedmen under Sherman's Special Field Order No. 15. This presidential mandate required the freedpeople who held "promissory" title to land they tilled on islands near Savannah—Ossabaw, Wassaw, and Skidaway—to relinquish the property.[79] This must have been a profound disappointment to those whose hopes for self-reliance were shattered upon the revocation of the special order.

When General Rufus Saxton, assistant commissioner of the Freedmen's Bureau in Georgia, defied President Johnson's order to return the "abandoned" lands to ex-Confederates, Johnson removed him and appointed General Davis Tillson to execute the new policy.[80] Now the ranking officer of the Freedmen's Bureau in Georgia, Tillson did continue his predecessor's policies of renovating or renting buildings for black classrooms and paying the salaries of school superintendents.[81] At the same time, Tillson moved expeditiously to return the "abandoned" lands to their former owners.

On Ossabaw Island, Tillson met with Tunis Campbell, an educated African American entrepreneur from New York and an agent of the Freedmen's Bureau. Later, Campbell wrote that, under Tillson's policy, "the people were driven off—unless they worked under contracts which were purposely made to cheat the freedmen out of their labor." Tillson believed that Campbell actively encouraged freedmen to resist white planters returning to claim their property on the islands and dismissed him from the Freedmen's Bureau. Campbell *had* in fact encouraged freedpeople on the sea islands to organize militias to protect themselves from planters seeking to retake their lands.[82]

Feeling betrayed by their government, some black former Union soldiers like Mustapha Shaw resisted the new policy on Ossabaw with bowie knives and pistols. Union soldiers were dispatched to the island to enforce the law. The vast majority of freedmen on the islands lost their opportunity to become landowners. Some like Shaw and Campbell moved to nearby McIntosh County where they purchased land—realizing their dream of being landowners. On Ossabaw many of those who had worked the island as slaves remained to work as sharecroppers for the returning planters. A generation later their children found a home just a few miles away on the mainland near Savannah at a place called Pin Point.[83]

About the time the Freedmen's Bureau revoked the land rights of blacks, Aaron Bradley found another cause. The light-skinned, long-haired, pistol-totting Bradley, often dressed in a top hat and white gloves, gave impromptu speeches on Savannah's street corners. He accused President Andrew Johnson, the Freedmen's Bureau, the military, local planters, and city leaders of colluding to deny African Americans basic rights and of conspiring to return them to slavery. A lightning rod for controversy, Bradley urged a mass meeting of blacks, who gathered in the Second Baptist Church in December to resist any attempt by the Freedmen's Bureau to remove them from their lands. Now the city's older black clergy started cutting their ties with Bradley and his militant politics.

In late December 1865, officers of the occupying army arrested, tried, and convicted Bradley in a military court for his use of insurrectionary language and sentenced him to imprisonment in Fort Pulaski for a year. He soon won parole, but when he continued to level charges of collusion between the city government and that of the United States to deny blacks their rights, the secretary of war, Edwin Stanton, passed sentence. He gave Bradley a choice: he could choose either imprisonment at Fort Pulaski or exile from the state for a year. Bradley chose the latter.[84] But he would return.

Amid the despair and disorder in the city, the Savannah Theatre reopened for the 1865–66 season on Saturday night, September 30, after a "thorough Renovation and Improvement." The local press noted that the "stars" of the stock company played to a capacity "audience comprised [of] the best classes of our citizens and many ladies." Theatergoers enjoyed such productions as *The Merchant of Venice* performed by "distinguished" thespians until the season ended in March 1866.[85]

By now the migration of blacks from across the southern countryside to the cities had increased. As in the antebellum period, whites for a variety of reasons remained uneasy over the large numbers of blacks residing in any southern city. The federal government, the Union Army, and the Freedmen's Bureau had urged the freedpeople to return to the countryside, and now the urban press took up the campaign to keep African Americans in their rural homes. The Montgomery, Alabama, *Daily Ledger* in late 1865 instructed blacks that they should "cultivate the soil, the employment God designed them for. . . . [The] city is no place for them; it was intended for white people."[86]

Freedpeople forced to give up "promissory" titles to lands on the South Carolina and Georgia sea islands soon returned to Savannah and, by the end of the 1860s, whites numbered fifteen thousand and blacks thirteen thousand (46 percent). One observer commented that poor whites and blacks alike crowded into "shanties" on the city's east and west sides. Here cholera spread and many suffered from malnutrition, even starvation. Based on records for Savannah in 1866, the black death rate was more than twice that of whites. But disease affected all races and classes.

George Mercer wrote in his diary that even the "best citizens" were dying—in November, forty-nine burials took place. People were seized with violent cramps and died within twelve hours. Savannahians believed that the "originating causes" of disease stemmed from "imprudence" in eating shrimp, oysters, pork and cabbage.[87]

Women and their children—many widowed or with severely wounded husbands and few if any relatives—found themselves without food or shelter. Some impoverished white women, the *Savannah Daily Republican* reported, engaged in "unseemly conduct" by day and enjoy "drunken revels at night" where destitute whites and blacks crowded together in hovels on the city's east and west sides. Rumors circulated that two thousand "respectable people" in and around the city were dependent on charity. Because Savannah's seasonal economy did not provide year-round work for white laborers, the ranks of the unemployed, especially Irish laborers and former Confederate enlisted men wounded in body, mind, and spirit, grew. Large numbers of these groups found it difficult to provide food for their families on a regular basis.[88]

Many of Savannah's young soldiers lay in unmarked graves near where they died on the battlefield; sons of the privileged class such as Francis Bartow, Charles Augustus Lafayette Lamar, the brothers Joseph and William Habersham, Edward Padelford Jr., and Thomas Purse Jr. were retrieved by mourning families. Among white middle-class Savannahians, a widow, Charlotte Branch, was devastated when she learned the fate of her three sons. The eldest son, Lieutenant John Branch, age twenty-three, was killed at Bull Run in Virginia; a younger son was captured and another wounded. Mothers like Charlotte grieved inconsolably. One Savannah woman wrote her husband, "Two such noble boys to have been thus sacrificed . . . rends my heart in despair. My anguish over the loss of my dear soldier boys fills my soul with sorrow." Some wives and mothers of soldiers turned to alcohol or morphine to ease the pain of loss.[89]

With employment opportunities few, some returning CSA officers opened schools for white children; others went to work for the federal government. Plantation owner Charles C. Jones Jr., lawyer, former mayor of Savannah, and a former colonel in the CSA, tired of negotiating with creditors and his former slaves, put two plantations up for sale and departed for New York City. Here he joined the firm of a former mentor and profited handsomely, assisting southerners seeking restitution for losses suffered in the war. Despite warnings from her husband, former CSA captain William W. Gordon, about asking favors of Yankees, Kinzie ("Nelly") Gordon called on her relative, a high-ranking Union officer, to expedite the paperwork for sale of the family's cotton. Kinzie's business acumen helped the Gordons recoup their wealth and prominence in Savannah society.

CSA officers and once well-to-do businessmen returned to their positions with the CGR and the Atlantic and Gulf Railroad (AGR). The young attorney George Mercer, who first bemoaned his "prospects," upon returning to Savannah quickly prospered from legal fees and temporarily recovered from his melancholia, a condition passed down to later generations of his family. He now believed that Savannah provided such good opportunities for "growth and prosperity" that he invested five hundred dollars in a local soap factory.[90] Former Confederate major William Basinger returned to the practice of the law, married, and within a few years derived enough from his professional earnings to build a substantial home in his mother's rear yard for $11,500.[91]

In Savannah there were the rich and then there were the super-rich. Mary Telfair, her sister Margaret, and Margaret's husband, William Hodgson, retained much of their wealth even after losing their property in slaves. Hodgson's frustration was evident as he described the loss: "perhaps the most ingenious and cruel device of the Federal [government] is that of destroying our system of labor, on which all values depend." Mary had little liking for the army occupying Savannah and told a friend: "We have all passed through a sad ordeal since subjugation." Yet she praised the "young men of the old aristocracy . . . supporting themselves by fishing and cutting wood for the government. I admire them as heroes. How nobly do they bear adversity!"[92]

Mary, the daughter of a former Georgia governor, prosperous in land and slaves, was the wealthiest woman in the city. With the bulk of the family's money in northern and London banks during the war, Mary and the Hodgsons could travel abroad like other wealthy Savannahians and the country's well-to-do. They sailed on July 14, 1866, for Le Havre.[93] Traveling in Normandy during the summer, then to Paris in the fall, Margaret reported that the city was "crowded with Americans," but "We only associate with Confederates." Margaret loved being in Paris, where she could sojourn "under the French flag which I *revere more highly* than I do the Stripes and Stars." They went to southern France in the winter and in the spring to Spain. After returning to Savannah, Mary traveled to Newport, Rhode Island, where many wealthy southerners spent their summers.[94]

Some of the well-to-do, like Susan Kollock, embraced the attitudes of Mary and the Hodgsons toward Yankees. On one occasion Susan confronted a "Yankee" officer telling him of the "injustice to us in robbing us of our property . . . our negroes." But Susan had no scruples about asking for assistance from Union officers who helped her secure her property, White Bluff Plantation, near the city and land on Ossabaw, previously given to freedpeople.[95]

Some Savannahians profited handsomely in property sales to northern speculators. The well-to-do former slaveholders John and Mary Stoddard sold a portion of Daufuskie, a sea island near Hilton Head Island, for $10 an acre; another well-heeled Savannah family made an offer, but planned to take no less per acre than the Stoddards. Ten dollars an acre was a good asking price. One visitor in 1866, A. G. C. Smits, found land in and around the city selling for $2.50 to $5 an acre, and he believed, "there is money to be made here." He considered groceries expensive—milk was twenty-five cents a quart—but he still thought about settling in the area and going into farming. The only drawback for him in living near Savannah permanently was "the terrific thunder storms which occur during the summer months."[96]

The influx of speculators and northern migrant workers as well as the continuing presence of Union soldiers and sailors boded well for those of the oldest profession, prostitution. As more black laborers returned from the sea islands and the hinterland to the city to look for jobs, they depressed wages for all workers. With living costs rising, prostitution offered black women without masters or husbands an opportunity to earn money to support themselves and their children.[97]

Mayor Anderson's Law-and-Order Campaign

On Sunday evenings especially, black and white prostitutes, in the words of William Wray, chief of the city's detectives, made "night hideous by their lewd and lascivious behavior," even in the city center where the privileged class resided. Johanna Anderson, who owned the largest brothel, brazenly advertised her entourage of "young girls, white and black," by parading them in the evenings through Savannah. A police report listed her as "the most *depraved and abandoned character* within the City Limits."[98]

When complaints over the incidence of prostitution again reached city officials in the summer of 1866, Mayor Anderson asked the Freedmen's Bureau for help in removing the "large number of shameless colored prostitutes who nightly infest our streets." His solution, "send them down to the islands" and hire them out as agricultural workers. The local white officials of the Freedmen's Bureau agreed: "Colored prostitutes are daily becoming worse, they insult people in the street & laugh at the punishment. . . . The jail is full of them."[99]

To white Savannahians, the large numbers of freedpeople seemed to have taken over the streets, where they enjoyed raucous dancing, carousing, and shouting to celebrate their freedom and taunt their former masters and mistresses. In response, angry city officials put more patrolmen on the streets and handed out harsher punishments. Anderson, a "law and order" mayor, remarked, "With a vagabond freed element in our midst, and constantly pouring in . . . it is a matter of necessity to keep up at any cost an efficient Police Force for our protection."[100] He might have added: And for the subordination of African Americans.

Anderson hired more men, reorganized the department, and increased its budget to $79,412 for the 1865–66 fiscal year. By late 1866, the police force numbered 116 members, including a special tactical unit. Because the City Council elected the officers and the mayor appointed the privates, city government exercised tight control over the police. In the late 1860s, 57 percent of the privates in the force of over 100 members were Irish. They now wore uniforms of butternut gray, the same color as those once worn by the army of the CSA.[101]

But at times in the 1860s, it seemed as if no one controlled the streets. When police arrested blacks, they were heckled by other blacks. Patrolmen themselves could not always be depended upon to subdue the street demonstrations as they occasionally joined in the disorder and willingly accepted libations and bribes. But far more blacks were arrested than whites, often for petty crimes like "having in possession a bar of soap he could not account for."[102]

When apprehended, blacks faced harsh punishments. Dominick O'Byrne, who served as a Savannah city councilman during the war and now as a Freedmen's Bureau judge, repeatedly sentenced black petty-criminals to months of hard labor on the streets, shackled in ball and chain. Aaron Bradley accused authorities of using the slightest offense to send blacks to the chain gangs. Nothing came of Bradley's efforts to stop the practice, and the notorious chain gangs spread across Georgia.[103]

Harsh sentences may have encouraged disorderly behavior, which spread to Forsyth Park. In June 1866 the council heard complaints that the "negroes" had taken "real possession of the Park" and occupied "all the seats and monopolize the walks around the fountain [so] that nobody likes to walk there." Hence a resolution was offered asserting that "negroes" had overrun the park, destroying trees and shrubbery, and that their foul language prevented use of the park by ladies and children. The council acted quickly to prevent such "nuisances" by posting guards at the gates of the park and instructing them to admit only those "Negroes" who were in charge of white children. In this case, General Tillson objected, calling the statute discriminatory, and the council responded by closing Forsyth Park to everyone. The civic-commercial elite loathed and feared social mixing of the races. The society of the Old South, founded on race or caste, persisted into the New.

Tensions between blacks and whites in Savannah and in other southern port cities appeared to rise with the temperature, escalating into open violence during the spring and summer of 1866. Racial clashes in Memphis and New Orleans left eighty African Americans and five whites dead, three of whom had sided with the blacks. In Savannah in midsummer two cart drivers, notorious for driving at breakneck speeds, slammed into each other—one driven by an unnamed black man and the other by Lawrence Craney, a white. The men exchanged angry words and, when the black man allegedly called Craney "a rebel son of a bitch," Craney leapt from his cart and began beating the black driver. Samuel Whitfield, a white teacher and a member of the local Colored Union League, intervened, whereupon Craney climbed back into his cart and with his friend, William Allen, started to pull away. To prevent their leaving, Whitfield and a growing crowd of blacks closed in and, when someone shouted for Whitfield to shoot Craney, Allen retaliated by firing at Whitfield, killing him instantly.

Within days, Allen stood before the magistrate's court on trial for murder. The well-connected William M. Russell Jr., clerk of the City Council since 1849 and now Judge Russell, heard the case. The jury decided in Allen's favor—justifiable homicide, essentially a verdict of not guilty. James Simms wrote to the National Freedmen's Relief Association that the local courts "Will Surely Justify Any White Man in Beating or Killing a Colored Man on a Trivial Offence . . . such is the state of Law and justice here."[104] Racial conflict also racked nearby Charleston in 1866.

During the summer, a black mob led by Scipio Fraser, a black, former Union soldier, attacked and killed a white man. Fraser bragged to anyone who would listen that he personally "killed the rebel son of a bitch and he is not the last I will kill." Violence continued for a week. A Boston visitor worried about the "growth of a bitter and hostile spirit between blacks and whites."[105]

Schools, Dredging, and Debt

By the late 1860s, real progress came in public schools for Savannah's children when the newly chartered Board of Education of the Savannah–Chatham County School System took control of the Massie School, and soon four county schools were brought under the auspices of the organization.

The first president of the Board of Education (BOE), the ubiquitous Dr. Richard Arnold, encountered daunting challenges as the tuition-free education system gained in popularity. Soon new constituent groups wanted to be brought under the public-school program, including African Americans. The AMA had provided education for black students since Reconstruction but could no longer keep up with the demand for classes and faced growing criticism over the quality and quantity of its offerings from the black community. After meetings and petitions by black adults seeking public education for their children, the BOE opened a school for African American children in the unused rectory of St. Stephen's Episcopal Church in December 1872. That same year, when black legislators in Georgia agreed to a separate-but-equal clause, the white, Democratic-controlled General Assembly quickly amended a bill on education providing separate systems that would be equal "as far as practicable."

Under a cooperative arrangement, the two free Catholic schools were brought under the BOE jurisdiction through an agreement between the BOE and the local Catholic bishop. The BOE paid faculty; the Catholic Church provided buildings and retained the right to offer religious education. Funding became so critical an issue that, when Chatham Academy became part of the system as a high school for white children, tuition was charged to defray costs.[106]

Other schools retained their private status, including the Savannah Hebrew Collegiate Institute, which had opened in the late 1860s. Led by Rabbi R. D. C. Lewin of Mickve Israel, and under the oversight of Octavus Cohen and the board president, Soloman Cohen, the institute followed the model of European-style high schools. The nondenominational institute quickly gained a reputation as the best academic institution in the city.[107]

In the years after the war, Savannah's economy appeared to be reviving. In 1866 the city's two major railroads, the CGR and the AGR, hauled to Savannah for export to the North nearly 257,000 bales of cotton, worth about $12 million, 30 percent more than the previous year. Such traffic tied the city to the hinterland and to a larger market economy. Imports also doubled, especially expensive coal and salt from Great Britain at $13 and $30 a ton respectively. Coasters drawing little draft brought in clothing, machinery, bricks, glass, and flour, sometimes meats and vegetables. Two pilot boats stood off the mouth of the river to help vessels avoid the navigational hazards that limited traffic. A local steamer was required to tow vessels up and down the river. There were few among the white civic-commercial elite who did not recognize that, to ensure the revival of Savannah's economy and to promote an image of growth, the navigability of the river must be assured. To accomplish this, it was imperative that the river be dredged and cleared of obstructions so that it could accommodate the largest draft vessels.

The river, known for its narrow channel, fast currents, silting, and sunken vessels, had been dredged, deepened, and cleared repeatedly since the 1750s. On occasion, the federal government had made generous appropriations for its maintenance. Now Savannah again asked Washington for funds. As the city in 1861 had supported the CSA in making war against the United States, it was not surprising that the federal government rejected the city's request. Savannah's City Council voted to buy dredging equipment and take on the job of keeping the river open to oceangoing traffic. In mid-1866, the city issued bonds to cover costs for a deeper and more navigable river. Boosters believed the expense was worth the price to insure commercial growth.

It seemed appropriate that the former naval officer, Mayor Anderson, should be given the authority to purchase the dredging equipment and to oversee the work. Anderson estimated that a dredge could be bought for $18,000 and optimistically predicted that the cost of the dredge would be minimal compared to the economic revival the city could expect when the port became accessible to larger vessels. Some predicted the port could become the "Great Atlantic Seaport." But the cost of the dredging exceeded the budget, and cost overruns of $40,000 may have dampened the enthusiasm of boosters. Eventually, deepening the channel and harbor did prove successful. Ships now drawing seventeen feet could enter and leave the city wharves. But it soon was clear that new business passing through the port came with significant costs. Within four years outlays for dredging equipment, contractor fees, and interest on loans topped $195,000.[108]

The city's indebtedness strained a city treasury already burdened by its financial obligations. Moreover, the costs were ongoing as the dredging had to continue at the city's expense since without it silting frequently caused ships to run aground. The *New York Times* reported that, while traffic moved up and down the river, at wharf side "accommodations are so poor as half the time the ships lie in the mud, and are barely floated at full tide."[109]

Voters returned Mayor Anderson and seven of his councilmen for a second term in the annual municipal election, October 1866. Five new council members joined the administration, including a former Confederate physician,

Dr. James Johnston Waring, a member of Savannah's civic-commercial elite. Among this class, he was one of only a few who befriended the freedpeople. Waring drew his main support from the city's white laboring classes, who earned meager wages and faced high rents and taxes. A member of one of the city's most prominent families, Waring attained his wealth from real estate investments. He rented property on Skidaway Island to blacks so they might learn "self-dependence"; an AMA teacher described him as "a firm friend of the colored people."[110]

Aaron Bradley, Reconstruction, and Violence

Disorder persisted as a rising chorus of discontent came from African Americans in the nearby countryside evicted or facing eviction from "promissory" title to lands originally granted them by the federal government. And as the year drew to a close, the U.S. Supreme Court invalidated the earlier conviction of Aaron Bradley in Savannah by declaring unconstitutional the military trials of civilians. In December 1866 Bradley reappeared in the city to the great chagrin of the city's leadership. About the time Bradley returned, black longshoremen walked off the job and, to make matters worse for the city's white leadership, an "insurrection" appeared to be brewing at Delta Plantation in South Carolina just across the river from Savannah.

Then in the midst of a slowly reviving economy in January 1867, three hundred black *and* white longshoremen walked off the job. A city-imposed $10 licensing fee unified the workers—blacks earned $1.25 to $1.50 daily, about half as much as whites. Both groups felt the license fee unfair. Many of the white dockworkers were Irish and most likely friends of the blacks—they fraternized and lived near each other. These unique circumstances brought them to strike together. Walkouts had occurred at other southern ports, but the Savannah dock strike was perhaps the first where blacks and whites joined in a common cause.

To break the walkout, local merchants and ship captains threatened to move cotton piling up on the quay from Savannah to Charleston for export. But the strikers stood firm for "their rights." Council member James Waring offered a plan to lower the licensing fee to $3; Council ratified it, but strikers refused the compromise and their sympathizers blocked access roads to the wharves. Mayor Anderson then sent in the police to end the strike, and a fight erupted. White strikers were neither beaten nor arrested, but blacks were. Nero Thomas, a black leader, cried out during the melee that he would rather die for the cause than surrender. Shot and wounded, the police arrested him along with eight others for disorderly conduct and possessing firearms; a judge sentenced the eight men to ninety days at hard labor and fined Thomas $100 and ordered him to jail for thirty days. About a year later, the white longshoremen, mainly Irish, formed a union of their own, the Workingmen's Benevolent Association of Savannah (WBA).[111] As for the black dockworkers, striking with their white friends was another effort by black men to stand up against overwhelming odds. Very likely they received encouragement from Aaron Bradley.

The most outspoken African American in the lowcountry, Bradley adopted various methods to prevent the subversion of the rights of the freedmen. In January 1867, he informed a Republican senator in Washington that General Tillson was evicting blacks from property granted under Sherman's Special Field Order No. 15 and permitting city officers to arrest and shackle blacks in ball and chain; he also applied for a license to practice law in Chatham County, where he could take his fight into the courts. But William Bennett Fleming, a member of Georgia's secession convention in 1861, now the presiding judge for the Eastern District of Georgia, turned down Bradley's request for a license, asserting that Georgia laws "do not authorize . . . the admission of persons of color to the Bar."[112]

Bradley persisted. In January, he crossed the Savannah River into South Carolina to advise the freedpeople of Delta Plantation. Here Freedmen's Bureau agents had ordered former slaves now working their own land to return it to the original planters and enter into contracts with them for employment. But the freedpeople resisted. They had planted crops, tilled the soil, paid taxes on the land, and they refused to give it up without a fight. Brandishing crude weapons, they faced down a Freedmen's Bureau officer, Captain Henry Brandt, and his small force. The freedmen informed Brandt that Bradley had told them that any effort made to seize their land should be resisted "at the point of the bayonet."

Rumors of an "insurrection" on Delta Plantation alarmed white Savannahians. Within days a larger military force sent from the city quelled any resistance. Some freedpeople signed labor contracts for subsistence wages to work the fields while others refused and moved on. But Bradley claimed one victory: his criticisms of General Tillson prompted Tillman's resignation from the Freedmen's Bureau. Meanwhile, the mother of Charles C. Jones Jr. relished defeat of the longshoremen's strike and the "insurrection" at Delta Plantation, which she viewed together as "a January revolution."[113]

Bradley continued his battle for the rights of those receiving "promissory" titles to land. No other black leader in Georgia or South Carolina developed a closer relationship with freedpeople who worked the rice fields than Bradley. No other person espoused their rights with greater "passion and militancy."[114]

In early 1867, a congressional Republican majority implemented their own policies for the reconstruction of the South. Angered by the violence against blacks in southern port cities, the leniency shown to rebels by President Andrew Johnson, and the failure of southern states to ratify the Fourteenth Amendment, Congress passed two major acts. First, with the exception of Tennessee, the southern states were required to hold elections in which blacks, former Confederate enlisted men, and their leaders not holding a federal post before 1861 would elect delegates to conventions to draft new state constitutions to give voting rights to all males and to ratify the Fourteenth Amendment, citizenship for African Americans, and equal protection under the laws. Second, the Military Reconstruction Act set up five districts, each with a military commander who would ensure implementation of the Congressional Reconstruction Acts. General John Pope assumed command of the Third Military District, embracing Alabama, Florida, and Georgia.[115]

The registration of blacks and whites took place in Georgia in April 1867; election of delegates to the federally mandated constitutional convention was scheduled for the fall. Aaron Bradley stood for election to the convention and spoke on street corners in Savannah and at mass meetings. He denounced Mayor Anderson for oppressing blacks and condemned "aristocratic mulattoes, bankers and millionaires" as part of the local power structure. He campaigned for the underdog, championing the cause of the lowcountry's African American rice workers and white and black longshoremen. This tactic split the newborn Republican Party and played into the hands of Mayor Anderson, who warned darkly of a growing "revolutionary" movement.

As the statewide elections of delegates to the constitutional convention approached in the fall, Savannah blacks registered to vote. The city's black male population, though numbering only slightly less than the white, registered in greater numbers, 3,091 to 2,240, and they turned out on the day of the election. A reporter for the *Savannah Republican* watched African American men "of every hue and shade . . . for the first time in the history of the state . . . exercising the greatest privilege of citizenship." The former slaves liked Bradley's style and confrontational politics, and he won election to the convention.[116]

The 169 delegates elected from across the state included Bradley and 36 other African Americans. They convened in Atlanta on December 9, 1867, and wrote a conservative document that met the demands of Congress. The delegates completed their work in early March 1868. Military officials directed that the state present the new constitution to the voters for their approval in April and at the same time hold elections for state officers and congressmen.[117]

Anger, enthusiasm, and fear coursed through Savannah as electioneering began by conservatives and the Chatham County Republican Party. Of course, Aaron Bradley ran for election—this time to the state senate. Whites called him, among other names, a "troublesome negro." Dr. Richard Arnold courted both blacks and whites to join a "Conservative Club." Curbside speeches in Savannah multiplied. An anti-Republican leaflet appeared, featuring crudely drawn daggers and a coffin circulated by a mysterious new organization which called itself the Savannah Group 90 of the Ku Klux Klan. Across Georgia between January 1 and November 15, 1868, there were 336 murders and assaults with the intent to kill against African Americans; 23 occurred in Savannah.

By way of response, the Republicans held a rally on April 6 in Chippewa Square, one of the largest multiracial political assemblies ever held in the city, 7,000 whites and blacks. Speakers like James Simms urged the crowd to work together for the success of the Republican Party in Georgia. Dr. James J. Waring explained to the large gathering that labor, long controlled by capital, was now free, and would bring "good results."

During the winter and spring, armed white policemen disrupted Republican political gatherings and randomly arrested blacks on charges of "vagrancy." Aaron Bradley responded by nailing up posters warning whites that anyone striking blows against blacks would be followed, and wherever they took shelter it would be "burned to the ground."[118]

On election day, April 20, 1868, great numbers of black men squeezed into the city's courthouse and stood in long lines waiting to vote. Fistfights erupted between whites and blacks. James Simms, editor of the *Freedmen's Standard,* reported that whites bent on intimidating Republican voters showed up at the polls with "bowie knives and revolvers." Nevertheless, the new voters carried the day by a bare majority in the city and county, with Republicans casting about 2,800 votes and Democrats with about 2,700 votes.

In Chatham County's Ogeechee District, eleven miles southwest of the city, black voters sent James Simms to Georgia's lower house and Aaron Bradley to the state senate. The balance of power in the legislature overwhelmingly favored whites, who outnumbered blacks 236 to 29. Statewide, voters narrowly approved the new constitution and elected Republican Rufus Bullock as governor. With the balance of power so skewed against them, black Republicans quickly became discouraged as they watched white Republicans in the legislature vote along racial rather than party lines. In Savannah, conservatives celebrated. They remained in firm control of the city government, and now they intended to exercise that control.

Mayor Anderson and the City Council named streets after local former Confederate supporters: Episcopal Bishop Stephen Elliott of Christ Church, Dr. James P. Screven, and railroad executive Richard R. Cuyler; the council ordered policemen to arrest black men and women on any flimsy pretext and hold them in the county jail for months without access to attorneys. The city diminished the role of the once-proud black fire companies by providing little or no public funding while purchasing a $4,800 steam fire engine for one company and providing other white units with $12,000 for maintenance and equipment. No invitation was extended to black firemen to join the white firefighters in a parade on May 1, 1868, though Mayor Anderson and his councilmen did march and afterwards raised toasts to white supremacy.[119]

Flush from their victory and trumpeting support for their candidates in the upcoming November elections, Democrats held a torchlight parade through the city. The next day, William Hopkins, twenty-two, son of Charles Hopkins, the white planter and Republican politician, entered a bar at the corner of Jefferson and Minis streets. He came face-to-face with Isaac Russell, twenty-three, a city deputy sheriff and son of a prominent Democrat, Judge William Russell. Hopkins moved toward young Russell, calling him "one of those G—d d—d . . . rebel sons of bitches" and attacked him with the butt of his pistol. Somehow, Russell managed to pull his own weapon and shoot Hopkins multiple times.

News of Hopkins's death rippled through Savannah; angry freedpeople rushed to the scene and carried the murdered man's body to his father's home. In the evening, frightened whites heard drums, which reminded them of rebellious slaves. Several thousand blacks carrying axes, clubs, and guns gathered outside Russell Sr.'s home. Some shouted, "Kill every Rebel that dares to shoot a Republican." But there was no violence, and the mob soon dispersed.

The noises, shouts, and sights of a black mob carrying fearsome weapons frightened the city's elite. Four black men were quickly arrested for participating in the "riot." Some days later, local authorities exonerated young Russell of wrongdoing. But prominent white citizens remained on edge by what they had perceived as a black mob on the verge of insurrection.[120]

The Georgia legislature ratified the Fourteenth Amendment in July (one of the last states to do so), guaranteeing African Americans citizenship and equal protection under the law. Then in early August, U.S. General Caleb Sibley officially ended federal military authority in Georgia and transferred power back to civilian authorities. This action, Savannah Republicans concluded, threatened their tenuous control over politics, and they introduced a bill in the legislature to extend for four miles in each direction Savannah's present corporate limits. This action would add a large population of blacks who could register as Savannah voters if the bill passed. Democrats in the legislature recognized this gerrymandering as a tactic for local Republicans to "perpetuate themselves in control," and they quickly killed the bill.[121] Next, the white, Democratic-controlled legislature focused its attention on the controversial, if not reviled, new senator from Savannah, Aaron Bradley.

Earlier in his career, Bradley had been convicted of the crime of female seduction in New York, and Democrats now used this to question his eligibility to serve. The legislature appointed a special committee to investigate the case, which became the focus of attention in the Senate during July and August. When it became clear that Bradley did not have the support even of the white Republicans, he chose to resign before officially being declared ineligible. Although he gave up his seat in the Georgia Senate, Bradley did not give up politics.

He was the first African American expelled from the legislature, but not the last. In September, white Republicans joined white Democrats in the legislature to expel the remaining black legislators. They based their action on the rationale that the new Georgia Constitution of 1868 gave blacks the right to vote, but did not explicitly give them the right to hold elective office. Subsequently, using the same reasoning, state lawmakers voted to exclude blacks from serving on juries. Anger flared in the black community, having been once more denied equal civil rights with whites.[122]

On presidential election day, November 3, 1868, about 1,000 black men waited patiently outside the courthouse while white authorities opened the city's lone polling place. Once the African Americans entered to vote, Democrat challengers met them and turned away every prospective black voter who had not paid the poll tax or other taxes, about 90 percent of the city's registered black voters.[123]

Denied the right to vote, outraged black men milled around the courthouse. Suddenly 50 white CGR employees arrived, saying they were permitted only a short time to vote; to make way for them, police shoved blacks aside and gunfire erupted. In the melee, 2 or 3 black men died, an estimated 17 were wounded, and 3 white policemen perished. A future mayor and city historian, Thomas Gamble, calling it "a riot," mentioned the deaths of police officers, but not those of the blacks killed and the many wounded. Though the number of blacks registered to vote in the city numbered 3,900, the Republican candidate, Ulysses S. Grant, received only 400 votes.[124]

That same day, Aaron Bradley, despite rumors that whites planned to kill him, appeared at a rally in the Ogeechee District southwest of Savannah. After his usual dramatic speech, he headed back to the city, escorted by the well-armed

Ogeechee Home Guard. Along the way, a white posse from Savannah confronted Bradley's group and demanded they disperse. Without warning, someone fired shots and both parties exchanged volleys. Twenty-four-year-old Samuel S. Law, son of Judge William Law, was killed. Savannah authorities charged Bradley with the murder and launched efforts to find him, but Bradley had vanished.

When his indictment for the murder of Law was quashed, Bradley returned to the city and stood for election to the U.S. Congress. In his usual flamboyant style, he campaigned on a large white horse, armed with his ever-present pistol and bowie knife. Of course, he failed to win office as the Democrats had successfully eliminated blacks from the city voting booth.[125]

Denied the right to participate in the political process and likely inspired by Bradley, blacks in Ogeechee District armed themselves and vowed to prevent anyone from taking away their land. Then in December, angry over contracts written by Freedmen's Bureau officials that gave the bulk of the harvested rice to white planters, freedmen ransacked several homes and seized and hid large quantities of the rice. A Savannah magistrate issued an arrest warrant for the perpetrators, but when a city sheriff and posse arrived to take away one of the leaders, Solomon Farley, the Ogeechee Home Guards arrived and disarmed the posse. The sheriff and his men had to walk part of the way back to Savannah. Apparently they spread frightening rumors that five hundred to eight hundred insurrectionists planned to march on the city, and the Savannah government readied cannon to use against them.

The freedmen in the Ogeechee Home Guards sent word that they wished to surrender, but only to U.S. military authorities. Union officers thought the situation overblown in the local press but nevertheless sent two companies of infantry to the Ogeechee District. Sixty-eight blacks were arrested and hustled back to Savannah and into confinement at Oglethorpe Barracks. Over the next few months the city spent thousands of dollars in lodging and trying the men. Six were convicted and sentenced to hard labor, and the state's Republican governor, Rufus Bullock, promptly pardoned them.[126]

After the so-called "Ogeechee Insurrection" and following persistent reports of violence against blacks and appeals by Georgia Republicans, Congress passed the Congressional Reorganization Act of 1869. The act called for the governor to reconvene the General Assembly in its original form as of 1868 and reseat African American legislators; Congress also required the legislators to ratify the Fifteenth Amendment as a condition for readmission to the Union. The Georgia legislature acted promptly and endorsed the measure, which prohibited anyone from being denied the right to vote because of "race, color, or previous condition of servitude." Congress acted quickly to readmit Georgia to the Union for the third and last time in July 1870.[127]

Republican control of the Georgia legislature was short-lived. Elections soon returned a Democratic majority; Governor Rufus Bullock left office and the state. In one of his last official acts, he appointed the black leader, James Simms, as district judge of the First Senatorial District sitting in Savannah. Bullock described Simms as "a colored man possessed of a fair education, excellent moral character . . . and natural ability" who brought "great credit to himself . . . and to his race." White lawyers of the Savannah bar harshly criticized the appointment and announced threateningly there were many "remedies" to terminate it.

Though the judgeship was a "first" for a black man in the state, rival black leaders also challenged the appointment. The new Democratic legislators took care of the matter; they simply moved the court out of the district. Afterwards, Simms was rewarded for his loyalty to the Republican Party and received a federal appointment as inspector at the U.S. Customs House in Savannah. He remained active as a senior statesmen in the city's African American community until his death at age eighty-nine in the early twentieth century.

Following Governor Bullock's resignation, the Democrats in the legislature called a special convention that chose one of their own, James M. Smith, as governor. With Smith sworn in, Democrats controlled the legislature, and Georgia was on a path to erase any "vestiges" of Republican influence.[128]

Democrats "Redeem" Savannah

By the time Savannah's municipal elections took place in the fall of 1869, local conservatives, now more frequently referring to themselves as Democrats, found new ways to suppress the black vote. In March, the City Council enacted a poll registration tax deemed legal by state law if revenue raised went to support the public schools; it disenfranchised most black and white laborers, who were unable to afford the tax. Next, the council devised a new plan that changed the tradition of at-large municipal elections. The City Council divided Savannah into four districts. Within each, conservative leaders gathered prior to local elections and nominated three candidates (twelve total) who would become the mayor's slate for election to City Council. Then seven representatives from each district would be selected (twenty-eight total) to choose the mayoral candidate. In municipal elections, voters would vote for the mayor and his slate or "ticket" of twelve. Authors of the new district system said it protected Savannah from "misrule and ruin." But, more important to the Democrats, it effectively disfranchised the city's black voters, nearly one-half of the city's electorate, and served as a model for the all-white primary in Savannah and the South until the mid-twentieth century.

In the first test of the new system, the Democrats nominated for mayor forty-two-year-old John Screven, a Confederate veteran, attorney, planter, and president of the AGR and a "ticket" of twelve businessmen and lawyers representing the city's civic-commercial elite. The *Savannah Morning News*, mouthpiece of the party, editorialized that "all were gentlemen of the highest social and commercial standing" who had the interest of "our people" at heart.[129]

Two "outside tickets" were put forward, the strongest headed by Republican Charles Hopkins and a slate of seven independent candidates. Hopkins's son, William, recently had been killed during a violent encounter in a Savannah barroom. The older Hopkins, who once owned a hundred slaves and *opposed* secession, was rather sui generis for the lowcountry. Like James J. Waring, he also became active in the Republican Party and befriended the freedmen when he rented his plantation, Belle Ville, in McIntosh County to a leader of the freedpeople, Tunis Campbell, whose yearly payments would be applied to the purchase price.

In the unlikely event that Hopkins's candidacy might be a threat to Screven, conservative leaders met with municipal authorities and agreed on tactics to insure their victory during the upcoming election. When the courthouse doors opened on October 11, 1869, black voters faced a daunting path to reach the ballot box. One hundred citizens had been deputized to assist the city police. A "challenging committee" of seventy-five men, including the jailer, Waring Russell; attorney George A. Mercer; and the mayor's son, Edward C. Anderson Jr., challenged potential black voters' eligibility on such grounds as residency requirements and paid poll-taxes. These tactics prevented many registered blacks from voting; intimidation discouraged others from exercising their franchise.

Screven and his ticket buried the opposition, winning 2,977 votes, with 967 votes cast for Hopkins and his slate. That evening the conservatives held a grand torchlight parade; Roman candles illuminated the night sky, and four marching bands accompanied the victors and city officials through the streets. They congratulated themselves for saving Savannah from the fate of other major southern cities like Savannah's "sister city," Charleston, where blacks were members of the City Council. Their celebration and self-congratulations proved prescient as no black would be elected to Savannah's City Council until the latter part of the twentieth century.

The political future must have seemed dim to the city's African Americans who were now deprived of the vote and legally prohibited from sitting on juries. They lived in a city where government was solely in the hands of a white mayor and council and where laws were enforced by an all-white police department—and it would remain so for the next seventy years. Another source of frustration was the federal government's seeming indifference to equal rights under the law for black citizens.[130]

Savannah's African American community, squeezed out of politics and harassed by city police, resisted white domination as best they could. Many found refuge in their own churches and in the more than one hundred political, social, and mutual-aid societies. Rather than trusting white bankers with their savings, black individuals and societies deposited their money at the local Freedmen's Savings and Trust Company that opened in a building on Bryan Street near Drayton. Their deposits served as a barometer of sorts for the African American community's economic progress. Between 1866 and the early 1870s, hundreds of black Savannahians deposited over $154,000 in the Savannah branch.[131] The deposits reflected the success and growing prosperity of Savannah's middle-class black artisans and businessmen.

The older prewar, property-owning black middle class was joined by a younger, upwardly mobile one, giving Savannah the largest black middle class in the state in 1870. By this time, sixty-six African Americans operated twenty-seven different types of businesses; ninety-six owned property. Forty-six families were said to be socially prominent leaders of the black community, noteworthy for their stability, literacy, and income; 90 percent of the women did not have to work, the young were at home, and the older children attended school or worked as apprentices. In Brownsville, a suburb of the city, African Americans owned almost all of the residences.[132]

Debt, Disorder, and Cleaning Up the City

When Mayor John Screven convened his councilmen for the first time in 1869, the city faced a huge and growing debt. Payments to the contractor of the dredging operations and interest payments on bonds siphoned off city revenues. Screven's administration, like the prior one, launched a campaign to ask Congress for funds for harbor improvements. Earlier harbor improvements had increased tonnage passing through the port from 820,991 tons in 1866 to over 1,000,000 tons in 1869. Efforts to find money to continue the dredging paid off three years later when the federal government appropriated $50,000. The amount disappointed city leaders, who had counted on twice that amount as the city was paying $20,972 annually just to fund the interest on public debt and some harbor improvements.

Between 1866 and 1870, the annual expenses of the municipal government rose 153 percent ($396,000 to more than $1,000,000) while revenue from taxes increased only 26 percent. The situation required the city to depend on additional bond issues and short-term loans to raise money for large undertakings and ongoing city expenses. But soon Screven became less concerned about the city's indebtedness and more concerned about improving the city's physical attractiveness and infrastructure, which he believed would woo investors and tourists. To accomplish this, he proposed costly, massive projects and asked the City Council for money and swift approval. Screven wanted a clean city, a new market, an adequate sewage and drainage system, repair of the wharves, paving of the streets, and improved municipal services.

Throughout the country, municipalities occasionally issued bonds for such projects and paid for them with tax revenue. Savannah hoped to do the same. Following the 1869 election, the Screven administration increased taxes and licenses for nearly everything and everybody. A license for a one-horse dray costs $16, a four-horse dray $60. To keep each of their dogs, owners paid a fee of $1.50; wholesale apothecary owners paid $50 to operate their business; "junk shop" owners paid $300, hucksters $10, and resident stevedores, $100. However, Savannah's population did not grow as it had in the 1850s, and despite the substantial rise in taxes and licensing fees, revenues actually declined. Nevertheless, the City Council gave Screven what he asked for. They approved, in early 1870, a $500,000 bond issue to fund Mayor Screven's beautification and infrastructure proposals.[133]

According to the U.S. Census of 1870, Savannah's population of 28,235 ranked it sixth among the South's ten largest cities. Here one might see not only grinding poverty but also dazzling displays of wealth. Those attending the wedding of Octavus Cohen's daughter, Fanny, who married her cousin, called it a "magnificent affair" where women wore the latest fashions and guests enjoyed a grand dinner with "every delicacy."

During the Christmas season, the affluent celebrated the consolidation of Democratic power in the city and state. They purchased gifts of toys and clothing imported from Europe; the ladies had their hair done at Madam L. Louis's salon in the latest and "highest style." On Christmas Day the churches were open, cotton brokers and bankers mingled in the streets, a brass band played. Others enjoyed sporting events, such as a "Yankee base-ball match," a pigeon-shooting contest, or a cockfight in Yamacraw.[134]

The well-to-do attended the Savannah Theatre to see one of the country's greatest, though aging, actors, Edwin Forest. Over a two-week period in November 1870, Forest played before capacity audiences in the role of Othello, Hamlet, and King Lear, which Col. J. H. Estill, owner of the *Morning News,* called a "masterpiece" performance. That same season, Edward C. Anderson, a past and future mayor of the city, confided to his diary that on one occasion the appearance of a "mulatto boy" in the dress circle of the theater "scandalized" Savannah's elite.

Likewise, white Charlestonians were angered by an antidiscrimination law passed by a legislature dominated by South Carolina Republicans that permitted African Americans unrestricted access to theaters, saloons and restaurants. It was an integrated audience that enjoyed opening night at the Academy of Music—the venue featuring a frescoed ceiling and red plush velvet seating for twelve hundred persons. The Charleston press effused over the play and remarked on the "large, enthusiastic and brilliant assemblage of ladies and gentlemen" attending. Of course, this new legislation now meant that members of the audience might suffer some embarrassment by the proximity of a former slave—or master.[135] But even during the theater seasons in the two cities, disorder and violence persisted.

In Savannah, Union soldiers and drunks sometimes assaulted people on the sidewalks; from time to time sailors and dockworkers had free-for-all brawls, attacking each other with knives. Poor white and black children picked pockets, and noisy accusations between husbands and wives occasionally spilled into the streets; inebriants passed out on sidewalks. Prostitutes carried on a lively business in the squares and in brothels on the east and west sides of the city.

Two brothels employed white and black women, ages sixteen to thirty-eight, from Georgia, New York, and Ireland. By 1870, 115 women worked as prostitutes, another 150 were "kept women," and city authorities knew the specific location of all the "Houses of Ill Fame." Prominent white men sometimes solicited prostitutes; indeed a rumor circulated in the early 1870s that the successor to Bishop Stephen Elliott of Christ Church, the mother church of Georgia's Episcopalians, resigned for "gross immoral conduct," likely with prostitutes. In sum, certain areas in Savannah did not give the impression that one was in a safe, refined, and orderly place.[136]

Considering the size of the police force, a future mayor and historian of the city, Thomas Gamble, wondered why the slums on the edges of the city received virtually no police protection when within these areas were "large numbers of worthless refugees and vagabonds, principally negroes without visible means of support and a terror to the more respectable white and colored neighbors." Retrenchment seemed the only alternative when the costs of maintaining the force increased and the city budget proved inadequate. The force reduced the number of police in 1871 and instituted pay cuts the following year.[137]

Appearances count and were certainly a priority for Mayor Screven. To make the city appear clean and healthy to visitors, not disorderly and odiferous,

Mayor Screven and his council passed laws warning people against throwing slops into the streets and regulated the storage of foul-smelling guano used in making fertilizer. To hide manacled prisoners from public view when moving them to or from their trials or punishments, the city government recommended demolishing the "dilapidated" integrated county jail on the edge of Forsyth Park. Apparently this was not a "county" priority as the county took no action even after a grand jury labeled the facility as shameful. By 1870–71, the jail, built to accommodate forty-eight prisoners, held on average eighty, including several "lunatics." The situation required the city jailer to crowd two or three prisoners at a time into the small cells, "giving them scarcely room to lie down." The city's jailer urged that a new jail be built as the present one was "wholly inadequate."

The mayor and council also wanted to remove from public view the "dying, the loathsome, and the unknown sick" found on the city's alleys and sidewalks. But when the Reverend Abraham Burke asked the city to join with local black charities in caring for infirm black men and women, Screven balked. He rejected the proposal because he thought the idea might lead to the establishment of a "home for the idle and malingering." But Screven enthusiastically endorsed the council's proposal that sought assistance from white philanthropists to create a shelter for the black ill and indigent. Apparently, Screven had Edward Padelford in mind, the wealthiest resident in antebellum Savannah and, like Waring and Hopkins, unique among the white lowcountry elite—his two sons died fighting for the CSA, which was especially tragic in that Padelford *opposed* secession. As Screven hoped, Padelford donated ten thousand dollars to build an infirmary for the city's African Americans. Over time, its directors received support from the city and the county.[138]

Mayor Screven and his council knew that Savannah's long history of disease and epidemics reflected badly on the city's population, reputation, and commerce. Previously, efforts to construct a drainage system for the city had been haphazard at best. Following the war, the city's Board of Health repeatedly warned that stagnant water bred "pestilence," and individual citizens petitioned for a drainage system.

The city let a contract for the sewer and drainage project and, by the spring of 1871, excavations were underway to drain all the "impure water" from the city through the West Broad Street line into the Savannah River below the waterworks. Problems plagued the project from the outset—including quicksand, logistics, and equipment failures—and sent costs soaring. Within the first six months, the project expended $500,000, the *entire* sum originally appropriated not only to fix the sewer and drainage problem, but also to construct a new market and improve the streets.[139]

The City Council also advertised for bids for a new market. The architects, encouraged by boosters to design a building matching their image of Savannah, came in with a plan for the market that featured an orchestra and concert hall, a gallery, and a price tag of $200,000. The council rejected the plan and demanded a radically redesigned building, eventually settling on a proposal with an estimated cost of $75,000. A wrecking crew demolished the old market on Ellis Square in late 1870. During construction of the new market, cost overruns, shoddy workmanship, and delays resulted in a final cost of $160,000, over twice the amount budgeted. Soon after its completion, the building needed major repairs.[140]

Clinging to the Old South

Mayor Screven ran and won a second term in 1870. In that same year, events in or near the city evoked life in the Old South rather than the New. Urged by his physicians to go south for his health, General Robert E. Lee arrived in Savannah on April 1. When he and his daughter stepped from the train, a large crowd cheered and the men waved their hats in the air. General Lee renewed friendships with former Confederate general Alexander R. Lawton and his wife and took lodgings with an English cotton broker, Andrew Low. Margaret Mackay Elliott visited with her "dear old friend" General Lee and marveled over him as "the highest type of manhood" and for "his nobility of soul." She was however disappointed that he did not remain until April 26, she wrote, "the day when the Confederate graves are dressed with flowers & when all Savh. turns out to do them honour." When Lee died six months later, the bells tolled in Savannah and the council chamber was draped in black. Despite the city's growing indebtedness, the Screven administration commissioned a "full-length portrait" of Lee by a Richmond artist for $391. It hung in council chambers for more than 130 years.[141]

In August 1870, two yachtsmen, Richardson F. Aiken of Darien and Ludlow Cohen of Charleston, were in Savannah with their racing sailboats. At the home of friends on the Vernon River and with the wind up, someone suggested that the two race. They agreed. Aiken won the race, but afterwards Cohen accused Aiken of cheating. As a point of honor Aiken challenged him to a duel and Cohen, a poor shot, accepted.

Four miles from the city, in a small cluster of trees on the Augusta Road as the sun came up on the morning of August 18, the two faced each other, holding smooth-bore dueling pistols. Their seconds looked on. Cohen and Aiken exchanged four shots, but drew no blood. With their pistols once more reloaded, they aimed and discharged their pistols. Cohen fell mortally wounded, a bullet penetrating his abdomen and slicing through his intestines. When the news reached the state's governor, he ordered the arrest of all parties "engaged in the affair of honor." The body of Cohen was returned to Charleston for burial. The grand jury never brought an indictment against Aiken, and he returned to his plantation near Darien.[142]

Ruinous Debt, Streetcars, and Equal Rights

As the 1871 budget year ended, the city was unable to meet its financial obligations. The indebtedness stood at $2,817,140, about one-half of the value of all the property owned by the city. The administration concluded that the only alternative to solving the problem was to issue more bonds, but before taking action they decided first to take the idea to the public.[143]

At the meeting, the property owners agreed to a bond issue to meet the city's "extraordinary demands," with the caveat that the bond or bonds be used solely to redeem the current "floating debt" for "harbor improvements, the drainage system, and the market" building. Acting on this advice, the city in January 1872 issued $500,000 in bonds. Yet, within a short time, the city again was in default.

Questions now arose over where the money raised went, why it disappeared so quickly, and who was paid what. Rumors circulated that Mayor Screven himself used the money to aid the ailing AGR, where he served as president. He may have. Evidence points in that direction. Curiously, about this time Screven brought in an old friend and confidant, the well-known attorney William Basinger, to handle litigation on another matter, the Brunswick and Albany Railroad.[144] Moreover, Screven, Basinger, and others had investments in the local horse-drawn streetcars in which the city had special interests, even control.

By the late 1860s, streetcars were running in many cities of the North and South, including Savannah's neighbors, Charleston and Augusta. In 1866, the Georgia legislature granted a charter to the Savannah, Skidaway and Seaboard Railroad (SSSR), founded by a small group of prominent Savannahians including James J. Waring, William Neyle Habersham, and Edward J. Purse. A city ordinance gave them the authority to lay tracks connecting Savannah's major thoroughfares. The line soon extended to resorts on the nearby rivers—the so-called "salts"—at White Bluff, the Isle of Hope, and Thunderbolt, where the SSSR also offered accommodations for vacationers. Here, boosters claimed, Savannahians and tourists alike might breathe the salt air and bathe in the salt water for their health. The cost of a ride to the "salts" was modest, 25 to 50 cents, and offered "luxuries" now "in the reach of everyone." The line also offered suburban junkets to Bonaventure Cemetery and the Bethesda orphanage.[145] The investors in the SSSR hoped to make money while the city government counted on the streetcars to raise much needed revenue. But controversy over the rights to ridership soon sparked open racial conflict.

In the late 1860s, African Americans in Charleston, inspired by their leaders, boarded and entered horse-drawn cars of the Charleston City Railway Company, which allowed black riders outside the cars but prohibited them inside. Twice they were physically removed by local police and federal troops before the company ended its whites-only policy. This successful effort for equal rights on Charleston's street railway likely encouraged Savannah's black leaders. In May 1870, following announcement of a policy by the SSSR that a car would run daily every forty-five minutes for the "Exclusive Convenience of the Colored People," black Savannahians challenged the new policy and a city ordinance mandating segregated seating.

On May 6, James Habersham, a black Chatham County constable who was highly regarded in the black community, boarded an SSSR car near the Exchange Building at the foot of Bull Street and took a seat by white passengers. The conductor immediately halted the streetcar and ordered Habersham off. He refused. Policemen soon arrived and carried him from the car. Two days later in the mayor's court, Mayor John Screven dismissed the case against Habersham, finding him an "ignorant . . . negro" who designing men encouraged to challenge local policies. Screven pointed out that Savannah blacks had equal accommodations under the law, but admonished Habersham and the blacks in the courtroom that "insolence and aggression [by blacks] in conflict with the white community will not be tolerated." In sum, whites believed that equality under the law for blacks brought social mixing, which to them was intolerable.[146] Two years later a similar, but bloodier, incident occurred as congressional Republicans in Washington debated civil rights legislation.

On a late and hot Saturday evening, July 27, 1872, a group of blacks, likely by design, entered cars reserved for whites by the SSSR at its Exchange Building stop. After the blacks rode south for several blocks to Liberty Street, three white men shoved them from the streetcar. Soon a large crowd of blacks surrounded the car to prevent its movement; when a black man grabbed the bridle of one of the horses hauling the rail car, a white man knocked him to the ground.

The following day, the city remained eerily quiet. Then around 6:00 P.M., Richard W. White, a light-skinned African American who attended Oberlin College, served with the Union Army, and held local office, boarded a car reserved for white women passengers. Whites quickly grabbed him and threw him off. Blacks began pelting streetcars with bottles, and white toughs beat any protestor they could find. Across the city more than one thousand blacks repeatedly entered the SSSR cars, only to be roughly removed. Then gunfire shattered the hot night air at Bull Street north of Anderson. Before the shooting stopped, three blacks lay dead and several wounded; bullets or shrapnel struck two white women and their children. A few days later, Avery Smith, an African American and federal customs employee, brought suit against three white men for violating his civil rights by forcing him from a streetcar. U.S. Commissioner Henry Wayne heard the case and ruled that Smith had violated streetcar regulations by entering a white car and thereby disturbing the peace. He exonerated the white men, decided the SSSR could segregate the races, but also ruled that the SSSR needed to supply more cars for blacks. Blacks boycotted the streetcars for two months and asserted their right to integrated seating.[147] Coincidentally, about this time, Savannah's antebellum white militias began reorganizing with their original names.

William Basinger, the close friend of Mayor Screven, in April 1872 was commissioned a major in the revived Savannah Volunteer Guards. The unit occasionally paraded with other reconstituted white militias like the Georgia Hussars, Irish Jasper Greens, Oglethorpe Light Infantry, and the Savannah Sabre Club. As in the years before the war, these militias served as social organizations, supporters of law and order, agents of intimidation, and on parade, exemplars of southern white masculinity.

Around the same time and for some of the same and other reasons, Savannah's black men organized militia companies. They were encouraged by the African Americans on the sea islands who had sought to protect their "possessory title" to lands by forming militias. Now Savannah's blacks wanted the same respect that the white militias enjoyed and recognition of their new citizenship and civil equality with white men. In 1872, they formed two militia companies, the Forest City Light Infantry and the Union Lincoln Guards.

The black militias made the city's leading white citizens uneasy, if not tense. Criticism came quickly. The Union Lincoln Guards were accused of siding with blacks during the streetcar sit-ins and violence during the streetcar "riots." Captain Richard D. Goodman, leader of the Lincoln Guards, in a letter to the governor of Georgia vigorously denied the charges. But this did not stop the local criticism. After the Lincoln Guards paraded through the streets in August, the *Morning News* charged that Captain Goodman of the "Linkums" hailed from New York, an outsider, and his leadership of the "colored militias" could be disruptive. At the time, however, no attempts were made to disband Savannah's newly formed black militias.[148]

As the fall state and presidential elections of 1872 approached, Democrats in Savannah and at the state level continued to employ laws to keep black voters from the polls. The *Morning News* reminded its readers that the election was "a contest between whites and blacks for supremacy. It is white civilization against anarchy. For a man to proclaim himself a [Republican] . . . is . . . a disgraced man."[149]

Such intimidation, of course, did not deter Aaron Bradley. He repeatedly denounced police abuse publicly and advised blacks to go to the polls with hatchets, which he believed were more effective than pistols in hand-to-hand combat. By now local whites referred to Bradley as "the great wahoo of the Ogeechee"; they reserved even more demeaning terms for ordinary black men like "bullet headed" or "ebony bipeds." During the election, the revived white militias, the Georgia Hussars and the Savannah Sabre Club, patrolled the streets on horseback while city police surrounded the courthouse, the city's sole polling station. When a black man, John Bryant, called the election a fraud, the police clubbed and arrested him for inciting a riot.

The white establishment used the same tactics in the November presidential election. There was one major change: the federal troops that now backed up the city police around the city polling place were led by an officer in Union blue alongside policemen wearing Confederate gray. The symbolism of blue and gray joining in the same cause, keeping blacks from the polling place, angered African Americans. Throughout the day, guns were fired. Bradley called the election process fraudulent, insulting to the rights of all, and urged his followers to take revenge and "*burn the city of Savannah.*" The entire state elected only three Republicans to Congress, the last Republicans elected for more than a century.

As for Bradley, over the next several years he gave occasional speeches in Savannah, and the *Morning News* noted that "the old negro Wahoo" was again speechifying in "favor of Democracy." Eventually, Bradley left for St. Louis, where he practiced law for a few years until one day he suddenly collapsed on the street and died, as one historian wryly noted, "remarkably of natural causes." By this time, the Republican Party of Georgia, divided, discredited, and deserted by blacks and most whites, retained little political power anywhere in Georgia.[150] Of Aaron A. Bradley, one historian wrote that no leader played "a more instrumental role" of inspiring lowcountry blacks to challenge the status quo than Bradley and that his influence persisted.[151]

As in Savannah, the Democratic Party controlled politics in both Atlanta and Nashville. Freedmen had surged into Atlanta after the war and, by supporting the local Republican Party, they threatened Democratic hegemony. However, a Democratic-controlled Georgia legislature allowed citywide elections, thereby diluting Republican voting strength, and conservative Democrats quickly took control of the city.

Many of these "sons of the South" engineered the move of the state capital from Milledgeville to Atlanta, which in itself launched a building boom. Atlanta's new leaders courted northern investors for assistance in rebuilding the city's commence and infrastructure. Northerner Hannibal I. Kimball built an opera house and a lavish, six-story hotel, the most renowned in the South, and named it for himself, Kimball House.

By the late 1860s, the central business district was rebuilt and Atlanta's mayor publicly celebrated its rebirth: "Atlanta fresh from her smoldering ruins of the past is again on the way to prosperity." Visitors in the early 1870s remarked on the new buildings and new money flowing into the city. Later in the decade, Atlanta's leaders hosted a cordial reception for none other than a figure reviled by Georgians into the twentieth century, General William Tecumseh Sherman.[152]

Like Atlanta, Nashville did not experience the grinding effects of racial political battles and a drawn out period of Reconstruction which left scars, bitterness, and even lethargy in other southern cities. The foundations of growth for both Atlanta and Nashville were finance, commerce, and manufacturing. Railroads transformed both cities into the major trading centers of the so-called "New South." Local capitalists and entrepreneurs took the initial steps in building each city's rail network, but within a decade, the rail lines were swallowed up by large railroad corporations with headquarters elsewhere.

Nevertheless, both Nashville and Atlanta continued as regional shipping centers. Wholesale merchants built warehouses and sent out armies of traveling sales agents to drum up buyers deep in rural areas west to the Mississippi and south to Key West. Within a few years the warehouses of the two cities bulged with food products, clothing, Coca-Cola, whiskey, tobacco, and furniture to satisfy the consumer needs of the growing southern market.[153]

The railroads out of Atlanta and Nashville and the wholesale merchants and their drummers spawned a new and unique business enterprise, the southern country store. The owner, usually a crossroads merchant-planter or local banker, or sometimes an undertaker, stocked his store with everything from cologne to farm implements and traded them for cotton, the coin of the realm.

The country-store owner then used the same new railroads that supplied his store to send his cotton or marketable products back to the big cities to be sold. These transactions completely bypassed the southern port cities.

The emergence of the Nashville and Atlanta railroad networks, the political atmosphere, a sizeable debt, a general malaise, and other factors led to the downward economic spiral of New Orleans, Mobile, Charleston, and Savannah. The new marketing systems and a devastating hurricane, epidemics of yellow fever, and a broken financial structure brought rapid decline to New Orleans. Its commercial activity atrophied, and the population dwindled.[154]

Mobile, the last major Confederate city to fall, on April 9, 1865, the same day General Lee surrendered at Appomattox, had gone unscathed during the war, but soon after its occupation, explosions and fires razed twenty blocks of the business district, killing two hundred to three hundred people. Northern journalist Whitelaw Reid, who watched a parade by the Union occupiers, described Mobilians as "seething with anger," withdrawn and sullen, "exhausted of force and energy." Nevertheless, Reid predicted that "New Men" would soon rebuild the city. Yet four years later, a Britisher described Mobile as "one of the . . . dirtiest . . . most depressed towns I had ever seen. The stores were mean, and the streets ill-lighted and filthily dirty."[155]

Unlike Atlanta, Nashville, or Savannah, Mobile experienced a long and traumatic Reconstruction. Mobilians were shocked by the great numbers of freedpeople who moved into the city. The black population soon climbed to 43 percent and provided a solid political base for the nascent Republican Party. As the Alabama state legislature moved closer to enfranchising the freedmen, racial tensions exploded. In May 1867, during a Republican rally of four thousand persons, shots were fired and a riot erupted, leaving one white and one black dead and twenty persons injured. Union officers imposed martial law, disbanded the City Council, and appointed Republicans to local offices. The new mayor gave several blacks city jobs and replaced white police officers with blacks, a move that outraged and humiliated white residents. The city remained under Republican influence through the 1870s. City indebtedness climbed, property values fell, and many Mobilians refused to pay their taxes. By the mid-1870s, the city government was headed toward bankruptcy.[156]

Charleston, Mobile, Savannah, and Norfolk as well as other southern urban centers all had to adjust to the vast numbers of ex-slaves who rushed into the cities after the war. White urbanites were generally unreceptive and unsympathetic to the new residents. In Charleston, former slaves occupied shanties along the waterfronts or squatted in the deserted mansions of the civic-commercial elite. Within a few years, the number of blacks in Charleston exceeded the number of whites. The sight of armed black soldiers angered and frightened white citizens.[157] Blacks strolling on the Battery, a place reserved for whites before the war, became a "nauseating sight" to one white resident. A well-to-do woman complained that "one cannot go out without having . . . 'Hang Jeff Davis on the sour apple tree'. . . shouted in your face."[158]

When riots erupted between black soldiers and angry whites in Charleston, Union officers seized the weapons of the African American troops and sent in white troops with clubs to keep order among them. White Charlestonians tried to defend white supremacy, but it was a campaign they initially lost. After passage of the South Carolina Constitution in 1868, which enfranchised black males, a Republican Party of white and black politicians controlled city government for most of the 1870s. White Charlestonians likened the proceedings of the City Council to scenes "which would have disgraced a brothel."[159] The city's debt soared, credit became difficult to obtain, property values plunged, and city services floundered. Commercial life slowed. Charleston's harbor remained for some years choked by wreckage. When South Carolinians sought funds to help clear the debris, they were refused. Northerners viewed South Carolina as the "Hell Hole of Secession."[160]

The Savannah and Charleston Railroad (CSR), destroyed by Union forces during the war, took five years to rebuild. During the antebellum years, it hauled vast amounts of rice and cotton into the city, which fueled Charleston's economy. But there was little cotton to be sold, and the railroad fell into receivership, as did the South Carolina Railroad, which had been reduced to ruins by General Sherman's army. The new railroads running out from Atlanta and Nashville siphoned business away from the merchants of the older Atlantic port cities. Furthermore, discriminatory rail rates came to favor New England and New York over Savannah and Charleston: a bale of cotton shipped from Alabama to New England or New York cost four dollars; if shipped from Savannah or Charleston and then north, the rate was five dollars.

As Charleston's economy deteriorated, fewer and fewer opportunities presented themselves for Charleston's young men. The city sent some fifty-five hundred into the war; of these nearly 30 percent were killed or maimed. When survivors found better prospects in urban centers elsewhere, they relocated. "Their departure drained the city of much of its vitality.[161]

A malaise settled over Charleston. It lacked the energy and optimism of an Atlanta or a Nashville. Seven years after Union troops marched in, much of the city remained in ruins. In 1872, a visitor described the one-time Capital of the Plantations as a center of "idle ragged negroes . . . of laborers . . . of widows and children of planters" living "in hopeless and unspeakable penury . . . of young men loafing in the saloons . . . and of utterly worthless and accursed political adventurers from the North . . . fattening on the humiliation of the South."[162]

As 1872 moved to a close, Savannah's economy reflected that of Mobile and Charleston more than Atlanta's or Nashville's. The city's debt rose to its highest levels ever. Many Savannahians thought Mayor Screven's administration incapable of dealing with its indebtedness and amended the city's charter to require the City Council to seek the advice of citizens before authorizing any future bond issues. Upon the council's request, the legislature increased the mayor's term from one to two years and moved municipal elections from October to January. The latter action may have been purely political in that it allowed the Irish migrants, who returned to Savannah every January for seasonal work, to vote. And they always supported the Democratic Party ticket.[163] Within a year, a severe nationwide financial panic, then depression and a yellow fever epidemic, swept the city, bringing economic paralysis and death along with a compounding of the city's debt crisis.

CHAPTER TWO

Depression, Neo-Confederates, Fevers, Society, and Labor

1873–1891

In January 1873, the city's Democratic Executive Committee selected a mayoral candidate "of known ability and independence," Edward C. Anderson, and together they agreed on a slate of twelve "easy to manage" council candidates to run with him. Anderson and his ticket won the election and assumed leadership of a city government mired in debt. The new governing team looked much like the former one, a civic-commercial elite of merchant-planters and ex-Confederates, which assured continuation of the status quo.

Politics and Depression

Initially, the new administration took little action to ameliorate the indebtedness. But late that year bank failures in the North and a sharp plunge on Wall Street precipitated a financial panic in much of the country. Thousands of businesses closed, leaving employees unable to pay their mortgages or rents. Evicted from their dwellings, they roamed the streets, looking for food. When the railroads and the textile mills cut wages, workers went on strike and violence flared in the Northeast.[1]

The *Morning News* assured local citizens that the economic unraveling in the North would remain there; however, the financial downdraft slipped into a prolonged depression and soon reached into the South. Railroads hauled less, some lines declared bankruptcy, and in Savannah white managers along with black and white laborers—who loaded cotton onto ships at dockside—lost their jobs. Georgia companies closed their doors. Banks stopped lending. In Savannah several financial institutions issued checks to depositors who wished to withdraw their money. Then with little warning, the local branch of the Freedmen's Savings and Trust Company (Freedmen's Bank) failed.[2]

Collapse of the Freedmen's Savings and Trust Company

Word reached Savannah on July 3, 1874, that the parent company of the Freedmen's Bank in Washington, D.C., had closed its doors, its capital plunging from $3,000,000 to $30,000. In the speculative fever of the times, officers of the bank had made unsecured loans to white-owned companies that failed and were unable to repay their debts. Curiously, the editors of the *Morning News,* rarely concerned about the manifold dilemmas facing Savannah's black citizens, found it "pathetic . . . that the modest earnings of years of patient toil" accumulated by "Negroes . . . should . . . suddenly and hopelessly be swept into the pockets of knaves who profess to be their friends." When blacks rushed to take their money out of the local bank, they were told that "no drafts or checks could be paid for the present." The *Morning News* reported that depositors had been at the very least "swindled out of $35,000" by the local Freedmen's Bank, and this caused "quite a stir among the colored folks and no little anxiety."[3]

The city's most vulnerable were distraught. Deposits of $800 to erect a new black church were gone; a skilled, black artisan with more than $1,000 in the bank became "demented" over the loss of "savings from years" of work. The white cashier of the bank, I. M. Brinckerhoff, repeatedly made announcements that the funds of depositors were safe, but no money was available for anxious customers. Now black Savannahians took matters into their own hands. Their leaders, James M. Simms, the Reverend Henry M. Turner, and Louis B. Toomer, called for a mass meeting in July at St. Phillip's Church on New Street. Here the Reverend Turner was elected to travel to Washington "in the interest of his race and ascertain what was the prospect of the Bank paying the depositors." Once in Washington, despite assurances that the bank's customers would be reimbursed ninety-five cents on the dollar, Turner was not "convinced that it will be done."[4]

Commissioners of the Freedmen's Bank in Washington as well as local officials continued to assure depositors that all was well. But in late September, the same commissioners issued an order closing all bank branches in the South. Anger exploded in Savannah's black community. In a letter to the *Morning News,* Butler Jones, "colored," wrote that he had "waited in vain" for a report from the commissioners of the Freedmen's Bank; if ever issued, he believed, it would show that while "poor men have become victimized . . . [others] have become fat by crime and false representations."

Deposits by thousands of local blacks in the Savannah branch of the Freedman's Bank had vanished. At one time these deposits reached $153,000. The *Morning News* waxed sympathetic, its editors asserting that the Freedmen's Bank was created purely for "robbery"; now the "swindle was complete" and will ever be known "as one of the most outrageous swindles ever perpetrated . . . upon a too confiding people."[5] Local boosters likely were more concerned about the effects of the lost capital on Savannah's struggling economy than the personal losses in the African American community.

The city's black artisans, businessmen, and proprietors of lunch counters, saloons, groceries, and barbershops sustained the heaviest losses when the Freedmen's Bank collapsed. Among them were members of the 84 well-to-do African American families. These families enjoyed financial assets, stability, good housing, literacy, and an active social life. Their numbers increased throughout the 1870s, rising to 648 families by decade's end. However, though the acreage they owned doubled, their per capita wealth declined due in part to the fall in property values generally throughout Savannah and money lost in the collapse of the Freedmen's Bank.

One cause of the dramatic increase in Savannah's black population (now 15,654) was the in-migration of ex-slaves from the countryside to the city after the Civil War. The same phenomenon occurred in Charleston, Memphis, and Atlanta. In the 1870s the number of blacks rose 20 percent and made up 51 percent of Savannah's population. Most were poor, illiterate, unskilled, and without jobs or job prospects. They moved into hovels on the peripheries of the city. The chief of police, Robert H. Anderson, a Savannah native and former Confederate cavalry general, kept a wary eye on them. He, like another Savannahian and former Confederate general, Alexander R. Lawton, wanted to insure that a government of law and order remained "in the hands of those who represent the native virtue and intelligence of the people."[6]

With this view prevailing, it was not surprising that, as the black population climbed, the number of blacks incarcerated did too. Although the population was almost evenly divided between whites and blacks by the mid-1870s, Chief Anderson annually reported more arrests of the latter. In 1873–74 there were 1,828 "Whites" arrested compared to 2,254 "Colored" (a 23 percent difference). Inexorably, the caste line tightened in Savannah and across the South.

Yet the pattern of integrated housing in antebellum Savannah continued for a while. In 1860, slaves lived in small quarters on the property or the ground-floor level of their master's home. Now in the postbellum years, it served the former owners' interest for ex-slaves to continue to work and live on the same property. Unlike Atlanta, where blacks were rigidly segregated immediately after the war, Savannah's housing pattern resembled that of New Orleans, where antebellum integrated housing persisted. But as concentrations of poorer blacks, many from rural areas, moved into settlements that resembled ghettos on Savannah's east and west sides, segregation became the norm. When the all-black Braham Musical Club performed at the Savannah Theatre in early 1876, the manager forced blacks to sit in the balcony because whites refused to sit with people of color. As there were no all-black theaters, African Americans became relegated to balcony seats, soon dubbed "the peanut gallery."[7]

Some African Americans in Savannah pushed back against the growing segregation of white and black in the city. They were especially encouraged by passage of the federal Civil Rights Act of 1875, specifying equal rights in public places. But the reaction of white southerners and white Savannahians was markedly different—they viewed the law as a threat to white supremacy. The *Morning News,* in a reprint from the *Eufaula Times,* condemned the federal act as one promoting "social equality . . . amalgamation and miscegenation."[8]

In 1875 Mary Telfair died. Savannah's wealthiest woman gave her vast fortune to friends and charities and left her mansion and its furnishing on St. James Square (renamed Telfair Square) for use as a public museum. It became the Telfair Academy of Arts and Sciences, the first such institution in the South. Mary's wealth came from her family's slave-trading and the production of vast rice fields worked by hundreds of slaves whom Mary characterized as "the sloth of the sable" population of the South. And she had no kind words for abolitionists. Upon reading William Ellery Channing's antislavery tract, she called it "as feeble as his own little body." Ironically, soon after Mary died, John H. Deveaux, a young man of mixed race, gave Savannah's ex-slaves a newspaper of their own.[9]

Deveaux's ancestors emigrated from Santo Domingo in the late 1700s. His grandfather served as pastor of the Second Baptist Church, and his maternal grandmother, Catherine, an immigrant from Antigua, and her daughter Jane, Deveaux's mother, conducted at their peril a clandestine school for African Americans in antebellum Savannah. Jane and Deveaux's father, a skilled artisan, were both free. In his early thirties, John Deveaux, with two light-skinned partners, Louis M. Pleasant and Louis B. Toomer, founded the *Savannah Colored Tribune.* All three were educated, active leaders in the local Republican Party and held political appointments in Savannah's federal post office or the customs house. They replaced the former, more aggressive leadership of men like Tunis G. Campbell, James Simms, and Aaron Bradley with a more nuanced style. Rather than staging street-corner rallies against the Democrats, they intended to use their four-page paper to promote equal rights under the law. In the first issue, Deveaux wrote: "The Character of the *TRIBUNE* will be the defense of the rights of the colored people, and their elevation to the highest plane of citizenship. . . . [A]ll other considerations shall be secondary."

Known for his tact, Louis Pleasant, a political manipulator and self-promoter like Deveaux, often spoke for the well-to-do Republicans, black and white. When factionalism threatened to divide Republicans, white Republicans maneuvered Pleasant's appointment as collector of internal revenue for Savannah and thereby retained the loyalty of Georgia's African Americans. Active in state and national politics, Pleasant became the most influential black Republican in Georgia; he was in fact called "Mr. Negro Republican." As the appointed collector of internal revenue, his salary would have been about $3,000 annually, approximately the same as that of the "appointed" head of the Postal Office at Savannah. Comparatively these were well-paying appointments—black deputy collectors or workers in more menial federal jobs had salaries that ranged from $150 to $400 yearly. Appointments as a U.S. federal marshal were reserved only for white Republicans; these positions paid $6,000 annually.[10]

Louis Toomer served as a Republican appointee in the Savannah Post Office for years. His integrity, fairness, attention to duty, and genuine concern for the welfare of African Americans won him wide respect from both Republicans and Democrats. When he ran for the post of magistrate in 1876, he had the endorsement of a black dockworkers' association which eventually became incorporated as the Workingmen's Union Association (WUA). Toomer won, unlike many other blacks who ran for local office. As the *Morning News* provocatively reported, Republicans might vote, but Democrats counted the ballots and decided which ones to accept.

Deveaux, Pleasant, and Toomer as owners of the *Colored Tribune* faced an uphill battle for equal rights. They founded a paper at a time when Democrats controlled elections locally and across the state, when Savannah's government forbade "dogs and negroes" to enter Forsyth Park, when blacks were relegated to the balcony of the local theater and were expected to walk on the east side of Bull Street while whites walked on the west. It was an era when the city court used separate Bibles to swear in black and white witnesses, a practice soon adopted by courts in Atlanta and other southern cities. Within a few years, the Georgia legislature even mandated the segregation of chain gangs.

During the first year of the *Colored Tribune's* circulation, Tunis G. Campbell returned to Savannah. A former black Union soldier, he had been appointed as an agent of the Freedmen's Bureau; he also organized and had led a militia to prevent whites from seizing land granted African Americans on Skidaway Island. Dismissed from the bureau for trying to prevent former white landowners from reclaiming property that had been promised to the ex-slaves, Campbell relocated to nearby McIntosh County, invested in land, and became a local magistrate. But when he arrested two white men and defended equal rights for African Americans, Campbell himself was incarcerated.

On January 12, 1876, blacks and whites watched Campbell, humiliated, marched through the streets of Savannah at age sixty-three, manacled in chains.

Taken to a plantation in middle Georgia, he had to work at hard labor and "keep up or die." After a year he was released and moved to Washington, D.C., where he referred to Georgia as "the Empire of Rascality" and urged people to assist Georgia blacks.[11]

African American editors, sometimes regarded as agitators, occasionally had to flee southern towns just a step ahead of lynch mobs. John Deveaux's editorials championed equal rights and challenged Savannah's segregation laws. The paper did not mince words when it chided the state legislature for passing a law that opened voter registration books only three months of the year—the same months farmers were planting their crops. Deveaux chastised blacks for failing to register to vote: "It is our own fault, and the remedy lies in our own hands." Deveaux's strategy of agitation and accommodation, of chiding the dominant white class and admonishing blacks to do better, probably lessened criticism of his paper. Yet his editorials hammered home the theme that African Americans must stand up for their rights, "be courageous, accumulate wealth and education . . . and learn to labor with perseverance, and wait with patience."

Very likely there was occasional collusion between Deveaux and other African Americans on the best ways to test the limits of the new Civil Rights Act of 1875. When a sign went up in the Savannah Court House over a water cooler, reading, "Exclusively for white people," blacks successfully demanded that it be removed and Deveaux publicized the incident.[12]

Indeed it was John H. Deveaux and other black activists and intellectuals like Garrison Frazier, Aaron Bradley, James M. Simms, Tunis Campbell, Emanuel K. Love, and Richard Wright who through their actions, petitions, speeches, sermons, essays, and literary works paved the way for twentieth-century leaders like Sol C. Johnson, J. C. Lindsey, W. G. Alexander, Mary L. Ayers, Rebecca Stiles Taylor, Ralph Mark Gilbert, and W. W. Law.[13]

Deveaux may also have encouraged Emil Pollard, "a Negro," to test the recent Civil Rights Act in Savannah. In early August 1875, Pollard, a Republican and an employee of the Savannah Post Office, and his wife boarded in downtown Savannah a streetcar of the Savannah, Skidaway and Seaboard Rail Road Company. The Pollards were no sooner seated than two white conductors, George Willett and George Alley, asked them to move to another car. Initially, they refused to leave, but then did so. Upon departing, Pollard told the conductors: "they would hear from him." Several days later, a U.S. deputy marshal served the conductors warrants charging them with violating the rights of the Pollards under the 1875 Civil Rights Act. On August 10, all parties appeared in court with their attorneys before the U.S. commissioner, A. N. Wilson, to present their case.

The *Morning News* predicted Wilson "will dismiss the case." But when court resumed on August 13, Colonel James Atkins, an attorney and collector of customs, spoke on behalf of the Pollards. The editors of the *Morning News* denigrated Atkins, saying he "made statements of an incongruous character." Five days later, Commissioner Wilson ruled that the conductors of the streetcar were "guilty of violating" the Pollards' civil rights and set bail at one thousand dollars. The defendants were to answer the charges at the fall term of the U.S. Circuit Court where, on November 15, a grand jury returned a "true bill" against the two conductors on the charge of violating the Civil Rights Act. But this was not the end of the matter.

Years passed. Justice moved slowly. As the federal government began drawing down all troops from the South, hostility toward blacks escalated, as did opposition to the Civil Rights Act. Five years after the Pollards brought their case, it again came before the U.S. Circuit Court. However, this time a former Confederate captain, George A. Mercer, acted as attorney for the defendants in the case of the United States vs. George W. Alley and George M. Willett. Mercer asked that the indictment be quashed, and the Hon. John Erskine demurred, ruling the indictment insufficient in law and the case closed.[14]

Even with escalating violence and widespread segregation, there was some fraternization among blacks and whites in Savannah. The interracial brothels that flourished in antebellum Savannah, Charleston, and other southern cities continued in the New South. In both Savannah and Charleston, interracial couples cohabitated and occasionally took marriage vows, though some in the white community viewed such sexual intimacy with disgust. And of course when it served their interests there was political fraternizing—Savannah's white politicians courted prominent blacks and one way or another won their support.

During the decade of the 1870s, more than four thousand African Americans living in Chatham County paid their poll taxes annually and were eligible to vote. They formed a large voting bloc. Long before the campaign began for election to the Georgia state legislature in October 1875, Lemuel Wade and Crawford Jones were "employed by" the brothers John and Peter Reilly "to solicit votes among their friends the Colored People . . . and use their influence in behalf of" Colonel Peter Reilly and Captain William W. Gordon. This they were able to accomplish because Wade, a highly regarded African American, served as president of the WUA and obviously exerted great influence among the city's black dockworkers.[15]

It now became commonplace for white politicians in Savannah, in Georgia, and throughout the South to offer bribes to blacks or to threaten them with the loss of jobs if they failed to vote the Democratic Party ticket. Henry W. Grady, the so-called "prophet of the New South," promoted the use of northern capital for the development of southern resources, and his ideas held great sway among white southerners. Grady occasionally spoke on politics and the "Negro." He argued that whites were superior to blacks and that white domination must endure forever as "self-preservation is the first law of nature." Besides economic coercion, bribes, and election frauds, physical brutality was another way to maintain white supremacy.[16]

Another Term for Anderson?

By the end of Mayor Edward C. Anderson's third term, indebtedness still threatened the city's solvency. Concerned over the administration's failure to reduce Savannah's debt, members of the city's Democratic Executive Committee and a group calling themselves the "Young Democracy" refused to support Anderson for another term. Rather they supported a popular Georgia state senator, Rufus Lester, to run for mayor. Another Anderson enemy, Dr. James J. Waring, also entered the race. Waring, one of the wealthiest men in the city, a friend of Savannah's black community, and one of only a few white Republicans, did not win. When ballots were counted, Anderson narrowly beat Lester by 214 votes. Waring polled just 31.

When Anderson took office for a fourth term in 1875, merchants, professionals, and laborers watched commerce continue to fall. The administration made the situation worse when it raised taxes in an attempt to reduce the city's burdensome debts. With the new increase, taxes paid by well-to-do Savannahians to the state, county, and city of Savannah reached an all-time high and sparked a taxpayer revolt. It began with the draymen.

Because these black drivers earned money only during the seven months when they hauled cotton and other products from the CGR yards to the wharves for export, they petitioned the city to pay taxes quarterly. The City Council denied their request, demanded immediate payment, and called out the police. The draymen had no alternative but to pay the tax. After attorneys won a temporary injunction from what they considered to be discriminatory fee increases by the city, other groups followed suit. Encouraged by the lawyers' success, property owners, artisans, and merchants took similar legal action; a number of citizens simply refused to pay their taxes, claiming them to be "illegal."

Revenues decreased, indebtedness increased, population growth slowed, and unemployment climbed. With fewer taxes coming in, city government had to make deep budget cuts. The police, one of Mayor Anderson's favorite departments, reduced salaries and slashed the staffing "from 112 to 68" officers. The City Council's austerity measures saved only $200,000, not even enough to pay the interest on the debt. The council now considered issuing more bonds—a plan than brought increased criticism from the well-to-do.[17]

Memorializing the Confederate Dead

Even in the grip of an economic depression, white southerners found the time, energy, and money to celebrate what they called "the Lost Cause." The movement mythologized the Old South by romanticizing the kindness of plantation masters and mistresses, the loyalty of slaves, the righteousness of the South's cause in the Civil War, the heroism of Confederate soldiers, and the steadfastness of white southern women. The myth was nurtured by evangelical religion and undergirded by a belief in white supremacy as the path to maintaining social stability. Focusing on the white citizenry's view of the recent war, it manifested itself in the creation of cemeteries and monuments and a yearly memorial day to remember the Confederate dead and their cause.[18]

The idea of the Memorial Day apparently originated with the women of Columbus, Georgia, and spread to communities across the South. By the late 1860s, on April 26 of each year, the Ladies Memorial Association of Savannah (LMAS) "dressed with flowers" the local Confederate graves and "all Savh. turns out to do them honour," one participant wrote. Local women met with former Confederate general Jeremy F. Gilmer to plan a permanent monument to the memory of Savannah's Confederate dead; the LMAS, Gilmer, and Robert Reid—an architect in Montreal—agreed to the construction of a monument in Canada made of Nova Scotia sandstone with the figures gracing it made of Carrara marble. When complete, it would be shipped to Savannah in a British vessel to insure that the monument never touched northern soil. The city government granted permission to erect the monument in Forsyth Park, where Confederate troops once camped.

To pay for the monument, estimated to cost twenty-five thousand dollars, the LMAS held bake sales. Other sponsors pledged money that local attorney Octavus Cohen invested. On Christmas Day 1874, a British schooner arrived at Savannah with the monument, but a U.S. Customs official seized the shipment for violation of regulations and threatened to put it up for auction. Once again the Savannah women raised money, paid the import fees and penalties, and the customs agent permitted the monument to be offloaded.

At the unveiling and dedication of the memorial in Forsyth Park on May 24, 1875, most of the crowd witnessed for the first time the elaborately carved Victorian monument. On top was the marble statue of a woman, *Judgment* or

Resurrection; in a cupola halfway down stood *Death* or *Silence,* a woman draped in white marble folds with a finger to her lips. Most of the public found the monument unacceptable; more importantly, it was not what the women of the Memorial Association had anticipated.[19]

A few years later, when George Wymberly Jones De Renne, a member of a founding family of Savannah, learned that the LMAS wished to change the monument by removing the two female figures, he took up their cause. At his own expense, he planned to cast "a colossal bronze statue of a Confederate soldier" to stand atop the monument—a "battle-scarred, weather beaten, poorly clad and worse shod" enlisted man "with only his weapons in perfect array . . . a figure of resolute endurance to the end—the type of men who sacrificed all to duty." It would be a lesson to others "that there is something nobler than success." The LMAS promptly accepted his offer.

Just over a year later, De Renne presented the bronze statue to the women, calling it "a tribute to the men of the Confederate Army who did their duty and to the women of the South who, true to the dead, have sought to save their memory from perishing."[20] The bronze soldier was positioned facing north atop the original sandstone monument. The inscription read: "TO THE CONFEDERATE DEAD," with the words of the prophet Ezekiel: "Come from the four winds, O breath, and breathe upon these slain that they may live." A female from one of Savannah's elite families was sure that many read the inscriptions "through a mist of tears."

Removed from the original monument, the female statue, *Silence,* stands today overlooking the Confederate dead at the Gettysburg Lot in Laurel Grove Cemetery. Local Confederate heritage societies hold ceremonies at both sites every April 26.[21] The statue *Judgment* was moved to the Laurel Hill Cemetery in Thomasville, Georgia. But, as the memory of the "Lost Cause" spread, so too did the economic crisis and epidemic disease.

Yellow Fever

Like other southern urban centers, Savannah's recovery was handicapped by war, the economic depression, and disease. The economy of New Orleans suffered from slow trade in cotton, the lack of adequate rail traffic, and a yellow fever epidemic in which thousands died. Upriver, the city of Memphis, which had boomed in the immediate postwar years, doubling its population to more than forty thousand, and becoming the country's largest cotton market saw its economy threatened as outbreaks of yellow fever in the 1870s killed thousands. Many of the well-to-do fled, never to return. Late in the decade, Memphis sought bankruptcy protection.[22]

The city of Savannah also remained deeply in debt to its bondholders. New rail lines running south of the Ohio River brought increased business to Norfolk, which became the country's third largest cotton port behind New Orleans and Galveston. Like Mobile and Charleston, Savannah's trade in cotton in the mid-1870s and its dollar value in imports slowed dramatically. Savannah did not recover until near the end of the decade. Then, in the midst of the economic depression, yellow fever swept the city.

Mild weather prevailed during the winter of 1876. Rains drenched the city, and "Vegetation . . . became luxuriant." In June, downpours over sixteen days reached eighteen inches. Most of the city's 3,366 privies overflowed. Of approximately five thousand dwellings in the city, only five hundred were connected to the sewer system, whose main arteries ran along Broughton and East Broad streets, finally emptying into the Savannah River—homes of the well-to-do were among the first to be connected. For those homes not connected to the sewer system, the city scavengers emptied their privies and sold the night soil to area farmers for fertilizer. In many southern cities, excreta flowed into porous privy vaults and cesspools rather than sewers.[23] Likewise, during heavy rains in Savannah, excrement and urine from were particularly dangerous and noxious. They bubbled through rain-saturated soil and overflowed on Savannah's eastern and western sides, flooding the "offal filled" stables, chicken coops, streets, and yards of the wooden, "decaying" tenements of the poor. Summer temperatures climbed to 100 degrees and higher.

That June and July disease broke out with fevers of victims sometimes reported to reach 108 degrees (likely overstated or misread). But it was not until August 21 that a doctor reported a death from yellow fever, sometimes called "black vomit." No public mention was made as to the cause of the patient's death.[24] In antebellum Savannah, the civic-commercial elite were slow to release information about disease. Any such acknowledgment, they reasoned, might harm business or cause unnecessary panic among the citizenry.

To make matters worse, on the night of August 25 a blaze started at Kelly's Wharf, located at the foot of Drayton Street. Flames raced along the river to Bull Street, "wrapping in flames" the "handsomest" block of buildings in the city and "burning out" merchants along the way. The *Morning News* reported that, after some months free from "the dreaded fire fiend," the city had suffered "one of the most disastrous" fires ever, concluding ominously, "the origin of the conflagration was either carelessness or design," hinting at arson.[25] The fear of firebrands in the night persisted among the elite from the Old South into the New.

Citizens along the route of the fire began cleaning up when new, troubling rumors circulated about the presence of thirty-nine cases of yellow fever in the city and nine deaths. When city officials finally acknowledged the presence of yellow fever, panic swirled through Savannah. As in Mobile and Memphis, the well-to-do fled. Without the wherewithal, most poor whites and blacks remained.

Former Confederate general Alexander Lawton typified the response of the elite: "the unexpected appearance of yellow fever as an epidemic brought with it inextricable confusion." Lawton and his family fled to Gainesville, Georgia, a "quiet retreat near the mountains." It was about as far as they could go from Savannah without leaving the state. Nelly Gordon, wife of the former Confederate captain William W. Gordon, took their four girls (Mabel, Alice, Daisy, and Nell) and son, Arthur, to Etowah Cliffs to stay with the prominent Stiles family of Savannah. To Nelly's dismay, her husband remained in Savannah.

As a member and volunteer of the Benevolent Association, William Gordon worked with priests and physicians to assist the poor, ill, and dying. Each morning after breakfast, he took a quinine pill and drank a glass of whiskey before beginning his rounds. Gordon provided basic and comforting services: mustard plasters, hot baths, medicines, and food. If necessary, he summoned a doctor. On entering one dwelling, he found the mother dead in one bed, the father dead in another, and several small children "sprawled on the floor crying with hunger."[26]

The disease reached epidemic levels from early September to early October and "raged with terrific violence." Torrential rains flooded fresh burial sites, and blacks used poles or sticks to keep coffins from floating upward while others shoveled fresh earth into the graves. Harriet Cumming wrote a friend on the evening of September 15, 1876, "Things go . . . from bad to worse." That very day she arrived at one dwelling to find the "husband dead and . . . being carried out." The mother was ill, the family had just buried one child, and another was "lying very low." Only a five-year-old child and a nurse remained ambulatory. Harriet lamented that the Benevolent Association hired black nurses for white families in desperate need. She doubted round-the-clock care could be provided by "an ignorant hireling" and speculated that "many . . . poor creatures die for the want of care."[27]

However, well-to-do Martha Gallaudet Waring praised the actions of "negroes" during the epidemic. Although many lacked work and food, they remained "as loyal and helpful as they have always proved to be." Martha acknowledged, "there was panic among the negroes," but added, "it speaks well for [them] that there were no riots." Fear of arsonist and rioting persisted in the minds of white elites across the South.[28] The number of blacks who stayed in Savannah during the epidemic far outnumbered whites and apparently this disparity troubled some of the white elite.

The usual white population of Savannah during the summers in the late 1870s was 16,000; during the epidemic there were far fewer. About 14,000 blacks resided in the city during the epidemic; approximately 12,000 were unemployed. The Benevolent Association's soup kitchens sustained over one-third of the population; blacks "were the most numerous claimants for public benevolence." The association also demanded that the city investigate the causes of the epidemic and thereby restore "the public happiness and welfare."

The municipal government responded by appointing a committee with several doctors, but for political reasons did not include James J. Waring. The irrepressible Dr. Waring offered his own proposal as to the cause of the disease and a plan for ending it quickly. The city and the Medical Society dismissed his ideas, and Mayor Anderson appointed another committee to advise him on how to end the epidemic; the committee promptly informed him that it was impossible to do anything now since an epidemic "must run its course."[29]

In late October, Dr. Waring told his wife in Charleston, where she had taken refuge with their children, that Savannah "is . . . dreadful looking," but the disease "mostly disappearing." He publicly criticized Mayor Anderson for his "indifference or incapacity . . . to alleviate or arrest the epidemic," calling him "a professional office holder and politician." Such criticism infuriated "Eddie" Anderson, the mayor's son. To defend family honor, he challenged Waring to a duel. But as Georgia law prohibited dueling, Waring refused to accept. Furthermore, he said, his feud was with the mayor, "the man who has so often misused me wantonly." No doubt, Waring must have had some concerns as he told his wife, if "anything serious arises, I will telegraph for you." The matter became moot when Eddie died of yellow fever.

A warming trend in early November suddenly brought a rise in the incidence of yellow fever. The disease was especially fatal to those who had fled weeks before and recently returned. Waring described conditions: "The situation here is as bad as it can be. Well-known people were "dying" or ill. A week later, "a heavy frost" enveloped Savannah and Waring informed his wife: "Now I think the disease is over here and you can return without the slightest risk."

To err on the side of caution, he suggested his wife and children stay beyond the city at their plantation, "Sedgebank," and black hired hands, Pinch and Ella, prepared for her return. Waring also mentioned "Old Susan," likely a former family slave, whom he described as "faithful beyond expectation." Susan was now unemployed with "no visible means of support"; Waring did admit to occasionally giving "her a dollar or two with rations and she feeds herself and dresses wonderfully well . . . [and] is so good and faithful that I am ashamed of myself." Exactly what he meant by this is not known.

Many white elites were paternalistic, like Waring. He had given ex-slaves land on Skidaway Island to farm, and they in turn trusted and admired him. Other local, prominent families retained former slaves as butlers and cooks, caring for them until they died and then laying them away "lovingly."[30] But to be treated paternalistically puts the receiver in a childlike association with the giver, and to suggest that these relationships helped foster a sense of self-worth and independence in black Savannahians is doubtful. One scholar recently pointed out that some of Savannah's best families used pejorative terms for blacks. Even the daughter of Nelly and William Gordon, Daisy, who founded the Girl Scouts, from youth to adulthood occasionally referred to African Americans as "niggers."[31]

In the city proper, 771 whites and 125 blacks died during the yellow fever epidemic, among them 138 white children and 21 black children under the age of thirteen. Unknown at the time, mosquitoes carrying yellow fever were native to Africa, and blacks had some level of resistance to the disease, which likely accounted for differences in the mortality statistics. Forty persons also succumbed to yellow fever in the suburbs—on the Isle of Hope and Thunderbolt. During the epidemic another 455 persons died of "undiagnosed fevers," bringing the number of fever-related deaths to more than 1,350.

Many Savannahians donned mourning clothes for months afterwards. Men wore black suits or a black cloth sewn on their left sleeve. Women wore a black dress trimmed with heavy black crepe, a small black bonnet tied under the chin, and a long veil covering the face. In time the colors of the dresses changed from black to white to gray, then purple, lavender, or lilac, and eventually all colors were deemed acceptable. It was not uncommon for a widow to wear black for the rest of her life.[32]

There were various theories within the city's medical community as to the cause of the epidemic. James Waring and other doctors agreed with the prominent physician Julius C. Le Hardy that a contributing factor was "filth" caused by an inadequate drainage system. Not until the end of the century did the medical community recognize that the *Aedes aegypti* mosquito carried the disease and that their favorite breeding ground was standing water in drainage ditches and stagnant pools.[33]

Savannah's yellow fever outbreak never reached the epidemic levels of New Orleans and Memphis in the 1870s—catastrophic for both cities in numbers of lives lost, the *permanent* exodus of the well-to-do, and a devastated economy.

However, the epidemic did remind local businessmen of Savannah's reputation as a sickly place.

It also slowed commercial life in a city already burdened by a nationwide depression. Alexander Lawton remarked upon fleeing the city that the epidemic "brought . . . the temporary abandonment of all business." At his cotton brokerage business "on the Bay," William Gordon found "the atmosphere so deadly that not even a policeman was stationed there"; twelve of his clerks fell ill from yellow fever. Dr. Waring, who fled the city for several weeks, returned to find "my business is in a deplorable fix." Income from his real estate investments atrophied; he complained, "No money from rents, the situation is horrible." The Benevolent Association declared that "industry was paralyzed" by the epidemic. Mayor Anderson in his annual report wrote that the disease caused "the sudden prostration of all business."[34]

Some years later, Thomas Gamble, a future mayor of Savannah and author of a history of the city government, analyzed the impact of the epidemic and concluded, "The ravages of this scourge had a disastrous effect upon all pecuniary interests." Indeed, he said, due to the "misfortune," the city's tax collection in 1876 fell short by $200,619, a sum that, if collected along with other taxes, could have reduced the city's floating debt significantly, despite "the paralyzing effects of the epidemic."[35]

Facing Down Bankruptcy

As the mayoralty elections approached in early 1877, Dr. Waring, who planned to run for City Council, became convinced that all Savannahians were now "thoroughly aroused against" Mayor Anderson. His assumption proved correct. City leaders chose Captain John F. Wheaton, a businessman active in the Chatham Artillery and the admired leader of the Benevolent Association.

Wheaton won the mayoralty race with fewer than eight hundred votes cast. Even though he was viewed by Democrats as a despised Republican, Waring was elected to the City Council, winning on a popular platform of permanently eradicating yellow fever. As the only Republican in city government, Waring was regarded by colleagues as an obstructionist, but they were forced to involve him in strategic decisions when the new administration learned that, because of the depression, the epidemic, and the refusal of citizens to pay their taxes, the city would not be able to meet its financial obligations.

Waring pushed the new government to face the situation head-on. He introduced a resolution declaring the city bankrupt and specifying that, with the exception of meeting current expenses, all liabilities would be deferred until the debts could be arranged to the satisfaction of creditors. Waring's resolution went to the finance committee, whose members issued a report describing the city as "embarrassed" by its indebtedness, but not "bankrupt." Every council member voted to approve the finance report, except Waring. The council did ask its creditors to bear with them as they worked to address with the city's $4 million debt crisis—a shortfall equivalent to 50 percent of the market value of all the real estate in Savannah. The council, in good faith, asked all citizens to pay any taxes not in litigation and in this way mitigate the city's "embarrassment." This action (or inaction) made the city government appear as much in denial about the serious financial situation as prior administrations.[36]

The city remained in default to its creditors, who soon sought restitution through the courts. Bondholders in New York warned Savannah government and business leaders against "dishonest intent" regarding its debts—in other words, do not follow the examples of Mobile and Memphis; both cities had repudiated their obligations. But, as the number of suits against the city continued to rise, city leaders themselves, in 1879, turned to the courts in an attempt to resolve Savannah's indebtedness, short of bankruptcy. Four years later the city's case reached the Supreme Court of the United States, which upheld a lower-court decision and ordered the city to work out a compromise with its bondholders. The administration soon did so. Savannah had jeopardized its credit rating and narrowly averted default. It appears the civic-commercial elite learned a tough economic lesson: borrowing heavily at high interest rates to enhance the image of the city in hopes of making it "the Great Atlantic Seaport" brought the city to the edge of bankruptcy and sullied Savannah's reputation. In the decade following, the city government severely curtailed building, borrowing, and expenditures by cutting personnel on the police force, the fire department, and the health department and by requiring the city jailer and city surveyor to use chain-gang labor to reduce costs.[37]

Savannah had offered generous interest rates to creditors in both the antebellum and postbellum years to build railroads and an elaborate city infrastructure. But in the long run it could not meet its financial obligations due to a number of factors: the catastrophe that befell the city as a result of its participation in the war against the Union, a tax structure that failed to raise enough revenue in a city with high unemployment and underemployment, a nationwide depression, and the yellow fever epidemic.

The Police and "A Riotous Mob"

With his police force reduced from 64 to 56 men, Savannah's long-serving police chief, former Confederate cavalry officer Robert H. Anderson, closely monitored the activities of the city's black population during the late 1870s and early 1880s. Arrests climbed markedly and, though the population remained almost evenly divided among blacks and whites, the number of blacks arrested was significantly greater than whites. Data from years for which records are available (1875–85) show "Disorderly Conduct" arrests, 653 whites, 1,480 blacks; "Suspicious Characters" arrests, 138 whites, 371 blacks; and "Larceny" arrests, 48 whites, 612 blacks.[38]

Mayor Edward C. Anderson admitted that rising crime rates and fewer policemen on the streets made it difficult to insure the "security of life and property within the city limits." He sympathized with citizens who complained "that an officer cannot be found when needed." Anderson's successor, Mayor John Wheaton, believed that the force had been reduced "to the lowest point compatible with the safety and good government of the city," and he pressed the City Council for additional funds to "properly protect the business and commercial interests." When Wheaton took office, the police force already received the largest budget of any city department, approximately $47,000 annually; police crime-reduction efforts were no doubt aided by the installation of additional gas lamps on the east, west, and south edges of the town, bringing the total to 588 lights maintained by the city.[39]

The police force did not receive the requested weapons. No money was appropriated for the purchase of new breech-loading rifles and pistols that Police Chief Anderson asked for in his budget request. Mayor Wheaton did acquire some weapons, but only through loans from local militia units when he declared an emergency in the city in September 1881.[40]

On the northwest side of Savannah, the railroad tracks of the CGR ran down to wharves on the river. Here black and white workers loaded cotton bales and naval stores into vessels of the Ocean Steamship Company, a subsidiary of the CGR. It was dangerous, demanding heavy labor. And in the late, hot summer of 1881, black wharf workers sought a modest increase in wages for a ten-hour day—they already earned much less than their white counterparts. Among the group were members of the WUA, an organization committed to provide "mutual aid and assistance" to those working "along the wharfs and on board ships."

When the supervisor of the dock laborers refused even to discuss the matter, they walked off the job on September 19. Robert Lucas, described by the *Morning News* as a "bright [in color] mulatto," spoke in the streets urging holdouts to join the strike. Ordered arrested for attempting "to incite negro strikers . . . to violence," Lucas was seized by police, who roughed him up for his "impudent and defiant" attitude. He seemed remarkably subdued, possibly injured, when he later appeared in the city's Police Court. Lucas was sentenced

Dockworkers at the wharf, Savannah, ca. 1880s. Courtesy of Georgia Archives, Vanishing Georgia Collection, image no. ctm333-84.

to thirty days at "hard labor" and fined one hundred dollars. He was unable to pay, so the court added additional days "equivalent" to his fine. Mayor Wheaton cautioned Lucas about his radical "speechifying." The reporter for the *Morning News* welcomed the news that Lucas "will not be seen in his usual haunts for many months."[41]

The strikers seized a CGR bridge leading to the docks and shut down loading operations. Mayor Wheaton, informed that the laborers had turned into a "riotous and disorderly crowd," ordered out the police. Sgt. H. H. Harvey rushed to the scene. As he tried to "suppress" the workers, he was shot and mortally wounded.

Fearing the strike might spiral out of control, Wheaton enacted his emergency powers and called for assistance from the Georgia Hussars and the Savannah Volunteer Guards; the militias also loaned the city new breech-loading weapons for use if needed. At the request of the CGR, the City Council deputized a twenty-one-member auxiliary, a uniformed police force subject to the rules of the regular force, but paid for by the railroad. During two violent clashes between the police and militias and the strikers, black laborers were beaten and four killed. Their deaths were never made public. Even with such an overwhelming show of strength by the police, the militia, and the deputized police auxiliary, it took five days to "suppress" the disorder. Colonel William W. Wadley, president of the CGR, met with representatives of "the colored workers" and told them "the business of a great port like Savannah could not be long retarded because a few hundred laborers refused to work."

City officials also requested help from black militia officers. Col. William H. Woodhouse, Major John H. Deveaux, and adjutant Louis B. Toomer met with the dockworkers and urged them to use peaceful means rather than the strike to address their grievances. The next day, the dockworkers began returning to work.

Once derided by the local press and the target of rock throwers when on parade, the local black militia officers were now praised by the *Morning News* for restoring order to the city. Ironically it was black leadership that helped end the "disorder"caused by striking black workers whose demand for an increase in wages failed.[42]

Caring for Indigents and Cleaning Up the City

Even during this time of strikes and violence, Mayor Wheaton praised municipal authorities for providing for the needs of the city's indigents, "irrespective of color." He boasted that the city annually appropriated fifteen hundred dollars to the Georgia Infirmary for the treatment and care of all "colored persons" without friends or family. It was a vastly inadequate expenditure considering the health needs of the black community. The mayor also reported that two white physicians paid by the city treated indigents, and the dispensary provided free medicine to the poor who presented a prescription. The mayor defended the cost of free vaccinations against smallpox and the relocation of the smallpox hospital as good investments because the outbreaks of smallpox that had occurred over the past three years no longer "prevailed in the city." These preventatives, however, proved insufficient; smallpox retuned a few years later with outbreaks in Yamacraw and "Old Fort." During this outbreak, about thirty-three thousand persons were vaccinated.[43]

The civic-commercial elite blamed irresponsible, "careless" citizens who failed to maintain "sanitary" premises and threw "offensive matter" into the streets as the cause of disease outbreaks. Mayor Wheaton expressed special concern over the great disparity in the mortality rates between the "white and colored races," twenty and forty-six deaths per thousand respectively. Wheaton attributed this disparity to the failure of the "lower class of colored persons to follow the laws of public hygiene" and their inadequacies in "ministering to the sick."

The stark contrast in mortality rates likely had many causes: access to health care, inadequate diets, poor living conditions in the sprawling hovels built on the east and west sides of the city, physically demanding—often dangerous—

work, and persistent unemployment. Similar conditions existed in other southern cities. Working-class blacks in Charleston lived in a low marshy area on the city's east side which flooded during heavy rains, an area the city's Board of Health referred to as a "dangerous and unhealthy region" and a breeding ground for disease.

On occasion, fires roared through such slums in Savannah and the jerry-built wooden structures exploded like fatwood lighter. During a conflagration in Yamacraw in the early 1880s, eight persons died when three hundred dwellings went up in flames, sending twelve hundred poor fleeing into the streets, now homeless.[44]

Savannah's health officer, Dr. J. T. McFarland, a civic booster like Wheaton, while acknowledging a mortality rate for blacks that was more than twice that of whites, offered his usual upbeat annual report. Savannah, "like many Southern cities," he wrote, had experienced an outbreak of dengue fever, but by "disinfecting and cleaning" the sinks and premises where it existed, the fever disappeared. More likely, cooler weather was the major factor. McFarland urged the City Council to initiate mandatory vaccinations and require all applicants to public schools to certify their inoculation before admission. Savannah's civic and commercial elite, like those in other major southern cities, knew that the city's image as a healthy, robust, prosperous urban environment was essential if Savannah wanted to attract outside investment and sustain growth.[45] And as the recession slowly receded, boosters once more touted Savannah as beautiful, healthful, and open for business.

The Depression Wanes, the Boosters Promote, and the Civic-Commercial Elite Cash In

During the year of the yellow fever epidemic a mere 171,416 cotton bales shipped from Savannah. However, beginning in 1877 the amount increased steadily; 410,237 bales left the port in 1882 and 502,649 seven years later. Over the same period, the value of shipments of naval stores (rosin, tar, and turpentine) and timber soared from $577,988 to $3,296,503, making Savannah the chief port in the world for the handling and shipment of these commodities.

The value of imports also increased from $511,528 in 1876 to $696,434 in 1885; but soon thereafter, imports dropped sharply, perhaps because of the lack of local purchasing power, especially among the black community. Most important was the fact that other rail lines were now bypassing the city of Savannah.[46]

But over time, as the national economic recovery gathered steam from the late 1870s through the 1880s, great wealth flowed to the civic-commercial elite of Savannah. All three young daughters of the wealthy Gordon family—Nelly (named after her mother), Daisy, and Alice—went away to boarding schools in Virginia, then attended the prestigious Mlle. Charbonnier's School in New York City, where the classes were in French. The school was designed to prepare young ladies for their debut. Nelly and Daisy had their "coming out" or introduction to society in Savannah. Alice died of scarlet fever while in New York; her death devastated the family, especially her mother.[47]

The city's elite enjoyed travel and visiting friends abroad. Near the end of the 1870s, former mayor of Savannah and former Confederate colonel Charles C. Jones Jr. decided to "run over to Europe for the summer months." His close friend, former Confederate general and Savannah attorney Alexander R. Lawton, happily provided Jones a letter of introduction to his friend the American minister in Vienna, a former Confederate general.[48]

Savannah's elite were a close-knit group; they traveled together, provided letters of introduction for each other, and often visited friends abroad. They founded the Oglethorpe Club in the mid-1870s on upper Bull Street; subsequent members had to be approved by secret ballot. They belonged to the Couper Boat Club and raced shells on the Vernon River at the Savannah Yacht Club in Thunderbolt, where sailing regattas attracted boaters from across the state and South Carolina.[49]

In spring, members of the elite like George Wymberley Jones De Renne of Wormsloe Plantation chartered steamers for day-long excursions to nearby Daufuskie and Tybee islands. While cruising they dined on "boned turkey, sandwiches, rolls, crab salad, chicken salad, orange sherbet, strawberries and strawberry ice cream, snowball pound cake," and the like, all prepared by black hands—their beverages, "6 bottles of champagne, 2 of sherry, 2 of whiskey." For the comfort of the guests, De Renne brought along "five rocking chairs (bamboo) for the ladies . . . napkins, plates, dishes, tumblers, wine glasses, knives, forks, spoons, saucers etc."[50] Some prosperous Savannahians, lured by the refreshing ocean breezes on Tybee Island, built dwellings on the island, well aware of the pace at which resorts were going up along the northeastern Atlantic seaboard.

A Horrible Hurricane!

By 1880, Tybee Island counted numbers of substantial homes and cottages and a forty-room, three-story hotel. A steamer ran from Savannah to the Tybee wharf, where a mule-drawn streetcar took owners and guests to the properties. Vacationers crowded the island during the summers, but on August 26, 1881, they worried about the weather as large swells crashed on the beach and scudding clouds and rain squalls swept the island. On the evening of the next day, a hurricane crashed into the island. Homeowners on Tybee's beachfront like John Estill, owner of the *Morning News*, and his family, friends, and two black servants were in the house when windows blew in and a tidal surge of twelve feet swept beneath the dwelling. Quickly they all leaped into the water and sloughed through to safety. Their neighbors were not so fortunate. A gas line exploded in Henry Soloman's home, killing three people; other houses and cottages disappeared into the sea.

Winds at Savannah smashed vessels against the wharves and peeled tin roofs from businesses and private homes. Savannahians described it as a night of "howling wind and fierce rain." Enormous oaks and elms fell onto telegraph wires which together choked city streets.[51] Huge waves swept up the Savannah River and inundated small islands and low-lying properties. Darkness made it difficult for former slaves living there in cabins to flee, and 335 persons perished, mostly African Americans who could not swim. Clara Waring told her husband Charles of "sad accounts of loss of life among the negroes." Estimates of the damages at Tybee Island, Savannah, and the vicinity reached $1.5 million—in twenty-first-century terms, over $37 million. The development of Tybee as a seaside resort temporarily ended at a time when the nationwide economy appeared to be recovering.[52]

Debutants and a Wedding

The year of the hurricane, the CGR earned $500,000 more than the previous year. Four black longshoremen had died in a failed strike that year seeking a modest raise to $2 a day; the CGR paid a dividend on its bonds and gave a raise to certain employees. This dividend windfall likely was welcomed by many well-to-do fathers as it helped defray some of the costs associated with the parties and debuts of their daughters—a practice essential to making a good match within their own privileged class.

Young ladies like Margaret Habersham moved quickly from debutant to bride—she married a local cotton merchant with a prominent lowcountry name, James Hamilton Couper, formerly of the Confederate Signal Corps. Likewise, Eugenia Johnston attended all the finest parties and dances like the Georgia Hussars' balls and traveled to Charleston for the St. Cecilia Ball, where she danced with all of the eligible young bachelors.[53]

Daisy Gordon, age twenty, made her debut at Savannah's prestigious Cotillion Club ball. After her introduction to society, Daisy rarely missed a party. Known for her style, grace, and wit, she became a full-time socialite, frequently traveling to visit distant relatives and friends and often meeting celebrities of the day. Travel clothes and entertainments so necessary for a young woman of her status were underwritten by her father, William W. Gordon.

Daisy's father owned Gordon & Company, Cotton Factors and Commission Merchants, located at 112 Bay Street. Though well-to-do, Gordon at the time was trying to sell some properties to raise money for his business and repair of the firm's wharves. Gordon received from the company one thousand dollars monthly, a princely income that few white or African American businessmen locally or elsewhere enjoyed. Nevertheless, Gordon worried about his expenses.

Gordon even asked his wife Nelly to reign in the "extravagant" lifestyles of their daughters, but Nelly seemed less worried with spending and more concerned that Daisy might become an "old maid" as she seemed to prefer the single life. But, when traveling in England in the early 1880s, Daisy met William Mackay Low, nicknamed "Willie." His father, Andrew, a Scotsman, had made a fortune in the cotton business in Savannah and knew Daisy's father; another connection for the young couple stemmed from the marriage of Daisy's aunt Eliza Gordon to Willie's uncle Henry Stiles.

As the courtship developed, Daisy and Willie kept their relationship a secret, perhaps due to his reputation as a playboy, heavy drinker, and gambler. When they decided to wed, the Gordons worried over their prospective son-in-law's stability. Even after Willie inherited great wealth following his father's death, the Gordons' doubts about Willie's character persisted even to the day of the high-noon wedding at Christ Church, Savannah, on December 21, 1886.

It was the premier social event of the season. The bride wore a dress of "corded silk . . . [with a] sash . . . looped with an elegant crescent of diamonds [and a veil that] . . . reached to the edge of the train . . . [and] a handsome diamond shoulder ornament." Soon after the ceremony, the couple departed for a six-day honeymoon in a "lovely" furnished home on St. Catherines Island with servants and provisions.[54]

After the nuptials, the wedding guests continued to celebrate. For weeks, guests were entertained with food and drinks in the Gordons' home at 10 East Oglethorpe Street. Daisy's mother, Nelly, had "18 people sit down to every meal." She supervised "the duties of 2 cooks, 2 butlers, 2 chambermaids and innumerable laundresses to keep 15 fires going all the time & 21 beds [made] every day!" Nelly confided, "I broke down once and went to bed." Despite the celebratory beginning, in the long run, the Gordons' doubts about the marriage proved well founded.

Following the wedding, Daisy's father escaped the many guests who remained in the Gordon home. As a member of the legislature, he traveled to Atlanta to fight efforts of competing railroads to "steal the property of existing . . . [railroads]." Gordon had his interests and those of other Savannahians in mind. Not only was he an investor in the CGR, but a cotton factor and merchant who now made a smaller net profit due to the discriminatory rail rates—rates that favored "New England and New York as against Savannah & Charleston."

Gordon next traveled to Manhattan to observe the outcome of an election for the board of the CGR, in which he and other Savannahians had an interest. Unfortunately, he learned that "the old board was defeated & the control . . . gobbled up by Wall Street speculators." He predicted correctly that the railroad's "prosperity and integrity may be . . . a thing of the past . . . [as] a Board of stockbrokers and riff raff" now controlled the CGR. It was the beginning of the end for the railroad his father had founded. Within two years, the Richmond Terminal Company gained control of the CGR.[55]

A Recovery for Some

The reviving economy of Savannah in the early 1880s brought out local promoters who sounded much like their antebellum counterparts. They distributed forty- to seventy-page publications describing the city as destined to be the "First Seaport of the South Atlantic and First Naval Stores Port of the World." Because the city was located on a river easily navigable by the largest vessels, steamship lines and railroads provided easy access to Savannah by sea or land; four streetcar companies carried passengers throughout a city "blessed" with good government; small industries abounded which were "powerful levers" to make Savannah "great and prosperous."

The real estate market enjoyed "a steady increase in values"; the climate was "favorable to vigor of mind and health of body" as the temperature in "January is as genial as Spring." Savannah's water when "filtered" is "excellent," and the healthfulness of the city is remarkable as "the tables of mortality (leaving out the negroes, who are, as a class, dirty and careless of their health and comfort)" demonstrate that Savannah "is one of the healthiest cities in the United States." With its "church-going and church-loving people, Savannah is second to few cities"; its citizens recognize that education "is the mortar that holds the social fabric together," which is why the city is "blessed" with a number of academies and schools, which are free, with the exception of a modest fee to matriculate in the high schools. To the boosters, Savannah possessed "extraordinary advantages" to become "one of the greatest, if not the greatest, of commercial and manufacturing cities in the South."[56]

From the beginning of the 1880s into the 1890s, Savannah showed signs of a sustainable recovery. The population grew, and new houses went up. The City Council extended the limits of the city south of Anderson Street to what is now Forty-second Street and Estill Avenue (now Victory Drive) and from the Ogeechee Road to East Broad Street and added a large slice of land on the western side of the city. Southern Bell Telephone & Telegraph Company found the city large and prosperous enough in 1883 to provide phone services as it had done in Richmond, Charleston, Augusta, Mobile, and other southern urban centers. About the same time, a power company began providing illumination for public places, and some homes and the city installed large engines to pump water from artesian wells through thirty-two miles of city pipes.

The new Chatham County–Savannah Jail on Habersham Street opened to receive inmates in early 1888. Frequent conflagrations prompted the city to provide the Fire Department with additional horses, firefighting equipment, hydrants, and hoses to fight fires in the rows of "thickly inhabited" tenement houses to the west of West Broad Street and south of Anderson Street. The city paved Whitaker, Gaston, Henry, Liberty, Hall, and Huntington streets and began to open new streets in Yamacraw; "sheet asphalt" was laid from Abercorn down Broughton to West Broad, and hundreds of new trees were planted in the squares, in Forsyth Park, and along Bay, South Broad, and Liberty streets. The surging economy of the late 1880s brought additional tax revenues, enabling the city to invest in these municipal improvements.

By mid-1888, more buildings were going up in Savannah than any previous year. The Oglethorpe Barracks was purchased by the Savannah Hotel Company for seventy-five thousand dollars. The barracks were torn down, and investors constructed the DeSoto Hotel, a five-story structure with 206 rooms, including a restaurant and a fountain in the form of a lion's head—a feature that remains part of the latest hotel on the site. The DeSoto opened to the public in early 1890; that same year the city issued construction permits for more than three hundred buildings.

In these boom times, an African American entrepreneur, Charles Baker, saw opportunities for a black neighborhood and bought up land on Savannah's east side. Likewise, Robert LePage, manager of the SF&W wharf, believed the time was right for offering housing on the east side for black railroad workers. From 1885 to 1888, LePage built a village of thirty-five houses. Their location just east of what is today President Street was within walking distance of the wharf, which made them especially desirable. The black neighborhood became known as LePageville. On the city's western side, beyond Yamacraw, African Americans were investing in and erecting dwellings in the community of Woodville.[57]

In the city, Savannah's health officer, Dr. J. T. McFarland, and his assistants disinfected stinking, stagnant ponds and privy vaults, adopted measures to insure that garbage and other filth did not accumulate in the yards of tenement houses, and remained vigilant for outbreaks of cholera, scarlet fever, and diphtheria. McFarland continued to be deeply concerned over the rising death rates of blacks, which by the late 1880s had climbed to fifty per one thousand, compared to twenty per one thousand for whites. McFarland attributed the dramatically higher rate for blacks to the "large numbers" who had congregated in Savannah after the Civil War and moved into overcrowded, squalid housing. He maintained that prior to emancipation the black death rate was lower than that of whites—where he found this statistic is unknown. McFarland ended his annual report by calling African Americans "an incubus population"; however, he stressed that his "remarks" did not apply to Savannah's "many excellent, worthy and thrifty colored citizens." McFarland believed the national practice of combining the death rates of whites and blacks "convey[ed] false ideas to white people who are disposed to seek homes in the South."

In sum, the city was growing, and with growth came the need for additional municipal expenditures. The civic-commercial elite wished to give businessmen beyond the city an image of Savannah as a clean and healthy place. When complaints arose from the well-to-do about the "heavy public debt," Mayor Rufus Lester urged the critics to invest money locally rather than abroad and thereby add to the "prosperity of their city."[58]

The Black Elite and the Laboring Classes

Few in Savannah could afford the accommodations and fashionable entertainments offered by families like Nelly and William Gordon. But as the economy improved nationwide, so too did the incomes of local white businessmen, the professional class, and their African American counterparts. Unfortunately the black and white laboring classes remained largely underpaid, underemployed, or unemployed and mired in poverty as the city's population increased from 30,709 in 1880 to 43,189 in 1890.[59]

The year Daisy Gordon married, John Deveaux resumed publication of the *Savannah Tribune*. The paper, started in 1875 as the *Colored Tribune*, had stopped publishing in 1878 but, in 1886, with a new partner, Richard W. White, the *Tribune* rolled off the presses again. No other newspaper for Africa

Americans published before and after the *Tribune* had the staying power of Deveaux's paper, perhaps due its emphasis on news, commentary, and promotion of education as the path to a better life. With offices at the corner of Market Square and St. Julian streets, the *Savannah Tribune* employed African American printers and offered public printing services to earn extra income. One of the skilled typesetters with only a rudimentary education, Sol Johnson, soon became editor and eventually the paper's owner.

Deveaux and White most likely subsidized the paper with their own money. Few African Americans could afford to buy the paper; fewer still could read, although the illiteracy rate for blacks in Georgia had dropped from 92 percent in 1870 to 52 percent in 1890. The newspaper business was not a big moneymaker. White along with his wife, Annie, and their four children lived next door to Deveaux and his wife, Fanny, and their four small children in the 1880s. White, a man of biracial parentage like Deveaux, was South Carolina–born, attended Oberlin College, and served in the Union Army. Active in the Republican Party at the state and local level, the two men held patronage jobs as federal appointees, White as a U.S. postal employee.[60]

Deveaux and White, like Louis Pleasant and Louis Toomer, counted themselves among Savannah's leading professional class, a part of its African American elite, yet their publication sought to serve the entire "colored" community. Many of Savannah's light-skinned African Americans remained clannish—Savannah's "mulatto clique," very similar to those in Charleston and New Orleans, held themselves aloof from darker blacks in socializing, marriage, and in their church, St. Stephen's Episcopal on Bull Street.

The black well-to-do included livery stable owners, barbers, grocers, carpenters, clergymen, teachers, newspapermen, doctors, dentists, and attorneys. During the final decade of the nineteenth century, fourteen black lawyers and five dentists offered professional services in Georgia. At the time fewer than five black attorneys had offices in Savannah. Most African Americans preferred to take their legal problems to white rather than black lawyers.[61]

Forty-three African American physicians practiced in Georgia, nine in Chatham County and another ten in the city of Savannah. The most prominent African American physician, Dr. Simeon Palmer Lloyd, was born in Savannah a year after the Civil War and graduated with distinction from Atlanta University and the University of Pennsylvania. In his first year of practice in Savannah in the early 1890s, Lloyd treated 6,712 Negro patients and 224 whites. Mayor Herman Myers appointed him as the first African American to serve as one of the four city physicians, Lloyd's reward for supporting Myers in his mayoralty race.

Another black physician and Republican politician, Dr. Floyd Snelson, may have been the most popular local doctor in the city. Whites sought him out for medical attention, and African American politicians like John Deveaux and Louis Toomer worked closely with him on political campaigns. Both Lloyd and Snelson likely enjoyed a lucrative a practice, as did their contemporary, Dr. R. D. Badger, an Atlanta dentist, who accumulated an estate of ninety-six hundred dollars, a considerable sum for the time.[62]

Black businessmen profited handsomely as livery stable owners in the last decades of the nineteenth century. John Monroe operated a stable at 97 York Street and held real estate valued at five thousand dollars. Another stable owner, the very popular Daniel Button, who could neither read nor write, accumulated an estate of twenty thousand dollars. By the end of the century, black draymen monopolized the transportation business. Black businessmen also operated a large number of groceries. Robert Green at his South Broad Street store did a thriving business in domestic meats and wild game. James Hart and Brothers sold meats, vegetables, liquor, and tobacco.[63]

Excluded from white social organizations, Savannah's upper-class African Americans enjoyed a rich social life, not unlike that of the white well-to-do. The Skidmore Club and String Band occasionally provided dance music for the Social Club of Savannah, the Union Coterie, the Ladies and Gents Social Club, and the Committee of Nine. Generally literate, the well-to-do participated in discussion groups and debated such erudite issues as: "Who did most in support of the Protestant Religion, Martin Luther or Queen Elizabeth?" The local black Masonic and Odd Fellows Lodges held frequent meetings and dinners and acted as benevolent organizations. The black upper class took steamboat and rail excursions, held picnics, played in pick-up baseball games and took the lead in special celebrations on Lincoln's Birthday, Emancipation Day, Independence Day, and the anniversaries of passage of the Fourteenth and Fifteenth amendments to the U.S. Constitution.[64]

African American workingmen constituted about 50 percent of all the artisans and laborers in Savannah at the beginning of the 1880s. Skilled black carpenters and plasterers dominated the building trades, and others worked as boat builders and saddlers. But by the middle of the decade their numbers began falling dramatically due to the competition for jobs, deteriorating race relations, and racial prejudice. White carpentry unions excluded blacks, and white employers favored whites over blacks. The pattern of caste discrimination in the trades became a pattern throughout the country.[65]

At times of high unemployment, black males represented about 70 percent of all unemployed males in the city. Excluded from carpentry and other trades,

Savannah's skilled blacks had to take work as draymen and laborers. By the end of the century, there were 518 black draymen and 94 white; the railroads employed 909 blacks and 373 whites. Over time many of these workers would be replaced by whites.

Many skilled black artisans, now denied opportunities to ply their trades, remained chronically unemployed, and their wives and children took whatever work was available. Some out-of-work artisans spent their time at gambling houses and saloons or loitered at the Savannah market on Saturday nights. Though the period was a time of prosperity for some blacks, for most neither their living conditions nor their health improved. With crime up, the police force made good use of its new jail on Habersham Street.

Hundreds of black women, about 60 percent of the city's black female population, found work as laundresses, seamstresses, nurses, cooks, and house servants. Others peddled goods, sometimes accompanied by their children. The *Morning News* described a group hawking their products in the streets during the late 1880s as "noisy, indolent, and indifferent . . . ranging in age from ten to sixty." They sell "many oddities, and the city to no small extent depends on these peddlers for fruit, fish, oysters, crabs, clams, and shrimp."[66]

Racial Tensions, Rising Violence

The exclusion of black artisans and laborers in Savannah during the 1880s came at a time of increasing racism. The Supreme Court of the United States in 1883 declared the Civil Rights Act of 1875 unconstitutional. The act had permitted African Americans equal treatment in public accommodations like retail establishments, educational institutions, and had prohibited their exclusions from juries. In sum, the federal government took a giant step in moving away from insuring blacks equal treatment under the law.

After the Civil Rights Act was struck down, segregation gained momentum. Within the decade and afterward, Savannah's government prohibited African Americans from using its bicycle paths; when Savannah's white doctors feared competition from black physicians, the city passed an ordinance requiring black and white doctors to treat only their own kind. The state legislature even enacted a law that segregated chain gangs by race. Whites and blacks were fast becoming segregated in nearly every aspect of life and even unto death—in 1888 Savannah's governing body required separate cemeteries for blacks and whites.[67] Of course, these were legal measures; extralegal methods also enforced segregation, including intimidation through brutal beatings and murder by gun, burning, or lynch rope.

The great "lynching era" of black Americans encompassed the years 1880 to 1930. During this period 3,343 lynchings were recorded; 80 percent took place in the South. Mississippi ranked first in the nation with 560 lynchings, followed by Georgia with 505. Whites of the ruling class clung to their antebellum fears of black uprisings and used violence to enforce segregation and white supremacy; sometimes the racist rhetoric of politicians encouraged lower-class whites to carry out murder. Blacks were often helpless to protect themselves against mob violence on a variety of trumped-up charges.

During the 1880s, Ku Klux Klan leaders used violence against black politicians and property owners in Macon, Georgia, and its environs; in Barnwell County, South Carolina, a mob broke into a jail, carried away eight black men accused of murdering a local white merchant, tied them to trees, and shot them, perhaps the largest mass "lynching" in the South.[68]

Most cases of violence against African Americans occurred in small towns and rural areas. But the news of lynchings quickly spread to urban areas like Savannah and brought to black communities the warnings intended. In addition to police brutality and harassment in the cities, intimidation came in more subtle ways, like celebrating the Confederacy and its "Ghosts."

"Ghosts of the Confederacy"

Jefferson Davis, president of the "Lost Cause," enjoyed enormous crowds on his tour of southern cities in the spring of 1886. Thousands turned out to hear him speak in Montgomery, and eighty thousand greeted him in Atlanta. From there Davis entrained for Savannah, a place he last visited in chains. Now ex-Confederate units from across the South, many in uniforms of Confederate gray, awaited him. Seventy thousand hat-waving, cheering spectators lined his parade route. Some three thousand schoolchildren gathered on the grounds of Chatham Academy to spread rose petals in his path and to hear "the great man speak," the *Morning News* reported. Davis praised the war's martyred soldier-heroes, who died fighting for "the noblest people who have graced the pages of history." Likely few if any blacks attended ceremonies that celebrated slaveholders and their defenders.[69]

On the day of the election of the Republican Benjamin Harrison as president of the United States in 1888, a torchlight parade led by blacks with a sprinkling of whites formed to celebrate at the corner of Lincoln and Oglethorpe. From here they wound through the city and into Yamacraw, shouting "Hurrah for Harrison." The city's police rushed to the scene, beat and overpowered the marchers, and apparently with no cause given, hustled them off to jail. About a year later, a policeman apprehended Abram Ward, an elderly black man, and repeatedly clubbed him until Ward's leg fractured.

The *Tribune* adopted a more militant tone in denouncing police brutality and racial injustice when Sol Johnson assumed the editorship of the paper after John Deveaux departed in 1889 to become the collector of customs at Brunswick, Georgia. Johnson on one occasion wrote a blistering editorial asserting that, when Savannah policemen "see a colored man in a crowd, they make it their indispensable duty to rout him out and if the least word is spoken in remonstrance he is clubbed into insensibility."[70] Given the fierce hostility directed toward African Americans at the time in Georgia and the nation, it is remarkable that such language could be used by an editor of a black paper in a southern urban center and not bring retaliation.

In the final decades of the century, a wave of strikes rippled across the nation and into the South. The Knights of Labor, a national union organization, defied the color line and supported interracial strikes. They successfully organized walkouts by miners in Alabama and Tennessee and cotton-mill workers in Augusta, Georgia. The Knights also became more politically active, helping to elect city and county officials in Macon and Mobile. In 1891, twenty-two strikes occurred in Georgia alone; the largest took place in Savannah.

The LUPA and the Strike of 1891

Restive dockworkers in the city in September 1891 no doubt remembered the strike of longshoremen ten years earlier against the CGR when four black men died in an unsuccessful attempt to win an increase in wages. Already feeling squeezed economically by the city's two railroads, the CGR and the Savannah, Florida & Western Railway, the African American wharf workers now faced the threat of pay cuts from fifteen to eleven cents per hour, arbitrary dismissals, and harassment by the police of the CGR. Such "unbearable wrongs" galvanized black wharf workers who, at the bottom of the city's wage scale, likely knew about union successes in upcountry Georgia; they decided to organize a union of their own, the Labor Union and Protective Association (LUPA). Workers choose a propitious time to make their demands known, September, the peak time for the arrival of millions of dollars worth of naval stores and cotton ready to be shipped out on waiting vessels of the CGR's Ocean Steamship Company.

On September 25, a committee of the LUPA met with CGR officials and asked for a five-cent increase in pay. The CGR representatives told the union men that, rather than increase their pay, the railroad would find others to take their jobs. The CGR men next met with John J. McDonough, the new mayor elected on the "Conservative Citizens Ticket" who, like his predecessors, pledged to see "law and order enforced." McDonough immediately told the city's militia officers to prepare for any "riotous disturbance" and ordered five thousand rounds of ammunition from the state arsenal.

Rebuffed by the CGR and angered by the city's response, the LUPA called on its members to strike and asked all laboring men in the city to join them. By September 28, some eleven hundred members of the union had walked off the job. The wharves of the CGR seemed deserted. Strike leaders advertised in the papers and in circulars, urging black men to refuse appeals by the railroads to act as strikebreakers. The city ordered twenty-thousand more rounds of ammunition as the potential for violence escalated.[71]

Carrying clubs, pistols, and rifles with fixed bayonets, railroad police patrolled CGR property day and night. Union leaders held prayer meetings and sang hymns and encouraged others to join their cause. Garbage rotted in the streets as the city scavengers joined the strikers; naval stores and cotton bales piled up in city rail yards, and Savannah seemed in the grip of "economic paralysis." Cotton merchants knew they faced financial ruin unless a settlement was reached, and a contingent of the civic-commercial elite agreed to negotiate for the LUPA with the railroads. Only after the city threatened lawsuits did the CGR agree to pay the union men two and a half cents more per hour. When union leaders refused the offer, the *Morning News* accused the strikers of believing "they had the business community by the throat and proposed to squeeze it."[72]

The little sympathy the LUPA had among the white community evaporated when the compromise was rejected and the civic-commercial elite came together. Mayor McDonough deputized fifty additional police officers, arming them with weapons to protect railroad property. The *Atlanta Constitution* and the *New York Times* reported that civil and military authorities appeared ready to "crush out . . . any mob" action whether it be by "one thousand or ten thousand desperate negroes."[73]

Hundreds of strikebreakers recruited by the CGR poured into the city and loaded the cotton and naval stores onto the vessels at the wharves. Seven days after leaders of the LUPA ordered the strike, union members started returning to work. The railroads gave them an increase in pay of two and a half cents an hour. The city scavengers resumed collecting the garbage. One businessman remarked, "the peril has been averted." A more determined group of strikers held out for recognition of their union and a labor contract, but the railroads refused to honor either request and threatened to blacklist the workers. When the holdouts did return to work, the rail lines told them they had no openings as strikebreakers held their former jobs.[74] Somewhat later, the general manager of the CGR remarked: "the strike never worried us. We knew we could get all the labor we wanted to take the place of the strikers. There are hundreds of negroes in [the South] . . . waiting now for the Savannah train, anxious to come here for work."[75]

The LUPA had been broken. Once more a walkout by black dockworkers failed, but this time none died. The press blamed the strike on outside agitators, a recurring shibboleth. One scholar offered a more positive appraisal of the situation, writing that the dockworkers showed "the unexpected possibilities of cohesion and unity in the face of overwhelming social and economic adversity."[76] Indeed, the strike encouraged longshoremen to form a new union within several years, and the experience taught them how to use this union to claim better wages and working conditions.

CHAPTER THREE

Murder, a Strike, a Swindle, and a Boycott

1892–1915

The number of business failures in the economic depression of 1891–95 was greater in the South than other areas of the nation. The Central of Georgia Railway (CGR) declared bankruptcy. Savannah's exports of naval stores and cotton declined sharply, as did its imports. Layoffs soared, contributing to the city's already high unemployment.

A "Horrible Crime"

Joblessness and desperation may explain why five black men gathered on Sunday morning, January 24, 1892, and conspired to rob a successful thirty-two-year-old Savannah businessman, August Meyer.[1] Meyer, who had emigrated from Germany ten years earlier, owned the local soda-water factory that adjoined his house and stable at Duffy and West Broad streets; the plotters were aware that Meyer usually carried "a roll of money" and that he routinely attended social gatherings on Sunday evenings. At nightfall, Gus Williams, Charles Bacon, Marion Heyward, James Gay, and Joe Blois (Meyer's twenty-two-year-old stable boy) met near Meyer's factory.

Following their plan, Blois unlocked the factory door and Heyward and Gay joined him inside. Bacon remained on the street as a lookout while Williams hid in the shadows to await the victim. When Meyer returned home, Williams followed him into the factory, where Blois rushed out of the darkness and with a soda bottle stunned Meyer by a blow to his head. Gay then bludgeoned him with an ax handle, fracturing his skull, and Heyward cut his throat. Meyer died without a sound.

Swift police work, made easier when some associated with the crime turned state's evidence, resulted in arrests within twenty-four hours. On Tuesday, January 26, the *Morning News* announced that the "murderous gang were behind bars" for "the commission of their horrible crime." The news galvanized members of Savannah's German community, who called for the gang's death by rope or faggot. Their cry for immediate "justice" by lynching, commonplace in the South, alarmed the local sheriff, who took the threats seriously and stationed four deputies and ten policemen inside the jail with double-barreled shotguns and Springfield rifles. According to the press, "a mob would have found an attack [on the jail] decidedly disastrous." The sheriff's quick action tamped down the passion for revenge, as did the state's call for a speedy trial. Two days later a grand jury indicted Williams, Bacon, Heyward, Gay, and Blois for the murder of August Meyer with the trial date for "the negro conspirators" set for March 28.[2]

A jury of twelve white men took only seven minutes to decide Gay's fate, guilty of murder. Subsequently, both Williams and Heyward were found guilty as charged. A reporter who watched the proceedings described the prisoners as "indifferent" to the charges; they stood "carelessly" and "lazily" before the court, "spitting tobacco juice." After Heyward was sentenced to death and removed from the courtroom to the jail, the reporter rendered his own verdict: "He will never again come forth except as a corpse."

While Heyward, Gay, and Williams were incarcerated in the new Savannah–Chatham County Jail on Habersham Street awaiting their execution, Heyward died suddenly of "complications arising from indigestion." He was buried in the county's "pauper's field." Deemed accomplices, Bacon and Blois received long prison terms in the state penitentiary.[3]

The robbery and vicious murder of August Meyer may have been one of the most sensational black-on-white crimes ever committed in Savannah. It was rare to have a black-on-white murder; usually blacks killed blacks and whites killed whites. There must have been talk in the city about the recent murder, but a visitor apparently did not hear it or chose not to comment on it, though during her visit she made several observations about the city and its people.

In late February, a well-to-do widow, Catherine Markell, arrived in Savannah to visit relatives. As a tourist she admired sights like the newly built DeSoto Hotel, comparing it to the Ponce de Leon in St. Augustine; at the Telfair Academy of Arts she met Karl Brandt, the curator, and admired his work. The Telfair Hospital, City Hospital, and St. Joseph's Hospital impressed Catherine, and she marveled at the city's monuments to distinguished military men. She took the streetcars to Tybee Island, which she thought "rivals Cape May." Her only remark about the African Americans was that "the letter carriers, sextons, ushers . . . brakemen, & delivery clerks are all negroes."[4]

Armed and Dangerous

Although Catherine did not mention the murder of Meyer, her hosts would have been well aware of escalating violence in Savannah during the early 1890s—indeed, such was the case across the whole South. A prominent historian of the

South has written that, like the Old South, "The New South was a notoriously violent place."

The long-held fears of whites escalated whenever black men gathered in numbers. In nearby South Carolina, Anne Simons Deas wrote in September 1893, "The negroes are in a very excited state. . . . [F]or two nights we have not slept much. I fear trouble is pending." Frequently white southerners expressed concern that blacks were dangerous and prone to violence; many white "young blades," carried with them daily "a pistol . . . knife, and . . . brass knuckles"—the same weapons used in the Old South—as protection against this perceived threat. But as whites feared black violence, so too did blacks fear white violence. According to Savannah police reports of the time, more blacks than whites armed themselves with concealed weapons. This culture of violence, the familiarity with and access to weapons, and a sense of impending threats to the social order may explain why homicide rates in the South were the highest in the nation.[5]

In Savannah from the 1890s into the twentieth century, a period when the black population fluctuated between 39 percent and 51 percent of the total inhabitants, black arrests were three to four times higher annually than white arrests. During the years 1892 to 1895, arrests for various crimes by race were reported as: abusing police or resisting arrest (477 white, 1,012 "colored"); assault with intent to murder (55 white, 166 "colored"); larceny (111 white and 1,133 "colored"). Over the next thirty years in Savannah the number of blacks arrested annually always exceeded that of whites.

To address high crime rates, Savannah increased the police force from 67 to 78 men in the early 1890s. And to the city police could be added another 24 private-duty police employed by the Ocean Steamship Company. All totaled, 102 policemen patrolled the city, and the local militia stood ready to preserve "law and order" in the event of any emergency.[6] The 1894 dockworker's strike gave them the opportunity to do just that.

A Strike and Revenge

The wages of Savannah's longshoremen decreased over time as the Ocean Steamship Company and the railroads more frequently employed nonunion labor. After the negotiations between the ship brokers and dockworkers failed during the busy shipping season, violence erupted. In their appeal the white stevedores union (WBA) and the black dock laborers union (WUA) joined forces to protest the use of nonunion labor and to petition for wages comparable to those paid in Charleston and other southern port cities.

On Friday, September 7, 1894, a contracting agent of the Ocean Steamship Company, Colonel Richard F. Harmon, known as "the chief agent of nonunionism and lower wages," began hiring nonunion men to load the British steamer *Bellisloe*. In short order, knife- and rock-throwing "rows" broke out between nonunion and union workers. Leaders of the longshoremen called a strike. Anxious cotton brokers asked Mayor John J. McDonough to order police protection for nonunion men, but the mayor ignored the request, though he did urge all parties to meet and settle their differences.

Worried about the festering tensions, McDonough alerted the police chief to prepare for unrest and ordered the militia to ready their commands. Formed in Old South Savannah, the militia units were led by the civic-commercial elite: Major Edward Karow, First Georgia Regiment; Captain Thomas Screven, Guards Battalion; Captain J. F. Wheaton, Chatham Artillery; and Lieutenant George C. Gaillard, Georgia Hussars. The *Morning News* offered up a bit of optimism tinged with sarcasm regarding the police and militia's ability to bring about a peaceful resolution: peace would prevail if dockworkers who lived in slums on the west and east sides of the city did not swill too much "Yamacraw and Old Fort liquor."[7]

"Rioting" broke out across the city in the early morning hours of Saturday, September 8. At Bay and Houston streets a few whites and a large number of blacks attacked a column of nonunion workers headed for the wharves to load cotton. A nonunion man remembered that a "dozen men with pistols . . . pointed [them] right at us" and fired. Blows were traded, and a nonunion foreman fell gravely wounded; two of his fellow workers sustained gunshot wounds. A black, union longshoreman suffered a gunshot to his thigh. Mayor McDonough rushed police and militia into the streets and posted them under arms around the city day and night. The move effectively put the city under martial law.

Some complained that McDonough overreacted. One observer witnessed "a sentinel in campaign uniform with loaded musket and fixed bayonet" guarding a local armory "to protect . . . [against an] attack by a mob trying to seize the guns," an attack he believed very unlikely: "There is about as much likelihood of the skies falling as of any such attempt."

The *Morning News* warned that, if violence continued, "the law will be enforced against the rioters vigorously." Jefferson Randolph Anderson, a young Savannah-born attorney and emerging politician, wrote in a September 11, 1894, letter to Miss Page, his sweetheart, "the union men have only two courses open to them. They must either begin a riotous attempt to prevent the loading of the vessels or they must create a general strike." He went on to say that everything was ready to "quell any disorder," that his militia company had been assured they would be "given full authority to fire and fire very early in the game. . . . [W]e will not stop to ask any questions but just as soon as we come in range of any unlawful assemblage we are to open fire upon them."[8] Antiunion passions were not confined to the South but swept across the country in the early 1890s. Clashes such as the one in Savannah between strikers and strike-breakers left many bloodied and dead, and it was the strikebreakers who won again and again.

Nelly Gordon called the "riot" of September 8 a "skirmish." She informed a relative that the nonunion men were "waylaid" by union men: "We are in a state of turmoil just now on account of the bad blood between the Union longshoremen and the non-Union ship loaders." Nelly blamed the mayhem on "the tyranny . . . of the Union men" who "demanded $6 a day; nothing would bring them to reason." She added, "There's no doubt the Non-Union men will hold their own as they have done in other cities."[9] Of course, Nelly spoke on behalf of the shippers and cotton merchants like her husband, William W. Gordon Jr., whose profits improved significantly with the use of nonunion labor.

Mayor McDonough called an arbitration conference where representatives of the unions met with James M. Barnard, spokesman for the ship brokers. The unions demanded an end to nonunion hires on the waterfront plus a living wage for their members, who worked only one hundred days a year during shipping season. The unions argued that they needed a pay raise to match the significantly higher wages of four to five dollars earned daily by dockworkers in nearby ports. When Barnard would not agree to any union demand, the longshoremen saw nothing to gain by continuing the talks and asked for an adjournment, which the mayor granted.[10]

Three African American men, alleged participants in the "riotous" attack on the nonunion men at Bay and Houston streets, were arrested, tried for "disorderly conduct," and sentenced to thirty days hard labor on the county chaingang. They were afterwards remanded to superior court for trial on another charge, "assault with intent to murder." For lack of evidence, the court released the only white man arrested for participation in the "riot." No nonunion men were charged, and they immediately resumed loading cotton onto ships at wharf side, escorted to and from the loading zones by heavily armed police.[11]

During the earlier arbitration conference, spirited exchanges had erupted between spokesmen of the unions and the ship brokers. During one, Sawney Wilson, president of the "colored" longshoremen's union, predicted that failure of negotiations would result in "the loss of life and property." The *Morning News* charged Sawney with making "a threat" even though Sawney had explained previously that he meant he lacked any control over "hotheads."[12]

With all their requests rejected, one hundred union longshoremen left Savannah for Charleston, Port Royal, Brunswick, and New Orleans, all of which paid better wages. Nelly Gordon was correct: nonunion labor came to dominate Savannah's waterfront jobs, earning 60 percent less than the previously unionized workers. The savings went into the pockets of ship and cotton brokers like Colonel Richard F. Harmon, James M. Barnard, William W. Gordon Jr., and owners of the Ocean Steamship Company. By October it was clear that the unions had suffered a total defeat, which left longshoremen and their sympathizers embittered and angry. As Sawney Wilson predicted, some "hot heads" struck back with well-coordinated, defiant acts of revenge.[13]

Cries of "fire" rang out at 6:22 P.M. in the gathering darkness of November 5, 1894. A watchman rang box 91 of the city's fire-alarm system to signal that smoke and flames were rising from the *Skidby,* the largest of the nine British steamships loading cotton destined for Liverpool, Bremen, and Barcelona. Earlier, nonunion laborers had wrestled ten thousand bales into the *Skidby*; now the chief engineer of the fire department, William B. Puder, and three city fire engines rushed to the scene and for hours aimed streams of water at the smoldering cotton, deep in the holds of the *Skidby.*[14]

A mile away from the *Skidby,* a watchman on the Gordon Wharf at 7:15 P.M. sounded an alarm from box 71. The *Baltimore City* was bellowing smoke from the cotton in its hold; the *Castlegarth* tied alongside had forty-five hundred bales on board smoldering or afire. Chief Puder hurried to fight these new blazes. Firefighters soon brought the blaze in the *Baltimore City* under control, but the fire in the *Castlegarth* required hours to extinguish. Most of the cotton burned or became soaked with water.

At 9:15 P.M., shortly after exhausted firemen returned to their stations, an alarm came in from box 53. Cotton in the *Delegarth* lying at the upper wharf was on fire. The tired firefighters were ordered to respond; soon some firemen were redirected south to the Gordon Wharf to fight a blaze aboard the *Stag,* a vessel loaded with twenty-six hundred bales. For over two hours they poured water into the *Stag,* damaging most of the cotton aboard. Fires erupted on several other vessels—the last shipboard fire call came in at 2:00 A.M. on November 6. The *Morning News* described the scene: "The firemen had a night . . . as never known before with a new fire breaking out every hour or less."[15]

Upon inspecting the damaged vessels, Chief Puder reported the discovery of phosphorous at the scene, which indicated "the fires . . . were of incendiary origin." The *Morning News* announced in bold print: "Traces of . . . [phosphorous] Found Everywhere Among the Damaged Cotton." Col. Harmon, who arranged for nonunion laborers to replace the union men, now spoke for the shipbrokers; he and the underwriters and insurers agreed that phosphorous was used as an accelerant and that the "fire bugs" knew how to use phosphorous to start a fire.[16] What was not said was that Fenians often employed phosphorous in acts of revenge in Ireland; a few of Savannah's immigrant-Irish longshoremen may well have known how to use this agent to exact revenge—no one was ever charged.

Whoever the arsonists were, the cleverly planned attack kept firefighters rushing from fires on the upper wharf to new fires on the lower wharves. Damages to cotton and the ships exceeded $100,000 (about $2,800,000 in 2016 dollars). Cotton brokers William W. Gordon Jr. and J. F. Minis & Company and shipbrokers Col. Richard F. Harmon and James Barnard sustained heavy losses; underwriters covered most of the damages.

Most of the civic-commercial elite agreed, "Nothing that has occurred here in recent years has aroused such deep concern as the firing of the cotton ships. . . . [T]he guilty parties should be uncovered and punished without delay." Private companies and individuals paid for men to stand guard aboard ships and patrol the wharves; the City Council offered a reward of $500 for the arrest and conviction of each and every arsonist. Members of the Cotton Exchange listened attentively as one of their most distinguished members, William W. Gordon Jr., addressed the issue.

Mr. Gordon said that not since the yellow fever epidemic of 1876 had Savannah faced "a pestilence which threatened . . . the city's growth [and] . . . the existence of the city. itself. . . . [Savannah's] life blood is commerce," and if the ships that carry its commerce "cannot be protected . . . businessmen will go . . . and wharves and offices and dwellings will lose their tenants and their value." Gordon's resolution that "no pains or expense should be spared in detecting and punishing the guilty" passed unanimously.[17]

At Savannah's Board of Trade meeting, Captain D. G. Purse offered a resolution with even harsher language: "An extraordinary outbreak of incendiarism has placed in jeopardy the entire commerce of this city." He urged that upon conviction the "criminals" be given the "severest penalties . . . [so] that lawlessness and violence may be summarily crushed out in this community forever."

Both Gordon and Purse asked the city, the Cotton Exchange, and the Board of Trade to offer substantial rewards for the capture of the arsonists. Gordon warned that "if cotton can be destroyed here there is no reason why businesses, houses and dwellings may not be destroyed in the same manner." Eventually the reward money reached over thirty thousand dollars; the city itself appropriated twenty-five thousand. Despite the generous offer, no one came forward with information leading to the arrest of those responsible.[18]

In the end the white power structure prevailed. Savannah's unions, the WBA and the WUA, were crushed. Many of Savannah's black longshoremen who did not or could not leave for work at other ports entered the ranks of the chronically unemployed, thus contributing to increasing rates of poverty and its consequences.

Not until the passage and protections of the Wagner Act by the federal government in the first third of the twentieth century could workers unionize and bargain collectively. This act resuscitated the union movement in Savannah. Local 1414 of the International Longshoremen's Association opened in Savannah, and African American workers quickly joined. The new labor union became almost exclusively black.[19]

Despite white domination of state and local government in the 1890s, the rise in lynchings across the South, and an increasingly segregated city, black Savannahians found support in their churches, social clubs, Emancipation Day celebrations, and local black militia parades. By this time some African American intellectuals were sources of pride and inspiration. Local black leaders cheered the arrival in Savannah of forward-looking black men and women like Richard Wright and the doctors Alice and Cornelius McKane.[20]

The Emergence of Dr. Richard Wright

Born into slavery near Dalton, Georgia, Richard Wright's mother enrolled him at the end of the Civil War in a Freedmen's Bureau school in Atlanta. A gifted student, he moved to the preparatory school of Atlanta University at age fourteen and after passing rigorous examinations was admitted to the College Department of Atlanta University, where he majored in the classics. In 1876 he received one of the first college degrees awarded to an African American in Georgia. He married a year later.

Wright's career moved at lightning speed. Two years after graduating, he founded a school for blacks in Cuthbert, Georgia, and a newspaper that became one of the most influential African American newspapers in the South. Wright, who was dark skinned, stood five feet two, and weighed 130 pounds, lectured across the region and was active as a political organizer. Because of his inspiring leadership, Wright was elected to the Republican National Convention in 1880.[21]

That same year he moved to Augusta, Georgia, where he established the first publicly supported high school for African Americans in the state and founded another newspaper. In writings and speeches, Wright opposed the convict lease system as well as segregation and discrimination in public transportation, hotels, restaurants, and theaters. His progressive ideas were developing as white attitudes toward blacks were hardening.

Efforts to separate blacks and whites moved apace in Georgia. Between 1889 and 1891 the state passed laws segregating chain gangs and streetcars and stiffened voting requirements for African Americans. Savannah's City Council passed laws prohibiting black bicyclists from riding in Forsyth Park, and the Savannah post office installed a restroom for "Negroes."[22]

The recently formed, primarily rural-based Populist Party was courting blacks, and Democrats feared this coalition threatened their control of the state. The *Tribune* accused Democrats of raising a "social equality scare" and of trying to turn white Georgians against the newly formed party and rekindle racism. Violence and discrimination against blacks surged as white opposition emerged to any form of black advancement, including education.

Disappointed at the growing opposition to equal treatment under the law for blacks, Richard Wright's Emancipation Day address in Atlanta in the early 1890s denounced the state legislature for its efforts to curtail the rights of African Americans, remove and restrict their political access, and deny them the same rights as whites.[23]Wright repeatedly challenged the status quo and in so doing galvanized the strong feelings of his friends and his enemies. Wright no doubt was aware of discussions regarding the establishment of a publicly supported college for African Americans in Georgia. Wright's friends urged him to seek the office of president.

The passage of the second Morrill Act by the federal government in 1890 made funds available to states to establish black colleges of agricultural and mechanical arts. The Georgia governor and legislature agreed to create such a school for "Negroes" as a part of the state university system. The Democratic Party, the party that controlled Georgia politics, wanted to ensure that the state received a share of the federal money provided by the Morrill Act, but opposed giving "Negroes" a "white man's education."[24] The first step in the funding progress was to establish a Negro College Commission.

The Negro College Commission and Peter W. Meldrim

Savannah attorney Peter Wiltberger Meldrim accepted the appointment as chairman of the Negro College Commission by Governor W. J. Northern, who charged the commission to find a location and a president for the institution. Prominent Savannah clergymen like the reverends Emanuel K. Love and James M. Simms appeared before the commission to urge that the college be located in Savannah and that Dr. Richard Wright be appointed its first president.

As chairman, Meldrim wielded a great deal of influence. A forty-four-year-old lawyer, Meldrim was a rare Savannahian for the times. Born and reared in a Savannah home "of comfort and refinement," Meldrim served in the Civil War. He later became commander of the Georgia Division, United Confederate Veterans. Meldrim attended the University of Georgia, won a Phi Beta Kappa key, earned a law degree, and returned to Savannah to practice. His wife, Frances, from Augusta, Georgia, was the "social belle of her day." Meldrim had wealth, family status, power, a beautiful wife, a successful law practice, and a curious mind. Meldrim remained throughout his life an "ardent friend of education," believing that "the preservation of our very liberties depend upon an educated citizenship."[25]

Blacks and whites alike characterized Meldrim as a pioneer in race relations. A presiding bishop of the African Methodist Episcopal Church, the Right Reverend J. S. Flipper wrote Meldrim: "For years I had always admired you for the interest that you have shown in my people."[26] Meldrim believed in education for the "Negro." He once told an integrated audience, "We are all Georgians irrespective of color. We are one people with the same past, present and future." Perhaps this last phase might have amused some African Americans in the audience who were well able to contrast Meldrim's past and present life to their own. Nonetheless, with support from "prominent" black Savannahians and white merchants, who believed the location of a "Negro" college would be good for business, Meldrim's Negro College Commission selected Savannah as the site for the college and Dr. Richard R. Wright its first president.

The Board of Trustees of the University of Georgia approved a budget of eight thousand dollars for the college, substantially less than both the chancellor and Meldrim's commission anticipated. This move suggests that the Board of Trustees had no intention of adequately funding the new college even though federal funds were available to do so. The pattern of underfunding the black college continued far into the twentieth century.[27]

The grounds of the "Warren Place," just southeast of Savannah, became the site of the Georgia State Industrial College for Colored Youth (GSIC). The campus of thirty acres included groves of oak trees and several dilapidated, wooden structures with neither indoor plumbing nor electricity.

The college opened on October 7, 1891. About a thousand visitors both black and some white attended the dedication of the college. By March, forty-two students had enrolled. Over the next dozen years, enrollments fluctuated between two hundred and five hundred. Near the end of the 1890s, female students were permitted to attend classes and the faculty increased from three to ten. The school became a cultural resource for Savannah's black community by sponsoring events such as an evening of music by the faculty in December 1894 at the historic Savannah Theatre.

Wright brought to campus lecturers who reinforced philosophies of racial pride, uplift, and accountability, including the Reverend Emanuel K. Love, the controversial abolitionist Frederick Douglass, Bishop Henry McNeal Turner, Booker T. Washington, and Mary McLeod Bethune.[28] President Wright clashed occasionally with Peter Meldrim. The two highly educated men, one black and born into slavery, the other white who represented the white elite, disagreed on the type of education needed for African Americans. Meldrim and the Negro College commissioners at first opposed a "white man's" education for blacks, but in debates with Meldrim, Wright argued that, in order to compete with whites in an increasingly complicated world, blacks needed a broad education. Wright won the curriculum issue and devised a plan of study like that of Atlanta University and New England colleges. Entering students for the 1892–93 academic year enrolled in agricultural and mechanical subjects as well as courses in Greek, Latin, algebra, natural science, and English. Over time those who attended GSIC and remained in Savannah constituted the core of the city's more educated black citizenry.[29] Like President Wright, other African American "outsiders" were welcomed to Savannah's growing community of black intellectuals.

The Doctors McKane

Alice Woodby, a native of Pennsylvania, became the first female physician in Georgia, where she met and married the African-born, light-skinned Dr. Cornelius McKane, a graduate of the Medical School of the University of Vermont who had opened an office in Savannah. Together they founded a nurse-training school at 202 Liberty Street for black male and female nurses. In 1895 the school graduated its first class.

For a variety of reasons, that same year and to the great disappointment of the African American community, the McKanes departed for Liberia, where they established a nurse-training school and hospital. However, their failure to change the political culture of that country and to earn an adequate income soon led the couple to return to Savannah. Cornelius, who once championed black emigration to Africa, now believed that the future of Africa lay in the hands of Africans. He advocated that American blacks remain at home to fight for their rights and "solve the Negro problem in America."

Welcomed upon their return by black professionals like President Wright; the Reverend Emanuel Love; Sol Johnson, editor of the *Tribune*; and William Royall, the city's pioneering black mortician, the McKanes founded the McKane Hospital for women and children at 644 West Sixtieth Street. The *Tribune* and black churches promoted the hospital and successfully appealed for funds to support it. Within a few years the McKanes relinquished control of the hospital to a group of black physicians who renamed the institution Charity Hospital. For years black and some white Savannahians struggled to raise money for the hospital. By the early twentieth century, about half of the total patients were charity cases—the hospital's new name appeared well chosen. In the early twenty-first century that hospital became the Heritage Place Apartments in the historic African American Cuyler-Brownsville neighborhood.[30]

The McKanes remained in Savannah as practicing physicians and Republican Party activists until they left for Boston in search of a better education for their two children. Three years after their arrival there, Dr. Cornelius McKane died at age fifty in 1912. Dr. Alice McKane remained in Boston until her death in 1948.[31]

Fissures among the Democrats

Disunity developed within Savannah's Democrat Party in the 1890s. Jefferson Randolph Anderson observed in early June 1894, "The local political pot is red hot and boiling over—a war of factions." Son of Confederate Colonel Edward C. Anderson Jr. and a graduate of the University of Virginia, Jefferson decided to enter a race for office. But in July he encountered attacks by an opponent that "reflected on my personal integrity, and wounded my sense of honor." This sent Jefferson into a "black rage," and he bought a "cow hide" whip to "thrash" his opponent. Only intervention by his friends prevented him from doing so.[32] The personal affront Jefferson felt from the words of his opponent triggered duels in the Old South. Indeed, devotion to the Old South remained very much alive in New South Savannah.

Anderson believed he lost his political campaign due to the "unfortunate factional feeling which has arisen" between the city's two wings of the Democratic Party—the "so-called" Tammany Club, most often associated with maintaining the status quo, and the Citizens' Club, more business-dominated and reform-minded. Usually the Citizens' Club voted against any candidate put forward by the Tammany Club and vice-versa.[33] One group of Democrats had formed the Citizens' Club, another the Tammany Club, another faction the Peoples Club, and yet another the Citizens Committee. These factions lobbied for various causes and/or candidates.

By late 1894, Mayor John J. McDonough and his Tammany Club had controlled City Hall for four years and citizens were tired of its perceived chicanery. On one occasion, during an October meeting of the City Council, Tammany members voted to override their own rules, prompting Councilman Herman R.

Myers to call the procedure "unlawful." He walked out to "hisses" from the Tammany Club members. Others called him a "hero," and thus Myers emerged as the leader of a movement to reform city government.[34]

The Rise of Herman Myers

Herman Myers immigrated with his Jewish family to Virginia from Bavaria when he was five. The family opened a tanning business, and at age fifteen young Myers came to Savannah and entered a partnership with a Jewish tanner. Within forty years he accumulated a significant fortune by successful investing. Businessmen sought his advice on financial matters. He became a Mason and a member of Mickve Israel Synagogue. While serving for ten years on the City Council, Myers came to understand the inside of Savannah politics.[35]

In late November 1894, at a meeting of the Citizens' Club, Herman Myers received its endorsement for the upcoming mayoralty race. However, another contingent of the club wanted to support former Confederate surgeon Dr. William Duncan rather than Myers, and they walked out and formed yet another faction, the People's Club, with Duncan as their nominee. During the mayoralty campaign, both Duncan and Myers called for economy in government and basic services for the city to accommodate the surge in population in the 1890s from 43,189 to 54,284.

On the campaign trail, Myers characterized himself as a "rags to riches" businessman; his opponent he called a "socialite." Myers ran with a "reform" slate of candidates, most of whom were young and new to government. The Myers campaign not only identified voters but also paid their back taxes so they could vote. The Duncan team came late to this tactic and sometimes physically collided with Myers's workers when they attempted to be first in line at the tax collector's office. One night in mid-December, armed thugs from both campaigns bloodied each other with "sticks and brickbats" before police arrived and restored order.[36]

In early January 1895, shortly before the election, the *Tribune* endorsed Myers, who it said would bring prosperity such that "the colored man will be able to secure work at living wages." The *Tribune* accused the "Duncanites" of having been associated with many injustices inflicted on the African American community, including the period "when our colored longshoremen were sentenced to jail for daring to try to better their condition as workingmen and . . . to take bread out of their mouths."[37]

When Myers gained a comfortable lead in the race, his opponents launched a smear campaign. They denigrated Myers as a foreigner, said he was "not a citizen of the United States," and accused him of bribery. On January 22, 1895, there were 4,504 voters who showed up at the polls on a very cold Tuesday to cast ballots. Herman Myers won the election by a margin of 633 votes and soon took office as Savannah's first Jewish mayor.

Bloc voting and other factors gave him the victory. Germans, Russian Jews, and Italians counted for approximately 25 percent of the total white vote, blacks about 22 percent of the total voters. The *Tribune* claimed that 90 percent of blacks voted for Myers; some might have been influenced by a little "street" money that changed hands during the campaign. In Precincts 13 to 20 at the south end of the city, dominated by middle-class whites of all ethnicities and some blacks, Myers won every precinct except one. His strong showing in the Irish and German community may have been because he was perceived as less strict on the enforcement of liquor laws than his opponent. As the city continued to expand southward over the years, the population in these precincts rose and became increasingly important in local politics.[38]

Myers believed that, by applying the principles and techniques of business, Savannah could be managed more effectively. As a booster he hoped to lure manufacturing, which would make the city "permanently prosperous." At the outset of Myers's administration, the City Council created the Citizen's Industrial Committee, dominated by businessmen who promoted the city through personal contacts. *Morning News* articles boasted the successes of manufacturers in the city, where 106 factories employed 2,383 people. The campaign resulted in several companies relocating to Savannah. And as success breeds success, the campaign also stimulated enthusiasm among local retailers, who wooed customers into Savannah from the hinterlands with a May Day celebration, modeled after similar events in Charleston and New Orleans. About 4,000 shoppers visited Savannah in 1895.

Myers wanted more exports of a greater variety. At the time, Savannah ranked as the world's largest exporter of naval stores, third in lumber, and fifth in cotton exports. Efforts to link Savannah and Manchester, England, paid off. Georgia commodities now went directly to Manchester, and from there English finished goods shipped out to Savannah. In a decade, Savannah's export and import trade doubled. Cotton shipments soared, and Savannah became the third largest exporter of cotton, behind New Orleans and Galveston. Tonnage of outbound shipments of fertilizer rose as naval stores shipments declined due to a sharp drop in the region's supply. Within a few years, the banks of Savannah held twice the capital of Charleston banks, which reflected Savannah's booming economy.[39]

Myers's administration brought new blood to city government, especially businessmen. The City Council terminated thirteen of the twenty-six hold-

Ships awaiting loading of rosin barrels in Savannah, ca. 1898–1900. Savannah was the largest rosin market in the world. Courtesy of Georgia Archives, Vanishing Georgia Collection, image no. ctm083.

overs from the prior administration and replaced important posts like city attorney, clerk of council, harbor master, and head of the police force with their own appointees.

The new police chief, Frank McDermott, employed enforcement tactics used by earlier administrations to improve the ambiance of downtown Savannah. Patrolmen chased tramps beyond the city limits and declared war on a gang of white and black thieves and "Negro boys" known as "petty pilfers." The newfound exuberance manifested by police apparently exceeded the mayor's expectations. After an incident in a black neighborhood resulted in wholesale arrests and beating a black man, Myers fired two patrolmen and gave them a public tongue lashing and ordered the release of the incarcerated African Americans. In spite of aggressive police tactics, Savannah remained a violent place. In 1895 there were sixteen killings, more than half of them black-on-black homicides.

Mayor Myers repeatedly found it necessary to remind Chief McDermott to arrest bar owners who violated liquor laws. Apparently, some officers overlooked offenders on their beats. But Myers resisted calls for prohibition of liquor sales and the closing of pool halls demanded by local Protestant clergymen. By ignoring the twin vices, he curried support from anti-prohibition voters—Irish, German, and Jewish ethnics.[40]

Aware that the black community gave him 90 percent of their vote, Myers made some gestures on their behalf. He appointed a black, Dr. S. Palmer Lloyd, to his staff of city physicians to serve "the unfortunate negroes who, even when well are unable to take care of themselves." The appointment was something his predecessor had refused to do. At the end of his first year, Dr. Lloyd recommended that the "unhygienic surroundings" of the houses and yards in the slums of Yamacraw on the west side and Old Fort on the east be given immediate attention because such "unsanitary conditions" caused diseases and death.[41]

By the end of Myers's first term more blacks were employed by the city than ever before. Yet from a business perspective, cost-cutting became a priority, and the target for this was indigent care. Free prescription drugs for the poor were now available only from two city-run dispensaries, and the city's contribution of four hundred dollars for indigent care in 1895 (a fraction of the monies allocated in Charleston and Atlanta) was, according to Mayor Myers, all the city budget could afford.

To raise money and eliminate favoritism in tax evaluations, the administration established a Board of Tax Assessors. Merely the threat of an audit brought many people in to pay taxes owed. Myers also appointed city commissioners to oversee the police, fire, and public works departments. The commissioners appointed included Myers's political allies Harry Willink and George J. Baldwin *and* political opponents William W. Gordon Jr. and George H. Stone. The businessman-mayor was also a good politician.

Under the commissioners, significant improvements were made in the city's financial health. Harry Willink, commissioner of public works, became one of the most successful and forward-looking members of the Myers team. He purchased land on the south and east side of the city for future development, opened and paved new streets, initiated the city's first house-numbering system, provided new stables and wagons for the scavenger department, added a new chimney to the city's crematory for waste, and initiated major improvements in the sewer system.[42]

In 1895, the city health officer said that Savannah's "combination system of sewers," built when "hygiene and sanitary engineering were in their ignorant infancy," needed immediate attention. "Our sewers . . . are 'elongated privy vaults,' good enough to be used for transportation of surface water but as conveyors of . . . excrementitious [*sic*] matter would be condemned by any sanitary engineer."[43] Other southern cities like Charleston, Memphis, and Atlanta faced similar problems with waste disposal.

In Atlanta during heavy rains in the 1890s, sewer conduits overflowed and poured into streams running through black neighborhoods, polluting the groundwater. Charleston and Memphis also had sewage issues. Luckily for the white population, Charleston's health officer, Dr. Henry Horlbeck, was an indefatigable sanitarian. He had a flush toilet in his living room at a time when people in Boston and Paris considered the indoor privy unsanitary. Horlbeck initiated the building of a modern sewer system for Charleston in the 1890s, as did other southern cities like Savannah.[44]

Savannah's city engineer designed a new, four-mile sewage line that emptied into the Savannah River—a house-drainage plan, debated for decades, was to be tied into the main line. Initially, the plan stirred controversy, especially from worries over sewage flowing into the river, the main source of the city's drinking water. The administration approved the plan, and construction took six years to complete.

Myers's first administration heralded the beginning of the Progressive Era in the city's history. Progressivism came to be characterized as a period of governmental reform and moral uplift, usually "for whites only." But Savannah's black community, as in the past, refused to be ignored. Often overlooked, even exploited economically by the white civic-commercial elite, Savannah's African Americans came together to overcome segregation and new Jim Crow laws, to improve their economic lives, to educate their children, to develop their own institutions, and to secure the same respect and opportunity accorded whites.[45]

Near the end of September 1896 a devastating hurricane slammed into Savannah. Seventeen people in and around the city perished, and nearly every private dwelling and public building suffered damage. Winds bowled over hundreds of trees; telephone and telegraph wires collapsed into tangled, splintered masses. The debris blocked streets, and floodwaters inundated certain sections of the city. Damage estimates reached $1 million, or more than $28 million in 2016 dollars. Recovery efforts cut deeply into the city's budget on the eve of a mayoralty election.[46]

Meldrim Takes on Myers

In the mayor's race of 1897 a new faction of the Democratic Party, calling itself the Liberal Club, nominated the articulate, wealthy, hard-nosed attorney and Irish politico Peter W. Meldrim, the same Peter Meldrim who had chaired the Negro College Commission. The Citizens' Club backed Mayor Myers for another term.

Meldrim charged Myers with filling City Hall with disreputable citizens. Myers trumpeted the success of his businesslike and reformed-minded administration. In sum, the candidates split the ethnic and silk-stocking vote, but the Liberal Club's better organizational skills and money to buy both black and white votes won the election for Meldrim.[47]

William W. Gordon Jr.'s observations about the 1897 mayoral campaign provide some provocative insights. He said the Liberal Club "hunted up every resident in Savannah not registered & paid their back taxes . . . on condition they would register." The Liberals "registered 1000 to 1200 voters at a cost of probably $10,000." Meanwhile, the Citizens' Club, using the same tactic, "bought about 300 to 400 negroes—many of whom . . . had previously been registered by the Liberals [but who] deserted to get a second price from the Citizens [*sic*] Club." Annoyed by the duplicity, the night before the election, the Liberal Club rounded up "800 to 900 [citizens they had registered], guarded them all night and lined them up at the polls at 7 am" and voted them before the Citizens' Club "could get at these voters." Gordon predicted, "the negro vote will decide." Gordon guessed correctly. Meldrim won.[48]

The Meldrim administration soon launched investigations of the commissions established by Myers, especially the police and fire commissioners, with the intent of replacing them with their own men. In the process of naming replacements, the City Council sometimes erupted into open and angry outbursts over the selections and, though the shouting matches embarrassed Mayor Meldrim, he seemed unable to quell the rancor.

Unlike the Myers administration, Meldrim's team did not work closely with the city businessmen. The council appeared to be less innovative and less efficient, having run up thirty thousand dollars of debt. Additionally, government also seemed tinged with racism and showed these leanings when one member of City Council proposed a whites-only primary because "[people are] disgusted with the corrupting of the negro vote." The council also passed a resolution prohibiting black doctors from treating white patients.

Such discrimination angered men like John Deveaux and Sol Johnson. As editors of the *Tribune*, they tried to raise awareness of disparities between the black and white experience among the paper's readership. They blamed the city's white government for the crowded and underfunded African American schools and condemned the segregated parks, theaters, soda fountains, public restrooms, and beach facilities. The editors urged blacks not to patronize businesses that discriminated. But the *Tribune* also chastised blacks for selling their vote, failing to pay poll taxes, and lacking loyalty to the Republican Party.[49] Occasionally discrimination manifested itself in public violence.

Virulent Racism Rising

On Emancipation Day, January 1, in Savannah and other southern cities, blacks celebrated their freedom and proclaimed their rights as part of the body politic. The local black militia, wearing smart uniforms, performed drills and on parade demonstrated racial pride and black masculinity. Much like the members of white militias, these young militiamen enjoyed comradeship, social events, and excursions. On parade, the GSIC band sometimes accompanied the black militia, followed by members of social clubs and black leaders riding in carriages. On occasion, white hostility toward this display expressed itself in confrontational encounters.

One such explosive event happened in the 1890s. While officers were inspecting a black militia company at the intersection of Liberty and East Broad streets, a horse-drawn vehicle driven by two white men ploughed through the unit at high speed. Two black militia sergeants fell injured. Lt. Colonel John Deveaux, founder of the *Tribune*, who witnessed the event, ordered a squad to pursue the carriage. During the arrest, the drivers were recognized as two city policemen. As the incident was unfolding, a white crowd gathered and roughed up Deveaux. Though the policemen in the carriage had broken the law and caused serious injuries, the two men, James McGuire and C. W. Dyer, received only brief suspensions without pay. Had the races of the perpetrators and victims been reversed, one can only speculate as to the outcome.[50]

Expressions of hostility to black soldiers came in more subtle ways. Whereas Savannah's white militia units received state and local funds for supplies, uniforms, summer training, medical units, a signal corps, and machine guns—black units did not. Evaluations by white officers frequently cited deficiencies in the training of black units, but none in white. Furthermore, petitions for aid sent to local, state, and federal sources by black militia leaders, including Lt. Colonel John Deveaux, were denied.

By the 1890s, as segregation increased, white militia units challenged the right of black units to use Forsyth Park for drills. Already the state had acted to reduce the number of black militia units in the state. Savannah itself had eight black militia companies, one cavalry company, and the only black artillery unit in the United States. Within a few years the legislature banned all black militia units in the state.[51]

America's declaration of war on Spain in 1898 was seen by men like Deveaux and Sol Johnson as an opportunity for black soldiers to win recognition and respect. When Georgia's governor responded to the national call for troops by asking for white volunteers only, the *Tribune* editorialized: "What honor will the colored man get for chivalrous acts in the present war? His manhood is curtailed by restricting his ambition and preventing him from being promoted higher than a sergeant." Other states did not restrict black volunteers, and the presence of black U.S. Army troops stationed in Georgia seemed to fuel racism.

The *Morning News* asserted: "Negro troops have shown a lawless spirit wherever they have been in camp near towns. They had no respect for civil authorities." The *Tribune* offered a different perspective, "The Negro's valor had intensified prejudice against him. His former friends are . . . silent and indifferent to his persecutions." The *Tribune* called Georgia's failure to recruit black volunteers "one of the most brutal and unjust [acts] ever . . . inflicted upon our people in this state."[52]

By late 1898, the attention of Savannah's white civic-commercial elite focused on another mayoralty race. Mayor Meldrim, who appeared to have lost control of the City Council, decided not to run again. It became a race of former mayors: John J. McDonough received the nomination of the Liberal Club; the Citizens' Club once more nominated Herman Myers.[53] That same year a scandal broke that unified the city's civic-commercial elite.

Scandal!

During the 1890s an Ohio-born West Point graduate, thirty-five-year-old Oberlin M. Carter, headed the U.S. Army Corps of Engineers Savannah District. He resided in a luxurious home at 112 Liberty Street with his beautiful wife, Marguerite. From his office on the third floor of the Southern Bank Building at the intersection of Drayton and Bryan streets, Carter could see a waterfront teeming with vessels. His responsibility was to keep Savannah's silting, shifting channel open to oceangoing ships, a challenge the federal and local governments had struggled with since the eighteenth century.

Carter and his wife enjoyed cycling, sailing, dinners, and the theater with Savannah's close-knit elite. Local professionals and businessmen marveled that Carter, an engineer, read great literature and spoke Spanish, German, and French and consoled him when his wife fell ill with typhoid fever and died. Sometime thereafter, President William McKinley rewarded Carter's highly touted work on the river by selecting him as the military attaché to the Court of St. James. A newspaperman applauded the appointment, reflecting the attitude of Savannah's elite when he observed that the handsome "brilliant and popular officer [is] a man people here will regret very much to see go."[54] Another West Pointer, Cassius E. Gillette, replaced Carter as head of the Savannah District Corps of Engineers. With the transition underway, Captain Carter offered

Gillette his home as temporary lodgings, a hospitable gesture that Carter came to regret.

In order to better understand his new job, Gillette immediately ordered a review of the Savannah River project and immersed himself in the details. While staying in Carter's home, he found and happened to read some of Carter's private papers. What Gillette discovered astounded him. Carter's financial records showed investments of more than $400,000—about $11 million in 2016 dollars—astonishing on a captain's pay.

After two weeks of reading through Carter's private records, Gillette met with General John M. Wilson, chief of the Army Engineer Corps, and presented a report accusing Carter of massive fraud. The evidence dumbfounded Wilson. When confronted, Carter "emphatically denied" the authenticity of Gillette's report, and friends among Savannah's elite branded Gillette a "liar" and ostracized him and his family. Carter was ordered to face a court-martial in Savannah in January 1898.

Defense attorneys recruited twenty-nine of the country's best engineers to inspect Captain Carter's work, which they found "very successful." Indeed, the engineers concluded that Carter's leadership had saved the government $1 million, and "not one cent was missing." Attorneys for the government presented a starkly different picture. They charged that Carter together with the Atlantic Contracting Company of Greene and Gaynor defrauded the government, that contractor profits were exorbitant, and that misappropriations totaled more than $1 million. In sum, they concluded Carter had become wealthy through embezzlement of the taxpayer's money.

The prosecution showed that the profits made by Carter, Green, and Gaynor came from the availability of cheap, black labor and abundant raw materials. Taken to nearby islands, black workmen collected "brush and dry leaves" and under atrocious working conditions fashioned retaining walls and jetties to improve the river's channel. The federal government had appropriated sizeable sums of money to the contractors to pay for labor and building materials. Of course, the materials cost nothing and the black laborers received only seventeen cents a day for their work. The vast amount of money saved was skimmed off the federal appropriations and into the pockets of Greene, Gaynor, and their "secret partner," Captain Carter.[55]

On the morning of April 30, 1898, officers of the court-martial found Captain Carter and his coconspirators guilty of fraud. Carter was fined, dismissed from the Army, and sentenced to federal prison for five years. The *New York Times* reported that, on his way to prison with a military escort, he wore an elegant dark suit, a turned-down collar, a bow tie, a black derby hat, an overcoat, and yellow kid gloves. He was imprisoned in a cell six feet high, just over three feet wide, and seven feet long; his possessions included a tin cup, wash pail, a cot with a straw mattress, and blankets, but no sheets.

Carter served three years of his five-year sentence. After appeals and delays, Greene and Gaynor fled to Canada where they remained until President Theodore Roosevelt took an interest in the case and announced publicly, "This affair fosters the idea that there is one law for the rich and another for the poor." Shortly thereafter Greene and Gaynor were extradited to Savannah, tried, and found guilty of a "carnival of graft" and imprisoned for four years.[56]

Until the end of his life, Oberlin Carter vigorously denied his guilt, blamed others for his conviction, and repeatedly appealed his sentence to the U.S. Supreme Court. Members of Savannah's finest families remained loyal to the dashing former army officer and accepted his version of events—that others had intrigued against him and caused his downfall. A prominent socialite and Savannahian, Juliette Gordon Low, founder of the Girl Scouts, believed passionately in Carter's innocence. On one occasion she wrote him: "You must have known we all sympathized with you"; there remains "a systematic tyranny . . . towards you . . . to persecute you." She concluded: "Your work [on the Savannah River] stands as a monument to your genius. . . . Some day you will have justice done you. That is what your friends hope and pray for you."[57] Sounding like an unreconstructed Rebel, Juliette Gordon Low blamed a conspiratorial government that brought about Carter's downfall!

One author recently concluded that Carter did in fact act fraudulently. He argued that the lavish lifestyle of Savannah's elite—bankers, railroad executives, and cotton brokers—influenced the lowly, underpaid Army captain. The inequities he perceived between the lives of the civic-commercial elite and his own life may have led him to embezzle a fortune. Indeed, in the decade Carter was in Savannah, he likely came to know that some of the elite bent and even violated the law to make their own fortunes.

After nearly forty years of appealing his case to various courts and losing, the former Army officer lost his final appeal. In the late 1930s, the Supreme Court of the United States once more refused to set aside his conviction for fraud. Carter always maintained his innocence and claimed he was "a victim of jealousy." He regained neither his rank in the army nor his honor. Frail and dispirited, Carter died of pneumonia at the age of eighty-eight.[58]

The Lives of the Well-to-Do

As the late nineteenth faded into the early twentieth century, Savannah's white elite appeared to enjoy the best of times. It took twenty-three pages to list the names of the city's elite in the New York–published *Social Register of Savannah*. For breakfast the well-to-do enjoyed eggs, bacon, and hot breads with Georgia syrup. An older patriarch, the cotton broker and politician William W. Gordon Jr., told a friend: "I get up at sunrise . . . and ride on horseback for about an hour and a half." The elite dined on rice birds served on silver platters until the birds became extinct due to overzealous hunters and the disappearance of the rice fields.

The "belles" born into the upper reaches of Savannah society were tutored locally and sent to schools in the Northeast though some matriculated in the local progressive school founded by Nina Pape. Young women attended cotillions and soirees and made their debuts at the "Germans" given in the Guards Armory, where they enjoyed "marvelous suppers" and dancing with their escorts or chaperones until the popular song, "After the Ball," ended the evening.

The belles "loved" the romance novels of Richard Harding Davis and played lawn tennis in wide hats and shirt-waists with pleated skirts that reached the ground. The introduction of the bicycle for recreational use changed the way well-to-do Savannah women dressed and began their emancipation from extensive layers of clothes. Young ladies sailed together with young men who enjoyed regattas on the nearby rivers or tinkered with their new "power boats."

The privileged class founded several women's clubs and a card club; Nelly Gordon's home served as the venue for the founding of the Georgia Society of Colonial Dames of America. At the end of the nineteenth century, one well-to-do woman of the city remembered it as a time of "widespread belief in the unchanging order of things, a satisfaction with things as they were." Of course, the privileged class had the time to enjoy their leisure. Only 18 percent of the city's white women worked outside the home, whereas 64 percent of the city's black women did.[59]

Mayor Myers' Second, Third, and Fourth Terms

In the mayoralty election of January 24, 1899, Herman Myers outpolled John McDonough by 224 votes out of 3,184 cast. Myers received a good number of Irish votes and won the black vote by a two-to-one margin. African Americans regarded the McDonough administration as unsympathetic to the needs of the black community. In the election, white and black "purchaseable" votes divided evenly. Myers again came to the aid of his black constituents, who now numbered over 51 percent of Savannah's population, the only city in Georgia where African Americans constituted a majority. With their help, Myers would be reelected without opposition in 1901, 1903, and 1905.

In the first few months of Myers's second term, the Town Council of nearby Thunderbolt passed an ordinance segregating passengers on the Savannah, Thunderbolt & Isle of Hope Railway. Sol Johnson's influential *Tribune* quickly reminded its readers of the success of their 1872 boycott and urged them to use the tactic again. Black Savannahians took up the challenge. Stockholders in the railway company, including Mayor Myers, as well as Savannah's black clergy, pressured the Thunderbolt Town Council to rescind its segregation policy. Whether the decision was economically motivated or simply a new spirit of interracial cooperation is not known—but it brought an end to the boycott. Around the same period, the editor of the *Tribune* raised an issue about another segregated venue.

He posed the question: why do "Many of our best . . . young men and women" sit in "the peanut gallery" (balcony) of the local theater? The editor wondered when will "our people . . . learn to have self respect and refuse to accept accommodation that is forced upon them?"[60] A year later, Johnson raised a question to the white elite about the incident of local violence toward blacks. A lynching near the city reflected the regional mentality.

In spring 1900, in the nearby community of Bloomingdale, a large white mob seized Allen Brooks for allegedly raping a white woman, hanged him, and fired an estimated five hundred bullets into his lifeless body. The *Tribune*'s editor demanded that the police arrest mob leaders and asked how could "the better element among the white citizens allow this stain against law and order to remain . . . without efforts to clear it?"[61]

This type of violence reflected a hardening of racial lines across the South in the late nineteenth century. Despite some racial comingling in Savannah's low-income neighborhoods like Oglethorpe Ward, where mixed-race brothels, taverns, and grocery stores were commonplace, blacks who challenged the white social order sometimes faced violence, arrest, and the chain gang.

Black employees on Savannah's railroads were paid half the usual wage of whites. Jobs for African Americans depended largely on the cotton trade, naval stores, truck farming, shrimping, and oystering—all of which paid low wages in the decades after emancipation. The jobs brought freedom if not prosperity. Some of these jobs, however, were disappearing.[62]

During Myers's second term there were other changes. The City Council fired the police and fire chiefs appointed by the Meldrim administration and appointed their own allies to the posts. In the long run, Myers brought the city's fractious Democrats together and ushered in "an era of good feeling" and prosperity. He created a modern Chamber of Commerce to promote tourism and to woo industry and investors. The chamber launched a publicity campaign and negotiated reduced excursion fares for tourists from the North.

Through the courts Myers won equal treatment on freight rates for cotton, naval stores, and other products from the four major railroads serving the city. Terminal facilities went up on Hutchinson Island, factories relocated to the city, and shipbuilding companies and warehouses sprang up along Savannah's waterfront. By the early 1900s, the traffic passing through the port exceeded the combined totals of all other South Atlantic ports. To accommodate the booming export-import traffic, Myers convinced the Army Corps of Engineers to deepen the channel to twenty-eight feet. Savannah now became a major *world* port. Myers appointed a second black physician. There were now five hospitals: St. Joseph's Infirmary, Savannah Hospital, and Park View Sanitarium served whites only. Georgia Infirmary and Charity Hospital were for black citizens.

Boosterism became contagious. The Chamber of Commerce called it the "Spirit of Savannah." Private groups urged construction of a city auditorium to attract large conventions; others called for making Savannah the auto racing center of Dixie. By the early 1900s the city attracted thousands of conventioneers who spent millions of dollars, to the delight of the local retail merchants.[63] Between 1897 and 1908. Savannah's population increased from fifty-six thousand to more than seventy-five thousand, ranking it among the top ten southern cities in population. This flood of new residents required Mayor Myers to redouble his efforts to provide basic services. In 1899 the city had about 117 miles of paved streets, totally inadequate, Myers believed. As he said, "A progressive city must have its streets paved." Within a few years, the administration increased the paved areas by 40 percent.

Myers pushed for a public library after the steel magnate Andrew Carnegie offered $100,000 if the city agreed to provide money annually for the building's maintenance. But political opposition, especially fears by some that African Americans might demand use of the new library, made the City Council wary of accepting Carnegie's largess. The council refused to appropriate money for day-to-day expenses. No money was available for a black library, so eleven African American men "formed the Colored Library Association of Savannah and established the Library for Colored Citizens." With private funding the modest library was constructed on Price Street in 1906. However, some projects moved forward without opposition. With a promise of city funding, the once private Georgia Historical Society opened its doors to white patrons.

The Myers administration completed the city's sewage-drainage system, doubled the waterworks' pumping capacity, and let a contract with the Savannah

Bustling Broughton Street, Savannah, ca. 1900. The stone, at lower right, was used when stepping from a carriage to the sidewalk. Sign, at right, reads "Kirby's—Nothing over 10 cents"; later, Woolworth's located here. Courtesy of Georgia Archives, Vanishing Georgia Collection, image no. ctm179.

Electric Company to transport garbage in closed trains for disposal beyond the city limits. This mitigated somewhat the foul odors wafting through Savannah's squares.

The city also spent money on sidewalks, curbing, and the improvement of wharf facilities. The administration was enthusiastic in its support of privately funded projects, such as the one that built the Union Railroad Terminal on West Broad Street. Private dollars also constructed office buildings and hotels and improved streetcar service. Myers promoted a new City Hall building that more truly reflected the standing of Savannah as a world-class city. The old Exchange Building was demolished, and on its site a new City Hall in the late Victorian style of architecture went up on the river at the foot of Bull Street. Its completion within a few years at a total cost of $270,050 seemed a testament to the capabilities of Myers as a progressive, a business executive, and a leader who envisioned a greater Savannah. Its copper-sheeted dome could be admired from a great distance.[64]

Savannah's rapid population growth brought a construction boom of office buildings in the city and single-family homes south of Savannah's Thirty-first Street. Property values rose in the inner city, which also experienced overcrowding. In the annual report of 1905, Mayor Myers worried that "Tenements, mainly for negroes, are being crowded on every bit of land with a reckless disregard of health conditions." The construction boom contributed to a rise in city taxes and city income from 1900 to 1906.

On social issues, the Methodist, Baptist, and Presbyterian ministers and their congregations were formidable enough by 1906 to lobby the City Council to pass "blue laws" that prohibited bars from selling liquor on Sundays. Police began crackdowns on barkeepers who remained open after 12:01 Sunday morning. But many church people wanted even stricter regulations. One member of the council complained: "There are in Savannah practically as many saloons as there are in all of the other cities in the state."

On occasion, religious leaders pushed Myers to abandon his hands-off policy on gambling rooms. After criticism from the *Atlanta Constitution* in an article, "The Gambling Dens of Savannah," the mayor ordered a police campaign against the gamblers, many of whom operated in Congress Lane. Periodic raids, some ending in shoot-outs, erupted in both black and white "dens." By Myers's last term in office many gambling sites were shuttered, which fitted in with his plans to make Savannah a reformed-minded, progressive city.[65]

The Myers administration passed a nine-hour workday for some public employees and increased support for hospitals and relief for the indigent. Some of the motivation for these changes came from a desire that Savannah not suffer by comparison to more progressive cities. Because Forsyth Park remained off-limits to blacks, Myers created Emmett Park in 1900, a small recreation area for blacks on the outskirts of the city.

In 1902 the City Council defeated a Jim Crow streetcar proposal by a vote of eleven to one. Local black leaders had succeeded in convincing the white elite to kill the measure at a time when Savannah's Southern Bank required blacks to stand in a segregated line to conduct business. The *Tribune* made the ironic comment: "When colored patrons go [to the bank] they will have to keep away from the other folks for fear that contamination will be the result, while the money will be gladly received." A few years later the local Superior Court Judge ruled "that white jurors were not required to eat at the same table with a Negro."

The image of the black man in the South promoted by the *Morning News* was that even with a surging economy a labor shortage existed because many blacks were lazy. During Myers's last term, he authorized police raids to arrest all "idle persons" in the city. On the first night, sixty-seven persons were taken into custody and, with one exception, all were black. In the South, in Georgia, and in Savannah racism rose, and favorable black opinions about Mayor Myers fell.[66]

Recognizing the threat, Savannah's well-to-do African Americans came together to push back against the tide of racism and to promote self-help for the good of their community. They were encouraged by a talk given by Booker T. Washington in Savannah after the turn of the century in which he stressed the need of "group economy"—the creation of a black business sector. The concept advanced the notion of keeping as much money as possible within the black community by building a social and financial infrastructure for blacks. Washington's idea led local black businessmen to come together to establish the Wage Earners Loan and Investment Company of Savannah, a savings bank for African Americans. Within a few years, deposits reached seventy-eight thousand dollars. The bank thrived throughout the Progressive Era and beyond.

The same enthusiasm motivated young blacks to form the Men's Sunday Club, whose members made it their business to look into "conditions which are of vital importance to the life and progress of the Colored citizen"; another men's group, the Success Club, promoted "the self-development of young colored men."[67] Even in a progressive administration like that of Myers, these black social organizations found it daunting to overcome a pervasive racism which continued even after death. During Myers's final year in office, a fence was erected in Laurel Grove Cemetery to separate black burial sites from white.

Despite pleas from the African American community, Myers did little to end overcrowding in the city's black schools, which met in a few rented facilities like Beach Institute and in churches. Finally, the school board did construct a permanent structure for black education, the Cuyler Street School, but still supply did not meet demand. African Americans now made up over 50 percent of Savannah's population; the inadequate classroom space left large numbers of black youth on the streets with little to do.[68]

During Mayor Myers's terms in office the usual four-to-one ratio of black arrests to white persisted. There were four black murders for every one white murder. There were three black deaths for every one white death; in 1904, 154 blacks died from tuberculosis, compared to 55 whites.

Dr. W. W. Brunner, in the city's health officer's 1906 report, gave some details about black and white morbidity and mortality. He reported that, though Savannah's population was made up of 33,000 whites and 39,000 blacks, blacks had abnormally higher disease, death, and incarnation rates. Brunner urged the city government to appoint a commission to look into the sociological and sanitary conditions confronting Savannah's black population. Brunner's recommendation to the commission sounds racist in today's context: "[Go] where he lives in colonies in this city" and observe "the food that he must eat"; ask why "his Tuberculosis rate [is] rising"; and understand "his surplus population is . . . dangerous to this community and must contaminate its health and prosperity." Brunner's admonitions appear both paternalistic and self-serving: "[It is] up to the white people to prevent him [blacks] from becoming a criminal and to guard him against Tuberculosis; . . . if he is tainted with disease you will suffer," and "if he develops criminal tendencies you will be affected." He concluded that because of the high death rate of the "colored . . . there is no chance for this city to be placed in the front rank of American cities from a health standpoint."[69]

The poor state of black health, Brunner hypothesized, would likely dissuade businesses from locating in Savannah. With Caucasian death rates of 16 per 1,000 and "Negro" death rates at 25–30 per 1,000, one could not continue to overlook differences in diet, housing, and work stress. Brunner's remarks were quoted verbatim in a national journal article in which Brunner asked the question, "Will not the white South . . . in order to save itself from disease, be forced to save its negroes from disease? It would seem an inevitable conclusion."[70]

A Gruesome "Carnival of Violence"

Health issues were not the only problems being confronted by Georgia's black citizens. By the early 1900s, Georgia was second only to Mississippi in the number of lynchings that occurred in the region. As a flood of poor whites moved into southern towns and cities like Savannah, lured by an improving economy and jobs, they brought with them long-held and deep-seated disdain for the black man. Such feelings were reflected in a heinous event in nearby Statesboro.

Two black men, Paul Reed and Will Cato, were accused of and arrested for the murder of five members of the Hodges family on July 28, 1904. Hearing of threats to lynch the two men, Georgia's governor dispatched Captain Robert M. Hitch and the Oglethorpe Light Infantry of Savannah to protect the prisoners. On the trial date, August 15, people from around the region arrived in Statesboro by buggy and wagon; the offer of half-price tickets by the Savannah and Statesboro Railroad lured large numbers of would-be spectators to jam the cars for Statesboro. Here they watched the jury of white men find Reed and Cato guilty. The judge sentenced them to hang. However, a mob quickly gathered and rushed into the courthouse jail. They overpowered Captain Hitch and hurled him outside; his militiamen, holding rifles with fixed bayonets, made no effort to stop the mob. They seized the two black men and took them a mile beyond the town, chained them to a pine stump, doused them with kerosene, and burned them alive. Suspecting that others besides Reed and Cato were involved in the murder of the white family, armed white men shot and beat African Americans in and around the Statesboro community.

The extralegal, gruesome "carnival of violence" in the Statesboro area even outraged some southern demagogues, but not Hoke Smith, who ran a virulent, race-baiting campaign to win the governorship in 1906. While in office he promoted a bill that aimed to diminish black voter registration, but the bill also disfranchised poor whites and illiterates. For more than fifty years this legislation sharply curtailed adult participation in this essential element of a democracy, voting. Other southern states adopted similar legislation.[71]

Segregation, Big Business, and the Boycott

In the 1890s the Georgia legislature enacted bills separating blacks and whites in railroad cars. Georgia cities like Atlanta, Rome, and Augusta soon followed suit by passing their own local ordinances mandating segregation on urban streetcars. In Savannah the competition between two electric companies over who controlled the city's electric power was at the heart of the streetcar controversy.

On January 11, 1905, City Councilman William L. Grayson and his business partner, Jacob S. Collins, enjoyed drinks in Savannah's downtown Suwanee Saloon with a representative of the newly formed Savannah Lighting Company (SLC). Councilman Grayson wanted to involve the two gentlemen in a scheme to undermine the Savannah Electric Company (SEC), a Boston-based firm that long held a monopoly on Savannah lighting and streetcars. Grayson knew that wresting the lucrative city contract from the SEC would not be easy; indeed, the struggle ignited a very public battle between members of the civic-commercial elite.

One reason the SLC had the audacity to challenge the entrenched SEC was due to influential support from Savannahians like Mills Lane, who wanted lower electric rates and better service from the new company. When the president of the established SEC, the prominent George Baldwin, learned about the upstart SLC, he began to batten down the hatches and called for advice from SEC founders and major stockholders like Mayor Herman Myers.

Already, local businessmen like George Tiedeman, Abraham Minis, J. H. Estill (the newspaper publisher), Leopold Adler, and B. H. Levy were selling their shares of SEC and buying shares of the SLC. Wanting to prevent damage to the company, Baldwin called on his political friends to submit petitions to the City Council that would impede the new electric company's ability to do business, such as restricting where poles could be placed.

The new SLC reacted with stinging criticisms in the press to the underhanded tactics and called attention again to the SEC's historically high rates and poor service record. The paper did not miss an opportunity to remind readers that the SEC was a "foreign," not a Savannah, company. Also Mayor Myers was accused of conflict of interest because of his financial association with the SEC. All of these charges and countercharges of corruption naturally spilled into the streets, and a violent shootout erupted in front of City Hall that left one dead and six wounded.[72]

Sensing that now was the time for the coup de grâce, Grayson presented a petition to City Hall demanding segregation of local streetcars—white riders had complained that blacks were often "drunk and disorderly" and carried disease. Because the streetcars were the property of the SEC, Grayson reasoned that the new ordinance would reduce ridership and that SEC resources would be siphoned off in trying to resolve the matter.

A quick response came from Sol Johnson's *Tribune* denouncing the bill. Emotions ran high. On the night of September 8, a black man stabbed and killed a streetcar conductor. Black leaders asked for a meeting with the City Council in order to air their grievance. But on arrival, they were met by a menacing-looking crowd of thirty-five white men, and they quickly departed. Grayson's streetcar-segregation ordinance passed unanimously amid raucous outburst and applause from a crowd of white onlookers in City Hall. The police would begin immediate enforcement.

Johnson's *Tribune* called on African Americans to censure the actions of the City Council. Black attorneys, physicians, and skilled artisans joined with local black ministers in mid-September to endorse a boycott of city streetcars. They were joined by black hack drivers who reduced their fees from twenty-five cents to a dime to transport riders wherever they wished to go. The *Tribune* urged readers to "walk! walk! . . . Do not trample on your pride by being 'jim crowed.' Walk!" The police harassed the walkers, but they were not deterred, even after news reached Savannah in late September that race-baiting politicians had unleashed four days of shooting, torturing, and murdering African American residents in Atlanta. The news jarred Savannah's boycotters, but they kept on walking.[73] Without its African American riders, the SEC bled money. Grayson's ploy worked. In less than six months the company lost 88 percent of its black ridership and $50,000.[74]

Baldwin, as president of the SEC, tried various tactics to stop the outflow of money caused by the boycott. Eventually Baldwin successfully bribed

Streetcar and conductor, Savannah, ca. 1907–8. This photograph was taken some months after the 1906 African American boycott protesting the company's segregation policies. Courtesy of Georgia Archives, Vanishing Georgia Collection, image no. ctm327-84.

"ten negroes of influence" whose job was to end the boycott. When Sol Johnson heard of this, the *Tribune* condemned any "traitorous men in the garb of preachers . . . [willing to] sell their manhood rights" for money. But Johnson's editorials were no match for fervent calls from black church pulpits to end the boycott. Soon streetcars carrying blacks and whites in *separate* cars began rolling through Savannah. For many African Americans, segregated railroads and streetcars simply affirmed again their second-class citizenship status.[75]

With the boycott solved, President Baldwin quickly moved to ensure the SEC would remain the Savannah electric company of choice. When banker and merchant George W. Tiedeman decided to run for mayor, Baldwin simply called on the huge financial resources of the SEC's Boston-based parent company, Stone & Webster. He also hired an advertising firm to refurbish the SEC's image, hired more black workers, and added relatives and friends of Tiedeman to the SEC payroll. On the eve of the City Council's decision as to who would receive the new city lighting contract, Baldwin offered the city $75,000 for repairs to its lighting and street-railway properties; to no one's surprise the SEC won the city contract. Baldwin's savvy political instincts and his access to the deep pockets of Stone & Webster secured an SEC monopoly in Savannah for many years to come.[76]

One curious event that occurred in the midst of the boycott was the arrival in Savannah of a virulently racist play, *The Clansman,* by Thomas Dixon to be performed at the Savannah Theatre. Shortly before the play opened, the segregated performance site mysteriously burned, leaving only charred walls standing. Not wanting to deprive any Savannahian of the opportunity to enjoy a special evening out, the SEC offered its Thunderbolt casino as a replacement venue. The SEC also assured the public that more streetcars would be added to the line, one leaving every five minutes, so that theatergoers could secure low-priced, round-trip tickets to this much-anticipated event.[77]

George Baldwin, Daffin Park, and Another Election

While involved in promoting his Savannah Electric Company, George Baldwin also took on city planning and beautification as two of his philanthropic interests. These passions perfectly merged when he encouraged P. D. Daffin, chairman of the city's Park and Tree Commission, to bring to the city John Nolen, a highly regarded young landscape architect from Boston. Baldwin wanted Nolen to design a grand park for Savannah. The park would be named for P. D. Daffin. Baldwin personally told Nolen that he might also receive a commission for drafting a full-scale city plan. Nolen began his work on the design of Daffin Park, which was to be created just beyond the city's southern limits, the first park developed since Forsyth Park, fifty years earlier. The City Council approved most of Nolen's design: a center promenade, angled tree-lined drives, a pine grove, and ample space for playing fields, which remained off-limits to African Americans for decades.

Now Baldwin asked Nolen to begin drafting a general plan for the city, which Nolen did. But when Nolen's plan was submitted to the Park and Tree Commission, the commissioners balked at such a grand design. There must have been many awkward pauses when Baldwin had to tell Nolen that the city no longer needed his services. Most certainly Nolen was disappointed. He received only five hundred dollars for designing Daffin Park, and his expenses alone were four hundred. Nor did Nolen receive any compensation for drafting his grand design for the city. Probably embarrassed, Baldwin sent a personal check for an additional four hundred dollars to Nolen, who went on to enjoy a spectacular career as an internationally recognized architect in "regional and city planning."

Without a plan, a design worthy of Oglethorpe's first grand efforts, Savannah came to resemble a down-at-the-heels city. As the city departed from Oglethorpe's original plan, failed to maintain the city's waterfront, and ignored blight, deteriorating structures, and decaying infrastructure, Savannah's appearance diminished. The city held little charm for tourists, and seamy and seedy businesses went up around neglected squares. Little headway was made in city planning until the 1960s.[78]

As the mayoralty election of January 1907 approached, Citizens' Club members on the City Council who wished to save their own political skins launched investigations of their own appointees! When they found corruption in the Police Department, the City Council asked for resignations and, if those were not forthcoming, they fired the offenders.

One resident, incensed by what was happening in the Police Department, wrote Colonel G. Arthur Gordon, complaining that slot machines taken in raids "by the authorities are placed in the hallways of the [police] barracks and played constantly (every day) by the police and detectives in plain sight of the chief." Mr. Horning, the letter writer, went on to express his dismay that the "target practice range at the barracks—built for the benefit of the police—"had not been used by police "since opening day." He also noted that "the police are docked for every day they lost except when electioneering," and finally he asked that this information not be publicized as the informant within the department was already suspected of leaking information.

Prominent politician W. W. Gordon Jr. spoke on behalf of the new People's Democratic League (PDL), accusing the incumbent Herman Myers administration of allowing "lawlessness and concealed weapons and gambling" to get out of hand. Moreover, they had not solved "the negro problem" at the polls. Gordon's daughter Daisy thought like her father, writing on one occasion, "The Negroes and other immigrants are a serious obstacle to votes being given to women." Her brother, G. Arthur Gordon, a rising political star, who chaired the PDL committee on registration, mailed out flyers urging Savannahians to vote for the PDL and against the Citizens' Club, "the party of tyranny [and] Bossism."[79]

Political posturing was in the air. The old Citizens' Club group wanted to be seen as more reform-minded than PDL nominee George W. Tiedeman, but they were too closely tied to the earlier shootout in front of City Hall. Black Savannahians, furious that the Myers administration failed to prevent the segregation of streetcars, pledged their support to Tiedeman. The Citizens' Club failed to nominate a candidate. The only person left to oppose Tiedeman was Col. William Garrard, nominated because of his "service to the Confederacy." But Garrard came too late to the contest and had too few supporters. A much larger group rallied behind the PDL. A festive atmosphere surrounded election eve with brass bands and speakers like Captain Richard J. Davant, who urged crowds to vote for Tiedeman—a vote against "crime and iniquity . . . so your wife and your daughter may walk on the streets without hearing blasphemy on every corner."

Of the 7,296 voters registered, 522 were "colored." Emotions ran high. Reports of fisticuffs and even weapons drawn appeared in the press. Tiedeman easily won a majority of the vote. Though Myers did not run in 1907, the election was really a rejection of Myers's policies, ending more than a decade of his progressive leadership. Savannahians, however, had elected another politician who fashioned himself as a champion of reform, George Tiedeman.[80] He was reelected to two consecutive two-year terms, leaving office in 1911.

Mayor Tiedeman Continues the Progressive Agenda

Near the end of his first term, Tiedeman publicly highlighted his most important accomplishments: ending public gambling, regulating the liquor traffic, and enforcing the prohibition of liquor sales on Sunday. His administration purchased Bonaventure Cemetery, reorganized the Police Department, beautified Daffin Park, and appropriated funds for a bacteriologist and laboratory. Ordinances passed banning all bicyclists from the public squares or sidewalks under penalty of fines. Those who drove automobiles while intoxicated or under the age of sixteen or at speeds over fifteen miles per hour could expect stiff fines.[81]

Despite the mayor's claims that the liquor trade had been curtailed following the state's prohibition amendment, one journalist who wrote about prohibition in Alabama and Georgia asserted otherwise. In a national magazine article published in March 1909, he alleged that Savannah city government "permitted ['blind tigers'] to operate openly (except on Sundays) and sell anything drinkable . . . on the understanding . . . [they] would be raided twice each year and fined in city court." Charleston had a similar arrangement whereby the police made "scheduled" raids on bars. The Anti-Saloon League of Savannah carried out its own investigation and, after finding drunks imbibing heavily, went to court twice to shut down city saloons. Their efforts failed. One writer was of the opinion that "the state-wide prohibition law has always been ignored in the city and will continue to be."[82]

Savannah's public schools remained underfunded and so overcrowded that repeatedly African American students were turned away. "The best colored citizens" again and again "reproached" school board members for "not providing facilities for their children." With too much time on their hands, black teenagers spent hours on the streets, unschooled and occasionally arrested for "vandalism." Disparities in facilities, transportation. and salaries were the norm; black principals made twelve hundred dollars per annum; white principals made two thousand.

One remarkably progressive area in Savannah's education system, the Kate Baldwin Free Kindergartens, was backed by George J. Baldwin. Because of his generous philanthropy, Baldwin was able to bring together the city's progressive-minded privileged class of ladies who taught in the schools and followed the principles promoted by nationally known educator Dr. John Dewey. The four kindergartens, located in separate areas of the city, sought to provide the "very poor" children, black and white, an education in English, the arts, nature studies, and moral training to improve their "social conditions," ameliorate suffering, and prepare them for subsequent schooling.[83]

The police force, headed now by Mayor Tiedeman's appointee, Chief W. G. Austin, numbered 110 officers, but with the rising population and the expansion of the city south of Fortieth Street, Austin asked for additional patrolmen. One crime deterrent that could be dispatched speedily to check disorder was the horse patrol. The budget for the police, $115,800, was the highest of any city department.

Dr. W. W. Brunner, the crusading carryover from the previous administration, continued to urge methods to control the spread of disease. One less conventional idea emerged when he discovered that 20 percent of the city's black population migrated from South Carolina's coastal regions and that this group had an "abnormally high death rate." His proposed solution was that the city enforce the Vagrant Law, authorizing the police to remove these undesirables to "benefit Savannah morally and hygienically."[84]

Mayor Tiedeman's first term served as a blueprint for his second. In many ways it resembled the progressive administrations of Herman Myers, progressivism mainly for Savannah's white population. Like Myers, Mayor Tiedeman focused on improving the sewer system, paving and opening new streets, providing clean water and good health.

Prosperity continued nationally and locally, due especially to the ever-increasing traffic on the Savannah River. By 1908 Savannah's exports, primarily cotton and naval stores, and imports were nearly as large as those of all the South Atlantic ports combined. The city's exports were greater than San Francisco's.

Savannah's population numbered about seventy-five thousand in 1907, which ranked it seventh among all southern cities. The value of real estate in the city increased from $26 million in 1900 to $35 million in 1908. The government's income from taxation exceeded $1 million for the first time.[85] Now money was readily available for investment in the city, and Mayor Tiedeman stepped up his campaign to promote Savannah. One venture under consideration was sponsoring local automobile races. Memphis and other southern cities had already begun their own love affairs with cars and racing.

The International Automobile Races at Savannah became one of the mayor's favorite events. For several years the races were held in Savannah on a winding track on the city's south side. Harvey Granger, president of the three-hundred-member Savannah Automobile Club, joined the mayor in promoting races where stock cars traveled at speeds of more than seventy-five miles per hour, setting records for the course. Prominent drivers and large crowds from across the country participated. The races and Savannah received glowing reviews in the *New York Times*. However, the city's clergy did not share the same enthusiasm. They adamantly opposed Thanksgiving Day races, and likely their opposition eventually led to the event moving elsewhere. Local football games on Thanksgiving Day came to take their place.[86]

Despite positive reports from the Police Department, the numbers of arrests increased every year. Patrolmen in night raids repeatedly shut down gambling houses and seized gamblers, even though police reports showed all "gambling dens" already had been closed. More arrests of black men and women (5,028) than whites (3,042) in 1908 followed a similar pattern as in years past: drunkenness and disorderly conduct accounted for over half of all arrests. Annually, Police Chief Austin asked for more police officers, his rationale being the expanding city limits, more property to protect, and the rising number of sailors on shore leave.

The Bacteriological Laboratory, designed for the diagnosis and prevention of disease, opened and, following a national search, the city hired Dr. Victor H. Bassett of Milwaukee as its head. Bassett's hire proved to be one of the most progressive acts of the Tiedeman administration. Like other southern cities, Savannah sought to improve its reputation as a healthy place to live and work. The city government soon passed a milk ordinance requiring that only pure milk be sold; this new law came at a time when it was not unusual to see a cow or two tethered in backyards.[87]

Dr. Brunner, the city's health officer, again called attention to disparities in death rates for whites (14 per 1,000) and blacks (24 per 1,000) for the year 1908. Brunner recommended a municipal commission be appointed to investigate, in Brunner's inflammatory language, the "contamination of the white race by the negro" and the "abnormal number of criminals" the race produced. Brunner again expressed his view that such conditions "place . . . [Savannah] in a bad light and . . . certainly immigration will not come our way," or business and industry.

Mayor Tiedeman, also concerned about Savannah's progressive image, asked for a bond issue to extend the sewage system to the entire city because "the health of any city is desirable and necessary from a purely commercial motive." But funding for health care facilities reflected a racial bias; the white hospitals were awarded $13,500 while the two "colored" hospitals, Charity and the Georgia Infirmary, received $900. Adequate hospital care for blacks in Georgia and other southern cities was rare.[88]

Mayor Tiedeman highlighted as one of his successes in 1909 the "removal of a negro settlement known as Sunnyside which has long retarded the growth of the city" southward. The city acquired the land from Messrs. Lattimore & Lattimore and then constructed streets, curbing, parks, water mains, and sewage-disposal lines on the property with money borrowed from the Lattimores at an agreed-upon interest rate. Sunnyside's destruction, likely the first example of gentrification in Savannah, made way for the birth of Ardsley Park, a handsome suburban development for well-to-do whites. So pleased was Mayor Tiedeman with the project that he announced his readiness "to undertake any similar work in any locality within the city limits."[89]

As the white elite began moving out of the city to suburban developments, middle-class black Savannahians moved to neighborhoods on the east side like LePageville and East Savannah. Rural blacks continued to migrate into the east and west edges of the city. These relocations led to fewer and fewer racially integrated streets and neighborhoods which in time became thoroughly segregated.[90]

The Mayor remained buoyant. He told City Council that Savannah was on the cusp of "unprecedented prosperity . . . and a greater, healthier, busier, more beautiful and more populous city."[91] It was an idealized view given other events that would transpire.

A "Diabolical" Act Shocks the City

One of the more "diabolical" and violent attacks occurred during daylight hours when an ax-wielding intruder crushed the skulls of three white women residing at 401 West Perry Street in early December 1909. The police threw a dragnet around the slums of Yamacraw and rounded-up 150 black men. All were released save one who police claimed planned to assault Maggie Hunter but murdered the other two so they could not identify him.

Local and national newspapers carried the story. Maggie who survived for a few hours after the attack, gave an account that implicated not the man arrested but her husband, J. C. Hunter, a once-wounded Confederate veteran who had served prison time as a horse thief and a bigamist. Despite Maggie's tip, the police did not arrest Hunter initially though they soon released the first black suspect for lack of evidence.

Subsequently, a local grand jury indicted Hunter for the murder and he was sentenced to death by hanging. But the Governor commuted his sentence and the administrator of the Confederate Home in Atlanta hired Hunter to serve out his term as a waiter. At age 77, Hunter was pardoned and returned to Savannah to live out his remaining years.[92]

Violence, another "Brunner" Campaign, and a Library

Police continued to confront violence in the years following the "diabolical" killings. In 1910 the police made 9,965 arrests—about half for "disorderly conduct," 16 for murder, 62 for attempted murder, 11 for keeping a house of prostitution, and 9 for maintaining a "gambling house." Sometimes the same people were arrested multiple times.

Law enforcement personnel faced increasing job risks. One policeman was shot and killed in the line of duty, and the city offered a reward for the arrest and conviction of a "negro" charged with shooting and killing the City Court Sheriff, J. W. McIntire Jr. Arrests and murder rates rose over the next several years.

Citizen concerns over flooding on the east, west, and south sides of the city during heavy rains led Dr. Brunner to urge the city to tackle these drainage problems as mosquitoes bred in pools of standing water. Brunner thought the current practice of using petroleum to control the insects to be a makeshift and costly solution. "The city which provides best for its citizens . . . will attract the best people," he wrote.

Brunner with characteristic paternalism and disparagement wrote about the African American citizenry: the "negro" is not "incapable of improvement," but if he is "allowed to remain here as he is, he will be a menace to himself and to us." Brunner seemed convinced of some sinister element innate within the black population as he again urged the administration to appoint a commission to determine "why he dies in excess of the whites and why he is a bad citizen in the eyes of the law."[93]

George Baldwin, philanthropist and friend of the mayor, chaired the board of managers of Savannah's small library. In 1910 Atlanta, Jacksonville, and even smaller southern cities "enjoyed [modern] libraries." In Baldwin's view nothing "more surely improves a city . . . [than] convenient and ready access to good books placed in a building of handsome . . . design." Within a few years, Baldwin's advocacy won support from City Council and $75,000 from the Carnegie

Foundation to construct a large classical-style building of granite at what is today 2002 Bull Street. In past years the city had declined an offer of $100,000 to build a library during Herman Myers's administration for fear that it would be used by blacks. The new library, built under Tiedeman's administration, was for decades open only to whites.[94]

While chairing the board of managers of the library and serving as president of the Kate Baldwin Free Kindergarten, George Baldwin also led the Associated Charities of Savannah, which opened in 1910. Akin to the today's United Way, the organization in its first year aided 730 persons with "instant relief in every case of apparent need" and stood ready to insure that no "human being in the city . . . will suffer from want of food." Associated Charities also worked with a group of "the most intelligent colored people in the city" to form an Anti-Tuberculosis Society and showed a "willingness to cooperate in helping colored cases," perhaps fearing that close contact with potentially consumptive "negro servants" increased white families' vulnerability.[95]

Davant Challenges Tiedeman and Loses

Upon the approach of the mayoralty election of 1911, Captain Richard J. Davant, previously a loyal supporter of Tiedeman, launched an "anti-administration insurgency." Davant told audiences he stood for "honesty in politics" and against the "illegal use of money" for "the corruption of voters." Those campaigning for Davant accused Tiedeman's current chief of police, Austin, with vote buying. Davant wanted a "progressive city," but not one whose "idea of progress is to rob the entire city . . . of hundreds of thousands of dollars for . . . a land scheme for a few . . . who are the beneficiaries." Clearly the friendship had soured as Davant charged Tiedeman with failing to "keep a . . . watchful eye on . . . expenditures." Davant's mention of "a land scheme for a few" hinted darkly at profiteering by some of the elite involved in the city's purchase of the property and financing of the development of Ardsley Park.

The campaign was spirited and, on the day of the election, "a number of arrests were made for fighting and disorderly conduct." Some in the opposing camps slugged it out with "billie" clubs, and a "Negro" was apprehended for attempting to vote using the name of someone who had been "dead for . . . months." In spite of Davant's charges, Tiedeman proved to be "popular with all classes," and he won reelection for a third term.[96]

During his last two years in office, Mayor Tiedeman asked for and Savannahians approved a referendum for a $600,000 bond issue to finish the sewage- and storm-drain system. With tax revenues trending upward, Tiedeman replaced horse-drawn fire equipment with motorized vehicles and boasted, perhaps with some hyperbole, "Savannah is the first city in the world to have a fully equipped automobile fire department."

The council also approved $39,000 for repairs to the City Market and $10,000 to promote the city nationwide. Ordinances passed requiring the use of receptacles for garbage and, in a forward-looking move, the mayor asked that terms for mayor and council be increased to four years rather than two. Because of the frequency of elections, he argued, the city was "seldom free of political agitation."

Police Chief Austin again requested more patrolmen and recommended that the Industrial Farm on the city's outskirts serve as a place to incarcerate "white women of questionable character and habits." After the death of a physician's child from the bite of a rabid dog, Dr. Bassett, the city bacteriologist, asked the City Council to address the problem of wandering dogs. He recommended that unlicensed canines be seized and destroyed and that the city establish a dog pound. Having witnessed the success of the milk ordinance, the city now passed a law which called for sanitary inspections and regulation of all hotels and restaurants in the city.[97]

Progressive legislation characterized the last year of Mayor Tiedeman's six years in office. The City Council passed a law amending the city charter to establish a commission form of government and a civil service system with elections every four years (on the fourth Tuesday of January). The mayor's salary was set at six thousand dollars; City Council members would be paid five thousand.[98]

Captain Richard Davant, Now Called Mr. Mayor

In the next mayoral election, Captain Richard J. Davant, longtime member of the City Council and a former supporter but later critic of Mayor Tiedeman, won a hotly contested and closely monitored race against Captain George P. Walker. Of nearly 6,000 votes cast, Davant won by 394. He took office in 1913 and was reelected two years later. Davant began his second term as the first mayor elected to serve a four-year term. Ironically, less than a year into this second term, Davant fell ill and died. Wallace J. Pierpont, chairman of the City Council, filled the remainder of Davant's term as mayor.

Pierpont remembered Davant as a "progressive and far-seeing spirit" who perfected the city's "obsolete" accounting system, urged creation of playgrounds for white children, pushed for a modern garbage "destructor" system, and extended the storm drainage and sewage lines.[99] Though Davant was credited with these accomplishments, it was sometimes his predecessors who had initiated the improvement.

By the time Pierpont succeeded Davant, black businessmen had relocated the Wage Earners Loan and Investment Company (later renamed Wage Earners Savings Bank) to West Broad Street. This energized their plan to create the sort of black enterprise zone or economic infrastructure that Booker T. Washington promoted. The bank's depositors now numbered in the thousands, and its assets were well over $500,000. With the Wage Earners Bank and two other African American–owned banks established, Savannah was the banking capital of black Georgia.

Sol Johnson also moved the offices of the *Tribune* to West Broad Street, where a growing number of black businesses were relocating. Johnson's *Tribune* trumpeted: "If anyone doubts the progressiveness of Savannah Negroes, let them take a stroll down West Broad Street, one of our most prominent business thoroughfares" and take note of the "excellent buildings and businesses" between the new, "costly and beautiful Union Station and Bolton Street"; it will "act as a panacea for the most pessimistic as to the future success among us."

Three black-owned theaters opened on booming West Broad Street—the Pekin, the Star, and the Air Dome. West Broad resembled Atlanta's "Sweet Auburn Street." Johnson, who had long agitated for civil rights, now appeared to view business development as a new way forward for the city's African Americans.[100]

By 1913 the Colored Library Association of Savannah had amassed a collection of books and periodicals from private donations, and the group asked the Carnegie Foundation for funds to construct a permanent facility. With the Carnegie Foundation's promise of twelve thousand dollars for construction of a library for African Americans, the City Council approved twelve hundred annually for its maintenance. Now Savannah's "better class" of blacks came together to raise money to purchase a site for the library on east Henry Street. Black ministers canvassed their congregations for donations. The campaign succeeded. Within two years the black Carnegie Library opened with books donated by blacks and whites. Token increases in appropriations by the city over time helped the financially struggling library, which appeared to be in "constant use," especially by black children. The library may have helped raise the literacy rate for the black population of Savannah as the illiteracy rate fell from 34 percent in 1900 to 20 percent in 1920. Literacy rates also improved in Atlanta, Memphis, and Charleston.[101]

Savannah's literacy rates improved too because Savannah's well-to-do African Americans pressed for a policy whereby *all* black children who wanted to attend the public schools would be able to enroll. Sol Johnson's *Tribune* applauded this groundswell of interest because he recognized, "For any community to make progress there must be cooperative efforts on the part of its inhabitants."[102] Even before the emancipation, African Americans viewed education as the way to improve their social and political status. By the 1912–13 school year and for several years following, the city provided five public schools for black students. In spite of this, many children were turned away for lack of space.

Black businessmen and ministers petitioned the Board of Education for more black schools, but the board said funds were not available to do so. In a few years, funds were unavailable to open *any* school, black or white! The financial crisis precipitated the decision to hold a referendum on a special tax so schools had sufficient monies to open as usual in October. Passing such a tax would require a "yes" vote by two-thirds of the registered voters. Although the "better class of blacks" and affluent whites usually enrolled their children in local private schools or sent them to distant private institutions, they favored the referendum. The school tax passed by an overwhelming margin, 4,469 to 34 votes.

When the public schools opened for the fall term, more black children than ever before were enrolled. Nonetheless, 732 were turned away for lack of space. But the new superintendent elected by the Savannah Board of Education, Carleton B. Gibson, found this unacceptable. He came up with a simple, cost-effective solution.

Gibson came to the post of superintendent following a remarkable education and career. A graduate of the University of Alabama and the University of Chicago, Dr. Gibson served as president of several small normal colleges in Alabama before he accepted the post in Savannah. His advocacy for vocational education for all children, rich or poor, was well known in academic circles.

Facing a shortage of classroom space for black students, Gibson, with approval of the Board of Education, simply instituted morning and afternoon sessions and thereby accommodated all children seeking to enroll. He doubled the number of black students without adding a single new building.

The following year the city was divided into four school districts which, using "double day" sessions, ensured a seat for every African American child who wished to attend school. Furthermore, a free book system was instituted for those unable to pay for school supplies. Atlanta's public schools did not provide free textbooks until the 1920s.

Gibson's innovations pleased the black community. His policies brought to fruition what they had so long sought. Mutual cooperation within the black community and progressive action by municipal government brought education and opportunities for self-help to black youth. It became the high point of progressivism for Savannah's African American community from 1912 to 1917, and it was led by a well-educated outsider, Dr. Carleton Gibson.[103]

During these years, too, black civic clubs and groups organized locally and nationwide to protect the rights of blacks, promote their social welfare, and improve sanitary and economic conditions. President Richard Wright of the GSIC and Sol Johnson pressed for more cooperative ventures between the black community and Savannah's city government. The Chamber of Commerce responded by inviting Wright and Johnson to serve on a biracial committee of the chamber. One outcome of the committee was the city sponsorship of "Clean Up Day" on May 4, 1912. Blacks as well as whites turned out to pick up trash and pile it onto carts to be hauled away. Wright and Johnson also organized the Civic League, which sponsored public addresses before integrated audiences on how white landlords could improve sanitation in and around their tenements.

During the holiday season of 1912, black women of the Civic League organized a Christmas fund that distributed hundreds of packages to the needy. A newly formed branch of the Negro Business League fostered cooperation among black businessmen, urged blacks to patronize black-owned businesses, and undertook charitable work. Of sixteen local chapters of the Business League in Georgia, Savannah's became the most active.

It was during this period that Savannah's "better class" of blacks formed the Urban League; Sol Johnson became its first president, and membership quickly grew to seventy-five. Although the national organization focused on improving living conditions of blacks who had recently migrated from the South to urban centers of the North in search of work, the local chapter focused on ameliorating substandard living conditions and providing education and recreation facilities for blacks. It organized a boys and girls club, secured a black probation officer for the juvenile court, organized a community club for black women, planned picnics for elderly blacks, and hosted lecturers on health and sanitation.[104]

Contemporary medical opinion that access to open-air areas improved the health of citizens prompted southern cities like Memphis and Charleston to join the nationwide playground movement. Savannah took much longer to embrace these ideas. In a city where the populations of black and white children were nearly equal in 1914, Savannah opened five playgrounds for whites and none for blacks. The city's Playground Committee had good documentation that white children who engaged in outdoor "vigorous games were healthier and hardier and more muscular and more vigorous."

Because the city failed to include black children in its planning for outdoor recreation, the local Urban League purchased property on the north side of Huntingdon Street between Price and East Broad and equipped what became the East Side Playground. It was an instant success. Five hundred black children showed up on opening day, some coming from the west side of the city. Eventually, the local government appropriated some money for the care of the playground, and the city director of playgrounds suggested creating one for black children living in the slums of Yamacraw. Within a few years the city-funded playground opened at Indian and Fahm streets.[105]

Year after year, Dr. Brunner's annual report pleaded with city government to improve living conditions in the black community, usually in language that was insulting to blacks and self-serving to white citizens: "If you allow [the Negro] to be herded into the basements of houses and . . . colonized in crowded districts you will suffer." The lower-class black "furnishes 80% of your household help. You cannot keep pace with modern sanitation without caring for him." Furthermore: "Without the sanitary and moral support of the . . . white people, [the Negro's] progress must be retarded."[106]

In spite his off-putting racist language, Brunner was one of the few southern health officers and nearly a lone voice among Savannah's civic-commercial elite who called for city intervention in behalf of the black community. He was supported by the city's African Americans, black civic organizations, and the *Tribune.*

Well-to-do blacks were of the mind that, if they stepped-up efforts to help their own, the municipal government would come to their assistance. When in early 1915 the National Negro Business League sponsored a National Health Week to raise awareness in the black community that good health fostered the progress of blacks in all endeavors, Savannah's Business League participated. The *Tribune* called Health Week a great success in that "every class" demonstrated concern for improving the living conditions of the African American community. Health Week became an annual event in the city. And, to address exceptionally high morbidity among black infants and children both black and white, civic organizations came together to sponsor "Child Welfare Week" and "Baby Welfare Week."[107]

Collaborative events such as those sponsored by both the black and white community suggest that some progress was being made in black-white relations in Savannah. Unfortunately, external events intruded. Between 1914 and

1918 the boll weevil crept into Georgia, the sea islands, and Chatham County, and the price of cotton plummeted. During this period the Ku Klux Klan revived, Savannahians screened the virulent anti-black movie *Birth of a Nation,* and World War I erupted in Europe.

Trouble Brewing at Home and Abroad

When Europe plunged into war in 1914, it came to Americans "like lightening out of a clear sky." Cotton dropped even more, from thirteen to five cents a pound. Some farmers hauled their crop to town, but unable to find a buyer, hauled it back home. The price collapse cut the value of the crop by $500 million, affecting growers and cotton merchants and those who depended on the commodity for a living. Within a year prices stabilized, and the commodity rose to postwar peaks.

From the outbreak of the World War I, both black and white southerners favored the Allies. The news of German atrocities in Belgium and in May 1915 of the torpedoing of the *Lusitania* fueled public opinion.[108] The elites' views on the war may have resembled somewhat those of Juliette Gordon Low, who wrote in a May letter, "We await President [Woodrow Wilson's] decision regarding the death rate on the *Lusitania.* . . . Wilson will, I feel sure, do nothing. . . . Teddy Roosevelt with his shouts for 'Instant Action' does voice the feelings of the true bred Americans." Juliette ended her letter with a rather caustic aside: "This city is full of Germans, most of them spies."[109]

During the war years, blacks from across Georgia headed North as part of the Great Migration. Some half-million black southerners departed the South in search of better living, better social and working conditions, better wages, equal treatment under the law, and escape from white violence. Black farmhands in the South earned less than $1.00 daily, and shops and factories paid $1.25. Wages in the North were two to four times higher. Labor agents, newspapers, and letters from friends or family living in the North promised opportunities there for a better life.

Black migrants in southwestern Georgia left cotton fields ravaged by the boll weevil; those in coastal counties departed areas where hurricanes had destroyed rice and cotton farming. At Georgia train stations in Albany, Americus, and Macon police harassed migrants. With the state's best rail and ship connections to New York, Newark, Philadelphia, Chicago, and points west, Savannah became the South's leading center for embarkation. Here some of the worst harassment of those attempting to leave took place. Although thousands passed through Savannah bound for the North, only three thousand locals departed.

Savannah's civic-commercial elite, like other southern power brokers, recognized that it was in their interest to keep a surplus of black laborers vying for a limited number of jobs. Oversupply and modest demand would keep wages low; this was especially important for the slowly resuscitating cotton industry, which relied on an abundance of cheap labor to keep profits up.[110] With American's entry into World War I, things changed. But the more things changed, the more they remained the same.

CHAPTER FOUR

World War I, Boom, Bust, and a New Deal

1916–1941

Fear swept American coastal ports in 1915 and 1916. Rumors circulated that fires on ships loaded with war supplies were likely set by German agents. Some prominent Savannahians believed that German spies operated in Savannah, actively courting sympathy among African Americans. Even the *New York Times* called Savannah "a stronghold of German sympathizers"; supposedly federal Secret Service agents had "a gang of bombmakers . . . under surveillance."

The war's effect on the economy alarmed Arthur Gordon, a wealthy cotton merchant, and others: "The cotton business is dead and will not be resurrected until this uncertainty [of war] is over." Whether the United States should join the war effort with the Allies was a source of nationwide and local debate. Prominent black leader Sol Johnson did not favor U.S. involvement, calling the war in Europe a "barbarous struggle" that the United States should avoid. On the home front another pressing issue affected the labor force and the local economy—the Great Migration of African Americans.[1]

Spies, Disharmony among the Democrats, and the Great Migration

The *Morning News* repeatedly ran articles to discourage those who might consider moving north in search of better-paying jobs; the articles depicted those who left as being disillusioned by the high cost of living in the North and able to save little. Mayor Wallace J. Pierpont and other city leaders characterized northern cities as unhealthy for blacks and asserted that many who relocated there died of pneumonia and other diseases. But one migrant from the coastal region now living in Philadelphia wrote a southern friend: "[Here] . . . I don't have to mister every little white boy [that] comes along [and] . . . I haven't heard any white man call a colored a nigger."[2]

Savannah's police sometimes became overzealous in their attempts to stop northern agents from recruiting blacks away from the city. On one occasion, Mayor Pierpont ordered police to arrest and jail two men who were signing up blacks to work for northern railroads. But the labor agents had already lured hundreds of black laborers from the Savannah area. Indeed, so many African

Americans recruits were trying to leave the city on July 31, 1916, that the *Morning News* described the scene as a "surging mob . . . of negroes," pushing into Union Station to board trains for the North. Police with clubs looked on menacingly but did not intervene.[3]

The day following, the Negro Business League, led by Lucius E. Williams, president of the Wage Earners Savings Bank, and other black leaders, met with Mayor Pierpont and the City Council to protest police harassment of blacks who wished to relocate away from the city. Pierpont denied any attempt to stop blacks from boarding trains and defended the police presence. Unconvinced, the Negro Business League created a defense fund to be used in case of future arrests related to entrainment.[4]

In May 1917, five black men were arrested for distributing a poem in Savannah titled "Bound for the Promised Lands." The doggerel began: "From Savannah's Stormy banks I go, / I'll bid the South goodbye; / No longer shall they treat me so, / And knock me in the eye." Their arrest on charges of threatening to incite a riot obviously violated their constitutional rights of free speech. Two of the men, James N. Chisolm and A. P. Walker, were charged with disorderly conduct and sentenced to thirty days of hard labor at the Brown Farm, a segregated labor camp in Chatham County. The word on the street was that corporal punishment for whites held there was less severe than that inflicted on blacks.[5]

The *Morning News* continued to report on Savannah's labor shortage, using it as a rationale for encouraging efforts to prevent migration. A *Tribune* editorial asked why, with such a dire labor shortage, "hundreds of Negroes [were] walking the streets in search of work." Ironically, Sol Johnson initially argued against migration. He saw it as detrimental to the black community—"depleting the churches" and hurting "Negro business and professional[s]" who were dependent on African American clientele. He attributed low wages to the growing exodus and believed that, with more competitive pay, men would not leave the South for points north. But Johnson's views changed radically over time, and his question became not why blacks were leaving but rather why they should stay. Why live and work in a community where they received low wages, endured the threat of mob violence and lynching, lived under "dismal social and economic conditions," and were "badly treated . . . [without] hope" for improving their circumstances.[6]

Southern blacks migrated primarily to five major northern industrial cities between 1915 and 1930: New York, Chicago, Detroit, Philadelphia, and Cleveland. During these fifteen years the combined black population of these five cities more than tripled, increasing from 234,460 to 973,173.[7] As southern blacks found jobs and resettled in the North, they encouraged other family members and friends to follow. But some of those who stayed behind found opportunities to celebrate. A brass band, male social clubs, black Union Civil War soldiers, and 1,000 African American longshoremen led a parade through Savannah on January 1, 1917, to honor Emancipation Day. Blacks of all classes turned out to demonstrate racial solidarity and to announce again that they were part of the body politic.

Two months later, sixty members of Savannah's black business elite welcomed to the city the Hon. James W. Johnson, organizer of the National Association for the Advancement of Colored People (NAACP), who delivered an address about the NAACP and its goal "to make sensible and respectful protest at injustice directed at the race." The audience eagerly embraced the purposes and established a Savannah chapter. The ubiquitous Sol Johnson agreed to serve on the executive committee. By the end of the year, chapters of the NAACP had organized in Charleston, Augusta, Athens, Macon, and Atlanta. These branches expressed the long-held interest of southern black leaders in coming together to secure their equal rights as Americans.[8]

World War I, a "Jim Crow" Army, and Two Red Crosses

Savannah loves a parade. On Flag Day, June 14, 1916, some seven thousand children and adult Savannahians turned out for a "Preparedness Parade" sponsored by the civic-commercial elite. Similar parades were going on all across the country as a way to inspire nationalistic ideals in anticipation of the United States' imminent entry into World War I. They marched "in a mighty protest" to the country's being lulled into the belief that it could avoid armed conflict."[9]

Less than a year later, in April 1917, America joined the Allies, in the words of President Woodrow Wilson, "to make the world safe for democracy." The following month, Congress passed the Selective Service Act, which ignored any opposition by southern whites to drafting African Americans for military service. The *Tribune* viewed the opportunity for military service as a step on the road to equality, but offered a caveat: "We are with you . . . but we are going to watch you to see whether our efforts are as much appreciated as they appear to be desired."[10]

Patriotism and the enthusiasm for the war effort brought Savannahians out for another parade on Labor Day 1917, when hundreds of black and white men marched together through Savannah streets. Among the marchers were the Sons of Confederate Soldiers. Such signs of racial goodwill lasted only briefly.[11]

Black draftees from Savannah entrained from Union Station on West Broad Street for Camp Gordon in Atlanta. Here they joined a "Jim Crow" Army. They were segregated at camp and in mess halls; provided the least desirable quarters and a different standard of health care; draftees were frequently referred to as "niggers" and were often punished by the military police for trivial offenses. Recruits were usually assigned menial tasks like loading and unloading cargo, kitchen work, and serving as stewards for white officers. With few exceptions black soldiers seldom had the opportunity to be involved in combat and, when sent to Europe to fight, were segregated aboard troop transports and on the front lines.[12]

Sol Johnson and his *Tribune* staff watched the discrimination the draftees endured and took every opportunity to praise the patriotism of each group leaving Savannah. Early in the war, the *Tribune* described 53 departing draftees as "the finest looking . . . most intelligent, neatest looking bunch" ever to board trains for Atlanta. About a month later, as another group of 124 black draftees prepared to depart, Johnson reflected philosophically on their future: "They go forth, lighthearted and enthusiastic—hurrying to the trenches and death, (For What?), that they may perpetrate a government and a people [who] would keep them in bonds?" The *Tribune* lashed out at the "uncouth policeman . . . [who] dogged" the draftees until their departure. To their credit, the young men ignored the policeman and "'went fourth . . . singing . . . 'We're With You Uncle Sam.'"[13]

Although a history of political feuding divided Sol Johnson and Georgia State Industrial College President Richard Wright on many issues, both vigorously supported the war effort. Wright established a U.S. Army Training School on the campus that enrolled 200 black men. After two months of training they were assigned to one of the "colored" divisions in the army. Georgia Governor Hugh Dorsey later appointed Wright as the historian of black troops in France.[14]

On the home front, white women of prominent Savannah families established a branch of the national War Camp Community Service to provide entertainment for white servicemen, including street dances, boat rides, and other amusements "of a wholesome character." The women had access to the Hussars Club at the corner of Bull and Liberty streets, which they decorated and used as a spot for entertaining visiting servicemen in the evenings. Nothing was more effective than "cheery conversation and music" to make the young soldiers "forget their homesickness." The secretary of the white service reported that the black branch provided the same services as the white and that the group was successful because "the [Negro] race purchased a building" and its services "are financed by themselves."[15]

The Savannah Chapter of the American Red Cross, reorganized after the outbreak of war in Europe, was led by some of the city's most prominent white citizens: Dr. A. J. Waring, J. Randolph Anderson, and Arthur Gordon, whose mother Nelly organized the first chapter in the city during the Spanish-American War. As the chapter needed more space, the organization moved from a city store to the rectory of Christ Church and then to the W. W. Gordon home on Oglethorpe Avenue. During the war, Arthur Gordon also chaired the local Liberty Loan Committee. With other prominent civic-commercial elites like Soloman Sheftall and Leon Adler, the committee raised $555,000. Gordon made a very generous personal contribution of $5,000.[16]

One problem facing the local Red Cross was "how to handle the negroes who desired to contribute their share towards the Red Cross work." After "serious thought," the all-white chapter "deemed it best to organize the negroes of Savannah into a colored branch." Thus the Toussaint L'Ouverture branch of the Savannah Chapter of the American Red Cross organized with Rebecca Stiles Taylor as its first president. The sixty-plus-member chapter, like many other service organizations chartered by black women in Savannah, gave "African American women a taste for leadership," and within these groups they honed organizational skills that would be put to use in service, politics, and civil rights.

With its own officers and committees, the new Toussaint L'Ouverture branch of the Red Cross, named for a black hero who liberated slaves in Haiti, set to work. They met regularly in the *Tribune* building on West Broad Street, offered assistance to any soldier's family in distress, and established knitting and surgical dressing groups. Serving troops was also a segregated activity. White Red Cross workers greeted trains carrying white soldiers; black Red Cross workers greeted "colored troop trains." On one occasion, the white chapter's Civilian Relief, Home Service and Rehabilitation Committee gave a class composed solely of "negro women . . . who volunteered to visit their own race." Apparently, it was the only time the white chapter integrated with the "colored."

Whereas the white chapter of the Savannah Red Cross received twenty-five thousand dollars from the local War Chest Fund to meet the needs of soldiers passing through the city, the L'Ouverture branch received nothing. By March 1918, a *Tribune* article praising the "good work" of the chapter said it had grown to 387 members. In Atlanta, African Americans were "rebuffed "in their efforts to open a Red Cross affiliate.[17]

Shipbuilding, Suburbs, and Sugar

World War I rejuvenated shipbuilding in coastal ports, saw military bases established, and brought boom times to numerous cities and towns across the South. In less than a year the population of Norfolk and nearby Hampton Roads increased from 67,000 to 167,000. Thousands migrated from the countryside

Members of the Toussaint L'Ouverture Chapter of the American Red Cross, Savannah, 1918. Front, left to right: Mamie George Williams, Rebecca Stiles Taylor, Mamie S. Belcher, Anna Honor Whitmore. Middle, left to right: Fannie Petty Goodall, Sarah A. Jackson, Helen Lee, Dr. Fannin S. Belcher (the instructor), Lottie Curley, Mariah Jackson Thomas. Back, left to right: Mae Stewart, Ophel Lee McIvy, and Willie Hill Powell. Courtesy of Georgia Archives, Vanishing Georgia Collection, image no. ctm096.

to work in shipbuilding and with dry-dock companies on the coasts of Mississippi, Texas, and South Carolina. The existing Naval Yard at Charleston was named headquarters of the Sixth Naval District, which hired 5,000 civilian employees along with 7,350 military officers and enlisted men who trained 25,000 recruits.[18]

Savannah grew more slowly. From 1900 to 1920 the population increased from approximately 54,000 to 83,000 and was 53 percent white and 47 percent black. Savannah now ranked thirteenth among the twenty-five largest cities in the South and had one of the highest percentages of black residents.[19]

By the early 1900s there was a flurry of suburban development for whites on Savannah's east side beyond the city limits. Wagner Heights went up between a large farm and Wheaton Street and accepted only white prospects. Nearby, the Twickenham Development Company offered fine homes to white buyers, touting its paved streets, city water connections, and streetcars—just fifteen minutes to Broughton Street, the city's business district.

The Twickenham subdivision was located near the prestigious Savannah Golf Club on Garrard Avenue (Gobel Street today). Nominees for golfing memberships, white males of the local elite, had to be voted up or down by the membership committee. In an early nod to gender equity, women had access to the course even though they could not attend meetings or vote on club issues. Golfers played over several hazards on the course, including Civil War fortifications. Subsequently, a new two-story stucco clubhouse sporting a red tile roof replaced the original clapboard clubhouse just north of East Gwinnett Street. The new facility included large locker rooms for men and women and public rooms for card games, banquets, and dances.

The club hired Donald Ross to design a new, eighteen-hole golf course, and the Chamber of Commerce promoted it as one of the many fine sporting venues in Savannah. The DeSoto Hotel arranged for its guests to enjoy a round of golf by paying the green fee set by the club. When Bobby Jones played the course during the Savannah Open Golf Tournament in 1930, the club drew the attention of professional golfers and duffers everywhere. Though Jones did not win *this* event, he never lost another. White boys from Wagner Heights and Twickenham and black youngsters from the neighborhood of East Savannah served as caddies.[20]

Black adults from the LePageville and East Savannah neighborhoods found employment on the eastside waterfront with the railroads and briefly with the Savannah Dry Dock and Repair Company during World War I. Later, Southern States Phosphate, the Mutual Fertilizer Company, the Texas Oil Company, and the Standard Oil Company employed workers at their petroleum storage tanks and wharves; other eastside employment opportunities for African American were jobs as docking pilots on the river or as fishermen, oystermen, and shrimpers who sold their abundant catches to the city market or local canneries. In the canneries, black women picked blue crabs and headed shrimp; white women worked there too, most in the packaging process.[21]

During World War I, Savannah did not receive the amount of federal money that poured into Charleston, but on the river commercial wharves and modest private shipyards sprang up near former plantations like Vale Royal and Brewton Hill, lands once worked by slaves. One company built minesweepers for the French government even before America joined the Allies. Another company, Terry Shipbuilding, received contracts from the U.S. government for five tankers weighting about fifty-two hundred tons each and composite ships, one named the *James Oglethorpe.* On Independence Day 1918, a cheering crowd watched the launch of the 287-foot *Oglethorpe,* which could carry thirty-six hundred tons of cargo to American troops fighting abroad; another *SS Oglethorpe* would be built in Savannah during WW II. As concerns lingered over spies or saboteurs, anyone wishing to visit the wharves on the river had to provide a pass for the armed guards.[22]

During the war, demand pushed cotton prices to their highest levels ever and brought jobs for longshoremen. Although Savannah's population did not surge like that of some coastal cities, the population grew from the influx of rural white and black migrants seeking work. Some of these newcomers pushed west beyond crowded Yamacraw and the city limits to find jobs in the factories and wharves going up along the river—fertilizer companies, the Hilton-Dodge Lumber Company, the American Can Company, and the Central of Georgia Railway. Most work for African Americans tended to be in low-paid laboring positions. Near this factory district more and more people settled and helped create the Hudson Hill, Woodville, and West Savannah neighborhoods. A new company upriver from the city, the Sugar Refinery, began hiring workers soon after the United States entered World War I.[23] For a time it was one of the largest employers in the factory district.

The move of the Adeline Sugar Company from New Orleans to Savannah was the brainchild of sixty-year-old Benjamin A. Oxnard and his partner and nephew, Richard H. Sprague, whose brother, Benjamin Oxnard Sprague, quickly agreed to the plan. A variety of factors—freezes, floods, droughts in Louisiana, and an act of Congress permitting the free entry of foreign sugar—influenced this bold and expensive decision. The relocation meant moving not only their own families but also 300 "Cajun" and French-speaking black workers hundreds of miles across country. Oxnard selected a site for the refinery, thirty acres on the south bank of the Savannah River near the town of Port Wentworth. Local blacks were hired to work side by side with the Cajuns. The company dropped the name "Adeline" and became known as the Sugar Refinery.

Locally, Oxnard received financial advice from Savannah banker Mills B. Lane, who, shortly before the plant opened with 350 employees in the summer of 1917, feted the new owners at a luncheon in his Citizens and Southern Bank in downtown Savannah. Raising a glass of wine, Lane said: "Savannah is an old town with old families, old traditions. . . . We feel honored to welcome people like yourselves who understand these things so well."[24]

Of all the industries along the river that provided rental homes for its workers, the Sugar Refinery provided some of the best affordable housing on the grounds of the plant itself—two separate villages of small frame cottages, one for the white employees and another for the African Americans. The cottages were not built to the same standards: the latter lacked indoor bathrooms. Even after the city of Savannah annexed the west-side neighborhoods in 1939, years passed before these homes had water and sewer access, paved roads, and sidewalks.

Well into the mid- to late twentieth century, everything remained segregated. Recreation and company social events for all the companies in the factory district were segregated. At barbecues, the tables for blacks were positioned close enough to the tables of whites to suggest their working relationships, but far enough apart to indicate their social distance. Segregation remained the norm on the west side, east side, in Savannah, the South, and the nation. African Americans by and large were restricted to menial jobs, stood in separate lines to receive their pay, used separate restrooms and water fountains, and dined at segregated eating establishments; they were expected to defer to whites, who had the prerogative of boarding busses first. These day-after-day reminders of second-class citizenship gnawed away at people, one of Savannah's African Americans reminisced.[25]

In July 1917, a Norwegian freighter carefully wound its way up the Savannah River, the first in an endless line of ships to unload tons of refined sugar at the Sugar Refinery's dock. Oxnard and Sprague needed more workers. The country's need for draftees took many laborers from the area and, seeing few options, management decided to advertise for black females to perform "light, sanitary and desirable work." When a representative of the *Tribune* toured the plant, he found that management's job description matched the work performed by the women.[26] The Oxnard and Sprague families and other investors made fortunes from the Sugar Refinery. Over time some of the founders used their wealth to provide generous support for the arts and education in Savannah.

Public Expenditures, Prohibition, Prostitution, and the Flu

In the first year of World War I, Savannah's city budget reached $1,127,710. As had been the case for decades, the Police Department received the largest allocation, $163,994. The Sanitation Department budget increased to $158,700, due largely to the construction of new sewer systems and storm drains. Other items in the budget included the Savannah Public Library (white), which received $14,000; the Carnegie Public Library ("colored"), $1,350; the white hospitals received $9,616, the colored hospitals $6,550. The city's interest on its bonded indebtedness, $166,645, was a sizeable portion (15 percent) of the budget. Mayor Pierpont reported city revenues "meager," just slightly over that of the previous year; therefore, the most "rigid economy is unavoidable in all municipal outlays."[27]

Despite this gloomy assessment, Pierpont remained enthusiastic about the sudden "growth in population at manufacturing plants . . . along the river." And he anticipated they "will continue to show a remarkable expansion in coming years." As for the present, the city would be ever vigilant and would "zealously enforce the statutes of the state directed at the iniquitous outlawed liquor traffic [and] would enforce measures for the protection of the army and navy . . . in campaigns for the suppression of vice." Here, of course, the mayor was referring to prostitution.

Pierpont concluded his report: "The war has served . . . to knit our people together . . . with the exception of that small minority [who] . . . put a check on moral and social betterment"—Pierpont likely was speaking of the city's anti-prohibition faction. But he ended on a high note: The city occupies a "unique position among the municipalities of America for its beauty and wealth and culture . . . integrity, honor, cleanness of life."[28] As for the traffic in liquor, the state went "bone dry" in 1917.

Georgia Governor Nathaniel Harris used "apocalyptic terms" when he spoke to a large audience in Atlanta to celebrate the prohibition victory: "Liquor arouses . . . race hatred . . . and if its use were not controlled . . . would . . . bring anarchy and race war." Mayor Pierpont also addressed the same audience: "The victory . . . we are celebrating is largely due to the awakening of the people in our churches to the power that they possess" over Savannah's "liquor dealers."[29] But the report of the Savannah chief of police that same year suggests that perhaps Pierpont's "victory" was overstated.

Police Chief B. S. Bryant found numerous violations of the Prohibition Law and questioned if it could be enforced. During the year, police arrested 7,893 persons, among them 1,888 for disorderly conduct, driving an automobile while drunk, or being drunk on a train. And alcohol was not the only vice undermining city morals. Nearly 300 persons were arrested for gambling, possessing a gambling device, or running a gambling house, including three women for "keeping a lewd house."[30]

Pressure on Savannah's city leaders came too from the federal government's desire to control prostitution in order to protect army and navy personnel from venereal diseases. When the results of annual examinations of soldiers were reported during 1917–18, red light districts were shut down across the South, including Storyville in New Orleans as well as those in Charleston and Savannah.[31]

Before the war, Charleston restricted prostitution to a "segregated area." When ordered by the federal government to shut down vice in the city, Charleston police and federal agents shuttered eight brothels. Some Charlestonians claimed that the anti-vice campaign had become too successful. This was not the case with alcohol. Charleston officials generally ignored national and state laws prohibiting consumption of alcoholic beverages; as one observer noted, during prohibition the city remained "wringing, sopping, dripping wet."[32]

Savannah's city government decided to take action when it learned that 200 of 600 Paris Island marines who visited Savannah admitted having had "sexual intercourse" with prostitutes.[33] The city's proposed solution was to move prostitution from the city's east side to the west side. If the plan had been carried out, prostitutes and houses of prostitution would have been relocated to the heart of the black business and residential district.

The West Broad Street area, where 95 percent of families were black, was also home to many of Savannah's black churches and social organizations. Upon hearing about the prostitution-relocation plan, prominent African Americans pushed back just as they had done on other issues in the past. The *Tribune* blasted the instigators: "We resent . . . the proposal . . . to establish the red-light district in the heart of a Negro neighborhood." It would bring a "cesspool of crime . . . and immorality" and "lewd [white] women." One of his arguments was that the move would undo the local policy of segregated black neighborhoods.

The NAACP joined the protest, and a Committee of Nine, composed of members of religious and civic organizations, appealed to whites to join their cause, which they did. A local white judge, Samuel B. Johnson, went before the City Council, told them he agreed with the protestors, and took the opportunity to call for treating blacks "justly, fairly and kindly," which he said might prevent the exodus of blacks to the North. Both the city's white and African American newspapers found something to champion in Judge Johnson's presentation. A shift began in white and black attitudes. The Committee of Nine appeared before the City Council and called on members to reverse their policy; the council acted immediately and ordered the police chief to stop any removal of prostitutes to the west side and to relocate elsewhere any "houses of ill-fame" presently on the west side.[34]

Though not always in agreement on political issues, both Sol Johnson and Richard Wright celebrated the news. Johnson regarded the reversal of city policy by the white power structure as a turning point in Savannah's history. It has also been suggested that the successful protest encouraged Savannah blacks to be more forceful in confronting injustices, a practice that culminated in the civil rights movement in the 1960s.[35]

Mayor Pierpont took the brunt of the criticism on this issue, and he defended himself near the end of this term when he said, "certain forms of vice . . . entrenched in the city since colonial days . . . have been outlawed and largely extirpated." It was the federal government that ordered the city to protect "the boys in uniform" from "the districts of immorality." For trying to address this concern, Pierpont said, he had faced "vicious opposition" and incurred "bitter political enmity" from both anti-prohibitionists and those opposed to his plan to "segregate the 'red light'" district into "Negro neighborhoods." In Pierpont's words, after "a storm of protest from enraged black and white citizens," the City Council "killed" his proposition.[36]

Though Pierpont apparently felt somewhat betrayed on the relocation issue, the outgoing mayor did praise City Council members for their help during his years in office as the city pursed a "progressive policy": new wells pumped purer water, an obsolete system of accounting had been replaced to prevent "waste and graft," a "purchase board" had been established to prevent "wasteful ... purchasing," and a "traffic bureau" now protected the city from "discriminating freight rates." In turn, the City Council congratulated the outgoing mayor for his "magnificent" years of leadership.[37]

Though Pierpont had implemented some progressive programs, the plight of blacks living in the city slums remained unaddressed and unmentioned. During the war years, the *Tribune,* like Savannah's health officer, Dr. William Brunner, repeatedly asked city government to address the "appalling conditions in Yamacraw." In the area lived some seven thousand African Americans (17 percent of the city's black population); "suffering and misery" abounded, as did poverty, ignorance, filth, and overcrowding—the "handmaidens of disease" and death. Well-to-do black leaders of Savannah's Urban League decided that, "if the city will not help, we must do it ourselves." We must "instill ... pride for better houses, cleaner yards, less dirt" and provide better foods and medicine. The *Tribune* labeled Yamacraw "a blot and disgrace upon the fair name of our city." One vital statistic affected by these deplorable living conditions was life span. According to local leaders of the time, average life span for white and black residents was dramatically different.[38]

Brunner also noted his concern for a growing "narcotic drug habit" in the city. He had written a paper on the matter regarding the local "persons addicted to its use," and those "individuals instrumental in its importation and distribution." He asked Savannah's Board of Sanitary Commissioners for permission to publish the paper in order to keep the public apprised of "full knowledge of the situation in the community." The commissioners agreed only to send the paper to the mayor so he might decide if there is "anything objectionable in it."[39] Apparently, the matter was dropped.

During and after World War I, the migration of blacks to the North continued. More than fifty thousand left Georgia in one year alone. Savannah's

African American leaders, who once encouraged the outflow, now became alarmed about the loss of depositors at black banks and insurance companies and the declining numbers of church members and patrons for black doctors, lawyers, dentists, and merchants. In some circles, Savannah's civic-commercial elite recognized that fairer treatment of blacks rather than repression might somewhat curb the exodus. City Council actions also reflected a shift in attitude as they began to fund several black social and charitable organizations in the war years and continued to do so into the 1920s.[40]

In September 1918, an outbreak of Spanish influenza spread to the United States. Before running its course worldwide, 50,000,000 people died. Fearing infection, schools, movie theaters, and churches closed and social gatherings were put on hold. The *Morning News* urged readers who contracted the disease to "go to bed, avoid others, take a purgative, eat and drink plenty and keep quiet." Plenty of remedies were touted in the ads of newspapers. Whiskey, used as the prime elixir in Charleston, failed to cure all. Four hundred fifty people died there. By late October, the number of deaths in Savannah had reached 19; seven "visiting nurses" tended 259 influenza patients in one twenty-four-hour period, and 3 of the 10 Red Cross nurses had themselves fallen ill. Whole families were sick as the flu in Savannah spread into the next year. Urgent appeals went out for more volunteers to tend the growing number of patients.

Despite the precautions to minimize spread of disease, crowds gathered to celebrate the signing of an Armistice in Europe on November 11, 1918. From dawn to midnight a "carnival-like" atmosphere swept the city. Bands played, church bells pealed, and citizens dressed in gaudy costumes sang the "Marseillaise" and lynched and burned an effigy of the German Kaiser.[41]

Homecoming Tensions, a Manhunt, and "the Courage to Speak Out"

American troops in Europe began returning home, including 200,000 black soldiers. Months in advance, plans had begun in Savannah's black community to celebrate the homecoming of African American soldiers. In early May 1919, black Savannahians held a "welcome home parade" for the "doughboys" of Savannah and Chatham County. The line of march through the city included about 5,000 persons led by the Knights of Pythias, their band, and 1,200 returning troops who were greeted with "uninterrupted applause" by spectators. Next came 500 longshoremen, the Young Boys' Aid and Social Club, the Friendly Brothers Aid Society and Social Club, Imperial Aid and Social Club, the Union Brotherhood Evening Call and Social Club, and 150 members of the Savannah Home Association dressed in matching Palm Beach suits, white shoes, and straw hats. One of the final displays in the parade was a massive "Gold Star" honoring those local black soldiers who made "the Supreme Sacrifice." The parade ended at a ballpark where everyone gathered to hear speeches, enjoy music, and eat barbecue.

Upon discharge, black soldiers were encouraged to wear their uniforms home with pride. However, in Georgia and throughout the country there were concerns among some of the rising aspirations of African Americans, especially the "colored troops." A *Tribune* editorial explained the hostility: "[whites] resent the presence of Negroes in uniform" for fear that the Negroes who served abroad "will forget their place" and thereby threaten white supremacy.[42]

Inflation, strikes, the arrest of thousands of alleged Bolsheviks, and deportations stirred fears nationwide. These factors and the recent rebirth of the Ku Klux Klan in Georgia and black militancy triggered interracial violence. "Christian" politicians, men and women, like Georgia's Tom Watson and Rebecca Felton, publicly and often promoted the murder of blacks. The Bible Belt became the lynching center of America.[43]

In nearby Charleston, two white sailors and a black man scuffled in a pool hall; the black man died and a sailor was injured. The year was 1919. The fight precipitated a riot. Hundreds of white sailors and civilians poured into the streets, attacking blacks and ransacking their neighborhoods and businesses. Three blacks died, and a large number were injured, as were several dozen sailors and civilians. Eventually, a squad of marines arrived in battle dress and restored order.

The violence in Charleston ushered in the so-called Red Summer. Riots broke out in twenty-five American cities, marking the highest incidence ever of interracial clashes in the country. The worst riots erupted in Chicago and Washington, D.C., where scores of blacks and whites died. In the small town of Millen, near Savannah, during an out-of-control riot, a white policeman and marshal were killed. Whites retaliated by killing five blacks and burning seven black churches. The Savannah police advised local retailers not to sell arms and ammunition to blacks as a "precautionary measure."[44]

Sol Johnson's *Tribune* manifest profound concern that Georgia blacks were being murdered; Georgia led all other states in the number of lynchings in 1918. The "terror and brutality" of the murders and the fact that authorities did not always apprehend the "suspected parties" left many feeling anxious and vulnerable. Although Savannah thus far had escaped mob violence, "hundreds of irresponsible young white men . . . are carrying guns on their hips every day," the *Tribune* reported. The editors predicted that, if mob action came, it would begin on "the street cars where Negroes are driven and dogged every day for little or nothing." This type of harassment would continue unless public opinion "rises up to counteract the spirit of lawlessness and relieves the tension of the times."

The Christmas season of 1919 proved to be "most disorderly . . . [with] three persons killed and several shot and cut . . . and many injured in fisticuffs." The *Tribune* speculated that some "had gotten hold of the 'fighting moonshine' that is floating around."[45] In nearby rural counties lynching sometimes occurred, a most extreme way of ensuring white supremacy. Apparently, Savannahians had not participated, that is, until the late spring of 1920.

In June a manhunt was underway in the marshes near Savannah for Phillip Gathers, a "Negro," alleged to have murdered a young woman in Effingham County, a county abutting Chatham. The *Tribune* characterized it as a hunt with bloodhounds by "bloody-thirsty . . . men . . . drunk with liquor . . . and hate." The mob finally ran Gathers to the ground and, with "brutality and barbarism," he was "beaten, oiled, burned and his body dissected for souvenirs." One rural countian congratulated "the good citizens of 'Old Chatham' who gave good service in the chase [for Gathers]." That night, "Many of the men [who] live in Savannah were on the streets . . . exhibiting parts of Gathers' body."[46]

Gather's lynching, typical of the violence against African Americans after World War I, alarmed Sol Johnson, who wrote about it frequently in the *Tribune,* as he did on December 4, 1920: "white men have run wild on a rampage of slaughter and lynching and burning. It seems many of these men are literally crazed and wild with hate." His editorial went on to describe the revival of "Ku Kluxism [and] . . . the burning of homes and churches and schools by the night riders . . . [and the plight of] . . . prosperous law abiding Negroes [who] are being driven from their farms, their crops and their stock being confiscated or sacrificed." Johnson wrote of African Americans "running helter-skelter through the woods and swamps for their lives . . . [and of the] terror of fleeing women, dragging their children behind them, seeking shelter from these Georgia Cossacks." Johnson lamented the "changes which have taken place in our own city . . . which threaten the peace and good record [of Savannah]." He specifically condemned the coroner's juries who found that victims of the mob "died at the hands of parties unknown," the grand juries who "fail to order investigations," and the juries who "fail to punish." Further, he expressed disappointment that "no voice has been raised against . . . this barbarism." And he chastised those "who would condemn the oppression behind closed doors [but] do not have the courage to speak out openly and publicly against the wrong. Herein is the moral depravity and degeneracy—and the danger to our civilization."[47]

A few weeks later, an editorial in the *Tribune* on December 18, 1920, described a meeting of the local NAACP that drew a large crowd. The paper reminded citizens that the NAACP was "aiding the defense of Negroes . . . throwing the white light of truth on lynchings . . . fighting Jim crowism . . . fighting disfranchisement . . . [and promoting] the general welfare of the people of our race." The paper's closing directive, "join."

De Renne, the West Broad Building Boom, and "All That Jazz"

The war brought a taste of prosperity to southern farms and cities alike. Money made during the war years and saved by individuals and banks found outlets for investments in buildings and land. Men like Arthur Gordon, Wymberley Wormsloe De Renne, and others who had served abroad during the war now came home to seek their fortunes. Gordon served as an officer with the Red Cross and De Renne as a first lieutenant in France. Before shipping out, De Renne and a local beauty from a prominent and wealthy family, Augusta Floyd, exchanged wedding vows in Savannah's Christ Church. De Renne's best man was Dr. Charles Norris, and ushers included George Nobel Jones and Dr. Craig Barrow. Following the war, Gordon and De Renne both wanted to profit from the anticipated influx of veterans and others moving to Savannah who would need housing.[48] De Renne, who wanted to become a "capitalist," saw this as his opportunity.

After his father's death, De Renne became master of Wormsloe, the family's historic homesite on the Isle of Hope, near Savannah. His father bequeathed a considerable estate to De Renne and his two sisters, and they received a monthly income from two apartment buildings on Liberty Street, just east of the DeSoto Hotel. De Renne, like his father, shopped at Brooks Brothers, walked the trails of his hunting club, and enjoyed the camaraderie of the Union Club. He also emulated his father by investing in real estate.

De Renne planned to buy land and build a large apartment building at the corner of Liberty and Drayton streets. His attorneys objected strenuously to such a risky venture in uncertain times, but paying no heed, De Renne invested $142,000 during 1919 and 1920 just to accumulate the property where he planned to build his apartment.

To finance the project, De Renne sold his father's two nearby apartment buildings and the De Renne wharf for $60,000 and offered for sale through Mills Lane's Citizens and Southern Bank $225,000 in bonds paying 6 percent interest, secured by a first mortgage on the new apartment building. Bond investors were told that the total investment in the apartment building would be $500,000, but were not informed that this amount nearly equaled De Renne's entire inheritance. Unbeknownst to his sisters, De Renne also took out a mortgage on Wormsloe Plantation. By 1920, a large apartment building was going up on his Liberty Street property.

The masonry, eight-story building in the Georgian Revival style would have forty-four units opening onto balconies. Residents and guests would approach the building through a large stone portico leading into a courtyard and then enter the building through wide glass doors that opened into the lobby. Elevators would whisk guests upstairs to the various levels. Long hallways opened into the individual apartments, a new feature in Savannah apartment design. The De Renne building was called "an ornament to Savannah" with "the last word in comfort and elegance." Unique for the times, the apartments had built-in appliances: gas ranges, refrigerators, and garbage disposals.[49]

As the De Renne building went up, so too did the Forsyth Apartments with six stories and sixty units overlooking Forsyth Park. Single-family dwellings were also being built in both black and white neighborhoods. By the end of 1920, the housing shortage had become a surplus in Savannah. Costs of living rose, rents dropped sharply, and the price of cotton plunged—this chain of events had a profound economic effect on the port city.

Interest payments and the cost of buying land and building and maintaining the De Renne apartments siphoned off Wymberley's fortune. No longer able to keep his financial situation and Wormsloe's mortgage a secret, and now trying to fend off his creditors, De Renne found himself in a very compromising situation that set off repercussions within the family and for the future of Wormsloe.[50]

At the time the De Renne went up, construction in Savannah skyrocketed 900 percent. On the east side, an Atlanta businessman, Arthur Lucas, built an ornate and architecturally significant theater of 28,514 square feet with seating for about seventeen hundred. Located on Abercorn Avenue just off Broughton Street and named after the builder, some called it the "Jewel of Savannah."[51]

A building boom surged in the three-block area of West Broad Street dominated by black businesses. Realty and financial firms, small stores, shops, and funeral homes located there. Investors bought a two-story building at the corner of West Broad and Maple streets for $20,000 and opened the sole black pharmacy in the city. The Fidelity Bank and the Mechanics Bank opened their doors on West Broad Street and became neighbors of the city's oldest black financial institution, the Wage Earners Savings Bank. All three catered to the African American community.

Lucius Williams, president of the Wage Earners Savings Bank, headed the only African American bank in the country whose assets topped $1 million in the 1920s. People from across the state and county had accounts at the bank. The bank purchased a whole block of property adjacent to Union Station on West Broad Street, where Williams planned to construct a huge business complex, estimated to cost $500,000. The bank also purchased a building on Seventh Avenue and 135th Street in New York's Harlem for $200,000. Walter Sanford Scott, another African American entrepreneur, established the Guarantee Life Insurance Company on West Broad. With other investors, Scott underwrote a four-story building costing $100,000 at West Broad and Gaston streets that included the Dunbar Moving Picture Theatre, the only fireproof theater in the city; the theater had seating for seven hundred in the mezzanine and two hundred in the balcony. The purchase of other theaters added to Mr. Scott's assets, and he soon came to control the movie business for black Savannah. Mr. Scott also became a millionaire.

When the Dunbar Theater opened in 1921, Scott made a political statement with his choice of the first feature film shown, *The Symbol of the Unconquer'd.* The plot of the movie with an all-black cast depicted murderous KKK night-riders forcing a black man off his oil-rich land and other blacks rallying to save him.[52]

"Hot jazz and hot jazz clubs" also found a home on West Broad Street or nearby in the early twentieth century. Savannah and New Orleans jazz emerged about the same time—the former influenced by a vibrant African tradition, the latter by the Creole culture. The Pekin was Savannah's jazz mecca. The thousand-seat theater founded by Josephine Styles and built at 625 West Broad Street from its opening attracted black jazz musicians, vaudeville, and musical comedies and usually enjoyed a full house. Legendary greats like ragtime jazz pianist James P. Johnston, Fletcher Henderson, and Gertrude "Ma" Rainey performed here. White Savannahians sometimes attended. The theater became so successful that it installed a luxurious, four-thousand-dollar iceless soda fountain for patrons. When fire gutted the theater in 1918, it was rebuilt within three months. One scholar noted that not since the 1920s has such an array of black talent appeared in Savannah.[53]

Across West Broad from the Pekin, the Star Theatre offered some brief competition, but it soon promoted silent movies. The Dunbar Theater showed movies, had a house band, sponsored theater parties, and held benefits for children sponsored by the Federation of Negro Women's Clubs and local churches. Savannah also had its own "Storyville." Along West Broad Street and just beyond, "hot jazz" spread into Savannah's largest red light districts, Frogtown and Yamacraw, where one could buy chicken, fish, and barbeque, enjoy "honky-tonk" by black piano players like Blind Charlie and Sammy Jackson, and purchase hard drinks in speakeasies and bordellos.

To appease some white Savannahians scandalized by the new jazz dancing, the City Council passed an anti-jazz ordinance in 1922, prohibiting "lascivious music" and its accompanying dancing. The city's official jazz inspector had no patience with the new shimmy jazz, warning that any dancing that brought "into play that part of the body from the waist up . . . [would] be considered a violation of the anti-jazz ordinance." The ordinance was short-lived.[54] Yet, even the national government worried over the city's purported vices.

Federal investigators who prowled the city in the 1920s reported that Savannah ranked among the nation's thirty most immoral cities. The city allowed legalized vice. Anyone, black or white, who wished to operate a brothel or a cabaret had only to apply for a license at City Hall. A like scheme in Charleston evolved when madams of brothels and the city police agreed that madams illegally maintaining houses of prostitution would post a hundred-dollar monthly bond; of course, the bonds were forfeited, the money flowed into the city treasury, and the madams continued their businesses.

The federal investigators in Savannah commented that the city had one of the few red light districts in the country segregated by race. It was bounded on the north by Gwinnett Street, on the south by Waldburg, on the east by West Broad, and on the west by Cemetery. But there were also other venues and other entertainments. When big-tent black circuses came to town, they located at the corner of West Broad and Thirty-second streets and drew thousands.[55]

Entertainment also emerged with the formation of local jazz bands. On weekends, open-air trolleys brought patrons to Lincoln Park just off East Broad Street to listen and dance to the music of the "Snappy Six," the "Jolly Five," or the "Golden Syncopators." These early, local jazz musicians of the 1920s opened the way for local dance orchestras and nationally known jazz bands to play at local black social clubs—the Harlem Club, the Golden Dream Club, and the Tybrisa Pavilion on Tybee Island.[56] Savannah's prominent white community also enjoyed the social life and boom times of the early 1920s.

The all-white Tomochichi Club planned four grand dances for the social season that ran November to February. The city's white elite enjoyed golf, tennis, and teas at the Savannah Golf Club; they held extravagant prenuptial parties and luncheons for locals and out-of-town guests. Debutants were "introduced" in various settings; one of the most creative occurred in January 1923 aboard the U.S. Coast Guard vessel *Yamacraw,* where Colonel and Mrs. William L. Grayson gave a party for their daughter and other debutants. With the deck enclosed in flags, the debs and their escorts danced and enjoyed punch in the cabin![57] But boom times did not continue uninterrupted, even for the well-to-do.

In the so-called "Roaring Twenties," Savannah's boom collapsed suddenly, recovered briefly, then continued downward again. Inflation, devastation of 30 percent of the state's cotton crop (90 percent along the coast), a status quo attitude among the civic-commercial elite, and a plunge in the port's export-import trade ended boom times. Between 1920 and 1921, import tonnage fell from 735,955 to 213,911 tons; export tonnage fell from 642,706 to 338, 000 tons. Only near the end of World War II did port trade approach the previous highs reached in 1920.

Aware of the dramatic decline in traffic at state ports, the Georgia legislature established the Georgia Harbor, Port and Terminal Commission. The commission selected Savannah over Brunswick and St. Mary's as the "state port" because of Savannah's reputation, land available for expansion, and the commercial base that was already established in the area. While Georgia debated the port site, other southern ports from Wilmington to Mobile were expanding their existing facilities. But there was no such push for quick action from Georgia legislators. Faced with declining revenues, they failed to see the need for speedy action, a decision that would have long-term consequences.[58]

A "League" of Their Own and Bitter Democratic Schisms

After passage of the Nineteenth Amendment to the U.S. Constitution, "The right of citizens to vote shall not be denied . . . on account of sex," both black and white women worked to get out the vote across the country. The Savannah Federation of Negro Women's Clubs, the black Republican League of Women Voters of Savannah, and the National League of Republican Colored Women joined forces. They conducted night schools, held mass meetings, and printed leaflets such as "Ten Reasons Why Negro Women Should Vote," which they sent home with African American children "attending Savannah's segregated public schools."

Though blacks still could not vote in white primary elections, they could vote in the general elections, and their vote would prove crucial. By October, nearly as many African American women as white women had registered to vote in Savannah. Ironically, the city's "all-white League of Women Voters" publically charged the registrar with failing to "enforce the voter qualifications" for the new black registrants. They were shocked by the black clubwomen's successful campaign: "We do not believe there are one thousand educated negro women in Chatham County, who can sign their names, who own property, who understand the laws, or who are descendants of Confederate Veterans." Despite the league's opposition, twenty-seven hundred black women's names were added to the voter rolls. Both black and white women became major players in elections of the 1920s as the Democratic Party of Savannah divided into factions.[59]

"A Conspiracy to Defeat the People's Will"

Party fissures grew as the economy worsened. In the fall of 1922, loyalists of the incumbent mayor, Murray M. Stewart, drafted him for a second term. Another wing of Democrats—local reformers and prohibitionists—endorsed another candidate, Captain James M. Rogers. The reformers sensed a strong undercurrent of opposition to Stewart and opened a campaign attacking the administration's "bossism," cronyism, and corruption. The local paper urged both factions to wage "a clean campaign": no casting ballots of "dead people" or former city residents and "no ringers." At a Rogers rally, speakers warned of the necessity of guarding against "fraud on election day."

"Widespread fighting" swept the city on the day of the "all white" primary election. The local League of Women Voters called it the "bitterest and closest municipal fight ever waged in Savannah . . . [a] shameful primary disgraced by vote buying[,] . . . [use of] ringers, slugging," and "missing ballot boxes." Stewart won by ten votes. Captain Rogers challenged the election results, but the local Democratic Executive Committee upheld Stewart's win in the primary.

Determined to prevent Stewart from returning to the mayor's office, the reformer faction persuaded a highly regarded local judge, Paul E. Seabrook, to run against Stewart in the general election, and they set about collecting signatures to have Seabrook's name added to the general election ballot.

The *Morning News,* now clearly on the side of the reform party, endorsed Seabrook. The paper declared that Captain Rogers lost the primary election because Stewart used "ringers" and thereby "cheated the people of Savannah" out of the election. Rogers and the reformers threw their support behind Judge Seabrook, and the race was on.

The movement for Seabrook reached out to prominent black citizens to campaign for the judge. In a surprising turn of events, a group of educated well-to-do African American women allied themselves with the local white League of Women Voters for a rare biracial alliance in the South. By early 1923, citizens had gathered a remarkable 6,893 signatures to get Seabrook's name on the ballot to run against Stewart in the mayoralty election of January 9.

A few days before the election, some fifty persons guarding the Seabrook petition marched to City Hall, accompanied by a large crowd. Now that the Nineteenth Amendment was law, prominent women like Mrs. Abram Minis and Mrs. Craig Barrow joined Mills B. Lane, Judge S. B. Adams, and Alexander R. Lawton to deliver the petition to Mayor Stewart. Judge Adams declared that the signatures represented the will of the people "against fraud and corruption."[60]

Then, only one day before the general election, the *Morning News* printed a letter to the editor by a prominent Savannahian, Arthur Gordon, who had learned that Mayor Stewart, the City Council, and the clerk of council had refused to place the name of Judge Seabrook on the ballot. This act, Gordon wrote, demonstrates the "viciousness" of the Stewart administration. Accompanying Gordon's letter, the paper ran an extra edition that declared in bold headlines: "Vote For Paul E. Seabrook Tomorrow. He Is In The Race To Stay And To Win." Just below were the words: "Conspiracy to Defeat People's Will [Is] Futile" and "Twelve eminent local attorneys" asserted that the rights of voters are "guaranteed under the U.S. Constitution."

The *Morning News* told voters to scratch out Stewart's name on the ballots and to write in the name Seabrook! Another page in the same paper showed a poster imprinted with a large "Skull and Crossbones" that the paper reported had been "nailed" to the doors of every black church in the city, with the warning: "This is a white man's fight—keep away." It was said to be an attempt by "Stewart supporters . . . to frighten Negroes away from the polls tomorrow"; however, a letter from the Ku Klux Klan, signed by the "Exalted Cyclops, Savannah Klan No. 41, Realm of Georgia," denied that the KKK "had anything to do" with distributing the "Skull and Crossbones." Revived in Georgia some years earlier, the Klan had reached the apogee of its political influence in the state. But the *Morning News* voiced confidence that Savannah's "colored people" would not be deterred; they "are well organized . . . and not afraid to vote."[61] Seabrook and his lieutenants prepared well. They registered about eleven hundred African American voters. Seabrook's white supporters seemed unfazed by Stewart's charge that the Seabrook reformers were "nigger loving."[62]

Unlike primary election day, the general election passed quietly with just one fistfight. An "excited crowd" gathered to await the election results. When word leaked that Mayor Stewart's poll managers had "refused to count ballots bearing Judge Seabrook's name," Superior Court Judge Peter W. Meldrim issued a "restraining order preventing Stewart managers from interfering with the work of tallying the votes."

The next day, with three boxes remaining uncounted, the *Morning News* headlined: "STEWART MEETS CRUSHING DEFEAT." Judge Seabrook won "perhaps by the greatest popular vote . . . ever accorded a mayoralty candidate." The editorial page congratulated voters: "The influence that has been directing affairs in this city for years was disrupted, and the air seems purer today in Savannah on that account."

The writer also praised the women of the city. No doubt the African American and white women's vote contributed to Seabrook's large margin of victory. The *Morning News* said that women's "presence at the polls was in the interest of good order, and their activity in the campaign proves that they may be expected to throw their majority to the cause that is right. The men in Savannah who still do not believe in woman suffrage . . . are few are far between."

In a less-heralded win in the election, voters sent Sarah Berrien Casey Morgan to the City Council, the first female ever to be elected to that office. The *Morning News* predicted that, if the election was a guide, women in the future will be the "deciding factor in Savannah politics." However, more than fifty years passed before another woman sought and won election to the City Council, Dr. Harris K. Lentini in 1978. The day following the 1923 general election, an editor of the hometown paper wrote: "Now that the people of Savannah have spoken . . . let there be peace"[63]

Progressivism, Health, and Policing the City

Mayor Seabrook hoped a "spirit of cooperation" and a move away from "factional politics" would be possible and endorsed the adoption of "a city manager form of government" as one step along this path. Seabrook viewed it as a way to speed up "our economic and civic progress"; other "progressive" cities had already adopted this governance model. For Seabrook, "progressive" was the au currant coin of the realm. In Georgia, progressive reform meant "urbanizing, centralizing, rationalizing, and modernizing." Typically these reforms were seen in the cities and big towns that had an adequate tax base to support change. The word "progressive" by now had come to stand for just about anything showing progress or deemed modern.

When Seabrook became mayor, the city's population numbered about 90,000 (50 percent "native-born white," 46 percent "colored" and 4 percent "foreign-born white"). Like previous mayors, he pointed out, "we have the problem of a larger negro population which keeps our mortality rate higher by comparison to the rest of the U.S." In his first year as mayor, 1923, the death rate of whites was 9.1 per 1,000 and that of blacks, 23.6. But whereas other mayors had recognized the problem but done little to address it, Seabrook in concert with his "progressive" health officer, Dr. Victor Hugo Bassett, took aggressive steps to improve the health of African Americans in Savannah.[64]

Born in Illinois, Bassett studied medicine at the University of Wisconsin and Johns Hopkins University, served at hospitals in Baltimore and Chicago, and was professor of pathology and bacteriology at the Milwaukee Medical School. Bassett won the city bacteriologist post in 1908 and served under the "progressive" city health officer Dr. William Brunner until Brunner's retirement in 1923, at which time the city appointed Bassett to the position.

In a paper rarely given to hyperbole, the *Morning News* years later paid tribute to Bassett's tireless "work to replace backward public health technique[s] . . . [with] modern, effective methods of waging a fight against disease in Chatham [County]." Dr. Bassett enjoyed a national reputation and could easily have moved to positions in far larger cities but "preferred to remain in Savannah."[65]

Under Bassett, Savannah's laboratory, located in City Hall, increased examinations for disease. He reinstituted a free drug dispensary to better serve charity patients and initiated a campaign by public health nurses to prevent the spread of hookworm and measles in children. Bassett targeted "infant welfare hygiene" to reduce the mortality rate of black infants, which was twice that of white infants, and put in place the first "systematic vaccination" program to prevent smallpox, inoculating 90 percent of the city's population. Because Savannah's typhoid death rate was twice as high as the nation's, Bassett called for a better means of garbage disposal and elimination of open privies.[66]

Pulmonary tuberculosis, a highly contagious disease, had been on the rise. Savannah had diagnosed 988 cases over a five-year period; rates for blacks were five times higher than whites, and Savannah's overall rate was significantly above the national average. Because the number of cases was increasing annually, Bassett urged city government to do more to prevent its spread. Currently, two nurses and two clinics funded by the city were doing a "fine job," but a city-funded tuberculosis sanitarium was needed for the long-term specialized treatment the disease required. Bassett declared that the financial support of the city hospitals was "inadequate" when compared to the support provided to hospitals nationwide.[67]

In Mayor Seabrook's first annual report, Dr. Bassett's section on the health of the city offered a final, blistering critique: "Savannah has an incomplete, unbalanced and unsafe water supply . . . from the standpoint of both fire risk and health risk." He "urgently" recommended that "work for improvement needs to begin." Occasional criticism of Bassett came from powerful individuals like Colonel C. E. Koerper, who apparently believed that Bassett, an outsider, was too critical of the city.[68]

But Seabrook stood by Bassett, supporting his public criticism of the city's lack of support for health care and his suggestions for improvements. Some had opposed Bassett since his appointment. They feared his transparency about the city's health status might turn away prospective business and industry. This likely was true. Furthermore, enacting Bassett's recommendations cost money at a time when the city government was experiencing falling revenues.

From the city budget for 1923, which totaled $1,491,100, the police requested $253,000. Chief of Police Enoch L. Hendry said an increase was called for to address the need for salary increases due to "the high cost of living." During the year the police arrested 4,554 blacks and 3,722 whites. Representing a city government bent on more reform, Chief Hendry informed the mayor of "special effort[s] to cope with the whiskey violators" by using a "raiding squad." Working in concert with federal officers, the police had arrested 1,034 persons, leading to 439 convictions.

The police also took into custody 1,163 drunk and disorderly persons, 318 gambling-law violators, and arrested ten persons for keeping a house of prostitution. Forty-two were arrested for carrying concealed weapons, 45 had been jailed for assault with intent to murder, and 11 had been arrested for murder.[69] One white-on-white homicide of the day seemed reminiscent of Old South Savannah.

Frederick W. Mock, a "trouble shooter" for the Savannah Electric Company, "had been friendly with" the sister of James A. Von Dolteren, a driver for the American Oil Company. James and his younger brother, Lawrence, warned Mock that, if he did not marry their sister, they would defend her reputation at any cost. But twenty-seven-year-old Mock had no intention of marrying Miss Von Dolteren, so he purchased a billy club for protection and then took out a marriage license to marry another woman, nineteen-year-old Edna Lee Floyd. James Von Dolteren learned about Mr. Mock's marriage plans within hours and, after purchasing a pint of moonshine, he borrowed his father's revolver and went in search of the man who had besmirched his sister's reputation.[70]

James found Fred Mock in Bay Street Lane, where he approached him and fired. One shot went wild; the second severed an artery. Mock staggered through the nearby doorway of his employer, the Savannah Electric Company, where he collapsed and died. Witnesses observed Von Dolteren calmly driving away from the scene. The police arrested James without a struggle, and he confessed. When the slayer's younger brother, Lawrence, heard of the murder, he responded that he only wished he "had done the shooting." Mock's body was taken to his residence at 516 West Forty-second Street; Von Dolteren lived nearby, at 504 West Forty-first Street. His attorney instructed him "to discuss the case with no one."[71]

As one historian has observed, "Southerners will be polite until they're angry enough to kill you." Perhaps this explains somewhat why the South "has the dubious distinction of being . . . the most violent region in an increasingly violent nation."[72] Indeed, in the 1920s, violence and disorder appeared to escalate as the economy atrophied.

The Economy, the Crash, and the Great Depression

Like many other civic leaders across the nation, Savannah's City Council and Mayor Seabrook seemed oblivious of gathering economic storm clouds. In mid-1926, the municipal government set aside land in Daffin Park to build an athletic stadium and planned to extend street paving beyond Victory Boulevard to Fifty-fourth Street. The council also proposed the issuance of bonds for house and storm drains, for improving the waterworks, for building a Bay Street Viaduct, and money to reduce the city's current debt. A public referendum to issue such bonds and notes and to pay dividends on them passed overwhelmingly and raised $2 million.[73]

Meanwhile, Wymberley De Renne's financial situation continued to deteriorate. He sold stocks, borrowed more money, and speculated in Florida real estate to keep his creditors at bay. He was especially worried about being able to keep the family estate, Wormsloe, and took steps to preserve it. With his wife, his sister Elfrida and her husband, Dr. Craig Barrow, a decision was made to promote the Wormsloe Gardens as a tourist site. Visitors would pay a modest fee to visit, and the local Chamber of Commerce promised to boost the gardens as a major tourist attraction. Over time this became a modestly successful business enterprise, and the estate remained in family hands. However, De Renne himself remained mired in financial difficulties for years.[74]

Harbingers of what lay ahead for many financially began with the failure of banks nationally and in Savannah. During the 1920s, five large banks owned by whites and four banks owned by blacks closed their doors in the city. Sol Johnson in 1927 described the black-owned Wage Earners Savings Bank, with resources of $1.5 million, as "the means" by which "thousands of black men and women [were] getting a foothold in life" and a testament "to Negro thrift and his managerial ability." Suddenly, without warning, on the evening of March 1, 1928, directors of the institution voted to turn over the bank to the state's bank examiners. The following day, the Wage Earners Savings Bank, the largest black-owned financial institution in the nation, shuttered its doors. The closure of the bank that had anchored the heart of the city's black business district shocked whites and blacks alike. On hearing the news, the institution's black janitor, who had served for many years, succumbed to "heart failure." Local depositors rushed to the bank, unbelieving that it had failed after more than twenty-five years in business. During the fall of the 1928 fifteen banks failed in two adjoining counties in South Carolina, and bank collapses continued across the country. Soon more than one hundred rural banks closed in Georgia and the value of farm real estate plunged by 40 percent.

Sol Johnson called the collapse of the Wage Earners Savings Bank a "catastrophe," saying "many have lost their all." Its closure had a devastating effect on "colored morale" and on all Savannahians, but we must "carry on," Johnson wrote. The immediate cause of the bankruptcy may have come from a run on the bank by depositors; however, a major contributing factor was the collapse in the value of speculative property the bank owned in New York's Harlem. Walter Scott, the entrepreneur and president of the Savannah Savings and Real Estate Corporation, watched his own bank fail, adding to the "calamity" facing Savannah's black community.[75] The state of Savannah's economy was reflected in the plight of the city's schools.

The city's public-school system remained, with few exceptions, in the hands of the local elite—based on wealth as in a plutocracy rather than an aristocracy based on linage—who favored the status quo. Or such was the case until Dr. Carleton Gibson became superintendent of schools. Alabama-born and educated at the universities of Alabama and Chicago, where he earned an LLD degree, Gibson was a progressive, unlike most holding similar posts.

Gibson saw that the local public-school population had jumped 66 percent in the 1920s while fiscal support for the schools fell sharply. Annual statewide funding for white children remained at $9.50 per pupil, and for black children, $1.76—amounts very similar to per-pupil funding rates across the South. A national report argued for better support for black schools across the region, and Gibson made it a point to inform Savannahians of such disparities in his own report, "Critical Situation Faces Schools Here." He told readers that, although white schools did have critical needs, the black schools were a disgrace to the community. "Common justice" demands "they . . . be rebuilt." Bonds were issued for $500,000 to fund the schools when $3,000,000 was needed. Gibson retired in 1926, disappointed with the failure of the city to provide even modestly for the schools.[76]

Two years later, with the local and national economy unraveling, a prominent local businessman, Colonel Sigo Myers, offered $100 in gold to anyone for an essay that would explain the causes of local business conditions and how they might be resolved. A committee of the civic-commercial elite awarded the prize to Dr. Benjamin F. Hubert, the African American president of Savannah's Georgia State Industrial College for Colored Youth, known by the acronym GSIC.

Dr. Hubert wrote that the city for too long had "let things be as they are." There had been too much reliance promoting Savannah to outsiders and too little on the education and health of its own citizens. If Savannah had spent as much money on the development of its youth as it had in attracting tourists, Hubert wrote, "we would get somewhere." The great cities of the country "are progressive and wide awake" because their public school systems have "the best educational methods, equipment and personnel" that turn out "keen and alert . . . boys and girls." Savannah needed to follow the lead of these cities in its own public schools and build a first-class junior college that offered opportunities for every youth, whatever their "condition and circumstances," so they could attain "their maximum capacity." In this way the best youths might plan for a "future in their city rather some distant place." Such an educational system also would attract people who "will add to the growing power and influence of the city." Hubert also argued that large numbers of unhealthy people are a "liability rather than an asset." Savannah was "inadequately prepared to take care of the health of its people" and therefore could not compete with healthier, progressive cities. The city too, "must lead in cultural . . . progress." Citizens who "lose sight of this . . . cannot be expected . . . to keep pace with modern civilization"; people "ought to look to Savannah for the best in art, music and other cultural phases of life."[77]

Like other outsiders, Dr. Hubert was not Savannah-born, but he was well educated with degrees from Morehouse College and Massachusetts Agriculture College and had studied at the University of Minnesota. In establishing a vision for what the city could become, it was frequently "outsiders," not Savannah natives—Dr. Hubert of Hancock County, Georgia; Sol Johnson of South Carolina; Dr. William Brunner of Beaufort; Dr. Victor H. Bassett of Minnesota; Dr. Carleton Gibson of Alabama; and Richmond-born Thomas Gamble—who were among Savannah's foremost progressives.[78]

"Professor Hubert's essay was judged on its merits and . . . the fact that he is a leader of the colored people did not enter into its selection for the prize," the *Morning News* editorialized. Like Hubert, other "Negro leaders are thinking of the advancement of the South as a whole and have not been so influenced by criticism of the South from outsiders who know nothing of conditions here."[79]

Some civic leaders, however, paid little heed to the advice of progressive Savannahians, who believed Savannah needed to address several significant problems: lack of a sizeable educated citizenry, poor health and slums, and the incidence of crime—all likely reasons some businesses failed to locate in Savannah. Savannah's inner city reflected some of the problems that a prominent historian of the time, W. J. Cash, observed in larger southern towns. When the gentry abandoned the downtown mansions for the suburbs, the black and white laboring class moved in, and soon they were "living in slum or semi-slum conditions." This described Savannah's downtown in the 1930s. Yet some of the civic-commercial elite ignored the profound problems that stalked the city and continued to use the same old bromides to promote Savannah as those before them.[80]

Even as the boll weevil devastated the cotton market and the naval-stores industry fell 40 percent due to the clear-cutting of trees across the region, Savannah promoters once again sought to lure industry. One touted that the city "is led by men of high intelligence . . . and trained experience" who will overcome "the effect of the startling shrinkage in the old staple goods on which its commerce so long relied." They will bring "new commodities" through the port and encourage "new industries" to relocate in Savannah. Thereby, the city will continue as "the chief port and market of the South Atlantic coast." These words of optimism failed to address the municipality's endemic problems raised by Johnson, Hubert, Brunner, Bassett, Gibson, and Gamble, all outsiders.[81]

In the 1920s and 1930s, the coastwise trade that once provided a reliable income for executives, managers, and labor atrophied. Passenger and cargo service between Savannah, Baltimore, Philadelphia, New York, and Boston ended. The income from city taxes shrank, limiting city services. Even so, the City Council found ample funds for the police raiding squad, whom the mayor congratulated for "rigidly enforcing the dry laws [and] seeking to clean the city of blind tigers and dealers in liquor."

Mayor Gamble, Two Views on Curriculum, and a "Wool Hat" Governor

When Thomas Gamble took the oath of Mayor in City Council chambers in early 1933, the city treasury for three years had taken in $200,000 less than in the three years previous; four years later, municipal income had decreased by $1,446, 000.[82] Gamble, another outsider, may be considered a progressive, especially with regards to his interest in education and the curriculum of Savannah's public schools.

A former superintendent of schools, Charleton Gibson, had urged the adoption of progressive measures in education, but the school board took no action. Now Mayor Gamble jumped into the debate over the relevance of progressive programs in the public schools. On one side, the grand jury and one of the eleven school board members, Dr. Walter S. Wilson, criticized the new "child-centered" concepts and demanded that only the "three Rs" be taught.

Wilson, once a teacher in the schools, had returned in midlife to attend Johns Hopkins University, where he took a medical degree. He was a formidable opponent. He clashed repeatedly with other school board members, especially Martha Gallaudet Waring, the second woman to serve on the board and the first woman vice-president.

From an old Savannah family, and the wife of a distinguished physician, Dr. Thomas Pinckney Waring, Martha had taught in the public schools and was a pioneer in the statewide kindergarten movement. During one school board meeting clash, Wilson asked Waring if she considered "everything that is old is no good." She responded that between radical and conservative she preferred the middle way, the path of the progressive. Waring advocated taking the best of the old and combining it with the best of the new: students could advance in their studies while acquiring both growth of character and good citizenship. Wilson and Waring both enjoyed considerable popular support. But, as the ideological divide widened between them, the debate took a "nasty" twist. Wilson turned to character assassination of school officials. At this point, Mayor Gamble stepped into the fray.[83]

In a letter to the editor of the *Morning News,* Gamble focused his criticism on recent grand juries that organized themselves into a "perpetual inquisition" or "vigilance committee" regarding the school board. He likened their reports to the opinions of Charles Dickens characters who "Don't imagine . . . that poor children. . . have any right to stray off onto the paths of beauty, glimpse the wonders of the skies . . . or loveliness of nature"; they "must be kept to the fundamentals," the "bread and butter courses." Sarcastically, Gamble added: "We must keep out of their foolish heads the nonessentials—the ideals of the poet who said if you have sixpence, spend three pence for bread and three 'to buy hyacinths to feed your soul.'" Gamble concluded: "facts will not save the America of the 1930s . . . but ideals . . . may."[84]

The public, acrimonious war of words became so offensive that the *Morning News* announced it no longer would publish articles on progressive education. With backing from a strong Parent Teacher Association, the school board on three occasions endorsed progressive education and the progressive curriculum of the city's public schools. It also censured Dr. Wilson for his personal attacks on progressive teachers.

As the curriculum evolved, and with some federal money, the Savannah School Board, beginning in the late 1920s and into the 1930s, embarked on a remarkable program of construction that included eleven new schools; one, a

$1 million high school, became for a time the largest in the state. At the end of the decade, board members were talking about the need for an expanded vocational guidance program to encourage youth to remain in school and complete their education.[85] That these dramatic changes came during a time of austerity is noteworthy. That progressive reforms were adopted when Eugene Talmadge governed Georgia is remarkable, considering that his opinions about curriculum were totally antithetical to the programs and policies being implemented in Savannah.

Talmadge's views on education may be summarized in his own words: "Education . . . ain't never taught a man how to plant cotton . . . or raise cows and chickens. You gotta git out and do them things, and no school education is gonna help ya." Indeed, Talmadge appealed to his agrarian base in Georgia, the "wool-hat boys" as he called them. He publicly disdained city dwellers and their politicians. Talmadge told his "boys": "Come see me at the Mansion. We'll sit on the front porch and piss over the rail on those city bastards."[86]

How extraordinary that, into the 1930s and beyond, progressive education survived in Savannah and produced those who contributed to the Southern Renaissance in literature and music—Conrad Aiken, Flannery O'Connor, and Johnny Mercer. Progressives hoped that providing a broader education for the city's children would overcome the view that Georgia and Savannah lacked an educated workforce. But local economic problems of long standing were exacerbated by the stock market crash that brought on the Great Depression.

An Increasingly Depressed Economy

Many southern white and black farmers and workers, managers, and executives had experienced a depressed economy for years. The economic collapse fell heaviest on the laboring classes. By the early 1930s, the number of families seeking relief in Savannah reached four thousand. The city government tried to meet the needs of the destitute by establishing an Employment Commission (EC), which hired the able-bodied for projects in the city; those unemployable received small stipends: white applicants were given $4.00 every eight weeks, and black males received $1.50 every fifteen to eighteen weeks.

The need soon outstripped city and private resources, and the municipality sought help from the federal government. Savannah officials' appeal noted that citizens had long enjoyed income from "the handling of cotton, naval stores and lumber," but such exports had all but evaporated.[87] Many of the laboring jobs in these industries were once held by African Americans. A Savannah visitor in 1930 noted: "The streets are filled with Negroes. Young boys . . . sing while rowing their boats . . . all day against the swift current" and take "people across the river for five cents a ride. A half-dozen boats rush eagerly to meet each [prospective] passenger."[88]

Blacks comprised about 45 percent of Savannah's population in the era of the Great Depression, with unemployment within this demographic approaching 70 percent. Finding work became increasingly difficult as the economy deteriorated and whites willingly accepted laboring jobs in the city and county.[89] At the outset of the Depression, Sol Johnson's paper complained repeatedly that blacks were often fired from even menial jobs and whites hired to replace them. An example of this occurred when one of the larger laundries in the city fired its black male workers and replaced them with white females. Aggressive opposition to hiring African American workers came from the Black Shirts, a white paramilitary group that publicly protested the hiring of black workers.

With African American unemployment came increases in the number of homeless and hungry. Without work, money, or shelter, blacks raided the city dump to find scraps of tin and other materials to construct one-room shacks on the ragged eastern edge of Savannah off Wheaton Street. This area came to be referred to by the *Morning News* as "Tin City"—a settlement born of the Depression. Sol Johnson himself witnessed one "heart rending" scene in the yard of the Savannah Boys Club at Price and Charlton streets where two thousand "men and women, old and young, sick and hearty" waited for their biweekly ration tickets from the government.[90]

Dr. Victor Bassett, the crusading health officer, in one of the last reports issued before his death in the late 1930s, called attention to the failing health among the city's poor. He attributed it "to the [economic] depression and high cost of food" that brought on "pellagra," caused by a lack of niacin in the diet, and other diseases. In two of the last years of the decade, nine people died of pellagra, six from typhoid fever, "due likely to consumption of food of doubtful quality." The "financial condition of the city," Dr. Bassett wrote, "has prevented any great extension of health work, in some instances much needed."[91]

During the 1930s, the *Tribune* continued to push back at what it viewed as a new era of Jim Crow—the white obsession with keeping blacks orderly and oppressed. On April 29, 1933, about 75 persons met in the Carnegie Library to form the Chatham County Colored Citizens Council, later referred to as the "5Cs." The organization's constitution included language that addressed its work for the general welfare and uplift of the race.

The council was especially concerned, like Johnson, about crowded conditions in the black schools and the prohibition of black children and adults from use of the city's most spacious playgrounds. The following year, the long moribund Savannah branch of the NAACP launched a drive that recruited 250 new members, and 40 African Americans organized the Black Democratic Club of Chatham County, a remarkable political event in light of the long association of blacks with the Republican Party.

Two years later, the local NAACP adopted a platform that demanded the same voting rights for whites and blacks, equality in education and employment, a fair trial, the right to sit on juries, equal rights for use of public parks, schools, and libraries—for which blacks paid taxes—and the right to live in any neighborhood they chose. Especially off-putting to Sol Johnson was that only a few black landowners were permitted on Tybee Island, and he criticized the island's officials for refusing to allow black visitors.[92] But local protestations had little effect. It took decisions by the U.S. Supreme Court to bring about dramatic changes for equal rights in the South.

In the case of *Hollins v. State of Oklahoma* (1935), the Supreme Court decided that exclusion of African Americans from juries violated the Constitution's Fourteenth Amendment. Two years later, the Chatham County Board of Jury Commissioners came in line with the court's ruling by naming nine local black leaders eligible for jury duty.[93]

The City Council responded to the Chatham County Colored Citizens Council's allegations of unequal facilities by agreeing to improve the African American Recreation Center and pool on Ogeechee Road at Thirty-ninth Street. By a resolution, the council was "affording rest, recreation and better health for its colored citizens."[94]

Old Fort, New Housing

The president of the GSIC, Dr. Benjamin Hubert, spoke out for change. After visiting Yamacraw on Savannah's west side, he called attention to the hundreds of dwellings in need of repair; only a few had electric lights, running water, and modern sanitary facilities. Hubert found the streets so deep in sand that they were unrecognizable as streets, and he cataloged equally deplorable living conditions in the nearby slums of Frogtown and Currytown. From Currytown's border westward to Brownsville were some of the "inevitable shacks," but here too were "good frame and brick houses" where more well-to-do African Americans lived—teachers, doctors, lawyers, and businessmen. In Old Fort on the extreme northeastern side of Savannah wound "dusty, windy lanes bordered with rows of squat wooden houses . . . [and the} the smells of river, fishboats, fertilizer plants and escaping gases." Overshadowing all stood "gigantic gas reservoirs."[95]

One author described Old Fort in the late 1930s as once a select quarter where in a mansion one might hear "the murmur of well-bred voices . . . [and within] a walled garden [one] breathed gently. But now, encroached upon by "the noisy vitality of shanty Irish and Negroes and a bastard architecture, . . . [on summer evenings] is heard the whining radios . . . auto horns . . . rupturing backfire blasts . . . and where a filling station exhales gas fumes and the cloying disinfectant from a rest room."[96]

Sol Johnson used even stronger language than President Hubert in writing about the slums: "[The city] must . . . improve sanitary conditions in every locality. The owners of [dwellings] . . . must share part of the blame." Johnson chided the municipal government for allowing "unsanitary shacks in many of the lanes and alleys of the city. It is up to the city to cause the razing of such houses."[97]

Health officer Dr. Victor Bassett sometimes pushed through changes, such as persuading Chatham County to inaugurate "the only compulsory vaccination law in the State." Other times he was not so successful, an example being his failed efforts to eliminate slums where tuberculosis thrived or to provide facilities for African Americans who fell ill with the disease.

Perhaps Bassett used a little reverse psychology in the last year of his life, 1938, when he warned the civic-commercial elite, in the fashion of Dr. William Brunner, that black "servants . . . carry the disease into white families." If infected, the servant may "endeavor to hide the same" for fear "he will lose his job . . . [knowing] there is no . . . provision for his care." If whites could be convinced that programs for blacks were in their own self-interest, perhaps these initiatives would be funded. Though sometimes criticized for his views, Bassett's job was never in jeopardy; other critics of the prevailing attitudes sometimes found themselves unemployed.[98]

When Professor Asa H. Gordon of the GSIC criticized Georgia's Jim Crow policies in a book published in Michigan, he was fired. The Board of Regents of the University System of Georgia refused to renew Gordon's contract. Governor Eugene Talmadge, an ex officio member of the board, a race-baiter and anti-Semite, thought the state's colleges and universities harbored "foreign" and "ultraliberal" professors. Because of Talmadge's interference, various accrediting agencies dropped their endorsements of the state's ten white institutions of higher education.[99]

In spite of problems, business and commercial life in some sectors of the African American community thrived. A survey by black Savannah attorney J. G. Lemon described a great deal about black business, employment, and life in the 1930s. During this period the number of black-owned businesses exceeded

175. Twenty-five black physicians, six dentists, and four lawyers served the African American community; one public high school and two junior highs were open to blacks. African American men worked as porters for the rail lines, and many black women worked in the steam laundries. Lemon noted, however, that where once black artisans enjoyed a monopoly, now whites had taken over many of the skilled carpentry and brick-masonry jobs. Whites also had taken over many jobs once held by blacks as common laborers.[100] Some relief came to both black and white communities with the election of Franklin D. Roosevelt and the launch of his New Deal.

A New Deal

Visiting Savannah on November 18, 1933, to celebrate the Georgia Bicentennial, President Franklin Roosevelt gave a rousing speech at the Municipal Stadium before an audience of forty thousand, where he said that, since visiting Georgia nine months earlier, "the lives of the people of this commonwealth . . . have undergone a great change. . . . [I]t has been a change for the better; . . . I come back to see smiles replacing gloom, to see hope replacing despair." Before leaving from Union Station, Roosevelt, his mother, Governor Talmadge, and others toured the city in an open car with the mayor. While touring, Gamble spoke of the Depression's effect on Savannah and likely mentioned the need for federal funding to raze local slums like Yamacraw and replace them with small rental homes and apartments. Such a project would provide healthier physical environments for citizens, something progressives Brunner, Bassett, Hubert, and Johnson had championed for years. Earlier, Gamble had held a meeting in City Hall in which the local architectural firm of Levy & Clark presented a renovation proposal to white property owners of rental units in Yamacraw; within a few years, the plan for urban renewal would move forward with federal and city funding.[101] One of the first "alphabet agencies" of Roosevelt New Deal was the Federal Emergency Relief Administration (FERA), headed by Harry Hopkins. FERA's goal was to provide wages for "useful work" on government projects for the unemployed and "relief payments" for those in "immediate and desperate need."

Through a local committee and with help some influential locals, FERA dollars provided work relief for seventeen thousand individuals in the Savannah area, distributing $150,000 monthly in work-relief wages. Fraud sometimes occurred when government commodities were resold on the black market by "entrepreneurs." There were complaints also by certain white-collar workers who thought their assigned tasks too menial—jobs like wielding a "bushhook" or an "axe" should have been, in their opinion, relegated to common laborers.[102]

Before-and-after photographs of Yamacraw: Above, Yamacraw Village Slum Clearance Project gets underway. Below, the second housing project in Savannah is finished, ca. 1941. Photographs made available by the Housing Authority of Savannah, Earline Wesley Davis, executive director.

Savannah's white managerial class complained that FERA wages were out of line with local pay standards. A government agent in Savannah in 1934 observed: "For these people to be getting $12.00 a week—at least twice as much as common labor has ever been paid before . . . is an awfully bitter pill for Savannah people to swallow."[103]

Concerned that the FERA would not achieve its employment goals, the New Deal created another agency, the Civil Works Administration (CWA), which paid even better wages. The CWA employed thousands of laborers in jobs such as paving streets, repairing schools, and making improvements to municipal buildings. Women were paid to tend farms, sew garments. and nurse the sick. Even unemployed artists and archivers found work with local cultural organizations. As one program waned, another took its place.

By now, Harry Hopkins, the national director of the relief agencies, had become furious with Governor Talmadge for his continuing criticism of the New Deal, and Hopkins relieved him of federal relief programs in Georgia. In April, Roosevelt abruptly ended the CWA. He did not want the country to become accustomed to permanent federally funded work relief. Work relief reverted to the FERA.

The end of the CWA meant that large number of government workers in Savannah and the county were unemployed by the spring of 1934, and the FERA once more became the major federal employer. Now Miss Rose Marie Smith, a former social worker, became the director of the local office. Drainage projects were continued, but when a prehistoric animal was unearthed, a state geologist rushed to Savannah to supervise extraction of the bones. Unfortunately the FERA did not provide funds for those who needed it most, the infirm and disabled. The cost of this care fell to the city. Between 1933 and 1937 Savannah's municipal government disbursed for charity and relief $140,000 annually. Eventually, Mayor Gamble alerted Washington to the city's plight. Income had fallen so drastically that it simply could not afford any longer to support the elderly.[104] The indigent and ill suffered, as did the city's youth. Frank Callen tried to help.

Callen, one of Savannah's black progressives, founded the Savannah Boys Club to get black juveniles off the street and to offer them vocational training. He succeeded in winning federal dollars from another agency, the National Youth Administration. Callen served as an important role model, though he did not challenge the stereotypes of the day. Young men were trained in manual skills, the girls in domestic work. Many males who participated in Callen's program became skilled tradesmen.[105]

Weathering the Great Depression: Social Life

Despite the persistent joblessness and deteriorating economy of the 1930s, both the black and the white well-to-do continued to enjoy parties, social clubs, and dinners—at least in the early years of the Depression. The black elite spent time at the Coconut Grove nightclub. Opened in April 1936 on six acres of land on Ogeechee Road–Highway 17, the club featured tennis courts, tourist cabins, eight dining rooms, and a dance hall. A month later, the Hollywood Casino opened to host jazz groups and dance music on Stiles Avenue north of Bay Street Extension. Black social clubs brought to Savannah jazz greats like Duke Ellington and Louis Armstrong and extended invitations to whites to attend performances at the Municipal Auditorium. Whites and blacks did attend but sat in segregated sections.[106]

In the early 1930s, a female member of the white elite attended a "golden wedding celebration" along with eighteen other relatives and friends: "We . . . entered the parlor, which was literally filled with flowers" and then crossed to the library where "cocktails in silver cups" were served "accompanied by hors d'oeuvres." Next the party moved to the dining room, where they enjoyed "shrimp bisque with whipped cream . . . broiled chicken and croquets, fresh asparagus, green peas, lettuce salad, hot rolls, and ended with ice cream and angel cake."[107]

Dr. Craig Barrow and his wife, Elfrida, of Wormsloe Plantation provided area horsemen use of their "splendid" Water's Avenue Polo Field on Sunday afternoons from mid-November to mid-May during the early 1930s. The local Artillery Polo Club sometimes invited over one hundred friends, providing reserved parking at a cost of ten dollars for the season. The fee defrayed expenses for local and visiting teams and maintenance of the field.[108] But by the 1930s even the elite began feeling the pinch of the persistent economic decline.

Dr. Barrow, chief surgeon of the Central of Georgia Railway in the 1930s, member of the Savannah Golf Club and the Oglethorpe Club, received a letter from the president of the latter organization in 1934: "The Depression has seriously affected the Club. It has sustained a grave impairment of revenue owing to the fact that so many members have been forced to resign." The president offered a proposal to the holders of "six percent First Mortgage Gold Bonds of the Oglethorpe Club." In sum, members were asked to accept a 2 percent rather than a 6 percent return for two years, after which a cash payment of $2,940,000 would be made to bondholders, and then the 6 percent interest would be reinstated. This proposal would provide the club with a capital reserve of $4,560,000. Eighty-eight percent of the Gold Bond holders accepted the recommendations of the club president, but Barrow questioned the decision. He resigned from the Oglethorpe Club in the late 1930s.[109]

While the 1930s and the beginning of the next decade were financially grim for many Savannahians, prominent members of the white elite, both women and men, enjoyed fine food and card games at the Oglethorpe Club and participated in drag hunts at the Savannah Riding and Driving Club. They arranged luncheons for visitors and gave elaborate bridal parties. The young men and women of the "smart set" continued to visit their favorite places. Even in winter they ventured to Tybee Island; carrying picnic suppers and accompanied by chaperones, they remained overnight in cottages of the well-to-do. During "the season"—November to February—especially around Christmas, the *Morning News* noted that the "Holiday Calendar Assures a Brilliant {Season]." There were rounds of "supper dances," "dinner dances," and "cocktail parties" for the debutants of the year and their many friends at the General Oglethorpe Hotel on Wilmington Island or the DeSoto Hotel in Savannah. The Cotillion Club opened its winter season with a dinner dance in late December.[110] However, during these same years, Mayor Thomas Gamble reported that the city government encountered "Four of the most difficult years in the history of our city."

Plunging Tax Revenue and a New College

Between 1930 and 1935, personal property tax returns to the city plunged from nearly $14,000,000 to $7,500,000; total revenues fell from $78,000,000 to $61,000,000; and the city's indebtedness grew to more than $400,000. In order to reduce expenses, the city cut municipal salaries by 20 percent. The city also adopted an "open records policy" regarding finances, "one of the safeguards of the taxpayer against waste, extravagance or corruption."

Sounding a note of progressivism, Gamble reported that the police had "largely suppressed the innumerable fixed slot machines . . . the lottery, and other rackets" that "filched daily enormous profits from the poor and ignorant." As well, the "vice" of prostitution had been "suppressed."

Always a promoter, Gamble enthused in his 1935 annual report that the junior college recently established in the Armstrong Mansion at Gaston and Bull streets now enrolled 335 students. He thanked Mrs. Lucy Moltz and her daughter for the gift of the mansion. Mills B. Lane provided funds to develop within the college a School of Finance and Commerce—a few years earlier, Dr. Hubert, president of GSCI, had suggested that just such a college be established.

Mayor Gamble touted the beautification of all the squares on Bull Street and the two northernmost squares on Abercorn, which now "reveal to our people what can be done with [all] the squares." At this time the Park and Tree Commission had "constant supervision of 25,000 trees" and over 9,000 flowering azaleas. Gamble believed that, when all the squares are beautified, "our citizens will not . . . permit their desecration." This work by the commission and the college would breath "new life" into the city, attract tourists, and "make Savannah more . . . attractive as a city in which to locate and live."

With a pension system for public employees established, streetcar fares reduced, and lower fees for the city's lighting contract in place, it seemed that Savannah was gaining control over its financial situation. In spite of noteworthy accomplishments, the Gamble administration gave little attention to the slums and poverty and, though the mayor recognized that a modern city needed to address these problems, the city lacked the money. How could Savannah move from the depths of the Depression? The mayor believed some opportunities were on the horizon.

The anemic export trade did worry Gamble somewhat. The cotton trade had shrunk to "a pitiful percentage," and the "naval stores" business posted a "greatly reduced volume." But Gamble, ever the optimist, wanted to put in place a foundation for growth, and he believed the local economy could be revived by deepening the harbor, adding new and adequate wharf facilities, and promoting tourism and new industry. Indeed, Gamble thought the major accomplishment of his first term was bringing to Savannah "the world's greatest paper pulp and bag plant."[111]

Let There Be Pulp and Paper

Gamble's administration had disbursed $213,000 annually to promote Savannah and bring industry to the city. The civic-commercial elite were convinced the investment had paid off when Union Bag and Paper Company of New Jersey decided to locate the world's largest paper-bag plant near the city. The company promised jobs for hundreds of workers and millions of dollars for the purchase of local materials. The terms negotiated by the local Savannah Port Authority and the city were very generous—the city built access roads, docks, and rail lines and leased the plant site, once the location of the Hermitage Plantation, to Union Bag for a mere pittance for years. When it opened in 1936, Union Bag projected it would employ 875 at the plant and 500 more in forestry and timbering. Ten years later, the company employed 4,200 people with a payroll of $10 million.[112]

The company, soon known as Union Camp (UC), brought sorely needed jobs and money to Savannah, but also liabilities. Less than thirty years after it began operating, one writer observed: "When UC used the [Savannah] River as its sewer, no one else could use it for anything." One author wrote how delightful to "Stroll through Savannah on a summer night when the wind is not blowing from the direction of Union Camp."[113] But in the 1930s the ends seemed to justify the means: creating jobs was on the minds of locals and Washington politicians.

In the mayoralty election of 1936, Mayor Gamble endorsed Robert M. Hitch, a local attorney, in an uncontested election. As Hitch took office, the *Morning News* praised outgoing Mayor Gamble for cracking down on "sinister" forces in the city—"racketeers, gamblers . . . illicit dives who hoped for a 'wide-open' town." The paper "fervently hoped that the vigilance of . . . Gamble in suppressing vice will not be relaxed" and had confidence the city would not "slump morally, physically or financially" under Hitch's leadership.[114]

Indeed, as a mayor, Hitch delighted local businessmen as his financial views were the same as Gamble's. The city operated on "a pay as you go" philosophy, the opposite of Washington's policy of deficit spending. But with the sharp fall in real estate prices and personal income, tax delinquencies soared to $500,000 and monies to assist the city's "unemployables" dried up. Savannah never resorted to the use of script to pay its employees as Charleston did, but budgets were very restricted.[115] As for federal programs, by the late 1930s Savannah officials and Washington were of the opinion that the FERA had failed in its mission to create jobs.

President Roosevelt, ever the pragmatist, called on another agency to replace the failed FERA. This time he convinced Congress to appropriate money for the Works Progress Administration (WPA), intended to find employment for the unemployed. The WPA, with some money appropriated by the city, funneled more than $1,250,000 to employ hundreds of workers. Even with black unemployment at 70 percent, WPA policy limited the number of blacks who could be hired because work assignments had to be based on the makeup of the city's population, which at that time was 40 percent black and 60 percent white. To some it appeared that white skilled workers received priority in hiring. When President Hubert of the GSIC complained about this, he was told by the WPA that "very little [black] skilled labor" was available. Hubert insisted he knew of "several hundred" skilled blacks, among them brickmasons and electricians, who were without work in Savannah. To placate Hubert, the federal government agreed to fund extensive renovations and to construct new buildings on the GSCI campus.[116]

President Hubert was not the only one with WPA grievances. A Savannah black labor union, the Workers Alliance of America, complained repeatedly to the Washington office about numerous cases of "discrimination in regards to race color." There were also complaints about poor treatment of black workers. A local newspaper reporter charged that black women working on a vegetable farm managed by the WPA were reduced to "slavery." The "women . . . lined up like convicts . . . push . . . wheelbarrows, carrying heavy articles and dig . . . new ground . . . under the watchful eyes of white bosses. Half the women are sick or too old to do any kind of work." Such complaints brought little change.[117]

WPA-paid workers repaired or paved more than forty miles of streets and erected six steel bridges in Savannah and Chatham County. The city and the WPA funded the construction and lighting of eighty-one hundred feet of runways at Hunter Air Field and the building of an administration building and one of the largest hangers in the Southeast. By 1940, Hunter Field was unsurpassed in the South.

The WPA repaired the city docks, built a new jail, and erected a municipal health building. The city provided modest funds to support the WPA, most of the money paid for labor and food to prepare school lunches. By the end of the 1930s several thousand gallons of soup and sandwiches were provided daily to six thousand hungry children, black and white, who attended city schools. Black women were hired by the city, with some funding by the federal government, to grow edibles for the school lunch program, and they produced about twenty thousand pounds of vegetables monthly. Eventually, Washington shut down the WPA, a casualty of World War II.[118]

The *Morning News* supported Roosevelt in his first presidential election, but Sol Johnson's *Tribune* backed the Republican candidate, Herbert Hoover. One of President Roosevelt's first acts was to close insolvent banks, but only temporarily. The press and the public supported this move. When Roosevelt had visited Savannah for the city and the state's two hundredth anniversary celebration, his local popularity soared, but not everyone was a Roosevelt fan.

Local executives of the national American Liberty League, Mills B. Lane the banker and the lawyer Mayhew Cunningham, denounced Washington's growing "bureaucracy" and called for a return to "state rights . . . and let the states handle and care for their needy."[119] Some years later, a well-to-do physician, Dr. Craig Barrow, wrote U.S. Senator Richard B. Russell to call his attention to public fears that "rightly or wrongly" a "dictatorship" is at hand and we are moving "towards omnipresent governmental control."[120] The *Morning News,* whose enthusiasm for Roosevelt had waned since his election, compared the New Deal's wage and hour legislation to the philosophies of "Mussolini and Hitler."

The *Morning News* "raged" again when the WPA approved the construction of the new city high school with a closed-shop agreement that excluded skilled nonunion labor. Wealthy elites nationwide, like Savannah's civic-commercial elite, denounced Roosevelt and his programs. In the 1936 presidential election the *Morning News* supported the Republican candidate, Alf Landon, rather than Roosevelt's "dreamers and theorists" in Washington. But the vast majority of Savannahians embraced Roosevelt's policies and gave him 89 percent of the vote.

On some issues the *Tribune* continued to support Republican nominees, but when the *Morning News* condemned Roosevelt for attempting to "pack" the Supreme Court, the *Tribune* defended his actions, arguing that if Roosevelt wanted change he could and should make these appointments because he enjoyed nationwide popularity. By the end of the decade, both the *Morning News* and the *Tribune* complained about Roosevelt's fiscal policies; though millions had been spent, "the average workers are in worse condition today than ever."[121] But as war threatened to engulf Europe, the local press united in opposing American involvement.

Changing Cityscape

By this time the U.S. Housing Authority in Savannah had begun a program of slum clearance, a program long sought by city progressives like Sol Johnson and health officials Brunner and Bassett. Ninety percent of substandard homes in Savannah were clustered in slums on the east and west sides of the city. For years some prominent citizens had called the slums "a disgrace to the city." But not until federal officials of the Housing Authority in Washington in 1939 announced plans to spend $5 million for low-income housing did Savannah's city government become actively involved.

The city agreed to raze the unsafe and unsanitary structures in the city slums where the federal government planned to build. In 1940 the first public housing for African Americans, Fellwood Homes, opened for occupancy near the West Savannah and Hudson Hill neighborhoods. Its construction accelerated slum clearance in other areas of the city.

Mayor Hitch ended his two-year term in January 1939. In his January 18 farewell address he prefaced his remarks to the City Council by noting: "Savannah has suffered severely from our business depression which came upon our country in the late fall 1929 and from which we have not yet emerged." But he went on to say that, in spite of this, the city had taken some positive steps forward during his term. He mentioned that Montgomery Street had been restructured to provide a new route for tourists and that Ogeechee Road had been improved to provide a favorable impression to people visiting the city. The slum-clearance program funded by several million federal dollars would reduce fire hazards and "remove many breeding grounds for criminals." Hitch said the administration had secured a wire-weaving plant, a gypsum plant, and an asphalt-products plant, which would bring added jobs. A new rail and vehicular bridge over the Savannah River would expand trade territory for city merchants. Hitch discussed the upcoming 1940 census and told his colleagues, "there is a noticeable seepage of business and population from Savannah to larger centers of population and no effort should be spared to check that tendency." It would be in the city's best interest to have a population of 100,000 as cities with that designation are at a distinct advantage.[122]

Thomas Gamble, certified as mayor for the third time on January 23, 1939, thanked outgoing mayor Robert Hitch for his service, especially his efforts regarding "the housing project" and "protecting the interests of the municipality." Gamble reiterated the importance of "comprehensive slum clearance" as a means to improve living conditions. Within several years, Savannah counted nearly one thousand new dwellings that could be attributed to these early urban-renewal efforts.[123]

More Than Gale Force Winds

On August 11–12, 1940, a hurricane came ashore in lower South Carolina, and gusts over seventy miles per hour ripped across Savannah, tearing roofs off houses, sending bricks and other debris flying, smashing plate glass in the business district, and downing power and telephone lines. It uprooted so many oaks and sycamore trees that the commissioner of the Park and Tree Commission "was on the verge of weeping." One person died after being struck by flying glass, and another dropped dead of a heart attack. Damages in Savannah reached over $4 million (about $68,000,000 in 2016 dollars).[124]

How concerns about storms affected population growth is not fully understood. At the turn of the century, Savannah ranked seventh in population among southern cities, but by 1940 the city had dropped to seventeenth place. By comparison, Charleston ranked twenty-fifth and Atlanta third.[125]

Mayor Gamble at age seventy-three remained a persistent and optimistic booster for Savannah. When he spoke to the Atlantic Deepwater Ports Association in Miami in November 1941, Gamble told his audience that Savannah "had enjoyed the greatest industrial development of any port between Baltimore and New Orleans, with a total annual value of products of 66 million dollars and payrolls of six million dollars." The old commodities of cotton and naval stores that had sustained Savannah's commerce for decades had suffered "tremendous losses"; that era was essentially over, Gamble said. But with more than a dozen new industries relocating to Savannah, the port would thrive on new exports. The output of pulp, kraft paper, and bags by the Union Camp Company alone in 1940 reached 265,000 tons.

Other companies dealt in petroleum products. Tankers arrived at wharves along the river, carrying thousands of barrels of fuel oil, gasoline, and kerosene, which were offloaded and carried by rail tank cars and tank trucks across the country. These industrial plants employed "thousands of men and women who enrich the community by their weekly payrolls." Five railroads and two airlines served Savannah. In 1940 the Savannah Airport was renamed Hunter Airfield after Frank O. Hunter, a heroic World War I flyboy from Savannah. Gamble concluded his address in Miami by saying this is how "Savannah is defeating the depression." He predicted that the city would become even more prosperous "with peace" abroad.[126] The next month, the Japanese attacked Pearl Harbor.

CHAPTER FIVE

From World War II to Rousakis's Last Term

1942–1991

Shortly after dawn on December 7, 1941, Japanese aircraft attacked American ships and air bases in the Pacific, with devastating effects. The day following, the *Morning News* carried the boldface headline: "Japanese Strike Initial Blow of War Great Loss of Life Reported in Hawaii." The paper accused the Japanese government of duplicity: while Japanese envoys in Washington promoted peace, their government at home plotted an attack on a United States territory; a similar tactic had been used by their "Axis partner, Adolph Hitler." President Franklin Roosevelt called the surprise attack a "date which will live in infamy" and asked for a declaration of war on Japan, which Congress approved.[2]

The *Morning News* celebrated news that the U.S. Maritime Commission (USMC) planned to launch a new merchant-marine vessel each day until victory over Japan and Germany was achieved. The production quotas encouraged workers and shipyard owners who, after twelve years of depression, knew a boom in local shipbuilding could resuscitate the local economy.

The War, Shipbuilding, and Jobs

Already the USMC had underway the construction of seven new shipways from Florida to Washington State and with war declared, the commission authorized construction of three more. One would be built at a private company, Savannah Shipyards, Inc. (SSI), two miles downriver from the city. SSI had received a federal contract to produce Liberty Ships that would be used to carry cargo to the Allies. But when the SSI failed to meet its obligations, the U.S. government seized the shipyard and signed a contract with Southeastern Shipbuilding Corporation of Savannah (SSCS) to take over the SSI yard and build Liberty Ships. The "Libertys" were designed to carry 9,149 tons, equivalent to a cargo of 2,480 jeeps, 440 light tanks, and either 230 million rounds of rifle ammunition or 3,000 to 4,000 C rations in addition to fuel.

The first contract between the USMC and SSCS specified that a Liberty was to be delivered by December 1942. That same year, on November 20, as winds blew a damp mist into the onlookers, a cheer went up from the workers.

Flags unfurled, speeches were made, a band played the "Star Spangled Banner," and Mrs. Lucy George, wife of Georgia's senior U.S. senator, smashed an 1857 bottle of champagne against the bow, thus launching the SS *James Oglethorpe.* After resolving some problems during sea trials, the *Oglethorpe* was delivered to the USMC in early 1943. It became the first of many Liberty Ships and eighteen smaller cargo ships launched by the SSCS, making the company the largest manufacturing entity in Savannah.[2]

By March the three major shipyards—SSCS, MacEvoy Shipbuilding Corporation, and Savannah Machine and Foundry Company—employed nearly sixteen thousand civilian personnel, and the search for skilled workers continued apace at these and other defense-industry contractors. The military populations of Hunter Army Airfield and nearby Fort Stewart surged. All this growth had a significant impact on Savannah.

The Population Surge and the Housing Shortage

From 1940 through 1945, the metropolitan population of four southern coastal cities increased dramatically: Savannah grew by 29 percent, Charleston 37 percent, Norfolk 57 percent, and Mobile by 61 percent. Georgia's inland cities—Macon, Milledgeville, and Atlanta—also witnessed an upsurge in population. As war sounded the death knell for the state's cotton-based agrarian economy, marginalized workers flocked to the cities. The South's urban population increased during the decade of the 1940s almost 36 percent, an increase 50 percent higher than the national average. The war ended the Great Depression and brought prosperity to many across the country. Boom times returned to Savannah and other southern cities, along with problems of accommodating expanding populations in such a short time.[3]

The SSCS recruited skilled workers from other shipyards as well as people who had never seen the inside of a factory or a ship. They came from nearby towns and from afar—farmers, salespeople, school principals, teachers, and even those once thought unemployable—southern white migrants, ex-convicts, the very young and the very old, the physically handicapped, women, and African Americans. Sometimes whole families were hired by the SSCS. One employee characterized the SSCS as "a magnet. It just drew people."[4] The search for housing in Savannah became extremely competitive as new workers tried to find living quarters.

Shipbuilding employees were not the only workers looking for housing. Other defense industries in Savannah included Union Bag and Paper Corporation, which turned out massive amounts of cardboard for the U.S. Army and cardboard products for the Allies. The Products Company, later known as Great Dane, manufactured about twelve thousand trailers for the army, and Southern States Iron and Roofing turned out thousands of bomb casings monthly. The Mexican Petroleum Company sent tons of asphalt to combat zones, and Pierpont Manufacturing produced wooden boxes for the Allies. City and federal officials scrambled to meet the critical housing shortage.[5]

The National Housing Authority built living quarters for white employees of the SSCS but none for African Americans. Moses Rogers Grove, a development with 150 units for white workers and their families, was so near the shipyard that residents could walk to work. Tattnall Homes, located south of Liberty Street along Pennsylvania Avenue, had 750 apartments. It was one of the most luxurious, with hardwood floors and the latest appliances. Rents in these whites-only developments ranged from $32.00 to $40.50 monthly, depending on the number of bedrooms. A third complex, Pine Gardens, consisted of hundreds of prefabricated units and was the most expensive option of the group.[6]

The African American neighborhood of East Savannah stood in stark contrast to the nearby whites-only dwellings with all modern conveniences being erected by the Housing Authority. Beyond the city limits, East Savannah had no electrical power, no running water, no indoor plumbing, and no delivery of home mail. Here kerosene lanterns, wood stoves, and outhouses were the norm. It was much the same in the black community of LePageville, built 40 years earlier as housing for railroad employees.[7]

West of the city, the Savannah Machine and Foundry Company rushed to complete its shipyard at Hudson Hill along with 600 dwellings next to the shipyard for white defense employees and their families. Immediately upon completion, Clearview and Bayview Homes were at full occupancy, and another "defense housing" development in West Savannah opened, Francis Bartow Place. The 150 units quickly filled, and it soon became a close-knit community.[8]

Residents of the defense contractor whites-only housing neighborhoods used various conveyances to travel to and from work. Some who had automobiles traveled on dirt streets that remained unpaved for years. They frequently carpooled to conserve rationed fuel and rubber or used public transportation, which soon reached maximum capacity. City government authorized Savannah Electric and Power Company to use its buses to transport workers to the three shipyards, but the power company soon reported it lacked enough seating to carry the ten thousand to fifteen thousand passengers who needed transport daily. Mayor Thomas Gamble and the City Council added other travel options, including trains and passenger boats, to get workers to and from the defense-industry jobsites.

Fear of German air raids prompted the federal government to camouflage the exterior of two housing developments, and Savannahians were required to install blackout curtains. Civil defense meetings at the municipal auditorium briefed citizens on how to respond to attacks by air or sea. Indeed, some coastal cities were warned they "may be attacked by German airplanes any night," and those fears escalated early in the war when bodies, oil slicks, and the flotsam and jetsam from vessels torpedoed by German submarines washed ashore at Virginia Beach. Off Charleston, submarines lurked and laid mines in the harbor. In March 1942, the port of Savannah shut down briefly, fearing submarines might torpedo shipping near the coast. Some of Savannah's shipyard workers found the potential for danger exhilarating, one called it "probably the most exciting time of my life."[9] For many women, defense-industry employment was their first opportunity to be part of a paid workforce and, even though they earned less than men doing the same jobs, they found the work challenging and liberating.

Women and Blacks Seek Work in the Defense Industry

As the draft swept millions of men into the armed services, the need for women in defense jobs climbed rapidly. National magazines, radio broadcasts, and movie newsreels promoted the image of "Rosie the Riveter." By the middle years of the war, two thousand women held jobs building ships in Savannah, representing 9.3 percent of the workforce. Many men did not at first welcome women to the jobsites, but over time, as women proved to be capable and conscientious workers, the atmosphere improved. Of course the new and often close work situations offered many temptations; as one woman remarked, "If you flirt you get flirted with."[10] These encounters sometimes led to on-the-job amorous liaisons. Johnny Mercer wrote a song about sex in the workplace, "On the Swing Shift." When a Liberty Ship neared completion, hidden places abounded. On one occasion, a carpenter recalled that he knew a shipfitter who discovered a well-concealed compartment where he enjoyed intimate afternoons with a welder.[11] Without question, women's contributions to the war effort were significant; as one shipyard official said, "America's wartime achievements in shipbuilding could not have been realized without women workers."[12]

Many black Savannahians who worked in defense industries such as those at the SSCS lived in the city's least desirable neighborhoods. One author wrote that the dwellings "would have to be improved to be called substandard."[13] When African American workers took a bus to their defense jobs, they had to sit in the back. Generally, black social life was relegated to West Broad Street, the heart of black Savannah, where they patronized businesses, theaters, bars, and nightclubs.

As part of the war effort, an interracial committee agreed to provide funds to buy the McKelvey Building on West Broad Street for a "Negro" USO-Army-Navy Club. Another segregated USO for blacks opened on Thirty-sixth Street, and still another opened off Ogeechee Road. Six whites-only USO clubs offered entertainment in the city. But the black and white soldiers had different experiences. If African Americans strolled east of West Broad, they encountered "white only" signs. By custom and law, black men and women were forbidden to eat in white restaurants. Drinking fountains, toilets, churches, schools, public transportation, motion pictures, pools, beaches, hotels, and waiting rooms left no doubt that one lived in a segregated Savannah. The separation of the races remained much the same inside the gates of Savannah shipyards and other defense contractors.[14]

Nationally, few African Americans were hired when American industries began recruiting workers in preparation for war. Seeing the racial discrimination in hiring practices, the president of the Brotherhood of Sleeping Car Conductors, A. Phillip Randolph, threatened a fifty-thousand-person march on Washington if Congress failed to remedy the inequity. When Congress refused to act, President Roosevelt issued an executive order prohibiting discrimination in defense plants and established the Fair Employment Practices Commission (FEPC) to ensure equitable treatment of federal employees.

Subsequently, in Savannah, USMC federal contracts included the words that the contractor agreed not to "discriminate against any worker because of race, creed, color or national origin." The SSCS signed such a contract, but ignored the clause. So did other southern defense plants. When complaints of discrimination were brought to the companies' attention, management simply argued that, if the federal government wanted armaments and supplies to win the war, it should not interfere in matters regarding hiring. Because the USMC needed all shipbuilders to meet stringent production quotas, its officers went to great lengths to protect shipbuilders and to insure that nothing interfered with this priority, including stalling or "derailing" the issuance of compliance orders by the FEPC.

Pushback from African American newspapers was swift, and they began promoting the "Double-V" symbol-victory over discrimination at home and victory over America's enemies abroad.[15] Complaints of bias brought by African Americans working in shipyards in Savannah were also ignored; most held menial jobs, were paid the lowest wages, and faced daily segregation and harassment.

Blacks entered the SSCS shipyard by the "Colored Peoples Gate"; though permitted to work in the cafeteria, they could not eat there. Watercoolers throughout the shipyard marked "Colored Only" never received an ounce of the 16 tons of ice which arrived daily for the white coolers. The *Sou' Easter,* the magazine of the SSCS, published only segregated photos of blacks and whites at work in the shipyard and occasionally ran cartoons which depicted caricatures of blacks captioned in "sho'nuff-style" dialect.[16] Perhaps most galling to black employees was management's refusal to consider the skills or former employment of African American workers or to provide them opportunities for advancement.

When Sam Williams, a young African American, completed an application for a diesel mechanic oiler job, a job he previously held elsewhere, a teller at the window tore it up. Williams said this affront was industry's way of telling him, "You are going to be a laborer no matter what skills you had." He wanted to be more than a laborer and soon left the shipyard and went into business for himself. For decades he remained bitter over this experience.

The SSCS's contention that black applicants lacked skills and therefore could not be hired for jobs other than laborers, porters, and helpers stemmed from what one historian called "The Vicious Circle of Training and Employment." At the Naval Yard in Charleston, black employees trained whites to serve as engineers on vessels, but never themselves advanced to the engine rooms—the union permitted white members only.[17]

The ongoing shortage of skilled labor in Georgia moved the City Council to propose a bond issue of $150,000 to build a school downtown to house the Vocational Education–National Defense (VEND) program. Officials actively courted both whites and blacks to support the bond referendum, and it passed. The school went up. Applicants applied, but no blacks were admitted. The rationale for this decision was that blacks could attend VEND classes at Georgia State College (formerly Georgia State Industrial College for Colored Youth) near Thunderbolt, four miles outside the city limits.

Unfortunately, GSIC's VEND program was inadequately staffed, could accommodate but 116 students, and was open only from 3:00 P.M. to 11:00 P.M. A vast gulf existed between the two training centers: the new downtown school was convenient to black neighborhoods, had space for eighteen hundred students, was open twenty-four hours a day, had adequate funding, taught a relevant curriculum for local needs, and students trained on the latest equipment. In early 1942, Savannah came under criticism from the U.S. Employment Service for failing to provide training for blacks. Without appropriate training for the skilled jobs that needed to be filled, blacks were relegated to positions as helpers or laborers.[18] The local NAACP and the *Tribune* believed the U.S. Employment Service had correctly identified the problem, and they intended to keep the issue before the public until something was done to correct the situation.

Mark Gilbert, a Resurgent NAACP, Johnny Bouhan, and Voting Rights

Near the beginning of the 1940s, the Reverend Mark Gilbert accepted a call from Savannah's First African Baptist Church. Born in Jacksonville, Florida, Gilbert was educated at Morehouse College, Howard University, the University of Michigan, and Western University where he received his doctorate in divinity. A charismatic leader and gifted orator, Gilbert was a man of many talents. He wrote and directed plays to teach black history, conducted elaborate musical events and, through his involvement in many aspects of community life, gathered information about conditions within the local black community.[19] Soon after his arrival, Reverend Gilbert staged a spectacular production of the *Passion and Triumph,* sung by a chorus of three hundred in City Auditorium; a block of seats was reserved for white patrons. The *Morning News,* usually mute on such events, gushed, "The choir sang its way into the hearts of music lovers."[20]

Having moved from Detroit to Jim Crow Savannah, Gilbert must have been surprised at the status of African American workers. Daily he would have seen blacks of all ages hawking their wares in the streets: shoeshine boys; peddlers; vendors of ice cream and baked goods; purveyors of vegetables, fresh fish, and shrimp. He must surely have heard about conditions in the overcrowded black schools—one condemned as unsafe, lacking adequate toilet facilities, washbasins, and electric lighting. Gilbert would have observed the onerous living conditions in some areas of his adopted city, where 42 percent of black rental dwellings had no running water. Although African Americans made up 45 percent of the city's population, a poll tax, literacy tests, and the white primary insured the maintenance of the white status quo. John J. Bouhan controlled local politics, and his lieutenants made sure the tactics that denied equal rights to African Americans were enforced. Anyone who defied Bouhan's political machine would pay the price.[21]

Bouhan, a second generation Irish-Catholic, perhaps personified a local saying about Savannah: "The Jews own it, the Irish run it, the Negroes enjoy it, and the Crackers pay for it."[22] Educated in local schools, Bouhan received a degree from Belmont Abbey College, attended law school at Georgetown University, opened a law office in Savannah, served in World War I, and then returned home, where he practiced law for more than fifty years. He was a partner in the prestigious law firm Bouhan, Williams and Levy, with offices in the Armstrong House at the corner of Gaston and Bull streets.

As attorney for Chatham County, Bouhan had absolute control of local politics. He gained loyal political followers when he handpicked fellow Irishmen to work as policemen, firemen, and in other government jobs. Few candidates could win political office without Bouhan's blessing. Bouhan used his office in the courthouse to send orders to City Hall. He was friendly, articulate, and smart, but also "ruthless" to any who crossed him. He "controlled the people that were elected to . . . the city [and] . . . county government and the state legislature." Bouhan described himself as a "Kingmaker." When told some of his political friends were "nasty" to their constituents, Bouhan agreed that some were ornery "sons of bitches. . . . But they're my sons of bitches, so I hafta take care of them." One prominent black Savannahian described Johnny Bouhan as "a mystery man. . . . [H]e controlled politics for twenty-five or thirty years." He was of medium statue, a "very refined guy," . . . "distinguished looking . . . very kind and soft spoken," not the sort of person you would think, "given his brand of politics." In the beginning Johnny Bouhan got the black vote and "became a real powerful guy." He could "give out a few dollars to blacks and they'd have fish frys . . . and he didn't even have to show up. . . . [H]e had his people, his lieutenants, who did that for him." Before the 1960s he was a very powerful man; "what got him was [that] the black vote became real powerful and he couldn't control that."[23]

Mark Gilbert, aware of Bouhan's well-oiled machine, told the national NAACP, "White supremacy forces of this city . . . have perfected an organization of over 400 members." He went on to say that the political machine led by Johnny Bouhan was entrenched in power, and he accused Bouhan of exploiting blacks though "manipulation of an illegal gambling racket." A popular and easily rigged Cuban game, bolita, attracted many black players who could ill afford to lose wages; the gamers frequently employed black "runners" to collect the bets.[24]

Gilbert saw a reinvigorated NAACP as a way to counter Bouhan's control, and he asked the national NAACP to renew Savannah's membership charter, which had been revoked in 1939 for inactivity. The national organization agreed to do so, and soon thereafter Gilbert, the local president, launched a membership drive. Remarkably, within a short time the local chapter had recruited more than 2,000 adult members, and its youth program recorded 609 young people on the membership roster.[25]

Officials at NAACP national headquarters marveled at Gilbert's success. The local chapter flourished under Gilbert's leadership and became the starting point for Savannah's modern civil rights movement. Gilbert used the chapter as

Political "Kingmaker" John Bouhan with shotgun and dog, December 1936. Mr. Bouhan dominated Savannah politics for three decades. Courtesy of Georgia Historical Society.

a pulpit to "out" the city's failure to train blacks for defense industry jobs. With Sol Johnson's *Tribune,* Gilbert made black citizens aware of how critical their support had been to the passage of the bond referendum that secured the new VEND training school in downtown Savannah—the same vocational program that now denied access to black students. He reminded them too of the city's promises that "Negroes would be taken care of, but like other promises this has . . . been broken." Both the NAACP and the *Tribune* described skill training for blacks at GSIC's VEND training school as a "farce." "When the shipyards asked the GSIC for 150 men skilled in ship building, the college failed to send a single student."

Finding no support for training blacks to work in the defense industry among the Bouhan-controlled politicos, the local NAACP turned to the federal government. Black leaders wanted a properly equipped and staffed VEND facility located convenient to black neighborhoods in the city. The NAACP claimed ninety black organizations in Savannah supported their position. Not surprisingly, opposition emerged from none other than the very influential president of GSIC, Dr. Benjamin F. Hubert, who vigorously defended his institution's federally funded training program. But most of Savannah's black community saw Hubert's program as ineffective and criticized him for putting the interests of GSIC over that of the larger community.[26]

In June 1942, the issue came to a head at a meeting with representatives of the Fair Employment Practices Commission in Birmingham, Alabama. The NAACP presented its grievances, pressing its claim that Savannah needed a new VEND training facility for blacks because GSIC remained inadequate in location, faculty, and equipment. The controversy boiled into a heated exchange. M. D. Mobley, who was there to support GSIC and the state's position, read a letter from President Hubert with "veiled references" denigrating the NAACP; Hubert later refuted these criticisms. Several prominent white officials endorsed President Hubert's position. The spokesman for the NAACP countered the accolades by pointing out that Southeastern Shipbuilding Corporation of Savannah, the largest employer in the city, would not hire blacks trained by GSIC because their graduates lacked the skills to do the work needed. The GSIC critics also pointed to the recent request for 150 men by local shipyards and GSIC's inability to provide one person adequately trained for a position. Because the shipyards had promised to hire these graduates if properly trained, the absence of GSIC graduates in the skilled workforce there served as an indictment of Dr. Hubert's program.[27] The *Tribune* praised the work of the NAACP officials and blasted Hubert, calling him a "czar" who should know he "cannot dictate the wishes of our people by appealing to his white friends."[28]

The debate between the NAACP and President Benjamin Hubert did not resolve the issue. Over time the SSCS hired 1,200 blacks, but none were trained for or employed in skilled jobs. Instead they worked in jobs classified as common laborers and were paid 63 to 75 cents per hour. White workers trained as skilled crane operators and mechanics received from $1.25 to $1.75 hourly. Despite efforts by the FEPC, black men in Georgia held few skilled jobs in the defense industries because of inadequate training. Without question, this deficiency affected their earning potential not only during the war but for many years thereafter.[29]

Gamble Leads Savannah in Wartime but Plans for Peace

Higher salaries paid to thousands of workers in the defense industries and the military, coupled with a surge in the export-import traffic, fueled the local boom. An American Farm Bureau Federation lobbyist described a war worker as having "so much money he doesn't know what to do with it."[30] In Savannah the war industries put more money in more pockets than ever before. At the port, between 1943 and 1945, exports rose from 511,542 to 858,623 tons, and imports almost doubled, climbing from 349,969 to 669,556 tons. Mayor Gamble reported payrolls increased during those years to over $5 million, which brought "a tremendous increase . . . in commerce and widespread prosperity."[31] But the newcomers and new industries required expanded city services, which increased city expenditures.

In his twelfth year in office, Mayor Gamble analyzed the city's fiscal situation: "the global war has had . . . favorable and unfavorable" effects on Savannah. Due to the lowering of tax rates during the Great Depression and [with] no tax increases since, the city's income, especially real estate and personal property tax revenue, fell 42 percent, from $26 to $15 million. During the war years, departmental budgets soared, and the city's bonded indebtedness saw a 38 percent rise, from $3,774,500 in 1940 to $5,207,250 in 1944. Four years later, the City Council with public approval issued $1 million in bonds for building an industrial and domestic water supply to furnish water for defense industries and Savannah's fast-growing population.

But Mayor Gamble also looked to the future, warning the City Council in March 1944 that, with the end of the war and the loss of well-paid civilian and military transients, "unemployment here will rise on a large scale; we will soon be facing what promises to be a very difficult time."[32] A year later, Gamble, wrote in even stronger terms about what lay ahead.

He projected that within two years the municipal government would have to authorize yet another bond issue to pay for the improvement of public works, for more officers for the understaffed police force, and for repairs to "dangerous sidewalks." Gamble then turned to an issue he likely had talked about with Dr. Victor Bassett. More money would be needed for additional slum clearance "to sweep away the horrible housing conditions . . . north, south and east of Yamacraw Village." This area and other "densely populated territory are a disgrace to Savannah . . . a continued menace to health, a breeder of noxious evils." He was concerned that few citizens realized "the conditions under which our Negro population continues to live . . . in dwellings without sanitary facilities"; his theme was echoed by the *Morning News* article that called Savannah's "Negro [housing] . . . a disgrace to the city." Despite looming financial challenges, Gamble did not advocate retrenchment; rather he told the council that, as Savannah approached a "most critical period in its history, "it cannot stand still," and the municipal government must remain an "alert and progressive agent . . . to ensure growth." Always the booster, Gamble envisioned Savannah moving "higher and higher in rank" among the nation's cities, but to do this, "its annual revenues and its services to its people must expand." To achieve this "move up," he recommended that the city grow by annexation and extend

Yamacraw slum dwellings photographed ca. 1939 as part of a comprehensive survey in preparation for the Yamacraw Village Slum Clearance Project. Most homes in Yamacraw had yard toilets, no baths, no lights, and used fireplace heating. Photograph made available by the Housing Authority of Savannah, Earline Wesley Davis, executive director.

"its territorial limits in all directions . . . to the great industrial areas" around Savannah.[33]

Mayor Gamble had charted a path for the city, but he would not live to see it traveled. The stress of governing and the wartime demands on his energy left Gamble so exhausted that he scheduled a brief vacation at a resort near Chattanooga. A few days after arriving, he suffered a coronary thrombosis and died July 13, 1945. When news of his death reached Savannah, Acting Mayor Peter R. Nugent closed City Hall, draped it in black mourning crepe, and directed that flags on public buildings be flown at half-mast.

At his death, the leading men of Savannah praised Thomas Gamble, the "outsider" from Virginia, as "a progressive [and] brilliant leader" and chronicler of the city's history. In September 1945, the City Hall Annex was renamed "The Thomas Gamble Building . . . a permanent memorial to perpetuate his name in tribute to the outstanding service rendered by him during his life-time to the City Government and the citizens of Savannah."[34]

Court Decisions, the Vote, and Bloodshed

During the war years, decisions by state and federal courts brought major changes for African Americans in the South. The local chapter of the NAACP, led by the Reverend Gilbert, seized the opportunities offered. Following the decision of the U.S. Supreme Court in *Alston v. Board of Education of the City of Norfolk,* which rejected racial pay differentials for colored teachers, the Savannah NAACP moved quickly to seek equal pay for black teachers. Gilbert seemed to be everywhere—recruiting new members for the local chapter, writing and directing religious dramas, serving as a principal speaker at Emancipation Day celebrations, and active in the local Democratic Party. With his wife and others, Gilbert helped established some fifty-one NAACP chapters across the state, which in turn recruited 13,595 members. The Savannah chapter alone counted 3,000 members by 1944. The organization was thriving at a period when federal courts were striking down the barriers to African American voting rights.[35]

On April 3 the U.S. Supreme Court ruled in the case of *Smith v. Allwright* (1944) that the whites-only primary in Texas "violated the Fifteenth Amendment." In Georgia, plaintiffs, aided by the ubiquitous Mark Gilbert, made the same argument in *King v. Chapman, et al.* (1945), and the Supreme Court ruled that Georgia blacks were entitled to vote in white primaries. These judgments and the elimination of the poll tax in Georgia in 1945 seemed to offer African Americans a promise of full participation in the state's electoral process. By now Gilbert, according to Sol Johnson's *Tribune,* was promoting the watchwords of black soldiers, the "Double V Pledge"—"Victory in Europe and also victory at home against segregation."

Gilbert worked with several hundred black veterans to found an organization called "Negro Veterans of All Wars" that pledged to work for better schools, housing, and street lighting. A like-minded group of Savannah's African American business and professional men formed the "Hub," a politically active group focused on providing a voice for the black community and registering voters. In the 1990s, Curtis Cooper described the Hub as being "like the black Kiwanians. . . . [T]hey often dabbled in civic matters and politics and the black leadership in those days were represented in the Hub." Most members were professionals, doctors, lawyers, business people—men like Eugene Gadsden, Bowles Ford, and Sam Brown. Excluded from white social and civic clubs, black men and women created their own.

Encouraged by the Supreme Court's decision ending the white primary and President Truman's creation of a national Committee on Civil Rights, members of the Hub, Savannah's Longshoremen Association, the Citizens Progressive League, and the NAACP registered nineteen thousand voters in 1945–46. Ministers of black churches escorted blacks to the courthouse, where they were assisted in registering by a local white attorney, Aaron Kravitch.[36]

With rising expectations over the Supreme Court's decision, some young African Americans in Deep South states tested white segregation policies—they sat in at soda fountains and in the dining cars of railroads. Appalled by these affronts to white supremacy, whites began circulating stories of blacks throwing kisses to white college girls in Birmingham, and in other cities rumors persisted that blacks were planning insurrections with ice picks and that they harbored sinister intentions to "take over" white women.[37]

In Louisiana, Mississippi, Texas, and Georgia race riots erupted. At a shipyard in Beaumont, Louisiana, stories that a black man had raped a white woman ignited a six-hour riot in which whites destroyed much of a black neighborhood. Two blacks and one white died, and hundreds were injured. The rumor proved false.

Rigid segregation and harassment at Camp Stewart near Savannah sometimes led to racial confrontations at the base. On occasion these hostilities spilled over onto Savannah's streets. In August 1943, a black soldier on West Broad Street came to the defense of a woman he judged to be unfairly arrested. When a policeman rushed at the soldier with a club, the serviceman ripped it out of his hands and beat the officer senseless. A melee ensued, but when the city's riot police appeared, they were confronted by a large number of black soldiers in a truck mounted with guns. It was one of the most dramatic incidences of black militancy in Georgia. The skirmish ended without bloodshed when police left the scene without a confrontation—a decision that likely prevented an explosive encounter.[38]

As the war abroad wound down, returning black veterans, all the wiser because of their overseas and military experiences, were often greeted with outright hostility. White anger over perceived black aggressiveness and challenges to Jim Crow laws led to two separate incidents in Georgia during spring 1946. In each, a young black soldier returning home in uniform took a seat in the front of the bus. Both were shot by the conductors.[39] The fact that blacks "appeared" to have forgotten their place posed a threat to white supremacy.

Lady Astor Comes to Town

As defense industries and military bases in and around Savannah began closing, the transient population in the armed services and civilian workers started leaving the city. Though some remained in Savannah, many more hurried back to homes beyond Chatham County. Within a short time the central city had been abandoned as a large number of wealthier citizens migrated to the suburbs. The well-to-do's nineteenth-century homes frequently were converted to boarding houses, and without costly maintenance many of these soon fell into disrepair. John Dos Passos described another southern city, Mobile, in the latter years of the war as looking "trampled and battered like a city that's been taken by storm."[40]

An often-quoted incident related to Savannah's deteriorating cityscape occurred in early 1946 when Lady Waldorf Astor and her husband took an unplanned tour of the city and afterwards Lady Astor publicly likened Savannah to a "beautiful woman with a dirty face"; the city "has been allowed to become run down, unkempt and dirty." She was especially dismayed by all the paper and trash scattered about. Some found her remarks offense, but many agreed with her frank, if unflattering, assessment. Captain Frank Spencer, a prominent civic leader, told the board of the Chamber of Commerce that Lady Astor was right, "the city is one of the dirtiest in the world." A guest columnist in the *Morning News* suggested that if Lady Astor pried beneath the surface she may also find "low wages . . . [poorly funded] educational facilities . . . [and the] lack of economic and political privileges and rights for a large group of citizens, both white and black," to be less visible but equally disturbing problems.[41]

Mayor Peter Nugent rushed to do damage control. He told the press, "Everything humanly possible was being done to get equipment to clean up the city," and the mayor sent the city's chief purchasing agent to Atlanta with a check to buy twelve garbage trucks. The Chamber of Commerce tried to defuse any negative publicity caused by Lady Astor's comment by publishing a brochure boosting the business, social, and cultural attributes of Savannah. Lady Astor, the former Nancy Langhorne of Danville, Virginia, and the first woman member of Parliament, subsequently issued a public apology to Mayor Nugent. Later, when she revisited Savannah, she was charmed by the city's improved appearance.[42]

Governor Eugene Talmadge, Johnny Bouhan, and Lillian Bragg

In 1946, race-baiting Eugene Talmadge ran for a fourth term as governor of Georgia. He personified the backlash coming from white supremacists. The *Atlanta Journal* condemned him as "a blatant demagogue this fomenter of strife, this panderer to the passions of the ignorant and to the fears of the timid . . . is a cheap fraud and menace to the security and welfare of us all." Talmadge's strongholds had always been in the rural parts of the state; he was a "scourge" of the cities. Because Talmadge's political opponents found their support in urban areas, his campaigns worked aggressively to neutralize the city vote by chicanery. The political machine of Johnny Bouhan helped Talmadge accomplish this in Savannah; Bouhan was one of his close allies.

Bouhan wielded such political power in Savannah that, when he asked a local banker to demand early loan repayment from Mayor Nugent if he ran for a second term, Nugent took the hint and bowed out of the race.[43] Bouhan was so sure of his control of Chatham County politics that on one occasion he told an audience in Atlanta that Chatham County always "played ball" with Ol' Gene. Bouhan recounted how in one campaign he "held out some boxes" of ballots until he heard from the Talmadge faction regarding how many extra votes they needed to put Talmadge over the top in Chatham County. Johnny Bouhan, the quintessential old-style political boss, was known throughout the state as the "voice of influence in Chatham County."[44] African Americans in Georgia, under former progressive governor Ellis Arnall, had made significant gains in voting rights during the 1940s. But now Talmadge staked out black disenfranchisement as the central plank of his campaign. He told audiences his agenda was to let "the people of this world know that Georgia is still a white man's state." He repeatedly reminded voters that his candidacy was based on preventing the danger of "a nigra takeover."[45]

Black leaders in Georgia thought "Talmadge's anti-Negro utterances . . . so vile and vicious . . . that many feared what might happen racially."[46] Talmadge's hate-filled campaign rhetoric encouraged white supremacists in the state, and as the gubernatorial election geared up, the Talmadge machine set about striking black names from voting lists across the state. A later FBI investigation found that, in approximately 50 of the 159 counties in Georgia, registered African Americans had been purged from the voting rolls. In a subsequent report, the FBI estimated fifty thousand blacks had been intimidated from registering or even appearing before county boards of registrars for fear of retaliation. Blacks who did appear were disqualified by various tactics, such as having to prove their residency or answer detailed questions about the state's constitution or define such concepts as "democracy." Registrars in a majority of the fifty counties that used these tactics to prevent blacks from voting never challenged a white voter.

The ubiquitous Savannah attorney Aaron Kravitch counseled African Americans in various counties who had been summoned before boards of registrars. Black and some white newspapers in the state charged the Talmadge machine with trying to "intimidate, embarrass, and harass the Negro voters." Complaints streamed into the offices of U.S. attorneys who, on July 9, eight days

Eugene Talmadge speaking at a Savannah political meeting, ca. 1940s. Courtesy of Georgia Archives, Vanishing Georgia Collection, image no. ge0091.

before the primary, announced that investigations would begin soon as to why qualified black voters in Georgia were prohibited from voting in white primaries. Despite FBI investigations, pushback by the black community, and outrage by many citizens, disqualification of blacks by boards of registrars in some Georgia counties continued until passage of the federal Voting Rights Act in the mid-1960s.[47]

A day before the gubernatorial election of July 17, 1946, crosses were burned in yards and automobiles sped past the homes of some African Americans, the white riders yelling obscenities. At one rally, Talmadge urged "every white Georgian . . . to strike a blow . . . for the security and racial integrity of unborn . . . Georgians." The evening before balloting began, he used the radio to remind Georgians: "We will reestablish white supremacy in tomorrow's election."[48]

Rain swept most of the state on election day; nonetheless dawn found blacks standing in long lines waiting to vote. Some faced physical harassment; others were turned away at voting booths by crowds of whites. Blacks in some fifty counties were not permitted to cast a ballot. Talmadge himself had warned: "wise Negroes will stay away from white folks' ballot boxes."[49] None of the one hundred still-qualified black voters in Schley County, Georgia, cast a ballot—perhaps because the state representative stood just outside the polling booth with a shotgun repeating: "if a nigger votes in this election, he'll be a dead nigger."[50] In Savannah, voting went ahead as planned by the Bouhan machine.

Early in the campaign, the Talmadge Club of Savannah, Johnny Bouhan, and about four hundred Savannah officials conspired to suppress the black vote. On election day, complaints surfaced that Savannah election officials had minimized the number of polling places, opened some late, and closed others early—resulting in some black voters waiting in line up to ten hours to cast their ballots, only to be told they were not registered.[51]

Another tactic used by Bouhan to insure victory at the polls involved the use of "street money" to pay voters who in return promised to vote for Bouhan's candidates. Policemen also were expected to see that the election went the right way. In a 1990 interview, former mayor Malcolm Maclean remembered this period in Savannah's history when city policemen sometimes arrived at the polling places, opened up the boxes, and filled out paper ballots "for everybody who hadn't gotten there" in time to vote. The captains of the boxes got "a prize like . . . fifty bucks for the one who carried the box by the biggest number . . . 2–1 or 3–1."[52] But, though powerful, Bouhan was not invincible, as a 1945 election illustrated.

During an election in August 1945, one Savannah poll worker, Lillian Bragg, appalled by what she had seen, described in a letter to the *Savannah Mooning News* how "one of the ladies in charge announced casually [that they] . . . "might as well begin," at which point names "of absentee voters were written on ballots and stuffed into the box with machine-like regularity." Her accusations came to be known as "the shot heard across Savannah." After the paper published her account, a Savannah grand jury found ballot tampering widespread and the Bouhan organization a major player in the chicanery. These revelations drove another nail in the coffin of the Bouhan machine.[53]

Though no ballot stuffing was reported in the July 1946 election, to the dismay of many African Americans, Eugene Talmadge won his fourth gubernatorial election. One scholar was of the opinion that "Talmadge would have lost without the benefits of the campaign against black voting."[54] But the governor-elect never took office. He died in December. His racist rhetoric, however, continued to nurture white supremacy in Georgia and brought a chill to African American communities. An investigative journalist who visited the state observed that, during "Ol' Gene's" run for governor, a "'season on niggers' . . . automatically opened and every pinheaded Georgia cracker and bigoted Ku Kluxer figured he had a hunting license."[55]

Backlash and White Supremacy

On July 25, 1946, eight days after the election, some twenty-five to thirty unidentified white men piled out of four automobiles and for no apparent reason seized two young African American couples in Walton County. After binding the black men, the white mob realized that a member of their group had been recognized by one of the wives—so all four were dragged to the banks of the Apalachee River and murdered in a hail of bullets. One of the men killed was a highly decorated World War II combat veteran, George Dorsey. The murders were denounced by newspapers in the state, country, and world, but the killers were never identified even though the crime had been witnessed by a white farmer.

The *Tribune,* whose editor closely monitored violence against African Americans in Georgia, called the massacre "one of the most brutal and most revolting crimes in the history of the state." The *Morning News* editorial page was more concerned that "the extremists in the North will seize upon this unfortunate incident to continue their attempted interference with the affairs of Georgia."[56] Even as violence continued in upcountry Georgia that year, progressives won elections in Savannah and Chatham County and chipped away ever larger pieces of Bouhan's machine.

The Citizens Progressive League and John G. Kennedy's Administration

The Citizens Progressive League, a wing of the local Democratic Party, defeated Bouhan's three Chatham County legislative picks and elected their own; they also elected their candidates for City Council. The Citizens Progressive League's legislative delegation also helped pass a bill mandating the use of voting machines in all future elections held in the county and city. In the mayoralty election, the league elected the progressive John G. Kennedy, who discovered a large operating deficit upon taking office. However, rather than curtail city services or stop improvements and pay off the city's indebtedness, Kennedy decided to make only a modest payment on the debt.

During his two-year term, 1947–48, Kennedy and the City Council together desegregated the police force. For several years Sol Johnson's *Tribune* had promoted the idea that "black officers stationed in the several densely populated black districts would [maintain] . . . better order and ferret . . . out crime more

The first nine African American members of the Savannah Police Department, May 3, 1947, with their soon-to-be chief, Truman F. Ward. In alphabetical order the original nine were: Howard J. Davis, Alexander Grant Jr., Milton Hall, Stepney Houston, William Malone, Frank Mullino, James Nealy, John A. White, and Leroy Wilson. Courtesy of Georgia Archives, Vanishing Georgia Collection, image no. ctm077.

promptly." After three months of extensive "secret" training in the "Masonic Temple," nine black police officers were sworn in on May 3, 1947, "in the presence of Rev. Ralph Mark Gilbert, pastor of the First African Baptist Church, John W. McGlockton, President of the Citizens Democratic Club, and many others."

The new recruits had to endure numerous indignities as they integrated the previously all- white department, even being told to use the back door to enter the station. John A. White, one of the black officers, a former marine, recalled in a 2002 interview that, soon after joining the force, he became aware that "a lot of the [police had] KKK affiliations." Mayor Kennedy wanted to help "Negroes help themselves," and when he discovered that posting black officers in African American communities had reduced crime, racketeering, and juvenile delinquency, he judged the "experiment" more "successful tha[n] could at first be imagined." Kennedy then took the unprecedented step of appointing an all-black committee of prominent citizens to advise him on the black community's needs. At the time this was such a progressive move that it attracted national attention.[57]

After a survey of conditions in southern cities, *New South* magazine in the late 1940s determined that the city where blacks got the most benefit from voter participation, "the city of the South which leads all others is not Richmond, Va., or Nashville, Tenn., but Savannah, Ga." The article went on to say those "benefits" came in the form of two black jail matrons, a new black school, swimming pool and recreation center, and especially the hiring of nine black police officers. The *New York Times* reported: "Savannah has always seen itself as a semi-autonomous republic in relation to the rest of the state and this framework has extended to racial relations according to workers in the field."[58]

Mayor Kennedy's administration, interested in luring industry to the city and increasing tonnage passing through the port, saw an opportunity to do both when the recently abandoned Army Quartermaster Depot on the Savannah River became available for purchase. Conditions of the sale required immediate action, and the process got underway quickly. The Savannah Port Authority asked the State Ports Authority (later renamed the Georgia Ports Authority) to inspect and fund the purchase of the four-hundred-acre site, which included railroad tracks, a dock, and warehouse space. A state audit determined the property to be worth millions and, with the backing of Governor Herman Talmadge, arrangements were made to purchase the tract for $808,100. This purchase was a milestone in the port's history; the investment paved the way for Savannah to become Georgia's major port city. The State Ports Authority began construction immediately on facilities of the Garden City Terminal, financed by a bond issue of $5,500,000. The terminal opened shortly thereafter.

Under Mayor Kennedy the city also purchased the Southeastern Shipyard property and announced that now, with Savannah's "strategically located water front property," the city was poised "for a great industrial expansion that will mean more employment and added income to our people." The new port seemed to be well accommodated; however, within a few years it became clear that even more modern facilities were needed, and the state purchased the Central of Georgia Railway and the Ocean Steamship Terminals for $2,760,000. The city also took control of Hunter Field.[59]

The New Mayor Fulmer Assumes Old Problems

Even in Mayor Kennedy's progressive administration, machine politics sometimes pushed back against progress. Such was the case when the City Council passed an ordinance stripping Mayor Kennedy of many of his mayoral powers and handed those over to the council. Mayor Kennedy vetoed the act, but the council had the votes to override his veto.

Following Kennedy, Olin F. Fulmer was inaugurated as mayor in front of a flower-festooned and bunting-draped City Hall on January 24, 1949. He was the first mayor to take the oath of office in an outdoor setting. At his inauguration, Fulmer told a crowd of five thousand that his administration would operate under the principle of doing "the greatest good for the greatest number." Fulmer pledged to rehabilitate city "finances" and improve city services, such as "streets and sewers," and to strengthen the "health and recreation of the people" so that "business and industry will be attracted here" to take the city to "new heights . . . of prosperity."

One of Fulmer's first orders of business was to pass an ordinance restoring all former powers to the mayor. A progressive and another "exceptional" outsider, Mayor Fulmer appointed Mrs. Louis J. Roos (Nola) as clerk of council, the first woman to reach a top-level position in Savannah government.[60]

From the outset, Fulmer had some involvement with the Bouhan machine. Shortly after his inauguration, he wrote Congressman Prince H. Preston, "You made business in Washington a distinct pleasure for us and my colleagues, John Bouhan [and] Spence Grayson." He expressed his appreciation for all Preston had done in "helping solve our problems." Other Savannahians kept in touch with their congressman. In the late 1940s, Frank M. Oliver wrote Preston informing him that some high official in Bouhan's network had told Gordon that "Grayson will not be put forward as a candidate against you [Preston]."

And Congressman Preston also got advice from conservative businessmen in Savannah, urging him to "vote against any increase in taxes or any increase in the federal budget." The writer continued in the same vein: "[Remember] what happened to Rome, Greece, France, and other countries and it can happen to this country if we overburden our people with taxes." Preston's letter of reply assured his constituent, "I can tell you that I . . . will vote against any increase in taxes. . . . [O]ur eventual destruction would be brought about through our over-spending."[61]

When Mayor Fulmer took the helm, Savannah had a population of approximately 130,000 and, as he soon discovered, a very large debt. The ambitious goals Mayor Fulmer set out in his inaugural address had to be put on hold when he learned, to his great dismay, that bills incurred by the prior administration, and now due, amounted to $1,274,000. More bad news came in the form of interest due on "several hundreds of thousands of dollars bonds" issued by the city in years past.

Simply to meet these bills alone, Fulmer and the City Council had to increase taxes on property and utilities and raise ad valorem and millage rates. These tax increases generated $500,000 for fiscal year 1950 but left many Savannahians unhappy. Nonetheless, the City Council persisted with their austerity measures. How, Fulmer questioned, when his taxing policies were criticized, could citizens believe "a city of 130,000 can be operated with the same sums of as a city of 90,000"—the population of Savannah eight years previous. And the mayor reminded Savannahians that generating revenue was only one part of the equation; to "meet the increasing costs of government," the city had to cut expenditures.[62]

Three months after Fulmer's inauguration, City Councilman Leo Griffin led a successful move to end what he called "Star Chamber" sessions by opening council meetings to reporters. Arguments that had taken place behind closed doors now headlined the morning paper. Sometimes the differences of opinion strained civility, such as when Mayor Fulmer asked the council to appoint Sanford Butler as police chief and was attacked by council members, who called him the "Dictator" of City Hall. Councilman Griffin, who had championed the idea of open meetings, now became a target. He probably was not amused to find his own words in the morning press regarding the police-chief appointment: "I have respect for the Mayor but no respect in his integrity and word." Subsequently, a vote of six to three affirmed the mayor's selection of Butler as Savannah's new police chief.[63]

In his December 1949 meeting with the City Council, Mayor Fulmer highlighted accomplishments of the past year. The city inaugurated a civil service system for city employees and planned for extension of the city limits. Suppressing crime and "practically eliminat[ing]" prostitution remained at the top of his list of achievements. He allocated funds for the Health Department as "there is a never-slackening need to be watchful of the health of the community." Perhaps extending an olive branch to some disgruntled councilmen regarding the police-chief appointment, Fulmer told the council he had no "lingering resentment against any member for the differences of the past" and suggested, perhaps tongue-in-cheek, that they adopt the public service motto "Not for ourselves but for others."[64]

By the early 1950s, Savannah's economy was back on track and city expenditures had been brought under control, likely reasons Fulmer won a second term. In 1952 the city reported the level of activity at the port to be the second highest ever achieved, with 1,699,583 tons imported and 262,884 exported. The city also met its budget obligations and, due to "economical handling of city affairs," reduced the city's indebtedness by 63 percent. Extensive paving operations and widening heavily traveled roads like Waters Avenue and Skidaway Road eased congestion, making commutes to the city easier for Savannah's "worthy citizens." Two new sewage disposal plants were nearing completion; one on the south side at Bacon Park, Fulmer boasted, would eliminate pollution and its discharge water would be "as pure as drinking water."

Overall, Fulmer reported, the city "is in far better shape in its underground and top ground facilities than it has been in years," but he reminded citizens that "Savannah's growing pains . . . necessitated close scrutiny of sewage, garbage, housing and rodent control." He also reported that the city and county had formulated plans for both budget and operations to be consolidated, a move Fulmer called "a distinctly forward step."[65] The plan apparently remained just that.

One problem continued to confound the city's leadership in the early 1950s, and that was crime. Apparently Chief Sanford P. Butler took a lot of criticism for the increasing criminal assaults: the count rose from fourteen to forty-eight in one year. The mayor and the City Council appointed Captain Sidney E. Barnes to replace Butler.[66]

Another Talmadge

Meanwhile, a bizarre series of events were taking place at the state level. The chaos had been precipitated by the untimely death of Eugene Talmadge in December 1946, a month before he was to be inaugurated for a fourth term as governor. This void and the ensuing fistfights, stolen ballot boxes, and guerrilla-style occupation of the governor's mansion resulted in three self-proclaimed governors serving simultaneously. The Georgia legislature stepped in and named Herman Talmadge, Eugene's son, as governor of the state. But lieutenant governor-elect M. E Thompson and outgoing governor Ellis Arnall both claimed that the office was rightfully theirs.

When Ellis Arnall refused to surrender the governor's office, Herman Talmadge had the adjutant general and state troopers "escort" Arnall off the premises. He then changed the locks on the doors and proceeded to govern for sixty-seven days. At that time, the Georgia Supreme Court intervened and ruled Thompson the legitimate governor with a special election set for 1948. Herman Talmadge won the special election, and his governorship ignited a resurgence of racial violence exceeding that in the rest of the South. One writer observed that black Georgians were living "through a veritable reign of terror." Talmadge refused to investigate the new outbreak of violence, insisting that "race relations were good in the state."[67]

Leaders of the NAACP within the state denounced the "terror." The Reverend Mark Gilbert urged the national NAACP to help Georgia launch a protest. "White supremacy is the main issue," Gilbert argued. The national NAACP ignored the petitions for assistance. Violence escalated around the state.

In Loganville, Georgia, all of the black churches and schools were burned to the ground. Such racial threats and acts of terrorism caused Georgia branches of the NAACP to lose members. The collapse of the state's NAACP branches—units Gilbert had invested so much time and energy to develop—likely contributed to his despair and mental breakdown. He wrote: "It is hard going . . . keeping up an active interest in the NAACP."[68]

Herman Talmadge's term as governor ushered in "a long, dark night for Georgia." One observer lamented, "Poor Ol' Georgia, first Sherman, and then Herman." Talmadge allied himself with a resurgent Ku Klux Klan and its leadership. He publicly acknowledged that he "won election on as white a primary as possible." Upon taking office, Talmadge immediately signed a new poll tax and a more stringent voter-registration law. In Savannah alone, five thousand black voters were required to provide the board of registrars with personal information or lose their voting rights. To ensure racial purity, Talmadge endorsed laws requiring hospitals to segregate black and white blood. His actions encouraged a resurgence of violence, often led by the KKK. A writer called Talmadge's election "a signal to these hooded devils to don their sheets."[69]

Over the next several years, violence against blacks remained unchecked, especially in rural Georgia. Yet even in Atlanta, African American middle-class homes were occasionally attacked by bomb throwers. The white-supremacy backlash scared away many black voters across the state. In Savannah, black ministers and attorneys bemoaned the "loss of countless thousands of registered voters in the southeast." The nascent statewide civil rights movement appeared to be quashed.[70]

The successful efforts by Herman Talmadge to undo gains made by African Americans left many dispirited. Political pressure caused black teachers to refrain from openly supporting the NAACP. Membership in the Savannah chapter dropped from 695 to 203 between 1948 and 1949. In the latter year, the Rev. Mark Gilbert resigned his membership. A twenty-seven-year-old Savannah native, Westley Wallace Law, succeeded him.

W. W. Law, a New Governance Model, and a "Pekingese" Takes on Bouhan

Over the years, Gilbert had served as a mentor to the young Westley Wallace Law. Law's grandmother and mother also greatly influenced him after the death of his father—his mother passing along her love of books and music and his grandmother likely inspiring his "ferocious quest for justice."

During the Great Depression, Law contributed to the family's meager income by carrying papers and mowing lawns. Described as "impatient and precocious," he soon became a leader of Savannah's NAACP youth movement. After graduating from high school, Law attended GSIC until he was drafted during World War II. In the army he learned more about the inequities of segregation. Mustered out at the end of the war, Law returned to college and earned a BA in biology. Turned down for a position to teach in Savannah's school system because of his affiliation with the NAACP, Law, at age twenty-seven, joined the local U.S. Post Office. In 1950 he became president of the Savannah NAACP, the youngest branch president in the nation and one of the youngest members of the National Board. He quietly began building a cadre of workers and coalitions locally.[71]

Despite the successful pushback by the Talmadge administration against equal rights in Georgia in the late 1940s, Savannah at the time appeared to be generally unaffected by his racist policies. The local NAACP opened a citizens-training course in which prominent African American leaders hoped to reach ten thousand blacks with an introduction to equal rights issues. A small advance came when white Savannahians selected Jesse Brinson as the first black foreman of a Savannah court jury.[72]

The City Council in Mayor Fulmer's administration remained divided over a range of issues, so much so that Johnny Bouhan took advantage of the opportunity to try to scuttle the proposal to reduce the council from twelve to six members and to institute a council-manager form of government for Savannah.

After years of overspending and deficit budgets, a report by outside consultants Griffenhagen and Associates strongly advocated more efficient management of city departments and finances. Eventually a public relations campaign in support of a council–manager system was spearheaded by local Jaycees, the League of Women Voters, and the *Morning News*. The campaign generated sufficient support for a local referendum on the issue. The council-manager option was overwhelmingly endorsed by voters, much to dismay of the entrenched administration, including Johnny Bouhan, who understood that these changes would dilute his role as a power broker. The vote on the referendum made it clear that citizens were "fed up with a strong council form of government, which many believed encouraged political favors in assigning city jobs and services."[73]

Another indication of Bouhan's declining influence occurred when a vacancy on the Chatham County legislative delegation created the need for a special election. Bouhan controlled the delegation and intended to do so in the future by deciding who would run for and win the Georgia House seat. Much to his surprise, Frank S. Cheatham Jr., a young progressive lawyer and an advocate for the council-manager system, decided to run. A victim of polio, Cheatham appeared frail, used crutches, and seemed an unlikely candidate to take on the Bouhan machine—so much so in fact that Bouhan said of this adversary, it is "[l]ike sending a Pekingese on a coon hunt." But when the new voting machines tallied the votes, Cheatham won. Cheatham's comment to the press: "Some Pekingese!"[74] Bouhan's control of local politics continued to ebb; Cheatham later became a Superior Court judge.

Mayor Fulmer and his team brought about remarkable changes during their tenure. Even with a divided City Council, Mayor Fulmer managed to rally enough votes to carry progressive legislation forward. But one issue still unresolved in 1952 was how to generate more money for city coffers. One option under discussion concerned the City Market and whether this city-owned property might have some revenue-generating potential.[75]

Mayor Fulmer began his report in 1953 by reminding constituents that in the coming year Savannah would move to a council-manager form of government, as approved by the city and state legislature. Based on revisions to the City Charter, the mayor and six City Council members would comprise the council. The mayor would remain the official head of Savannah's government, but the city manager would oversee departments, budgets, daily operations, and employees; in essence, the position would be responsible for the proper administration of the government and implementation of the plans of the mayor and council. The city manager could make recommendations to the council for new programs, but those recommendations would only be adopted after review and approval by the council.

One reason for the reorganization was to end the "financial mismanagement" that had plagued city government for years. In 1953 the city had a $1.2 million deficit. From a list of one hundred applicants, Mayor Fulmer appointed Frank A. Jacocks as the first city manager of Savannah, with his annual salary set at fifteen thousand dollars.[76]

A Growing City

As Savannah's population grew, the city approved new subdivisions and building permits, and the administration scrambled to meet demands for an improved city sewage system, sidewalk repairs, and a massive paving program to change "the face of street surface in Savannah." More pressure came too for enlarging the Scavenger and Sanitary Department. To fund these initiatives the city established cost-cutting measures that included a deep retrenchment in personnel.

The number of city workers dropped from 1,464 to 1,088 (26 percent) between 1948 and 1953, saving the city about $350,000. Savannah also increased its sale of water to domestic and industrial users; water was one of the few commodities the city had to sell, and it found ready buyers in Union Bag and Paper, Certain-Teed Products, and Savannah Sugar Refining Corporation, who were among the largest consumers. Another cost savings came from consolidating the city and county health departments.[77]

In his annual report the mayor informed his constituents that heart disease and cancer were the major causes of death among the white population but noted with regret that death rates for some diseases were often twice as high in the "colored" population. The mayor announced his pleasure in being able to report that "Savannah was blessed with having no major outbreaks of communicable diseases."[78] Epidemics and the overall health status of citizens continued to be recognized as factors that could hamper future growth.

The NAACP and the Campaign for Better Schools

During the early 1950s the local NAACP, the Hub, and *Tribune* editor Sol Johnson came together to promote better schools, accusing the local school board of passing over the educational needs of "black children to provide for the less pressing needs of white children." In 1950 the U.S. Supreme Court nudged along a like idea in two cases: *McLauren v. Oklahoma State Regents* and *Sweat v. Painter,* which held that separate but equal facilities in graduate schools did not guarantee equal educational quality.

When African Americans filed a suit in Atlanta to end segregation in public schools, the *Morning News* warned that such action "is extremely regrettable because . . . the relations between the races in Georgia will suffer as a result." Two years later, Westley Law's NAACP and Hub backed twenty-seven black families who petitioned the Chatham County School Board demanding that schools for blacks and whites be equalized or that white schools admit black children. The Board of Education argued that it spent more proportionally on black than white schools. Members of the NAACP and the Hub members received threatening calls from the Ku Klux Klan.[79] But such threats did not deter local protesters.

Sol Johnson's *Tribune* asked rhetorically, had it occurred to City Council "that it has been unfair to Negroes, when they spent over a million dollars on a junior college for whites and not one comparable dime on the education of Negro children[?]" And, with all the tax dollars spent on street paving, "very little [is] done in Negro sections" where in "rainy weather . . . residents cannot leave their houses “without walking in water or mud.” In sum, these things “make colored citizens feel they are forgotten or ignored.”[80]

The local NAACP president, W. W. Law, invited Clarence Mitchell, national director of the NAACP, to Savannah; apparently Mitchell gave a “passionate” pep talk on registering to vote, and Law continued to grow the local chapter. The Ku Klux Klan took notice of young Law, and its members were seen walking around his neighborhood; his family received threatening calls from the KKK suggesting they “get some place to bury him because he was stirring up too much trouble.” Law was not dissuaded but challenged; to him this backlash underscored “why I must continue to fight to destroy segregation and discrimination.”[81]

Still brooding over Savannah school inequities, Law and local NAACP attorneys paid an “uninvited visit” to the state Board of Education in Atlanta to ask for equality in schools for Savannah children and an end to racial segregation in the public schools. That same year the U.S. Supreme Court affirmed by a unanimous vote that separate but equal education was unconstitutional in *Brown v. Board of Education of Topeka, Kansas* (1954). The local NAACP celebrated the decision; the *Morning News* “deplored” it, as did Governor Herman Talmadge, whose solution to the integration predicament was to suggest that Georgia may need to convert all public schools into private ones. At this time Georgia law prohibited the use of public funding for schools unless they were segregated.[82]

Mayor Mingledorff, the Preservationists, and Urban Renewal

Mayor Fulmer left office after serving three terms. With the near unanimous support of the Citizens Committee, a new faction of the Democratic Party, Lee Mingledorff won the mayoralty election in 1954 without engaging in Bouhan-bashing tactics. Mingledorff’s father had been a Bouhan friend, and the young candidate wanted to avoid a rough-and-tumble campaign against him. Mingledorff’s opponents characterized him as high society, with little sympathy for the common man. A graduate of Georgia Tech, Mingledorff had served briefly in the war as an officer until being discharged to manage the Mingledorff shipyard, Savannah Machine and Foundry, a company that built minesweepers for the Navy.

Following the war, Mingledorff impressed many as a fresh, young talent who was not afraid to criticize Savannah’s “lethargic attitude.” As an outspoken, reform-minded president of the Chamber of Commerce, Mingledorff quickly moved from the sidelines onto center stage in the political arena. In 1955 he took office as mayor.[83]

Mingledorff was the first mayor to serve under the new Savannah charter, which specified the council-manager form of government and reduced the number of council members from twelve to six. All six were members of the new Democratic faction, the Citizens Committee. A new businesslike atmosphere came to pervade city government. With the leadership and assistance from the new city manager, Frank Jacocks, Savannah reduced its deficit and adopted a new civil service system based on merit. The new system replaced an era of cronyism and political patronage and ended Bouhan's "reign."[84] There also emerged a new enthusiasm for preservation, restoration, and urban renewal.

The first preservation and restoration efforts in downtown Savannah began before the end of World War II when Marmaduke Floyd, a local engineer-historian, purchased a derelict tavern near the intersection of Bay and East Broad streets. Known as the Pirates' House because of legends that it once was a place where men were shanghaied to serve on the vessels of buccaneers, Floyd turned it into a museum, and today tourists know it as a restaurant. Nearby was the Savannah Gas Company, a business purchased by Louisianan Hansell Hillyer soon after the war.

When Hillyer and his wife, Mary, moved to Savannah to run the business, they began restoring numbers of rundown houses in the Old Fort area near the gas company and Trustee Garden on the east side of the city. Here Savannah's first settlers tried unsuccessfully to grow such crops as grapes for winemaking and white Mulberry trees to be used as food for silkworms in the silk-production enterprise they planned to start. The Hillyers turned the slum area into sixty-one desirable offices and houses for the well-to-do. So devoted were they to Savannah preservation and so pivotal were their ideas regarding restoring areas of the city that, in 1999, their ashes were scattered in Trustee Garden.[85]

Although the first major preservation movement was not led by locals, the Hillyers, as "outsiders," inspired Savannahians who in the mid-1950s seized leadership of the city's modern preservation and restoration movement. More than three decades earlier, Savannah's "sister city," Charleston, became the first urban center in the Southeast to push for the preservation of its historic properties. Charleston's movement began on April 21, 1920, when Susan Pringle Frost, a progressive-minded real estate broker, met with the city's elite to formulate plans to prevent the threatened demolition of several early Charleston homes.[86] A similar event ignited Savannah's preservation passion.

By 1955, Savannah's government had a solution for what to do with the old City Market. A decision was made to tear down the city-owned Italianate marketplace on Ellis Square in order to build a more profitable entity, a parking garage. Savannah lost money yearly on City Market. Some thought it a filthy,

Over the centuries, various city markets stood on Ellis Square at Congress and Barnard streets. The old Italianate City Market, shown here ca. 1900, was demolished in 1954 to make way for a parking garage. The destruction of this beloved icon was the catalyst that launched the preservation movement in Savannah. Courtesy of Georgia Archives, Vanishing Georgia Collection, image no. ctm200.

rat-infested and odiferous nineteenth-century eyesore. And as Broughton Street was reviving, merchants desperately needed more parking for customers. City Market's location made it an ideal site. A demolition date was set. But many Savannahians had a deep affection for the property, and it did not take long before a "Save-the-Market" campaign gained momentum. Unfortunately, local preservationists came too late to the party. When the Save-the-Market coalition realized they were going to lose the fight, they cleaned up the market and staged a huge goodbye ball. Seven hundred showed up for the party dressed as fruits, vegetables, sacks of fertilizer, and the like, costumed to pay homage to the market's history.

The money raised at the ball went into the nonprofit Historic Savannah Foundation (HSF). When foundation supporters scanned the inventory of properties, they were alarmed to discover that one-third of the city's historic structures had been destroyed for one reason or another between 1930 and 1950. The HSF decided its resources would be best used to buy homes threatened by decay or destruction and then resell these to buyers who agreed not to tear down the structure but to restore it for a residence, office, or business. Elinor Adler and local art critic Anna Colquitt Hunter were among the seven women who were early promoters of the HSF. Ironically, Adler's husband, who owned a downtown store, had been among the group of businessmen advocating the City Market site as a parking garage.

The cadre of seven downtown Savannah women used their connections with the local garden club, the Junior League, and the Colonial Dames, among others, to save the Davenport House (1821), a decaying gem of English Regency–style architecture at Habersham and State streets. It was the first major property "saved" by the HSF. After decades of neglect by absentee owners who had moved to the suburbs or by native Savannahians who stood by passively as historic structures fell to the wrecking ball, the preservationists prevailed. Soon businessmen, realtors, the *Morning News,* the Chamber of Commerce, and city officials endorsed the "progressive spirit of preservation" and supported efforts to reinvigorate the downtown and expand tourism by saving the built environment and enhancing public squares.

In the late 1950s, the city government published a master plan for the "preservation of the original pedestrian-oriented atmosphere" of the city and prohibited any future construction that would destroy the historic "pattern, scale, and atmosphere" of downtown Savannah. Over the next several decades, the HSF saved and restored more than eleven hundred historic structures. The National Park Service designated a 2.5-square-mile area of the city as a Registered National Historic Landmark of "exceptional value"; gentrification with federal loans increased rapidly, and tourism soon became a major factor in the economic life of the city.[87]

Around the time the HSF was founded, Savannah city government sought and received federal funds for the largest urban-renewal project in the Southeast, the West Broad Street Project. Eighty percent of the area was slated for demolition; a historian of the urban South observed that Savannah's "energetic and innovative" white preservationists saved the city's downtown, but showed no concern over the threat urban renewal posed to black neighborhoods.[88]

West Broad Street, the thriving heart of the African American social, business, and entertainment district, was home to more than two hundred black-owned businesses, making Savannah one of the South's centers of black capitalism. But after urban renewal gutted the area, business owners were forced to relocate; they often failed to retain their customers or find new ones. Apparently, some businessmen were paid a pittance for their properties. The demolition on West Broad Street began in the late 1950s.[89]

One of the significant buildings to fall to the wrecking ball was Union Station. Built in 1902, Union Station was the centerpiece of West Broad Street. It served as the "gateway to Savannah," the symbolic entrance and exit to the city, a sign of Savannah's importance to the southeastern railway system and a reminder to passengers that Savannah was a prosperous and cosmopolitan place. The eclectic Spanish renaissance structure designed by Frank P. Milburn featured two towers and an eighty-foot octagonal rotunda spanned by a glass and iron roof. Building Union Station provided jobs for local black construction workers and later employment opportunities for porters and other service workers. More than ten thousand people visited the station on opening day to marvel at the new building. Many businesses sprang up along West Broad to serve those who disembarked on the commercial corridor; it was a hub of activity for all races and classes. Union Station also reinforced the notion of a segregated South with clearly marked racially divided waiting areas, ticket windows, and dining options.

By the 1950s, because of deferred maintenance and costly upkeep, Union Station had fallen into neglect. Outdated, lacking modern conveniences, and needing many repairs, the historic landmark was sold to the highway department in 1961 for approximately $775,000. It was demolished in 1963 to make way for Savannah's new "gateway," Interstate 16.[90]

Historian Charles Elmore recalled, "It made me sick when they tore [Union Station] down."[91] Besides razing the architecturally significant train station, wrecking crews in the name of urban renewal demolished other historic structures in the area like Saint Phillips Monumental Church and Saint Paul CME Church. Hovels in nearby Currytown and Frogtown that lacked indoor plumbing and other properties marked "dilapidated" came down as well.

Captain Frank Bynes's son, Raleigh, remembered the demolition of West Broad Street. Raleigh's father left the army at the end of World War II and purchased a funeral home at the corner of West Broad and Gaston streets. Nearby were restaurants, the Dunbar and another theater, physicians' offices, and a hotel. When urban renewal began, the city and federal government designated the terminus of Interstate 16 to empty into West Broad and Gaston: "They gave my daddy $28,000 to move from there and sold the property for two and a half million. That was a rip off."[92]

Leroy Beavers also grew up on West Broad Street—he said it was a "mecca" for Savannah's blacks. To him the razing of Union Station was "the beginning of the decay of West Broad [as] it was the hub of what was going on"; it was "terrible . . . in the 1960s [as] . . . I saw the decay start setting in [and] businesses

Union Station, gateway to Savannah, was built in 1902. Located on what was then West Broad Street, the elegant and eclectic Spanish-styled structure, one of the landmarks of Savannah, was torn down in 1963 to make way for another gateway to the city, Interstate 16. Courtesy of Georgia Archives, Vanishing Georgia Collection, image no. ctm184.

closing down."[93] Over time, fast-food restaurants, service stations, and a supermarket replaced the once substantial businesses, physician offices, theaters, restaurants, and bars on West Broad, today renamed Martin Luther King Jr. Boulevard.

A future and the first black mayor of the city, Floyd Adams Jr., son of the founder of the black weekly *Savannah Herald,* said of the experience, "Urban renewal came through here and cleared us out."[94] Adams believed the city fathers saw urban renewal as a good thing for all concerned. But it also "destroyed quite a few of the black businesses" and "displaced the black population who lived on the dirt streets of Currytown. And like the people in Yamacraw and Frogtown, they were dispersed and moved into public housing. Reflecting on the period, Adams said that "the initial urban renewal project moved black people away from their churches, from where they shopped and into public housing which mixed middle class blacks with the poor." In sum, Adams believed, if it could be done over again, a better option would have been to provide rental duplexes and single-family homes rather than the type of "projects" that were first built.[95]

Frustration within the black community grew as more black neighborhoods were destroyed. The white newspapers and city government justified the indiscriminate destruction, arguing the need to connect I-16 to downtown Savannah and to preserve city money drained by "slums." Proponents also expressed concern for tourists who had to walk through "diseased" and "crime-ridden" neighborhoods to reach downtown. The white-owned *Savannah Evening Press* said these African American neighborhoods were a "black shadow" over Savannah.[96]

Why did Savannah's African American community of the 1950s go along with urban-renewal programs? Certainly city and federal mandates would have been difficult to contradict; then too urban renewal created alternative housing options for some of the city's most needy. There is also the possibility that some segments of the African American community may have thought that being a cooperative partner in this venture might provide a path forward to address other long-standing grievances.

One aspect of urban renewal did concern white preservationists: they worried that blacks displaced by the wrecking ball might move closer to the city's historic edge, taking over deteriorating dwellings and curbing the revival of downtown Savannah. To prevent this, part of the city's redevelopment plans included federal funds to build low-cost public housing that would channel displaced blacks beyond Savannah's Historic District. Black neighborhoods within the Historic District on the east side received quite different treatment.

Here restoration, not demolition, became the goal. The HSF "exploited" generous loans from the federal government and worked with the city to restore a line of historic row houses in Troup Ward on the eastern edge of the Historic District. Of course, the displaced blacks could not afford to rent the renovated row houses, and the neighborhood became "gentrified" as upper-class whites bought them and moved in. The success in Troup Ward encouraged preservationists who, hand in hand with the city government, doubled the size of the Historic District by pushing southward into Victorian-era neighborhoods.[97] Within a few years, a second wave of Savannah's preservation and restoration movement began.

Other southern cities had their West Broad Street counterparts, Auburn Avenue in Atlanta, Fulton Street in Richmond, Market Street in Greensboro, Beale Street in Memphis—all experienced Savannah's initial brand of urban renewal. Savannah's African American residents, like some of their displaced colleagues in other cities, initially supported urban renewal, but some views changed as they saw and experienced the repercussions of the relocations for many families.

Savannah blacks readily acknowledged important milestones and accomplishments: they comprised about 40 percent of the population; half of eligible black voters were registered; black policemen patrolled black neighborhoods; a committee of prominent black citizens now advised the mayor, and the city's aggressive NAACP chapter was thriving under the leadership of its "charismatic" president, W. W. Law.[98]

The African American community's relationship with Mayor Lee Mingledorff appeared cordial. He convened black leaders, listened to their concerns, and tried to solve problems. Mingledorff collaborated with the NAACP to address concerns about police abuse of black citizens, supported building two black schools, approved hiring of five women as the first African American street-crossing guards, removed the segregation signs in Union Station, and supported garbage workers when they struck for higher wages in July 16, 1956. As tons of smelly garbage piled up around the city in the hot summer sun, Mayor Mingledorff negotiated with representatives of the union and secured modest pay raises for strikers who returned to work within three days. Subsequently, the City Council increased the minimum wage of all city laborers to one dollar an hour.[99]

To some black Savannahians, Mingledorff seemed to be an ally who was willing to work with them to solve long-held grievances. But frustrations grew. When it became apparent that efforts to gain equal rights under the law had failed, when discrimination and subtle harassment continued, when the West Broad Street community found itself torn apart in the name of urban renewal, when displaced black businesses found themselves closing, when black businesses owners discovered they had been paid significantly less than their properties' value, when uprooted black families found their refurbished homes sold to the white elite, when news of civil rights violations and demonstrations were reported daily in local media, a younger, less patient generation of African Americans stepped forward fully prepared to use more aggressive tactics in the fight for equal rights under the law.

Community Leadership Seminar of Savannah

In May 1958, Savannahians voted to approve the four- rather than two-year terms for mayor and City Council members. On October 6, Lee Mingledorff was sworn in for a second time. The following year in the interest of urban renewal, city government ordered thirty-six black families to vacate their substandard homes.[100] In 1960 the Savannah Metropolitan Area included Savannah, Thunderbolt, Garden City, and Port Wentworth. Even with 24,000 persons added to the demographic by expanding the city limits, Savannah's population of 150,000 no longer ranked it among the top twenty southern cities in population. Central-city Savannah experienced more white flight to suburbia. Chatham County could already envision problems related to this decrease in population.

To the credit of local leaders, city government and the Chamber of Commerce supported Dr. John W. Fanning of the University of Georgia who, in the 1950s, proposed and established the Community Leadership Seminar of Savannah. The purpose of this group was to develop potential city leaders. Members came from civic, business, education. and social and cultural communities. Over an intense one-year orientation, this "select group," initially all men, participated in seminars, discussions, and other experiences that were structured to make them better informed about all aspects of community life—demographics, the economy, cultural life, poverty, health, education, and the city's assets and detractors. Leadership Savannah served as a training ground for future leaders, the expectation being that the group would become effective and progressive agents of change in the community. Leadership Savannah became both the inspiration and the model for Leadership Georgia.[101]

Since the late 1950s, one important training opportunity for Leadership Savannah was an annual seminar that brought participants and business and civic leaders together with University of Georgia faculty to study the city and to explore ways to chart a better path forward. Academic specialists in economics, culture, accounting, sociology, and architecture presented papers on issues that did, could, or would affect the quality of life in Savannah.

In the early 1960s, lecturers congratulated the city for its Metropolitan Planning Commission and commitment to ongoing urban renewal, but expressed concern about "blight" and the large number of substandard structures (roughly 40 percent of the city) and unpaved streets.[102] The faculty who spoke on architectural issues told the audience that Savannah visitors today see "the sad face of a city once well built" and now "scared." Only one-third of the original squares were "free of blight," and most were surrounded by "vacant lots, derelict buildings . . . used car [dealerships]" and were crisscrossed "by utility lines." Venerable buildings like the Telfair Academy were "confronted by a display of commercial squalor . . . its façade reduced to . . . a poor surrealist joke." Several faculty made reference to another neglected resource, the disused riverfront, "cut off by a wall of warehouses. . . . [It] should be visually linked" to the city to create "a dramatic symbol of the source of the city's prosperity."[103]

Other deficiencies noted in the presentations were a lack of adequate recreational facilities, substandard ratings of 154 school classrooms and forty school sites, nine schools in such poor condition they needed to be abandoned, hospitals able to meet only one-third of the needs of citizens, inadequate public welfare facilities, and many crowded city administrative offices in need of repair. And the list went on: libraries were "badly located," the city fire-alarm system was obsolete, and most industrial areas just outside Savannah received inadequate fire-protection services.[104]

A professor from UGA's School of School of Social Work identified the cycle of poverty as one of the city's greatest challenges; he expressed concern that local government may be unable to fund investments to address this need because such a large portion of city revenue was required to pay down its debt service and operating costs.[105]

Another speaker said that Savannah must find ways to reduce racial tensions; otherwise the city might follow the path of "Little Rock and New Orleans," cities that paid dearly "for their handling of the integration issue, not only in lost industry, but in other ways." Recurring themes were to "broaden the tax base," recruit new industry, expand the ports, seize the "enormous potential source of income in import-export trade," and aggressively develop Savannah's "tourist and recreation business." The city's "rich history" is a strategic advantage that places Savannah "in an ideal position to attract large numbers of tourists."[106]

Why Mayor Mingledorff and subsequent mayors Maclean and Lewis did not move expeditiously to tackle the issues identified in this academic conclave might have been the reluctance to spend, the pushback from citizens who did not want substantive changes or higher taxes, and the fact that the mayors now devoted a good portion of their energies to rising racial tensions in the 1960s.[107]

Civil Rights

In 1957 the Savannah and Chatham County Christian Ministerial Association protested the ban of blacks at Tybee Beach and asked the governor and Chatham County commissioners to set aside a section of the beach for blacks. There was no response. The next year, prominent black leaders again asked the city and county to appoint African Americans to the Board of Education. No action was taken.

It was then that NAACP President W. W. Law announced that the local organization planned to support anyone who wished to bring suit against the school board's segregation policies. In 1959 the local NAACP issued a formal request asking the Savannah School Board to make public its plans for integrating the local schools in light of the earlier Supreme Court decision in *Brown v. the Topeka Board of Education.* During the same year, black students tried without success to enroll in the all-white Groves High School. Black citizens continued to be denied the use of the Bull Street Library, and eleven blacks were prohibited from playing on Savannah's Municipal Golf Course.[108]

On February 1, 1960, around 4:45 P.M., four African American college students in Greensboro, North Carolina, took seats at the whites-only lunch counter of F. W. Woolworth's. Ignored by the waitress, they remained seated until the store closed at 5:30 and then departed. Little did they know that this action had launched the "modern" confrontational phase of the civil rights movement.

Within two months, sit-ins occurred in seventy-eight cities in thirteen southern states. By this time, the national Student Nonviolent Coordinating Committee had called also for the desegregation of parks, swimming pools, museums, and art galleries.[109] White Savannah guardedly watched the movement emerge.

Although the virulent hostility of whites toward blacks that existed in many rural towns was not as prevalent in Savannah, the discrimination and white-supremacist views experienced in the city resembled those of the Old South. Savannah's long history as an urban center and a major port contributed somewhat to a more cosmopolitanism outlook. Nonetheless in Savannah there was a remarkable level of African American protest, even though the violence was restrained somewhat by the influence of local black leaders like W. W. Law and Eugene Gadsden.[110]

Decades of African American protest in Savannah for civil rights contributed to the city's leadership of the movement in Georgia. In the 1960s, Otis Johnson, a local student activist and future mayor, observed: "This community has a very sophisticated form of racism, it is not nigger-nigger racism like in Alabama or Mississippi." Another protest leader of the period, nineteen-year-old Benjamin Van Clark, described local racism as a "tokenism and do-nothingism of white people when confronted."[111]

A reporter in the *Atlanta Journal* seeking to account for white Savannah's attitudes observed in June 1960: "Savannah society is traditionally self-contained and aloof from the rest of Johnny-come-lately Georgia. Savannah aristocrats nod coolly to Atlanta, smile at Charleston, but bow only to London and Florence."[112] Mayor Malcolm Maclean perhaps had a more pragmatic view as he dealt with the era's unrest: "preserve Savannah's good name."[113]

Learning of the sit-ins in Atlanta, the *Morning News* warned they are harmful and may cost the "Negro" important gains. In contrast, Savannah's black press, the *Tribune* and the *Herald,* praised the young people "who are willing to endure the humiliation of arrests. . . . The nine white students and the Negro students who submitted to arrests in the sit-down strikes along with the fellow Negro students will some day be acclaimed as the champions of liberty."[114]

All was quiet in the city until the St. Patrick's Day eve, March 16, 1960, when three local black students sat down at the whites-only lunch counter in Levy's Department Store on Broughton Street, among them Carolyn Quilloin, a member of the local NAACP Youth Council. The group was denied service and asked to leave. When the students refused, they were arrested. Apparently, the students presented several demands: desegregation of the lunch counters as well as water fountains, bathrooms, and dressing rooms as well as employment of African American salespeople and an end to arrests of demonstrators. W. W. Law later admitted that the NAACP trained and supported the students in a nonviolent approach to integration. The organization also arranged for a local beauty culturist to post a three-hundred-dollar bond for each student. The *Morning News* once again sounded a warning: "These sit downs pose . . . the possibility of violence."[115]

When asked how the sit-ins started, Curtis Cooper, a local activist at the time, said that the Savannah "NAACP Youth Council here wanted to start sitting in." Cooper was on the board of the local NAACP, and that board told the Youth Council, "no, don't do it because if you get in jail we have no assurance that we can get you out." Nevertheless, "the kids were making plans to do it . . . and they did it on their own." But when they went and "sat in and got put in jail, [we had to get them out]."[116]

One of those involved in training the young protesters was Hosea Williams, who had seen violence up close when fighting in Europe in World War II. A trained chemist who worked in Savannah, Hosea Williams believed his commitment to civil rights came from a transforming experience in the trenches during the war. An exploding shell killed all of the soldiers near him and ripped open his stomach, but when he returned to Savannah on crutches, he was "roughed up" in the bus terminal when he tried to drink from a water fountain. Like other black veterans, he was angry, "eager and unafraid." As one of the trainers for the nonviolent protest movement, he described the training experience: they slapped the kids, kicked them, spit in their faces, and "we did it to one another, so when we went down town we were prepared for anything."

Five more young black students sat in at Levy's lunch counter on March 18. They were denied service, refused to leave, and were arrested. Other arrests followed as more sit-ins occurred. Sidney Barnes, Savannah's chief of police, worried things were spiraling out of control. He asked the governor to send twenty state troopers to the city, which the governor did.

Ministers march, Savannah, ca. 1960s. W. W. Law may be on the far left. 1121-100_0070. W. W. Law Photograph Collection. Courtesy of the City of Savannah, Research Library & Municipal Archives.

Six days after the first arrests, NAACP President W. W. Law held a mass meeting at the Bolton Street Baptist Church, where he asked for the moral and financial support of the black community. It was forthcoming.[117] The determination of Law, Williams, Eugene Gadsden, Carolyn Quilloin, Mercedes Wright Arnold, Curtis Cooper, and countless others fostered the success of the Savannah movement. In an interview, Cooper remembered growing up in segregated Savannah. He described three restrooms at the Chatham Service Station: there was one for "white men, white ladies and then colored." Cooper had vivid memories of walking by Broughton Street restaurants, where he would "see foreigners who would get off the ships on the waterfront and they could come and go to the restaurants and . . . and Levy's Department Store." These sailors had "more privileges than those of us who were registered voters and citizens of this country. . . . [T]his really got under our skin and we got together and started the sit ins."[118]

Mr. Cooper described also "a boycott to try to make the merchants negotiate" and traveling to all the surrounding towns and black churches and schools, asking them not to shop in Savannah. Cooper spoke of the black community's reliance on the Spiegel catalog for shopping during the year-and-a-half boycott and of the picketing on Broughton Street, but then "the police got so mean and nasty they would let people beat us up." Cooper said, "We knew they [the police] were part of the conspiracy—they'd spit on us, beat you up," and so the protesters resorted to "silent pickets"—people would not carry signs but would wear ribbons; people wearing a ribbon "we knew to be a friend." One of their jobs was to "take the names of people who violated the boycott and we would call them out at the churches on Sunday"—they had a "traitors list."

One of the coleaders of the boycott was Mercedes Wright Arnold, who in a 1990 interview shared similar memories of the sit-ins, the boycott, and push-back from the white community. Described as a "grass roots" leader of Savannah's civil rights movement, light-skinned Mercedes Wright Arnold was born in Washington, D.C., on November 2, 1933. She grew up in Savannah in the large Bolton Street home of her foster mother, Georgia Reid, after the deaths of her own parents and grandparents. Ms. Reid "mothered" Mercedes, inspiring her to be a "voracious reader" and teaching her some life lessons about private protest, such as to shop only at one of the two Jewish groceries in the neighborhood, Myer Tannenbaum's, because he always addressed blacks using courtesy titles, unlike the other store's proprietor. Georgia Reid told Mercedes, you "don't pay to be insulted."

As a young child Mercedes came face-to-face with blatant racism at the Old Factor's Walk public library. She entered, browsed, and selected a book, but when she attempted to check it out, an older woman told her, "Little niggers cannot carry books out." This was Mercedes's first encounter with discrimination, and she never forgot the incident.[119]

Georgia Reid planned for Mercedes to attend college, but at sixteen she ran away to marry Daniel W. Wright Jr., "an industrious man," and remained married for twenty-eight years, rearing three children. With boundless energy, she volunteered for a variety of causes, such as welfare clinics for African American women.

One day in the late 1950s, as Mercedes's children played on the swings at Forsyth Park, a policeman sauntered toward them, brandishing a nightstick "in a menacing fashion." He told her the park was reserved for whites only. Enraged, Mercedes screamed at the policeman that the swings were for the taxpaying citizens of Savannah, that she probably paid more taxes than he did, and did not give a damn what the law was. She swept up her children and left the park. Her growing awareness of racial inequity and her anger over this indignity propelled her into the civil rights movement.[120]

Woman participating in Bargain Corner boycott demonstration, Savannah, May 1963. 1121-100_0659. W. W. Law Photograph Collection. Courtesy of City of Savannah, Research Library & Municipal Archives.

When the sit-ins began, Mercedes volunteered at NAACP headquarters, located at 1216 West Broad Street. She joined the picket lines, where she saw "young toughs" with blackjacks rough up picketers at Woolworth's Five and Dime and Levy's Department Store; in one incident, the jaws of two young black men, Ben West and James McMillan, were broken. Policemen occasionally overlooked such incidents and sometimes themselves waded into the fray against the picketers with billy clubs. Bloody racial fights among teenagers broke out in Forsyth Park.

Some well-to-do and middle-class black business and professional men opposed the sit-ins and boycott. They feared for the tranquility of their community and told Mercedes: "You are going to get children killed . . . your husband fired . . . and your children are going to starve." She responded that she "had to follow her heart, mind and conscience."

Mrs. Arnold remembered some of the well-to-do African Americans, like dentist Dr. J. W. Jamerson Jr. and businessmen Bowles Ford, who provided financial support for the movement, as did members of the Jewish community; she recalled especially Leo and Miriam Center and Aaron and Esther Buchbaum.

As the protests continued, Mrs. Arnold observed, working people of the African American community become so enraged by the treatment of black youngsters, who only sought their "Constitutional rights," that they too became enthusiastic supporters of the movement. At one of NAACP President W. W. Law's Sunday mass meetings, twenty-five hundred supporters voted to undertake a total economic boycott of downtown businesses until charges against the students were dropped.

Mercedes Arnold and Curtis Cooper were appointed cochairs of the Boycott Committee. The eighteen-month boycott was said to have been 99 percent effective.[121] In April 1960, the City Council passed an anti-picketing ordinance. Mercedes took to the phones to make sure the black community knew "what was being done and why." A Savannah attorney, Eugene Gadsden, called her "a moving spirit who had a really good common touch with the people and [she was] a good speaker."[122]

On August 17, 1960, Mercedes organized what likely was the country's first successful "wade in." She transported a dozen students to Tybee Island, the local beach resort, where the group, including some nonswimmers, waded into the Atlantic Ocean, singing the black spiritual "Wade in the Water," until chased away by white bathers. Police briefly detained Mercedes, but the mayor of Tybee Beach declared the beach open to all. Mercedes also participated in "kneel-ins" at Savannah's white churches—at most, black worshipers were turned away—and in "bus-ins" on the city transit system.[123]

Backlash, the Boycott, and Angry Protests

Occasionally, the local White Citizens Council and other extremist groups threatened the boycotters. The Ku Klux Klan burned eighteen-foot crosses near the town of Bloomingdale, at a field in Port Wentworth, and on the lawn of Hosea Williams's home in Thunderbolt. Over 250 robed Klansmen marched down Broughton Street. Klan intimidation escalated when its members hurled bricks into the homes of Savannah's NAACP leaders with a note warning, "Sit in and we will blow you to hell. Nigger stay in your place." The *Tribune* shot back: "The colored community refuses to be intimidated by men who parade under the disguise of hoods."[124]

Mayor Lee Mingledorff, who favored a "law and order" approach, told the police to "clamp down" on the protesters. He appointed a biracial committee to negotiate some resolution between businessmen and the boycotters, but the NAACP refused to meet with Mingledorff's committee, calling it "stacked," handpicked to achieve his ends, not those of the black community. What the NAACP wanted was every privilege whites had, "nothing more or nothing less," complete desegregation. The *Morning News* charged that "outsiders" and communist sympathizers were leading the local movement.[125]

Regarding the city's April 1960 antipicketing ordinance, Mercedes Wright Arnold commented that it "took away our constitutional rights." She believed Mayor Mingledorff repressed black efforts to secure equal treatment under the law. Indeed, when confronted by an Atlanta newspaper about the legality of the ordinance outlawing picketing by "two or more persons," Mayor Mingledorff commented, "I don't especially care whether it's constitutional or not."[126]

After the anti-picketing ordinance was passed, the boycott and the civil rights movement went underground. Mercedes and her committees telephoned nightly and distributed leaflets during the day to keep the people informed and committed to the movement. Instead of carrying picket signs (now outlawed), the protesters wore black ribbons and walked up and down Broughton Street in silent protest. At church meetings W. W. Law appealed to congregations to put up their property as collateral to obtain bail money to free young boycotters who had been arrested and jailed. Meanwhile, attorney Eugene Gadsden challenged the anti-picketing law and took the case to the U.S. Supreme Court, where the law was declared unconstitutional.

Sales of Broughton Street merchants continued to plummet. Stores hemorrhaged money. The silent boycott continued. Mercedes Wright Arnold described Mayor Mingledorff as "recalcitrant [and] hateful" toward any negotiation. She attributed his attitude to precipitating the founding of the Chatham County Crusade for Voters (CCCV), a black voter-registration movement that grew from 3,500 in 1960 to 22,000 in 1964.

Although blacks comprised only one-third of the city's population, 57 percent of eligible blacks were registered voters, a higher proportion than in the white community.[127] Curtis Cooper said in an interview that, to him, Mayor "Mingledorff was totally uncooperative, he was against integration." And so, when Mr. Mingledorff stepped down as mayor in May 1960, ostensibly to run for a seat on the County Commission, Curtis Cooper said that blacks united to vote against him, "and he lost that race." Mingledorff, in Cooper's view, "was against the sit ins and had us put in jail. . . . [W]hen he said he was going to run for the county commission . . . the blacks "decided that [it] was time to retire him from public service. . . . [W]e stood in the rain, blacks were there dripping

Voter-registration demonstration, Savannah. 1121-100_0657, W. W. Law Photograph Collec-tion. Courtesy of the City of Savannah, Research Library & Municipal Archives.

with water, waiting to get in to vote against this man." Through this experience, the black community learned that "if you put your votes together you can stop something, you can change something."

By bloc voting, blacks played a major role in electing a moderate slate in 1960 after Mingledorff resigned. Many suspected that Mingledorff left office because of his frustration in dealing with the seemingly irresolvable civil rights conflict and with trying to placate both the white and the African American communities. With Mingledorff's resignation, the president pro-tem of City Council, Malcolm Maclean, automatically assumed the office of mayor. Eugene Gadsden told the author that Maclean "made all the difference in the world."[128]

Maclean, born on Long Island, New York, grew up in Savannah, a city where some of his ancestors first settled. Educated in private schools, as well as at Yale and Harvard, Maclean served in World War II and then practiced law in Savannah. After assuming the mayorship, he immediately appointed an advisory board and opened a dialogue with black community leaders like W. W. Law, Curtis Cooper, Eugene Gadsden, and Mercedes Wright Arnold.[129] But a setback to these new efforts to find common ground could have developed when federal charges were leveled against the NAACP president, W. W. Law.

The Campaign against W. W. Law

The local campaign against Law had been going on for more than a year. Many white citizens, incensed especially by the business boycotts and sit-ins, saw Law as the primary instigator. Letters to Congressman Preston informed him of the "deplorable" situation in Savannah, "due the active part being played by negro agitators led by a certain negro postal carrier by the name of W. W. Law. . . . [B]usiness in this county has been seriously curtailed by the selfish, unlawful acts led by this uncouth character. . . . I respectfully demand through you that the Post Office Department bring charges against [him]." To which Preston replied, "I join you in deploring the illegal sit-down protests. . . . [T]hese activities accomplish nothing but only serve to promote racial strife." The congressman wrote that he was heartened that "a large segment of the negro population in Savannah is not joining these activities which have been inspired and promoted by northern racial extremists." He assured his constituent that he had been "looking into the illegality of the activities of the Savannah postal service employee, W. W. Law."

In corresponding with another Savannahian, Preston expressed his feelings about the 1960 Civil Rights Bill's recent passage, "I think it is tragic, indeed, that such a bill was passed at all because it definitely is not needed." He blamed its passage on his left-wing colleagues from the West and North who, he said, "delighted in passing legislation punitive to the South.[130]

On July 11, 1961, the U.S. Post Office dismissed Law ostensibly for code violations, more specifically for urinating in public. The NAACP declared the charges against him were "trumped up." Law claimed that the local postmaster, Marcus Stubbs, "put a tail on . . . him" and followed Law around in "an effort to get him." Law admitted that during his sixteen years as a postman he had stood behind trees in parks to relieve himself because there were no "black-only" restrooms on his route.

Political motivations were soon revealed when the pubic learned that the top aide of Postmaster General Edward Day had promised First District

Congressman C. Elliot Hagan that Law would be dismissed. In his congressional campaign Hagan said, "If I was a member of Congress there is one particular NAACP bigwig right here in Savannah who would cease to work for the U.S. Post Office Department." The firing of Law "violated every federal regulation." A three-member committee heard the charges against Law and recommended his reinstatement. Postmaster Day did so, but asserted that he would not "want a person of Law's record of conduct delivering mail to my family home."[131]

Both blacks and whites were outraged at Day's remarks. President John Kennedy made Day retract his comments and soon thereafter fired the postmaster general. Briefly, Law became a celebrity. The whole matter enhanced his own reputation and attracted more people to the local NAACP. The *Morning News* wrote that "Law was returned to duty so that he would not become a martyr." Congressman Hagan and Senator Talmadge called for a full investigation, but nothing came of their demands.[132]

Negotiating an End to the Boycott

Talks continued between Mayor Maclean, his advisory committee, and the Broughton Street businessmen who increasingly felt the economic pinch from the boycott. Blacks wanted lunch counters opened to African Americans, black clerks to be hired by businesses, restrooms to be desegregated, and to have courtesy titles used when being addressed. Some businessmen worried that, if they gave in to the black boycott, a white boycott might follow. But after losing over a million dollars and with sales still plunging, the Broughton Street businessmen agreed to integrate their lunch counters and to implement other requests for changes. In July 1961 lunch counters were desegregated in the city and in the growing businesses on the south side of Savannah.[133] That fall, Mayor Maclean, his advisory committee, and the City Council succeeded in integrating the Bull Street Library, public parks, the municipal golf course, the bus drivers of the Savannah Transit system, and the bus-station and airport cafes.[134]

Meanwhile, the white Chatham County Citizens Council urged the governor to send the state patrol to Savannah to enforce segregation laws, and they voted to boycott any integrated schools. Other setbacks occurred. When young blacks were arrested on the basketball courts at Daffin Park and charged with and found guilty of unlawful assembly, the local NAACP posted their bonds and attorney Eugene Gadsden took their case to the Georgia Supreme Court. He lost there but won the case before the U.S. Supreme Court in *Wright v. Georgia*.

During the 1962 mayoralty campaign, Maclean promised to hire more blacks at City Hall, to add more black firemen, to increase the number of black policemen and give them the authority to arrest any offender. Despite charges that he had allowed "Communist outsiders" to take over the local government, Maclean beat Grady Darby in the mayor's race. The bloc votes of the city's African American community no doubt helped secure his election.

True to his word, once in office Maclean hired African Americans for positions in the city's Revenue and Personnel departments. Previously, blacks had held jobs in City Hall only as custodians and messengers. And Maclean added other black employees to the city payroll as well. Hosea Williams, who had recruited and registered large numbers of black voters, wrote after Maclean's victory: "so [as] the *Negroes* go," so goes the election.[135]

Upon the recommendation of Mayor Maclean's advisory committee of prominent blacks and whites, Maclean asked the owners of the downtown theaters—the Lucas, Weis, and Savannah—to open their doors to blacks. They agreed to do. However, shortly after opening on June 4, 1963, Albert Weis announced: "Due to the tremendous number of messages and calls from the [public], the Weis and Savannah theaters will not be integrated until all other public and private concerns also . . . integrate."[136] Since one theater owner had reneged on his agreement to desegregate, Hosea Williams seized the opportunity to launch an even more aggressive wave of protests.

Mercedes Arnold once described Williams as an "unguided missile," not a team player.[137] As the leader of the Chatham County Crusade for Voters (CCCV), he declared his group "independent" of any other organizations. Williams clashed with W. W. Law over the tactics of protests. Williams was something of a firebrand—he favored dramatic speeches, bold confrontations, protest marches, and public demonstrations. Law pursued a low-key approach in settling matters with the city government. Law opposed the night marches, which he believed escalated the violence. Mr. Law also wanted to insure that the local NAACP continued to be recognized as the voice of the local black community. Whatever their differences privately, publicly Williams and Law appeared united during the summer of 1963.

In early June, Williams and Benjamin Van Clark launched a series of mass marches into Johnson Square in the heart of the business and commercial district of the city. Here Williams's speeches whipped up the crowd. City Manager Arthur A. "Don" Mendonsa said "the city never attempted to stop [the] marching though we did ask that they tell us . . . their route . . . so we could ensure where they were going for the safety of all concerned." Usually, Mendonsa and the city attorney were present to make sure "the police did not overreact" and conducted "themselves within the law."[138] Mendonsa described one "tense" situation when about one thousand demonstrators marched into

W. W. Law, right, and others examine 1962 NAACP membership banner, Savannah. 1121-100_0069. W. W. Law Photograph Collection. Courtesy of City of Savannah, Research Library & Municipal Archives.

the intersection of Bull and Broughton streets around lunchtime on June 11 to protest the slow pace of desegregation. Helmeted police looked on but did not interfere when several hundred demonstrators broke away and marched on City Hall. There Mayor Maclean agreed to meet with some in City Council chambers. Their spokesman, Benjamin Van Clark, told the mayor he had twenty-four hours to give the demonstrators their "freedoms." Unsure of what was meant by their "freedoms," Maclean responded by saying he could not force private businesses to conduct business if they did not want to do so. Maclean explained that his duty was "to maintain law, order, and public services."

That same evening, several hundred demonstrators attended a three-hour "freedom rally" at St. Philip Monumental AME Church. Afterwards they joined about three thousand "chanting protesters" who marched along city streets and around Johnson Square, which had been closed that day by the city. Again, police units monitored the events but did not interfere. Chief of Police Sidney

B. Barnes Jr. said of the incident, "We had a real riotous situation . . . here today." That same day National Guard troops provided escorts for two black students entering the University of Alabama, and in Charleston black students began their second day of sit-ins at white lunch counters.[139]

Demonstrations continued in Savannah. Hosea Williams reported that the police had arrested more than six hundred black citizens by June 14, 1963. As the heat of the approaching summer rose, so did the frustration level of the demonstrators. In the early morning hours of June 20, the Fire Department headquarters received a call from "an unidentified Negro man" who reported "a box was on fire" at the rear of the Firestone Building at West Broad and Broughton streets. By the time firemen reached the scene, portions of the roof were ablaze, and the intense heat in the interior of the building caused a side of the large brick building to collapse. It took several hours to bring the blaze under control. A firefighter told the press that "the building was gone before we got there." One fireman was injured, and estimates of the damage reached $500,000. Following the blaze, the city's fire inspector investigated reports that "Negro boys" were seen near the store just before the fire, and he began "working under the idea that it could have been arson."[140]

Two days after the fire, the Reverend Ralph Abernathy, secretary-treasurer of the Southern Christian Leadership Conference (SCLC) arrived in Savannah. During a rally of one thousand at the First Bryan Baptist Church at Bolton and West Broad streets, he told the audience that the SCLC pledged "all-out financial and moral support" for Savannah's "anti-segregation movement." That same day the Cavalcade of White Americas picketed outside stores that had opened their lunch counters to blacks. Their signs urging people not to trade at integrated stores read "Buy White" and "Segregation or Mongrelization."[141]

On June 25, after a series of protest marches, Mayor Maclean hosted a meeting at City Hall between white businessmen and representatives from the African American community with the hope of negotiating a time frame to begin the integration of certain businesses in the city.[142] Their inability to agree upon a speedy desegregation timetable only increased frustration among the demonstrators, and their protests gathered momentum and led to more arrests.

After assembling at Mt. Tabor Baptist Church at Henry and East Broad streets late on the night of July 6, Hosea Williams led some 450 demonstrators to a point opposite the jail on Habersham Street, where some of the boycotters were incarcerated. Here Williams led a forty-minute song-and-prayer meeting. Protesters imprisoned inside showed their appreciation by lighting small makeshift torches. Williams announced another march the following day. City officials, he said, were "getting tough," and he was tired of the city manager,

Don Mendonsa, "telling me what to do." Williams promised to speed up the pace of demonstrations, and he did.[143]

Georgia's U.S. senators, Richard Russell and Herman Talmadge, condemned the Civil Rights Bill pending in Congress, claiming that extremist "left wing Democrats, the NAACP, and the Americans for Democratic Action" were behind it. Talmadge said publicly that, if the bill passed, it "would destroy the United States as we have known it for nearly 200 years." First District Congressman Elliott Hagan voiced the same opinion. Apparently this rhetoric inspired leaders of the Ku Klux Klan. In Atlanta the Klan announced plans to launch a large-scale campaign of white resistance to racial integration.[144]

Hosea Williams was arrested for the third time at 3:00 A.M. on July 9 on warrants sworn out by downtown white residents who charged that they lived in constant fear because of the demonstrations. With Williams now in jail, leadership of the CCCV passed to young Benjamin Van Clark, who organized the ongoing protests.[145]

At noon on the day of Williams's arrest, some 150 demonstrators marched through downtown Savannah. At Bull and Broughton streets, 26 "negroes," mostly juveniles, left the march and lay down at the intersection of Broughton and Bull, blocking traffic. Police immediately arrested them for violation of a city ordinance. In the evening, Benjamin Van Clark; Juanita Williams, Hosea's wife; and the Rev. C. T. Vivian, who had been sent to Savannah by Martin Luther King Jr., addressed hundreds of demonstrators at the Flamingo Recreation Center on West Gwinnett Street. Vivian excoriated the black ministers who disapproved of the protest tactics, telling them they "are going to have to serve God for freedom or serve elsewhere." After Van Clark issued an "ultimatum" to Mayor Maclean to end segregation, some 900 African Americans marched to City Hall. The demonstration did not end until the early morning hours.[146]

Williams's arrest triggered violence at the police station on July 10 when protestors lay down at the intersection of Habersham and Oglethorpe. They threatened to join Hosea Williams in the nearby Chatham County Jail, but City Manager Don Mendonsa persuaded them to do otherwise. According to the *Morning News,* "the demonstration of about 1,000 was different and wilder than in the preceding weeks." Hundreds of "shouting, singing Negro demonstrators . . . slashed automobiles tires [and] broke windows" in downtown Savannah; state troopers rushed to the city to aid local police, who were using tear gas and water hoses to disperse massed demonstrators. At one point a mob faced down the police and threw bricks at them. Several policemen were injured, and a young protester was shot in the foot, but by 2:00 A.M. the violence had subsided.

The day following, the lead editorial in the *Morning News* called for a "Crack Down on Disorders," saying the "community's patience with lawless demonstrators is at an end. . . . [T]he streets . . . must be made safe. . . . Lawlessness must end—and it must end now."[147] Various tactics were used to control rioting crowds. One of them was tear gas, which both protestors and residents loathed. Mayor Maclean expressed more tolerance for the use of gas because it "does discourage people from running around on the streets, so they all go home after awhile." During this same period, Charleston police were threatening to use fire hoses to bring similar protest under control.[148]

In spite of calls for calm, violence erupted again in Savannah. This time on the west side of the city during the early morning of July 11 an estimated 1,000 "rioters" smashed windows, slashed tires, blocked traffic, started fires, and threw stones at police and motorists. Flames enveloped a portion of the Bible Baptist Church on Waters Avenue—a church whose minister championed segregation—and flames gutted a vacant building on West Broad Street. In both cases investigators suspected arson. Reverend W. R. Tally, minister of the Derenne Baptist Church, placed "men armed with automatic shotguns" to guard his church and moved his wife and two children to the homes of members of his congregation because of threats. A rock smashed the windshield of City Manager Don Mendonsa's vehicle as he and Mayor Maclean tried to assist police struggling to keep the protesters from reaching the downtown business district. Demonstrators pulled large refuse cans into intersections to block streets on the west side.[149]

Mayor Maclean was present also when the protesters massed near dusk at the foot of the Talmadge Bridge. Here they began pulling dumpsters into the paths of cars coming off the bridge into the city. Maclean had a front-row seat for observing several crashes and wondered to himself what kind of "nonviolent" protest this was. When the mayor saw Andrew Young, then leader of the SCLC, he asked him, "What are you doing in Savannah?" Young replied: "We're sending a message to Senator Dirksen" to support the Civil Rights Bill pending in Congress. When Maclean asked Young why he wasn't doing this in Chicago, Young replied that Dirksen "will hear it from here," too. As Young rounded "up his troops" to leave, police began arresting the demonstrators, including Young and Benjamin Van Clark. With city jails now jammed with protesters, Young and Van Clark were taken to holding cells at Travis Field. Later that night, Maclean sent cars and brought Young and Van Clark to his office, where they talked until "three or four" in the morning about how to resolve the situation in ways that would be mutually beneficial to all.[150] The *Morning News* account of the demonstrations fueled a growing backlash among white and some black Savannahians.

"Rioting Negroes Stone Cars, Set Fires, Smash Windows," blared the headline of the *Morning News* on July 12, 1963. A photograph showed the image of a fire-gutted building and a front-page article, "Bond for Williams Placed at $30,000," described how the bond amount had been increased because of additional warrants sworn out against him and because Williams had been arrested twice before. His lawyers were unable to get his bond reduced or charges dismissed. Williams remained in jail for more than two months—at the time, the longest term of incarceration of any civil rights activists. The *Morning News* expressed the opinion of many in the community that "lawless demonstrators" must be brought under control.[151]

Mayor Maclean now adopted a tougher stand. He announced that whatever steps necessary would be taken to "keep down violence" in the city. Chatham County Sheriff Carl Griffin thought it was "past time to enforce or enact laws" to protect citizens and no doubt applauded Governor Carl Sanders's promise to "curb racial violence" and "protect life and property." Another fifty state troopers were dispatched to assist the two-hundred-member police force, and National Guard troops were placed on standby "to meet any new mass violence."

W. W. Law asked the leaders of "those doing mischief to bring them under control." Twenty-four local clergy, including three bishops, called for racial peace and announced a "truce" had been reached. Some reasoned that, if the police continued to stand by and watch "vandalism, arson and violence" occur, Savannah "could become another . . . Birmingham."[152] Meanwhile, biracial talks continued in the city.

On July 14 the temporary peace was threatened when a Cavalcade of White Americans rally took place in Forsyth Park, followed by a march on the city led by a former city detective, Henry S. Brooks, who wore a revolver on his hip. City police stopped the marchers at Bull and Jones streets on the charge of "unlawful assembly." Motorists accompanying the group were not stopped as they drove through the city waving Confederate flags. The local press urged the authorities to "deal as promptly with white troublemakers as with Negroes."[153]

Four days later, responding to concerns over life and property, the City Council unanimously agreed to ban marches by black or white demonstrators "until conditions improve." The resolution asserted that Savannah "is in a state of severe racial unrest" and appealed to all citizens to refrain from violence as it was doing "irreparable damage to this community." Speaking at the St. Philip AME Church, W. W. Law deplored the recent outbreak of rioting in the city. He told his audience that blacks must become registered voters and cast their ballots on election day to achieve their rights.[154]

Except for occasional incidents of vandalism, order prevailed. By early August, a hundred-person committee, working to achieve a compromise desegregation plan, announced that an agreement had been reached. Theaters, public accommodations, and such would be open to black patrons; in return, black demonstrations would be halted temporarily. This compromise helped "alleviate racial tension in the community," though some continued to stir up unrest.[155]

The agitator Henry S. Brooks, a leader of the Cavalcade of White Americans, urged an audience of about one hundred to "start working now to defeat" the current city administration. Along with businessmen, "they have sold out the Chatham County white people." He characterized white leaders as hypocrites who will "no more integrate the fashionable Oglethorpe Club than they will send their children to school with Negroes." Brooks's inflammatory speech came as plans were surfacing for integrating the local public schools. The white well-to-do, seeing the future, had already launched plans to raise funds to open another private institution, Savannah Country Day School. By 1990 there were twenty-three private schools operating in the county.[156]

Nearly a dozen years after *Brown v. Board of Education in Topeka*—when the U.S. Supreme Court ruled that racial segregation in public schools violated the Equal Protection Clause of the Fourteenth Amendment—the Chatham County Board of Education (BOE) in 1963, with the help of the federal government, adopted a plan for the desegregation of public schools. Repeatedly the judge of the U.S. District Court for the Southern District of Georgia, Frank Muir Scarlett, had summarily dismissed cases relating to desegregation. Scarlett had been recommended for the judgeship by his cousin, segregationist Senator Richard Russell. President Harry Truman appointed him. Scarlett, born in 1891, was related to the commanding officer of the last embattled troops in Savannah before General Sherman occupied the city. One writer referred to Scarlett as "a living relic of the Old South."[157]

The year the BOE wrote its plan for desegregation, Scarlett allowed a case to be brought forward by white interveners on behalf of *all* white children in Savannah. Their attorneys argued that based on certain evidence—pseudoscientific at best—white children would be "irreparably harmed" by attending schools with blacks, and they asked Scarlett to deny local plans to integrate Savannah's public schools. Scarlett made his decision on June 18, 1963, in favor of the interveners. However, the U.S. Fifth Circuit Court of Appeals reversed his decision and ordered another desegregation plan for the local schools. In early August 1963 the BOE offered a plan calling for the desegregation of the twelfth grade in the upcoming year and thereafter integration of one grade per year. The Fifth Circuit Court ordered desegregation of schools at a faster pace. Because of the legal maneuvering to prevent integration, implementation of the BOE plan did not go into effect until the following year. After several nasty fistfights between black and white students in the newly integrated schools, desegregation moved ahead.[158] With passage of the Civil Rights Act of 1964, integration of public facilities became the law of the land; only then did Savannah restaurants desegregate. Soon after Hosea Williams was released from jail, he departed Savannah for Atlanta to join the SCLC.

The demonstrations of African Americans in Savannah for their civil rights and the outbreak of violence by hundreds of protesters had raised fears among the city's leadership and brought white and black negotiators to the table to accept social change for social stability.[159] A prominent member of an old Savannah family, George Arthur Gordon Jr., remarked: "Listen! The tide's coming in and you may as well be ready for it!"[160]

The level of violence in many southern cities far exceeded that in Savannah.[161] Here, it seems that cooler heads prevailed on both sides and that Mayor Maclean, City Manager Don Mendonsa, W. W. Law, and others were calming influences during the passionate days of the civil rights movement.

Resistance and Savannah's First Republican Mayor

At the beginning of the 1960s, the *Morning News* changed hands. For some years, Alvah H. Chapman and Mills B. Lane Jr., the local banker, owned the *Morning News.* Chapman, who came from a progressive Florida paper, served as managing editor and Lane as a silent partner. Initially welcomed by Savannah's white elite, Chapman became a crusader for a better life for all Savannahians, especially poor whites and blacks. But he became too progressive for the elite, who urged Lane to buy out Chapman, and he did. A local newspaper man said Chapman "took a lot of Mills Lane's money with him" when he left and joined the prestigious Knight-Ridder chain of papers. William Morris of Augusta, Georgia, at the time owner of several papers, bought the *Morning News* from Lane in 1960.[162] The tone of the paper reverted to its politically right-of-center position.

On the issue of public schools, the *Morning News* editorialized: "If forced segregation is wrong, is forced integration right? Discrimination is wrong, but if forced is school integration itself a form of discrimination?"[163] Both in editorials and in articles the *Morning News* also stirred emotions among Savannahians who blamed Maclean's administration for the economic disruptions and violence which racked the city in the early 1960s. Now the paper featured on its editorial pages conservative columnists like Holmes Alexander and Barry Goldwater, who occasionally wrote columns charging that "Today's Liberals [Are] Bankrupt."

Aware of attitudes held by many Savannahians, Goldwater found fertile ground in the city for his conservative views and ambitions. In 1964, he opened an office in Savannah for his run for the presidency, a run that ultimately failed. In an interview Curtis Cooper reflected on black politics and their reactions to Goldwater's candidacy. Blacks had been Republicans before that time and "might still be if it hadn't been for Goldwater. They just literally kicked all the blacks out of the party. I think the Republicans are still suffering for that."[164]

Forty-year-old J. Curtis Lewis oversaw the "financial details" of Goldwater's local campaign in 1964. Lewis, a graduate of the prestigious Woodberry Forest School and the University of Georgia, served in the navy during World War II and following the war became a car dealer and real estate mogul. He was seen as a good candidate to run against Maclean and was being courted to do so by many in the business community as well as by some who were disgruntled with how integration policies were being implemented.

Animosity toward the Maclean administration grew among a group of wealthy churchgoers, especially after Bishop Albert Stewart directed St. John's Episcopal Church to admit African Americans. The Reverend Ernest Risley, rector of St. John's for twenty-nine years, refused to do so. Instead, Risley resigned his Episcopal ministry in 1965 and departed, taking some parishioners with him. Risley refused to admit Negroes to worship "except for servants attending a family wedding or funeral" because he felt they were trying to make a "political statement" rather than to worship. Four blacks had been barred by ushers from entering the church on Easter Sunday—Risley told Georgia Bishop Rhett Stuart, "I'll resign as a minister before I'll allow Negroes in St. John's." And he did. This protest and others were dramatic evidence of many white Savannahians' opposition to Maclean's administration. How strong these feelings were came to be known when J. C. Lewis ran as a Republican against Maclean in a city historically controlled by the Democratic Party.[165]

Ed Perkins, an executive with Savannah Bank and Trust Company, talked Lewis into running. The banker believed city leaders were too complacent about luring industry to the city and that Lewis, with his business orientation, would understand how to entice new industry and entrepreneurs like himself. Perkins also had concerns about the ports and did not feel that the "local boys" who ran the Ports Authority had the know-how to grow the ports into their potential; Finally Perkins believed Lewis would bring a much-needed business-like approach to city government.

Lewis agreed to put his hat in the ring for mayor, and he chose a slate to run with him that included Jewish, Irish, and Protestant representation. When a supporter told Lewis that a man had agreed to distribute "street money" to buy votes, Lewis declined to follow the path of some of his predecessors and refused the offer.[166] The election of 1966, the first two-party mayoralty race in the city's history, resulted in the election of Savannah's first Republican mayor.

Even though backed by nearly 100 percent of the black community, Maclean lost the election because of the small turnout of black voters and a larger-than-expected turnout of white voters. Lewis carried all but fourteen of the city's forty-five precincts to win 16,630 (54 percent) votes to Maclean's 14,069. Some Democrats changed allegiances to vote for Lewis. Likely Maclean's "weak showing" in the election could be attributed in part to the perception that he failed to "respond sternly enough" during the civil rights demonstrations.

Maclean himself recognized that the enmity of many white Savannahians toward his administration ran deep, especially due to his failure to "diffuse" the civil rights movement. But Maclean felt his work was unfinished, and he wanted to run for mayor again, or as he said, "give it one more try." To Maclean, the election of Lewis represented a "backlash" to the growing influence of blacks and to progressivism in local government.[167]

Interestingly, the conservative *Morning News* had endorsed Maclean but, following the election, pledged support to Lewis and predicted a "brighter future" for Savannah. The paper's analysis of the election outcome was that the vote may have turned on opposition to the increase in property taxes during Maclean's administration. The voters had spoken, and "the people wanted a change." Bringing about that change, the paper observed, would be a "herculean task."

The African American community was unhappy with the outcome of the election. Despite a pledge by candidate Lewis that he and his slate of councilmen planned to manage Savannah's government "in a manner equitable to all our people, regardless of race, creed, color or their station in life," the local NAACP and its president remained skeptical.[168]

Outside the black community, Savannah's affluent white residents generally divided themselves into two camps. One, families of the "cultural[ly]" rich who looked on themselves as the New South's version of Old South planters—patrons of art, history, and music. Their wealth flowed usually from inheritance and/or the city's large industries and banks, like Citizens and Southern.

The other group, called by one writer the "Elks Club" rich, was composed of insurance salesmen, real estate brokers, contractors, business owners, and such. Lewis appealed to both groups. He was a conservative businessman, a family man, a philanthropist whose entrepreneurial interests included car dealerships, land development, media (WJCL-TV), the Avis franchise, shopping centers, a supermarket, insurance, a restaurant, and motels like the Downtowner Inn.[169]

One of the first orders of business for the new mayor was to control crime. According to FBI reports, the crime rate soared in Savannah during the 1960s. Soon after taking office, Mayor Lewis commented that the city would enjoy "good law enforcement" once we ousted the "bad cops." And improved policing would be needed; between January and June 1966, the crime rate increased 11.4 percent over the same period in 1965 while rates fell in Georgia cities with similar-sized populations. To address sharp increases in robbery, larceny, and aggravated assault, the police and city government immediately launched a crime-abatement program. A month after release of the FBI report, a black employee fired by the Coca-Cola Bottling Company shot and killed a superintendent in front of a dozen witnesses.[170]

Gambling remained endemic. Mayor Lewis discovered that numerous illegal games persisted, especially the Cuban game bolita, in which one hundred numbered balls are placed into a bag with bets taken on what numbers would be drawn. Bolita was a popular game among blacks; easy to rig, the game also attracted "racketeers." Police revived the use of "undercover people" and took on the growing "drug scene." Local liquor distributors, some of them Lewis's friends, put pressure on him to allow black "dives" on the west side of town to remain open on Sundays. Lewis refused. He knew some of these bars traded in stolen goods and drugs and decided instead to enforce a curfew beginning at 2:00 A.M. In an interview some years after he left office, Lewis said he believed his efforts to suppress drug dealing likely led to a threat on his life—after which he carried a .38 detective special.[171]

During the first half of 1968, violent crime in Savannah jumped 50 percent over the same period the previous year. Murder was up 50 percent, forcible rape 71 percent, and aggravated assault 157 percent. Comparatively, nationwide crime increased only 21 percent, according to FBI statistics. When the *Morning News* asked Police Chief Leo B. Ryan the reason for the dramatic spike in local crime, he replied that it "is just on the rise [and] can't be attributed to anything in particular."[172] Curiously, Ryan ignored a seismic event that might have contributed to the upsurge in local violence, the assassination on April 4, 1968, of the Reverend Martin Luther King Jr.

Mayor Lewis and his wife had just left a sporting event at Grayson Stadium when they were informed of the murder of King in Memphis. Rumors that Savannah might be "burned" by rioters alarmed Lewis and all those charged with protecting the city. Meeting with police officials, Lewis told them to use "minimum force" to maintain law and order. But when the police told Lewis about threats to burn down his home, he returned there and armed his oldest boys, eight and ten, with shotguns. "Luckily," no attempts were made against his home or family.[173]

As racial violence spread across the nation, Mayor Lewis called for calm and ordered a voluntary 8:00 P.M. curfew. He told citizens that "it would be a sad turn of events if this tragedy were used to stimulate violence and disorder . . . [and] a poor tribute to a man who advocated non-violence." Similar pleas came from W. W. Law; the local Roman Catholic bishop, Gerard L. Frey; Don Kole, chairman of the Savannah Jewish Council and the steering body of the Committee of 100 chaired by James Lentz, an officer with Union Bag.

The Chatham Council on Human Relations, led by the Rev. James L. Hooten, called on civic leaders to "correct the ills of the community" and "keep King's dream alive" by enacting an open-housing law, establishing a permanent commission on civil rights, desegregating and improving public schools, and implementing a program for hiring and promoting African Americans on a nondiscriminatory basis in all public institutions.[174] Despite the pleas of black and white leaders, some vandalism took place.

Rock throwing in black neighborhoods and "destructive acts" in the central city broke out the day following the assassination. Early Friday morning, someone threw a "fire bomb" through the display window of the store Yachum and Yachum at 328 West Broad Street. Opened in 1921 and operated by Hymie and Morris Perlman, who served in World War I, the department store employed "28 negroes." Ironically, it was "the first white-owned store in Savannah to employ blacks to wait on white customers."

On Friday evening, crews extinguished fires at the Bay Street Lumber Company. Another arson attempt failed when a canister of gasoline did not ignite when tossed into a store at Montgomery and Thirty-seventh Street. Windows were smashed in some sections of the city. Taking advantage of the melee, two white men broke into the home of Aaron Kravitch, a civil rights attorney, brutally pistol-whipped him, bound his wife and daughter, and made off with thirteen hundred dollars. A day later someone shot and killed Claude Roberts in his home on Walberg Street.[175]

On Saturday, police cars patrolled the city, racing to areas when crowds gathered. The *Morning News* headlined, "Irresponsibility Must Stop—Rock throwing, arson and assaults have no more place on the American Scene than the cowardly shooting of Dr. King."

On Sunday, memorial services were held at several churches. The local NAACP president, W. W. Law, spoke at St. John's Baptist Church. Christ Church, crowded with *both* blacks and whites, including Mayor Lewis and other officials, hosted an interfaith memorial service for Dr. King. Cries of "amen" swept the sanctuary as ministers black and white delivered eulogies and pleaded for unity. Monsignor John Toomey, whom Malcolm Maclean credited with contributing significantly to "the making and maintaining of racial peace," called for a "practical eulogy" to Dr. King that he described as an active agenda that would include hot running water in Yamacraw Village, paving dirt streets, faster integration of schools, and inviting "Negroes" to join the white churches and civic clubs. Some wondered if Toomey's remarks might be the reason the Catholic bishop soon relocated him to Macon. Although a few incidents of "violence" persisted in the county, the community was sufficiently peaceful that Mayor Lewis soon lifted the voluntary curfew.[176]

Resurgent Racism

An NAACP-prepared paper for the Savannah Community Leadership Seminar titled "Some Major Problems in Race Relations" asserted that Savannah blacks lived in substandard dwellings due to discrimination in rental properties and public housing projects. In 1968, NAACP President Law publicly criticized the slow pace of promotion in the police department; some who had served on the force for twenty-one years remained among the lowest paid. Law declared, "Black citizens are living in utter hopelessness due to the negative attitude of city officials and discrimination against blacks by the police."[177] Such expressions of discontent soon triggered a backlash from the far right.

The National States' Rights Party (NSRP) established a branch in Savannah in 1968. Members occasionally waved the Confederate flag without the stars and with a white circle and thunderbolt in its center that symbolized the power and fury of the white race. Founded as a Christian organization, the NSRP wanted to deport all Negroes and Jews as they "will marry into our race and adulterate it."[178] The venom spewed by some politicians that blacks had come too far too fast inflamed racist attitudes.

NSRP activists in the town of Thunderbolt, near Savannah State College and the city, occasionally published the *Thunderbolt*, a paper of a few pages that was circulated to members and potential members of the NSRP. In the late

1960s the editor opposed integration, communists, liberals, radical blacks, Jews, and the FBI. The paper used crude diagrams to illustrate similarities between "the facial angles" of "Negroes" and "gorillas" and printed pseudoscientific studies about the Negro's "under-developed brain" which the article contended proved the race to be "retarded in mental development."

Amid articles with headlines such as "Scientific Tests Prove Negro Children Inferior Hold White Back in Mixed Race Classes" and "Negroes Mentally Behind Whites" were interspersed racial caricatures. The *Thunderbolt* repeatedly called for donations and a pledge from its readers: "I am a loyal White Christian and wish . . . to save our Race, Nation and Faith from Communism and mongrelization." In a 1969 issue, the paper called for establishment of "citizen patrols . . . to aid the police in keeping our city safe [from crimes] . . . by Negroes." The article warned of an "increasing wave of unprovoked attacks against innocent White people [by Negroes] on our streets" and charged that the "*Morning News* . . . [and] *Savannah Evening Press* have imposed a total blackout on this growing danger."[179]

Savannah's Revitalization

Near the end of the decade of the 1960s the academic speakers who addressed the Community Leadership Seminar on Savannah's current problems and opportunities again noted great gaps in welfare services, health problems, insufficient skills to support gainful employment, the breakdown of family structures, and the inability "to finance the level of expenditures necessary for the correction of problems."[180] Whatever the influence, over recent years local businessmen and city government had laid out a more focused agenda for development of the city, a task made easier by Savannah's improving economy.

The river continued to be the city's "lifeline" and the "economic base for its development." Over two hundred manufacturers and processors provided "diversified economic strength." Unemployment stood at about 4 percent. The income of the average factory worker had climbed to $6,122 (better than the pay in Atlanta, Charleston, Charlotte, and Jacksonville). Construction was up almost 12 percent, and department-store sales reflected a 4 percent increase. The *U.S. News and World Report* described Savannah as one of the "Cities in the U.S. Where Business is Best." City government and business interests appeared to be moving in sync to promote Savannah's economic opportunities, historical charm, and its potential as an education, tourist, convention, and cultural center. Leadership Savannah's academic consultants also made the observation that "the impulse to inhibit and prevent change . . . seems to have modified."[181] The *Morning News* trumpeted the city's new direction.

The paper celebrated plans to implement a citywide beautification program at a cost of $1.4 million, and the Beautification Committee of the Chamber of Commerce joined with the city for enforcement of Savannah's anti-litter ordinances. The local press also praised the great success of the 1968 five-day Savannah Arts Festival, "a highlight of the city's cultural year." The only recommendation offered was that "the mosquito fogging machine be run through the park" before next year's event to "keep down gnats and other predatory insects."[182]

John D. Burke, an arts consultant with the Leadership Savannah Seminar, was both optimistic and cautionary about the city's cultural life. Burke observed numerous empty seats at concerts by the Savannah Symphony Orchestra and viewed the recent resignation of its talented conductor as a terrible loss. He wondered if Savannah could afford a first-class conductor and orchestra. The local Little Theatre, also without a director, was one of only four community theaters in the state. Burke said community theaters in Columbus and Macon enjoyed "great progress" compared to Savannah. He praised the work of the city's Art Council, only in its third year of existence and enthusiastically endorsed the council's sponsorship of an upcoming festival that would include a lecture by writer and poet James Dickey—he called this "the greatest attraction on the calendar."[183]

Burke pointed to another positive step: the city's fine-arts groups now worked in tandem with the school board to increase arts education in the city's elementary and secondary schools. In sum, Savannah "is moving ahead [and] making progress." However, he offered a few words of advice, saying the arts in Savannah "will never . . . grow if the arts do not give the people what they want." Anything else would lead to failure as in Atlanta, where, in his words, a "cultural coterie considered art was never meant to be enjoyed by the people" and catered its offerings "to a distinctive, aristocratic class" who then blamed the masses for not supporting "art" at the box office.[184]

The 1968 Leadership Seminar participants were encouraged to hear that a "feeling of optimism beyond any the city had experienced in two full generations" now coursed through Savannah. Finalization of plans to build a new civic center, expansion of the port, development of Skidaway Island, and restoration of deteriorating housing in the central city provided a new sense of affluence. A widened tax base and "outside" investment in expanded hotel accommodations in expectation of a "substantial increase" in tourism were further indications of brighter days ahead.[185]

One seminar speaker, Dr. Paul Deuschberger, brought up some issues that could undermine the city's hope-filled forecast such as the "threadbare financing of social welfare services" and the failure to coordinate "efforts in dealing with the community's pressing social needs."[186] By the end of the 1960s there were opportunities and challenges, but overall, feelings of optimism and economic well-being prevailed.

Even as the city enjoyed high employment, increased construction, and new business ventures, more than 30 percent of the population reported annual incomes of less than three thousand dollars; about 35 percent of citizens over age twenty-five had less than an eighth-grade education; and 25 percent of housing units were classified as substandard with nearly 6 percent being labeled "dilapidated."

The Savannah Plan, created by the Community Development Corporation, took a new approach to urban renewal. The corporation loaned money to citizens to purchase or renovate their homes. Sponsored by the city's business interests, the corporation aimed to "help people help themselves" by addressing some of the displacement and gentrification problems that earlier urban renewal efforts had created. The concept promoted the idea of "urban *renewal* rather than urban *removal.*"[187] It would face its own challenges as the program moved forward.

Political squabbles sometimes flared, slowing projects such as the civic center. Design, parking and location of the new facility were issues of conflict among city government, downtown Jewish merchants, and the Historic Savannah Foundation (HSF). In the compromise, the HSF won the argument on location-the new facility would be built on the site of the old city auditorium (demolished in 1971) that had fronted Barnard and was bounded by Perry and Jefferson streets—Mayor Lewis and the City Council prevailed on the facility's design.

Differences of opinion between the city and the HSF also arose over the fate of downtown structures. Lewis believed the HSF "wanted to save everything." When the city wished to raze "dilapidated buildings" whose owners had paid no taxes for years, the HSF protested. Without demolishing historic structures, how would the business community find more parking near Broughton Street? Another controversial proposal on the table concerned the proposal for a high-rise hotel on the riverfront. All these issues would surely be topics for discussing in the mayoralty election of 1970.

Reflecting on the Lewis administration, local political activist Curtis Cooper said Lewis turned his attention to business development and, though Lewis brought in the Model Cities Program, "blacks remained rather cold to [Lewis] because they were afraid of Republican leadership. But now in hindsight, he wasn't a bad mayor." Mayor Edna Jackson said that Lewis had not been given enough credit for his accomplishments while in office.[188]

Rousakis Runs with Bowles Ford on the Ticket

Savannah native John P. Rousakis, a forty-one-year-old Democrat and seasoned politician, served six years on the Chatham County Commission before resigning his post to run for mayor in 1970. An insurance executive, Rousakis was the son of Greek immigrants and an army veteran with a hail-fellow-well-met persona. The Political Advisory Council of the Savannah Chapter of the NAACP backed his candidacy and his council slate.[189]

Union Camp and the Citizens and Southern Bank enjoyed a cozy relationship with the Chatham County Commission. Since the days of the self-styled "kingmaker," Johnny Bouhan, the political "boss" of Chatham County, bank executives like Robert F. Lovett and Union Camp officers like James Lientz served as county commissioners and influenced politics within a "friendly little group." One example of how this relationship was good for business concerned a land sale.

For several years Union Camp had owned 7,200 acres near Savannah on Skidaway Island; the property had been assessed at $20 per acre, but in 1969 when the state wanted to buy 109 acres for a park, the land appraised for around $2,000 per acre; its sales price $212,500. One investigative journalist wrote, "there is certainly no excuse for scandals like Skidaway." Subsequently, Union Camp sold off all its holdings on the island, which eventually became a high-end gated community. The sale generated a windfall for Union Camp's stockholders.[190]

As the mayoral campaign got underway, Rousakis decided to include a black community leader on his slate even though his advisors told him he would lose white votes. Nonetheless, he believed the time was right. Subsequently he met with the city's black leadership and asked for a candidate to run with him. The overwhelming majority suggested Bowles C. Ford. A college graduate, an insurance executive, and a Savannah resident for thirty-three years, Ford had good working relationships with the white leadership of Savannah. But the NAACP's W. W. Law was not satisfied. As Rousakis recounted the story in an interview with the author, Mr. Law reminded him that, with almost 40 percent of Savannah's population being African Americans, Rousakis should run with "at least two black candidates," to which Rousakis replied, "Mr. Law, do you want two black candidates or one black [member of City Council]?" Rousakis added Ford to his ticket. A few of Rousakis's insurance clients called Rousakis a "Negro lover" and canceled their policies.[191]

When Rousakis and his team embarked on their campaign they found that the city, under the Lewis administration, had practiced frugality to the point of delaying construction of a modern sewage-treatment system to prevent the city from discharging raw sewage into the Savannah River. Local study groups and the U.S. Public Health Service for some years had urged the city to address this issue. One environmental critic, James Fallows, charged that Mayor Lewis had failed to act because he was "running his [own]. . . enterprises" and devoting an "embarrassingly small amount of time . . . [to] being mayor." Fallows criticized the administration's "profound naiveté in the art of governing."

It was no secret whom Fallows supported; he called Rousakis a progressive and commended his "enthusiastic [support] of sewage treatment." He knew too that electing Rousakais would not guarantee that the problems would be addressed; Rousakis would have to "convince the tax-paying voters that curbing the pollution is worth the dollars it will cost."[192]

The Rousakis campaign attacked the conservative Lewis administration for failure to enact new taxes, which had left Savannah departments without adequate resources. In a later interview, Rousakis said, the city was in bad shape: "It was filthy with trash piled up all over the city; . . . policemen rode around in pickup trucks and the spirits of employees were down." He remembered it as a time when Savannah "wasn't developing new business . . . and people were leaving the city.[193] Henry Moore, an assistant city manager to Don Mendonsa, noted the trend.

Moore observed a "shrinking tax base," in large part caused by "white flight" to the suburbs to get away from "increasing crime and violence and . . . [a] growing underclass [whose use of] . . . crack cocaine really accelerated the process of blight and flight." Savannah's demographics "clearly reflected the tragic tale of an urban community in trouble."[194]

The Rousakis team rolled out a campaign platform to resuscitate and rebuild Savannah. A significant component of his plan embraced his promise to Savannah's African American community to enact an "equity agenda." Rousakis's campaign for equity was founded on political pragmatism. It aimed to improve public services and infrastructure in the inner-city neighborhoods long neglected because of segregationist policies. The campaign was remarkably comprehensive and progressive. It proposed growth by annexation, the cultivation of additional revenue sources, fairer taxes, and more economy in government.

One way to achieve more efficiency and to save money was to combine overlapping city-county services. Rousakis promised something for everyone—more paved streets, better garbage pickup, improved traffic control, street drainage, and better housing and recreation facilities—especially to keep "youth active and away from drugs." And the Rousakis platform's to-do list continued: enhanced educational facilities, better water treatment and sewer systems, pollution abatement, and a "strong program designed to control and prevent crime." Funding these initiatives would be accomplished by attracting new industry, improving airline services, and upgrading harbor facilities to attract "cruise ships."[195] It was an exhaustively comprehensive proposal; some might characterize it as overly ambitious.

Meanwhile, Mayor Lewis, urged to run for a second term by the local Republican leadership, appeared indecisive. During the campaign Rousakis and his promoters missed no opportunity to call attention to Lewis's apathy and lack of enthusiasm for another term. Three months before the mayoralty election, Lewis told the *Morning News* that although "under pressure" from friends and politicians he had not decided whether to enter the race; in fact he was "still hoping the Republicans can find someone else." The paper ran the interview under the headline, "Lewis Hints Again He Wants Out." Asked years later if he enjoyed being mayor, he answered, "No, I really didn't." It "felt like it was something I had to do." In spite of his own ambivalence, he did run for a second term though he admitted he "never cared much about campaigning."[196] But his opponent did.

Rousakis and his well-connected political team spent many days campaigning from May to August. Several days before the mayoral election, the *Morning News* urged citizens to turn out for a "crucial" vote and to vote for "growth and economic progress," which sounded like the Rousakis platform. Indeed, on election day, August 4, 1970, the Rousakis team swept the election, polling 14,556 votes (55 percent) to Lewis's 11,855 (45 percent). Lewis was gracious in defeat: "we lost because . . . we took for granted people would turn out . . . and Rousakis ran a good race." A Republican strategist attributed the loss to "apathy on the part of white voters."[197]

Changing the Culture and Landscape of Savannah

With Rousakis's win, Bowles Ford became the first black member of the City Council, indeed the first African American to win any elected city post. His inclusion on the slate of the Rousakis team turned out large numbers of black voters. White voters also backed Ford, which indicated to Rousakis and others that Ford enjoyed good support across the community. On inauguration day, however, Bowles Ford was not present. Recuperating from a heart attack, he took the oath of office via phone on a specially arranged line.

In 1970 elections were citywide. Seven years later and under outside pressure, the City Council passed a bill creating voting districts and increased the number of council members from six to eight—two at-large members were added. The majority of black leaders supported the plan, believing it assured black representation on the City Council—which it did.[198]

In the mayoral race of 1970, Rousakis won twenty-six of the fifty-five precincts—a majority of which were in predominantly African American areas. In those precincts won by Lewis the margin of victory was much smaller than in those won by Rousakis; for example, in predominantly black polling areas like Yamacraw Village, Rousakis received 348 votes, Lewis 20 votes.[199] The Democratic Party had regained control of City Hall.

Following the announcement of the election results, a reporter found Republicans in the "Lewis camp solemn . . . subdued and quiet" at the Downtowner Motor Inn and in "sharp contrast to the fevered pitch of the winning Rousakis celebration" at the Hellenic Center. As mayor-elect Rousakis made his way to the celebration, a thousand-plus crowd of supporters reached out to congratulate him. Mayor Lewis and four of his City Council members came over to greet the new mayor-elect and pledge their support. As Lewis watched the Greek dancers, an aide attempted to assuage his disappointment by stressing their frugality in office: "take a good look at [our] financial statement. . . . It'll never look like this again." About that time, Rousakis bounded onto the stage and made a "V" for victory sign as he promised a wildly cheering crowd, "We're going to build Savannah again." Rousakis would be elected for four consecutive terms (twenty-one years) without opposition to become the city's longest-serving mayor.[200]

Cleaning Up the River and the Air

Rousakis had promised to bring the city together but, in the first months of his administration, consensus remained elusive after "Nader's Raiders" came to town. By the late twentieth century, shrimpers in Savannah were complaining: "Them paper bag people is fiddlin' with our livelihood. . . . What's more important, a damn paper bag or us keepin' our living?" Shrimp harvests were off more than 50 percent since industry moved in along the river. Harvests of red snapper, blue fish, trout, and oysters had also declined dramatically.

The downturn was attributed to industrial pollutants which now suffused the once pristine Savannah River. Among the polluters were American Cyanamid, Continental Can, and the city itself which discharged raw sewage into the river. Union Camp Bag and Paper Company, the "world's largest paper mill" and the largest polluter locally, also belched from a huge smokestack sulfur-smelling emissions that pervaded the city. When the wind blew from the northwest, a rotten-egg odor swept over Savannah.

During the Great Depression of the 1930s everything had been subordinated to bringing jobs to Savannah. City government lured industries by providing "miniscule rent for land and greatly reduced tax bills for companies, but for private citizens, taxes soared." For years Savannahians would "prostitute . . . their civic pride to a belief that Union Camp saved the town from ruin" even as the company flushed massive amounts of toxins into the river that shared the city's name. As fears spread that the nation's rivers and streams were becoming polluted with mercury, Ralph Nader, author of *Unsafe at Any Speed,* a book that triggered major reforms in the automotive industry, sent a team of scientists, attorneys, and student volunteers to the city in the summer of 1970 to determine the level and causes of the Savannah River's toxicity. They soon issued a devastating report.[201]

The resulting book, by the project director James M. Fallows, *The Water Lords: Ralph Nader's Study Group on Industry and Environmental Crisis in Savannah, Georgia,* explained how out-of-state companies passed on costs that burdened the city treasury and small taxpayers while "ravage[ing] the environment." In a foreword to the book, Nader described how the "massive contamination" of the river had a direct effect on the city's drinking water, fish stocks, recreation, and health. Union Camp's "voracious pumping of water for its industrial use" exposed the "precious ground water to saline intrusion." The river was no longer "suitable for human use." Nader posed the question: what right, "legal or moral, do these companies [have to] destroy the property and health of innocent neighbors" and to jeopardize the natural resources held in "trust for future generations?" In sum, he concluded, "These Savannah-based companies are outlaws." Nader called for industrial companies on the river and around the country "to pay their taxes and their environmental way" like ordinary citizens do. The "double standard that coddles corporations breeds immense cynicism and disrespect for the law and permits industries to . . . corrupt political processes, and to manipulate the law in order to be permitted to continue destroying . . . natural resources." This environmental destruction helps industry to generate handsome profits.[202]

Project director and author of the report, James Fallows, a Harvard graduate (1970) and later Rhodes Scholar, used equally harsh words, holding Union Camp accountable for 80 percent of the industrial pollution of the river. His conclusion: "When Union Camp used the Savannah as its sewer, no one else could use it for anything." No other polluter effused the "torrent of filth that came from the paper mill."

A year after the Union Bag Company located up river from the city, in 1935, Savannahians knew they had a problem. A local civic committee warned of the rising industrial development in the area and recommended that a study be made of "industrial waste pollution" in the river and that "a constant check [be] maintained on this potential menace." Yet with a cozy town-industry relationship no action was taken, and the pollution continued unabated for decades. Curiously, Mayor J. C. Lewis remarked on one occasion: "Most of us thought it was a dirty old stream, without any hope."[203]

Dumped into the Savannah River daily were pulp-mill wastes from Union Camp, poisons from Continental Can, and the untreated raw sewage of 100,000 people; by the time the river, saturated with contaminants, reached City Hall, it sometimes boiled as "pockets of hydrogen sulfide and methane gas [rose] from the waste on the river bed." Several miles downriver, the American Cyanamid factory flushed nearly 700,000 pounds of sulfuric acid daily into the river, adding to its toxicity.

Every twenty-four hours, about 100 million gallons poured into the river from Savannah's major polluters. The effect on the ecosystem was devastating. The toxic mix killed fish, flowed into the marshes that nurtured fish stocks, and sometimes even burned the fingers of small children who dangled their hands in the water. The Georgia Water Quality Control Board closed the lower portions of the river due to industrial and municipal pollution; fishermen were unable to sell catches taken from the lower hundred miles of the Savannah River, and for years oyster beds of the Savannah estuary remained closed because of sewage contamination.[204]

Despite pressure by federal and state authorities to reduce pollution by 85 percent in the early 1970s, the industrial polluters made only "meager" progress. Indeed, "notoriously," it appeared that Union Camp dumped into the river *more* waste than previously. The city of Savannah, having been told in 1965 to build a modern sewage-treatment system, had not yet broken ground for one.

Fallows identified weakness of the state legislature, deception by industrialists, technical problems of sewage treatment, and the cozy company-town arrangements as reasons for the river's continued deterioration.[205] He concluded: "So far the polluters have acted with remarkable ingenuity in delaying the sewer system . . . in hiding the facts about their pollution [and] in manipulating the tax structure." He also added, if "the people of Savannah show anything resembling this ingenuity, they can turn the city around," and he praised the local press for keeping the "environmental issue before the citizens."[206] To counter this criticism, spokesmen for the polluters pushed back with an aggressive public-relations campaign.

On October 19, 1970, John E. Ray III, a Union Camp official, addressed the Savannah Rotary Club. He began by saying that his company recently "has been the target of inflammatory charges relating to the deterioration of the Savannah River." We have been "placed in the role of arch polluter and despoiler of the natural resources of the Savannah community." Some "charges . . . are wrong in fact and in substance [and] some have been stated out of context. . . . others are scientifically meaningless [and] the . . . publicity and notoriety are unjustly damaging . . . to Union Camp [and] . . . the Savannah community."[207]

In the face of deadlines and the threat of fines ordered by the Georgia Water Quality Control Board to cease dumping toxins into the river, Union Camp and American Cyanamid among others continued to pollute, and indeed such was the support from local business and political leaders that the Savannah government passed a bond issue of more than $32 million to assist the companies in finding ways to mitigate their pollution of the river and air. Some referred to air pollution as "the smell of money," but a Savannah grand jury compared the smells wafting over Savannah to that of a "high class sewer."[208] Indeed, by the 1970s and into the twenty-first century, Georgia led several other southern states in befouling the air and water with carcinogens while offering tax exemptions on the costs related to pollution abatement by polluting industries.[209]

Near the end of the twentieth century, air quality in Savannah was among the worst in the Southeast. And pollution affected other issues. Some residents complained about nausea and headaches. "Savannahians who recently met with EPD officials to talk about pulp mill odors . . . want the often sickening smell to go away." Death rates from lung cancer were disproportionally high. Local industry thwarted efforts by the state to regulate air pollution, arguing that the restrictions would be "crippling" to the economy. The fouled river and the smells emitted by Union Camp had become increasingly offensive to both Savannahians and visitors. Tourists stayed away, and many citizens relocated. In the decade of the 1960s, Savannah's urban population fell by about 32,000 to 118,344; "between 1960 and 1970 the City lost more than 20 percent of its population, while the county population remained almost stable." Industrial pollution now obstructed progress and threatened the city's growth.[210]

Rousakis and Mendonsa, the "Yin and the Yang"

John P. Rousakis and his slate of City Council members were sworn in on October 5, 1970. Once in office, they moved quickly to act on campaign promises, one of which was a pledge to address the historic "bias" toward the "black neighborhoods [which] got things last." In these communities, Rousakis said, "garbage is picked up last, there are no street lights . . . sidewalks . . . parks [or] playgrounds."

With the aid of a federal grant, the city moved forward to build a long-needed sewage treatment plant which also helped "clean up the river." More money now came into city coffers because of annexation, which ended a taxation system whereby municipal residents subsidized the cost of services provided to unincorporated areas of the county.

The administration soon rehired Arthur A. "Don" Mendonsa as city manager. After serving in the job for eighteen years, Mendonsa had been pressured to resign during the Lewis administration because certain council members thought he exercised too much control and they believed they had the public's endorsement "to run the city government." Lewis replaced Mendonsa with native son Picot Floyd, whose philosophy was more in line with that administration's vision for city governance.[211]

Rousakis had a progressive agenda, and he now had a progressive city manager to implement it. Their work styles were so complementary that it was referred to as a "yin-yang" partnership—a perfect match. Soon after Mendonsa returned to the position, a national publication ranked him as "one of the top three city managers in the country." Rousakis's comment on his right-hand man: "He is good."[212]

The mayor changed the "complexion of city offices" by hiring blacks as secretaries and clerks, and he continued Maclean's policy of appointing blacks to boards and commissions. Curtis Cooper said of this period in a later interview that the black community had wanted to see more policemen appointed to high-level positions and that there was "a yearning to see a black serve as mayor in Savannah . . . and it is something I think will eventually come about."

Mendonsa worked closely with the Chatham County–Savannah Metropolitan Planning Commission to secure federal grants for urban renewal. Faced with a decaying, seedy riverscape, the administration used funds from the Savannah Port Authority and the federal government to expedite a massive restoration of the city's waterfront, which was completed in late 1970s. Because of this initiative and Rousakis's role in it, visitors now stroll through John P. Rousakis Riverfront Plaza. After his first four years in office, the mayor cited his greatest accomplishment as "The change of spirit in the city."[213]

It was around this time that Malcolm Bell Jr., a prominent local banker and historian, addressed members of the elite Madeira Club and praised the recent progress of the city. Bell began by saying that the river remained "truly Savannah's greatest reason for being," not only because it supported a vital import-export trade, but also because it was now a place where people could gather. He commended those who had called attention to the pollution issues and expressed confidence that, because of federal and state laws, no longer

Before-and-after views of Savannah's Riverfront: Above, River Street looking east as the Riverfront Project is under construction, October, 1975. A portion of City Hall is visible in the distance. Below, the completed Riverfront Project, with old Talmadge Memorial Bridge in the distance. The Riverfront Urban Renewal Project was designed by Gunn & Meyerhoff A.I.A., Architects. Work started in 1975 and was completed in 1977. Courtesy of the City of Savannah, Research Library & Municipal Archives.

will "industry be free . . . to commit relentless environmental violence by discharging their waste in untreated form." He went on almost lyrically: "Now the fish and fisherman are returning. Once again the waterfront will be fashionable. A handsome embankment will extend from the foot of East Broad Street, beneath the fine old harbor light, on past the big bronze Waving Girl . . . and run beneath the balconies of the buildings that face old Factor's Walk and back up to River Street." It will extend "to the aging Savannah Electric plant at West Broad Street" and become the "newest park in a city of parks . . . perhaps where Savannahians might share with visitors a new found pride in the city's greatest source of strength."[214]

School Desegregation

Despite the physical progress in the city and public enthusiasm for the riverfront project, people remained bitterly divided over court decisions affecting the public schools. Less than a year into office, Rousakis met a hostile crowd gathering before City Hall. In early 1970 a district court ordered the desegregation of the Savannah–Chatham County Public Schools. Subsequently, the Board of Education adopted a policy of desegregation by busing. Court orders and mandates and busing plans and mounting racial tensions were very much on the mayor's mind on September 8, 1971, as he came down the steps of City Hall to meet a crowd of about seventy-five protesters who opposed elementary-school desegregation. When he appeared, the crowd chanted, "Down with Rousakis." The mayor issued a written statement saying he opposed busing, adding, "It won't do a bit of good to march against anyone." Amid shouts of "Rousakis won't help," the crowd accused him of enrolling his children in private schools, although at the time all of the Rousakis children attended public schools. The protestors soon turned away, marched south on Bull Street, and joined another anti-busing group at the Board of Education.[215]

Over the next several months, hundreds of cars participated in anti-busing motorcades through downtown Savannah. Violent episodes at some schools left students injured; vandals smashed furniture and ignited fires. A crowd of five hundred gathered to burn an effigy of Julian Halligan, school-board president. Churches held meetings on how to oppose the most recent court order, and about fifteen thousand students boycotted the public schools. White parents rushed to enroll their children at local parochial and private schools like Savannah Country Day. Within a few years, ten thousand white students had left the public school system, reversing the racial composition: black students now outnumbered white.[216]

The busing policies, political infighting at the BOE, threats of lawsuits, turnover of superintendents, and a local paper focused on failings of schools contributed to a negative image of public education in Savannah. By the 1980s about 25 percent of the Chatham County children attended private schools compared to 7 percent statewide. Change came slowly. Decades passed before the "public schools [went] from being the community sore spot to the hot spot." After the public agreed to add an extra penny in sales tax for ten years, the public school system experienced "unprecedented growth and popularity" due to the system's "major effort to reform academics, behavior and facilities." Long-time Superintendent Thomas Lockamy in the early twenty-first century also named a downturn in the economy as part of the motivation for some families returning to the public schools—private school was just too expensive.[217]

End of the Talmadge Era and Rebirth of the Victorian District

In 1980 Senator Talmadge, who had served for twenty-four years in Congress, was challenged by Matt Mattingly. The *Morning News* "strongly urged the return of Herman Talmadge to the Senate." It was a tough campaign. His admitted alcoholism, the death of a son, allegations of financial misconduct, and his former wife's testimony against him before the Senate Ethics Committee were all factors that weakened Talmadge's popularity. He nonetheless won 53.4 percent of the vote in Chatham County but lost most of the state. The Talmadge era had ended.[218] Around the same time, preservation continued to move apace.

City leaders like Lee Adler II, Mills Lane, and City Manager Mendonsa recognized that low-income blacks and whites displaced by initial urban-renewal efforts and the preservation movement often had nowhere to go. Many moved into the low-income rental units in the Victorian District south of the city. Here slumlords, some owning as many as four hundred apartment units, rented to low-income blacks and a few whites. Numerous dwellings in the fifty-one-block area were substandard, some dilapidated to the point of posing health and safety risks. Adler, one of the early leaders of the Historic Savannah Foundation (HSF), urged the foundation to support a program for the Victorian District that would restore homes and allow the residents to remain in them. When the HSF failed to support his idea, Adler founded the Savannah Landmark Rehabilitation Project (SLRP) and adopted the slogan: "Preservation is for people."

The goal of the SLRP was "preserving the neighborhood's racial and economic mix, its social fabric," so that the "benefits of preservation can be shared by the rich and the poor." The SLRP was a courageous effort. Adler once said,

"We don't think it's fair, decent or anything else to shove a whole bunch of people out. . . . Black people built a lot of this town." Many had lived in the Victorian District for thirty years. In the long run, the SLRP aimed to provide decent rental housing for the "responsible poor" and maintenance of the property. Some white critics said that the poor would just "tear up" the renovated housing.

The city's leading civil rights leader, Westley W. Law, was initially suspicious of the SLRP's plans because he feared "gentrification" of the neighborhood. However, Law soon recognized that Adler's plan coincided with his own agenda, which was to prevent displacement and to identify and save historic black properties. Law became an avid supporter of the SLRP. Indeed, Mr. Law had initiated his own project to preserve black properties, and he not only saved structures in the Victorian District, but others across the city including the splendid old bank building on Martin Luther King Jr. Boulevard that was once the Wage Earners Bank, Through Law's efforts, it became the home of the Ralph Mark Gilbert Civil Rights Museum, named to honor a local civil rights icon.[219]

Adler recruited a cross-section of the city for the SLRP board and, with grants from private, city, and federal sources as well as low interest loans from local banks, the project moved forward in its restoration efforts and soon gained the advocacy of leading citizens. It was described in a *New York Times* article as one of "the most innovative in the United States." Prestigious national organizations like the Ford Foundation and the National Trust for Historic Preservation and HUD heartily supported the SLRP concept and appropriated funds for the SLRP to buy, renovate, and rent more historic properties in the Victorian District.

Mayor Rousakis, who served as head of the National League of Cities, had been instrumental in securing some of the funds that poured into the SLRP. Within a few years, the Victorian District was placed on the National Register of Historic Places.[220] Rousakis, a supporter of the SLRP from the beginning, said on one occasion that the restoration of the Victorian District was the "most rewarding project in preservation in Savannah. It has assisted low-income families while at the same time preserving a significant portion of Savannah's heritage."[221]

But over time the SLRP vision was undermined somewhat by its success as real estate developers began acquiring hundreds of properties and renovating them and advertising them for sale or rent at prices affordable only by middle- and upper-middle-class families. W. W. Law's suspicions about black displacement and "gentrification" appeared well founded.

The HSF in the 1970s oversaw the restoration of more than a thousand historic structures and transformed decaying historic properties into upper-middle-class homes, and blighted areas into much-sought-after neighborhoods. The city itself poured millions of dollars into downtown Savannah, helping to transform much of the Historic District. Beginning in the 1970s and into the 1980s the SLRP renovated four hundred houses, rehabilitating much of the Victorian District. *Southern Living* magazine raved: "One year, a house remains forlorn with neglect; the next year, it sparkles with renewal." The author urged visitors who wished to learn more about Savannah to visit the Savannah Visitors' Center and Museum. Tourism became a new "industry." Revenue created by a flood of visitors rose from $200,000 in the late 1950s to more than $300 million in 1985.

Yet for all the vast progress of Savannah from the 1950s to the 1980s, Price Street on the east side of the city and Gwinnett Street on the west remained dividing lines between endemic poverty and upper-middle-class livelihoods. The SLRP Board in the 1980s always had a long waiting list for rehabilitated housing in the Victorian District, but many who needed housing could not afford even modest rents. For a city of Savannah's size there were too many poor people unable to afford housing in the Historic District. Among U.S. cities with the highest rates of poverty, Savannah ranked tenth.[222]

About half of Savannah's black community lived below the poverty line according to Henry Moore, Savannah's assistant manager for development in the 1980s, who estimated that "sixty-seven percent of the black households earn less than $14,000 [and] 50 percent less than $10,000." Although blacks now made up nearly 50 percent of the population, only "194 households . . . earned more than $50,000," whereas 1,275 white families enjoyed that level of income.[223]

The magazine *Travel* promoted the city in an article typical of those appearing in national publications. The president of the HSF, Betty Lee, spoke with journalists as she sat in her walled garden, "banked with flowers," about "Savannah's charms, Savannah's buildings, squares . . . especially in the spring when the azaleas are out. . . . all combine to make Savannah a wonderful place both to visit and to live in." Such promotional pieces brought new people to town looking for property, as did the book *Midnight in the Garden of Good and Evil,* a phenomenon that spent a record-setting 216 weeks on the *New York Times* best-seller list.[224]

The city continued to pursue nonpolluting industries, but lost out often to Jacksonville, Macon, and other places in the bidding for many desirable companies. By the late 1980s, the director of economic opportunity, John Finney, said with some urgency: "Now we need whatever we can get; if it's non-polluting, OK, if it's not. . . ."[225]

Crime, Drugs, and the Mercer Murder

In the late twentieth century, violent crimes across the country were on the rise. Young males were committing these crimes at younger ages, and frequently their behavior was linked to an intensely addictive drug, crack cocaine. Between the 1960s and 1980s criminal activity in Savannah rose 400 percent, and even local media warned the public about unsafe streets—but the public already knew, especially in some neighborhoods like Hitch Village where one resident said, "we just don't go out at night." Indeed, in the mid-1970s Savannah's crime rate increased more than twice that of the national rate increase. Most crimes were black-on-black and occurred in low-income areas.[226]

Savannah hired David Gellatly as its new chief of police in 1980, a time when violent crime was on the rise. In a March 1982 interview, Gellatly attacked crime statistics, television's emphasis on violence, and the judicial system as all contributing to Savannah's unacceptably high crime rate—the sixth highest in the nation. He warned that the city would suffer from publicity about the high crime numbers. As in the past, and as would hold true in the future, the remedy was to put more police on the streets. Unfortunately this tactic appeared to have little effect. Mayor Rousakis was stunned when an FBI report showed that Savannah in 1986 had earned the title "the murder capital of the U.S."[227]

In the late 1980s drug-related crime spiked and six additional police were added to the Metropolitan Drug Squad to focus on large-scale drug dealers in the area. The police department reactivated the police horse patrol disbanded in 1937 for reasons of economy. Such efforts had the support of City Manager Don Mendonsa, Mayor Rousakis and Chief Gellatly but crime continued to "fester and breed" particularly in the usual geographical areas that had for so long been plagued with violence.[228]

Around the time Gellatly took office, a high-profile murder occurred. The Mercer family of Savannah included themselves among the "blue bloods." They traced their genealogy in America from Hugh Mercer of Aberdeen, Scotland, who served as an aide to General George Washington during the American Revolution. The twentieth-century Mercer family manufactured Great Dane truck trailers and were members of the elite Oglethorpe Club—"a kind of family that can ordinarily sort out any difficulty with a phone call." But on this occasion they could not. They called the FBI and waited.

Young George Mercer IV, a great-grandnephew of Johnny Mercer, the world-renowned songwriter, was a sometime college student who wrote lyrics,

Savannah Police Department Horse Patrol, ca. 1930s. Disbanded shortly thereafter, the mounted patrol was reorganized in 1989. Courtesy of Georgia Archives, Vanishing Georgia Collection, image no. ctm071.

played the guitar, and also dabbled in "get-rich-quick" schemes. Shortly after young Mercer met Michael Harper, the two made plans to set up an audio business. But to do this they needed quick cash and, as Harper later recounted the story, the two acquired forty thousand dollars' worth of marijuana on credit planning to resell it for a profit. But thieves stole the drugs and, when the young men could not repay the forty thousand, their lives were threatened. According to Harper, the two hatched a plan to extort the cash from Mercer's father.

The details of what happened next are not clear. What is known is that young George Mercer vanished on January 29, 1980, and soon thereafter the Mercer family began receiving ransom notes. The family tried to keep publicity about the incident out of the papers for fear of putting their son's life in jeopardy, but a new Savannah publication, the *Georgia Gazette*, insisted on publishing details of the case. In April, the decomposed remains of young George Mercer IV, with two bullet holes in his body, were found in a shallow grave near the campus of Armstrong State College. Harper went on trial for murder. His past involvement with drug dealers, probation violations, and threats to kill former neighbors did not help his case. Harper pleaded not guilty, but a jury found otherwise and he was sentenced to life in prison. The best days of the Mercer family of Savannah were over.[229]

The Deaths of Officer Mark MacPhail and Attorney Robbie Robinson

On the night of August 19, 1989, Officer MacPhail, a twenty-seven-year-old white male in uniform, was providing security in an off-duty job on the premises of a Burger King near the Greyhound bus station on West Oglethorpe Avenue. A former Army Ranger, married, and the father of two children, MacPhail found his attention attracted by a loud altercation between two black men outside the bus terminal. He saw what appeared to be a homeless black man being pistol-whipped by another black man over a can of beer. MacPhail ran to intervene but was shot in the face and then shot again "execution-style." Witnesses named the shooter, Troy A. Davis. Shortly thereafter, Davis turned himself in and was subsequently tried and convicted by a jury, a majority of whom were African Americans, who deliberated only two hours. Davis was sentenced to death.

After the trial, many former witnesses recanted their testimony, saying they were coerced by the police to implicate Davis. The incident opened another schism between the white and black communities. Worldwide appeals for clemency followed over the next twenty years. After a ruling by the U.S. Supreme Court that "Mr. Davis is not innocent," he was executed on September 21, 2011.

A few years later the scars were reopened when a debate emerged among politicians and in the press over whether a modest public memorial should be erected to honor slain officer MacPhail. The deaths of the two young men, MacPhail and Davis, stirred deep emotions. One Savannahian wrote in the local paper, "there is a long and sordid history of racially motivated injustice in our criminal justice system." But now, even if one believed "Troy Davis was innocent" or his prosecution "racially motivated," the writer urged joining with the "community of people for whom Mark MacPhail gave his life in an effort to memorialize and express our gratitude for his courage and sacrifice on behalf of all of us—black and white." He concluded: "But if there must be blame, blame me." The author was Spencer Lawton, the prosecutor in the case against Troy Davis.[230]

Blind vengeance might have been the cause of another death that shocked the city in 1989. It was the Christmas season. After an exhausting day in court, Robbie Robinson, a local black attorney and city councilman representing the Fifth District, was in his downtown office opening the mail. He probably assumed the brown paper-wrapped box, taped and tied with string, was a Christmas gift. But it turned out to be a pipe bomb. Shrapnel blew the windows out of his office. Robinson died a painful death three hours later at a local hospital. The community was mystified. A mild-mannered family man, Robbie Robinson seemed an unlikely target.

Mayor Rousakis said "Robbie was not a radical." He was however the chief attorney for the local NAACP and had argued a 1988 desegregation case before the Eleventh Circuit Court. As the investigation unfolded, the bombing was linked to a similar mail bombing in Alabama that killed a federal judge, Robert Smith Vance, and two attempted bombings—one at the Eleventh Circuit Court in Atlanta and another at the office of the Jacksonville NAACP.

In December 1990 a jury found Leroy Moody guilty of the murders of Vance and Robinson. After numerous appeals, Moody was sentenced to death in 1997. He continued to appeal the verdict while on death row in Alabama. Moody's motives were complex; some believe he may have killed Robbie Robinson as a diversionary tactic, his real target being the courts and Judge Vance.[231]

Crime Is on My Mind

A study done in 1989 found crime concentrated on the east side of the city and the Victorian District, where drug sales and other crimes were especially high. Within these boundaries resided about 10 percent of the city's population. The spike in criminal activity terrified residents. The outcry was loudest when crime targeted tourists or the well-to-do. Even with 323 policemen, with black officers now making up about 35 percent of the force, the manpower seemed inadequate relative to the needs of some neighborhoods. "Use of force" had been required in 133 incidents, most associated with drugs or alcohol consumption. During 1989, five police officers used "lethal force," meaning they discharged their weapons in the line of duty.[232]

By the late 1980s, members of the local Crime Commission reported to the City Council that the high crime rate was due to the city's failure to provide drug treatment facilities, education programs, and more policemen. John Finney, director of Savannah's Economic Opportunity Authority, offered another perspective; he attributed the rising crime rate to the "lost hope" of people to find gainful employment: "We need jobs so people won't have to resort to crime."[233] The Rousakis administration's failure to control the escalating crime and the continued decline of Broughton Street, once the main shopping area of the city, brought new criticism of the mayor's leadership.

The Lucas, SCAD, and the Campaign to Save Broughton Street

As department stores like Maas Brothers and J. C. Penney departed Broughton Street for the malls on the city's south side, and storefronts boarded up, many took notice. To save the commercial center, private investors and the city launched a redevelopment effort, "Back to Broughton." It did not prove successful until the Adlers put their considerable influence behind the effort. It started when Emma Adler became the founding president of the Lucas Theatre. With others like Benjamin and Elizabeth Oxnard, Emma and Lee Adler made a personal investment and undertook fundraising for restoration of the theater by bringing together prominent citizens to form the nonprofit Lucas Theatre for the Arts.

Having closed as a movie house in 1976 and with the theater's owners threatening to demolish the Lucas to make way for a parking garage, local preservationists scrambled to save the historic "neoclassical movie palace." What followed was a decade-long multimillion dollar project that saved the theater and began the "restoration of the [the east] end of Broughton Street."

At about the same time, the expanding Savannah College of Art and Design (SCAD), noted for its investment in historic properties, purchased the eighty-five-thousand-square-foot Maas Brothers Department Store, which had been vacant for some years. Following extensive remodeling, the building became a state-of-the-art college library. Just across the street, SCAD restored and reopened the historic Weis Theater in 1989, renaming it the Trustees Theater. Such purchases with private money assured the resurgence of East Broughton Street.[234]

SCAD and the Savannah Renaissance

When Paula and Richard Rowan, described as "entrepreneurs," discovered the dearth of private art schools in the southeast, they resigned their jobs in Atlanta and established the Savannah College of Art and Design (SCAD). Never mind that the city's major shopping center, Broughton Street, was dreary or that dilapidated buildings abounded or that both businesses and schools had moved away from the city to the suburbs—the Rowans saw Savannah, with its "rich stock of unused buildings" as an ideal setting for their art college. Savannahians also discouraged them, perhaps fearing that a downtown campus would destroy both the ambiance and atmosphere of the city. Paula remembered that they were met with incredulity: "Most people thought they were being kind to discourage us."[235]

With Richard as president and Paula as provost, they purchased the Savannah Volunteer Guard Armory on Madison Square for $250,000 in 1979 as their first college building and spent $700,000 on renovation. That same year they hired faculty and admitted SCAD'S first freshman class.[236] In 1984, SCAD received accreditation from the Southern Association of Colleges and Schools, and three years later the association accredited the college to award master's degrees; shortly thereafter, the National Association of Architectural Boards accredited the school's bachelor of architecture program, only the second in Georgia. With each new accreditation, the college added more faculty to accommodate a growing student body, and the Rowans continued to purchase and renovate historic buildings, adding considerable real estate to their thriving academic enterprise.

SCAD's nonprofit status gave the school tax relief, allowed for tax-deductible donations, and protected the founders from organizational debt liability. The school's library, formerly the Mass Department Store, added significantly to its holdings when a New York university donated ten thousand books to its collection. By the end of 1993, SCAD had grown from seventy-one students and one building to "more than 2,400 students and 35 buildings."[237] But trouble was brewing beneath the surface calm.

Lawsuits, zoning issues, student protests, faculty unrest, and an IRS investigation provided challenges to the SCAD administration. When student and faculty would-be reformers were dismissed, the American Association of University Professors became involved, and the U.S Department of Education intervened when large operating deficits came to light.[238]

Students demonstrated for more rights, a student constitution, and a student government; faculty members protested the lack of tenure and a faculty senate. On April 6, 1992, "a small blast" occurred "in front of the administration building." School officials believed it to be linked to disgruntled student protesters, and several were barred from registering for the fall term. Four of those accused subsequently brought a $12.4 million dollar lawsuit against SCAD. Faculty criticism of school policies led to the dismissal of twelve teachers. Students rallied to their support and demanded instead the resignation of SCAD's president, Richard Rowan. On May 28 another pipe bomb detonated, this one outside Savannah's Civic Center Auditorium, site of SCAD's May 30 graduation. The formal ceremony was promptly cancelled.[239]

In the midst of these profoundly troubling days for SCAD, the *Morning News* praised the school as "a bona fide miracle. . . . its founders . . . deserve the credit." The institution had made a major contribution economically and culturally. John Rousakis told the paper that SCAD "has put us on the map and . . . its economic impact is in the millions" and that the school provided "some 400 jobs."[240]

But difficulties continued, leading to investigations by accrediting agencies. Suits brought by faculty, trustees, and students against SCAD on various issues and countersuits by the college relating to the events of 1992 went on for several years before settlements were reached. The suits by professors and trustees against SCAD for their wrongful dismissal were settled out of court. The records of these cases and those regarding other litigants were sealed, thus preventing the public from knowing who won, who lost, and why.

In February 1993, SCAD filed a $103 million lawsuit against the New York–based School of Visual Arts that was "attempting to establish a branch in Savannah." Among the many allegations, suits, charges, and countersuits were: "civil racketeering," damage to "reputation" and business interests, "scare tactics," and such. In 1996 the School of Visual Arts announced that it would leave Savannah within three years as part of an out-of-court settlement. A Savannah paper viewed the resolution: "Richard and Paula Rowan . . . managed to chase their New York based competitor . . . from town [in] . . . the confidential settlement." The paper also noted that the "settlement [was] eyed as vindication for some, [the] art community's loss" for others.[241]

But SCAD's second decade was not all conflict, controversy, and countersuits. School officials were delighted when in 1994 the institution received in Boston the National Preservation Honor Award from the National Trust for Historic Preservation. The award paid tribute to SCAD's restoration efforts that "helped revitalized Savannah's Historic District" by transforming "34 abandoned and boarded-up buildings . . . into state-of-the-art educational facilities." That same year the Historic Savannah Foundation honored SCAD with its Preservation Award, and the school library became the Jen Library, named in honor of Jim and Lancy Jen, its major benefactors.[242] In April 2000, Paula assumed the role of SCAD president. Within a year, Richard Rowan resigned from SCAD and left Savannah. Paula married former SCAD interior-design student and staff member Glenn Wallace Jr. in a private Thanksgiving Day ceremony in 2000.[243]

By the early twenty-first century, SCAD offered an international film festival that drew thousands of patrons; the institution now graciously accepted substantial endowments and donations, including Earl W. Newton's gift of rare seventeenth- and eighteenth-century English and American art and a priceless collection of African American art from Walter and Linda Evans, the second-largest collection of such art in the world. At the same time, SCAD was buying and renovating buildings along Martin Luther King Boulevard; preservationists, politicians, and the public credited this effort with helping to resuscitate the area, as did the National Trust, which awarded the school the 2003 "National Trust Main Street Leadership Award for Civic Leadership."

Lee Adler, one of Savannah's foremost preservationists, said of SCAD: the school provided "increased vitality and economic benefit . . . from its presence and that of its faculty and students . . . [it] put a floor under the downtown real estate market and streets became safer as students populated them at all hours." Adler's praise for SCAD continued when he said that the college had been "the single most significant benefit to Savannah's National Historic District in recent years."[244]

SCAD's most extensive renovation was unveiled in October 2011. The SCAD Museum of Art, a $26 million complex, was built on the ruins of the historic Central of Georgia Railway Depot. It was the largest building project in the school's history. The SCAD Museum anchored a growing art corridor on the city's west side.[245] SCAD by 2014 enrolled twelve thousand students and had campuses in Atlanta; Lacoste, France; and Hong Kong. The school also offered an "eLearning" option.[246] The attitude of many Savannahians who thought a downtown art school would ruin Savannah's ambiance now credit SCAD with playing a major role in Savannah's Renaissance.

Rousakis's Final Term as Mayor

By the beginning of the 1990s, City Manager Don Mendonsa as well as political opponents were aware that Mayor Rousakis's "equity agenda" had not resolved the disparities in quality of life between predominantly white and predominantly black neighborhoods. High rates of poverty persisted. Critics blamed Rousakis too for the large number of homeless in the city and high crime rates. Even City Council member Floyd Adams, known to criticize friends and foes alike, publicly told his friend Mayor Rousakis that he was "looking through rose colored-glasses at Savannah's crime problems."[247]

A defensive Rousakis told critics that the city was not responsible for certain social problems and that some issues should be addressed by the county and the state, not the city. He spoke of efforts to address the "homeless" by supporting several social agencies, and of increased funding for health services and hospitals. More importantly, the mayor reminded his critics that the budget of the city was in the black, that the city had an AA bond rating, and that there were no plans for a tax increase in 1991.

Rousakis did acknowledge that "crime-wise or murder-wise . . . we are in a bad year." But he defended the police by saying "the police can't prevent murders"; the lack of jobs and "the housing problem . . . contribute to the crime rate." Rousakis never forgot that "bad news burns," meaning that bad publicity can hamper growth and progress, and he defended his record, saying that when he took office citizens lacked "spirit," that Savannah was "dirty," and now the city is "aggressive and exciting" with "things happening" like a new waterfront, civic center, and the renewed life of the "parks and squares." The mayor was especially proud of having been able to secure Community Development Block Grant monies to improve the infrastructure of some of Savannah's poorest neighborhoods.[248] But an anti-Rousakis attitude pervaded the city, as was reflected in a "voter approved" measure mandating a maximum of two four-year terms for mayors. At the end of this term, Rousakis would have served for twenty-one years.

Crime became a rallying point for change. The Citizens Crime Commission, a private group formed a few years earlier, pressed for more police on the streets, bicycle patrols, extra security in the schools, and state funding for a youth detention center. In spite of all the police efforts and citizen input and new social initiatives, the number of murders in the city reached an all-time high of fifty-nine—not good news for Rousakis as he geared up for the mayoralty race of 1991.[249]

And there was more bad crime news to come when a member of local drug lord Ricky Jivens's gang, as part of an initiation rite, shot and killed John Thackston and his dog as they strolled through Ardsley Park. When Mayor Rousakis failed to move quickly enough to apprehend the murderer, the city's white leadership roundly criticized him. And when he did act, black leaders chided him for giving this single murder more time than he gave black homicides in the city.[250]

In June 1991 the Rousakis team rolled out a long-anticipated report on crime, identifying issues to be addressed: add more police officers, combat blight, reduce unemployment, stop drug trafficking, and reorganize the police to target a four-square-mile section of central Savannah—the city's worst crime area.

The reorganization plan divided the city into four precincts, putting officers in closer contact with the community they served. Officers would patrol on bicycles, attend community meetings, and interact with citizens—"all efforts designed to build trust and help police become part of the community." It was a crime-fighting tactic that would be used again and again in the years that followed.

Some progress occurred in several precincts. However, the precinct bounded by Victory Drive, Liberty Street, Waters Avenue, and Ogeechee Road, historically the area with the "worst" crime rates, saw virtually no improvement in "homicides . . . and drug offenses." Police Chief Gellatly had confidence in the new precinct program. Others did not.[251]

An especially vocal critic was Savannah newcomer and Republican Party member Susan Weiner. Weiner pounded the Rousakis administration for the high level of crime in the city. She and others were well aware of comparisons being made between "sister cities" Charleston and Savannah. Charleston's Ruben Greenberg, the innovative, roller-skating new police chief, had significantly reduced crime there. This success made Savannahians worry about being labeled a crime-ridden city.

Less than one hundred miles apart, both cities had urban centers, historic districts, ports, a military presence, and tourists. Always a little competitive, Savannah and Charleston now appeared to be moving along different paths. Charleston seemed to be thriving, with a larger population, more high-income residents, and safer streets. Of Savannah one observer said, just beyond the city's "horticulturally manicured squares," lurked a "combat zone" on the city's perimeters. If Savannah was to grow, public officials needed to curtail the "'Jack City' mayhem of Savannah's streets and neighborhoods and enliven its nearly extinguished public . . . life.'"[252]

Soon the city's crime rate and its leadership became major issues in the mayoral race between John Rousakis and Susan Weiner. But, in the months leading up to November 1991, Savannahians had something to distract them from the election hoopla. A new bridge across the Savannah River opened in March. The old cantilever bridge, now more than thirty-five years old, was hazardous to the large vessels coming into the port. With 185 feet of navigable clearance, the nearly two-mile-long bridge was supported by gleaming fan-like cables. From a distance in reflected light, the soaring cables resembled graceful iridescent sails. The structure became an iconic symbol for Savannah. Its name, the Eugene Talmadge Memorial Bridge, became a source of controversy that continues to this day.[253]

CHAPTER SIX

From Susan Weiner to Edna Jackson

1992–2016

Susan Weiner, age forty-five, a native of Albany, New York, former actress and business consultant, had lived in Savannah for six years when she decided to be a candidate in the 1991 mayor's race on the Republican ticket. Two liberals managed Weiner's campaign in the black community—votes that would be essential to an election victory. During a bitter contest Weiner promised to get rid of "the good old boy politics of city hall," to reduce crime, and put more police on the streets. Her billboards were designed to appear riddled with "bullet holes" hammering home her point about crime being out of control.

As a political newcomer, Ms. Weiner had to develop a thick skin. A pamphlet from the opposition described her as "racist," and Weiner once told an interviewer that "someone out there [called me] a communist, a lesbian, an ex-con racist from a family of racists." Incumbent Mayor Rousakis, now running for a sixth term, blasted Weiner's "campaign of lies."[1] Mudslinging was in the air.

In a city of 137,000 people (53 percent black and 46 percent white), 55 percent of eligible voters cast ballots and Weiner won by 2,600 votes, soundly defeating Rousakis 54 percent to 46 percent. To supporters, Susan Weiner dispelled the myth that "a woman, Republican, Yankee, a Jewish person who's from outside can't be elected." Her "stunning" victory surprised Savannah's Democrats; one even likened it to the "coming of Moses." Blacks who crossed over to vote the Republican ticket helped seal the election. Some years later the *Morning News* called Weiner's win "as much an anti-incumbent vote as a pro-Weiner mandate."

In the same election, four black City Council members were voted into office: Floyd Adams, for another term representing the city's First District; Clifford Hardwick; David Jones; and Gwendolyn Goodman. Dana Braun and Elizabeth Sheehan carried over from the Rousakis administration. Mayor Weiner and two other Republicans, Judi Ross and Ellis Cook, comprised the nine-member City Council. From the beginning it was a bitterly divided administration.[2]

At Susan's victory party she stood on a podium celebrating her win as her supporters pressed close, whooping it up. Her somewhat older husband, Al, a Yale PhD and university drama professor, suddenly grabbed the microphone. As the television cameras rolled, he shouted, "[Rousakis] is a pig." The cheering stopped, replaced by hisses and boos. Al later justified his remarks, saying the opposition had spread gossip that Susan was a Communist, a lesbian, or a convicted felon. Somewhat later he committed another *faux pas* when he told a reporter: "[if the IQs of] four city aldermen were added up, their combined IQs would not equal mine." Though Mr. Weiner did not state which City Council members' IQs would be tabulated, the four black Council members "took the insult personally."[3]

Floyd Adams Jr. was one of those insulted and he later characterized Al Weiner's comment as "another smartass remark to the black person." A native Savannahian, a protégée of W. W. Law during the civil rights movement, a graduate of a local Catholic high school and Savannah State College, Adams owned the *Savannah Herald*, an African American weekly newspaper. After 13 years on City Council, he knew city politics and he became the Mayor's most vocal and frequent critic.[4]

In response to mayor-elect Weiner's comments about crime, Rousakis's outgoing City Council voted unanimously to appoint its own "Crime Control Collaborative" with Dr. Otis S. Johnson as chair. The incoming mayor countered by appointing her own "Public Safety Issues Committee." Both committees were charged with investigating ways to battle crime.[5]

After being sworn in, one of Ms. Weiner's first acts as mayor was to veto the City Council's approval of funds to rehabilitate Broughton Street. She opposed using tax dollars to fund what she called "a commercial venture" and was confident the "majority of Savannahians" agreed. Not since the 1940s had a mayor overturned an act of the City Council.[6]

Next she tried to fire the long-time city manager, Don Mendonsa, and the city attorney. An indignant City Council—the most diverse ever, four blacks and five whites—instead gave both a vote of confidence and then cut the salary of the mayor's assistant. Weiner said she faced a "brick wall" from six of the nine City Council members. She did get support for two collaborative efforts between government and civic leaders, the Downtown Redevelopment Authority and a "Weed-and-Seed" program that brought together law enforcement and social agencies to clean up blighted neighborhoods.[7]

The new mayor's "Task Force" soon issued a report that made a number of observations and recommendations regarding crime in the city: Over the past twenty years more than a dozen studies had investigated "Savannah's protracted crime problems." Their review found that citizens had "a legitimate fear for their safety . . . [and that] the same trouble spots continue to exist." The "crime problem" has been "overstudied without producing sufficient tangible results" because of the city's unwillingness to make an "unequivocal commitment to the objective that crime will not be tolerated in this city." The report cited police for failing to "saturate areas repeatedly identified as high crime areas." More police needed to be hired, a minimum of thirty-four. Charleston with its "enviable crime rate [had] . . . 25 percent more officers per capita" than Savannah. The report concluded that city management had failed to give "the Savannah Police Department the functional and operational autonomy and sufficient resources to successfully accomplish" its mission.[8]

Years later Tom Barton of the *Morning News* provided his own assessment of Mayor Weiner's administration. Although he viewed her as a "dynamic woman with forward-looking ideas," Barton wrote that Weiner or any mayor by the 1990s needed five votes "to get anything done" on the nine-member City Council—she had "only one council member she could reliably count on." This handicap and "a goofball husband," Barton concluded, resulted in "Four lost years for local government and the community."[9]

Mayor Weiner and Councilman Floyd Adams continued their feud when they faced one another in the mayoralty contest of 1995. Adams gave her low marks on leadership, crime, and economic development and accused her of "regressive policies which divided the city racially." Adams had selected the "right time" to run. He was well known and popular at a time when Savannah's black population had recently become the majority.[10]

High priorities for both candidates included fighting crime, the city's drug problems, juvenile violence, and economic development. Weiner accused the opposition of again using a "whispering campaign" against her; though Adams denied any "mudslinging," the local press charged him with numerous counts of it. When Weiner's supporters circulated photographs of Adams emphasizing his wide girth (Adams weighed over three hundred pounds), his campaign manager shot back, "if the worst they can say about you is that you're too . . . fat, then that's not bad."[11]

On election day in early November, no mayoral candidate received 50 percent of the vote. In addition to Weiner and Adams, former mayor John Rousakis had joined the race along with one other candidate—state law mandated that a runoff take place on November 28, but one candidate was noticeably absent. The "election marked a milestone in area politics, Rousakis, the city's Mayor for 21 years, could not generate sufficient votes to be in the runoff." Subsequently Rousakis came out in support of Adams and for doing so received anonymous death threats. It was not the first time Rousakis had donned a bullet-proof vest.

In the runoff campaign, Adams emphasized that he planned to go after every vote in the community, "not just the black vote, or Greek vote or the Irish vote." Weiner stressed her commitment to "use positive campaigning."[12] In the runoff, Adams received 15,912 votes to Weiner's 15,656, winning the recount by 256 votes to become one of 417 black mayors in the country. Weiner called the election results "tainted" and demanded another recount. But the runoff vote results were certified and upheld.[13] Floyd Adams became Savannah's sixty-third and its first African American mayor.

Adams told a *Washington Post* reporter that he attributed his victory to "African-American women who ran a grass-roots campaign and increased voter registration among blacks by almost 25%." Black women themselves accounted for 65 percent of the registered black voters. Adams needed "85% of the black vote and 15% percent of the white to win," which is about what he got.

Mayor-elect Adams reflected on his victory: "Some looked at me as a militant. But now they have to deal with me. It will be okay. They'll see it will all work out." In the final analysis Adams recognized too that "race" was an issue. He was right. A local antique dealer said many whites were stunned by Weiner's loss: "they could not comprehend it."

Weiner's campaign workers blamed the loss on Weiner's overreliance on "a handful of rich people." Years later a *Morning News* editorial presented a different view: "White voters were responsible for electing Savannah's first black mayor. Enough of them were disgusted with then-Mayor Susan Weiner (and more annoyed with her husband) that they threw their support behind Adams." But, following the election, Savannah's African American community spoke as one: "It's about time."[14] W. W. Law looked to the times and the candidate to explain this monumental shift in the political landscape.

As a leader of Savannah's civil rights movement, Law said: "[The reason we never] had a black mayor is because blacks have no hesitation voting for whites, but whites have reservations about voting for blacks; . . . in Floyd Adams we had a candidate so experienced, so sensible, that he won some of their support." Correctly, the reporter for the *Washington Post* observed: "people of color do not have the power here. . . . when compared with many other southern cities, such as Atlanta, New Orleans or Birmingham . . . few occupy positions of [power] . . . in the business world." Nevertheless, in the "increasingly GOP-controlled South," Adams bested an incumbent Republican mayor running "on an anti-crime platform" with his "Democratic idea that the government should help black Savannahians get a larger slice of the pie."[15]

A former City Council member, future mayor, and then director of the Chatham County–Savannah Youth Futures Authority, Otis Johnson, hoped Adams would combine "rebuilding the physical structure of parts of the city and its social structure as well." Adams took on this challenge by continuing the "equity agenda" first launched by the Rousakis administration.

Mayor Floyd Adams: "We Are One Savannah"

On January 2, 1996, Floyd Adams Jr., a lifelong Democrat, was inaugurated as mayor. A native Savannahian, reared in a brick house in an upper-class black neighborhood on Newell Street, Floyd Jr. learned his strong work ethic from his father, founder of the *Herald,* an African American weekly. His father paid young Floyd ten cents an hour to clean up the press room rather than give him an allowance and urged him to meet various challenges head on. The new mayor, reporters found, was "difficult to pigeonhole. . . . He crosses party lines . . . in political battles as the need arises . . . and endorses Republicans when he thinks they're better candidates, and sometimes fights Democratic leaders." *USA Today* congratulated the city: "Savannah, renowned for preserving the symbols of its past claims a new level of political maturity . . . when it inaugurates its first black mayor."[16]

As he said he would, Adams set a goal of uniting all the people, black and white. Soon after taking office he attended Confederate Memorial Day ceremonies in Forsyth Park, the only black face in a crowd of reenactors dressed in Confederate gray.[17] Two years later, at the same event, he said that, regardless of our ethnicity, "We are one America, we are one Georgia and—most of all—we are one Savannah."[18] And he never hesitated to speak up for a position he believed in.

Some months after his election, when white Savannahians frowned on the inscription to be engraved on the new African American Family Monument on River Street, he took their side. The tribute, written by renowned poet Maya Angelou, read: "We were stolen, sold and bought together from the African continent. We got on the slave ships together. We lay back to belly in the holds of the slave ships in each others excrement and urine together, sometimes died together, and our lifeless bodies thrown overboard together." Because of community reaction, Ms. Angelou agreed to fashion a concluding sentence: "Today, we are standing up together, with faith and even some joy."[19]

Adams's vision for the city included attracting new industry, maximizing the booming tourist trade, creating a new black-and-white middle class, and revitalizing and making safer downtown neighborhoods. Luckily for Adams, the economy of the nation and Savannah surged in the late 1990s. SCAD's renovations of downtown buildings and burgeoning student body, movies like *Forest Gump*—filmed partly in the city—and Savannah's hosting of the 1996 Olympic yachting events attracted national and international attention—and tourists.[20]

But one of the main attractions that lured people to the city then (and now) was "the book," John Berendt's best-selling *Midnight in the Garden of Good and Evil,* "a true-crime story, a comedy of manners, and a wonderful evocation of the eccentricities, beauties, and legends of a grand old city, gone to seed and then reborn." The book was made into a 1997 movie starring John Cusack and Kevin Spacey. One prominent Savannahian, like others of her class, was upset about the book's characterization of the city and bemoaned, "the book told untruths about us. . . . It may be a good read for people who do not know about Savannah, but for us it was like a drive-by shooting. It upsets me to this day."[21]

Travelers to the city often romanticized it. One 1995 visitor to the gravesites of composer Johnny Mercer and poet Conrad Aiken at Bonaventure Cemetery on the banks of the Wilmington River said he "felt like lingering amid its moss-draped oaks forever. . . . [Here] a palpable sense of mystery . . . hangs in the cool night air."

Because of such images and with Savannah now frequently mentioned in the popular press, the city hosted nearly one million visitors in mid-1995. Expanding downtown real estate sales and home restorations created jobs for the middle class, but tourists rarely saw those who did not benefit from the boom times. By the late 1990s, 22 percent of Savannahians lived at or below the poverty level, a rate significantly higher than the state (13 percent) and the nation (12 percent). The percentage of persons living in poverty in Savannah's city center was reported to be 33 percent. And these rates were disproportionate by race: African Americans made up 58 percent of the population but comprised 76 percent of those in poverty. Those seeking to work their way out of poverty found options limited as the primary growth occupations were in service jobs such as "food preparation and related occupations"—the average weekly wage for these being "among the lowest at $252 a week."[22]

And there were other issues. In April 1995 the explosion of a storage tank full of turpentine at the Powell Duffryn Terminal caused a toxic chemical fire that burned for three days; whole neighborhoods had to be evacuated—some for as long as a month. An analysis of local industry found 175 companies with hazardous or extremely hazardous materials on site. The local paper warned, "The area's industrial history and status quo zoning leaves [*sic*] thousands, especially the poor and minorities, with Toxic Neighbors."[23]

Hoping to find ways to reduce the devastating effects of chronic poverty on individuals and the community, the Adams administration formed the "Anti-Poverty Task Force" and adopted a mini–Urban Redevelopment Plan, a blueprint for the reclamation of neighborhoods. Though other rehabilitation programs had been implemented, "the poverty rate in five . . . inner-city Census tracts had not changed in over 30 years."[24]

The city partnered with private developers and federal agencies to bring major changes to blighted communities like Cuyler-Brownville on the west side. Once a middle-income community with a diverse population, it became over time "raggedy with rundown houses, alcohol, drugs, guns, fights, and strangers going in and out of abandoned houses." Here stood Charity Hospital (founded as McKane Hospital in 1896), among the first to serve the black community.

Over the next few years city, federal and private funds rebuilt the hospital that had been gutted by fire in the 1990s and named it Heritage Place. The former hospital now provided eighty-eight apartments at affordable prices on Thirty-second Street, the heart of Cuyler-Brownville. Nearby, other units and dozens of homes went up, streets were paved, and water and sewer lines installed. Millions of federal dollars went into the area. In 1997, after a rigorous review process, Cuyler-Brownville was designated by local ordinance as a "Historic District," as were Thomas Square, Daffin Park, and Gordonston.[25]

On the city's east side, the Garden Homes housing project needed extensive renovation, and the city received a $16 million federal grant to rebuild homes and apartments. The city itself spent $2 million for new sidewalks, streets, and pipelines on this site and to revitalize Benjamin Van Clark Park, an adjoining neighborhood.

Aggressive Annexation and New Industry

The Adams administration also pursued an aggressive annexation program. Twelve small areas and the thirty-six-hundred-acre Godley Tract, all west of the city, were annexed. Savannah provided sewer and water lines to these areas and over time received from them significant property and sales taxes.[26] Adams continued to market Savannah to potential business and industry and never lost an opportunity to promote Savannah as a "visitors' destination."

In the first six months of 1998, Savannah-area manufacturing jumped 5.2 percent, well above Georgia's 0.4 percent. The retail sector rose 4.6 percent, the state 2.8 percent. Savannah enjoyed a diversified economy made up of manufacturing (40 percent), tourism (25 percent), the export-import trade (15 percent), the local army bases (10 percent), and business services (10 percent). The largest manufacturers included the Gulfstream Aerospace Corporation, a company that produced corporate jets and employed 4,300 personnel, and Union Camp with 2,200 on its payroll.

The Adams administration continued to bring more conventioneers and their money to Savannah. Revenues increased significantly after the city raised the tax on hotel-motel accommodations to 6 percent; within a few years, more than 5 million visitors annually were pumping $1 billion into the local economy. Plans were underway by private firms to add two thousand hotel rooms to meet the growing demand of tourists. A $116 million Savannah International Trade and Convention Center went up on Hutchinson Island, just north of the city across the Savannah River.

Problems and Partnerships

Georgia Trend featured Savannah in an article, "Oldest City, New Momentum." For all the successes of Adams and his city manager, Michael Brown, the city confronted a daunting array of problems: persistent poverty, inadequate resources to train a local workforce, and a mandate to reduce city water use by ten million gallons a day due to saltwater intrusion into the Florida Aquifer. More controversy emerged after the Georgia Ports Authority (GPA) declared a need to deepen the Savannah River channel. Doug Marchand, executive director of the GPA, made compelling arguments: "If it [the river channel] isn't deepened, Savannah and Georgia become less competitive." Already Norfolk's channel was fifty feet; Charleston anticipated deepening its channel to forty-five feet while Savannah's channel depth remained at forty-two feet—the GPA wanted to deepen the channel to forty-eight feet.[27]

Funds for major accomplishments during the Adams administration came from several sources, including property taxes and a Special Purpose Local Option Sales Tax (SPLOST) that had been approved again by voters in 1997. Much of the SPLOST money paid for infrastructure improvements such as drainage and roads. It also funded projects to make the city more attractive, including renovations to Colonial Cemetery and the Confederate Monument in Forsyth Park. SPLOST dollars also helped to defray a portion of the cost of the African American Monument on River Street.

City government continued partnerships with organizations like the Annie E. Casey Foundation, which underwrote the Chatham-Savannah Youth Futures Authority with a $10 million grant to provide support for family, health, social, and cultural services in some of Savannah's poorest neighborhoods. The city, the Chamber of Commerce, and the United Way became major funders of the Youth Futures Authority. Everyone recognized that poverty and its associated problems were not good for economic development.[28]

Police Scandal: "Busted Trust" and Crime

Adams also had to contend with unanticipated distractions, especially a scandal within the police department—in the making for some years—that erupted in 1997. On September 11, boldface headlines in the *Morning News* blared: "Busted Trust." Eleven police officers had been indicted on federal drug charges. In return for cash payments, the officers conspired to escort and provide protection "for shipments of cocaine into and out of the area." A tip from a convicted drug dealer initiated an undercover operation by the FBI and police. All those charged were African American officers. If convicted, fines ranged from $4 million and life in prison to a $250,000 fine and ten years in prison. Ten of the eleven officers were found guilty and sent to federal prisons.

Rick Pryor, a member of the local Citizen Crime Watchdog Group, said his organization had "concerns about corruption . . . in the police department" for years and had asked for an investigation. Chief of Police Gellatly called it "one of the most serious breaches of public trust" but reminded citizens that the other hundreds of police officers employed by the county and city had done "nothing . . . to tarnish the badge."[29] Following the convictions, the police budget went up dramatically.

In 1998 the budget for the Savannah Police Department reached $26.4 million or 28 percent of the general-fund budget for the city of Savannah. The mayor launched another collaboration on police-citizen relations, the Community Oriented Policy (COP)—a program that asked citizens to cooperate with police to solve problems in their neighborhoods and to help police identify criminal activity.

Chief Gellatly stepped down in 1999 after nearly twenty years of service. During his tenure the city force had grown from 250 to 450 officers; civilian employees had doubled to more than 100, the number of police cars increased from 75 to 245, and the department now had a computer on every desk. Such additions came at a cost as the budget increased from $6 million to $30 million. The following year, a search began for Gellatly's successor, and the department issued yet another report on strategies to reduce crime, "Violence Reduction Plan: A Cooperative Effort to Combat Violence in Savannah."[30]

Hurricane Floyd, a New Monument, and a New Chief of Police

Mayor Floyd Adams ran unopposed in November 1999 for a second term. One of his biggest concerns as the election approached was the threat of a hurricane, ironically named Hurricane Floyd. The massive storm, with winds projected at 110 to 155 miles per hour, potentially threatened a large portion of the southeastern coast. City government ordered a mandatory evacuation at noon on September 15. More than half a million people queued up in slow-moving traffic to leave Georgia's coast. "All lanes on Interstate 16, the main route out, were made westbound for 90 miles." On some sections, "walking was faster" than driving.[31] The Georgia coast was spared as the storm veered and made landfall in North Carolina. This massive exodus proved a good "dry run" for those who would make evacuation decisions when another storm threatened

The election of Adams for a second term as mayor and African American Edna Jackson as an at-large member of the City Council resulted in the first black majority council under the first black mayor in Savannah's history. A decade later, Jackson used the recognition received and the experience gained as a member of the City Council to make a successful run for mayor.[32]

Early in his second administration, Mayor Adams hosted a delegation of Haitian Americans interested in the preservation of the site of the 1779 siege of Savannah located just off Martin Luther King Jr. Boulevard near the Visitor Information Center. Members of the local Haitian-American Historical Society appeared before the City Council to propose that a monument be erected to the Chasseurs Volontaires, a Haitian unit that helped defend Savannah during the British siege. Subsequently, Mayor Adams led a delegation to Haiti, and eventually a modest sculpture went up in Franklin Square, one of the first monuments to blacks in Savannah; it was unveiled more than one hundred years after the erection of monuments built to celebrate white military heroes.[33] These efforts by Adams reflected his interest, like those of W. W. Law, in promoting the contributions of African Americans to Savannah's history.

On one occasion, after the City Council took a guided tour of Savannah, the mayor summarized what troubled them about the experience: "Our concern is [that] . . . tour guides could get more information on African American contributions to this community," and he requested them to "Please consider expanding your scope." The director of the largest tour company expressed reservations about the idea, calling it "a challenge."[34]

During the early 2000s, the global, national, and local economy soured. Thousands of job losses came to Savannah's construction and manufacturing sectors. Almost simultaneously violent crime spiked upward, and the city again rushed to combat it with several programs. The Savannah Impact Program focused on close supervision of high-risk offenders on parole or probation who perpetrated most of the violent crime. The city also implemented the Career Offender Tracking Unit that by year's end removed 130 violent criminals from Savannah's streets. Helping to accomplish this was a CrimeStoppers program that gave cash awards to citizens for information leading to the apprehension of criminals.[35]

Dan Flynn, a veteran of Miami's police force, was sworn in as Savannah's new chief of police during Adams's second term. After a two-year study, Adams, Chief Flynn, the City Council, and Chatham County officials supported a merger creating the Savannah–Chatham Metropolitan Police Department (SCMPD), envisioned as a more efficient system of fighting crime. The City Council voted for the merger in October, and a subsequent vote by the Chatham County Commission created the new, combined force. SPLOST funds were used for start-up costs for the six-hundred-member SCMPD—an image of General Oglethorpe appeared on the shoulder patches of its officers.[36]

No Third Term Possible

If Savannah's charter had permitted Adams to run for a third term he likely would have won, but the City Council in 1990 had imposed a two-term limit (eight years) for mayors. Adams sought to have the council undo the provision, but it refused. He decided to run for a congressional seat instead and was "hurt" when the business community failed to provide funding for his candidacy.

Adams had gone out of his way to court the Chamber of Commerce so "the entire community could move forward." It is unclear why the business community did not support Adams's political ambitions, but he was known to hold strong opinions that some may have found off-putting. Adams also came under criticism from African Americans; as one critic observed: "He should have been more of a mayor for black folks than he was." Occasionally he blundered by mixing personal and business life and, as one journalist reminded readers, Adams sometimes had "missteps—lapses in judgment and problems with staffing," and his bullying led to high turnover in personnel. But writers also praised the mayor for leading Savannah "through unprecedented economic growth." The *Morning News* editorialized that Mayor Adams "can be proud of his eight years as mayor." And he won a major personal battle: while in office he dropped 130 pounds![37]

In his final state-of-the city address, Adams returned to the theme that marked his tenure in office—the unity of all Savannahians. He told constituents he had hoped to remove the barrier to "racial division" and replace it with "racial harmony" but admitted, "I have done that [only] to a point." He went on to say, "We can achieve our destiny together—one voice, one city, one Savannah connecting each of us to one another . . . and face our challenges together." Adams acknowledged hurtles ahead: "we must build stronger families, reduce neighborhood blight, improve the condition of housing and reduce poverty." One of the city's greatest tasks, Adams declared, was "to take back our streets from crime, gangs and drugs."[38]

Adams died at age sixty-eight in February 2014. Community leaders reflected on his legacy as the city's first black mayor, though Adams always described himself as "everybody's mayor, not the first black mayor." His participation in the civil rights movement of the 1960s and in public service inspired young people. He never stopped "speaking out for the impoverished and others who were not being adequately served."[39] And his successes paved the way for Dr. Otis Johnson's run for the office in 2003.

Dr. Otis S. Johnson and the "Equity Agenda"

Surrounded by well-wishers outside City Hall in late January 2003, Johnson was introduced by Aaron Buchsbaum, local attorney and civil rights activist. Here he announced his candidacy for mayor: "Savannah . . . needs a person who is both practical and visionary. My record of service shows I can work well with all segments of the community [and] . . . I am not afraid to advocate for improving conditions [for] people of all races and classes." Businessman Pete Liakakis, a member of the City Council for eight years and realtor Richard "Dicky" Mopper already had entered the race when Johnson announced he would run. Eventually three more candidates joined the field.

A sixty-year-old native Savannahian, Johnson graduated from Beach High School, attended Savannah State College, and then transferred to Armstrong College, where he became the first African American to enroll and graduate. His heroes were W. W. Law and W. E. B. DuBois, the legendary civil rights author and advocate, an "activist-intellectual" whom Johnson emulated. After two years of active duty and several years in the naval reserves, he earned another undergraduate degree from the University of Georgia, a degree in social work from Clark-Atlanta University, and in 1980 a PhD in social welfare and management from Brandeis University. Elected to two terms on the City Council, Johnson spent ten years as executive director of the Chatham-Savannah Youth Futures Authority, an initiative that helped at-risk children and families. In 1998 he became a dean at Savannah State University, a post he retained until retiring in 2002. Subsequently Johnson ran unopposed for the Savannah–Chatham County Board of Education, where he served a four-year term. Johnson served on national boards and took on leadership roles in social and service organizations. A man of many talents, he played the clarinet and oboe, enjoyed jazz, blues, and spirituals, and found it therapeutic to cruise the open sea with the stars overhead and the wind in his face.[40]

Johnson's campaign Web site posted his ideas for Savannah's future. Like his predecessors, he made crime a major issue, favoring a "multi-disciplinary" approach and proposing a citizen's committee to develop a plan to make the community safer. As the campaign gathered speed, the Savannah Police Department issued yet another report on crime, "Analysis of the Risk Factors That Contribute to Youth Violence," that buttressed Johnson's positions. He advocated a Savannah that reflected its own "social, cultural . . . diversity." A serious man, Johnson understood the benefits of attracting environmentally friendly industry, of creating a qualified workforce that would be paid a living wage, of diversifying the economy, of promoting tourism and creating a "vibrant entertainment district." He also wanted to continue the strong flow of trade through the port and to make sure public-school students had a mastery of basic skills and access to "skill-up" programs such as one being developed by the city, the Chamber of Commerce, and the local technical college to reduce school dropouts and build career ladders for the underemployed and unemployed.[41]

Mayor Adams privately supported his friend Otis Johnson, but other influential members of the black community favored Pete Liakakis, a Greek American, city councilman, and former bodyguard for Burt Reynolds. Zaphon Wilson, a political scientist at Savannah State University, said Liakakis had paid his dues, having "been at every major event, wedding and funeral in the black community for years." A splintered vote in the black community and the large number of candidates on the ballot resulted in a runoff between Johnson and Liakakis.

Less than two weeks before the election, the *Morning News* described candidate Johnson as the person who can "address the one local issue that affects all others: public education." The endorsement also mentioned Johnson's life of service to the community, his efforts to combat crime, his willingness to discuss the "city's social ills," and the fact that he was not "afraid to blaze a new trail" as reasons "Our nod [for Mayor] goes to Otis Johnson."[42]

It was a "horse race." As votes came in on election night, it appeared that Liakakis might win. But as hopes ebbed at one headquarters, they soared at the other. When the 23,048 votes cast were tallied, the count showed Johnson had won by 502 votes (Johnson 51.1 percent, Liakakis 48.9 percent). Upon hearing the news, Pete Liakakis said to his supporters: "My God, I've lost." By phone he conceded the election around 9:45 P.M. Johnson's followers burst into cheers when the winner said, "I want to be the head coach and chief cheerleader" who leads Savannah forward.[43]

A post-election analysis of the outcome found that some black ministers, who had not declared their support for either candidate, in the waning days of the campaign came out publicly for Johnson. So too did Mayor Adams. Voters in Districts 1, 2, and 5, all heavily African American districts that Liakakis won in the November 4 general election, went for Johnson in the runoff. Additionally, Johnson gained votes throughout the city, some of them in Liakakis's strongholds. Perhaps this group was influenced by the *Morning News* endorsement. The close election prompted City Council member Tony Thomas to say, "The city is very divided. We need to . . . bring everybody together, or nobody will be together."[44]

The *Morning News* congratulated both Johnson and Liakakis for running "clean campaigns" founded on real issues and "hopes for Savannah's future." The new City Council that Johnson inherited from the Adams administration provided him with the "best of both worlds"—four "seasoned members," Edna Jackson, Clifton Jones, Ellis Cook, and Tony Thomas, as well as four "fresh faces"—Van Johnson, Mary Osborne, Jeff Felser, and Kenneth Sadler. The council was younger (average age fifty-two), well educated, diverse, and represented various faith communities: four white members (Jews, Catholics, and Protestants) and five black members (Episcopalians and Baptists). The council retained "a black majority, a reflection of the city's black demographic."[45]

On Sunday, January 4, 2004, more than 700 people assembled in the Johnny Mercer Theatre to see Otis S. Johnson sworn in as "Savannah's 64th Mayor." Upon the introduction of the mayor-elect, the crowd exploded into cheers, which Johnson acknowledged with a thumbs-up. He promised to take aim at the "twin evils" of poverty and racism, "[the roots] of many of our social problems that plague our community . . . [and to build] a better Savannah for all." Because of the exuberance of the crowd, both Mayor Johnson and Adams, the former mayor, found it difficult to bring the inauguration ceremonies to a close.[46]

Removing the Generals and Addressing Poverty and Blight

Almost immediately after moving into the mayor's office, Johnson took an action that pleased some and angered others. When the new mayor found offensive remnants of the Old South hanging on the walls of City Hall, he ordered them removed. Workers soon took down portraits of Confederate Civil War Generals

Robert E. Lee and John F. Wheaton. This action was perhaps an attempt by Johnson to move beyond the atmosphere of the Old South, and it brought a quick response from the local Confederate Heritage group, who compared him to the Taliban, describing Johnson as a "hypocrite . . . nothing but political correctness run amok."

The following year, Johnson attended Confederate Memorial Day in Forsyth Park; with hat over heart he listened as uniformed marchers played "'Dixie' and as they pledged allegiance to the Confederate Flag." Black community leaders criticized him for participating. Two years later, Johnson's niece chided him for refusing to offer an official apology for slavery. She wrote in the *Morning News,* "If the descendants of slaves have risen to the helm of the city . . . they have the opportunity to lead that institution to apologize for its historical wrong." Later, Johnson philosophically observed, "My public life helped me to moderate my idealism."[47]

In one of his first presentations to the City Council in 2004, Mayor Johnson outlined challenges facing the city's equity agenda: poverty rates of 33 percent in the poorest black neighborhoods, persistent lower incomes among blacks, and disproportionately fewer businesses owned by African Americans. Major roadblocks handicapped city progress in fighting poverty, such as federal and state governments' disinterest in rescuing inner-city neighborhoods and the refusal of Georgia lawmakers to enact a living-wage law for workers under city contracts or to approve a higher statewide minimum wage—initiatives essential to the Savannah Anti-Poverty Reduction Action Plan.[48]

Yet Johnson remained optimistic, as did City Manager Michael Brown, who spoke "passionately" about keeping the city's focus riveted on reducing poverty. By now the equity agenda was institutionalized in City Hall and endorsed and supported by more than seventy organizations. City government, the Chamber of Commerce, faith-based and educational groups were all collaborating to reduce poverty in Savannah.

With African Americans now 57 percent of the city's population, the highest ever, Johnson called attention to the new demographic milestone, saying, "[this] gets the attention of the powers that be." Even the business-focused Chamber of Commerce championed the equity agenda and efforts to "to promote the general welfare for everyone." Savannah's economic development director, Robert Keber, confirmed the expanded involvement when he said, "the wider community supports the equity agenda."[49] Mayor Johnson cautioned, "[it was] a lack of public policy that allowed our neighborhoods to deteriorate and we're just not going to let that happen again."[50]

Johnson moved aggressively to pursue Adams's policy of annexing property west and southwest of Savannah; especially noteworthy was the so-called "land grab" of sixty-five hundred acres mostly owned by International Paper situated between I-95 and I-16. The city once again spent millions to install sewer and water lines. And in the long run Savannah benefitted—property and sales-tax returns from the area being far greater than the investment costs.[51]

Following up on a campaign promise, Johnson held quarterly town hall meetings where he talked about changes needed to turn the community around. He wanted graffiti quickly eradicated, vacant lots cleaned, sold, or built on, and derelict vehicles removed. These efforts were part of his administration's "Operation Clean Sweep: A Blight Eradication Plan." The mayor also challenged the Savannah–Chatham County Schools to reduce the number of black male dropouts and the high rate of truancy. Repeatedly, Johnson reiterated that Savannah's biggest social problems stemmed from blight and juvenile crime.[52]

Murder, The Public Safety Taskforce and Chief Flynn's Resignation

In the early morning hours of February 7, 2004, two young black men approached West Bay Street's Church's Fried Chicken managed by Sean Abraham and after a botched robbery attempt, chased Abraham into an alley, forced him to kneel and beg for his life and then killed him "execution–style." Sean, a 25 year old black male and a 2002 business graduate of Alabama State University, had a promising future. The murderers, 17 year old Charles Hill and 19 year old Derek Horne received multiple consecutive life sentences for the crime.

Just over two months later, in broad daylight in a strip mall parking lot on the south side of the city, Gloria Peloquin, was shot and killed by a 16 year old black male during a robbery attempt. The young man received a life term for killing the 43 year old white homemaker. These slayings shocked the public and spurred the Mayor to appoint a task force to investigate the local law enforcement and justice systems and make recommendations for "change and improvement."[53]

Mayor Johnson chose a diverse forty-person group—neighborhood activists, a retired FBI agent, a gay activist, and a criminal justice expert—all "known for their expertise or passion." A cautionary *Morning News* reminded the public that three task forces had been appointed over the past twenty years and yet "crime was still a problem." The mayor was urged not to let the work of this task force "end up on a shelf somewhere gathering dust."[54]

Since taking over as chief of police in 2000, Dan Flynn had his hands full. He was the "architect" and implementer of the city-county police merger that created the Savannah-Chatham Metropolitan Police Department, and he played a key role in local security for the G8 Summit (meetings occurred on Sea Island though there were some protests in Savannah). In 2004–5 Flynn struggled with what some characterized as "micromanaging" by a mayor and council who were unhappy about those troublesome crime statistics.

The chief's crime-reduction efforts had focused on drug trafficking, which he said "[was] a major contributing factor in a high percentage of our crime, perhaps as much as 75 percent. . . . [It is] a major problem we have struggled with for years." Flynn also supported a Safe Streets–Safe Kids program targeting truancy, gangs, drugs, and underage drinking. But the perception remained that something was broken and needed to be fixed. Sixty percent of residents viewed crime as their biggest concern, and 40 percent did not feel safe in the city. The mayor and council's patience was wearing thin. At the November 2004 budget meeting, Mayor Johnson put it bluntly, telling Flynn there is a "crisis of confidence [in the police department]."[55]

The Public Safety Task Force's May 15, 2005, final report put the crime problem in perspective and offered some recommendations. After a year-long review, a twelve-member subcommittee issued a stinging report. Crime was unacceptably high: homicide rates in Savannah were 17.5 per 100,000 compared to 9.6 in Charleston and 6.9 in New York City. The report especially chastised police leadership for low expectations of crime reduction and for failure to allocate resources to the precincts in order to ensure a fully staffed cadre of officers on the streets.

In December 2005, Chief Flynn retired from his $112,000-a-year position. When asked why, he answered, "It's a business surrounded by conflict." Both City Manager Brown and County Manager Russ Abolt expressed regret at his departure. Brown said that Flynn had been "an excellent strategic chief." In his resignation letter, Flynn defended his record on crime, writing that "violent crime was the lowest it had been in twenty-seven years."

The mayor and council viewed Flynn's retirement as an opportunity to hire a new chief, one who would be more responsive to the recommendations of the Public Safety Task Force. City Manager Brown appointed Major Willie Lovett as interim chief; Councilman Clifton Jones predicted there would likely be lobbying for a black chief "by some members of council [and] . . . the public."[56]

In interviews, Mayor Johnson spoke candidly about his dissatisfaction with the Police Department. He said that he and the City Council had asked for a more "aggressive community-oriented policing style" and for more officers on the street, but neither was forthcoming. The mayor pointed out that the former chief not only failed to embrace the "Public Safety Task Force Report" but also had become defensive about the numbers, which created an atmosphere of conflict.

The mayor acknowledged that he and council had been accused of "micromanaging," but said by way of explanation, "we were looking for results." If the job is not getting done, it is "the elected people who are accountable for the good or the bad of the city. When crime is up, the public doesn't run to the City Manager, they say Mayor, you got to do something about the crime, but in reality the Mayor can't hire or fire the Police Chief." When asked if there was anything in the "Public Safety Task Force Report" that he did not agree with, the mayor replied with wry humor, "I'm not an opponent of the to-go cup. I don't see that as a big purveyor of evil."

Questioned as to whether Savannah had a "crime problem or a perception of a crime problem" the mayor answered, "Both. . . . crimes are far too high for a city of this size. But I think that the people who express the most fear of crime are the safest in the city. . . . people who live in the poor neighborhoods are far more likely to be a victim of crime than the people who live in the more affluent parts of the city, with the exception of the historic district where there is a tremendous interaction between rich and poor."[57] The mayor's interview was prompted in part by a recent murder that shocked the city.

"A Woman Dead, a City Wounded"

In the early morning hours of December 24, 2005, Jennifer Ross and three friends were walking in the downtown Historic District. Earlier that evening, Jennifer, a Mercer University student, had been one of ten debutants presented at the local Christmas Cotillion Club Ball. After celebrating the festivities with her family, she had gone out with three friends to a City Market jazz bar. When the bar closed around 3:00 A.M., the foursome set off on foot for a nearby apartment to call a cab. Near Orleans Square they were attacked by three black males in a robbery attempt. Brad Finley, who was walking with Jennifer, was pistol-whipped and, when Jennifer refused to give up her purse, she was shot in the back. Taken to Memorial Hospital, she died on January 1. Jennifer's father was senior vice-president and senior council for the hospital.[58] A manhunt ensued. Based on tips from the perpetrators' family and friends, shooter Michael "Turtle" Thorpe and two others were apprehended. Eventually all were sentenced to life plus consecutive-year prison terms. Their appeals were denied by the Georgia Supreme Court.[59]

The *Morning News* reflected on the recent tragedies: "too many Jennifer Rosses and Sean Abrahams," both shot down in the streets, one white, one black, both with bright futures and loving families. Savannah is "a beautiful city with an ugly crime problem that has for too long been denied lasting relief or solutions."[60] Another headline captured the mood of the city: "A woman dead, a city wounded. Shooting shocks a community into action." Save Our Savannah and other citizen-led groups quickly formed in response to the many local calls for action.[61]

Savannah State Professor Dan Lockwood's survey of crime in Savannah from 1993 to 2004 found that the census block that embraced the Historic District experienced more robberies and violent crime than any other census block in the city. Robbery and mugging rates here were 50 percent higher from Thanksgiving through Christmas, and those arrested usually had home addresses within easy walking distance of the crime. The census tract Lockwood described embraced the city's wealthiest residential neighborhoods, flanked by two of its poorest—on the east, Hitch Village, and on the west, Yamacraw.[62]

A "Disquieting" Crime Rate

Willie Clinton Lovett, the first African American assistant chief of police in Savannah, had been on the force for more than thirty years; he was appointed interim chief when Dan Flynn retired in 2005. The search now underway for a new chief would take a year; in the meantime, the department was short staffed and crime seemed to be on the upswing. Gangs reappeared, and violent crime pushed beyond its usual locations.[63]

Speaking to a group of four hundred at a Windsor Forest neighborhood meeting, Mayor Johnson said, "do not give up your streets to the thugs." The "thugs" he referenced were gang members. Interim Chief Lovett told a reporter that "at least 20 organized gangs [were] expanding throughout all areas of Chatham County." One organization that partnered with the police to address this problem was the Board of Education. Teachers were trained to look for gang symbols: body art, clothes, hat tilts, and graffiti. The *Morning News* called the gangs "cancers that can grow and destroy [neighborhoods]." Finally, "after years of denying that gangs have a foothold, police officials are now playing catch-up."[64]

As crime moved into the suburbs, more citizen groups formed. In November in broad daylight in the middle of West Forty-fourth Street someone shot and killed Quentin Clark, apparently in a turf battle. That same week in Ardsley Park, Frederick Brockway Gleason III, a former New York investment banker, was shot as he stood in front of his columned mansion on Washington Avenue, talking to his wife, Ann.

It was the first murder in the upscale neighborhood in fourteen years. Ann was the only witness. She first told police that two black males in their twenties had driven up in a white car; later she changed her story to a dark-colored car. One investigator called her "wishy-washy," saying her account "leaves a lot of what she said in doubt." Subsequently, Mrs. Gleason refused to talk to police. Investigators discovered that "abuse and affairs" had plagued the Gleasons' relationship.[65]

The Police Department quickly assigned a task force of six to the neighborhood to assuage demands for action by Gleason's friends and neighbors. When residents in much higher-crime areas complained that they never received such prompt response, interim chief Lovett answered, "we treat all crimes the same no matter where they're located."[66]

Local crime statistics released in 2006 showed violent crime rates up 5 percent from 2004 to 2005. A survey of eighteen hundred residents, taken between October 2005 and February 2006, found 69 percent of respondents believed "crime was the biggest issue facing Savannah over the next five years." Interim chief Lovett called the "crime rate 'disquieting.'"[67]

Dr. Lockwood, a Savannah State professor familiar with crime-data analysis, described the situation as more "grave" than disquieting. Lockwood maintained that the best way to evaluate crime statistics was to look at trend data, and he chose two violent crimes—robbery and murder, the most likely to be reported—as topics for his study. He concluded that Savannah's violent crime "may not be up but it is not getting a whole lot better." Savannah's murder rate was twice that of Jacksonville, Macon, and Charleston and "three times the state average." Lockwood asked rhetorically, "Is Savannah a dangerous place? Compared to other cities, it is." And there was mounting concern about the young age of criminals.[68]

The Savannah Youth Futures Authority's 2006 "Community Profile Report Card" showed the city's juvenile crime rate increased 22 percent between 2003 and 2004. Mayor Johnson made an observation about the eighteen-to-twenty-five-year-old perpetrators: "[It's] the macho part of a male's life. If you can get past 25 without being . . . [arrested] or being a victim of a violent act, you're fortunate." Professor Lockwood reasoned that children, unskilled in conflict resolution, with ready access to guns, sometimes used those weapons to solve disagreements. Mayor Johnson also called out parents who fostered aggressive behaviors: "Unfortunately, we have parents who tell their kids if they get into a confrontation to fight." No doubt the lack of job opportunities and feelings of hopelessness sometimes pushed youngsters into an early life of crime.[69] Whatever the reason, youth problems were deeply troubling to the mayor and may have contributed to his failing health.

A Heart Attack and a Second Term

On April 29, 2006, Mayor Johnson suffered a heart attack in Memphis while attending the Conference of Black Mayors. He was rushed to a Memphis hospital, where doctors installed three stents, and Johnson spent over two weeks there recovering. His heart had suffered "significant damage." He returned to Savannah on a Gulfstream jet with his friend Shevon Carr and his brother Paul. City Manager Brown noted that Gulfstream offered the jet "not for free," but at a cost of about $3,000.

When Mayor Johnson returned to Savannah, the *Morning News* "wished . . . the mayor a speedy recovery" and advised him to "throttle . . . back a bit" and over the next several weeks to share more of his workload with council members and the mayor pro tem, Edna Jackson. The paper recognized it was in Johnson's nature "to be personally involved in everything . . . [which] can be a blessing and a curse." Despite the advice and with a donated defibrillator in his office, Mayor Johnson soon announced that he planned to run for a second term. His salary was $42,000; City Council members were paid $14,500.[70]

One of the mayor's most pressing concerns on his return to work was the search for a new police chief. Interim chief Lovett himself applied for the job, but some members of the political and business community did not support him because of his association with former chief Flynn and department policies that had tolerated a hundred vacancies in the department and a 70 percent turnover rate for new hires.[71]

In September 2006, Lovett's application became moot when City Manager Michael Brown offered the post to Michael Berkow, a fifty-one-year-old deputy chief of police in Los Angeles with degrees from Johns Hopkins and a Juris Doctor from Syracuse University. Brown described Berkow as an "absolute dynamo." The new chief was on board officially by November 2006. Some criticized Brown's choice and the incoming chief's salary, $158,000. Berkow launched an "aggressive, on-the-street approach" to fighting crime—an approach very much in sync with the mayor's own thinking.[72]

Michael Berkow was hired to "to rock the boat," to change a culture "resistant to new ideas," because clearly the old ways of doing business "were not working." Some members of the local press characterized him as "brash, impatient and a workaholic"; criticism also came because he "wasn't from around here, which was . . . enough to arouse a little suspicion" and because he "beat out a favorite son," Willie Lovett.

From the outset, a number of veteran police officers opposed Berkow's approach to policing. But in three years Berkow overhauled the recruitment process, built a streamlined criminal investigations division, upgraded intelligence units, and established a technologically advanced patrol force. Toward the end of his tenure, he organized a "Most Violent Offenders" squad of "tough cops" who constantly were on the lookout for known troublemakers.[73]

Revitalizing Communities and "Velvet Racism"

Surveys showed increasing public approval of the city's targeting of run-down homes and overgrown lots. Millions of dollars had been invested in areas like Cuyler-Brownville, which "pleased" the mayor, who had long emphasized the connectedness of "neighborhood quality, public safety, poverty reduction and economic development." Early in his administration the mayor and City Council agreed that blight must be eradicated. City policy now required any gang graffiti to be removed within three days, and workers were kept busy cleaning up 330 vacant lots and removing 2,170 abandoned automobiles.[74]

As the mayor worked to reduce poverty and boost the local economy, he remained concerned about a bifurcated black community: "one segment is doing well and is benefiting from the results of the civil rights struggle . . . [even as the other part of the community] is becoming more and more dispossessed, with no good education, marketable skills or work ethic. They're basically alienated from the mainstream." With regard to black-white relationships, it was Johnson's view that generally "Savannah remains racially segregated and racism remains a problem. . . . we have velvet racism. It's institutional rather than individual. Go to your corporate offices and see who's there." In law firms there was "tokenism at best. White privilege is pretty intact."

Johnson's special talent, observed one reporter who interviewed him frequently, was to combine "an academic's ability to analyze community problems in the abstract with the political skills to move those ideas toward action." When asked what made him do what he was attempting to do, Johnson responded that he was driven to "improve . . . conditions for the people in Savannah–Chatham County."[75]

Johnson enlisted citizen assistance in the rehabilitation of "drug-infested and crime-ridden" communities. On the west side, the neighborhoods of Hudson Hill, West Savannah, and Woodville fit this pattern—high unemployment, high poverty rates, and high rates of homicides, rapes, robberies, and aggravated assaults. Using this data as a benchmark, Johnson's administration hired a Boston firm in 2005 to design a plan to revitalize West Savannah. After six months of dialogue with residents, the firm advised that a commercial center be revived and that parks, new homes, and apartments be created along with a job-training center. Generous grants from a private trust, United Way, and city

SPLOST monies were applied to the revitalization of these formerly interracial communities on Savannah's west side.

Johnson's administration, like those of Rousakis and Adams before him, supported the equity agenda and with public and private funds spent millions to end poverty. The development director, Robert Keber, explained why the investment was important: "The underlying rationale for government is not only security, but to promote the general welfare for everyone."[76] Promotion of the equity agenda won praise for Mayor Johnson and his administration. A flourishing economy also helped.

An Economic Boom and Johnson's "Cultural Tourism"

Nationally and locally in the early years of the twenty-first century, the economy accelerated. The city had a population of 131,510, an unemployment rate of 3.2 percent, and a median household income of $42,845. The port was flourishing, and estimates for its growth over the next fifteen years reached 150 percent. City and business leaders pushed to attract "Knowledge-Based Business" to Savannah, anticipating such operations to be a "high-tech/high-dollar growth magnet."

Creative Coast recruited artists and students from SCAD who pioneered and revitalized areas beyond downtown's Historic District. Eric Winger, president of the Savannah Economic Development Authority (SEDA), said that "diversity" drove the local economy—military facilities, hospitals, the port, manufacturing, and tourism. Bill Hubbard, president of the Chamber of Commerce, reported that Savannah was attracting more affluent and culturally sophisticated tourists.[77]

For art lovers, a remarkable contemporary venue opened in 2006, the Jepson Center for the Arts, designed by Moshe Safdie. With the nearby Telfair Museum, it dramatically expanded art exhibitions and art education for tourists and Savannahians. The city also began demolishing a high-rise parking garage located on Ellis Square, one of the city's earliest squares and site of the old City Market. Here revitalization would include an underground parking garage built in collaboration with private businesses that planned to construct aboveground a hotel and condominiums. Other projects to improve the cityscape continued apace near the gateway to Interstate 16 and on the east to Tybee Island, a destination for many tourists. Some of these improvements, however, rekindled discussion of issues related to "gentrification vs. revitalization."[78]

Mayor Johnson's administration drew praise from Savannah's boosters in his first term. They applauded his efforts at revitalization, the partnerships between the city and private entities, the increasing diversity of the economy, and improvements to the city's infrastructure.

Johnson's Second Term and the Imperial Sugar Fire

In a six-candidate field, Mayor Johnson ran for a second term and took a remarkable 70 percent of the vote on November 6, 2007. The City Council remained basically unchanged; seven of the nine council members returned. Another enthusiastic crowd greeted Johnson's second inaugural at the Civic Center on January 3, 2008. He urged his audience to work with his administration on a variety of problems and called on the African American community to show more responsibility. He added that he would be "off the leash" in this his second and last term. The *Morning News* gave him a "solid B plus" and applauded his "passion" for the job.[79] About a month after his second inauguration, a disaster rocked the community.

Savannahians remember well the deadly inferno that ultimately took the lives of fourteen people and injured many more at the Imperial Sugar Refinery in nearby Port Wentworth on February 7, 2008. The mayor ordered flags on city buildings flown at half staff. On Saturday, February 23, 2008, "10 wreaths of carnations, white as pure sugar, stood at the front of the [Civic Center] stage, a reminder [at that time] of the 10 Imperial workers killed in the fiery dust explosion." In his opening remarks Mayor Johnson said the tragedy was personal for him—his fifty-six-year-old first cousin, Eric Barnes, died in the blast.[80]

"Federal investigators found that combustible sugar dust—which workers said sometimes clouded the air and stood knee-high—fueled the conflagration." The Imperial Sugar Company and the Occupational Safety and Health Administration (OSHA) reached a settlement by July 7, 2010. The company agreed to a $6 million fine for infractions at its Port Wentworth and Gramercy, Louisiana, plants. Imperial Sugar admitted no wrongdoing but accepted three years of OSHA oversight at its Port Wentworth refinery. The company no longer contested OSHA's 124 citations.[81]

Two federal investigations found that "company officials knew for years about deadly hazards at the Port Wentworth site." Additionally, the U.S. Chemical Safety Board identified other hazards, including a nonfunctioning fire-alarm system and sugar-dust coatings on electrical wires. Nonetheless, U.S. Attorney Edward Tarver decided not to charge the company with criminal violations because, he said, no federal laws existed "specifically addressed to the safety of workers within the sugar industry at the time of the Imperial Sugar explosion."[82]

As more allegations and photographs of refinery conditions became available, public sympathy for Imperial's position waned—especially when the company asked for a five-year exemption from real and personal taxes. A *Morning News* editorial titled "No sweeteners" took the corporation to task: "The deadly event occurred because Imperial Sugar was running a dirty operation. . . . Imperial Sugar abused the trust of its employees by failing to provide a safe work environment. . . . The company should not be rewarded for bad behavior by shifting a $2.8 million burden onto [Chatham] county taxpayers." In 2012, Louis Dreyfus Commodities bought Imperial Sugar for about $78 million in cash.[83]

"Festivalizing" across the Year

A jazz lover, Mayor Johnson made personal efforts to boost cultural tourism, helping to build Savannah's reputation as "the city of festivals." One of the main groups assisting the city in this effort was the Cultural Affairs Commission, composed of eighteen volunteers appointed by the mayor and City Council who made recommendations for funding events to enhance the cultural life of residents and tourists. The Chamber of Commerce, Visit Savannah, and other groups joined the city as festival boosters, recognizing that affluent tourists spend more, stay longer, and often become ambassadors for Savannah.

City funding for a variety of festivals increased markedly over the years. The Savannah Music Festival received $50,000 in 2003 and, four years later, $150,000. Private sponsors and ticket sales contributed significantly more. The fifteen-day festival in the spring offered opportunities for music lovers of all genres to enjoy world-class talent. Critics raved, and the festival boosted the city's cultural prestige. When the City Council recommended $75,000 for the festival in 2007, somewhat less than the year before, Mayor Johnson raised the amount to $95,000, emphasizing the festival's very favorable impact on local businesses.[84]

One sometime Savannah resident wrote that spring usually begins in mid-January, and a "flowerfest" starts with Japanese magnolias; in March "a stunning azalea explosion" opens along with "fragrant wisteria vines" while in May and June gardenias and white magnolias reach their "magnificent peak." Now people came to Savannah for both the Music Festival and the heralded spring.

In 2009 the Music Festival director, Rob Gibson, spent eleven months luring "world-famous" musicians to Savannah and courting donors. The now eighteen-day event hosted more than one hundred shows in multiple venues. There was something for everyone, and the festival continued to expand its offerings—a vocalist's tribute to Savannah's Johnny Mercer, along with bluegrass, the Atlanta Symphony, Zydeco, Salsa, country, pop, Fado, gospel, rock, folk, jazz, tabla drums, cabaret, chamber, shape-note singing, and the list goes on. Attendance climbed despite the arrival nationally of the Great Recession, and the *Times* of London selected the Music Festival as one of the "Top Events of 2009"—the single U.S. event chosen.[85]

SCAD was among the private organizations winning funding from the city in 2003 of $10,000 and four years later $50,000 to support the Savannah Film Festival. "What the Savannah Music Festival is to the spring, the Savannah Film Festival is to the fall." In 2008 more than 40,000 persons attended to hear lecturers on film and cinematography; view classic movies, student productions, animation, independent films; and screen new releases like *Slumdog Millionaire.*

Other annual festivals and organizations receiving financial support from the city included the Savannah Jazz Festival, Asian Festival, and Shakespeare Festival and cultural institutions like the Telfair Museum of Art, the Jepson, the Georgia Historical Society, the Live Oak Public Library and religious groups.[86]

Tara Feis, St. Patrick's Family Festival, held during the celebration of St. Patrick, draws more than 20,000 people; it received $54,000 in 2003 and $70,000 in 2007 from the city. A child-friendly, alcohol-free event filled with Celtic music and dance, Tara Feis stands in stark contrast to other St. Patrick's Day festivities. With attendance figures second only to New York's parade, Savannah's St. Patrick's Day Parade is likely the oldest in the country.[87]

Parade day begins with a Mass at the Cathedral of St. John the Baptist. Bells toll as tens of thousands of spectators line downtown streets and squares to watch hundreds of marching units, dignitaries, bands, firefighters, Irish families, and other groups on parade. The event itself sets the mood for a few more days of revelry.

First celebrated in Savannah with a public procession in 1824, the parade brings between 300,000 and 700,000 revelers to the city—depending on whether March 17 falls on a weekday or a weekend. In 2007 a shortage of portable toilets created an emergency for some celebrants, and "Chippewa Square had to be sanitized three times." That year police kept busy, arresting 31 for urinating in public, 26 for under-age drinking, 43 for disorderly conduct, and others for drunk driving. About 125 celebrants spent at least one night in the Chatham County Jail, less than in years past.[88]

Coping with the "Great Recession"

Mayor Johnson began his first term with the national and local economy flourishing; however, as the mayor and council took office in 2008, the economy ebbed. Most businesses felt the impact, especially the import-export trade. The number of twenty-foot containers moving through Savannah's port increased by 55 percent between 2002 and 2007, making it the fourth-largest container port in the country. The Georgia Ports Authority executive director, Doug Marchand, and Dick Knowlton, SEDA head, together had marketed the port to shippers (like Walmart) and to shipping lines and, over time, this effort fueled remarkable growth. New cranes were installed, additional berthing space was built, and more personnel were hired. By 2008, however, the number of ship calls and overall cargo tonnage dropped through November.[89]

Auto sales, retail sales, and hotel occupancy rates fell. Tour-bus, carriage, and trolley operators saw a 15 percent decline in riders from the previous year. Among major manufactures, Great Dane Trailers closed its Savannah plant in 2008 and JCB Incorporated laid off 120 workers. Small businesses struggled, and real estate sales fell.[90]

In the face of an anemic economy, Mayor Johnson, City Manager Michael Brown, and the City Council nevertheless charted a bold course in 2008. Johnson liked sailing and used a quote from Oliver Wendell Holmes as a metaphor for his second term: "We must sail sometimes with the wind and sometimes against it, but sail we must and not drift nor lie at anchor." The mayor's charted course, he said, was to make Savannah the "world-class city we all deserve."

The administration continued economic development through its Minority and Women-owned Business Enterprise Program to help these groups participate more in city contracts. The Step-Up Poverty Reduction Collaborative and non-profits joined in efforts to make small, low-interest loans to help residents with basic needs. Capital infrastructure projects continued. The city was on track to complete the massive Ellis Square project that would restore one of Savannah's original squares.[91]

Change in Police Leadership and "Heat Wave, Crime Wave"

Berkow served as police chief less than three years, resigning in 2009 to accept a job as president of a global security firm. Some called his resignation "a tough loss" for the city and viewed Chief Berkow "a victim of politics." Business leaders Brian Foster, Gary Parker, and Chamber of Commerce President Bill Hubbard praised the chief for his changes and believed "Berkow's shoes [would be] hard to fill." Berkow advocates saw the Police Department as "much improved" and warned that it must not "backslide."

Most members of the City Council supported Berkow; his opposition came from within the police force itself and from some black community leaders. The

Morning News reported that "behind the scenes, an intense lobbying campaign is under way to name Assistant Chief Willie Lovett as interim chief." The city-county Police Policy Committee, comprised of County Commission Chair Pete Liakakis, County Manager Russ Abolt, City Manager Michael Brown, and Mayor Otis Johnson quickly came together and appointed Willie Lovett as interim chief of the SCMPD—it was Lovett's second time in this role. The search for a new, permanent chief began once more.

Lovett took over at a time when the SCMPD had become a technologically advanced department with state-of-the-art crime detection and analysis equipment. So sophisticated were its resources that it was ranked as one of the best-equipped police units in the country. But violent crime was not abating; it was in fact increasing.[92]

By mid-2009, metropolitan Savannah counted sixteen homicides. Ten remained unsolved. The police "solve rate" of 38 percent frustrated investigators. Why was it that witnesses and sometimes victims themselves refused to identify the assailant? One young man, killed in a "hail of bullets" at the intersection of Henry Street and Martin Luther King Jr. Boulevard before some three hundred witnesses at 2:30 A.M., illustrated the challenge. His mother agonized when no one came forward to provide information to police about his murder or those involved.[93]

The overall crime rate dropped in Savannah in 2009, as it did from time to time, though violent crime rose 12 percent over the previous year. Shoplifting rose 8 percent, but residential burglary declined 5 percent, and street robbery fell 23 percent. When asked why the overall crime had decreased, the interim police chief, Willie Lovett, responded, in an attempt at humor perhaps, "Let's just say it was a change in management." He also believed department morale had improved significantly.[94]

However, not everyone felt that crime was on the wane. One resident of the Victorian District wrote in a letter to the editor: "Victorian District residents face drug dealers and users daily acting fearlessly and blatantly." She went on to describe graphically the nightly "music-vibrating cars . . . metal-chair-throwing-fights of twelve or more people . . . yelling, groups congregating, and gunshots." And then there were "child-men hanging [out] on stoops where they do not live . . . [urinating] next to houses in broad daylight . . . wakes and welcome-home-from-prison parties with buffet tables and grills on the sidewalk." The letter writer had bricks thrown at her house, windows broken and, even though she had contacted city, state, and federal authorities, the problems continued. She concluded, "When the housing market strengthens enough to sell, forget profit, many people will leave so fast there will be skid marks from here to I-16."[95]

Willie Lovett: From Interim to Chief, SCMPD

The six-month search for a permanent police chief following Michael Berkow's resignation finally ended in April 2010 with the appointment of the interim chief, Lovett, as the new permanent head of SCMPD. Police chiefs in surrounding communities like Bloomingdale, Port Wentworth, Pooler, and Garden City responded as one to the news: "They . . . should have done this about five years ago. He's a home grown guy . . . [who] knows all the players. . . . He was the right one all along." The local paper hoped Chief Lovett would follow the "valuable reforms that Michael Berkow . . . implemented."[96] However, what transpired during Lovett's tenure as permanent chief changed the minds of many former supporters.

Police Chief Willie Lovett, a thirty-six-year veteran of the department and twice interim chief, was formally sworn in as Savannah-Chatham Metropolitan Police Department chief on April 17, 2010. Selected for the position by the Police Policy Committee (city manager, county manager, chair of the County Council, and mayor), he was the first black chief of police in Savannah's history. Lovett had risen from the ranks of street cop to become the department's top cop.[97] Beset by problems from the outset, his tenure would be brief.

A sharp decrease in crime in 2010—a 15 percent decrease in total crime and a 25 percent decrease in violent crime—encouraged city residents. However, violence and property crimes climbed with the temperature during 2011 and, by September, violent crime was up 9 percent over the previous year. Precincts emphasized different approaches and targeted various categories of crime, dependent on the needs of their precinct area. Shoplifting, home invasion, auto and motorcycle thefts were main targets; posting more plainclothes and uniformed officers on the streets was a frequent strategy. Officers in the department praised Lovett's "hands off approach" to management.[98]

Interviewed about the summer crime wave, an analyst in the Police Department pointed to studies that "found links between temperature, aggression and crime." Chief Lovett's explanation, an oft-repeated theme, was the failure of the justice system to handle recidivists who received short sentences and were soon back on the streets causing mischief. Of the fourteen homicides in the first half of 2011, the chief said ten were drug related. He characterized the young drug dealers as having little respect for parents, the police, or themselves. They are a hard-to-reach group who "have no fear of what might happen to them. . . . [We are] to the point we can't just arrest our way out of the situation that we are in."[99]

Alice Goffman, a researcher who studied the relationship between drugs and violence in another metropolitan area, found that residents there, much like Savannahians, blamed spiraling levels of violence on "bad parenting, absent fathers, or a lack of moral fortitude in the young." Though this may be true, she writes, "the roots of crime and violence were also found in economic hardship and in particular a profound dislocation from the legal labor market." Young black men unable to find jobs lose hope, turn to trade in drugs, are arrested, and soon become recidivists. A new director of Step Up Savannah, a city anti-poverty program, found that about 25 percent of residents lived at or below the poverty level; "reducing this troubling statistic," she said, "[requires] jobs and affordable housing."[100]

In the summer of 2011, over a one-week period, nine shootings occurred. Thirteen people were shot, one fatally. Mayor and council were inundated with calls. What was going on? Mayor Johnson told the council, "We have a broken criminal justice system." Chief Lovett explained what police were up against: "[Police make arrests] only to see those charged released in a matter of days." Juvenile offenders are "often turned away because there are no beds available at the youth detention center." Reviewing three recent cases, Lovett said, "one man had 17 priors in 2010; [two others] had 14 and 15 [previous] arrests." As council member Larry Stuber put it, "They go in the front door of the jail and out the back the same day." Lovett's summation left little room for optimism: "There's no way we can win at this"[101] And "this" was not Chief Lovett's only concern.

A brouhaha erupted when a videotape surfaced showing conditions during a rainstorm at the historic Police Headquarters at Oglethorpe and Habersham streets. Water poured through light fixtures and splashed onto desktops; trash cans collected drips from ceiling tiles, and several officers were confirmed to have contracted "mold-related illnesses." In an interview with the press in July, Chief Lovett called police headquarters "a hell hole."

Apparently, the chief's whistle-blowing was not appreciated by the new city manager, Rochelle Small-Toney, who said if it happened again "this person will be looking for a job." Though some backpedaling took place about the situation, council member Jeff Felser called the city manager's reaction "a gag order. . . . I think he's been reprimanded for openly telling the truth." Mayor Johnson, also upset by Lovett's interview, suggested that, "if the city manager had not been responsive to Chief Lovett's request [for improved facilities], . . . he should have reached out to council members." The need for a new police headquarters had been on the agenda of four former chiefs.[102]

In 2011 more people died in Chatham County from homicides (thirty-one) than from auto accidents (twenty-seven). Overall, crime for 2011 showed a 4 percent increase, violent crime a 5 percent increase, and homicides a 30 percent increase. Aggravated assault with a gun was up 24 percent. When analyzed by area, crime dropped for the Islands, Downtown, and West Chatham precincts but was up 18 percent in Southside Precinct and 9 percent in Central Precinct.[103]

Neighborhood Development and the Equity Agenda

Mayor Johnson in his second term continued to look for ways to increase affordable housing in Savannah. On the east side, the city partnered with the nonprofit Community Housing Services Agency to redevelop Strathmore Estates—once a crime-ridden neighborhood—into mixed-use, mixed-income affordable housing. It was renamed "Savannah Gardens." West of the city, Sustainable Fellwood, a twenty-seven-acre site near the downtown Historic District, was planned for 220 apartments, thirteen private homes, and one hundred senior units. Built as an affordable, energy-efficient, green community with organic gardens and large parks, Sustainable Fellwood became one of the first projects of its kind in the country.[104]

The city's Property Maintenance Department continued eradication of blighted properties by tearing down dilapidated structures and clearing overgrown lots. Citizens now participated in the war on blight by alerting city officials to down-at-the heels property, and the city continued to publicize its "100 worst properties" list.[105]

As the economy stalled in the Great Recession and crime increased, the mayor nevertheless continued his role as the city's number-one cheerleader. At the first town hall meeting in his second term, Mayor Johnson told the crowd that Savannah "will be bold in uncertain times." As to crime, he said, we "must keep career criminals off the street longer . . . but while they are in prison we need to teach them legitimate skills." He also emphasized the links between poverty and crime, which created heightened vulnerability in a city where "22% of the population" (twenty-seven thousand) lived at or below the poverty level.[106]

As public housing needs outstripped available resources, fifty-five-year-old dilapidated Hitch Village was razed in 2010 to make way for new mixed-use, mixed-financed housing. To bring the existing housing up to HUD standards would have cost $10 million. The new planned development was to transform the Wheaton Street Corridor, an area of the city that had long needed to be integrated more successfully into the downtown. The Housing Authority of Savannah planned to partner with the city, private developers, the federal government, banks, and underwriters to create a mixed-income community that would have various housing options interspersed among parklike spaces with neighborhood access to health services, education, training, transportation, and recreation.[107]

Despite such positive promotion of Savannah's future and the city's efforts to build and renovate homes, some communities remained on the brink of collapse. The blocks of East Fifty-first through Fifty-fifth Street of the Edgemere-Sackville neighborhood, bracketed by Waters Avenue and the Truman Parkway, remained dogged by blight and plagued by break-ins and shootings. Pleas by residents eventually led the police to assign mounted units, K-9 officers, and narcotics investigators to the area. Here over time the city's Operation Clean Sweep gathered tons of debris, removed derelict cars, and mowed lawns; the city budgeted more than $1 million for construction of curbs and gutters. Yet a few years after these efforts, drive-by shootings, assaults, and illegal drugs had neighbors asking for even more police assistance.[108]

In the downtown Historic District, another public space opened in 2010, Ellis Square. This transformational project took four years to build at a cost of $32 million. The finished project created a parklike space on the 1.5-acre site that was once one of General Oglethorpe's four original squares, then named Decker Square. With a fountain, shops, restaurants, bars, jazz clubs, and a life-size bronze statue of Johnny Mercer by local sculptor Susie Chisolm, the square quickly became a favorite gathering spot for tourists and locals alike. Though rain dampened plans for a grand opening, the enthusiastic response to the new space must have been encouraging to Mayor Johnson who, in reflecting on his accomplishments, said this was one of his proudest achievements.[109]

Schools and Youth

Mayor Johnson, perennially concerned about the problems of Savannah's young people, asked for advice from the religious community, parents, social and service organizations, the education system, and law enforcement to help identify those factors that appeared to set children off on a path to destructive lifestyles.[110]

One group that took the mayor's challenge to heart was the all-volunteer African American Male Achievement Group, who met with the Savannah-Chatham School Board to discuss racial bias in disciplinary issues. The group was concerned that black male suspensions began as early as kindergarten and that the "vast majority" of these suspensions were for minor infractions—"tardiness and dress code violations," not "weapons or drug violations." Indeed, the Board of Education's own data confirmed that black students made up 64 percent of the school population but constituted 87 percent of the suspensions.

Mayor Johnson, who attended the meeting, said, "When those children are not in school, they're *my* problem."[111]

Dr. Thomas B. Lockamy Jr., superintendent of the Savannah-Chatham County Public Schools, after a series of intensive town hall meetings, released a plan for redesigning public education which he titled *Passport to Excellence.* Essentially, the phased-in plan called for the construction of new schools, redistricting, and expanded educational options such as schools that focused on specific career or technical areas—for example, fine and performing arts, international education, medical sciences, or schools that used E. D. Hirsch's nationally known core-knowledge curriculum. Also, one school was to be open to young men only and would offer "a gender specific program designed to instill values of self-determination, character development and service." In keeping with his promise to address parent concerns, Lockamy's plan attempted to give students the option of attending a school "close to home."

Subsequently, the school board met to vote on the *Passport to Excellence* reorganization proposal. With more than thirty-four thousand students in the system, there were reservations and discontent and questions about the plan from parents, board members, and public officials. Even Mayor Otis Johnson, who endorsed the proposal, let it be known that he expected it to be "fair" to all concerned. After heated discussion, the board overwhelmingly endorsed the *Passport to Excellence.* Within a few years new schools were under construction, and the school board had crafted a new code of conduct and had established a certified police department for the schools to deter bad behavior and to patrol "problem schools."[112]

E-SPLOST funds—Special Purpose Local Option Sales Tax dollars used specifically for education—underwrote much of the costs of new and remodeled schools. With eight hundred new students entering the system each year and with county population shifts, adequate facilities remained a major challenge. Another E-SPLOST-funded improvement was erecting fencing to provide a single point of entry to each school, a modification to enhance security.[113]

Lockamy and others had hoped that *Passport to Excellence* might help slow the exodus of students who had been leaving public schools for private ones. Apparently it did. One reporter wrote in 2014 that schools had gone from being "a community sore spot to the hot spot." Dr. Lockamy remarked that "the economy played a part in some families returning to the system, but . . . they're staying because they've found some satisfaction." And Lockamy was staying too. In making the announcement he said, "The district is right at the point of a breakthrough. . . . I'm staying here as long as the people need me."[114] Lockamy remained, but City Manager Michael Brown did not.

City Manager Small-Toney: A Lightening Rod for Controversy

Michael Brown resigned his position as city manager in 2010 for unexplained reasons. Though no one acknowledged exactly why Brown stepped down, Mayor Johnson speculated in a later interview that Brown was uncomfortable with the shifting priorities and with the mayor and the council's conviction that they had both "a right and an obligation to set the agenda."[115]

A protégé of former city manager Don Mendonsa, Brown served the city for fifteen years. The *Morning News*'s Tom Barton observed that Brown aged perceptively during Johnson's first term: "The activist Council under Mayor Johnson may or may not have run Brown out of town. But it wasn't itching to show its heartfelt appreciation either. . . . [You] can't blame him for packing his suitcase." Barton wondered if a "fractured" City Council could "get it together to recruit a qualified, apolitical, colorblind city manager for this diverse city."[116]

Rochelle Small-Toney, an African American woman, moved into the acting city manager role as Brown's replacement. Ms. Small-Toney, who had worked for the city since 2007, quickly became a subject of controversy. One editorial writer questioned whether the fifty-four-year-old had "the talent to run a $277 million operation with 2,550 employees," but acknowledged, "I can see how a black-majority City Council in a black-majority city would like the opportunity to name a black city manager." It was obvious that Small-Toney had sufficient votes on the council to win the appointment. The writer's parting jab was that the mayor and the council must have "confidence in her. . . . otherwise they wouldn't have . . . bumped up her annual salary to $190,000."[117]

The initial vote for Small-Toney, the first African American to hold this position, found the City Council divided five to four along racial lines. A troubled council member, Van Johnson, called the situation "toxic and unhealthy but workable." During Mayor Johnson's seven years of leadership, the City Council had prided itself "on presenting a united front." This vote was a seismic shift that "laid bare a changing political landscape." It signaled a new age in Savannah's history—now a city governed by its new black majority. Journalist Lesley Conn observed its significance: "[It] will require the former white majority to learn how to operate as a minority."[118]

Perhaps white members recognized this because the council ended the search with a unanimous vote for Ms. Small-Toney. But acrimony remained. During a council meeting, one member told another to "shut up," there were charges that it was racist to spend tax money mostly for blacks, and Councilwoman Mary Ellen Sprague lamented that constituents thought the workforce was "all black."[119]

Press leaks, perhaps from Council members, concerning Ms. Small-Toney's bonding issues infuriated Mayor Johnson and he moved Council into a closed session where one member called for an investigation by the GBI to locate the source of leaked "confidential information." And then there were bad feelings generated by Small-Toney's $7,500 meet-and-greet reception where $1,000 of the budget was spent to pay for keepsake wine glasses engraved with Small-Toney's name and title.

Subsequently, the state attorney general "alleged" that the City Council violated Open Meetings and Open Records laws during the search for Small-Toney. When members of the council initially balked at signing an agreement with the attorney general to comply with the laws, Mayor Johnson told them that they could refuse to sign but that he was signing because he was not going to jail for them. The council agreed unanimously and followed the mayor's lead.[120]

Mayor Johnson's Last Days in Office

Developments on the city's west side, like the beautiful new SCAD Museum, no doubt encouraged the mayor. The community also added to its list of special events and festivals. Savannah's Rock 'n' Roll Marathon, inaugurated in 2011, attracted 23,000 runners, nearly 90 percent of whom came from out of town. Event coordinators said the race had an $18 million impact on the local economy.[121]

During Mayor Johnson's second term he became more concerned about the "evils" of leaking city business to the press: "If you play with snakes, you're going to get bit," he scolded the City Council. He was observed to be more aloof, "less patient and perhaps more bullying at times, affecting how he governed." *Morning News* editorial writer Tom Barton thought Johnson's heart attack had changed him, made him "more crotchety." Mayor Johnson agreed that the near-death experience was "life changing"; said he, "My tolerance for B.S. went to zero." Johnson also began work on an autobiography which he would title, "My Journey from the N Word to Mr. Mayor."[122]

Much of Johnson's second term was spent dealing "with acerbic exchanges among council members." The once cohesive group had "descended into name calling and finger pointing."[123] As the Great Recession loomed over Johnson's second term, the city he "loved" faced a surge of homelessness, poverty, persistent blight, and increasing violent crime—all affecting his ability to sail his charted course.

In the final weeks of his second term, Johnson gave a forty-minute keynote address to the local NAACP, sharing highlights from his two terms: the "renovation of Ellis Square . . . quarterly town hall meetings, and . . . the Healthy

Savannah Initiative." What would be next? The mayor said he planned a week-long jazz cruise and then a return to Savannah to finish his book.[124]

In a 2014 interview, the former mayor described his biggest challenge while in office as confronting the diminished power of mayor and council under the council-manager form of government. Though he hastened to say that the city had been blessed to have strong and ethical city managers, he believed that the elected council and mayor had over time relinquished their responsibility to create policy and set priorities.

His goal as mayor was to build a team of council members who would establish a set of priorities that would then be given to the city manager to implement. Asked about building the council team, Mayor Johnson said that, during his first term, "we had a very harmonious working group. We had our differences [but we] had created an environment where those differences were freely expressed in an environment of respect." In the second term, the mayor said, the "[chemistry] changed and it became more cantankerous and it began to break down along Democrat and Republican lines as well as along racial lines."

This was a period of tough decisions, involving the recession and the need to raise taxes to cover shortfalls. Five is the magic number as the City Council is made of up eight members and the mayor. As Johnson put it, "[Whatever] we did it took five, it took a minimum of five agreeing on these things and we were able to hold that together for my eight years."[125]

"Pumped Up" for Edna Jackson

The mayor's race geared up in fall 2010. Edna Jackson, a sixty-six-year-old retired Savannah State University administrator, was feted with a reception at the Mulberry Inn, hosted by one hundred movers and shakers including Howard Morrison, Arnold Tenenbaum, Annette Brock, Greg Parker, Otis Johnson, Pat Shay, and Mary Ellen Sprague. The *Morning News* predicted that, when Otis Johnson stepped down as mayor, "the person stepping up to be sworn in will be wearing pumps, not wing tips."[126]

The crowded field of six mayoral candidates included at-large council member Jackson, former mayor Floyd Adams, former councilman Ellis Cook, former state senator Regina Thomas, James Dewberry, and council member Jeff Felser. Jackson and Felser ended up in a December 6 runoff in which Jackson emerged victorious with 56 percent of the vote to become Savannah's sixty-fifth and first black female mayor.[127]

In early January, a "radiant" Edna Jackson took the oath of office in a packed Johnny Mercer Theatre. Her inaugural remarks stressed her desire to create a climate of good will and a pledge to work for "unity, diversity," and programs that moved "the whole community forward." Achieving that unity would not be easy. City Council member Van Johnson likened Mayor Jackson's inaugural ceremony to a wedding: "Anybody knows the work is in the marriage never in the wedding."[128]

One Jackson support group, confident she could make the "marriage" work, called itself the Mandingo Socio-Civic Club, a cadre of twelve women involved in mentorship and philanthropy. The tightly knit group, who regularly scheduled shopping trips to Atlanta and Jacksonville, knew they would be called on to criticize, advise, and commiserate as only those who have shared a nearly forty-year friendship can. They, like many in the community, emphasized Edna Jackson's kindness, dignity, and her ability to turn "ill will into good will."[129]

As she moved into her new role, Mayor Jackson may have found some humor in Tom Barton's characterization of the City Council as "one big mosh pit." Mayor Jackson will have her "hands full in building a consensus," Barton editorialized. But consensus building and the ability to use "a gentle insistence" were skills Ms. Jackson learned in the civil rights movement.[130]

She first joined the NAACP Youth Council in Savannah at age nine. As a protégé of W. W. Law and Judge Eugene Gadsden, she participated in sit-ins at downtown Savannah businesses, kneel-ins at various local churches, and a wade-in at Tybee Beach, where she was arrested before she even reached the ocean. Young Jackson was imprisoned for a night in the Tybee Island Jail. Years later, Jackson was presented a brick from the old jail to "honor her work in the Civil Rights Movement" and to commemorate her overnight stay at the beach. In making the presentation, Tybee Mayor Jason Buelterman said, "It's a way, in a way to apologize for something a long time ago that shouldn't have happened." When only eighteen, "Jackson took an integrated group of students from Tampa, Florida to the 1963 March on Washington where Dr. Martin Luther King Jr. made his famous 'I Have a Dream' speech."[131]

Personnel Issues: Small-Toney and Lovett

One of the first issues to require Mayor Jackson's finely-honed diplomatic skills concerned City Manager Rochelle Small-Toney, whose controversial appointment and continuing missteps provided great fodder for the media and the *Morning News*'s "Vox Populi" writers. Eventually, revelations about a $6 million backlog in purchasing operations, questions about hiring an acquaintance with a falsified resume, violations of travel reimbursement procedures, and declining staff morale prompted Mayor Jackson in October to ask for Small-Toney's resignation. Though in her city manager position for only eighteen months, Small-Toney had supporters both on and off the council, but the die was cast, and the beleaguered city manager resigned with a $97,123 severance package. Within a few months she was hired as deputy city manager in Fayetteville, North Carolina.[132]

Another brewing personnel matter soon required Mayor Jackson's attention: new disclosures about Police Chief Willie Lovett. An investigation into activities of two officers—subjects of a major federal and local narcotics probe—found Lovett's performance to be "inadequate" and "unprofessional." The report accused him of withholding information from Internal Affairs (IA) and of instructing IA to prepare a report with "patently false and incorrect information."[133]

Subsequently, Lovett learned of a sexual harassment suit being brought against him by one of his female officers, Detective Trina Mayes. Married to another officer on the force, Ms. Mayes's portrayal in the press raised quite a few eyebrows, especially her long-term relationship with a convicted felon, Rocky Sellers. A grand jury indicted her on "seven counts of making false statements about her association with criminals," including Sellers. In November 2014, Ms. Mayes was found guilty and sentenced to six months in prison. As news of the Mayes-Lovett relationship became public, the chief abruptly announced his retirement. It would not be a quiet one.[134]

In June 2014, a seven-count federal grand jury indictment charged the former chief with providing protection for and extorting money from a small-time gambling operation owned and operated by "Red Roach," his son Randy, and Kenny Blount. The group usually set up games at fairs and in downtown Savannah during holidays such as those for St. Patrick, Martin Luther King Jr., and W. W. Law. The games allegedly generated gross revenues of about two thousand dollars daily.[135] In a signed affidavit, Lovett said he would plead "not guilty" to the charges.[136]

In August a new federal indictment added two charges, alleging that Lovett lied to the FBI and that the charges could be substantiated by "video and audio surveillance of the former chief not only at the illegal gambling operation, but taking money directly from 'Red' Roach." One council member, Tony Thomas, offered a very direct assessment: "In the end, I felt he was a complete failure as chief. . . . I was as disappointed as the rest of the community, but I'm not shocked. I think there are other things that will come out."[137]

In June, an updated analysis of turnover in the SCMPD discovered that the department lost 229 officers out of a force of 600 between 2012 and 2013 and that "many of the resignations . . . were the result of dissatisfaction with the climate of favoritism."[138] And who would be the chief's replacement? Wearing the requisite "white dress shirt" of the chief's position, and affirming that she would not "seek the position on a permanent basis," interim chief Juliette Tolbert took over until a national search could be completed.[139]

The Rebounding Economy, Festivals, Tourism, and Jobs

Forbes Magazine in August of 2013 ranked Savannah 124 out of 200 in its "best places for business and careers." The lackluster ranking reminded civic leaders that growing "the local economy was job one." The previous year, *Forbes* had ranked Savannah 145th, but the uptick was hardly "something to crow about." An editorial on the topic said the ranking "points this community in the right direction but we still have a long way to go."[140]

As the economy improved, national and international marketing of the city ramped up for a burgeoning number of festivals and special events—among them, Savannah Fashion Week (SFW). Mayor Edna Jackson, who cites her guilty pleasure as "shopping," is known for her impressive array of corsages, one pinned to her lapel at what seems like all times. In 2014 she was given an addition to her corsage collection along with the inaugural Savannah Fashion Advocate Award for her "ardent support of Savannah's design and retail community." The award kicked off the fifth annual SFW, a period during which boutiques and designers showcased their wares in a variety of events. The 2014 SFW highlight, an outdoor runway show in Forsyth Park, had to be moved from under the oaks to under the tent due to inclement weather. No data were immediately available on whether retailers had seen an uptick in sales during the April 28 to May 3 event.[141]

The Savannah Music Festival in 2014 had more than thirty-seven thousand attendees, who generated $1.4 million in local tax revenues and pumped more than $10 million in direct spending into the local economy.[142] In addition to the high-profile major festivals, smaller, more specialized celebrations like the Craft Brew Festival, Savannah Book Festival, Tour of Homes, Oktoberfest, Savannah Black Heritage Festival, Jewish Food Festival, and at least fifty others were scheduled across the year; it seemed that "festivalizing" had become a "mighty economic engine that fuels spending throughout the community."[143]

Hotels rooms were at a premium. A study by Visit Savannah found the 2013 city visitor profile changed. Guests were younger; they stayed longer and spent more money. Savannah's tourism industry in 2013 counted 13 million visitors who spent $2.29 billion and contributed almost $18 million in local taxes.

Tourism had become the "chief job creator for the region." Armstrong State University economist Mike Toma placed the number of jobs generated by tourism at 24,100.[144]

The Savannah Economic Development Authority (SEDA) Web site indicates that the Savannah area boasts of "a flourishing economy balanced on a strong foundation that includes a thriving port, increasing tourism, a stabilizing manufacturing sector and significant military presence."[145] And it was this diversity that helped Savannah weather the Great Recession of 2008. Despite losing more than 13,000 jobs during the downturn, by 2013 Savannah had reclaimed half of its job losses.

One of the hardest-hit industries, construction, was predicted to rebound as residential and commercial projects appeared to be on the horizon. The construction industry lost 45 percent of its jobs during the recession, but with pent-up consumer demand for new homes, along with several very large development projects planned for downtown, there was optimism about the job sector.[146]

According to April 2014 estimates from the Georgia Department of Labor, "the Savannah metro area had 24,600 payroll jobs in leisure and hospitality, 23,900 in education and health services, 21,200 in professional and business services and 19,100 in retail trade, a sector significantly supported by tourism." Manufacturing jobs were slow to return to the area. By 2014, jobs in this sector had only climbed back to 2007 levels. Gulfstream Aerospace Corporation had been responsible for many of these additional employment opportunities.[147] But the port remained the great economic engine of Savannah.

The Growth of the Port

On Wednesday, June 5, 2013, as onlookers huddled in the rain, the heavy-equipment carrier *Teal*, loaded with four of the world's largest cranes, slipped under the Talmadge Bridge with only ten feet to spare. A $10 million price tag dangled from each crane—perhaps inexpensive considering that they could reach across twenty-two containers, lift almost 150,000 pounds, and carry that load to a height of 136 feet. The Garden City Terminal now had twenty-five of these lifting giants, more than "any other single terminal in the US."[148]

The Georgia Ports Authority operates two deepwater terminals in Chatham County, Garden City Terminal and Ocean Terminal. Garden City, the fourth-busiest container-handling facility in the United States, is located on a twelve-hundred-acre site. Ocean Terminal, Savannah's roll-on/roll-off facility, sits on a two-hundred-acre site and provides customers with more than "1.4

million square feet of covered versatile storage." Among the top exports are scrap metal and "saccharine and vanillin." The three top imports are furniture, chemicals, and "olive, palm and peanut oil."[149]

Business headlines in the Savannah papers reported a banner year for the Georgia Ports Authority. When figures were tallied, ending the 2014 fiscal year, records had been set in all categories, including a special milestone: handling more than three million TEUs (twenty-foot-equivalent container units) in one twelve-month period.[150] The good news continued.

After nearly fifteen years of contentious debate between two states (Georgia and South Carolina), environmentalists, economists, politicians, and the U.S. Army Corps of Engineers, the plan to dredge the Savannah River channel from forty-two to forty-seven feet appeared to have a green light for funding.[151]

Georgia's deepwater ports support more than 352,000 jobs across the state (37,319 in Chatham County alone) and contribute $2.5 billion in state and local taxes. Aware of this impact, the General Assembly approved $266 million of the cost-share of the river-dredging project. The total cost of the Savannah Harbor Expansion Project is estimated to be $652 million. Without expansion, Savannah ports would be unable to accommodate mega-ships now in production that are designed to take advantage of an enlarged Panama Canal. By 2015, dredging was underway.[152]

Candid Camera: Osborne and Bordeaux

Communication presents unexpected challenges for everyone, and local elected officials are no exception, especially when there are sharp differences of opinion between partisan colleagues. Such was the case on May 29, 2014, during a contentious City Council discussion on amending building-height restrictions for a planned River Street development. In a much publicized incident caught on camera by city government's Channel 8, Councilwoman Mary Osborne accused Councilman Tom Bordeaux of "head butting" and calling her "an asshole."

Complying with the city's commitment to transparency, the confrontation was "posted in unaltered form on the local government's website, as all public meetings are." According to WTOC-TV reporter Don Logana, who reached Osborne by phone for a comment, Ms. Osborne conceded she was not sure Bordeaux had intentionally head-butted her, but was convinced he had invaded her personal space and he did call her "that name." She described the incident using a sports analogy, "If this was basketball what he did would be a personal foul." Both Bordeaux and Osborne apologized for the disruption.[153]

Container ship moving up the Savannah River toward the port, December 5, 2014. Courtesy Richard H. Burke.

Gangs, Crime, and Violence: "Unacceptable"

Around 10:45 P.M. on Saturday, November 3, 2012, the crowded midway of the Exchange Club Coastal Empire Fairgrounds exploded in a hail of bullets; when it was over, eight people had been shot, all but one a teenager. It was the first high-profile violent incident in Mayor Jackson's term. For a while, chaos swept the grounds as families tried to reunite with loved ones. The injured were taken to a local hospital; none of the injuries proved fatal. Throughout the night, officers canvassed the area, questioning witnesses and looking for evidence or cell-phone videos that might have captured the shooting. The fair opened the next day as planned but with additional security, and the Exchange Club donated five thousand dollars to CrimeStoppers as a reward for information leading to the arrest and conviction of the perpetrators. Within a short time, police concluded that the barrage of gunfire involved a shootout between rival gangs—"Hellhole" and "Tatemville."[154]

About a month later, a Police Department detective told a reporter, "there's no need to be alarmed. . . . the majority of the people involved in these crimes know each other. . . . they're not attacking anyone they don't know, and it's not random violence."[155] But the newspaper had a different view: "when innocent fairgoers are caught in the crossfire, police must fight back. The same goes when a pattern of violent behavior destroys neighborhoods."[156]

"We do have a gang problem," the police told the press; at least thirty gangs were in residence in Savannah. Most gang members self-selected into membership because of where they lived: "38th Street Boys," the "Cann Park Goons," the "Hitch Village Posse." Local gangs were described as being very territorial with violent incidents often arising because of failure to observe certain geographic boundaries or for "disrespect, or just "look[ing] at you funny."[157] With their *modus operandi* being intimidation and fear, and drug trafficking their primary trade, gangs often terrorized whole neighborhoods.

At a preliminary hearing for four young men allegedly involved in the fairgrounds incident, detectives acknowledged the difficulty in getting people to come forward to describe what happened. Of the fairgrounds shootout, one officer told the court: "Probably the thousands of people out there saw it but nobody has come forward." An incredulous defense attorney asked, "You all don't have a witness that actually saw the shooting?" The answer was, "No sir."[158]

In September 2013, the Chatham County Grand Jury issued a ninety-seven-count indictment against nine "gang members . . . all of whom had some involvement with the fairground shootings as well as other crimes in the city." The Police Department called it a "major strike against gang violence that has plagued Savannah." The Exchange Club soon offered for sale the nearly seventy-acre Coastal Empire Fairgrounds for a price of $3.45 million. If the property did not sell, the club said the fair would go on as planned in 2014. In August 2016, the City Council voted to purchase the Coastal Empire Fairgrounds for $2.9 million.[159]

Police Department investigations, probes into misconduct, and lawsuits were stacking up on the desk of the new city manager, Stephanie Cutter, as she coordinated the search for a new police chief. She was also under fire to purge cronyism, restore professionalism, and remove politics and race from the equation. The attention-grabbing headline in the *Morning News* left no doubt about the paper's perspective on the need for change: "Police department needs an enema."[160]

During the first six months of 2014, fourteen homicides occurred in Chatham County; two were teenagers, ages fifteen and sixteen. All but one took place "within the city limits of Savannah." In one incident two young men argued over a trivial issue outside a restaurant. When one young man pulled a gun, the other pulled his own weapon and chased the victim down the street, firing nine shots into his back, including the *coup de grace,* a bullet to the back of the head. Explaining what transpired, the shooter said: "I was afraid for my life. . . . I couldn't believe what had happened, you know, everything happened so fast." Events like this are familiar occurrences in cities like Baltimore, Philadelphia and Chicago. Ta-Nehisi Coates, national correspondent for the *Atlantic,* recounted a similar incident with a happier outcome. He was confronted by a young boy who reached into his pocket and pulled out a gun, and "in his small eyes" Nehisi saw a "surging rage that could, in an instant, erase my body. . . . I remember being amazed that death could so easily rise up from the nothing of a boyish afternoon."

When another eight shootings occurred over one week in mid-July 2014, Mayor Jackson called a news conference. Flanked by City Council members and interim police chief Julie Tolbert, the mayor called the shootings "unacceptable" and urged residents to stand together: "[People] in the eastside community where many of the shootings have taken place . . . don't deserve to live in fear caused by a handful of kids too dumb to sort out their problems without guns." She implored parents to get involved in their children's lives, to know where they are, to "search their rooms," to know their children's friends, and to know the community's precinct officers. "It's time for tough love." Councilwoman Osborne echoed some of these sentiments: "There are parents who know what's going on, and there are witnesses that won't even testify against who shot them."[161]

If one week and eight shootings were not bad enough, statistics for the month of July 2014 were equally alarming: twenty-four people shot in twenty-one shooting incidents that left two dead. Interim chief Tolbert provided some background on the cases. In eleven incidents, victims and suspects knew each other. Most shootings were in inner-city neighborhoods. Six of the people shot refused to cooperate with police—either because they intended to "handle it themselves" or they "don't like the police." The *Morning News* editorialized: "The fact that the shootings were confined to inner city neighborhoods, or that most of the victims knew the gunmen who shot them is of no comfort. That's because violence does more than kill people. It can be fatal to a city's reputation."[162]

Operation Ceasefire promised a new approach. Police and other service providers would intervene personally with "known offenders who are the source of the most violent crime." This high-risk group would be required to meet with teams composed of police, city representatives, and trainers and would be offered education and employment as a way to lift them "out of a life of crime." Those who elected not to participate or who violated the terms of participation should consider themselves forewarned that they would be dealt with harshly if involved in further illegal activity. Similar programs had been successful in Boston, Chattanooga, and other cities.[163]

And there were other deterrents, including six prized horses that were part of the mounted patrol unit. Trained to deal with loud noises, like "gunshots and sirens," the horses were able to "run down criminals" in places patrol cars could not go. Mounted police can be very intimidating—an officer on a horse is fourteen to fifteen feet tall.[164]

The Savannah business community's concern about crime brought a standing-room-only crowd to the July meeting of the Downtown Business Association. Attendees were there to hear criminologist David Kennedy, who told the group: "If you are born black and male, there is a one in three chance that you will be locked up at some point during your lifetime. . . . [For a black male who does] not finish high school that possibility jumps to 70 percent." Kennedy had some encouragement; it was a remarkably small group committing the crimes. "In Savannah, we're talking about 300 people." He recommended interventions like Operation Ceasefire.[165]

Changing the Landscape of the City

A rebounding economy brought a boom to Broughton Street. Once the major downtown retail thoroughfare, the street by 1991 had become a veritable wasteland with 40 percent of the first-floor properties vacant. But as high-end retailers like Marc Jacobs and Kate Spade opened next to local boutiques and specialty shops and national chains with a more bohemian vibe like Free People, Anthropologie, and Urban Outfitters moved in, Broughton evolved into an eclectic shopping mecca.

In 2014, Atlanta developer Ben Carter informed the City Council that he had contracts to buy twenty-two properties as part of his Broughton Street plan, a $75 million project designed to "further transform Broughton into a shopping and dining hub." His successful track record in other cities appears to have persuaded the council to consider upgrading the "Broughton streetscape" and to investigate strategies to solve parking issues.[166]

Savannah native and hotelier Richard Kessler announced plans for a $200 million project, Plant Riverside, that would add four hundred hotel rooms, "26,000 square feet of retail, restaurant and entertainment space and 65,000 square feet of outdoor communal space to the waterfront"; the centerpiece of the project would be the hundred-year-old power plant on the west end of River Street. Christian Sottile, dean of SCAD's Building Arts program, who would have major architectural responsibility for the renovation, envisioned the project as bringing new life to the west end of River Street, an area "which has been dormant for so long." Extending the Riverwalk promenade westward would require city funding.[167] However, objections were raised by some preservationists who believed new developments could "threaten Savannah's historic character."

Reed Engle, a veteran member of Savannah's Historic Review Board, published his concerns in the *Morning News* during summer 2014. He wrote that the Historic District Ordinance of 1973 and its amendments until now had checked "inappropriate and incompatible development." Recent decisions by the Metropolitan Planning Commission, the City Zoning Board of Appeals, and the City Council, Engle asserted, "appear to threaten the stability of predictability and to turn Savannah's historic district over to out-of-town developers with very deep pockets and no understanding of the city's historic character."[168]

It was a quiet opening with little fanfare. After twenty-four years, the final phase of the Truman Parkway, an eleven-mile, $182 million, multilane highway that runs from Abercorn Street on the south side of the city to President Street, a main artery into downtown, opened for traffic in mid-March 2014. The Truman was expected to relieve congestion and to significantly reduce driving time between many areas of the city. Thirty-five thousand drivers are expected to travel the parkway daily. Most residents seem happy to have another route for maneuvering around Savannah.[169]

Also in the summer of 2014, Dulany Industries purchased a sixteen-hundred-acre waterfront tract off East President Street. The first order of business would be a two-year environmental cleanup of the property, former site of chemical companies Tronox and Kerr-McGee. The new venture, the SeaPoint Industrial Terminal Complex, would structure the property into multiuse sites for high-tech manufacturing tenants. With one mile of deepwater frontage and dual-rail access, it would be the largest private industrial site on the Savannah River. One veteran commercial broker called it the most "exciting site I have seen" in thirty years "of marketing industrial real estate in the Savannah area."[170]

The improving economy appeared to be breathing some life into the fifty-four-acre Savannah River Landing site. Envisioned as an eastern expansion of downtown with two thousand feet of riverfront, the original master plan of 2006 had specified single-family homes, townhomes, condos, a hotel, restaurants, and retail and office space all built around squares and public parks. After the city invested money into the project's infrastructure, foreclosure issues, pending lawsuits, and a collapsing Riverwalk extension threatened to undermine the planned development. By 2014 virtually no progress had been made, but deals were being discussed and developers were buying or building nearby in anticipation that a resuscitated River Landing project would soon come to fruition.[171] Government funded projects were on the drawing board that would also change the downtown landscape south of Broughton.

The City Council approved a $1 million purchase of property at Thirty-fourth Street and Martin Luther King Jr. Boulevard for a new SCMPD Central Precinct station. Construction was expected to be fast-tracked. The 1.6-acre plot addressed several selection criteria: it was in a high-crime area so its presence could have an immediate impact; it had good access from multiple roads; and it could serve as a catalyst for future area development.

Another benefit of this particular property was that the city could negotiate with one rather than multiple owners. But not everyone embraced the site chosen. A writer in the *Savannah Herald* lamented in a July 23, 2014, letter to the editor: "What would Mr. Law say about the demolishing of historical homes to build a midtown precinct? I think that he would be turning in his grave. . . . black leaders of the city of Savannah are planning to destroy homes rented for 130 years by working class black families and replace those homes with a police station." Ellen Harris of the Metropolitan Planning Commission said the houses, part of what was once called Meldrim Row, "are not within a designated local historic district."[172] Transformation of the Martin Luther King Jr. corridor was also in process.

Opened first in November 1967, the I-16 flyover off-ramp—which passed over Martin Luther King Jr. Boulevard into Savannah—was hailed as a great addition, allowing for easy access into downtown Savannah. In 2008 the Georgia Department of Transportation conducted a study of the flyover question, the review likely stimulated by public advocacy that began in the mid-1990s for revitalizing this area of downtown Savannah. W.W. Law said in 1996: "If the street is named after a great leader like Martin Luther King, Jr., then we should be compelled to make the street live up to all of its potential."[173]

In 2014 the I-16 off-ramp remained a topic of forums, debates, and study. The route had destroyed the black-owned business community already in decline along West Broad Street (now MLK Jr. Boulevard) and wiped out entire neighborhoods. The concrete ramp came to represent more than a physical barrier as it had effectively devastated what was once the heart of Savannah's African American community—a vibrant, prosperous center of commerce and entertainment.

By 2014, funds had not yet been budgeted for flyover demolition, though some beautification efforts in the area such as the installation of pavers on some medians and sidewalks had begun. The Metropolitan Planning Commission maintained a project manual for public review; Savannah resident Ardis Wood said of the concepts presented, "This plan will change that MLK area from a vast, empty wasteland of concrete . . . to tree-lined streets [with] a vibrant collection of new commercial and residential buildings graced by green spaces."

Not everyone thought the flyover should be removed. There were suggestions for transforming it into a pedestrian bridge and park. Preservationist Emma Adler in a May 2014 letter to the *Morning News* offered other reasons for opposing the flyover demolition, including "the cost and the inconvenience. The flyover is in a perfect location for entrance or exit into or out of downtown Savannah. Leave the situation as it is."[174]

Mayor Jackson's State of the City Address: 2014, 2015

Mayor Jackson received a standing ovation at the conclusion of her February 2014 State of the City Address, in which she outlined four initiatives that she said "were key to Savannah's future." These included: the "Canal District" with its $120 million arena centerpiece; a $20 million arts center, and $750,000 to support local organizations that promote educational and cultural events, thus enhancing quality of life for residents and tourists alike; infrastructure improvements for drainage and road projects such as revamping President Street; and "improving public safety by uncovering all the problems with the Savannah-Chatham police department"—a process she described as "painful."

Jackson applauded Savannah for surviving five years of the Great Recession. The city not only survived but appeared to be thriving, and the mayor's announcement left no doubt of that. The year 2013 had brought in "record breaking . . . [numbers] of tourists, new businesses and construction projects."[175] Though wearing flats, not heels, Mayor Edna Jackson was clearly "pumped" about Savannah's future.

Mayor Jackson's February 2015 State of the City address had a much different tone. This time she focused on public safety. She reminded her audience of some positives: "Flooding is down, taxes are low, the economy is up"; the city had seen "more commercial investment the past two years than at any point in our history." Here she paused. "But none of that matters when our young people are shooting each other in our streets . . . teenagers shooting each other over drugs, money or disrespect. . . . Until every one of us IS and FEELS safe, it is ALL of our problem."

The mayor described Savannah as having "persistent, generational crime occurring in the same neighborhoods—and same families—year after year." She mourned the death of "all 32 of Savannah's homicide victims last year," almost all young men with a "lifestyle that put them in harm's way." She continued, "What keeps me up at night is the constant threat of gunfire . . . and the innocent children unlucky enough to live with these criminals."[176] The mayor refuted claims that crime was "at an all-time high." Likely she was remembering the fifty-nine homicides that occurred during 1991, the last year of the

Rousakis administration. But she acknowledged that three shootings a week were too much.

How was the city to reduce violent crime? She spoke of some efforts underway in the Police Department, but she first discussed the department itself. Several police officers "who had no business wearing a badge" had left the department. One she did not mention by name was the former chief, Willie Lovett, now incarcerated at Hazleton Federal Penitentiary in West Virginia, serving a 7.5 year term on charges of obstruction of justice, extortion, and protecting an illegal gambling operation.

Next she hailed the hiring of sixty-five-year-old Joseph "Jack" Lumpkin Sr. as the new chief of the Savannah-Chatham Metropolitan Police Department. Lumpkin, former chief of the Athens–Clarke County Police Department, brought to the job forty-three years of law-enforcement experience, and he would need every day of that experience to deal with a department understaffed and under pressure from outsiders.[177]

To help Lumpkin in his challenging job, the mayor called for a fully staffed Police Department, which at the time had about "70 vacancies" in a force of 605. Officers in Savannah's "sister city," Charleston, enjoyed higher salaries, and 90 percent had earned bachelor's, master's, or law degrees. Mayor Jackson wanted the city "to explore" making local police salaries "the highest of any department in the southeast." The department's new investments in technology, such as body cameras and data terminals in police cars and surveillance cameras on the streets, were heralded as important tools and deterrents.

The mayor praised the efforts of Operation Ceasefire. Developed by policing expert David Kennedy, the initiative would focus on "a few key neighborhoods with persistent violent crime" and would attack the gang issue from another perspective—pulling young men away from gangs, giving "gang members an honorable exit from street life." The mayor acknowledged that in the final analysis the city's crime problem would not be solved unless the community addressed such issues as jobs, education, and persistent poverty. In closing, Mayor Jackson said, "It's time for things to change in Savannah."[178]

Apparently others were of the same mind. As the election season of 2015 heated up, opinion pieces began to appear in the *Morning News.* One editorial hinted at "lingering rumors of corruption and cronyism"; another argued that "the lack of sufficient police on Savannah's streets is . . . a stain on the records of Mayor Edna Jackson, members of City Council and the city's management." In September 2015 the *Morning News* stated very bluntly, "It's time for the winds of change to begin blowing through Savannah's city government."[179]

Despite the leadership of Chief Lumpkin, crime remained at "unacceptable" levels. Shootings continued almost nightly; the *Morning News* reported in September 2015 that "violent crimes" were up over 20 percent and property crimes up 9 percent compared to the same time period in 2014. In fact, Savannah's murder rate of 9.8 per 100,000 was nearly double the national rate of 4.5. Even more bleak were statistics from the cities of Detroit and St. Louis with murder rates of 44 and 50 respectively.[180]

One member of the local press described Savannah as a "spiritually fulfilling and culturally rich place to live"; however, the writer noted, "Savannah is just one of many crime-ridden cities in America with stark economic, racial, and cultural divides. It will likely take years . . . before we see significant progress in reducing . . . senseless shootings."[181] Only time will tell. In the interim, with a growing economy, unemployment at 5.7 percent and falling, a port that is the "economic horse" of the region, a summer of record-breaking tourists visits, and with conversations underway about equity, race, violence, incarceration—there was hope that Savannah's best days were yet to come.[182]

Conclusion

For more than a hundred years, slavery endured in Savannah. As in other southern urban centers, the "peculiar institution" appeared to most as the normal way of life. Slave codes in the region characterized black people as akin to beasts of burden, and frequently they were treated as such. It took a Civil War and the deaths of 700,000 young men, North and South, to end an institution that was devastating for the enslaved and in very different ways profoundly affected the masters and the nonslaveholding class.[1]

Emancipation brought an economic and political sea change to Savannah and the South. Former slaves now expected wages, voting rights, and freedom and no longer felt compelled to show the deference required in the past. These expectations and behaviors promoted increasingly antiblack attitudes and encouraged violence toward blacks and intensified racism. One Savannahian's comment reflected the views of many whites: "There is one thing that I will not submit to that the negro is our equal."[2]

Both before and long after the Civil War, Savannah continued to be governed by a civic-commercial elite who repressed, often with the help of the city's police, any effort by blacks to gain equal rights under the law. Savannah like other southern cities became a bifurcated society where racism prevailed.

In the fight for rights denied, blacks used the pulpit, the pamphlet, and the press. From the end of the Civil War into the twenty-first century, African American leaders emerged in Savannah to champion equal treatment under the law, and blacks began to organize through their churches, service organizations, social clubs, and unions. When the elite refused to negotiate, the disenfranchised sometimes borrowed a tactic used in the antebellum years, arson. They also used strikes and boycotts with limited success; not until the mid-twentieth century and only after the decisions of lower courts and the U.S. Supreme Court and passage of the civil rights acts of the 1960s did justice begin to be served.

In an apartheid-like climate, Savannah blacks protested with marches, sit-ins, wade-ins, pray-ins, and even occasional acts of violence to achieve their ends. The long-dormant local NAACP led the quest. As in Greensboro, Atlanta, and Charleston, Savannah's black leaders called on the power of the boycott to demand that lunch counters be integrated, that blacks be addressed with courtesy titles, and that retail establishments hire black clerks and managers. African Americans wanted beaches, golf courses, libraries, schools, and theaters opened to people of all races; they asked for "the same rights as whites, nothing more, nothing less." And the boycotters did not hesitate to challenge their own. When members of Savannah's African American community continued to patronize or accept home deliveries from boycotted stores, their names were called out at churches and NAACP meetings as part of a "traitors list."

For eighteen months, protests, human barricades, marches, occasional confrontational demonstrations, vandalism, and arson swept the city. But the violence in Savannah never reached the levels that immobilized some other urban centers in the South. The city's ability to confront the demonstrations with little loss of life and property was the result of a group of remarkable black and white leaders who worked together to negotiate an acceptable resolution; this was a seminal event in Savannah's history.

By the end of the twentieth century and into the twenty-first, Savannah's registered black voters reached numbers that enabled them to elect consecutively three African American mayors and eventually a majority of City Council members, though not without the support of white voters. African Americans now sat where once the white civic-commercial elite had governed for more than 250 years.

Urban renewal that began with slum clearance in the late 1930s gained momentum and appeared initially to be a boon for the quality of life of black citizens, but it also displaced many black families and their businesses. Moreover, an "equity agenda" adopted by the city failed to end endemic poverty that persists to this day for about 25 percent of residents; in some census tracts, over 50 percent have incomes at or below poverty level. The relationship between poverty and crime has been a much discussed topic by sociologists, criminologists, and psychologists.

A recent mayor commented on Savannah's seemingly intractable crime problem, saying the city suffers "from a legacy of neglecting the long term interests of the black community, especially education, jobs and opportunities for social mobility." Where "intergenerational poverty" persists and youngsters grow up in the "toxic environment of low income neighborhoods," they often drop out of school; unable to find jobs, they quickly become "marginalized" members of society. Their growing "sense of alienation and frustration and anger" develops into "misplaced aggression." Many become involved in gangs or use drugs or commit petty crimes (or not-so-petty crimes) and, once arrested, their prospects for employment become even bleaker. Often these individuals become recidivists, the life of crime being the only life they know.[3]

Legal scholar and civil rights advocate Michelle Alexander argues that the criminal justice system targets young black males, a new type of "Jim Crow-ism." This perhaps explains the distrust of the police by many in Savannah's African American community and the reluctance of victims and witnesses to assist police in identifying perpetrators of crime.[4]

Historically, cops were distrusted. Police brutality when attempting to crush crime from the Civil War into the twenty-first century contributed to this legacy. Even with an integrated police force and the appointment of Savannah's first black chief of police, Willie Lovett, these attitudes persisted. Mr. Lovett's tenure was brief. He retired in 2013 after allegations of sexual misconduct and soon thereafter became indicted by the federal government for extortion, participation in an illegal gambling operation, and conspiracy to obstruct the enforcement of state criminal laws. He was convicted and is now serving a seven-and-a-half-year term in federal prison in West Virginia.[5]

In late 2014, the spike in shootings and criminal activity reached such levels that the *Morning News* warned that tourists now avoided Savannah. Savannah risked "being defined as . . . a city of danger . . . where tacit acceptance of random violence becomes part of the fabric of the community." With a murder rate nearly double the national average, citizens were anxious for a new chief to be hired.[6]

In early November 2014, Savannah welcomed a new chief of police, Joseph "Jack" Lumpkin, an African American, age sixty-five, with forty-three years in police work. At his swearing-in ceremony, Lumpkin said, "No chief is a silver bullet that is going to solve all the challenges and problems." And he was right. Even with a department that is one of the largest in the country for the size of the population it patrols, gangs, lack of community cooperation to identify perpetrators, and internal issues persist.[7]

In one of her last addresses, Mayor Edna Jackson expressed confidence that the new chief was "the right man for the job." And she was also encouraged by other signs of optimism and prosperity. More tourists than ever before slept in new hotels and dined in the many downtown restaurants—when they spent, they also paid a special-purpose local-option sales tax (SPLOST), a 1 percent tax that can be used to fund the building of parks, schools, roads, and other public facilities. Visitors contribute approximately 40 percent of all SPLOST dollars, not insignificant when one considers that, since 1985, this tax has funded more than one billion dollars in local projects. In 2013 voters agreed to extend SPLOST until 2020.[8]

And Mayor Jackson took great pride in the changing cityscape. Redevelopment of downtown areas by private investors seemed to promise continued revitalization of Broughton Street and River Street. The city government agreed to spend $14 million to extend westward the walk along the river, which currently ends at a defunct power plant soon to be converted by a private developer into a $220 million complex that will include a hotel, shops, restaurants, and public spaces. In the words of one City Council member: "[the project] changes the dynamics of the entire west end of River Street." Another entrepreneur put forward plans to develop part of Broughton Street and anticipated spending about $75,000,000 to create a shopping-and-dining hub.

The City Council continued to support plans long on the drawing board to build a new City Arena in Savannah's Historic West Boundary Canal District. Although the proposal was somewhat controversial, proponents claimed that it would rejuvenate yet another area of the city.[9] The Savannah College of Art and Design continued to preserve and beautify Savannah as it acquired and renovated historic properties. The revitalization plan for West Broad Street still awaits a decision on the fate of the I-16 flyover ramp. On the east side, hotels and other developments and redevelopments are attempting to revitalize long-neglected areas.

As Savannah's landscape changed, so did its demographics. The 2013 Census Bureau tabulation of population by race found the city to be 55 percent "Black or African American," 38 percent "White," 5 percent "Hispanic or Latino," and 2 percent "Asian."[10]

Four candidates entered the contest for mayor in 2015: the incumbent Democrat, Edna Jackson; "Republican-leaning" Eddie DeLoach, owner of a landscaping company; and two other white businessmen, Murray Silver Jr. and Louis Williams. The *Morning News* soon entered the fray, touting its picks for the mayoralty and City Council races scheduled for November 3.[11]

The *Morning News* blamed Mayor Jackson for failing "the community on public safety" and endorsed Eddie DeLoach as the city's "best hope for change." With the Savannah area now "riding the crest of a crime wave," curbing crime became the top priority for most of the candidates. On November 1, an editorial in the *Morning News* urged voters to elect DeLoach, citing skyrocketing "violent crime" and the rampant "incompetency" of the current administration.[12]

The election had a light voter turnout, about twenty-seven thousand. When the votes were counted, two candidates received the largest percentages: Jackson took 44 percent and DeLoach 42 percent. Because no candidate received 50 percent, a runoff was scheduled for December 1. Some contested City Council seats also were forced into the runoff.[13] Campaigning heated up again and focused on gun violence as a major theme, appropriately so, because before the year ended, Savannah–Chatham County reported fifty-three homicides, the highest incidence of homicides in Savannah since 1991.

A spokesperson for the current administration acknowledged the problem: "There are lots of guns on the streets of Savannah and people are not afraid to use them." Some local criminals now carried weapons with greater firepower than the police; Chief Lumpkin recommended arming officers with assault rifles, and the *Morning News* enthusiastically endorsed the plan. Gun violence was not limited to Savannah or the South; homicide rates were rising in New Orleans, Baltimore, Cincinnati, St. Louis, Los Angeles, Chicago, and other cities.[14]

As the runoff date neared, criticism persisted from Mayor Jackson's opponents for the administration's failure to end gun violence or defuse the "self-defeating culture" of young black men who were both the victims and perpetrators of many violent incidents. DeLoach supporters recognized that crime weighed heavily on the minds of Savannahians; they remembered how violent crime had affected the outcome of the mayoral election in 1991 when Susan Weiner, a political newcomer to Savannah and its politics, "rode a tidal wave of disgust [to defeat] . . . five term incumbent Mayor John P. Rousakis over the city's failure to address violent crime." Weiner's campaign used billboards riddled with bullet holes to drive home the point that local crime was out of control.[15]

On the day of the December 2015 runoff election, a full-page ad in the *Morning News* pictured silhouettes of homicide victims with the caption: "127 People . . . murdered since Edna Jackson Became Mayor of Savannah in 2012. These lives Mattered. Enough already. It's time for a change. Vote Eddie DeLoach Mayor of Savannah December 1 runoff." A curious disclaimer appeared at the bottom of the page: "Paid for by a concerned citizen. Independent expenditure not affiliated or approved by any campaign"[16] When the polls closed and the votes were tallied, an era ended. For two decades African Americans had served as mayor of Savannah.

The *Morning News* announced a "New dawn at city hall." Eddie DeLoach, with vigorous promotion by the newspaper, scored an upset victory, winning 53 percent of the votes to incumbent Mayor Jackson's 47 percent. The new City Council members, also backed by the *Morning News,* changed the composition of the council to five white and four black members in the black-majority city. Obviously, some black voters who supported Jackson in the November 3 election defected to DeLoach in the December runoff.[17]

"Eddie, Eddie," cheered hundreds of supporters during the victory celebration at the SoHo Restaurant on Liberty Street. He told his followers: "We are all here for the same reason. We want a better Savannah." The *Morning News* bluntly observed that the city government "will look . . . different from the current council, which is a good thing." DeLoach won, the paper concluded, because a majority of voters "craved change," concerned that "Savannah was lurching in the wrong direction and becoming too dangerous, too mired in poverty and other social ills and too wedded to the status quo." Now "new leaders will take the city in a different direction."[18]

But crime continued to plague Savannah citizens and embarrass politicians. Despite efforts locally to curb homicides through programs such as "End Gun Violence," internships and pre-apprenticeships for 600 youth, prosecuting firearms cases in federal court (where, if convicted, there would be no option for parole), and the use of street cameras and license plate readers, the success rates were far from encouraging.[19]

A CNN feature entitled *Southern Charm, Deadly Streets* juxtaposed the city's "homicide rate with descriptions of the peaceful, leisurely image of a southern city that draws millions of tourists each year." Mayor Eddie DeLoach apologized and told the *Savannah Morning News,* "We are working hard to make our streets and our neighborhoods safer." Lumpkin, echoed the mayor. At year's end, Savannah-Chatham police had investigated 50 homicides, compared to 53 in 2015 and 33 in 2014. But in a city where 13.9 million tourists spend $2.8 billion, these words were hardly soothing.[20]

Preservationists like Emma Adler have occasionally chided local tour guides for telling "outlandish tales" that characterize Savannah "as a 'spooky town.' How degrading," Mrs. Adler once wrote. Though their age, income and length of stay changed, tourists could not get enough of Savannah and to accommodate them, developers added more luxurious hotels, bars and restaurants.[21] One visitor from New York observed recently that, intentionally or not, Savannah has long appeared "stuck in its own kind of gauzy ante-bellum bubble." The legendary Savannah born songwriter and singer, Johnny Mercer, reflected the local atmosphere when he crooned: "I know I'm old fashioned / But I don't mind it / That's how I want to be / As long as you agree /To stay old fashioned with me." The visitor continued: "old school Savannah is gradually becoming . . . a thing of the past," and a "cultural renaissance is underway in this otherwise sleepy town . . . that now attracts scores of artsy intellectuals."[22]

Everyone's attention was diverted from tourism, crime and building projects when in early October a hurricane threatened the southeast coast. On

October 8th hurricane force winds buffeted Tybee's south end and roared across Savannah. The governor had earlier ordered a mandatory evacuation, likely saving lives. One person died on the Isle of Hope. Century old trees inflicted great damage and several tornadoes twisted 100 year old pines into kindling. It took months for work crews to remove the debris. The cost of Hurricane Matthew was reported to be more than $36 million.[23]

But Savannahians returned and started to think about the holiday season. A *Savannah Morning News* editorial on the first day of 2017 might have helped some reflect on challenges in year ahead. It was a cautionary tale. Fifty murders were too many. Mayor DeLoach and two city council members had won election promising to "halt the rising rate of violence . . . throughout the city." Were the new programs to combat crime really working? How much patience would voters have? The editorial writer went on to say "too much poverty and homelessness still plaque the city." The new 128 square foot "tiny houses" for homeless veterans seemed to be a step in the right direction. Schools had improved under the leadership of Thomas Lockamy who was retiring in 2017 after twelve years as superintendent. Dr. Lockamy won high praise from the press and his staff. The *SMN* acknowledged that it would be a challenge to find a person of his talent who could enhance the public schools' performance and also quell a contentious board whose meetings sometimes dissolved into acrimony.[24]

And the editorialist also mentioned a challenge perhaps less familiar to taxpayers though it had been discussed and debated for 25 years—the need to consolidate city and county government. "Savannah-Chatham is the only metro area outside Atlanta that maintains separate city and county governments." Consolidation would require a referendum but advocates believe it would help a city like Savannah which "remains divided by racial and partisan politics.[25] Some suggested that consolidation had always been considered a "non-starter" because of "the political assumption that the city's black majority and largely Democratic population would never give up any of its hard-won power . . . to a consolidated government with a county that historically has been majority white and Republican." But with changing demographics and the county now having a "minority" majority, perhaps the plan would find more support. Most agreed that consolidation would not be an easy transition to achieve.[26]

But there was also encouraging news: the growth and success of the port, a rebounding economy, a declining unemployment rate, a vibrant tourist industry, SCAD's student growth and preservation efforts, well-attended festivals across the year, huge construction projects at every compass point and people's interest in and affection for the city they called home.

A former mayor liked to quote Oliver Wendell Holmes: "We must sail sometimes with the wind and sometimes against it but not drift or lie at anchor." Perhaps the line that introduces this quote best describes Savannah today: "Greatness is not in where we stand, but in what direction we are moving." Charting this course is Savannah's great challenge.[27]

Notes

Preface

1. Jones, *Saving Savannah,* 408–9.

Introduction

1. Fraser, *Savannah in the Old South*, 1–12; Harris and Berry, eds., *Slavery and Freedom in Savannah*, 1–2.

2. Fraser, *Savannah in the Old South*, 45–46.

3. Fraser, *Savannah in the Old South,* 79–80.

4. Fraser, *Savannah in the Old South*, 37, 45–46, 49–50, 79–80; Harris and Berry, eds., *Slavery and Freedom in Savannah*, 3; Morgan, *African American Life in the Georgia Lowcountry*, 15–19, 22, 24, 26.

5. Harris and Berry, eds., *Slavery and Freedom in Savannah,* 11–13, 25; Morgan, *African American Life in the Lowcountry,* 89–97.

6. Harris and Berry, eds., *Slavery and Freedom in Savannah,* 23, 54–55; Fraser, *Savannah in the Old South*, 191–92, 310; Morgan, African American Life in Savannah, 81. Wood, Betty. "Slavery in Colonial Georgia." *New Georgia Encyclopedia*, 24 September 2014. http://m.georgiaencyclopedia.org/articles/history-archaeology/slavery-colonial-georgia (accessed January 13, 2017).

7. Fraser, *Savannah in the Old South*, 113–14, 126.

8. Harris and Berry, *Slavery and Freedom in Savannah,* 26–41; Fraser, *Savannah in the Old South,* 144–45.

9. Fraser, *Savannah in the Old South*, 91–8, 137, 139.

10. Fraser, *Savannah in the Old South*, 145–48; U. S. Bureau of Census, *The Population of the 33 Urban Places: 1800,* https://www.census.gov/population/www/documentation/twps0027/tab03.txt; Gillespie, *Free Labor in an Unfree World*, 27.

11. Fraser, *Savannah in the Old South*, 199–201, 241.

12. Fraser, *Savannah in the Old South*, 231–32, 243–46, 254.

13. Fraser, *Savannah in the Old South*, 291–92.

14. Fraser, *Savannah in the Old South*, 179–80, 255–56, 260–61.

15. Fraser, *Savannah in the Old South*, 216–71, 258–59; Jones, *Saving Savannah*, 88.

16. Jones, *Saving Savannah*, 88–89; Fraser, *Savannah in the Old South*, 49, 151.

17. Jones, *Saving Savannah*, 48; Fraser, *Savannah in the Old South*, 288–90.

18. Fraser, *Savannah in the Old South*, 151–52, 179–80.

19. Fraser, *Savannah in the Old South*, 316–17.

20. Fraser. *Savannah in the Old South*, 313, 320.

21. Fraser, *Savannah in the Old South*, 320–32.

22. Fraser, *Savannah in the Old South*, 321–23; *Jones, Saving Savanna*h, 126, 129–30, 132.

23. Fraser, *Savannah in the Old South*, 327, 30; Jones, *Saving Savannah*, 152–53.

24. Fraser, *Savannah in the Old South*, 334; Jones, *Saving Savannah*, 153.
25. Fraser, *Savannah in the Old South*, 338.
26. Fraser, *Savannah in the Old South*, 339–40; Jones, *Saving Savannah*, 206.

Chapter 1: Reconstruction, Ruins, and Revival: 1864–1872

1. City Council members—officially known as aldermen—I have referred to throughout as councilmember, councilwoman and councilman, terms I find to be more descriptive of the office held. The size of council has varied over the years. As of 2014, the City Council was composed of nine members, one elected from each of Savannah's six districts, two at-large members, and the mayor.
2. Qtd. by Harold Holzer, "Review of Mark M. Smith, *The Smell of Battle, the Taste of Siege*," *Wall Street Journal*, Saturday–Sunday, December 6–7, 2014.
3. Qtd. in Simms, *First Colored Baptist Church*, 137; see also Fraser, *Savannah in the Old South*, 339–40; Lawrence, *Present for Mr. Lincoln*, 206–14; Shryock, *Letters of Arnold*, 7–9.
4. King, ed., "Fanny Cohen's Journal," 411, 414; Myers, ed., *Children of Pride*, 1238–47.
5. Qtd. in Smith, "Cotton from Savannah," 495; see also Lawrence, *Present for Mr. Lincoln*, 213.
6. Conway, *Reconstruction of Georgia*, 16; Lawrence, *Present for Mr. Lincoln*, 213.
7. Golay, *Ruined Land*, 48–49; Campbell, *When Sherman Marched*, 27.
8. Lawrence, *Present for Mr. Lincoln*, 222.
9. Golay, *Ruined Land*, 49–51.
10. Gamble, *History of the City Government*, 264–65; Lawrence, *Present for Mr. Lincoln*, 220–22.
11. Gatell, ed., "Yankee Views the Agony of Savannah," 429; Conway, *Reconstruction of Georgia*, 17.
12. Golay, *Ruined Land*, 49; Reid, *After the War*, 147.
13. Campbell, *When Sherman Marched*, 18, 26.
14. Elliott, *Vain in the Help of Man*, 13.
15. Ibid., 26–28; King, ed., "Fanny Cohen's Journal," 411, 413, 414; Berger, "Sherman's Occupation of Savannah: Two Letters," 109–15.
16. Qtd. in Fraser, *Charleston! Charleston!* 279.
17. Campbell, *When Sherman Marched*, 20–21; see also Avary, *Dixie After the War*, 155.
18. Qtd. in Goldfield, *Cotton Fields and Skyscrapers*, 81–82.
19. Byrne, "'Uncle Billy' Sherman Comes to Town," 92–94.
20. Ibid., 93–95.
21. Qtd. in Drago, *Black Politicians and Reconstruction*, 8.
22. Byrne, "'Uncle Billy' Sherman Comes to Town," 97; Drago, *Black Politicians and Reconstruction*, 8–9.
23. Myers, ed., *Children of Pride*, 1338; see also Hargis, "For the Love of Place," 830.
24. Qtd. in Byrne, "'Uncle Billy' Sherman Comes to Town," 98.
25. Shryock, *Letters of Arnold*, 117–18, 119n1, 125.
26. Ibid., 115n1; Lawrence, *Present for Mr. Lincoln*, 218–21; Lee and Agnew, *Historical Record*, 99.
27. Qtd. in Byrne, "'Uncle Billy' Sherman Comes to Town," 105; Lawrence, *Present for Mr. Lincoln*, 262.
28. Qtd. in McFeely, *Yankee Stepfather*, 44; Mahaffey, "Carl Schurz's Letters from the South," 243; Rabinowitz, "Continuity and Change," 93, 99; Trowbridge, *The South*, 509;

Jones, *Saving Savannah,* 215; Fraser, *Savannah in the Old South,* 284; Reidy, "Aaron A. Bradley," 282.

29. Qtd. in Golay, *Ruined Land,* 69; qtd. in Tuck, *We Ain't What We Ought to Be,* 28–29.

30. Drago, *Black Politicians and Reconstruction,* 15; Jones, "Spirit of Great Enterprise," 205–6; Jones, *Saving Savannah,* 229; Fraser, *Savannah in the Old South,* 334.

31. Cimbala, *Under the Guardianship of the Nation,* 168; Hoskins, *The Trouble They Seen,* 28–29; Dorsey, "Great Cry of Our People," 226.

32. Foner, *Forever Free,* 3–6, 88.

33. Qtd. in Jones, *Soldiers of Light and Love,* 73; see also Hoskins, *The Trouble They Seen,* 30; Jones, *Saving Savannah,* 213, 216; Trowbridge, *The South,* 510.

34. Perdue, "Negro in Savannah," 127–28; Owens, "Negro in Georgia During Reconstruction," 133; Drago, *Black Politicians and Reconstruction,* 27.

35. Qtd. in *The Savannah Republican,* March 25, 1865; see also Abbot, "Republican Party Press," 726–28, 734–35; Talmadge, "Savannah's Yankee Newspapers," 68; Perdue, "Negro in Savannah," 127–28; Hoskins, *The Trouble They Seen,* 30.

36. Reidy, "Aaron A. Bradley," 281–82; Blassingame, "Before the Ghetto," 479; Jones, *Soldiers of Light and Love,* 73–75.

37. Jones, *Soldiers of Light and Love,* 73–75, 92; Taylor, *Reminiscences of My Life in Camp,* 29–30, 33–34, 124–28.

38. Qtd. in Bowden, *Two Hundred Years of Education,* 264–65; Grant and Grant, eds., *Way It Was in the South,* 228; Blassingame, "Before the Ghetto," 472; Jones, *Saving Savannah,* 296.

39. Qtd. in Jones, *Saving Savannah,* 226.

40. Qtd. in Owens, "Negro in Georgia During Reconstruction," 161–62.

41. Qtd. in Fraser, *Charleston! Charleston!* 274.

42. Qtd. in Conway, *Reconstruction of Georgia,* 86.

43. Reid, *After the War,* 152.

44. Ibid.; Dorsey, "Great Cry of Our People," 234; Lawrence, *Present for Mr. Lincoln,* 233.

45. Qtd. in Fraser, *Charleston! Charleston!* 269.

46. Ibid., 275.

47. Doyle, *New Men, New Cities, New South,* 67–68.

48. John M. Glidden to William H. Gardiner, January 29, 1865, qtd. in Gatell, ed., "Yankee Views the Agony of Savannah," 29–31; Lawrence, *Present for Mr. Lincoln,* 239–40.

49. Talmadge, "Savannah's Yankee Newspapers," 71–72.

50. Lawrence, *Present for Mr. Lincoln,* 215.

51. Fraser, *Savannah in the Old South,* 192–93, 260–61; Overstreet, "History of the Savannah Theater [*sic*]," 9–10, 12, 42–43.

52. Qtd. in Jones, *Saving Savannah,* 228.

53. Qtd. in Fraser, *Charleston! Charleston!* 284.

54. Reid, *After the War,* 212, 213–14.

55. Qtd. in Conway, *Reconstruction of Georgia,* 30.

56. Qtd. in Fraser, *Charleston! Charleston!* 274.

57. Jones, *Saving Savannah,* 223–24, 229, 245; Talmadge, "Savannah's Yankee Newspapers," 72.

58. Fraser, *Charleston! Charleston!* 273; qtd. in Lawrence, *Present for Mr. Lincoln,* 243; qtd. in Jones, *Saving Savannah,* 230; Basinger, *Personal Reminiscences,* 270.

59. Shryock, *Letters of Arnold,* 119n1; Simms, *First Colored Baptist Church,* 139–40.

60. Jones, *Saving Savannah,* 231–32.

61. Lawrence, *Present for Mr. Lincoln,* 244.

62. George Anderson Mercer Diary, 1851–1889, vol. 4: 13, Southern Historical Collection (hereafter cited as Mercer Diary); Sheehy, Wallace, Goode-Walker, *Savannah,* 267–68.

63. Lawrence, *Present for Mr. Lincoln,* 244–45.

64. Mercer Diary, vol. 3: 230.

65. Qtd. in Lawrence, *Present for Mr. Lincoln,* 246.

66. Mahaffey, "Carl Schurz's Letters from the South," 245; Shryock, *Letters of Arnold,* 122; "Parade of the Colored Fire Companies," *Savannah Daily Herald,* July 5, 1865.

67. Mahaffey, "Carl Schurz's Letters from the South," 244–45.

68. Qtd. in Fraser, *Charleston! Charleston!* 285.

69. Shryock, *Letters of Arnold,* 123–24.

70. DeCredico, *Patriotism for Profit,* 147.

71. Shryock, *Letters of Arnold,* 124; Jones, *Saving Savannah,* 239–40.

72. Denmark, "'At the Midnight Hour': Economic Dilemmas and Harsh Realities," 356n10; "Minutes of Savannah City Council," August 23, 1865.

73. Hunt, "Organized Labor along Georgia's Waterfront," 178.

74. Bailey and Fraser, *Portraits of Conflict,* 319.

75. Coleman, ed., *History of Georgia,* 208; Bartley, *Creation of Modern Georgia,* 47; qtd. in Conway, *Reconstruction of Georgia,* 55.

76. Mahaffey, "Carl Schurz's Letters from the South," 243–45; Jones, "Spirit of Great Enterprise," 208–9.

77. Fraser, *Savannah in the Old South,* 297, 306–7, 334, 336; Jones, "Spirit of Great Enterprise," 208–9.

78. Fraser, *Savannah in the Old South,* 297, 306–7, 334, 336; Jones, "Spirit of Great Enterprise," 208–9; Mayor Anderson as qtd. in Gamble, *History of the City Government,* 267.

79. Dorsey, "Great Cry of Our People," 232–33; Cimbala, "Freedmen's Bureau," 597–632.

80. Dorsey, "Great Cry of Our People," 234–35.

81. Ibid.

82. Ibid.; Cimbala, *Under the Guardianship of the Nation,* 169.

83. Cimbala, "Freedmen's Bureau," 617–21, 625; Dorsey, "Great Cry of Our People," 224–25, 234–35, 246–47.

84. Reidy, "Aaron A. Bradley," 284–86; Jones, "Spirit of Great Enterprise," 206–7.

85. Overstreet, "History of the Savannah Theater [*sic*]," 44–50.

86. Qtd. in Goldfield, *Cotton Fields and Skyscrapers,* 104.

87. Blassingame, "Before the Ghetto," 464; Reidy, "Aaron A. Bradley," 302n4; Shryock, *Letters of Arnold,* 131; Conway, *Reconstruction of Georgia,* 30; Mercer Diary, vol. 4: 22.

88. "Minutes of Savannah City Council," July 6, 1865; Simms, "Comment on Savannah in 1866," 459–60; *Mayor's Annual Report 1867,* 15; Reidy, "Aaron A. Bradley," 302n4.

89. Bailey and Fraser, *Portraits of Conflict,* 76, 373; Rosa to My Dear Husband, May 16, 1865, in *Georgia Historical Quarterly,* March 1966, 114; Sheehy, Wallace, Goode-Walker, *Savannah,* 250.

90. Myers, ed., *Children of Pride,* 1568; Clarke, *Dwelling Place,* 486; Jones, "Spirit of Great Enterprise," 209–10; Jones, *Saving Savannah,* 243–46; Lees, *Portrait of Johnny,* 190–96, 268–69; Mercer Diary, vol. 3: 244, vol. 4: 16, 36.

91. Basinger, *Personal Reminiscences,* 289.

92. Hodgson and Mary qtd. in Johnson, *Mary Telfair,* 354.

93. Qtd. in Johnson, *Mary Telfair,* 354.
94. Margaret qtd. in Johnson, *Mary Telfair,* 356.
95. Susan qtd. in Kollock, ed., "Letters of the Kollock and Allied Families," 5: 317–18.
96. Ibid., 318; Fraser, *Savannah in the Old South,* 302; Simms, *First Colored Baptist Church* [A.C. G. Smits to Daniel Scanland, April 25, 1866], 458–59.
97. Farmer-Kaiser, "Are they not in some sorts vagrants?" 49.
98. Qtd. in Jones, *Saving Savannah,* 259.
99. Qtd. in Farmer-Kaiser, "Are they not in some sorts vagrants?" 46; Fraser, *Savannah in the Old South,* 164–65, 289–90.
100. Qtd. in Drago, *Black Politicians and Reconstruction,* 109.
101. *Mayor's Annual Report 1871,* 46–49; Gamble, *History of the City Government,* 279.
102. Qtd. in Jones, *Saving Savannah,* 261.
103. Reidy, "Aaron A. Bradley," 285; Jones, "Spirit of Great Enterprise," 209.
104. Owens, "Negro in Georgia During Reconstruction," 223; Drago, *Black Politicians and Reconstruction,* 109; Jones, *Saving Savannah,* 261–64.
105. Fraser, *Charleston! Charleston!* 279–80.
106. *Annual Reports of the Superintendent of Public Schools for the City of Savannah and Country of Chatham for the Years 1866–7 and 1867–8,* 8–31; Gamble, *History of the City Government,* 280–84; Shryock, *Letters of Arnold,* 139; Hoskins, *The Troubles They Seen,* 33; Drago, *Black Politicians and Reconstruction,* 98.
107. Rubin, *Third to None,* 158–59.
108. Ibid., 99–100, 212–13, 247; Conway, *Reconstruction of Georgia,* 132; Denmark, "'At the Midnight Hour': Economic Dilemmas and Harsh Realities," 353–62, 360n19; *Mayor's Annual Report 1871,* 78; Gamble, *History of the City Government,* 272–73.
109. *New York Times* qtd. in Denmark, "At the Midnight Hour: Optimism and Disillusionment," 67.
110. Jones, *Saving Savannah,* 269–72.
111. Ibid.; Hunt, "Organized Labor along Savannah's Waterfront," 182–84; Litwack, *Been in the Storm too Long,* 441.
112. Reidy, "Aaron A. Bradley," 287; *Savannah Daily Republican,* January 18, 21, 23, 1867; Myers, ed., *Children of Pride,* 1522.
113. Jones, *Saving Savannah,* 271–75.
114. Reidy, "Aaron A. Bradley," 290.
115. Coleman, ed., *History of Georgia,* 211–12; Jones, "Spirit of Great Enterprise," 210.
116. Qtd. in Drago, "Georgia's First Black Registrars," 787.
117. Reidy, "Aaron A. Bradley," 290–94; Drago, "Georgia's First Black Registrars," 786; Coleman, ed., *History of Georgia,* 211–12.
118. Coleman, ed., *History of Georgia,* 210–11; Conway, *Reconstruction of Georgia,* 174; Jones, *Saving Savannah,* 236–38, 305–7.
119. Jones, *Saving Savannah,* 308–10; Jones, "Spirit of Great Enterprise," 211–12; Owens, "Negro in Georgia During Reconstruction," 112–13.
120. "Fatal Shooting Affair," *Savannah Morning News* (hereafter *SMN*), July 22, 1868; "Arrest of the Ringleaders," *SMN,* August 11, 1868; [Letter to the Editor] "To the Law Abiding People of Savannah," *SMN,* July 23, 1868.
121. Gamble, *History of the City Government,* Bull Street Library copy newspaper clipping in frontispiece.
122. Reidy, "Aaron A. Bradley," 296; Jones, "Spirit of Great Enterprise," 211–12.
123. Reidy, "Aaron A. Bradley," 296; Jones, "Spirit of Great Enterprise," 211–12; Drago, *Black Politicians and Reconstruction,* 76–77.

124. Drago, *Black Politicians and Reconstruction,* 76–77; Gamble, *History of the City Government,* 280.

125. Jones, *Saving Savannah,* 320–22, 357–59.

126. Ibid.; Bell, "The Ogeechee Troubles," 376–97; Drago, *Black Politicians and Reconstruction,* 123–24; Reidy, "Aaron A. Bradley," 296; Perdue, "Negro in Savannah," 37.

127. Bailey and Fraser, *Portraits of Conflict,* 319.

128. Ibid.; Jones, *Saving Savannah,* 372–76, 389, 394–95, 404.

129. Jones, *Saving Savannah,* 337–40.

130. Ibid., 286–87, 337–41; Fraser, *Charleston! Charleston!* 285–86; Jones, "Spirit of Great Enterprise," 214–15; Rabinowitz, "Continuity and Change," 101.

131. Blassingame, "Before the Ghetto," 468, 474, 476; Jones, *Saving Savannah,* 250–51.

132. Blassingame, "Before the Ghetto," 466–67, 476; Grant and Grant, eds., *Way It Was in the South,* 248.

133. *An Ordinance to Assess and Levy Taxes and Raise Revenue. . . for 1870,* 3–15; Denmark, "'At the Midnight Hour': Economic Dilemmas and Harsh Realities," 362–66.

134. Rabinowitz, "Continuity and Change," 92; Jones, *Saving Savannah,* 342–43, 359–60.

135. Overstreet, "History of the Savannah Theater [*sic*]," 88–90; Owens, "Negro in Georgia During Reconstruction," 220; Fraser, *Charleston! Charleston!* 289.

136. Jones, *Saving Savannah,* 349–51, 375; *Mayor's Annual Report 1871,* 42.

137. *Mayor's Annual Report 1871,* 46–49; Gamble, *History of the City Government,* 279.

138. "Minutes of Savannah City Council," January 24, February 2, March 2, May 11, May 26, June 18, and July 7, 1870; *Mayor's Annual Report 1871,* 50–51.

139. Fraser, *Savannah in the Old South,* 293–94; Denmark, "'At the Midnight Hour': Economic Dilemmas and Harsh Realities," 366–68.

140. Denmark, "'At the Midnight Hour': Economic Dilemmas and Harsh Realities," 368–70.

141. Margaret Mackay Elliott to My Dear Lucy, April 27, [1870], in Smith, ed., *Savannah Family,* 265–66; Jones, *Saving Savannah,* 368; Waring, "Striving 'Seventies in Savannah," 154–55.

142. Gamble, *Savannah Duels,* 260–69.

143. *Mayor's Annual Report 1871,* 4–5.

144. Denmark, "'At the Midnight Hour': Economic Dilemmas and Harsh Realities," 368–72nn43–44; Denmark, "At the Midnight Hour: Optimism and Disillusionment," 205n47; Gamble, *History of the City Government,* 288–89.

145. Lee and Agnew, *Historical Record,* 147–49, 197–99; Larsen, *Rise of the Urban South,* 128–29.

146. Fraser, *Charleston! Charleston!* 285; Owens, "Negro in Georgia During Reconstruction," 218–19; "Mayor's Court," *SMN,* May 7, 1870; "Mayor's Court," May 10, 1870. The *Savannah Daily News* changed its name to the *Savannah Daily News and Herald* on April 2, 1866, and to the *Savannah Morning News* on September 20, 1868.

147. "Street Car Difficulty," *SMN,* July 29, 1872; "Proclamations of the Mayor," *SMN,* July 30, 1872; "Negroes Jubilant," *SMN,* July 31, 1872; "Causalities of the Riot," *SMN,* July 31, 1872; "The Riot," *SMN,* July 31, 1872; "The Alleged Violations of the Civil Rights Bill," *SMN,* August 2, 1872; Alleged Violations of the Civil Rights Bill," *SMN,* August 3, 1872; "Street Car Question," *SMN,* August 5, 1872; Drago, *Black Politicians and Reconstruction,* 100.

148. Smith, "Black Militia in Savannah," 16–21; Basinger, *Personal Reminiscences,* 289–90; Taylor, "Reconstructing Men in Savannah," 1–24.

149. "The Democratic Meeting Tonight," *SMN,* September 17, 1872; Wingo, "Race Relations in Georgia," 20.

150. Wingo, "Race Relations in Georgia," 21; Jones, *Saving Savannah*, 383–84, 397; Reidy, "Aaron A. Bradley," 300–301; Matthews, "Negro Republicans," 145, 157–58.

151. Reidy, "Aaron A. Bradley," 301.

152. Doyle, *New Men, New Cities, New South*, 36–39; Goldfield, *Cotton Fields and Skyscrapers*, 85.

153. Doyle, *New Men, New Cities, New South*, 39–47.

154. Goldfield, *Cotton Fields and Skyscrapers*, 86–87.

155. Qtd. in Doyle, *New Men, New Cities, New South*, 62, 67–70.

156. Ibid., 61–62, 68–70.

157. Fraser, *Charleston! Charleston!* 268, 272.

158. Qtd. in Fraser, *Charleston! Charleston!* 275.

159. Fraser, *Charleston! Charleston!* 275, 289; Parramore et al., *Norfolk*, 228–29.

160. Doyle, *New Men, New Cities, New South*, 75–76; Fraser, *Charleston! Charleston!* 268.

161. Doyle, *New Men, New Cities, New South*, 58, 59, 60–62, 71–75; William Gordon to [Nellie] "My Darling Wife," December 6, 1886, Gordon Family Papers, 1810–1968, Southern Historical Collection.

162. Qtd. in Doyle, *New Men, New Cities, New South*, 58.

163. Denmark, "'At the Midnight Hour': Economic Dilemmas and Harsh Realities," 372–73; Gamble, *History of the City Government*, 272.

Chapter 2: Depression, Neo-Confederates, Fevers, Society and Labor: 1873–1891

1. Denmark, "'At the Midnight Hour': Economic Dilemmas and Harsh Realities," 373–74; DeCredico, *Patriotism for Profit*, 151; Zinn, *People's History of the United States*, 242–51. With regard to Savannah, I favor the case for the continuity of the antebellum South into the new rather than the discontinuity argument of the renowned C. Vann Woodward in his enduring classic, *Origins of the New South*. See also Moore, "Redeemers Reconsidered," 357–78; Wyatt-Brown, "C. Van Woodward and the Confessions of a 'Continuitarian,'" 294–305.

2. Denmark, "'At the Midnight Hour': Economic Dilemmas and Harsh Realities," 374; DeCredico, *Patriotism for Profit*, 151; Rabinowitz, *First New South*, 58; Rabinowitz, "Continuity and Change," 102.

3. "The Freedman's Bank Take or Pay No Deposits," *SMN*, July 2, 1874; "The Bubble Burst," *SMN*, July 3, 1874; "The Freedman's Bank—A Suggestion to the Colored People," *SMN*, July 6, 1874; "The Banking Question and the Colored People," *SMN*, July 10, 1874; "A Hard Case—A Depositor of the Freedman's Bank Crazed By His Loss," *SMN*, July 25, 1874.

4. "The Banking Question and the Colored People," July 10, 1874; "A Hard Case—A Depositor of the Freedman's Bank Crazed by His Loss," *SMN*, July 25, 1874; "The Freedman's Bank," *SMN*, August 11, 1874.

5. "The Freedmen's [*sic*] Bank," *SMN*, September 26, 1874; "The Burst Bubble and the Swindled Freedmen," *SMN*, September 29, 1874; Letter to the Editor, *SMN*, 16, 1874; Blassingame, "Before the Ghetto," 468.

6. Blassingame, "Before the Ghetto," 464, 468, 476, 480, 483–84; A. R. Lawton to Charles P. Greenough, September 11, 1876, Sarah Alexander Cunningham Collection, Georgia Historical Society.

7. *Mayor's Annual Report 1873*, 29; *Mayor's Annual Report 1874*, 34; Blassingame, "Before the Ghetto," 480–81; Perdue, "Negro in Savannah," 50–51.

8. "Ostracism," *SMN*, July 8, 1874.

9. Johnson, *Mary Telfair*, 159, 212, 392–402; Fraser, *Savannah in the Old South*, 77, 91–92, 140.

10. Perdue, "Negro in Savannah," 110–22, 163; Jones, *Saving Savannah,* 392; Shadgett, *Republican Party in Georgia,* 32, 78, 95, 129, 200; Bacote, "Negro in Georgia Politics," 72–74.

11. Waring, "Savannah of the 1870's," 60; Perdue, "Negro in Savannah," 99–105, 109; "Chatham County Does Her Duty," *SMN,* November 4, 1874; "How Now?" *SMN,* November 5, 1874; Grant and Grant, eds., *Way It Was in the South,* 220; Taylor, "Reconstructing Men in Savannah," 1–24; Duncan, *Freedom's Shore,* 89–91, 100–109.

12. Turner, "Agitation and Accommodation," 1, 5, 6, 8–13, 14–18. The *Tribune,* also known as the *Savannah Colored Tribune* and *Savannah Tribune,* ceased publication within three years of its founding. Likely financial problems and political differences with the white-owned printing office forced Deveaux to suspend publication. In less than a decade, the paper resumed publication and its efforts in behalf of equal rights for blacks.

13. Bryant, "'The Fighting Has Not Been in Vain," 185–212.

14. Ibid.; "A Question to Be Tested," *SMN,* August 9, 1875; "The First Case Under the Civil Rights Bill," *SMN,* August 11, 1875; "So-Called Civil Rights Case—Declaration Reversed," *SMN,* August 14, 1875.

15. Blassingame, "Before the Ghetto," 469, 480; Powers, *Black Charlestonians,* 254; Gordon Affidavit, 1875, Gordon Papers, Southern Historical Collection; Hunt, "Organized Labor along Savannah's Waterfront, 184–85.

16. Wingo, "Race Relations in Georgia," 32–33, 52, 59, 79, 154–55, 158–59.

17. Denmark, "'At the Midnight Hour': Economic Dilemmas and Harsh Realities," 375–78; Waring, "Savannah of the 1870's," 61.

18. Foster, *Ghosts of the Confederacy,* 37–38; Bartley, *Creation of Modern Georgia,* 105, 108; Rabinowitz, *First New South,* 174–75.

19. Margaret Mackay Elliott to My Dear Lucy, April 27 [1870] in Smith, ed., *Savannah Family,* 265–66; Piechocinski, *Men of Iron,* 189–92.

20. G. W. J. De Renne to the President of the Ladies Memorial Association of Savannah, April 25, 1878 and May 21, 1879, in the "Ladies Memorial Association of Savannah," Southern Historical Collection; Mrs. Octavus Cohen to G. W. J. De Renne, April 26, 1878 in the "Ladies Memorial Association of Savannah," Southern Historical Collection.

21. Piechocinski, *Men of Iron,* 193–94; Waring, "Striving 'Seventies in Savannah," 157.

22. Capers, *Biography of a River Town,* 189, 192–204; Rabinowitz, *First New South,* 55, 63; Goldfield, *Cotton Fields and Skyscrapers,* 95–96; Doyle, *New Men, New Cities, New South,* 70, 77.

23. Larsen, *Rise of the Urban South,* 124.

24. Le Hardy, *Yellow Fever,* 2–6; Waring, *Communication to the City Council on the Privy System,* 3–27.

25. "A Terrible Fire," *SMN,* August 26, 1876.

26. Lawton to Greenough, September 11, 1876, Sarah Alexander Cunningham Collection, Georgia Historical Society; Nellie Gordon, "Yellow Fever," [1876], Gordon Family Papers, Duke University.

27. Nellie Gordon, "Yellow Fever," [1876], Gordon Family Papers, Duke University; Le Hardy, *Yellow Fever,* 6; Harriet Cumming to Emma Barnett, September 15, 1876, qtd. in Waring, "Striving 'Seventies in Savannah," 169–70.

28. Le Hardy, *Yellow Fever,* 6; Waring, "Striving 'Seventies in Savannah," 169.

29. Sholes, *Chronological History of Savannah,* 81–82; Le Hardy, *Yellow Fever,* 6; Farley, "Mighty Monarch of the South," 56–57, 65; Gamble, *History of the City Government,* 301, 302.

30. James J. Waring to "My Dearest Wife," October 30, November 6, 8, 12, 1876, Waring Papers, Georgia Historical Society; Gamble, *Savannah's Duels,* 287; James J. Waring to "My Darling Daughter," October 30, 1876, Waring Papers, Georgia Historical Society.

31. Biegert, "Woman Scout," 45.

32. Waring, *Epidemic at Savannah*; *Mayor's Annual Report 1879,* 160; Otto, *Yellow Fever Record*; Waring, "Striving 'Seventies in Savannah," 170–71; Gamble, *History of the City Government,* 300.

33. Waring, *Epidemic at Savannah,* 21–37; *Mayor's Annual Report 1879,* 161.

34. Lawton to Greenough, September 11, 1876, Sarah Alexander Cunningham Collection, Georgia Historical Society; Nellie Gordon, "Yellow Fever" [1876], Gordon Family Papers, Duke University; Waring to "My Dearest Wife," October 30, November 6, 1876, Waring Papers, Georgia Historical Society; Gamble, *History of the City Government,* 303.

35. Gamble, *History of the City Government,* 293.

36. Gamble, *History of the City Government,* 293–304; Waring, "Savannah of the 1870's," 61; Denmark, "'At the Midnight Hour': Economic Dilemmas and Harsh Realities," 384–90.

37. Gamble, *History of the City Government,* 298–300; Denmark, "'At the Midnight Hour': Economic Dilemmas and Harsh Realities," 383–89; *Mayor's Annual Report 1875,* 11, 30; *Mayor's Annual Report 1877,* 12–15, 74; *Mayor's Annual Report 1881,* 9.

38. *Mayor's Annual Report 1875,* 33; *Mayor's Annual Report 1877,* 45–46; *Mayor's Annual Report 1880,* 41; *Mayor's Annual Report 1885,* 57.

39. *Mayor's Annual Report 1875,* 10–11; *Mayor's Annual Report 1877,* 7–11; *Mayor's Annual Report 1880,* 9 14; *Mayor's Annual Report 1881,* 9–10.

40. *Mayor's Annual Report 1877,* 74; *Mayor's Annual Report 1880,* 14–15, 43; *Mayor's Annual Report 1881,* 15, 68–70.

41. "The Labor Riots—Effective Action Necessary," *SMN,* September 20, 1881; "An Exciting Day," *SMN,* September 21, 1881; "The Strike," *SMN,* September 22, 1881; "How Impetuous Debaters Settled Their Argument," *SMN,* September 22, 1881; "A Ringleader of the Strikers Punished," *SMN,* September 22, 1881; Hunt, "Organized Labor along Savannah's Waterfront," 184–85. In 1885, the WUA petitioned the Chatham County Superior Court for incorporation.

42. *Mayor's Annual Report 1880,* 43; *Mayor's Annual Report 1881,* 9–10, 68–70; "The Labor Troubles," *SMN,* September 26, 1881; Werthington, "Savannah Negro Laborers' Strike," 5–7; Stewart, "Survival of the Fittest," 39–65; Smith, "Black Militia in Savannah," 27–34.

43. *Mayor's Annual Report 1877,* 14–15; *Mayor's Annual Report 1880,* 20; *Mayor's Annual Report 1891,* 163–71.

44. *Mayor's Annual Report 1880,* 20; Rabinowitz, "Continuity and Change," 93; Powers, *Black Charlestonians,* 251.

45. *Mayor's Annual Report 1881,* 72–73; Rabinowitz, "Continuity and Change," 103–4, 111; Goldfield, "Business of Health Planning," 569–70.

46. Carnes, "Georgia Deepwater Ports," 33, 37, 39, 42; Stewart, "Survival of the Fittest," 64–65.

47. Biegert, "Woman Scout," 48, 52, 54.

48. A. R. Lawton to Brig. General Benjamin, CSA, U.S. Minister to Austria, May 27, 1879, Alexander Robert Lawton Papers, Southern Historical Collection.

49. Smith, ed., *Savannah Family,* 270–71.

50. Ibid., 269–70.

51. Fraser, *Lowcountry Hurricanes,* 147–51.

52. Ibid., 150–51, 153.

53. Stewart, "Survival of the Fittest," 61; Smith, ed., *Savannah Family,* 271; "Invitations to Miss Eugenia M. Johnston," in Colonial Dames of America, Edith D. Johnston Collection, Georgia Historical Society.

54. Biegert, "Woman Scout," 57–67; [William W. Gordon] to "My Darling Wife," September 17, 18, 1882, Gordon Papers, University of North Carolina, Chapel Hill.

55. William W. Gordon to "My Darling Wife," December 6, 1886, Gordon Papers, Georgia Historical Society; "Your Loving Nell" to Laura, January 13, 1887, Gordon Papers, University of North Carolina, Chapel Hill; "Politics and the Railroads," *SMN,* December 22, 1886.

56. Bryan, *Savannah: A Brief Sketch*; Jonathan E. Land, *Savannah: Her Trade, Commerce and Industries.*

57. Waring, ed., "Charles Seton Henry Hardee's Recollections," 47–48; *Mayor's Annual Report 1884,* 7, 9, 11, 81–82, 87–93, 99–103; Sholes, *Chronological History of Savannah,* 84, 86, 87, 88, 90; Keber, *Ebb and Flow,* 15–16; Keber, *Low Land and the High Road,* 28.

58. *Mayor's Annual Report 1886,* 9, 13, 88–90.

59. Rabinowitz, "Continuity and Change," 93.

60. Turner, "Agitation and Accommodation," 17–21; Bacote, "Some Aspects of Negro Life," 210; Jones, *Saving Savannah,* 176, 308, 380, 392; Bacote, "Negro in Georgia Politics," 53–57.

61. Perdue, "Negro in Savannah," 158–63; Dittmer, *Black Georgia,* 61.

62. Bacote, "Some Aspects of Negro Life," 196–97; Perdue, "Negro in Savannah," 203, 216, 218, 221–23, 230–31.

63. Perdue, "Negro in Savannah," 202–3, 206, 211.

64. Ibid., 154–56.

65. Ibid., 191, 199–201; Wingo, "Race Relations in Georgia," 233.

66. Perdue, "Negro in Savannah," 156, 192, 208–9; "People Who Sell Truck," *SMN,* May 21, 1888.

67. Grant and Grant, eds., *Way It Was in the South,* 218–21.

68. Manis, *Macon Black and White,* 19, 56; Dittmer, *Black Georgia,* 131–32; Edgar, *South Carolina,* 579–80.

69. "Vicksburg Southrons," *SMN,* May 4, 1886; "A Day in Camp," *SMN,* May 5, 1886; "The Tented Field," *SMN,* May 6, 1886; "The Davis' Reception: Scenes and Incidents at the City Exchange," *SMN,* May 6, 1886; "Tramp of Troops: Gay Soldiers Drilling," *SMN,* May 7, 1886; Jones, *Saving Savannah,* 398; Foster, *Ghosts of the Confederacy,* 94–97.

70. Gadsden, "Negro's Political and Civic Life," 8; Perdue, "Negro in Savannah," 182–83, 232; Turner, "Agitation and Accommodation," 50.

71. Werthington, "Savannah Negro Laborers' Strike of 1891," 4–21.

72. Ibid., 9–11.

73. Qtd. in Werthington, "Savannah Negro Laborers' Strike of 1891," 12.

74. Werthington, "Savannah Negro Laborers' Strike of 1891," 13–15.

75. Qtd. in Werthington, "Savannah Negro Laborers' Strike of 1891," 15.

76. Werthington, "Savannah Negro Laborers' Strike of 1891," 16.

Chapter 3: Murder, a Strike, a Swindle, and a Boycott: 1892–1915

1. Woodward, *Origins of the New South,* 264; Carnes, "Georgia Deepwater Ports," 41, 42.

2. "Aug. Meyer Murdered," *SMN,* January 25, 1892; "Murderers Caught," *SMN,* January 26, 1892; "The Murderers Plot," *SMN,* January 27, 1892; "True Bills Against Five,"

SMN, January 28, 1892; "The Meyer Murder," *SMN*, January 29, 1892; "The Trial of Meyer Murderers," *SMN*, January 30, 1892.

3. "The Meyer Murder," *SMN*, January 29, 1892; "The Trial of Meyer Murderers," *SMN*, January 30, 1892; "Gay Guilty of Murder ," *SMN*, March 30, 1892; "On Trial For His Life," *SMN*, March 29, 1892; "Williams At The Bar," *SMN*, March 31, 1892; "The Rope For Williams," *SMN*, April 1, 1892; "Seven Weeks To Live," *SMN*, August 4, 1892; "Another For The Rope," *SMN*, August 3, 1892; "Another of August Meyer's Murderers Gets His Reward," *SMN*, September 14, 1894.

4. Coulter, ed., "Visit to Savannah, 1892," 100–104.

5. Ayers, *Promise of the New South*, 153, 155–56.

6. *Mayor's Annual Report 1892*, 71, 73; *Mayor's Annual Report 1893*, 58–59; *Mayor's Annual Report 1894*, 55–56; *Mayor's Annual Report 1895*, 57, 59; Matthews, "Studies in Race Relations," 141.

7. Hunt, "Organized Labor along Savannah's Waterfront," 193–95; "Mayor McDonough to Preserve the Peace at All Hazards," *SMN*, September 8, 1894; "Police Still In Reserve," *SMN*, September 10, 1894; "Rocks for Longshoremen," *SMN*, September 7, 1894.

8. J. Randolph Anderson to "My Dear Miss Page," September 11, 1894, King and Wilder Family Papers, Georgia Historical Society; "Union Men Sentenced," *SMN*, September 13, 1894; "Clash of Union and Non-Union Forces," *SMN*, September 9, 1894; Hunt, "Organized Labor along Savannah's Waterfront," 195–96; Zinn, *People's History of the United States*, 276–81.

9. Nellie Gordon to "My Dear Uncle," September 10, 1894, Gordon Family Papers, Southern Historical Collection.

10. Hunt, "Organized Labor along Savannah's Waterfront," 195–97, 197 n54.

11. "Union Men Sentenced," *SMN*, September 13, 1894.

12. Ibid.; "The City Well Guarded," *SMN*, September 14, 1894; "No Compromise Reached," *SMN*, September 12, 1894.

13. Hunt, "Organized Labor along Savannah's Waterfront," 198.

14. "Eight Ships On Fire," *SMN*, November 6, 1894; *Mayor's Annual Report, 1895*, 94.

15. "Eight Ships On Fire," *SMN*, November 6, 1894.

16. Ibid.; "Phosphorus In The Ships," *SMN*, November 7, 1894; *Mayor's Annual Report, 1895*, 97, 98.

17. "Eight Ships On Fire," *SMN*, November 6, 1894; "Phosphorus In The Ships," *SMN*, November 7, 1894; Federal Reserve Bank of Minneapolis, Consumer Price Index (estimate) 1800; *Mayor's Annual Report 1895*, 97, 98.

18. "Determined to Get Them," *SMN*, November 8, 1894; "The City Will Pay $2,500 To Convict The First Of The Ship Incendiaries," *SMN*, November 9, 1894; *Mayor's Annual Report 1895*, 98; Hunt, "Organized Labor along Savannah's Waterfront," 198.

19. Hunt, "Organized Labor along Savannah's Waterfront," 198–99.

20. Turner, "Agitation and Accommodation," 22–23.

21. Elmore, *Richard R. Wright, Sr.*, 17–18, 21–22; Patton, "Major Richard Robert Wright, Sr.," 111–13, 117.

22. Patton, "Major Richard Robert Wright, Sr.," 164, 167, 176–77, 232–34, 241–42; Matthews, "Studies in Race Relations," 137–38.

23. Patton, "Major Richard Wright, Sr.," 239, 241–42.

24. Ibid., 243, 247, 261.

25. William W. Gordon to P. W. Meldrim, April 13, 1888, Meldrim Family Papers, Georgia Historical Society; "Judge Meldrim Passes Away," *Savannah Evening Press*, December

13, 1933; "Judge Dickerson Praises Dead Jurist," *Savannah Evening Press,* December 13, 1933; "Meldrim's Death Grieves Talmadge," *Savannah Evening Press,* December 13, 1933; John T. Boifeuillet, "Judge Meldrim as Lecturer," *Atlanta Journal and Constitution,* February 28, 1928.

26. J. S. Flipper to Judge P. W. Meldrim, August 3, 1920, Meldrim Family Papers, Georgia Historical Society.

27. Elmore, *Richard R. Wright, Sr.,* 24, 32; Patton, "Major Richard Robert Wright, Sr.," 291–93, 298–99; Governor W. J. Northern to P. W. Meldrim, January 20, 1891, Meldrim Family Papers, Georgia Historical Society.

28. Patton, "Major Richard Robert Wright, Sr.," 299, 300–301, 305, 316, 339, 348; Elmore, *Richard R. Wright, Sr.*, 31, 33–34.

29. Elmore, *Richard R. Wright, Sr.*, 29, 31; Patton, "Major Richard Robert Wright, Sr.," 349, 350–60; Elmore, *Savannah, Georgia,* 82.

30. Elmore, "Black Medical Pioneers," 189–96; Mercy Housing, www.mercyhousing.org/featured-profile-heritage-place-apartments (accessed December 17, 2014).

31. Parker, "Doctors McKane," 6–11.

32. J. R. Anderson to My Dear Miss Page, June 3 and 23, July 1 and 8, 1894, Wilder and Anderson Family Papers, Southern Historical Collection; "[J. Randolph Anderson Obituary]," *SMN,* July, 18, 1950.

33. The Talk of the Ticket," *SMN,* July 1, 1894; "The Primary," *SMN,* July 11, 1894; William W. Gordon to "My Darling Wife," September 26, 1896, Gordon Family Papers, Georgia Historical Society.

34. Goldberg, "Administration of Herman Myers," 2–3.

35. "Friends of Myers and Schwartz Planning to Capture the Citizens [*sic*] Club Meeting," *SMN,* November 11, 1894; "The Schwartz and Myers Factions Alert for To-night's Meeting," *SMN,* November 12, 1894; "After Two and a Half Hours, Warring Citizens [*sic*] Club Reached a Conclusion," *SMN,* November 13, 1894; "[Myers and Schwartz Primary] for Mayor To-day," *SMN,* November 14, 1894; "The Schwartz Men Charge That the Voting Lists were Doctored," *SMN,* November 15, 1894; Goldberg, "Administration of Herman Myers," 1–5.

36. Goldberg, "Administration of Herman Myers," 1–5.

37. Ibid., 21–22.

38. Ibid., 17–20, 23–28.

39. Ibid., 29–42.

40. Ibid., 43–44, 61–64; *Mayor's Annual Report 1895,* 61.

41. *Mayor's Annual Report 1895,* 213–14, 267.

42. Ibid., 46–51, 55–56, 61.

43. *Mayor's Annual Report 1896,* 5–10, 294–302.

44. Elmore, "Hydrology and Residential Segregation," 43–45; Miller, *Memphis during the Progressive Era,* 66–68; Fraser, *Charleston! Charleston!* 330–31.

45. Goldberg, "Administration of Herman Myers," 58–59; Dittmer, *Black Georgia,* xi.

46. Fraser, *Lowcountry Hurricanes,* 189–90; Federal Reserve Bank of Minneapolis, Consumer Price Index (estimate) 1800.

47. Goldberg, "Administration of Herman Myers," 75–77.

48. William W. Gordon Jr. to "My Darling Wife," October 6, 7, 9, 1896, Gordon Family Papers, Georgia Historical Society.

49. Matthews, "Black Newspapermen," 363–64; Goldberg, "Administration of Herman Myers," 96–102.

50. Brundage, "Whispering Consolation to Generations Unborn," 346–47; Smith, "Black Militia in Savannah," 43–44, 53, 55.

51. Mixon, "Black Militia in Postbellum Georgia," 193–94.

52. Smith, "Black Militia in Savannah," 63–68, 70–74, 80–81.

53. Goldberg, "Administration of Herman Myers," 64–65, 73–77, 84–85, 87–96.

54. Perkins, "Oberlin M. Carter," 153–56, 159, 161; *Mayor's Annual Report 1892,* 22.

55. Perkins, "Oberlin M. Carter," 159–66.

56. Ibid., 166–69, 176–77.

57. Juliette Gordon Low qtd. in Perkins, "Oberlin M. Carter," 177.

58. Perkins, "Oberlin M. Carter," 171, 177–78.

59. William W. Gordon Jr. to Philip Younge, October 5, 1904, Gordon Family Papers, Georgia Historical Society; Waring, "The Gay Nineties in Savannah," 364–71, 373, 376; "Ladies in the Yachts," *SMN,* July 9, 1892; Social Register Association, *Social Register . . . 1908,* 150–73; Pressly, "Educating the Daughters of Savannah's Elite," 247–54; Matthews, "Studies in Race Relations," 226.

60. Murphy, "Right to Ride," 204–6; Matthews, "Studies in Race Relations," 225; Campbell, "Profit, Prejudice, and Protest," 202–3, 219; Goldberg, "Administration of Herman Myers," 106–8.

61. Turner, "Agitation and Accommodation," 39, 47–48.

62. Finlay, "The Postbellum Transition from Agriculture to Industry," 188–91.

63. *Mayor's Annual Report 1899,* 1–10; *Mayor's Annual Report 1906,* 163; Goldberg, "Administration of Herman Myers," 111–13, 117–19, 121–23, 126–27, 130–32.

64. "Dedication ceremony held at East Henry site," *SMN,* November 14, 2014; Goldberg, "Administration of Herman Myers," 134–37, 141–45, 167; *The Birth of City Hall, 1903–1906,* 1–5.

65. Goldberg, "Administration of Herman Myers," 147–54, 159, 161–65.

66. Perdue, "Negro in Savannah," 25–26; Bacote, "Negro Proscriptions," 482; Goldberg, "Administration of Herman Myers," 166–76; qtd. in Bacote, "Negro Proscriptions," 47n20; qtd. in Sineath, "Passing Through a Crucible," 13.

67. Sineath, "Passing Through a Crucible," 24–26; Hoskins, *The Trouble They Seen,* 59.

68. *Mayor's Annual Report 1904,* 67, 80; Gadsden, "Education of the Negro," 7.

69. *Mayor's Annual Report 1906,* 46, 162–64, 200–202, 239; Adams, "Guardians of Public Health," 251.

70. Adams, "Guardians of Public Health," 251.

71. Bacote, "Negro Proscriptions," 477–78; Mosley and Brogdon, "Lynching in Statesboro," 105–16; Grey, *Hand Me My Travelin' Shoes,* 109; Dittmer, *Black Georgia,* 133–34; Bartley, *Creation of Modern Georgia,* 152–53; Matthews, "Studies in Race Relations," 97, 107.

72. Bacote, "Negro Proscriptions," 477, 482; Murphy, "Right to Ride," 195–96; Campbell, "Profit, Prejudice, and Protest," 197–98, 200–206, 208–10; Goldberg, "Administration of Herman Myers," 175, 189; Meier and Rudwick, "Boycott Movement Against Jim Crow," 756–60, 763; "One Killed and Four Wounded," *SMN,* February 10, 1906; Goldberg, "Administration of Herman Myers," 1.

73. Murphy, "Right to Ride," 213–16, 223–25, 227–29, 231–33; Campbell, "Profit, Prejudice, and Protest," 209–19, 218n48.

74. Campbell, "Profit, Prejudice, and Protest," 221–30.

75. Murphy, "Right to Ride," 247–48, 256.

76. Campbell, "Profit, Prejudice, and Protest," 221–25, 228–30.

77. Ibid., 383–84.

78. Hanchett, "John Nolen," 810–27.

79. Letter from Jas. W. Honing to G. Arthur Gordon, May 4, 1906, Gordon Family Papers, Georgia Historical Society; [Speech of W. W. Gordon] in Gordon Family

Papers, Georgia Historical Society; D[aisy] Gordon to Mabel Gordon Leigh, May 2, 1915; G. A. Gordon to "Dear Sir," March 1906, Gordon Family Papers, Georgia Historical Society.

80. G. A. Gordon to "Dear Sir," February 2006, Gordon Family Papers, Georgia Historical Society; Goldberg, "Administration of Herman Myers," 194–209; "The Next City Administration," *SMN*, January 9, 1917; "Tiedeman Forces Out in Strength," *SMN*, January 8, 1907; "Garrard Men Met In Full Force," January 8, 1907; "7,296 Voters Registered," *SMN*, January 8, 1907.

81. *Mayor's Annual Report, 1907*, 15–29, 387, 391.

82. Ball, "Prohibition in Georgia," 701; "Sidelight on Georgia," leaflet.

83. *Mayor's Annual Report 1907*, 329–43; Otto, "Public School System," vols. 1 and 2, Bull Street Library; *Mayor's Annual Report 1902*, 237–41, 244.

84. *Mayor's Annual Report 1907*, 31, 47–59, 223–24.

85. *Mayor's Annual Report 1908*, 20, 346, 350; Brownell, "Urban South Comes of Age," 128.

86. *Mayor's Annual Report 1908*, 18; *Mayor's Annual Report 1910*, 529; Miller, *Memphis during the Progressive Era*, 183–84; "Savannah Auto Races," *New York Times*, January 26, 1908; "17 Racing Cars on Savannah Circuit," *New York Times*, November 14, 1908; "Three Cities Want Grand Prize Race," *New York Times*, October 8, 1910; "Scene on Savannah's Grand Prize Course—Prominent Drivers in Big Race," *New York Times*, November 6, 1910; "Racing Aids Good Roads Propaganda," *New York Times*, October 29, 1911; "Visitors Leaving Savannah," *New York Times*, December 11, 1911; "Savannah Abandons Classic Auto Races," *New York Times*, March 9, 1912.

87. "Meeting of the Board of Sanitary Commissioners," March 16, May 25, 1915; February 1, July 11, August 8, 1916; September 4, 18, 1917, Victor H. Bassett Papers, Georgia Historical Society.

88. *Mayor's Annual Report 1908*, 20, 36, 57, 60, 73–78, 190, 192–93; *Mayor's Annual Report 1909*, 27, 45, 51; *Mayor's Annual Report 1910*, 20; Sineath, "Passing Through a Crucible," 29; Matthews, "Studies in Race Relations," 228.

89. *Mayor's Annual Report* 1909, 14, 16–17, 19, 273, 297–98; *Mayor's Annual Report 1912*, 34.

90. Keber, *Ebb and Flow*, 16; Dittmer, *Black Georgia*, 10–11.

91. *Mayor's Annual Report 1910*, 22.

92. "Negro Strikes Down Women," *New York Times*, December 11, 1909; Linda Sickler, "Ghosts haunt city's 'most diabolical crime'" *SMN*, November 11, 2012.

93. *Mayor's Annual Report 1910*, 37–39, 66–67, 217, 232–33, 522; *Mayor's Annual Report 1912*, 70, 73, 236.

94. *Mayor's Annual Report 1910*, 321–31; Johnson, "History of the Savannah Public Library," 7.

95. *Mayor's Annual Report 1910*, 362, 382–83.

96. "Davant Asks For Pure Election," *SMN*, January 10, 1911; "Tideman is Re-elected Mayor," *SMN*, January 11, 1911; "The Municipal Election," *SMN*, January 11, 1911.

97. *Mayor's Annual Report 1911*, 16–24, 69, 248, 396.

98. *Municipal Report, 6th Annual Report of the Honorable George W. Tiedeman, Mayor Together with the Reports of City Officers of the City of Savannah, Georgia, for the year ending December 31, 1912*, 505–16.

99. "The Next Mayor," *SMN*, January 15, 1913; *Mayor's Annual Report 1915*.

100. Editorial, *Tribune*, January 27, 1912; Turner, "Agitation and Accommodation," 128–30; Gessel, "Nowhere But Heaven," 12; *Mayor's Annual Report 1912*, 370.

101. *Mayor's Annual Report 1916,* 412, 354, 470, 503–7; Sineath, "Passing Through a Crucible," 78, 80; "Dedication ceremony held at East Henry site," *SMN,* November 14, 2014.

102. "Central Parks School Makes Appeal," *Tribune,* January 24, 1914; "Carnegie Library Building to be Ready July 1," *Tribune,* January 24, 1914.

103. Sineath, "Passing Through a Crucible," 85–89, 91; Thompson, "Progressive Education," 110, 112–13.

104. Sineath, "Passing Through a Crucible," 46–50, 52–55; Dittmer, *Black Georgia,* 63; Matthews, Studies in Race Relations," 363–64.

105. Sineath, "Passing Through a Crucible," 74–77; Fraser, *Charleston! Charleston!* 362; Gessel, "Nowhere But Heaven," 202.

106. *Mayor's Annual Report 1913,* 377; *Mayor's Annual Report 1915,* 479–80.

107. Sineath, "Passing Through a Crucible," 71–73; *Mayor's Annual Report 1914,* 360.

108. Tindall, *Emergence of the New South,* 33–39.

109. Daisy [Juliette Gordon Low] to Mabel [Gordon Leigh], May 7, 1915, Gordon Family Papers, Georgia Historical Society.

110. Gessel, "Nowhere But Heaven," 28–33, 35–39, 94–95, 97, 99–100.

Chapter 4: World War I, Boom, Bust, and a New Deal: 1916–1941

1. "Close Watch in Savannah: Suspected for Months That Bomb Plotters Were Working There," *New York Times,* April 15, 1916; Dittmer, *Black Georgia,* 191; Arthur Gordon to Wayne Parker, June 5, 1915, Gordon Family Papers, 1810–1968, Southern Historical Collection.

2. Gessel, "Nowhere But Heaven," 31–32, 59, 61.

3. Ibid., 35, 37.

4. Dittmer, *Black Georgia,* 186–89; Gessel, "Nowhere But Heaven," 39–40.

5. Gessel, "Nowhere But Heaven," 63–64 n96.

6. Ibid., 35, 41, 48–53, 129.

7. Smith, "Redistribution of the Negro Population," 155, 160.

8. Sineath, "Passing Through a Crucible," 60; Mathews, "Black Newspapermen," 379; Matthews, "Studies in Race Relations," 366; Gessel, "Nowhere But Heaven," 142; Brundage, "Whispering Consolation to Generations Unborn," 347.

9. "It Is for Freedom," *SMN,* June 15, 1917; "Flag Presented," *SMN,* June 15, 1917; Spracher, *Century of History,* 20–21.

10. Qtd. in Dittmer, *Black Georgia,* 192.

11. Matthews, "Studies in Race Relations," 351.

12. Ibid., 195–97, 200.

13. "America's Changing Heart," *Tribune,* March 2, 1918; "53 Negro Draftees Depart for Camp," *Tribune,* March 2, 1918; "124 Negroes Go To Camp Gordon," *Tribune,* April 6, 1918.

14. Elmore, *Richard R. Wright, Sr.,* 50–51.

15. "War Camp Community Service Club Papers," Georgia Historical Society.

16. Freeman, *History of the Savannah Chapter American Red Cross,* 3–16; G. A. Gordon to William Murphy, October 23, 25, 1917, Gordon Family Papers, Georgia Historical Society.

17. "Rebecca Stiles Taylor," Georgia Women of Achievement, www.georgiawomen.org/2014/04/taylor-rebecca-stiles/ (accessed September 5, 2014); Dittmer, *Black Georgia,* 196 n52; "Colored Red Cross Doing Good Work," *Tribune,* March 16, 1918.

18. Tindall, *Emergence of the New South,* 54–55; Fraser, *Charleston! Charleston!* 359–61.

19. Tindall, *Emergence of the New South,* 54; Brownell, "Urban South Comes of Age," 158; Gessel, "Nowhere But Heaven," 89–91.

20. Keber, *Ebb and Flow,* 18–19, 93–95.

21. Ibid., 41–42, 52–56.

22. Cope, *On the Swing Shift,* 5, 27, 194; "Port of Savannah Waterfront Pass," 1918, Georgia Historical Society.

23. Keber, *Low Land and the High Road,* 8–9.

24. Gordon, *How Sweet It Is,* 2–12.

25. Keber, *Low Land and the High Road,* 12–13, 36–37, 39–40; Cooper interview.

26. Ibid., 13–14; "Sugar Refinery To Employ Colored Women," *Tribune,* March 2, 1918.

27. *Mayor's Annual Report 1917,* 1–28, 31.

28. Ibid., 31–34.

29. Pierpont, "Practical Effects of Prohibition," 1–6; Dittmer, *Black Georgia,* 113–14.

30. *Mayor's Annual Report 1917,* 177–78, 183, 184.

31. Ibid., 354; Tindall, *Emergence of the New South,* 62.

32. Fraser, *Charleston! Charleston!* 361.

33. "Minutes of the Board of Sanitary Commissioners," January 8, 1918, Victor Hugo Bassett Papers, Georgia Historical Society.

34. Gessel, "Nowhere But Heaven," 139–40, 152–57.

35. Ibid., 156–57, 176–77.

36. "Proceedings of City Council," January, 15, 1919; "Editorial," *Tribune,* February 1, 1919.

37. "Proceedings of City Council," January 15, 27, 1919.

38. "Cheap Milk and Ice," *Tribune,* February 23, 1918; "Health Bulletin No. 1," Victor H. Bassett Papers, David M. Rubenstein Rare Book & Manuscript Library, Duke University.

39. "Meeting of the Board of Sanitary Commissioners, October 27, 1914," Victor Hugo Bassett Papers, Georgia Historical Society.

40. Dittmer, *Black Georgia,* 189, 190–91, 201; Gessel, "Nowhere But Heaven," 157–74.

41. Fraser, *Charleston! Charleston!* 363; "To use Serum in the Fight," *SMN,* September 29, 1918; "Spreading in Many Sections," *SMN,* October 13, 1918; "12 Cases of Spanish Influenza," *SMN,* October 27, 1918; "Spanish Influenza Spreading; General Crowder Cancels Calls," *SMN,* October 27, 1918; "'Flu' Cases Show Decrease of 113," *SMN,* February 14, 1920.

42. "Welcome Home Soldiers," *Tribune,* January 4, 1919; "Welcome Home Celebration Wednesday Grandest Parade Ever Held In Savannah," *Tribune,* May 10, 1919; "Negroes Will Honor Service Men To-Day," *SMN,* May 7, 1919; "5,000 Negroes March in Welcome Parade," *SMN,* May 8, 1919.

43. Manis, *Macon Black and White,* 56–57; Matthews, "Studies in Race Relations," 157; Dittmer, *Black Georgia,* 203–4; "Racial Clashes," *Tribune,* July 26, 1919.

44. Fraser, *Charleston! Charleston!* 363; Dittmer, *Black Georgia,* 204–5; Brundage, *Lynching in the New South,* 279.

45. "Racial Clashes," *Tribune,* July 26, 1919; "Pistol Totters," *Tribune,* October 18, 1919; "Several Killings Christmas Day," *Tribune,* December 27, 1919.

46. "The Man-Hunt," *Tribune,* June 19, 1920; "Lynching Encouraged," *Tribune,* June 26, 1920; "Editorial [dated July 10, 1920]," *Tribune,* July 16, 1920; Brundage, *Lynching in the New South,* 279.

47. "Editorial," *Tribune,* December 4, 1920.

48. Tindall, *Emergence of the New South,* 69; Bragg, *De Renne,* 318–19, 323.

49. Bragg, *De Renne,* 318–19, 323–25.

50. Ibid., 324–25; [Wymberley W. De Renne] to [Elfrida] Mrs. Craig Barrow, June 3, 1936, and Elfrida Barrow to Wymberley, De Renne Papers, June 4, 1936, George Wymberley Jones De Renne Family Papers, Hargrett Rare Book and Manuscript Library.

51. Kreuzwieser, "Raising the Curtain," 33–35, 60.

52. "Wage Earners Passes [*sic*] Million," *Tribune,* August 7, 1920; "Editorial," *Tribune,* August 7, 1920; Elmore interview; Hoskins, *W. W. Law and His People,* 94–98; Hoskins, *The Trouble They Seen,* 59; "Wage Earners Savings Bank," *Tribune,* March 15, 1919; "Plans for Big West Broad Street Theatre and Hotel Being Worked Out by Architects," *Tribune,* September 13, 1919; Elmore, *All That Savannah Jazz,* 41–42, 57–58; "Editorial," *Tribune,* September 11, 1920.

53. Elmore, *All That Savannah Jazz,* 20, 27, 32, 47.

54. Ibid., 49–51.

55. Elmore interview; Elmore, *All That Savannah Jazz,* 42, 49, 50–51; Fraser, *Charleston! Charleston!* 373.

56. Elmore, *All That Savannah Jazz,* 57, 60, 62.

57. "Tea on 'Yamacraw,'" *SMN,* January 7, 1923.

58. Thompson, "Progressive Education," 33–39; Carnes, "Georgia Deepwater Ports," 49–50.

59. Schuyler, *The Weight of Their Votes,* 50–51, 116, 130.

60. "Economy in Municipal Affairs," *SMN,* November 8, 1922; "James M. Rogers tells where he stands in race for Mayor," *SMN,* November 7, 1922; "No Ringers Need Apply," *SMN,* November 6, 1922; "About 2000 More Names Than Needed," *SMN,* January 4, 1923; "Movement a Protest against Fraud, Judge Adams Declares," *SMN,* January 4, 1923; "Swell the Seabrook Majority," *SMN,* January 4, 1923; Schuyler, *Weight of Their Votes,* 68, 130–31.

61. "Skull and Crossbones Nailed to Every Negro Church in Savannah," *SMN,* January 8, 1923; "Conspiracy to Defeat People's Will Futile," *SMN,* January 8, 1923; "Speakers to Assert Rights of Voters," *SMN,* January 8, 1923; "Candidate's Rights Are Fully Protected, *SMN,* January 8, 1923; Bartley, *Creation of Modern Georgia,* 171.

62. Qtd. in Matthews, "Studies in Race Relations," 334–35.

63. Ibid.; "Court Order to Count Votes Thwarts Administration Plan," *SMN,* January 10, 1923; "Decisive Majority Given Judge Seabrook in Every Box Counted," *SMN,* January 10, 1923; "Good Order at the Polls," *SMN,* January 10, 1923; "[Judge Paul E. Seabrook] Officially Declared Mayor," *SMN,* January 11, 1923; "Let Us Have Peace." *SMN,* January 11, 1923; Schuyler, *Weight of Their Votes,* 130; Spracher, *Century of History,* 38; "Dr. Harris K. Lentini passes away," WTOC television, September 18, 2013, www.wtoc.com/story/23469828/career-educator-dr-harris-k-lentini-passes-away (accessed September 2, 2014). Berrien Casey Morgan was elected to complete the unexpired term of George R. White in 1923 and served four days; "her term represented an honorary measure."

64. "Annual Message to City Council, Honorable Paul E. Seabrook, December 31, 1923," 32–33, 396–97; Thompson, "Progressive Education," 75–76.

65. "Savannah's Health Officers Die," *SMN,* November 4, 1938.

66. "Annual Message to City Council, December 31, 1923," 28–30, 399–401, 407–10.

67. Ibid., 410–12, 418.

68. Ibid., 413; "What Are the Specifications," *SMN,* July 3, 1922.

69. "Annual Message to City Council, December 31, 1923," 191, 196, 226–27.

70. "Mock Shot to Death after Getting License to Marry," *SMN,* November 10, 1922.

71. Ibid.

72. Qtd. in Reed, *Enduring South,* 45, 55.

73. “Minutes of Savannah City Council,” March 17, June 16, June 29, 1926.

74. Bragg, *De Renne,* 326–58.

75. Hoskins, *W. W. Law and His People,* 104–6; Kalmar, “Savannah and the New Deal,” 2–3; see also Kalmar, “Southern Black Elites and the New Deal,” 341–55; Tindall, *Emergence of the New South,* 354.

76. Thompson, “Progressive Education,” 39, 61–62, 115–19; Gessel, “Nowhere But Heaven,” 182; Bowden, *Two Hundred Years of Education,* 302.

77. Hubert, “Savannah Present and Future,” 5–7, 14–15.

78. Hall, *One Hundred Years of Educating at Savannah State College,* 33–34.

79. [Sigo Myers Prize Awarded], *SMN,* March 17, 1929.

80. Cash, qtd. in Tindall, *Emergence of the New South,* 331; Cash, *Mind of the South,* 272–73.

81. Gamble, “Changing Currents in Savannah's Commerce,” 11–21.

82. *Annual Message of the Mayor 1925,* 28; “Minutes of Savannah City Council, 1929,” 168; “Minutes of Savannah City Council, 1930–1936,” [February 26, 1930, 168; January 23, December 3, 1933], 26, 478–80; *Mayor's Annual Report* [1935], 15–21; Kalmar, “Savannah and the New Deal,” 106.

83. Thompson, “Progressive Education,” 175, 178, 183–88.

84. Ibid., 73, 74–75.

85. Ibid., 188–90.

86. Qtd. in Thompson, “Progressive Education,” 73; see also Bartley, *Creation of Modern Georgia,* 175.

87. Kalmar, “Savannah and the New Deal,” 5–8.

88. Anderson, “Adrift in Georgia: Savannah,” 121–24.

89. Ibid., 86–91.

90. Hoskins, *W. W. Law and His People,* 121–26; Savannah Unit, Georgia Writers' Project, *Drums and Shadows,* 12.

91. [Victor Bassett], “Health Department, September 25, 1937,” Victor H. Bassett Papers, David M. Rubenstein Rare Book & Manuscript Library, Duke University.

92. Hoskins, *W. W. Law and His People,* 128, 129, 130, 131, 132, 137.

93. Ibid., 128, 131.

94. “Minutes of Savannah City Council,” April 13, 1938.

95. Hoskins, *W. W. Law and His People,* 128–31; Savannah Unit, Georgia Writers' Project, *Drums and Shadows,* 1, 23, 32, 46.

96. Excerpt from *The Damned Don't Cry* by Harry Hervey in Allen, *Literary Savannah,* 127–42.

97. Clipping from *Tribune,* [September 29], 1936, Victor H. Bassett Papers, David M. Rubenstein Rare Book & Manuscript Library, Duke University.

98. “Joint Meeting of Committees Advisory–State Board of Health,” Atlanta, April 28, 1935; [Victor Bassett] to Ernest A. Lowe, April 4, 1938, both in Victor H. Bassett Papers, David M. Rubenstein Rare Book & Manuscript Library, Duke University.

99. Bartley, *Creation of Modern Georgia,* 193–94; Gordon, *Georgia Negro,* 100.

100. Kalmar, “Savannah and the New Deal,” 130, 131, 136, 137.

101. Spracher, *Century of History,* 40; Franklin D. Roosevelt, “Roosevelt's Georgia bicentennial speech at Savannah, Georgia on November 18, 1933,” Project at the Pare Lorentz Center at the FDR Presidential Library, www.fdrlibrary.marist.edu/daybyday/resource/november-1933-2/ (accessed September 9, 2015).

102. Hopkins, “Harry Hopkins and Work Relief”; Kalmar, “Savannah and the New Deal,” 9–19.

103. Qtd. in Tindall, *Emergence of the New South,* 547.

104. Kalmar, "Savannah and the New Deal," 22–32, 109, 113–14. "Minutes of Savannah City Council," January 20, 1936; *Mayor's Annual Report* [1935], 14–15 (this was one of the few annual reports published in the 1930s).
105. Kalmar, "Southern Black Elites and the New Deal," 346–47.
106. Elmore, *All That Savannah Jazz,* 67–69, 85–86, 90.
107. [A. Leopold] Alexander to Eleanor, April 28, 1932, Alexander and Hillhouse Family Papers, 1758–1976, Southern Historical Collection.
108. E. S. Trogdal to Dr. Craig Barrow, November 29, 1929, and Col. Sheftal B. Coleman to Dr. Craig Barrow, September 27, 1933, Craig Barrow Family Papers, Hargrett Rare Book and Manuscript Library.
109. "A Proposal to Bondholders," to [Craig Barrow], February 19, 1934; Craig Barrow to the Oglethorpe Club, November 21, 1939, Craig Barrow Family Papers, Hargrett Rare Book and Manuscript Library.
110. "Week-End Parties and Outdoor Events Featured—Young Equestrians Enjoy Drag Hunt at Riding and Driving Club," *SMN,* February 1, 1930; "Group to Enjoy Picnic Supper This Evening [at Tybee]" and "Informal Luncheon," *SMN,* January 26, 1937; "Luncheon Party: To Be Given at Oglethorpe Club Tomorrow," *SMN,* March 10, 1938, "Christmas Calendar," *SMN,* December 7, 1941.
111. "Minutes of Savannah City Council," January 20, 1936; *Mayor's Annual Report* [1935], 4–11, 20–21.
112. Kalmar, "Savannah and the New Deal," 115–16; Dick and Johnson, "Smell of Money," 308–23; *Mayor's Annual Report* [1935], 18.
113. Fallows, *Water Lords*, xv, 7.
114. "Savannah Changes Mayors," *SMN,* January 25, 1937.
115. Kalmar, "Savannah and the New Deal," 105–7.
116. Ibid, 86–87.
117. Qtd. in Kalmar, "Savannah and the New Deal," 93, 96–100.
118. Kalmar, "Savannah and the New Deal," 32–36, 54–59, 62–64, 66, 68.
119. Ibid., 117–19; see also "A Clarifying Statement," *SMN,* January 9, 1936.
120. Craig Barrow to Senator Richard B. Russell, April 14, 1938, Craig Barrow Family Papers, Hargrett Rare Book and Manuscript Library. Dr. Barrow's progressive side became apparent on occasion when he urged that "academic freedom and the right of free speech on the campus were essential "at the University of Georgia"; see Craig Barrow to Editor, *Alumni Record*, March 17, 1932; see also Craig Barrow to H. N. Old, March 7, 1932, Craig Barrow Family Papers, Hargrett Rare Book and Manuscript Library.
121. Kalmar, "Savannah and the New Deal," 120–26.
122. "Communication from Mayor [Robert M. Hitch] to Aldermen," January 18, 1939, 431–33, Clerk of Council Chambers, City Hall, City of Savannah.
123. Kalmar, "Savannah and the New Deal," 102–3; "Minutes of Savannah City Council," January 23, 1939; Keber, *Low Land and the High Road*, 42.
124. Fraser, *Lowcountry Hurricanes*, 224.
125. Brownell, "Urban South Comes of Age," 128.
126. Gamble, "Changing Currents in Savannah's Commerce," 11–21; "Savannah Offers Transportation Facilities by Land, Sea, and Air," *Savannah Evening Press*, November 19, 1941.

Chapter 5: From World War II to Rousakis's Last Term: 1942–1991

1. "Japanese Strike Initial Blow of War Great Loss of Life Reported in Hawaii," *SMN,* December 8, 1941.

2. Cope, *On the Swing Shift*, 1–7, 21–25, 125–26; Keber, *Ebb and Flow*, 42–44; see also Veasey, "Liberty Shipyards," 159–81.

3. Butler, "Vicious Circle," 16; Goldfield, *Black, White, and Southern*, 35; Haas, Edward F., "Southern Metropolis, 1940–1976," in Brownell and Goldfield, eds, *City in Southern History*, 160–61; Tindall, *Emergence of the New South*, 703; Tuck, *Beyond Atlanta*, 30.

4. Cope, *On the Swing Shift*, 25–27.

5. Ibid., 27, 194; Keber, *Ebb and Flow*, 44.

6. Cope, *On the Swing Shift*, 27–31, 34–37; Keber, *Ebb and Flow*, 22–26.

7. Keber, *Ebb and Flow*, 29–30.

8. Ibid., 40–41.

9. Cope, *On the Swing Shift*, 39, 46, 50; Fraser, *Charleston! Charleston!* 387–88, 389; Parramore et al., *Norfolk*, 337–38, 339; Keber, *Ebb and Flow*, 26–28.

10. Cope, *On the Swing Shift*, 40–43.

11. Qtd. in Cope, *On the Swing Shift*, 43.

12. Ibid., 47.

13. Cope, *On the Swing Shift*, 48.

14. Ibid.; Hoskins, *W. W. Law and His People*, 142.

15. Butler, "Vicious Circle," 9–10; Tindall, *Emergence of the New South*, 713–14; Cope, *On the Swing Shift*, 48–49.

16. Keber, *Ebb and Flow*, 46–47; Cope, *On the Swing Shift*, 49–50, 53–55.

17. Cope, *On the Swing Shift*, 49–50, 56; Butler, "Vicious Circle," 11; Goldfield, *Black, White and Southern*, 35.

18. Butler, "Vicious Circle," 17–18.

19. Tuck, *Beyond Atlanta*, 44–47.

20. Qtd. in Hoskins, *W. W. Law and His People*, 135.

21. Hoskins, *W. W. Law and His People*, 137; "John J. Bouhan," *Savannah Evening Press*, January 12, 1971.

22. Qtd. in Coffey, *Only in Savannah*, 24.

23. Ibid., 26, 31; Cooper interview; Maclean interview; "John J. Bouhan," *Savannah Evening Press*, January 12, 1971; "Savannah Bar Association Memorial to John Joseph Bouhan," Vertical File, Bull Street Library, Kay Kole Genealogy and Local History Room, Savannah; Hoskins, *W. W. Law and His People*, 136; Maclean interview.

24. Qtd. in Tuck, *Beyond Atlanta*, 46.

25. Hoskins, *W. W. Law and His People*, 134–37.

26. Tuck, *Beyond Atlanta*, 46–47; Butler, "Vicious Circle," 20–23.

27. Butler, "Vicious Circle," 23–25.

28. Editorial, *Tribune*, June 25, 1942.

29. Butler, "Vicious Circle," 11, 16, 29, 103.

30. Qtd. in Tindall, *Emergence of the New South*, 710.

31. Carnes, "Georgia Deepwater Ports," 55; "Proceedings of City Council," March 8, 1944.

32. "Proceedings of City Council," March 8, 1944; *Message to City Council*, February 21, 1945.

33. "Proceedings of City Council," February 21, 1945; Hoskins, *W. W. Law and His People*, 139.

34. "Thomas Gamble," *SMN*, July 14, 1945; Spracher, *Century of History*, 54.

35. Hoskins, *W. W. Law and His People*, 136–45.

36. Ibid., 144–46; Goldfield, *Black, White and Southern*, 33–34; Novotny, *This Georgia Rising*, 172.

37. Tindall, *Emergence of the New South*, 716–17.

38. Goldfield, *Black, White and Southern*, 36; Tuck, *Beyond Atlanta*, 26–27.

39. Tuck, *Beyond Atlanta*, 27–28.

40. Qtd. in Tindall, *Emergence of the New South*, 701–2; see also Davidson, "Savannah's Amazing Grace," 32.

41. Qtd. in "Filth of City Draws Attacks," *SMN*, February 20, 1946; Bill Fielder, "Savannah Like Beautiful Woman With Dirty Face, Lady Astor Says," *SMN*, February 20, 1946; "Clean-up Drive Begins In City In Wake of Two-pronged Blast," *SMN*, February 21, 1946; Letter to the editor, "Suggests 'Good Cleaning Up,'" *SMN*, March 1, 1946; Letter to the editor, "Lady Astor Spoke Truly," *SMN*, March 2, 1946; "Lady Astor's Cleanup Ideas Have Spread," *SMN*, March 2, 1946.

42. "Filth of City Draws Attacks," *SMN*, February 20, 1946; Bill Fielder, "Savannah Like Beautiful Woman With Dirty Face, Lady Astor Says," *SMN*, February 20, 1946.

43. Qtd. in Bartley, *History of the New South*, 16, 161; Coffey, *Only in Savannah*, 26.

44. Coffey, *Only in Savannah*, 27; "Savannah Bar Association Memorial to John Joseph Bouhan," Vertical File, Bull Street Library, Kay Kole Genealogy and Local History Room, Savannah.

45. Qtd. in Tuck, *Beyond Atlanta*, 66–67, and in Novotny, *This Georgia Rising*, 195; White interview.

46. Qtd. in Tuck, *Beyond Atlanta*, 68.

47. Novotny, *This Georgia Rising*, 176–77, 179, 180, 181, 184–85, 190–91; see also Bernd, "White Supremacy," 492–513.

48. Novotny, *This Georgia Rising*, 196.

49. Tuck, *Beyond Atlanta*, 67.

50. Qtd. in *Beyond Atlanta*, 66–67.

51. Bartley, *History of the New South*, 16; Hoskins, *W. W. Law and His People*, 146–47; Novotny, *This Georgia Rising*, 197–98; Tuck, *Beyond Atlanta*, 67.

52. Maclean interview.

53. Coffey, *Only in Savannah*, 27–28; "Election Under Investigation—Probe by Grand Jury—Action Follows Charges by Mrs. Lillian Bragg," *SMN*, August 9, 1945; "Punish Ballot Box Stuffers!" *SMN*, August 9, 1945.

54. Tuck, *Beyond Atlanta*, 67.

55. Ibid., 68.

56. Novotny, *This Georgia Rising*, 202–15.

57. Coffey, *Only in Savannah*, 28–29; White interview; *Mayor's Annual Report 1948*; Hoskins, *W. W. Law and His People*, 140, 142, 148; Hoskins, *Out of Yamacraw and Beyond*, 130.

58. Tuck, "A City Too Dignified to Hate," 558, 557–58.

59. *Mayor's Annual Report 1948;* Carnes, "Georgia Deepwater Ports," 57–58.

60. "Proceedings of City Council," January 24, 1949; Spracher, *Century of History*, 57.

61. Olin F. Fulmer to Prince H. Preston, February 26, 1949; Frank M. Oliver to Prince H. Preston, March 26, 1949; Clarence D. Pederson to Prince H. Preston, March 5, 1949; Prince H. Preston to Clarence K. Pedersen, March 30, 1949, all in Richard B. Russell Papers, Richard B. Russell Library for Political Research and Studies.

62. "Proceedings of City Council," December 30, 1949.

63. Spracher, *Century of History*, 58.

64. "Proceedings of City Council," December 30, 1949.

65. *Mayor's Annual Report 1951*; "Proceedings of City Council," March 7, 1952; *Annual Report of the Mayor 1953*; Carnes, "Georgia Deepwater Ports," 56.

66. *Annual Report of the Mayor 1953*.

67. Qtd. in Tuck, *Beyond Atlanta*, 70; Talmadge interviews.
68. Qtd. in Tuck, *Beyond Atlanta*, 72.
69. Ibid., 77.
70. Tuck, *Beyond Atlanta*, 74–79.
71. Ibid., 72; Hoskins, *W. W. Law and His People*, 150–51, 162–63.
72. Hoskins, *W. W. Law and His People*, 153.
73. Spracher, "History & Highlights," 2–3, 7–9; Michael Homans, "Savannah's Charter Gives Mayor Vote on City Council, but Limited Authority," *Savannah News Press*, November 3, 1991.
74. Qtd. in Coffey, *Only in Savannah*, 30.
75. *Mayor's Annual Report 1952*.
76. *Annual Report of the Mayor 1953*; Spracher, *Century of History*, 63; Spracher, "History & Highlights," 2–3.
77. *Annual Report of the Mayor 1953*.
78. Ibid.
79. Hoskins, *W. W. Law and His People*, 162–68.
80. Ibid., 169.
81. Qtd. in Hoskins, *W. W. Law and His People*, 169–70.
82. Hoskins, *W. W. Law and His People*, 171–72.
83. Coffey, *Only in Savannah*, 31–32.
84. Ibid., 32–33.
85. Basso, "Savannah and the Golden Isles," 53–56; Joe Ryan, "Preservationist Mary Hillyer Dies," *SMN*, March 18, 1999.
86. Fraser, *Charleston! Charleston!* 366; Davidson, "Savannah's Saving Grace," 32, 34; Said, "Factors Contributing to the Success of Historic Preservation and Restoration," 74–76; Coffey, *Only in Savannah*, 16–18; Brundage, *Southern Past*, 255–58.
87. Gratz, *Living City*, 38–39; Chuck Mobley, "Ellis Square comes full circle," *SMN*, March 11, 2010; Leslie Conn, "Downpour, ribbon cutting officially christen Ellis Square," *SMN*, March 12, 2010.
88. Brundage, *Southern Past*, 255–56.
89. Ibid., 259–60; White interview.
90. Acosta, "Union Station," 4, 6, 35–46, 48–64.
91. Elmore interview.
92. Bynes interview.
93. Beavers interview.
94. Qtd. in Brundage, *Southern Past*, 259–60.
95. Adams interview.
96. Brundage, *Southern Past*, 258–59.
97. Ibid., 259–61.
98. Ibid., 260–63; Hoskins, *W. W. Law and His People*, 172–74.
99. Hoskins, *W. W. Law and His People*, 172–74; Spracher, *Century of History*, 68.
100. Spracher, *Century of History*, 70; Hoskins, *W. W. Law and His People*, 179.
101. J. W. Fanning Institute for Leadership Development, www.fanning.uga.edu/about-us/tradition-history (accessed October 19, 2014); By-laws, Community Leadership Seminar of Savannah, Inc., Article II.
102. Wood, "The Metropolis: An Overview," 1–11; Pikl, "Savannah's Economic Health, 1–28.
103. Dobereiner, "Planning: Why, How, How Much?" 1–17.
104. Pikl, "Savannah's Economic Health," 1–28.

105. Deutschberger, "Social Welfare Services: Present Realities and Future Prospects," 1–13.
106. Pikl, "Savannah's Economic Health," 1–28; Drewry, "Savannah's Economic Health," 1–28; Silverman, "The Growing Metropolis," 1–10; Ott, "Savannah's Economic Health," 1–13; Gibson, "Savannah: An Overview," 1–17; Tuck, *Beyond Atlanta*, 129.
107. Gibson, "Savannah: An Overview," 1–17.
108. Hoskins, *W. W. Law and His People*, 175–79.
109. Turner, *Sitting In and Speaking Out*, 45–47; Tuck, *Beyond Atlanta*, 107–10.
110. Tuck, *Beyond Atlanta*, 129.
111. Qtd. in Tuck, *Beyond Atlanta*, 131.
112. Ibid.
113. Ibid., 130.
114. Editorial, *SMN*, March 18, 1960.
115. Hoskins, *W. W. Law and His People*, 180–82; Tuck, *Beyond Atlanta*, 132–33.
116. Cooper interview.
117. Hoskins, *W. W. Law and His People*, 180–82; Tuck, *Beyond Atlanta*, 7, 127, 134–35; Tony Brown, "The Summer of '63," *SMN*, September 11, 1983; "Oral Histories Complement Photo Exhibit," *SMN*, September 11, 1983.
118. Cooper interview.
119. Arnold interview.
120. Ibid.
121. Ibid.; Hoskins, *W. W. Law and His People*, 183.
122. Gadsden interview; Tuck, *Beyond Atlanta*, 131.
123. Arnold interview.
124. Ibid.; Hoskins, *W. W. Law and His People*, 182–84.
125. Spracher, *Century of History*, 85; Arnold interview.
126. Arnold interview; qtd. in Tuck, *Beyond Atlanta*, 131.
127. Arnold interview; Cooper interview.
128. Gadsden interview; Lewis interview.
129. Maclean interview; Arnold interview.
130. James H. Byington Jr. to Congressman Preston, April 27, 1960; Prince H. Preston to Mr. J. H. Byington Jr., May 5, 1960; Prince H. Preston to Mr. R. S. Maylon, May 18, 1960, all in Richard B. Russell Papers, Richard B. Russell Library for Political Research and Studies.
131. Qtd. in Tuck, *Beyond Atlanta*, 132; Lewis interview.
132. Tuck, *Beyond Atlanta*, 133; qtd. in Hoskins, *W. W. Law and His People*, 188–89; Jan Skutch, "Stories from the Savannah News Archives Published in 1996," *Savannah Now*, savannahnow.com/features/wwlaw/commitment.shtml (accessed December 4. 2014).
133. Davis, *Weary Feet*, 179–91; Maclean interview.
134. Tuck, *Beyond Atlanta*, 128; Hoskins, *W. W. Law and His People*, 186–90.
135. Maclean interview; Arnold interview; Gadsden interview; Hoskins, *W. W. Law and His People*, 185–87; Spracher, *Century of History*, 85; Tuck, *Beyond Atlanta*, 127, 128, 134; Cooper interview.
136. "Theaters Integrate, Then 2 Withdraw," *SMN*, June 4, 1963.
137. Arnold interview.
138. Qtd. in Spracher, *Century of History*, 85–86.
139. Ibid.; "Thousands Join 'Freedom' March," *SMN*, June 12, 1963; "Charleston Sit-Ins Visit Three Stores," *SMN*, June 12, 1963.
140. "Arson Is Suspected In Firestone Blaze," *SMN*, July 5, 1963.

141. "Negroes Threaten Protest Speed-Up," *SMN*, July 7, 1963; "King Group Backs Savannah Negroes," *SMN*, July 6, 1963.
142. Spracher, *Century of History*, 86; Hoskins, *W. W. Law and His People*, 193.
143. "Negroes Threaten Protest Speed-Up," *SMN*, July 7, 1963.
144. Ibid.; "Talmadge, Russell Say Rights Bill Would 'Destroy U.S.'" *SMN*, July 8, 1963; "KKK Plans Resistance Campaign," *SMN*, July 10, 1963; "Rep Hagan Opposes Measure," *SMN*, April 11, 1968.
145. "Negro Integration Leader Arrested," *SMN*, July 10, 1963.
146. Ibid.; "900 Negroes Gather Downtown," *SMN*, July 10, 1963.
147. "Tear Gas, Hoses Rout Negroes Here," *SMN*, July 11, 1963; "900 Negroes Gather Downtown," *SMN*, July 10, 1963; "Crack Down on Disorders," *SMN*, July 12, 1963.
148. Maclean interview; Fraser, *Charleston! Charleston*, 416–17.
149. "Rioting Negroes Stone Cars, Set Fires, Smash Windows," *SMN*, July 12, 1963; "Arson Is Suspected At Church," July 12, 1963.
150. Maclean interview; Spracher, *Century of History*, 85–86.
151. "Rioting Negroes Stone Cars, Set Fires, Smash Windows," *SMN*, July 12, 1963; "Bond for Williams Placed at $30,000," *SMN*, July 12, 1963; "Crack Down on Disorders," *SMN*, July 12, 1963.
152. "Rioting Negroes Stone Cars, Set Fires, Smash Windows," *SMN*, July 12, 1963; "Crack Down on Disorders," *SMN*, July 12, 1963; "The Negro's Responsibility," *SMN*, July 13, 1963; "Irate Lady Lambasts Officials," *SMN*, July 12, 1962.
153. "Role of White Citizens," *SMN*, July 13, 1963; "Police Turn Back March of Whites," *SMN*, July 14, 1963.
154. "Negroes Call Off Savannah March," July 15, 1963; "City Council Bans Racial Marches," *SMN*, July 18, 1963.
155. Maclean interview; "Group Says Basis Is Set for Harmony," *SMN*, August 3, 1963.
156. "Defeat of Savannah Officials Is Urged," August 6, 1963; "Committee Regrets Agreement 'Report,'" *SMN*, August 10, 1963; Billy Vaughn, "Private Enrollments Stable in '89," *SMN*, March 4, 1990.
157. Jenkins, *Blind Vengeance*, 69–71.
158. Ibid., 72–75; "Group Organized To Help Schools," *SMN*, August 4, 1963; Hoskins, *W. W. Law and His People*, 187–93, 198.
159. Tuck, *Beyond Atlanta*, 128–37.
160. Qtd. in Tuck, *Beyond Atlanta*, 136–37.
161. Tuck, *Beyond Atlanta*, 128, 129, 137.
162. Coffey, *Only in Savannah*, 44–48.
163. Qtd. in Hoskins, *W. W. Law and His People*, 191, 193.
164. Barry Goldwater, "Crack Down On Disorder," *SMN*, July 12, 1963; Cooper interview.
165. Maclean interview; Lewis interview; Hoskins, *W. W. Law and His People*, 200, 202; "Episcopalians: Secession in Savannah," *Time*, May 7, 1965.
166. Lewis interview.
167. Ibid.; Maclean interview; Cooper interview.
168. Maclean interview; Archie Whitfield, "Lewis Wins Over Maclean In Historic City Election," *SMN*, August 3, 1966; "Pledge of Support," *SMN*, August 4, 1966; "Quality Standards for Water," *SMN*, October 10, 1966.
169. Fallows, *Water Lords*, 29–30.
170. Ibid.; John Carroll, "Bottling Official Shot to Death," *SMN*, July 26, 1966; "6-Month Crime Rate Up 11.4 Per Cent Over 1965 Period," September 15, 1966; "To Abate Crime," *SMN*, September 16, 1966.

171. Lewis interview.
172. "Crime Rate Rises," *SMN*, August 29, 1968.
173. Lewis interview.
174. "City Holds Curfew; Chiefs Urge Calm," *SMN*, April 6, 1968.
175. Ibid.; "We remember: Murray Pearlman," *Savannah Now*, April 3, 2004; "Trouble Hit, Miss," *SMN*, April 6, 1968; "Bandits Slug, Rob Attorney," *SMN*, April 6, 1968.
176. Joe Ryan, "Curfew Extension Not Yet Definite," *SMN*, April 7, 1968; "Irresponsibility Must Stop," *SMN*, April 6, 1968; "Scattered Violence Reported in County," *SMN*, April 9, 1968; Joe Ryan, "Clergyman Urges Unity," *SMN*, April 8, 1968; Rita H. DeLorme, "Monsignor John Downey Toomey: the man behind the 1968 'practical eulogy' at Christ Church, Savannah," Catholic Diocese of Savannah, January 8 2007, diosav.org /sites/all/files/archives/S8706p03.pdf, (accessed September 24, 2014); Maclean interview.
177. Qtd. in Hoskins, *W. W. Law and His People*, 201–2.
178. Ibid., 203.
179. *Thunderbolt*, 1966, 1969, David M. Rubenstein Rare Book & Manuscript Library, Special Collections, Duke University; NSRP Membership Application, University of Georgia Special Collections.
180. Gibson, "Whither Savannah?"
181. Green, "Economic Signs in Savannah."
182. "Get Concerned About Litter," *SMN*, April 9, 1968; "A Good Festival," *SMN*, April 10, 1968; "Good Ground Work," *SMN*, April 7, 1968.
183. Burke, "The City and Its Culture."
184. Ibid.
185. Deutschberger, "Social Welfare Services," June 4, 1968, address.
186. Ibid.
187. Brewer, "Social Welfare Services."
188. Lewis interview; Nancy Ancrum, "Rousakis Ticket Backed by Council," *SMN*, May 5, 1970; "Lewis Hints Again He Wants Out," *SMN*, May 4, 1970; Nancy Ancrum, "Rousakis Slate Issues Its City Race Platform," *SMN*, May 4, 1970; Cooper interview; Jackson interview.
189. Rousakis interview; Barbara Dlugozima, "Rossiter Top Man For Council Post," *SMN*, May 13, 1970.
190. Fallows, *Water Lords*, 182–87; for additional information on Skidaway Island, see Kelly, *Short History of Skidaway Island*.
191. Nancy Ancrum, "Rousakis Ticket Backed by Council," *SMN*, May 5, 1970; Rousakis interview.
192. Fallows, *Water Lords*, 30, 36.
193. Rousakis interview.
194. Qtd. in Cunningham et al., *Tapping the Power of City Hall*, 248–50.
195. Rousakis interview; Fallows, *Water Lords*, 30, 36; Nancy Ancrum, "Rousakis Ticket Backed by Council," *SMN*, May 5, 1970; Joe Ryan, "Rossiter's Vote Largest," *SMN*, August 5, 1970.
196. "Lewis Hints Again He Wants Out," *SMN*, May 4, 1970; Lewis interview.
197. "Few Surprises," *SMN*, May 14, 1970; Nancy Ancrum, "Rousakis Slate Issues Its City Race Platform," *SMN*, May 4, 1970; Barbara Dlugozima, "John Rousakis Nominated for Mayor in One-Sided Demo Primary Victory," *SMN*, May 13, 1970; "Close Race Seen in City Hall Vote," *SMN*, August 2, 1970; Joe Ryan, "Voters Choose Rousakis Over Lewis In Savannah's Election For Mayor," *SMN*, August 5, 1970; Nancy Ancrum, "'Lewis Offer [*sic*] 'Usual Way,'" *SMN*, June 26, 1970; Lewis interview.

198. Rousakis interview; Albert Oetgen, "Annexation Is Shoe-in: Voting Decisive," *SMN*, April 20, 1978; Spracher, *Century of History*, 101.

199. Joe Ryan, "Voters Choose Rousakis Over Lewis in Savannah's Election for Mayor," *SMN*, August 5, 1970.

200. Ibid.; Kathy Haeberle, "Lewis Camp Solemn," *SMN*, August 5, 1970; Barr Nobles, "Jubilant Rousakis Winners Hold Hellenic Center Party," *SMN*, August 5, 1970; Lewis interview.

201. Fallows, *Water Lords*, ix–xi, 6, 175, 236–40; Coffey, *Only in Savannah*, 220–21, 254.

202. Fallows, *Water Lords*, x–xi.

203. Ibid., 1, 6–7, 10–11.

204. Ibid., 8–12, 224.

205. Ibid., 11–12.

206. Ibid., 253.

207. Qtd. in Fallows, *Water Lords*, 256.

208. Barbara Dlugozima, "Deadline out—Cyanamid," *SMN*, February 17, 1972 ; Lantham Davis, "Industries Get Notices," *SMN*, January 3, 1973; "State Orders $500 Fine," *SMN*, January 13, 1973; Jan Skutch, "Air in Chatham Called Sewer by Grand Jury," *SMN*, November 30, 1973; "Water Act Will Lead To Specific State Guidelines," *SMN*, January 2, 1975; Shannon Lowry, "Cyananid Must Upgrade Its Waste Systems," *SMN*, Aug. 29, 1980; Cobb, *Selling of the South*, 248.

209. Cobb, *Selling of the South*, 247, 273; Cobb, *South and America*, 217.

210. Tom Barton, "Pulp Mills Get Break on Odor Deadline," *SMN*, December 2, 1981; Cobb, *Selling of the South*, 231; *Draft Environmental Statement, Harry S. Truman Parkway*, Department of the Army Permit Application 074–YN 003846," Georgia Department of Transportation, U.S. Army Engineer District, Savannah, Corps of Engineers, for Department of Army Permit, March 1979.

211. Rousakis interview; Spracher, "History & Highlights," 29–42.

212. "Savannah's best friend," *SMN*, December 12, 2000.

213. Rousakis interview; Spracher, *Century of History*, 102, 107; "In His Element at Mayor's Dinner," *SMN*, February 23 and 25, 1977; Rice, "Urbanization," 56–57; Cooper interview.

214. Bell Jr., "Isundiga."

215. Spracher, *Century of History*, 105–6.

216. Hoskins, *W. W. Law and His People*, 204–11.

217. Hepburn, ed., *Contemporary Georgia*, 333; Jenel Few, "Savannah-Chatham Schools: From Sore Spot to Hot Spot," *SMN*, April 6, 2014.

218. "Re-elect Talmadge," *SMN*, October 3, 1980; Scott E. Buchanan, "Herman Talmadge (1913–2002)."

219. Adler and Adler, *Savannah Renaissance*, 67–74, 77; Sies and Silver, eds., *Planning the Twentieth-Century American City*, 372–75, Hepburn, ed., *Contemporary Georgia*, 326, 328.

220. Adler and Adler, *Savannah Renaissance*, 67–74.

221. Qtd. in Adler and Adler, *Savannah Renaissance*, 75.

222. Hepburn, ed., *Contemporary Georgia*, 325–27; Debra Ellington, "Victorian District, street car suburb," *SMN*, February 6, 1983; Charles Craig, "Group Reassesses Historic District," *SMN*, March 3, 1985; Ford, "Seeing the New in Old Savannah," 20–22.

223. Qtd. in Hepburn, ed., *Contemporary Georgia*, 330.

224. Dennis and Dennis, "Savannah: The South's Greatest Comeback," *Travel*, July 1974, 26–31; *New York Times* Best Seller List, www.nytbestsellerlist.com/book/best selling (accessed September 23, 2014).

225. Hepburn, ed., *Contemporary* Georgia, 330.

226. Don Wilson, "Hitch Village Encased in Violent Atmosphere," *SMN*, February 14, 1971; Kathy Haeberle, "Anti-crime Drive Backed," *SMN*, February 18, 1971; Kathy Haeberle, "Support War Against Crime, Mayor Asks," *SMN*, February 24, 1975; Hepburn, ed., *Contemporary Georgia*, 330; McLaughlin, *Police and the Use of Force*, 6.

227. John Goyer, "Mendonsa Receives Report on Crime," *SMN*, October 23, 1980; "New Chief Says City Not 'Crime Riddled,'" *SMN*, October 23, 1980; Todd Glasenapp, "Gellatly Looks At Problems Surrounding Crime," *SMN*, March 24, 1982; Herbert Buchsbaum, "Savannah in '81: Crime, drug trafficking hog the headlines during year," *SMN*, January 3, 1982; Betsy Neal, "Crime news held headlines in 1986," *SMN*, January 4, 1987.

228. "Summary Report of the Issues Force Task Force, 1992," 358, Municipal Archives; Derek Smith, "Savannah Continues the Battle," *SMN*, March 4, 1990.

229. Lees, *Portrait of Johnny*, 331–33; *Harper v. Supreme Court of Georgia*, No. 38480 (June 2, 1982); editorial, *SMN*, September 16, 1992; Calvin Trillin, "Among Friends," *New Yorker*, February 2, 1981, 65.

230. McLaughlin, *Police and the Use of Force*, 87; Spencer Lawton, "Opposition to police officer's memorial is all about race—and it shouldn't be," *SMN*, April 13, 2014; excerpt from the decision of the U.S. District Court, Southern District of Georgia, Judge William T. Moore, *In re Troy Davis*, No. CV409–130 (August 24, 2010), Criminal Justice Legal Foundation, www.cjlf.org/files/DavisExcerpt.html (accessed December 27, 2014); see also Tom Rose, "Off-duty Policeman Shot to Death," *SMN*, August 20, 1989; Jan Skutch, "Davis Convicted: Jury Quick to Render Guilty Verdict in Murder of Officer," *SMN*, August 29, 1991; Jan Skutch, "Troy Davis' final day," *SMN*, September. 21, 2011; Charleston Montaldo, "The Shooting of Officer Mark MacPhail," crime.about.com/od/murder/a/The-Shooting-Of-Officer-Mark-Macphail.htm (accessed October 26,2014).

231. Jenkins, *Blind Vengeance*, 24–27, 100–112, 201–7, 320; Mary T. Schmich, "In Savannah, An Unlikely Target," *Chicago Tribune*, December 20, 1989; Jan Skutch, "Mailbomber Moody Faces Alabama Trial," *SMN*, October 27, 1994.

232. Hepburn, ed., *Contemporary* Georgia, 330; McLaughlin, *Police and the Use of Force*, 45, 47, 62, 64, 81, 83.

233. Rousakis interview; Hepburn, ed., *Contemporary Georgia*, 330.

234. Adler and Adler, *Savannah Renaissance*, 77–78; Benjamin Oxnard Biography, Vertical File, Bull Street Library; Kreuzwieser, "Raising the Curtain," 33–35, 60; Hardin, "Georgia No Longer a Secret to the World," 68–69.

235. Larry Peterson, "College thrives; city too," *SMN*, February 22, 2009; Larry Peterson, "SCAD president looks to school's future," *SMN*, February 22, 2009.

236. *Atlanta Weekly*, December 26, 1982.

237. Adler and Adler, *Savannah Renaissance*, 78; Kevin Meredith, "School draws praise, students to downtown," *SMN*, June 14, 1992; Peter Applebome, "Art and Commerce: a College's Turbulent Tale," *New York Times*, August 23, 1992, www.nytimes.com/1992/08/23/us/art-and-commerce-a-college-s-turbulent-tale.html?pagewanted=1 (accessed September 20, 2015); Kevin Meredith, "Several agencies keeping watch on school," *SMN*, June 14, 1992; Julius C. Muller, "A Thirty Year History of the Savannah College of Art and Design," *Savannah Now*, February 22, 2009, savannahnow.com/julia-c-muller/2009–2–21/30-year-history-savannah-college-art-and-design (accessed September 19, 2015).

238. "Several agencies keeping watch on school," *SMN*, June 14, 1992.

239. Ibid., Kevin Meredith, "But Protests Frequent This Spring," *SMN*, June 14, 1992; Peter Applebome, "Art and Commerce: a College's Turbulent Tale," *New York Times*,

August 23, 1992, www.nytimes.com/1992/08/23/us/art-and-commerce-a-college-s-turbulent-tale.html?pagewanted=1 (accessed September 20, 2015); Julius C. Muller, "A Thirty Year History of the Savannah College of Art and Design," *Savannah Now*, February 22, 2009, savannahnow.com/julia-c-muller/2009-2-21/30-year-history-savannah-college-art-and-design (accessed September 19, 2015).

240. Kevin Meredith, "School draws praise, students to downtown," *SMN*, June 14, 1992.

241. Julia Muller, "25 Years of SCAD Highlights," *Savannah Now*, September 28, 2003; "SCAD's impact on Savannah after 25 years," *SMN*, September 28, 2003; Jan Skutch and David Donald, "Settlement eyed as vindication for some, art community's loss," *SMN*, February 18, 1996; Jan Skutch and David Donald, "College's court dates continue in other suits," *SMN*, February 18, 1996; "SCAD vs. School of Visual Arts lawsuit," *Savannah Now*, March 10, 1998, savannahnow.com/stories/031098/LOCscadsvabox.html#.Vf66H5eYF2A (accessed September 20, 2015).

242. Julius C. Muller, "A Thirty Year History of the Savannah College of Art and Design," *Savannah Now*, February 22, 2009, savannahnow.com/julia-c-muller/2009-2-21/30-year-history-savannah-college-art-and-design (accessed September 19, 2015).

243. Jennifer Rose Marino, "SCAD president to wed today," November 23, 2000, *Savannah Now*, savannahnow.com/stories/112300/LOCturkeywedding.shtml#.Vf7P8ZeYF2A (accessed September 20, 2015).

244. Larry Peterson, College thrives; city too," *SMN*, February 22, 2009; Jenel Few, "National Trust recognizes SCAD's civic leadership," *SMN*, May 24, 2003; Adler and Adler, *Savannah Renaissance*, 9, 78.

245. "New Center at SCAD to Be Named for Walter Evans," *Savannah Tribune*, January 27, 2010; Adam Van Bremmer, "SCAD buys building on MLK," *SMN*, December 29, 2011; Chuck Mobley, "Abolitionist's Papers Attract Attention," *SMN*, April 11, 2011.

246. Larry Peterson, "College thrives; city, too," *SMN*, February, 22, 2009; Larry Peterson, "SCAD president looks to school's future," *SMN*, February 22, 2009.

247. John Cheves, "A veteran of city hall politics, Adams becomes mayor today," *SMN*, January 2, 1996; Rousakis interview; Cunningham et al., *Tapping the Power of City Hall*, 249–50.

248. Rousakis interview; Cunningham et al., *Tapping the Power of City Hall*, 249–50.

249. "Summary Report of the Issues Group Task Force of Mayor Susan Weiner," 358; Scott M. Larson, "Anti-crime groups silent at town hall," *SMN*, January 26, 2006; see also Tom Rose, "Feds Arrest City Police Sergeant," *SMN*, April 24, 1992.

250. Bret Bell, "A Tale of Two Responses," *SMN*, December 25, 2005.

251. Michael Homans, "Add Officers, Reorganize City Police, Report Urges," *Savannah Evening Press*, June 20, 1991; Tom Rose, "Mixed Reviews: New Police Precinct System Getting Fair to Good Grade From Community, City," *SMN*, May 13, 1993.

252. Willems, "A Tale of Two Cities," 50–54, 67–68.

253. "The History of the Georgia State Road and Tollway Authority and Its Predecessor Organizations," May 20, 2005, www.georgiatolls.com/assets/docs/copy_history.pdf (accessed December 22, 2014); Sean Horgan, "Talmadge Bridge keeping its name—for now," *SMN*, February 28 and March 1, 2013, savannahnow.com/news/2013-2-28/talmadge-bridge-keeping-its-name-now (accessed December 22, 2014).

Chapter 6: From Susan Weiner to Edna Jackson: 1992–2015

1. John Cheves, "Candidates Plot Early Agendas," *SMN*, November 26, 1995; Michael Homans, "Weiner Upsets Rousakis" *SMN*, November 6, 1991; Richard Fogaley, "Weiner Win Broke Tradition," *SMN*, November 10, 1991; Norman, "Herzoner!"

2. Amy A. Swann, "Woman at Helm of City Ship Finds First Year Stormy," *SMN*, January 24, 1993.

3. John Cheves, "If Mud's Flying, It Must Be Time for an Election," *SMN*, November 6, 1995; "The Trouble With Al," Vertical File, Bull Street Library; Amy A. Swann, "Weiner Earns Mixed, Mostly Positive Marks," *SMN*, January 24, 1993; Jennifer Moroz, "Controversial Husband of Former Mayor Dies," *SMN*, June 7, 2002.

4. "The Trouble With Al," Vertical File, Bull Street Library; William Booth, "Tide Turning in a City Slow to Change," *Washington Post*, January 14, 1996; Jennifer Moroz, "Controversial Husband of Former Mayor Dies," *SMN*, June 7, 2002.

5. Michael Homans, "Council Appoints 31 to Anti-Crime Panel," *SMN*, December 21, 1991; "Crime Control Collaborative: Recommendations to Control Crime in the Community, July 1993," Municipal Archives.

6. Richard Fogaley and Michael Homans, "Weiner Still Opposes Public Funds for Project," *SMN*, November 8, 1991.

7. Ibid.; Amy A. Swann, "Woman at Helm of City Ship Finds First Year Stormy," *SMN*, January 24, 1993.

8. "Summary Report of the Issues Group Task Force of Mayor Susan Weiner June 1, 1992," Municipal Archives, 354, 357, 359, 360, 361.

9. Ibid.; Tom Barton, "Edna Needs a Team," *SMN*, January 4, 2012.

10. John Cheves, "A Veteran of City Hall Politics, Adams Becomes Mayor Today," *SMN*, January 2, 1996.

11. Tom Watson, "Savannah to Get First Black Mayor," *USA Today*, January 2, 1996; William Booth, "Tide Turning in a City Slow to Change," *Washington Post*, January 14, 1996; Amy Swann, "Woman at Helm of City Ship Finds First Year Stormy, *SMN*, January 24, 1993.

12. John Cheves, "We Get to Vote Again," *SMN*, November 8, 1995; Associated Press report, *Rome News Tribune*, December 7, 1995; Tom Watson, "Savannah to Get First Black Mayor," *USA Today*, January 2, 1996; Rousakis interview.

13. "It's Official: Adams Is Still the Next Mayor," *SMN*, December 1, 1995.

14. William Booth, "Is Savannah Ready for Floyd Adams?" *Washington Post*, National Weekly edition, January 22–28, 1996; John Cheves, "Adams Makes History," *SMN*, November 29, 1995; John Cheves, "Working-class Support Played a Big Role in the Victory," *SMN*, November 30, 1995; Jane Fishman, "Adams' Victory Called Boost to African-Americans' Morale," *SMN*, November 30, 1995; "It's Official: Adams Is Still the Next Mayor," *SMN*, December 1, 1995; John Cheves, A Veteran of City Hall Politics, Adams Becomes Mayor Today," *SMN*, January 2, 1996; John Cheves, "'first and foremost, we are Savannahians,'" *SMN*, January 3, 1996; Donald Adderton, "Adams is steering Savannah to new era"; William Booth, "Tide Turning in a City Slow to Change," *Washington Post*, January 14, 1996; Tom Watson, "Savannah to Get First Black Mayor," *USA Today*, January 2, 1996; Tom Barton, "What Savannah owes Floyd Adams," *SMN*, February 5, 2014.

15. William Booth, "Tide Turning in a City Slow to Change," *Washington Post*, January 14, 1996; John Cheves, "A veteran of city hall politics, Adams becomes mayor today," *SMN*, January 2, 1996.

16. Spracher, *Century of History*, 148; "What Makes a Mayor?" Vertical File, Bull Street Library; John Cheves, "A veteran of city hall politics, Adams becomes mayor today," *SMN*, January 2, 1996; Tom Watson, "Savannah to Get First Black Mayor," *USA Today*, January 2, 1996.

17. "The People's Mayor," *SMN*, February 3, 2014.

18. Doug Gross, "Southern Pride on Display at Confederate Memorial Day," *SMN*, April 27, 1998.

19. Kate Wiltrout, "City to Build African-American Monument's Foundation," *SMN*, May 17, 2002.

20. Hardin, "Savannah No Longer a Secret to the World," 68–69; Tony Wilbert, "Tourism attraction," *Savannah News Press*, April 27, 1996; Garner, "Savannah on My Mind," 215–18, 238; Richard Fogaley, "Tourism in the Garden of Good and Gump," *SMN*, June 11, 1995.

21. Daniel Wattenberg, "Midnight in the Garden of Fact and Fiction," 18–23; letter to the editor, *SMN*, February 5, 2014.

22. Tony Wilbert, "Tourist Attraction," *SMN*, April 27, 1996; Garner, "Savannah on My Mind," 215–18, 238; *From Vision to Action: Savannah's Poverty Reduction Initiative*, April 2005, 7–8, 10, Municipal Archives.

23. "How Safe Is Safe?" *SMN*, June 11, 1995; "Toxic Neighbors," *SMN*, June 11, 1995.

24. Cunningham et al., *Tapping the Power of City Hall*, 250.

25. Ed Lightsey, "Reclaiming a Neighborhood," Johnson qtd in, *Georgia Trend*, February 2005, 25; Chatham County–Savannah Metropolitan Planning Commission, *Historic Review*, January 2002, 1–5. The Cuyler-Brownville area is roughly bracketed by Ogeechee Road, Victory Drive, and Montgomery and Anderson streets.

26. Bret Bell, "The Legacy He Painted," *SMN*, December 28, 2003; Bret Bell, "The City According to Adams," *SMN*, January 14, 2003.

27. Berryman, "Oldest City, New Momentum," 81–92; "City of Excellence Awards," 24; "Old and New Join Forces in 'Working Savannah,'" 49–50.

28. Cunningham et al., *Tapping the Power of City Hall*, 256–68; "The SPLOST News," *SMN*, March 29, 2009.

29. Keith Paul, "Busted Trust," *SMN*, September 11, 1997; Ann Hart, "Mistakes of Fallen Cops Teach Lessons," *SMN*, September 10, 2002.

30. Fulford, "Farewell to the Chief," Vertical File, Bull Street Library; "Violence Reduction Plan: A Cooperative Effort to Combat Violence in Savannah, Draft: Dated March 9, 2000," Municipal Archives; Richard Fogaley, "Police Gain Public Allies in Budget Talks," *Savannah Now*, November 12, 1997, savannahnow.com/stories/111297/NWSbudgettalks.html (accessed August 11, 2014).

31. David Firestone, "Slowly and Testily, Savannah Empties," *New York Times*, September 15, 1999.

32. Tom Barton, "What Savannah Owes Floyd Adams," *SMN*, February 5, 2014.

33. Spracher, *Century of History*, 170–71; "Floyd Adams Jr., Mayor City of Savannah Biography," Vertical File, Bull Street Library.

34. Keala Murdock, "Mayor Adams Calls for Diversity in Tour Speeches on Savannah," *SMN*, August 8, 2003.

35. Bret Bell, "The City According to Adams," *SMN*, January 14, 2003.

36. "Savannah Chatham Metropolitan Police," merger document, November 2003, Municipal Archives.

37. Kate Wiltrout, "A Revolving Door in the Mayor's Office," *SMN*, September 15, 2000; Bret Bell, "The City According to Adams," *SMN*, January 14, 2003; Bret Bell, "Otis Johnson Steps into Mayoral Contest," *SMN*, January 28, 2003; Tom Barton, "On Balance,

Adams Can Be Proud of His Eight Years as Mayor," *SMN*, December 14, 2003; Kate Wiltrout, "Mayor listens to heart, wallet," *SMN*, June 11, 2002.

38. Tom Barton, "On Balance, Adams Can Be Proud of His Eight Years as Mayor," *SMN*, December 14, 2003; Bret Bell, "The Legacy He Painted," *SMN*, December 28, 2003.

39. Eric Curl, "Everybody's Mayor," *SMN*, February 2, 2014; Eric Curd, "City Mourns Loss of Its First Black Mayor," *SMN*, February 2, 2014.

40. Swope, "Progress Report: The Mayor's First Year"; Bret Bell, "Otis Johnson Steps into Mayoral Contest," *SMN*, January 28, 2003; "Otis S. Johnson, PhD, Mayor City of Savannah Biography," Vertical File, Bull Street Library.

41. "Analysis of the Risk Factors That Contribute to Youth Violence in Savannah," August 27, 2003, Municipal Archives; Scott M. Larson, "Is Johnson's Next Label Mayor?" *SMN*, October 12, 2003.

42. Russ Bynum, "Genteel Savannah Mayoral Race Heats Up in Final Days," *On Line Athens*, November 11, 2003, onlineathens.com/stories/110103/new_20031101060.shtml (accessed August 2, 2014); Bret Bell, "Otis Johnson Steps into Mayoral Contest," *SMN*, January 28, 2003; editorial, "Johnson for Mayor," *SMN*, November 16, 2003.

43. Scott M. Larson and Bret Bell, "Mayor Johnson," *SMN*, November 26, 2003.

44. Scott M. Larson and Bret Bell, "How Johnson Became Mayor," *SMN*, November 27, 2003.

45. Editorial, *SMN*, November 28, 2003; Scott M. Larson, "Johnson to Fight Poverty, Racism," *SMN*, January 4, 2004; Bret Bell, "In With the New," [*SMN*, n.d.],Vertical File, Bull Street Library.

46. "The Johnson Administration," *SMN*, January 4, 2004; Scott M. Larson, "Johnson to Fight Poverty, Racism," *SMN*, January 4, 2004.

47. Jordan, "Bully Pulpit," 144–49.

48. Cunningham et al., *Tapping the Power of City Hall*, 263–65.

49. Ibid., 260, 262–68; Lesley Conn, "Council to Review Racial Diversity," *SMN*, April 11, 2011; "The Johnson Administration," *SMN*, January 4, 2004; Scott M. Larson, "Johnson to Fight Poverty, Racism," *SMN*, January 4, 2004.

50. Ed Lightsey, "Reclaiming a Neighborhood," Johnson qtd in, *Georgia Trend*, February 2005, 25.

51. Bret Bell, "City Targets Gigantic Southwest Land Grab," *SMN*, November 10, 2004.

52. "Operation: Clean Sweep, A Blight Eradication Plan," November 2004, Municipal Archives; "Savannah's Public Safety Task Force Final Report, May 15, 2005," Municipal Archives.

53. "Two Teens Indicted in Killing of Restaurant Manager," *Savannah Now*, May 13, 2004, savannahnow.com/stories/051304/LOC_indictments.shtml (accessed August 3, 2014); "Second Plea Offer Rejected by Second Man Charged in Connection with Slaying," *Savannah Now*, July 19, 2005, savannahnow.com/stories/071905/3170711.shtml (accessed August 3, 2014); Tom Barton, "City Must Find Ways to Reverse a Criminal 'Youth Movement,'" *SMN*, May 16, 2004; Tom Barton, "Drying Up 'Fountain Of Youth' that Nourishes Crime is a Must," *SMN*, January 15, 2006; *Petty v. The State*, Supreme Court of Georgia, No S07A14338, March 10. 2008.

54. Editorial, *SMN*, May 16, 2004.

55. "Safe Streets–Safe Kids: Improved Community Safety through Aggressive Enforcement and Youth Control," Savannah, June 7, 2005, Municipal Archives; Scott Larson, "Mayor: Fighting Crime Starts at Home," *SMN*, January 8, 2006. "CNT Drug Enforcement Plan," by Dan Flynn, Chief, SCMPD, February 3, 2004, Municipal Archives; "Savannah's Public Safety Task Force Final Report, May 15, 2005," Municipal Archives, 2; Bret Bell, "Mayor to Chief: 'Get angry,'" *SMN*, November 11, 2004. Crime data are

difficult to analyze because reports are by county, by city, by MSA, by crime category, by six-month report, by year-to-date report, by year-to-year, by raw numbers, by rates, by trending data, and so forth.

56. Megan Matteucci, "'I have. . . surpassed all my commitments,'" *SMN,* November 3, 2005; Scot M. Larsen, "From a Crime-obsessed Council, a Quiet, Subdued Reaction," *SMN,* November 3, 2005; "Savannah's Public Safety Task Force Final Report, May 15, 2005," Municipal Archives; Megan Matteucci, "Counter Narcotics Team: A division apart," *SMN,* February 25, 2006.

57. Scott Larson, "Mayor: Fighting Crime Starts at Home," *SMN,* January 8, 2006.

58. Jan Skutch, "Tears as Testimony Starts at Ross Trial," *Savannah Now*, December 8, 2006, savannahnow.com/news/2006–12–8/tears-testimony-starts-ross-trial#.U-SynLGa_04 (accessed August 8, 2014).

59. Scott M. Larson, "Mayor: Crime Efforts Ignored," *SMN,* December 30, 2005; Tom Barton, "Shooting Is Catalyst for Action," *SMN,* January 3, 2006; Megan Matteucci, "Orleans Square Shooting Victim Dies," *SMN,* January 2, 2006; Jan Skutch, "Court Upholds Conviction," *SMN,* June 30, 2009.

60. Tom Barton, "Shooting Is Catalyst for Action," *SMN,* January 3, 2006.

61. Bret Bell, "A Woman Dead, a City Wounded," *SMN,* January 29, 2006.

62. "Robbing the Historic District," *Savannah Now*, December 31, 2005, savannahnow.com/stories/123105/3527685.shtml (accessed August 13, 2014); Bret Bell, "Report Looks at Crime Over Time," *SMN,* May 28, 2006.

63. "Savannah's Public Safety Task Force Final Report, May 15, 2005," Municipal Archives; Megan Matteucci, "I have. . . surpassed all my commitments," *SMN,* November 3, 2005; Megan Matteucci, "Counter Narcotics Team: A Division Apart," *SMN,* February 25, 2006.

64. Megan Matteucci, "About 400 Residents Turn Out for Southside Crime Meeting," *SMN,* August 22, 2006; Megan Matteucci, "20 That's How Many GANGS There are in Chatham County," *SMN,* August 18, 2006; editorial, *SMN,* August 31, 2006.

65. Bret Bell, "A Tale of Two Responses," *SMN,* December 25, 2005; Megan Matteucci, "Police Say Wife of Ardsley Park Victim Not Cooperating," *SMN,* January 31, 2006.

66. "Same Crime Different Attention," *Savannah Now,* December 24, 2005, savannahnow.com/stories/122405/3516723.shtml (accessed August 13, 2014).

67. Bret Bell, "Groups Look for Solutions to Crime in Downtown," *SMN,* December 31, 2005; Bret Bell, "New Groups Tackle Old Challenges," *SMN,* January 14, 2006; Jan Skutch, "Attack Root Causes of Crime, Local Group Urges," *SMN,* January 14, 2006; Bret Bell, "A Woman Dead, a City Wounded," *SMN,* January 29, 2006; Bret Bell, "Chief Calls Crime Rate 'Disquieting,'" *SMN,* January 21, 2006; Scott M. Larsen, "Mayor: Crime Efforts Ignored," *SMN,* December 30, 2005.

68. Scott M. Larsen, "Good Life, But Safe?" *SMN,* September 1, 2006; Bret Bell, "Report Looks at Crime Over Time, *SMN,* May 28, 2006.

69. Jan Skutch, "This Is a Shake-Up Call," *SMN,* April 27, 2006; Eric Williamson, "Declining Numbers Offer Little Comfort," *SMN,* February 22, 2004; Johnson interview.

70. Scott M. Larsen, "Mayor Johnson Returns to Savannah in a Gulfstream Jet," *Savannah Now,* May 16, 2006, savannahnow.com/stories/051606/3887287.shtml (accessed August 20, 2014; editorial, *SMN,* May 20, 2006; Scott M. Larson, "Mayor to Refocus His Attentions," *SMN,* May 20, 2006; Eric Curl, "Mayor, Aldermen Consider City Council Salary Increases at Retreat," *Savannah Now,* February 11, 12, 2014, savannahnow.com/news/2014–2–11/p-nodehl1mayor-aldermen-considering-city-council-salary-increases-p#.U_SiXGNpG8w (accessed August 20, 2014).

71. "No backsliding," *SMN,* September 6, 2009.

72. Scott M. Larson, "From a Crime-Obsessed Council a Quiet, Subdued Reaction," *SMN*, November 3, 2005.

73. Ibid.; Arek Sarkissian II, "Berkow resigns," *SMN*, August 26, 2009; Lesley Conn, "Of love, pain, and other things," *SMN*, August 30, 2009; Jan Skutch, "'Tough cops' after bad guys," *SMN*, August 3, 2009; Lesley Conn and Eric Curl, "Savannah Chatham officials react to chief's resignation," *SMN*, August 26, 2009; "Build on Berkow," *SMN*, August 30, 2009.

74. Swope, "Progress Report: The Mayor's First Year," 52–54; Scott M. Larson, "Comfort Zone Is Close to Home," *SMN*, May 27, 2005.

75. Swope, "Progress Report: The Mayor's First Year," 52–54; Scott M. Larson, "Comfort Zone Is Close to Home," *SMN*, May 27, 2005; Johnson interview.

76. Keber, *Low Land and the High Road*, 122–23; Keber qtd. in Cunningham et al., *Tapping the Power of City Hall*, 267–68.

77. Young, "New Directions, Old Standbys," 45–53, 55; SEDA, www.seda.org/home (accessed June 3, 2014).

78. Young, "New Directions, Old Standbys," 45–53, 55.

79. Ibid.; "Passionate Platform," *SMN*, January 4, 2008.

80. Russ Bynum, "Community Mourns 10 Killed in Refinery Fire, Thanks Heroes," *Spartanburg Herald Journal*, February 24, 2008; Barbara Herring, "City Flags at Half Staff for Sugar Refinery Victims," WSAV-TV, February 23, 2008, www.wsav.com/story/20695789/city-flags-at-half-staff-for-sugar-refinery-victims (accessed August 10, 2014).

81. "Imperial Sugar Tragedy Unfinished Business," *SMN*, February 8, 2013; Larry Peterson, "Imperial Sugar Settles for $6 Million, Admits No Wrongdoing," *Savannah Now*, July 8, 2010, savannahnow.com/news/2010-7-8/imperial-sugar-settles-6-million-admits-no-wrongdoing#.U9vWW7Ga_04 (accessed August 1, 2014).

82. Larry Peterson, "Exec: Yearly Upkeep Shelved" *SMN*, October 26, 2009; Larry Peterson, "Imperial Sugar Settles for $6 million, Admits No Wrongdoing," *Savannah Now*, July 8, 2010, savannahnow.com/news/2010-7-8/imperial-sugar-settles-6-million-admits-no-wrongdoing#.U9vWW7Ga_04 (accessed August 1, 2014); Sean Horgan, "Imperial Sugar: No Prosecution," *SMN*, February 27, 2013.

83. "No Sweeteners," *SMN*, September 30, 2010; Mary Carr Mayle, "Imperial Sugar to Be Sold, " *Savannah Now*, May 2, 2012, savannahnow.com/news/2012-5-2/imperial-sugar-be-sold#.U9v4Y7Ga_04 (accessed August 1, 2014).

84. John Stoehr, "23 Arts Groups Ask for $962,000," *SMN*, August 25, 2006; John Stoehr, "Cultural Affairs Commission's List of Funding Recommendations Suggests Greater Accountability," *SMN*, August 25, 2006; Joel Weickgenant, "Festival Closes on a High Note," *SMN*, April 6, 2008.

85. K. W. Oxnard, "Savannah's Rites of Spring," *SMN*, March 24, 2009.

86. Peter Bart, "Savannah Film Festival Begins Tonight," *Savannah Now*, October 28, 2008, m.savannahnow.com/news/2008-10-25/savannah-film-festival-begins-tonight#gsc.tab=0 (accessed July 5, 2014); Orlando Montoya, "Savannah Film Festival Interviews and Highlights," *SMN*, August 25, 2007.

87. Arek Sarkissian II, "A kid-friendly Irish Frenzy," *SMN*, March 15, 2009.

88. Arek Sarkissian II, "St. Pat's Revelry Has Begun," *SMN*, March 15, 2009; Billy DeYoung, "Savannah Goes Green," *SMN*, March 18, 2009; Dana Clark Felty, "Honoring St. Patrick's Legacy," *SMN*, March 18, 2009; Dana Clark Felty, "Rumor vs. Reality," *SMN*, March 16, 2010. Some sources place the attendance range as 150,000 to 500,000.

89. Mary Carr Mayle, "No Trade Deficit at Ports," *SMN*, August 5, 2007.

90. Mary Carr Mayle and Lauren Mardella, "A Soured Economy Comes Home to Roost in 2008," *SMN*, December 14, 2008.

91. "Citizens' Report," Municipal Archives, 1–5; Lesley Conn, "Mayor: City will Be Bold in Uncertain Times," *SMN*, February 11, 2009.

92. Mary Carr Mayle, "Berkow's Shoes Hard to Fill, Say Business Leaders," *SMN*, August 26, 2009; Arek Sarkissian II, "Berkow Resigns," *SMN*, August 26, 2009; "No Backsliding," *SMN*, September 6, 2009; Arek Sarkissian II, "For Second Time, Lovett Ascends to Acting Chief," *SMN*, September 16, 2009.

93. Arek Sarkissian II, "10 Killings this year unsolved," *SMN*, August 2, 2009.

94. Arek Sarkissian II, "Crime drops in 2009," *SMN*, January 22, 2010.

95. Letter to the editor, "Victorian District Inundated by Crime," *SMN*, October 27, 2009.

96. Lesley Conn, "Finally—Lovett's Official," *SMN*, April 12010; editorial, *SMN*, May 8, 2010.

97. "Assistant Chief Willie Lovett Is Savannah Interim Chief Again," WSAV-TV, September 10, 2009, www.wsav.com/story/20696351/assistant-chief-willie-lovett-is-savannah-interim-chief-again (accessed August 5, 2014); Christy Hutchings, "History in the Making," WTOC-TV, March 31, 2010, April 2, 2010, www.wtoc.com/story/12238542/history-in-the-making (accessed August 5, 2014).

98. Corey Dickstein, "In 2010 Crime Down 15 pct.," *SMN*, January 13, 2011; editorial, *SMM*, January 14, 2011; Constance Cooper, "Metro Police Captains Respond to Crime Wave," *SMN*, September 18, 2011.

99. Constance Cooper, "Heat Wave, Crime Wave," *SMN*, July 10, 2011.

100. Alice Goffman, "This Fugitive Life," *New York Times*, June 1, 2014; editorial, *SMN*, July 27, 2014.

101. Lesley Conn, "Chief Details Crime Causes," *SMN*, September 2, 2011.

102. Lesley Conn, "Downtown Police Station a 'Hellhole,'" *SMN*, July 12, 2011; Lesley Conn, "City: 'Chief Free to Talk,'" *SMN*, July 16, 2011; Lesley Conn, "Savannah City Manager Threatens Police Chief's Job," *Savannah Now*, July 15, 2011, savannahnow.com/news/2011–7–15/savannah-city-manager-threatens-police-chiefs-job#.U-fBn2NpG8w (accessed August 10, 2014).

103. Constance Cooper, "Police Prepare for New Year's Eve," *SMN*, December 30, 2011; Constance Cooper, "Crime up in 2011," *Savannah Now*, January 15, 2012, savannahnow.com/news/2012–1–15/crime-2011#.U_TgYWNpG8w (accessed August 20, 2014).

104. "New Affordable Housing in Savannah." WTOC-TV, October 14, 2011, www.wtoc.com/story/15698631/first-person-moves-into-citys-largest-afforable-housing-community (accessed August 10, 2014); Tuquyen Mach, "Sustainable Fellwood Now Open," WSAV-TV, May 28, 2009, www.wsav.com/story/20699635/sustainable-fellwood-now-open (accessed August 10, 2014); New affordable housing in Savannah," *SMN*, October 7, 2008.

105. Lesley Conn, "Council targets property upkeep," *SMN*, March 5, 2009; Keber, *Low Land and the High Road*, 122–24.

106. Lesley Conn, "Mayor: City Will Be Bold in Uncertain Times," *SMN*, February 11, 2009.

107. Jan Skutch, "Hitch Village Faces demolition with stimulus funding," *SMN*, April 8, 2009, m.savannahnow.com/jan-skutch/2009–4–8/hitch-village-faces-demolition-stimulus-funding#gsc.tab=0 (accessed December 27, 2014); Housing Authority of Savannah, Robert Hitch Village Redevelopment, www.eastsavannahgateway.com/a-neighborhood-by-design/ (accessed December 27, 2014).

108. Lesley Conn, "Neighborhood on the Brink," *SMN*, March 12, 2009; "Mayor Calls for Review of Savannah's Edgemere/Sackville Enforcement," *Savannah Now*,

June 18, 19, 2012, savannahnow.com/news/2012-6-19/mayor-calls-review-savannahs-edgemeresackville-enforcement (accessed December 27, 2014); "2009 Great Savannah Cleanup," WTOC-TV, April 24, May 26, 2009, www.wtoc.com/story/10242951/2009-great-savannah-cleanup (accessed December 27, 2014).

109. Chuck Mobley, "Mercer Statue Ready for the Next Step." *SMN,* April 17, 2009; Johnson interview; Chuck Mobley, "Ellis Square Comes Full Circle," *Savannah Now,* March 11, 12, 2010, savannahnow.com/news/2010-3-11/ellis-square-comes-full-circle (accessed September 23, 2014).

110. "Citizens' Report," 1–5.

111. Linda Sickler, "Zero Tolerance?" *Connect Savannah,* April 3, 2009, www.connectsavannah.com/savannah/zero-tolerance/Content?oid=2130745 (accessed August 10, 2014).

112. Ibid.; "Best laid plans," *SMN,* May 10, 2011.

113. *Passport to Excellence,* Savannah–Chatham County Public School System (SCCPSS), April 13, 2010, internet.savannah.chatham.k12.ga.us/district/AcademicAffairs/PassporttoExcellence/Documents/P2Emaster.pdf (accessed August 24, 2014); Thomas B. Lockamy Jr., "Responding to Your Requests for Change," SCCPSC Superintendent's Column, internet.savannah.chatham.k12.ga.us/district/AcademicAffairs/PassporttoExcellence/Pages/Superintendent%27sColumn.aspx (accessed August 24, 2014).

114. Thomas B. Lockamy Jr., "School Plan Touches Everyone," *SMN,* March 2, 2009; Jenel Few, "Savannah–Chatham Public Schools Superintendent Lockamy Is Here to Stay," *Savannah Now,* August 3, 4, 2014, savannahnow.com/news/2014-8-3/lockamy-here-stay#.U_okVGNpGfc (accessed August 24, 2014); Jenel Few, "Savannah-Chatham Public Schools: From Sore Spot to Hot Spot," *Savannah Now,* April 5, 2014, m.savannahnow.com/news/2014-4-5/savannah-chatham-public-schools-sore-spot-hot-spot#gsc.tab=0 (accessed August 24, 2014).

115. Lesley Conn, "A History of Firsts," *SMN,* December 18, 2011.

116. Tom Barton, "Clouds Over City Hall," *SMN,* April 7, 2010.

117. Editorial, *SMN,* March 27, 2011; Tom Barton, "Merit Should Trump Race," *SMN,* September 9, 2010.

118. Lesley Conn, "A Diverse and Divided City," *SMN,* January 30, 2011.

119. Larry Peterson, "Council's Racial Chasm Still Wide," *SMN,* April 11, 2011.

120. Lesley Conn, "Savannah City Council Considers City Manager's Bond," *Savannah Now,* June 6, 2011, m.savannahnow.com/news/2011-6-17/savannah-city-council-considers-managers-bond#gsc.tab=0 (accessed August 10, 2014); Don Logana, "Small-Toney Offered City Manager Position," WTOC-TV, February 24, 2011, and December 24, 2012, www.wtoc.com/story/14135834/council-votes-unanimously-to-end-city-manager-search (accessed June 4, 2014); Lesley Conn, "Savannah City Council 'toxic . . . but workable,'" *SMN,* February 8, 2011; Lesley Conn, "Rochelle Small-Toney Bonded at $50,000," *Savannah Now,* January 20, 2011, m.savannahnow.com/news/2011-1-20/rochelle-small-toney bonded at 50000#U-j (accessed August 10, 2014); "City Council, Mayor Must Obey Open Records, Meetings Laws," *SMN,* June 19, 2011; Lesley Conn, "Alderman Wants GBI Investigation in Savannah Acting City Manager Leak," *Savannah Now,* January 18, February 2, 2011, savannahnow.com/news/2011-1-18/alderman-wants-gbi-investigation-savannah-acting-city-manager-leak?page=1#.U-j4rmOa_04 (accessed August 10, 2014).

121. "Inaugural Rock 'n' Roll Savannah Marathon Exceeds Economic Impact Projections," Visit Savannah, January 20, 2012, www.visitsavannah.com/press-and-media/press-releases.aspx?prid=7943 (accessed August 24, 2014).

122. Lesley Conn, "A History of Firsts," *SMN*, December 18, 2011.

123. Tom Barton, "New Broom Sweeps Clean," *SMN*, January 8, 2012; Edward Fulford, "Just Call Me 'Snake,'" *SMN*, April 4, 2009; editorial, *SMN*, January 2, 2012; Mary Carr Mayle, "Tourists Boost Economy in 3Q," *SMN*, November 28, 2010.

124. Chuck Mobley, "Mayor Defends His Record," *SMN*, November 28, 2011.

125. Johnson interview.

126. Tom Barton, "Pumped for Mayor's Race," *SMN*, November 21, 2010.

127. Larry Peterson, "Jackson, Felser Lead Polls," *SMN*, October 12, 2011.

128. Tom Barton, "Team Players Wanted," *SMN*, January 4, 2012; Lesley Conn, "Jackson Takes Oath," *SMN*, January 4, 2012; Jackson interview.

129. Leslie Conn, "A Mayor for All," *SMN*, January 1, 2012.

130. "Actions for Jackson," *SMN*, December 7, 2011.

131. Eric Curl, "Savannah Mayor's Stay in Tybee Jail Recognized," *SMN*, December 10, 2014; City of Savannah Council Biographies, savannahga.gov/index.aspx?NID=909 (accessed June 2, 2014); Elect Edna Jackson Mayor, www.ednabjackson.com/ (accessed June 12, 2014).

132. Lesley Conn, "State AG: Council Broke Law," *SMN*, June 17, 2011; Lesley Conn, "Savannah City Manager Rochelle Small-Toney's Travel Reports Violate City Policy," *Savannah Now*, August 19, 2012, savannahnow.com/news/2012–8–19/savannah-city-manager-rochelle-small-toneys-travel-reports-violate-city-policy#.U8aK-7Ga-pg (accessed August 19, 2014); Lesley Conn, "Savannah's Rochelle Small-Toney Hired Deputy City Manager," *Savannah Now*, March 14, 2013, and March 15, 2014, savannahnow.com/news/2013–3–14/savannahs-rochelle-small-toney-hired-deputy-city-manager#.U8bfbrGa-pg (accessed August 14, 2014); Don Logana, "Small-Toney Offered City Manger Position," WTOC-TV, February 24, 2011, and December 24, 2012, www.wtoc.com/story/14135834/council-votes-unanimously-to-end-city-manager-search (accessed August 11, 2014); Meredith Ley, "Shakeup at Savannah City Hall, Rochelle Small-Toney Asked to Resign," WSAV-TV, September 26, 2012, www.wsav.com/story/21208771/shakeup-at-savannah-city-hall-rochelle-small-toney-asked-to-resign (accessed August 14, 2014); Tuquyen Mach, "Rochelle Small-Toney Officially Out as Savannah City Manager," WSAV-TV, October 4, 2012, www.wsav.com/story/21209313/rochelle-small-toney-officially-out-as-savannah-city-manager (accessed August 14, 2014).

133. Jan Skutch and Eric Curl, "Investigation Blasts Former Savannah-Chatham Police Chief, Willie Lovett, *SMN*, December 12, 2013; Independent Review SCMPD "Investigation of Former Savannah-Chatham Former Police Chief Willie Lovett," savannahnow.com/investigation-former-police-chief-willie-lovett (accessed June 11, 2014).

134. Jan Skutch, "Documents: Sexual Harassment Complaint Final Chapter In Lovett's Reign," *Savannah Now*, October 5, 2013, m.savannahnow.com/news/2013–10–5/sexual-harassment-complaint-final-chapter-willie-lovetts-reign#gsc.tab=0 (accessed August 3, 2014); Andrew Davis, "Special Report: Investigating Savannah-Chatham Police Allegations," WSAV-TV, November 20, 2013, and January 1, 2014, www.wsav.com/story/24027296/special-report-investigating-savannah-chatham-police-allegations (accessed August 8, 2014); Jan Skutch, "Former Local Cop Indicted," *SMN*, February 27, 2014; "Former Police Officer Faces Six Months in Prison," *SMN*, November 21, 2014.

135. U.S. District Court, Southern District of Georgia, Savannah Division, *United States of America v. Willie Clinton Lovett, Randall Wayne Roach Aka "Red," Randle Wayne Roach, Jr., Aka "Randy" Kenny Amos Blount Defendants*, filed June 4, 2014 (accessed August 20, 2014).

136. Jan Skutch, "Lovett: Excuse Me from Court," *SMN*, July 15, 2014.

137. Jan Skutch, "Lovett co-defendant: 'I Paid Mr. Lovett Cash,'" *SMN,* June 12, 2014; WTOC-TV staff, "New Federal Indictment Filed Against SCMPD Police Chief Willie Lovett," WTOC, August 6, 2014, www.wtoc.com/story/26218216/new-federal-indictment-filed-against-former-scmpd-police-chief-willie-lovett (accessed August 10, 2014); Don Logana, "Reactions Mixed in Willie Lovett Indictment," WTOC-TV, June 5, July 5, 2014, www.wtoc.com/story/25706791/reactions-mixed-in-willie-lovett-indictment (accessed August 10, 2014).

138. Jim Morekis, "Editor's Note: Where Does Buck Stop in Lovett Case?" *Connect Savannah,* June 10, 2014, www.connectsavannah.com/savannah/lovett-case-the-buck-stops-where/Content?oid=2457933 (accessed August 24, 2014).

139. Marcus Howard, "Acting-chief Tolbert Won't Seek Top Cop Job," *Savannah Now,* October 12, 2013, savannahnow.com/news/2013–10–12/tolbert-won-t-seek-top-cop-job#.U8fnHLGa-pg (accessed August 9, 2014).

140. Editorial, *SMN,* December 22, 2003.

141. Eric Curl, "Mayor Jackson Fashion Activist," *Savannah Now,* April 28, 2014, savannahnow.com/share/blog-post/eric-curl/2014–4–28/mayor-jackson-fashion-activist#.U868ırGa-pg (accessed June 15, 2014); Bill Dawers, "Ambition Pays Off for Savannah Fashion Week 2014," *Savannah Now,* May 5, 6, 2014, savannahnow.com/exchange/2014–5–5/dawers-ambition-pays-savannah-fashoin-week-2014#.U87Bi7Ga-pg (accessed August 1, 2014); see also Fernanda Smith Fraser, "Edna Jackson and Fashion Week," paper in possession of the author.

142. Economic Impact of Savannah Music Festival as per SMF website. http://www.savannahmusicfestival.org/about-smf/advertise-with-smf/ (accessed January 19, 2017).

143. Bill Dawers, "A Quick Look at the Economic Impact of the Savannah Music Festival," *Savannah Now,* April 8, 9, 2009, savannahnow.com/exchange/2013–4–8/quick-look-economic-impact-savannah-music-festival#.U8z7e7Ga-pg (accessed August 1, 2014); Savannah Music Festival, www.savannahmusicfestival.org/ (accessed August 5, 2014); Allison Hersh, "Savannah Music Festival Celebrates Silver Anniversary," *Do Savannah,* March 17, 2014, www.dosavannah.com/article/mon-03172014–1451 (accessed July 22, 2014).

144. Julia Ritchey, "Savannah Tourism Industry Shows Gains, 13 Million Visitors in 2013," *Savannah Now,* June 14, 2013, and June 15, 2014, savannahnow.com/exchange/2014–6–13/savannah-tourism-industry-shows-gains-13-million-visitors-2013#.U9ED2LGa-pg (accessed August 3, 2014); WTOC-TV staff, "Visit Savannah Sees Increase in Tourism," WTOC, June 13, 2014, www.wtoc.com/story/25770569/visit-savannah-sees-increase-in-tourism-numbers (accessed August 2, 2014).

145. Savannah Economic Development Authority Web site. http://www.seda.org/home (accessed January 19, 2017).

146. Mary Carr Mayle and Adam Van Brimmer, "The Local Economy in 2013: A Look Ahead," *Savannah Now,* January 5, 6, 2013, savannahnow.com/exchange/2013–1–5/local-economy-2013-look-ahead#.U8-_D7Ga-pg (accessed August 3, 2014); Adam Van Brimmer, "Job Market Looks Positive for Metro Savannah," *BIS,* January 25, 2013, businessinsavannah.com/bis/2013–1–25/job-market-looks-positive-metro-savannah#.U9EKobGa-pg (accessed August 28, 2014).

147. Bill Dawers, "Tourism Booming But What About Other Things?" *SMN,* June 17, 2014.

148. Mary Carr Mayle, "Largest Cranes to Aid Larger Vessels," *SMN,* June 6, 2013.

149. Georgia Ports Authority, www.gaports.com/ (accessed August 22, 2014).

150. Mary Carr Mayle, "Georgia's Ports See Record-Setting Year: Tonnage, Containers, Auto Units All Post Gains," *SMN,* July 29, 2014.

151. Mary Carr Mayle, "Deepening Continues to Gather Momentum," *SMN*, September 13, 2014; Georgia Ports Authority, www.gaports.com/ (accessed September 1, 2014).

152. Mary Landers, "Harbor's Benefits Debated," *SMN*, December 15, 2010; Georgia Ports Authority, www.gaports.com/ (accessed August 1, 2014). Office of the Governor, "UGA Study: Georgia Ports," gov.georgia.gov/ (accessed 8/1/2014).

153. Don Logana, "Heated Exchange Leads to Altercation between Aldermen." WTOC-TV, May 20, June 29, 2014, www.wtoc.com/story/25654862/heated-exchange-leads-to-altercation-between-aldermen (accessed August 22, 2014); Eric Curl, "Alderman Offers Apology," *SMN*, June 4, 2014.

154. Russ Bynum, "Savannah Fair Shooting: Several Hurt During Violence at Georgia Fair," *Huffington Post*, November 4, 2012, www.huffingtonpost.com/2012/11/04/savannah-fair-shooting_n_2072000.html (accessed August 11, 2014); "Exchange Club Offers Cash Reward to Crimestoppers to Use for Information in Fairground Shooting," *Savannah Now*, November 7, 2012, www.savannahnow.com/crime/2012-11-7/exchange-club-offers-cash-reward-crimestoppers-use-information-fairground-shooting#.U-053mOa_04 (accessed August 11, 2014).

155. Cyreia Sandlin, "SCMPD Detectives Work to Stop Gang Activity," WTOC-TV, December 3, 2012, and January 8, 2013, www.wtoc.com/story/20252094/scmpd-detectives-work-to-stop-gang-activity (accessed August 12, 2014).

156. "Savannah Crime: Rage against Gangs," *SMN*, November 30, 2012.

157. Andrew Davis, "Savannah-Chatham Police Cracking Down on Gangs," WSAV-TV, December 3, 2012, www.wsav.com/story/21213274/savannah-chatham-police-cracking-down-on-gangs December 3 (accessed August 13, 2014).

158. Lynda Figueredo, "Fairground Shooting Suspects Appear in Court," WTOC-TV, January 23, February 8, 2013, www.wtoc.com/story/20663177/fairground-shooting-suspects-in-court-for-preliminary-hearing (accessed August 12, 2014); "Seventeen Defendants Convicted on Federal Charges in Connection with Savannah Anti-Gang Initiative," FBI, August 19, 2013, www.fbi.gov/atlanta/press-releases/2013/seventeen-defendants-convicted-on-federal-charges-in-connection-with-savannah-anti-gang-intitiative (accessed September 2, 2014).

159. "Final Fairgrounds Suspect Indicted," *Connect Savannah*, February 5, 2014, www.connectsavannah.com/savannah/final-fairgrounds-suspect-indicted/Content?oid=2333315 (accessed August 13, 2014); Mary Carr Mayle, "Coastal Empire Fairgrounds for Sale," *Savannah Now*, March 3, 4, 2014, savannahnow.com/exchange/2014-3-3/coastal-empire-fairgrounds-sale#.U-u8U2Oa_04 (accessed August 13, 2014); Eric Curl, "Savannah City Council reverses course, approves $2.9 million fairgrounds purchase," *Savannah Now*, August 5, 6, 2016, http://savannahnow.com/news/2016-8-5/savannah-city-council-reverses-course-approves-29-million-fairgrounds-purchase (accessed January 23, 2017).

160. Tom Barton, "Police Department Needs an Enema," *SMN*, October 5, 2013.

161. Dash Coleman, "Homicide Cases Never Come to an End," *SMN*, July 13, 2014; Jan Skutch, "Man Gets 25 Years in 2013 Slaying," *SMN*, June 6, 2014; "Mayor Edna Jackson Speaks Out on Savannah's Gun Violence," *Savannah Tribune*, July 23, 2014, www.savannahtribune.com/news/2014-7-23/Front_Page/Mayor_Edna_Jackson_Speaks_Out_On_Savannahs_Gun_Vio.html (accessed August 14, 2014); Ta-Nehisi Coates, "Letter to My Son," *The Atlantic*, September 2015; Katie Martin, "Mayor: 'Shootings . . . . Totally Unacceptable,'" *SMN*, July 22, 2014.

162. Dash Coleman, "24 Shot Over Last Month," *SMN*, August 6, 2014; editorial, *SMN*, August 7, 2014.

163. Eric Curl, "Officials Eye Anti-violence Moves," *SMN*, May 19, 2014; Katie Martin, "Mayor: 'Shootings . . . .Totally Unacceptable,'" *SMN*, July 22, 2014.

164. Karson Brandenburg, "Mounted Patrol Unit Celebrates 25 Years," *SMN*, July 23, 2014.

165. Mary Carr Mayle, "Crime Solutions Detailed," *SMN*, July 9, 2014.

166. Julia Ritchey, "Carter's Past a Clue to Future," *SMN*, February 9, 2014; editorial, *SMN*, February 9, 2014.

167. Julia Ritchey, "Project to 'Reboot' Old Power Plant on Savannah's River Street," *Savannah Now*, March 4, 5, 2014, savannahnow.com/exchange/2014-3-4/project-reboot-old-power-plant-savannahs-river-street#.U8_DTrGa-pg (accessed July 15, 2014).

168. Reed Engle, "City Council, Developers Threaten Savannah's Historic Character," *SMN*, July 17, 2014.

169. Marcus E. Howard, "Savannah's Truman Parkway Finished? Almost," *Savannah Now*, February 28, March 1, 2014 savannahnow.com/news/2014-2-28/savannahs-truman-parkway-finished-almost (accessed December 22, 2014); Marcus E. Howard, "UPDATE: Truman Parkway Expansion Open to Traffic," *Savannah Now*, March 13, 14, 2014, savannahnow.com/news/2014-3-13/truman-parkway-expansion-opens-traffic-friday (accessed December 22, 2014).

170. Mary Carr Mayle, "Dulany Industries to Develop Former Tronox Site," *SMN*, July 13, 2014.

171. Eric Curl, "$1.5M for Savannah River Landing Site," *SMN*, May 3, 2014; Julia Ritchey, "Hints of Activity at Savannah River Landings," *Savannah Now*, August 9, 11, 2014, savannahnow.com/news/2014-5-2/settlement-provides-funds-savannah-river-landing#.U-9MoGO8H5c, (accessed August 15, 2014).

172. Eric Curl, "Savannah-Chatham Central Precinct Moving to MLK, 34th," *Savannah Now*, May 29, 30, 2014, savannahnow.com/news/2014-5-29/city-may-buy-property-police-precinct#.U87TL7Ga-ph (accessed August 15, 2014); letter to the editor, *Savannah Herald*, July 13, 2014; Eric Curl, "Plans for Future Trump Historic Past for Savannah's Precinct Project," *Savannah Now*, June 14, 16, 2014, savannahnow.com/news/2014-6-14/plans-future-trump-historic-past-savannahs-police-precinct-project#.U-8wN2O8H5c (accessed August 16, 2014).

173. *I-16 Terminus/MLK Jr. Blvd Flyover Analysis & Concept Development Study*, Georgia Department of Transportation, September 2008, reclaimingoldwestbroad.files.wordpress.com/2014/04/i-16-terminus-mlk-flyover-analysis-concept-development-study.pdf (accessed August 16, 2014).

174. Julia Ritchey, "I-16 Flyover Removal Enters New Phase," *SMN*, April 27, 2014; Arlinda Smith Broady, "The I-16 Flyover: Its End Draws Near," *SMN*, February 21, 2010; *I-16 Terminus/MLK Jr. Blvd Flyover Analysis*, sec. 1: 1; "Restoring the Land Use and Transportation Connection After the I-16 Ramp Removal," 34; letter to the editor, *SMN*, May 22, 2014; Arlinda Smith Broady, "Ideas to Raze I-16 Flyover Revealed," *Savannah Now*, October 12, 2010, savannahnow.com/exchange/2010-10-12/ideas-raze-i-16-flyover-revealed#.U-ypsGNpG8w (accessed August 14, 2014); letter to the editor, *SMN*, May 12, 2014.

175. Eric Curl, "Mayor Lays out Plans for City," *Savannah Now*, February 18, 19, 2014, savannahnow.com/news/2014-2-18/mayor-lays-out-plans-city#.U_nwnmNpGfc (accessed August 24, 2014).

176. Mayor Edna Jackson, "Mayor Jackson—State of the City—February 11, 2015," City of Savannah, February 12, 2015, savannahga.gov/CivicAlerts.aspx?AID=686 (accessed October 8, 2015).

177. Jan Skutch, "Former Savannah-Chatham police chief, Willie Lovett sentenced to 7.5 years in prison," *Savannah Now*, February 6, 7, 2015, savannahnow.com/news/2015-2-6/former-savannah-chatham-police-chief-willie-lovett-sentenced-90-months-prison (accessed October 8, 2015); Eric Curl and Dash Coleman, "UPDATE: Joseph Lumpkin hired as Savannah-Chatham police chief," *Savannah Now*, October 14, 15, 2014, savannahnow.com/news/2014-10-14/alderman-lumpkin-selected-savannah-chatham-police-chief (accessed October 8, 2015); "Mayor Jackson—State of the City—February 11, 2015," City of Savannah, February 12, 2015 savannahga.gov/CivicAlerts.aspx?AID=686 (accessed October 8, 2015).

178. Dash Coleman, "Lumpkin strives to rebuild trust, hope," *SMN*, April 26, 2015; Mayor Edna Jackson, "Mayor Jackson—State of the City—February 11, 2015," City of Savannah, February 12, 2015, savannahga.gov/CivicAlerts.aspx?AID=686 (accessed October 8, 2015).

179. Mark Murphy, "We can do better: It's time to clean the pipes of City Hall," *SMN*, April 12, 2015; Tom Barton, "Stop playing catch and release with criminals," *SMN*, September 13, 2015; Tom Barton, "Healthy laxative for constipated government," *SMN*, September 6, 2015.

180. "And a small child shall lead them," *SMN*, September 10, 2015; Mark Murphy, "Here at home, it's like living in the Wild, Wild West," *SMN*, October 9, 2015.

181. Bill Dawes, "Savannah highlighted at its best—and worst," *SMN*, September 15, 2015.

182. Ibid.; Mary Carr Mayle, "Local Economy Gaining, Growing," *SMN*, June 28, 2015; Katie Martin, "Tourism Having Hot Summer," *SMN*, September 12, 2015.

Conclusion

1. Qtd. by Eric Foner in a review of Edward E. Baptist, *The Half Has Never Been Told: Slavery and the Making of American Capitalism* (New York: Basic Books, 2014), *New York Times Book Review*, October 5, 2014, 21.

2. Byrne, "'Uncle Billy' Sherman Comes to Town," 93–95.

3. Johnson interview.

4. Alexander, *New Jim Crow*, 178–220.

5. U.S. District Court, Southern District of Georgia, *United States of America v. Willie Clinton Lovett . . .*, June 4, 2014.

6. "Gun Violence—A threat to all of us," *SMN*, October 15, 2014; "Vox Populi," *SMN*, October 10, 2014.

7. Erik Curl, "Lumpkin Sworn in as Police Chief," *SMN*, November 11, 2014; Katie Martin, "Savannah's New Chief Settles In," *SMN*, November 11, 2014.

8. Mayor Jackson—State of the City—February 11, 2015, www.savannahga.gov/DocumentCenter/View/6863 (accessed September 2015); City of Savannah, www.savannahga.gov/SPLOST (accessed May 7, 2016).

9. Eric Curl, "Transforming West River Street," *SMN*, October 5, 2014; Tom Barton, "Holy Cow! Don't Get Stuck on One Site," *SMN*, October 5, 2014.

10. U.S. Census Bureau, Savannah, Georgia, Quick Facts, quickfacts.census.gov/qfd/states/13/1369000.html (accessed December 27, 2014).

11. Eric Curl, "Mayor candidates sound off," *SMN*, November 1, 2015; Tom Barton, "Conventional wisdom wrong in city's mayoral race," *SMN*, August 29, 30, 2015, savannahno.com/2015-8-29/convential-wisdom-wrong-citys-mayoral-race (accessed February 14, 2016).

12. Tom Barton, "Conventional wisdom wrong in city's mayoral race, *SMN*, August 29, 30, 1915, savannahno.com/2015-8-29/convential-wisdom-wrong-citys-mayoral-race

(accessed February 16, 2016); Eric Curl, "Six contenders put crime first," *SMN*, October 25, 2015; Eric Curl, "Mayoral candidates sound off, *SMN*, November 1, 2015.

13. Editorial, "DeLoach for change," *SMN*, November 1, 2015; Eric Curl, "Edna Jackson, Eddie DeLoach will square off December 1," *SMN*, November 4, 2015.

14. Dash Coleman, "Homicide rate highest since '91," *SMN*, December 9, 2015; editorial, "A bang up idea," *SMN*, November 24, 2015; Heather MacDonald, "Trying to hide the rise of violent crime, *Wall Street Journal*, December 26–27, 2015.

15. Tom Barton, "Mayor's crime speech: More blah blah blah, *SMN*, November 19, 2015; Tom Barton, "Conventional wisdom wrong in city's mayoral race," *SMN*, August 29, 30, 2015, savannahno.com/2015-8-29/convential-wisdom-wrong-citys-mayoral-race (accessed February 1, 2016).

16. Ad, "127 People . . . Murdered," *SMN*, December 1, 2015.

17. Lou Phelps, "New Mayor for City," *Savannah Business Journal*, December 2, 2015, www.savannahbusinessjournal.com/index-php/news-categories/savannah-2015-municipal-elections.html (accessed February 3, 2016); editorial, "New dawn at City Hall," *SMN*, December 3, 2015.

18. Editorial, "New dawn at City Hall," *SMN*, December 3, 2015.

19. Dash, Coleman, "Officials: Antiviolence program needs, time, patience," *SMN*, June 26, 2016.

20. Ibid.; Brittini Ray, "Chief Lumpkin addresses city violence amid national media attention," *Savannah Now*, May 20, 21, 2016, http://savannahnow.com/news/2016-5-20/chief-lumpkin-addresses-city-violence-amid-national-media-attention (accessed February 1, 2016); Brittini Ray and Will Peebles, "Savannah Area Homicides Fall I 2016," *SMN*, January 11, 2017; Katie Nussbaum, "Savannah visitors spending more money, staying in town longer," *BiS*, June 28, 2016, http://businessinsavannah.com/bis/2016-6-28/savannah-visitors-spending-more-money-staying-town-longer (accessed February 2, 2017).

21. Emma Adler, letter to the editor: "Homeowner Provides Her Home's History, But Tour Guides Ignore It," *SMN*, October 25, 2014.

22. Ron Stodghill, "Savannah, Both Sides," *New York Times*, October 5, 2014.

23. Brittini Ray, "Isle of Hope resident killed during Hurricane Matthew," *SMN*, October 8, 2016; Kelly Quimby, "Chatham County storm recovery costs now top $36 million," *Savannah Now*, January 27, 30, 2017, http://savannahnow.com/hurricane-guide-news/2017-1-27/chatham-county-s-storm-recovery-costs-now-top-36-million (accessed February 3, 2017).

24. "Editorial: 2016 in review: A year of challenge," *Savannah Now*, December 31, 2016, January 1, 2017, http://savannahnow.com/opinion-editorial/2016-12-31/editorial-2016-review-year-challenge (accessed February 2, 2017); Jenel Few, "Savannah-Chatham public schools Superintendent Thomas Lockamy announces retirement, *Savannah Now*, November 9, 10, 2016, http://savannahnow.com/news/2016-11-9/savannah-chatham-public-schools-superintendent-thomas-lockamy-announces-retirement (accessed February 1, 2017); "Editorial: End the discord on the school board," *Savannah Now*, January 23, 24, 2017, http://savannahnow.com/opinion-editorial/2017-1-23/editorial-end-discord-school-board (accessed February 1, 2017); "Thank you, Dr. Lockamy: retiring schools superintend will be missed" *Savannah Now*, November12,13,2016,http://savannahnow.com/opinion-editorial/2016-11-12/thank-you-dr-lockamy-retiring-schools-superintendent-will-be-missed (accessed February 1, 2017).

25. "Editorial: 2016 in review: A year of challenge," *Savannah Now*, December 31, 2016, January 1, 2017, http://savannahnow.com/opinion-editorial/2016-12-31/editorial

-2016-review-year-challenge (accessed February 2, 2017); Eric Curl, "Crime, funding challenges still plague Savannah City Council, *SMN*, January 1, 2017.

26. "Consolidated government an encouraging sign for taxpayers," *Savannah Now*, December 13, 14, 2016, http://savannahnow.com/opinion-editorial/2016–12–13/editorial-consolidated-government-encouraging-sign-taxpayers (accessed February 3, 2017); Eric Curl, "Merger study for Savannah, Chatham eyed for 2017," *Savannah Now*, December 12, 13, 2016, http://savannahnow.com/news/2016–12–12/merger-study-savannah-chatham-eyed-2017 (accessed February 3, 2017).

27. Johnson interview; "Oliver Wendell Holmes Quite," Wisdom Quotes, http://www.wisdomquotes.com/quote/oliver-wendell-holmes-3.html (accessed February 3, 2017).

Select Bibliography

Archival Sources

Bull Street Library, Kaye Kole Genealogy and Local History Room, Savannah. Gamble Collection.

Georgia Historical Society, Savannah. Victor Hugo Bassett Papers; Sarah Alexander Cunningham Collection; Gordon Family Papers; Edith D. Johnston Collection; King and Wilder Family Papers; Meldrim Family Papers; Mercer Family Papers; War Camp Community Service Club Papers; Waring Papers.

Hargrett Rare Book and Manuscript Library, University of Georgia Libraries. Craig Barrow Family Papers; George Wymberley Jones De Renne Family Papers.

David M. Rubenstein Rare Book & Manuscript Library, Duke University. Durham, N.C.: Victor H. Bassett Papers; Gordon Family Papers.

Richard B. Russell Library for Political Research and Studies. University of Georgia Libraries: Prince H. Preston Jr. Papers; Richard B. Russell Papers.

Southern Historical Collection, University of North Carolina, Chapel Hill. Gordon Family Papers, 1810–1968; Alexander and Hillhouse Family Papers, 1758–1976; Ladies' Memorial Association Papers, 1878–1879; Alexander Robert Lawton Papers, 1774–1952; George Anderson Mercer Diary, 1851–1889; Wilder and Anderson Family Papers, 1837–1938.

University of Virginia. Special Collections, Alderman Library. Charlottesville, Georgia leaflet.

Books, Edited Books, Book Chapters

Adler, Lee, and Emma Adler. *Savannah Renaissance.* Charleston: Wyrick & Co., 2003.

Alexander, Michelle. *The New Jim Crow: Mass Incarceration in the Age of Colorblindness.* Rev. ed. New York: New Press, 1912.

Anderson, Sherwood. "Adrift in Georgia: Savannah." In *Literary Savannah,* ed. Patrick Allen, 121–24. Athens, Ga.: Hill Street Press, 1998.

Avary, Myrta Lockett. *Dixie After the War.* New York: Doubleday Page and Co., 1906.

Ayers, Edward L. *The Promise of the New South: Life After Reconstruction.* New York: Oxford University Press, 2007.

Bailey, Anne J., and Walter J. Fraser Jr. *Portraits of Conflict: A Photographic History of Georgia in the Civil War.* Fayetteville: University of Arkansas Press, 1996.

Bartley, Neuman V. *The Creation of Modern Georgia.* Athens: University of Georgia Press, 1990.

———. *History of the New South.* Baton Rouge: Louisiana State University Press, 1995.

Basinger, William Starr. *The Personal Reminiscences of William Starr Basinger: 1827–1910.* [New York: J. G. Basinger, 1936].

Blackmon, Douglas A. *Slavery by Another Name: The Re-enslavement of Black Americans from the Civil War to World War II.* New York: Anchor Books, 2009.

Bowden, Samuel Haygood. *Two Hundred Years of Education; Bicentennial, 1733–1933, Savannah, Chatham County, Georgia.* Richmond, Va.: Dietz Print Co., 1932.

Bragg, William Harris. *De Renne: Three Generations of a Georgia Family.* Savannah: Wormsloe Foundation Publications, 1999.

Brownell, Blaine A. *The Urban Ethos in the South, 1920–1930.* Baton Rouge: Louisiana State University Press, 1975.

———. "The Urban South Comes of Age, 1900–1940." In *The City in Southern History,* ed. Brownell and Goldfield, 123–58.

———, and David R. Goldfield, eds. *The City in Southern History: The Growth of Urban Civilization in the South.* Port Washington, N.Y.: Kennikat Press, 1977.

Brundage, W. Fitzhugh. *Lynching in the New South: Georgia and Virginia, 1880–1930.* Urbana: University of Illinois Press, 1993.

———. "Whispering Consolation to Generations Unborn." In *Warm Ashes: Issues in Southern History at the Dawn of the Twenty-First Century,* ed. Winfred B. Moore Jr., Kyle S. Sinisi, and David H. White, 341–56. Columbia: University of South Carolina Press, 2003.

———. *The Southern Past: A Clash of Race and Memory.* Cambridge, Mass.: Harvard University Press, 2008.

Bryant, Jonathan M. "'We Defy You!' Politics and Violence in Reconstruction Savannah." In *Slavery and Freedom in Savannah,* ed. Harris and Berry, 161–84.

Buchanan, Scott E. "Herman Talmadge (1913–2002)." New Georgia Encyclopedia. September 11, 2014. www.georgiaencyclopedia.org/articles/government-politics/herman-talmadge-1913-2002.

Campbell, Jacqueline Glass. *When Sherman Marched North from the Sea: Resistance on the Confederate Home Front.* Chapel Hill: University of North Carolina Press, 2003.

Capers, Gerald M., Jr. *Biography of a River Town—Memphis: Its Heroic Age.* New Orleans: Hauser-American, 1966.

Carretta, Vincent. "'I began to feel the happiness of liberty, of which I knew nothing before': Eighteenth-Century Black Accounts of the Lowcountry." In *African American Life in the Georgia Lowcountry,* ed. Morgan, 77–102.

Cash, W. J. *The Mind of the South.* New York: Vintage Books, 1991.

Cimbala, Paul A. "'The People Go to Their Work Early and Gladly': Sherman's Reservation and the Freedpeople's Quest for Land." In *Under the Guardianship of the Nation: The Freedmen's Bureau and the Reconstruction of Georgia, 1865–1870.* Athens: University of Georgia Press, 1997.

Clarke, Erskine. *Dwelling Place: A Plantation Epic.* New Haven, Conn.: Yale University Press, 2005.

Cobb, James C. *The Selling of the South: The Southern Crusade for Industrial Development, 1936–1990.* Urbana: University of Illinois Press, 1993.

———. *Redefining Southern Culture: Mind & Identity in the Modern South.* Athens: University of Georgia Press, 1999.

———. *The South and America Since World War II.* New York: Oxford University Press, 2011.

Coffey, Tom. *Only in Savannah: Stories and Insights on Georgia's Mother City.* Savannah: Frederic C. Beil, 1994.

Coleman, Kenneth, ed. *A History of Georgia.* Athens: University of Georgia Press, 1991.

Conway, Alan. *The Reconstruction of Georgia.* Minneapolis: University of Minnesota Press, 1966.

Cope, Tony. *On the Swing Shift: Building Liberty Ships in Savannah.* Annapolis: Naval Institute Press, 2009.

Cunningham, Kiran, Phyllis A. Furdell, and Hannah J. McKinney. *Tapping the Power of City Hall to Build Equitable Communities: 10 City Profiles.* Washington, D.C.: National League of Cities, 2007.

Davis, Townsend. *Weary Feet, Tested Souls: A Guided History to the Civil Rights Movement.* New York: W. W. Norton & Co., 1998.

DeCredico, Mary A. *Patriotism for Profit: Georgia's Urban Entrepreneurs and the Confederate War Effort.* Chapel Hill: University of North Carolina Press, 1990.

Dittmer, John. *Black Georgia in the Progressive Era, 1900–1920.* Champaign: University of Illinois Press, 1980.

Donaldson, Bobby J. "'The Fighting Has Not Been in Vain': African American Intellectuals in Jim Crowe Savannah." In *Slavery and Freedom in Savannah,* ed. Harris and Berry, 185–212.

Dorsey, Allison. "'The Great Cry of Our People Is Land!' Black Settlement and Community Development on Ossabaw Island, Georgia, 1865–1900." In *African American Life in the Georgia Lowcountry,* ed. Morgan, 224–52.

Doyle, Don H. *New Men, New Cities, New South: Atlanta, Nashville, Charleston, Mobile, 1860–1910.* Chapel Hill: University of North Carolina Press, 1990.

Drago, Edmund L. *Black Politicians and Reconstruction in Georgia: A Splendid Failure.* Athens: University of Georgia Press, 1992.

Duncan, Russell. *Freedom's Shore: Tunis Campbell and the Georgia Freedmen.* Athens: University of Georgia Press, 1986.

Edgar, Walter. *South Carolina: A History.* Columbia: University of South Carolina Press, 1998.

Elliott, Stephen. *"Vain is the Help of Man" A Sermon Preached in Christ Church, Savannah on Thursday, September 15, 1864.* Macon: Burke, Boykin & Company, 1864.

Elmore, Charles J. *Richard R. Wright, Sr., at GSIC, 1891–1921: A Protean Force for the Social Uplift and Higher Education of Black Americans.* Savannah: Atlantic Printing Co., 1996.

———. *All That Savannah Jazz: From Brass Bands, Vaudeville, to Rhythm and Blues.* Savannah: Savannah State University, 1999.

———. *Savannah, Georgia.* Charleston: Arcadia Publishing, 2002.

Fallows, James M. *The Water Lords.* New York: Grossman Publishers, 1971.

Finlay, Mark R. "The Postbellum Transition from Agriculture to Industry." In *Slavery and Freedom in Savannah,* ed. Harris and Berry, 188–91.

Foner, Eric. *Forever Free: The Story of Emancipation and Reconstruction.* New York: Alfred A. Knopf, 2005.

Foster, Gaines M. *Ghosts of the Confederacy: Defeat, the Lost Cause, and the Emergence of the New South, 1865–1913.* New York: Oxford University Press, 1987.

Fraser, Walter J., Jr. *Charleston! Charleston! The History of a Southern City.* Columbia: University of South Carolina Press, 1989.

———. *Savannah in the Old South.* Athens: University of Georgia Press, 2003.

———. *Lowcountry Hurricanes.* Athens: University of Georgia Press, 2009.

———. "James Oglethorpe and the Georgia Plan." In *Slavery and Freedom in Savannah,* ed. Harris and Berry, 2–3.

Freeman, Cynthia A. *A History of the Savannah Chapter of the American National Red Cross.* Savannah: Armstrong State College, 1979.

Friend, Craig Thompson, ed. *Southern Masculinity: Perspectives on Manhood in the South Since Reconstruction.* Athens: University of Georgia Press, 2009.

Gamble, Thomas. *Savannah Duels and Duellists 1733–1877.* Spartanburg: Reprint Co., 1974.

Gamble, Thomas, Jr. *A History of the City Government in Savannah from 1790 to 1901, Compiled from Official Records by Thomas Gamble Jr., Secretary to the Mayor Under Direction of the City Council, 1900.* Savannah: n.p., 1901.

Gillespie, Michele. *Free Labor in an Unfree World: White Artisans in Slaveholding Georgia,* 1789-1860. Athens: University of Georgia Press, 2004.

Golay, Michael. *A Ruined Land: The End of the Civil War.* New York: John Wiley & Sons, Inc., 1999.

Goldfield, David R. *Religion, Race and Cities: Interpreting the Urban South.* Baton Rouge: Louisiana State University Press, 1977.

———. *Cotton Fields and Skyscrapers: Southern City and Region.* Baltimore: Johns Hopkins University Press, 1989.

———. *Black, White and Southern: Race Relations and Southern Culture, 1940 to the Present.* Baton Rouge: Louisiana State University Press, 1990.

Gordon, Arthur. *How Sweet It Is: The Story of Dixie Crystals and Savannah Foods.* Savannah: Savannah Foods and Industries, 1992.

Gordon, Asa Hines. *The Georgia Negro.* Ann Arbor, Mich.: Edwards Brothers, Inc., 1937.

Grant, Donald L., and Jonathan Grant, eds. *The Way It Was in the South: The Black Experience in Georgia.* Athens: University of Georgia Press, 2001.

Gratz, Roberta Brandes. *The Living City: How America's Cities Are Being Revitalized by Thinking Small in a Big Way.* New York: Simon and Schuster, 1989.

Grey, Michael. *Hand Me My Travelin' Shoes: In Search of Blind Willie McTell.* Chicago: Chicago Review Press, 2009.

Hall, Clyde W. *One Hundred Years of Educating at Savannah State College.* East Peoria, Ill.: Versa Press, 1991.

Harris, Leslie M., and Daina Ramey Berry, eds. *Slavery and Freedom in Savannah.* Athens: University of Georgia Press, 2014.

Harvey, Harry. "*The Damned Don't Cry.*" In *Literary Savannah,* ed. Patrick Allen, 127–42. Athens, Ga.: Hill Street Press, 1998.

Hepburn, Lawrence R. ed. *Contemporary Georgia.* Athens: University of Georgia, Carl Vinson Institute of Government, 1987.

Hoskins, Charles Lwanga. *The Trouble They Seen: Profiles in the Life of Col. John H. Deveaux, 1848–1909.* [Savannah]: C. L. Hoskins, 1989.

———. *Out of Yamacraw and Beyond: Discovering Black Savannah.* Savannah: Gullah Press, 2002.

———. *W. W. Law and His People: A Timeline and Biographies.* Savannah: Gullah Press, 2013.

Jenkins, Ray. *Blind Vengeance: The Roy Moody Mail Bomb Murders.* Athens: University of Georgia Press, 1997.

Jenkins, Wilbert L. *Seizing the New Day: African Americans in Post–Civil War Charleston.* Bloomington: Indiana University Press, 1998.

Johnson, Charles J. *Mary Telfair: The Life and Legacy of a Nineteenth-Century Woman.* Savannah: Frederic C. Beil Publishers, 2002.

Jones, Charles C., Jr. *History of Savannah, Ga., from its Settlement to the Close of the Eighteenth Century* and *From the Close of the Eighteenth Century* by O. F. Vedder and Frank Weldo. Syracuse, N.Y.: D. Mason & Co., 1890.

Jones, Jacqueline. *Soldiers of Light and Love: Northern Teachers and Georgia Blacks, 1865–1873.* Athens: University of Georgia Press, 1992.

———. *Saving Savannah: The City and the Civil War.* New York: Alfred A. Knopf, 2008.

———. "A Spirit of Great Enterprise: The African American Challenge to the Confederate Project in Civil War-Era Savannah." In *African American Life in the Georgia Lowcountry,* ed. Morgan, 188–223.

Keber, Martha L. *Low Land and the High Road.* Savannah: Department of Cultural Affairs and Leisure Services, 2008.

———. *Ebb and Flow.* Savannah: Department of Cultural Affairs and Leisure Services, 2011.

Kelly, V. E. *A Short History of Skidaway Island.* Privately published by the author, 1980.

Kole, Kaye. *The Minis Family of Georgia, 1733–1992.* Savannah: Georgia Historical Society, 1992.

Larsen, Lawrence H. *The Rise of the Urban South.* Lexington: University Press of Kentucky, 1985.

Lawrence, Alexander A. *A Present for Mr. Lincoln: The Story of Savannah from Secession to Sherman.* Macon, Ga.: Ardivan Press, 1961.

Lee, F. D. and J. L. Agnew. *Historical Record of the City of Savannah.* Savannah: J. H. Estill, 1869.

Lees, Gene. *Portrait of Johnny: The Life of John Herndon Mercer.* New York: Hal Leonard Publishers, 2004.

Litwack, Leon. *Been in the Storm So Long: The Aftermath of Slavery.* New York: Vintage Books, 1980.

Manis, Andrew M. *Macon Black and White: An Unutterable Separation in the American Century.* Macon: Mercer University Press, 2004.

McFeely, William S. *Yankee Stepfather: General O. O. Howard and the Freedmen.* New Haven, Conn.: Yale University Press, 1968.

McLaughlin, Vance. *Police and the Use of Force: The Savannah Study.* Westport, Conn.: Praeger, 1992.

Miller, William D. *Memphis during the Progressive Era, 1900–1917.* Memphis: Memphis State University Press, 1957.

Mixon, Gregory. "Black Militia Units in Postbellum Georgia." In *Slavery and Freedom in Savannah,* ed. Harris and Berry, 193–94.

Mohr, Raymond A. *On the Threshold of Freedom: Masters and Slaves in Civil War Georgia.* Athens: University of Georgia Press, 1986.

Moore, James Tice. "The Historical Context for "Redeemers Reconsidered." In *Origins of the New South Fifty Years Later: The Continuing Influence of a Historical Classic,* ed. John B. Boles and Bethany Johnson, 131–43. Baton Rouge: Louisiana State University Press, 2003.

Moore, Winfred B., Jr. and Kyle S. Sinisi, and David H. White, Jr., eds. *Warm Ashes: Issues in Southern History at the Dawn of the Twenty-First Century.* Columbia: University of South Carolina Press, 2003.

Morgan, Philip. "Lowcountry Georgia and the Early Modern Atlantic World, 1733–ca. 1820." In *African American Life in the Georgia Lowcountry,* ed. Morgan, 1–12 and 13–47.

———, ed. *African American Life in the Georgia Lowcountry: The Atlantic World and the Gullah Geechee.* Athens: University of Georgia Press, 2010.

Myers, Robert Manson, ed. *The Children of Pride: A True Story of Georgia and the Civil War.* New Haven, Conn.: Yale University Press, 1972.

Novotny, Patrick. *This Georgia Rising: Education, Civil Rights, and the Politics of Change in Georgia in the 1940s.* Macon, Ga.: Mercer University Press, 2007.

Parramore, Thomas C., with Peter C. Stewart and Tommy L. Bogger. *Norfolk: The First Four Centuries.* Charlottesville: University Press of Virginia, 1994.

Piechocinski, Elizabeth Carpenter. *Men of Iron, Men of Stone, Feet of Clay.* Savannah: Oglethorpe Press, 2006.

Powers, Bernard E. *Black Charlestonians: A Social History, 1822–1885.* Fayetteville: University of Arkansas Press, 1999.

Rabinowitz, Howard N. "Continuity and Change." In *The City in Southern History,* ed. Brownell and Goldfield, 92–122.

———.ed. *Southern Black Leaders of the Reconstruction Era.* Urbana: University of Illinois Press, 1982.

———. *The First New South, 1865–1920.* Arlington Heights, Ill.: Harlan Davidson, Inc., 1992.

Reed, John Shelton. *The Enduring South: Subcultural Persistence in Mass Society.* Chapel Hill: University of North Carolina Press, 1986.

Reid, Whitelaw. *After the War: A Tour of the Southern States, 1865–1866.* New York: Harper Torchbooks, 1965.

Reidy, Joseph P. "Aaron A. Bradley: Voice of Black Labor in the Georgia Lowcountry." In *Southern Black Leaders of the Reconstruction Era,* ed. Howard N. Rabinowitz, 281–308. Urbana: University of Illinois Press, 1982.

Rubin, Saul Jacob. *Third to None: The Saga of Savannah Jewry, 1733–1983.* Savannah: S. J. Rubin, 1983.

Russell, Preston and Barbara Hines. *Savannah: A History of Her People Since 1733.* Savannah: Frederic C. Beil, 1992.

Savannah Unit, Georgia Writers' Project, Work Projects Administration. *Drums and Shadows: Survival Studies among the Georgia Coastal Negroes.* Photographs by Muriel and Malcolm Bell Jr. Athens: University of Georgia Press, 1940.

Schuyler, Larraine Gates. *The Weight of Their Votes: Southern Women and Political Leverage in the 1920s.* Chapel Hill: University of North Carolina Press, 2006.

Shadgett, Olive Hall. *The Republican Party in Georgia: From Reconstruction through 1900.* Athens: University of Georgia Press, 2010.

Sheehy, Barry, and Cindy Wallace with Vaughnette Goode-Walker. *Savannah: Immortal City.* Austin: Emerald Book Co., 2011.

Sholes, A. E. *Chronological History of Savannah: From its settlement by Oglethorpe down to December 31, 1899, together with a complete record of the city and county, and Savannah's roll of honor.* Savannah: Morning News Press, 1900.

Shryock, Richard H., ed. *Letters of Richard D. Arnold, M.D., 1808-1876.* New York: Ames Press, 1929.

Sies, Mary Corbin, and Christopher Silver, eds. *Planning the Twentieth-Century American City.* Baltimore: Johns Hopkins University Press, 1996.

Simms, James M. *The First Colored Baptist Church in North America: Constituted at Savannah, Georgia, January 20 A.D. 1788, with Biographical Sketches of the Pastors.* New York: Negro Universities Press, 1969.

Smith, Anna Habersham Wright, ed. *A Savannah Family 1830–1901.* Milledgeville, Ga.: Boyd Publishing, 1999.

Social Register Association. *Social Register: Richmond, North Carolina, Charleston, Savannah, Augusta, Atlanta, 1908.* New York: Social Register Association, 1907.

Spracher, Luciana M. *Birth of City Hall, 1903-1906, Savannah City Hall Centennial, 1906-2006.* Savannah: City of Savannah Research Library & Municipal Archives, January 2006.

———. *A Century of History: Savannah City Hall Centennial, 1906–2006.* Savannah: City of Savannah, Research Library and Municipal Archives, 2006.

Taylor, Karen. "Reconstructing Men in Savannah, Georgia, 1865–1876." In *Southern Masculinity,* ed. Friend, 1–24.

Taylor, Susie King. *Reminiscences of my Life in Camp with the 33rd U.S. Colored Troops, Late 1st South Carolina Volunteers, A Black Woman's Civil War Memoirs.* Ed. Patricia W. Romero. Princeton, N.J.: Markus Wiener Publishing, Inc., 1992.

Tindall, George B. *The Emergence of the New South, 1913–1945.* Baton Rouge: Louisiana State University Press, 1967.

Trowbridge, J. T. *The South: A Tour of Its Battle-fields and Ruined Cities.* New York: Arno Press and New York Times, 1969.

Tuck, Stephen G. N. *Beyond Atlanta: The Struggle for Racial Equality in Georgia, 1940–1980.* Athens: University of Georgia Press, 2003.

———. *We Ain't What We Ought to Be: The Black Freedom Struggle from Emancipation to Obama.* Cambridge, Mass.: Harvard University Press, 2014.

Turner, Jeffrey A. *Sitting In and Speaking Out: Student Movements in the American South, 1960–1970.* Athens: University of Georgia Press, 2010.

Werthington, Mark V. "The Savannah Negro Laborers' Strike of 1891." In *Southern Workers and Their Unions, 1880–1975,* ed. Merle Reed, Leslie S. Hough, and Gary M. Finke, 4–21. Westport, Conn.: Greenwood Press, 1981.

Wilkerson, Isabel. *The Warmth of Other Suns: The Epic Story of America's Great Migration.* New York: Vintage Books, 2011.

Woodward, C. Vann. *Origins of the New South, 1877–1913.* Baton Rouge: Louisiana State University Press, 2006.

Wyatt-Brown, Bertram. "C. Van Woodward and the Confessions of a 'Continuitarian.'" In *Origins of the New South Fifty Years Later: The Continuing Influence of a Historical Classic,* ed. John B. Boles and Bethany Johnson, 294–305. Baton Rouge: Louisiana State University Press, 2003.

Zinn, Howard. A *People's History of the United States.* New York: Harper Perennial, 2005.

Journal and Magazine Articles

Abbott, Richard H. "The Republican Party Press in Reconstruction Georgia, 1867–1874." *Journal of Southern History* 61, no. 4 (November 1995): 725–60.

Adams, Samuel Hopkins. "Guardians of Public Health." *McClure's Magazine* 31 (July 1908): 241–52.

Bacote, Clarence A. "Some Aspects of Negro Life in Georgia, 1880–1908." *Journal of Negro History* 43 (1958): 186–213.

———. "Negro Proscriptions, Protests, and Proposed Solutions in Georgia, 1880–1908." *Journal of Southern History* 25, no. 4 (November 1959): 471–98.

Ball, S. Mays. "Prohibition in Georgia: Its Failure to Prevent Drinking In Atlanta And Other Cities." *Putnam's,* March 1909, 694–701.

Basso, Hamilton. "Savannah and the Golden Isles." *Holiday* 10 (December 1951): 44–57, 169, 171.

Bell, Karen B. "'The Ogeechee Troubles': Federal Land Restoration and the 'Lived Realities' of Temporary Proprietors, 1865–1868." *Georgia Historical Quarterly* 85, no. 3 (Fall 2001): 308–23.

Berger, Homer H. "Sherman's Occupation of Savannah: Two Letters." *Georgia Historical Quarterly* 50, no. 1 (March 1966): 109–15.

Bernd, Joseph L. "White Supremacy and the Disenfranchisement of Blacks in Georgia, 1946." *Georgia Historical Quarterly* 66, no. 4 (Winter 1982): 492–513.

Berryman, Anne. "Oldest City, New Momentum—Everything's on the Rise with Deeper Harbor, Hutchinson Island Looming in the Future." *Georgia Trend,* October 1998, 81–92.

Blassingame, John W. "Before the Ghetto: The Making of the Black Community in Savannah, Georgia, 1865–1880." *Journal of Social History* 6 (Summer 1973): 463–88.

Byrne, William A. "'Uncle Billy' Sherman Comes to Town: The Free Winter of Black Savannah." *Georgia Historical Quarterly* 79, no. 1 (Spring 1995): 91–116.

Campbell, Walter E. "Profit, Prejudice, and Protest: Utility Competition and the Generation of Jim Crow Streetcars in Savannah, 1905–1907." *Georgia Historical Quarterly* 70, no. 2 (Summer 1986): 197–231.

Cimbala, Paul A. "The Freedmen's Bureau, the Freedmen, and Sherman's Grant in Reconstruction Georgia, 1865–1867." *Journal of Southern History* 55, no. 4 (November 1989): 597–632.

"City of Excellence Awards." *Georgia Trend,* February 2000, 24.

Coulter, E. Merton, ed. "A Visit to Savannah, 1892." *Georgia Historical Quarterly* 50, no. 1 (March 1966): 100–104.

Davidson, Carla. "Savannah's Amazing Grace." *American Heritage* 40, no. 1 (February 1989): 32, 34.

Denmark, Lisa L. "'At the Midnight Hour': Economic Dilemmas and Harsh Realities in Post–Civil War Savannah." *Georgia Historical Quarterly* 90, no. 2 (Fall 2006): 350–90.

Dennis, Landt, and Lisl Dennis. "Savannah: The South's Greatest Comeback." *Travel,* July 1974, 26–31.

Dick, Susan E., and Mandi D. Johnson. "The Smell of Money: The Pulp and Paper-Making Industry in Savannah, 1931–1947." *Georgia Historical Quarterly* 84, no. 2 (Summer 2000): 308–23.

Drago, Edmund L. "Georgia's First Black Voter Registrars during Reconstruction." *Georgia Historical Quarterly* 78, no. 3 (Fall 1994): 760–93.

Elmore, Bartow. "Hydrology and Residential Segregation in the Postwar South: An Environmental History of Atlanta, 1865–1895." *Georgia Historical Quarterly* 94, no. 1 (Spring 2010): 30–61.

Elmore, Charles J. "Black Medical Pioneers in Savannah, 1892–1909: Cornelius McKane and Alice Woodby McKane." *Georgia Historical Quarterly* 88, no. 2 (Summer 2004): 179–96.

Farley, M. Foster. "The Mighty Monarch of the South: Yellow Fever in Charleston and Savannah." *Georgia Review* 27 (Spring 1973): 56–70.

Farmer-Kaiser, Mary. "'Are they not in some sorts vagrants?' Gender and the Efforts of the Freedmen's Bureau to Combat Vagrancy in the Reconstruction South." *Georgia Historical Quarterly* 88, no. 4 (Spring 2004): 25–49.

Ford, Gary. "Seeing the New in Old Savannah." *Southern Living,* July 1985, 20–22.

Garner, Dwight. "Savannah on My Mind." *Harper's Bazaar,* March 1995, 215–18, 238.

Gatell, Frank Otto, ed. "A Yankee Views the Agony of Savannah." *Georgia Historical Quarterly* 43, no. 4 (December 1959): 428–31.

Goldfield, David R. "The Business of Health Planning: Disease Prevention in the Old South." *Journal of Southern History* 42, no. 4 (November 1976): 557–70.

Hanchett, Thomas W. "John Nolen and the Planning of Daffin Park, 1906–1909." *Georgia Historical Quarterly* 78, no. 4 (Winter 1994): 810–27.

Hardin, Marie. "Georgia No Longer a Secret to the World." *Georgia Trend,* April 1999, 68–69.

Hargis, Peggy G. "For the Love of Place: Paternalism and Patronage in the Georgia Lowcountry, 1865–1898." *Journal of Southern History* 70, no. 4 (November 2004): 825–64.

Hunt, Monica. "Organized Labor along Savannah's Waterfront: Mutual Cooperation among Black and White Longshoremen, 1865–1894." *Georgia Historical Quarterly* 92, no. 2 (Summer 2008): 177–99.

Jordan, Michael. "The Bully Pulpit." *The South Magazine,* August–September 2007, 144–49.

Kalmar, Karen L. "Southern Black Elites and the New Deal: A Case Study of Savannah, Georgia." *Georgia Historical Quarterly* 65, no. 4 (Winter 1981): 341–55.

King, Spencer B. Jr., ed. "Fanny Cohen's Journal of Sherman's Occupation of Savannah." *Georgia Historical Quarterly* 41 (December 1957): 407–16.

Kollock, Susan M., ed. "Letters of the Kollock and Allied Families, 1826–1884, Part V." *Georgia Historical Quarterly* 34, no. 4 (December 1950): 313–21.

———. "Letters of the Kollock and Allied Families, 1826–1884, Part VI." *Georgia Historical Quarterly* 35, no. 1 (March 1951): 60–75, 222–57.

Kreuzwieser, Mark. "Raising the Curtain." *Savannah Magazine,* May–June, 1996, 32–35, 60.

Lightsey, Ed, "Reclaiming a Neighborhood." *Georgia Trend*, February 2005, 22-25.

Mahaffey, Joseph H. "Carl Schurz's Letters from the South." *Georgia Historical Quarterly* 35, no. 3 (September 1951): 222–57.

Matthews, John M. "Negro Republicans in the Reconstruction of Georgia." *Georgia Historical Quarterly* 60 (Summer 1976): 145–64.

———. "Black Newspapermen and the Black Community in Georgia, 1890–1930." *Georgia Historical Quarterly* 68, no. 3 (Fall 1984): 356–81.

Meier, August, and Elliott Rudwick. "The Boycott Movement Against Jim Crow: Streetcars in the South, 1900–1906." *Journal of American History* 55, no. 4 (March 1969): 756–75.

Moore, James Tice. "Redeemers Reconsidered: Change and Continuity in the Democratic South," *Journal of Southern History* 44, no. 3 (August 1978): 357–78.

Moseley, Charlton, and Frederick Brogdon. "A Lynching in Statesboro: The Story of Paul Reed and Will Cato." *Georgia Historical Quarterly* 65, no. 2 (Summer 1981): 104–18.

Norman, Tyler. "Herzoner!" *Savannah Magazine,* January–February, 1992, 28–30.

"Old and New Join Forces in 'Working Savannah,'" *Georgia Trend,* February 2000, 49–50.

Perkins, Robert Donald. "Oberlin M. Carter and the Savannah River Swindle of 1898." *Georgia Historical Quarterly* 94, no. 2 (Summer 2010): 153–78.

Pressly, Paul M. "Educating the Daughters of Savannah's Elite: The Pape School, the Girl Scouts, and the Progressive Movement." *Georgia Historical Quarterly* 80, no. 2 (Summer 1996): 246–75.

Rabinowitz, Howard N. "Black Teachers in the Negro Schools of the Urban South, 1865–1890." *Journal of Southern History* 40, no. 4 (November 1974): 565–94.

———. "Southern Race Relations, 1865–1890." *Journal of Southern History* 63 (September 1976): 325–50.

Rice, Bradley R. "Urbanization, 'Atlanta-ization,' and Suburbanization: Three Themes for the Urban History of Twentieth-Century Georgia." *Georgia Historical Quarterly* 68, no. 1 (Spring 1984): 40–59.

Simms, Moody L. "A Comment on Savannah in 1866." *Georgia Historical Quarterly* 50 (December 1966): 459–60.

Smith, George Winston. "Cotton from Savannah in 1865." *Journal of Southern History* 21, no. 4 (November 1955): 495–512.

Smith, T. Lynn. "The Redistribution of the Negro Population." *Journal of Negro History* 51, no. 3 (July 1966): 155–73.

Stewart, Dorothy Houseal. "Survival of the Fittest: William Morrill Wadley and the Central of Georgia Railroad's Coming of Age, 1866–1882." *Georgia Historical Quarterly* 78, no. 1 (Spring 1994): 48–65.
Swope, Brad. "Progress Report: The Mayor's First Year." *Savannah Magazine,* January–February 2005, 50–55.
Talmadge, John E. "Savannah's Yankee Newspapers." *Georgia Review* 12 (Spring 1958): 66–73.
Tuck, Stephen. "A City Too Dignified to Hate: Civic Pride, Civil Rights, and Savannah in Comparative Perspective." *Georgia Historical Quarterly* 79, no. 3 (Fall 1995): 539–59.
Veasey, Ashley. "Liberty Shipyards: The Role of Savannah and Brunswick in the Allied Victory, 1941–1945." *Georgia Historical Quarterly* 93, no. 2 (Summer 2009): 159–81.
Waring, Martha Gallaudet. "The Gay Nineties in Savannah: Notes On The 'Fin De Siècle' And Its Ways." *Georgia Historical Quarterly* 18 (December 1934): 364–77.
———. "The Striving 'Seventies in Savannah." *Georgia Historical Quarterly* 20, no. 2 (June 1936): 154–71.
———, ed. "Charles Seton Henry Hardee's Recollections of Old Savannah." *Georgia Historical Quarterly* 13 (March 1929): 13–49.
Waring, Thomas P. "Savannah of the 1870s." *Georgia Historical Quarterly* 20 (1936): 52–64.
Wattenberg, Daniel, "Midnight in the Garden of Fact and Fiction." *Weekly Standard,* December 30, 1996–January 6, 1997, 18–23.
Westwood, Howard C. "Sherman Marched—and Proclaimed 'Land for the Landless.'" *South Carolina Historical Magazine* 85, no. 1 (January 1984): 33–50.
Willems, David M. "A Tale of Two Cities." *Savannah Magazine* 3 (January–February, 1992): 50–53, 67–68.
Young, Ben. "New Directions, Old Standbys." *Georgia Trend,* April 2005, 45–55.

Theses and Dissertations

Acosta, Rubin A. "Union Station: Architecture and the Gateway in the South." MFA thesis, Savannah's College of Art and Design, 2010.
Bacote, Clarence A. "The Negro in Georgia Politics, 1880–1908." PhD diss., University of Chicago, 1955.
Biegert, Melissa Ann Langley. "Woman Scout: The Empowerment of Juliette Gordon Low, 1860–1927." PhD diss., University of Texas at Austin, 1998.
Butler, Todd L. "The Vicious Circle of Training and Employment: Black Employment in Defense Industries in Georgia, 1941–1945." MA thesis, University of Georgia, 1985.
Carnes, Lon Melson. "The Georgia Deepwater Ports and Their Role in the Economy of the State." PhD diss., Georgia State University, 1971.
Cooper, Neloweze Williams. "The History of Public Library Service to Negroes in Savannah, Georgia." MS thesis, Atlanta University, 1960.
Denmark, Lisa Louise. "'At the Midnight Hour': Optimism and Disillusionment in Savannah, 1865–1880." PhD diss., University of South Carolina, 2004.
Gessel, Elizabeth Anne. "Nowhere But Heaven: Savannah, Georgia during the Era of the First Great Migration." PhD diss., University of California, Berkeley, 2003.
Goldberg, David J. "The Administration of Herman Myers as Mayor of Savannah, Georgia, 1895–1897 and 1899–1907." MA thesis, University of North Carolina, Chapel Hill, 1978.
Kalmar, Karen L. "Savannah and the New Deal, 1932–1939: A Case Study." MA thesis, University of Georgia, 1970.
Matthews, John Michael. "Studies in Race Relations in Georgia, 1890–1930." PhD diss., Duke University, 1970.

Murphy, Blair Lynne. "'A Right to Ride': African American Citizenship, Identity, and the Protest Over Jim Crow Transportation." PhD diss., Duke University, 2003.

Overstreet, Robert Lane. "The History of the Savannah Theater, 1865–1906." PhD diss., Louisiana State College and Agricultural and Mechanical College, 1970.

Owens, James Leggette. "The Negro in Georgia During Reconstruction, 1864–1872: A Social History." PhD diss., University of Georgia, 1975.

Patton, June Odessa. "Major Richard Robert Wright, Sr., and Black Higher Education in Georgia, 1880–1920." PhD diss., University of Chicago, 1980.

Perdue, Robert Eugene. "The Negro in Savannah, 1865–1900." PhD diss., University of Georgia, 1971.

Said, Asad Abdelkarim. "Factors Contributing to the Success of Historic Preservation and Restoration in Four Historic American Cities." PhD diss., Texas A&M University, 1987.

Sineath, Mary Shannon. "Passing Through a Crucible: Savannah's 'Better Class' of Blacks During the Progressive Era, 1897–1917." MA thesis, Georgia Southern University, 1998.

Smith, Frances. "Black Militia in Savannah." MA thesis, Georgia Southern College, 1981.

Thompson, Larry James. "Progressive Education and the Savannah Public School System." EdD diss., University of Georgia, 1986.

Turner, Jeffery Alan. "Agitation and Accommodation in a Southern Black Newspaper: The Savannah Tribune, 1886–1915." MA thesis, University of Georgia, 1993.

Wingo, Horace Calvin. "Race Relations in Georgia, 1872–1908." PhD diss., University of Georgia, 1969.

Interviews

Floyd Adams Jr. by Kieran W. Taylor, August 16, 2002. Southern Oral History Program Collection, Manuscripts Department, Southern Historical Collection.

Mercedes Wright Arnold by Walter J. Fraser Jr. and Esther Mallard, June 14, 1990. Special Collections, Zach S. Henderson Library, Georgia Southern University.

Leroy Beavers by Kieran W. Taylor, August 2, 2002. Southern Oral History Program Collection, Manuscripts Department, Southern Historical Collection.

Raleigh D. Bynes by Kieran W. Taylor, August 6, 2002. Southern Oral History Program Collection, Manuscripts Department, Southern Historical Collection.

Curtis Cooper by Esther Mallard, n.d. Special Collections, Zach S. Henderson Library, Georgia Southern University.

Charles Elmore by Kieran W. Taylor, August 9, 2002. Southern Oral History Program Collection, Manuscripts Department, Southern Historical Collection.

William Fonvielle by Kieran W. Taylor, August 2, 2002. Southern Oral History Program Collection, Manuscripts Department, Southern Historical Collection.

Eugene Gadsden by Walter J. Fraser Jr., June 1990. Special Collections, Zach S. Henderson Library, Georgia Southern University.

Mayor Edna Jackson by Walter J. Fraser Jr. and J. Lynn Wolfe, December 2014. Interview to be deposited with Special Collections, Zach S. Henderson Library, Georgia Southern University.

Mayor Otis S. Johnson by Walter J. Fraser Jr. and J. Lynn Wolfe, November 6, 2014. Interview to be deposited with Special Collections, Zach S. Henderson Library, Georgia Southern University.

Mayor J. C. Lewis by Walter J. Fraser Jr. and Esther Mallard, December 14, 1988, and May 23, 1990. Special Collections, Zach S. Henderson Library, Georgia Southern University.

Mayor Malcolm Maclean by Walter J. Fraser Jr., May 16 and 12, 1990. Special Collections, Zach S. Henderson Library, Georgia Southern University.

Mayor John J. Rousakis by Walter J. Fraser Jr., July 17, 1990. Special Collections, Zach S. Henderson Library, Georgia Southern University.

Herman Talmadge. "Oral history interview with Herman Talmadge, 1985 September 4." Georgia's Political Heritage Program oral history interviews. Annie Belle Weaver Special Collections, Irvine Sullivan Ingram Library, University of West Georgia, dlg.galileo.usg.edu/uwg/phc/do:talmadge1 (accessed October 1, 2014).

Herman Talmadge. "Herman Talmadge comments on the Three Governor's Controversy," published November 7, 2007. https://www.youtube.com/watch?v=8Zgc_7QypHo, (accessed January 20, 2017).

John A. White by Kieran W. Taylor, August 8, 2002. Southern Oral History Program Collection, Manuscripts Department, Southern Historical Collection.

Public Reports, Government Documents, and Conference Presentations

"Analysis of the Risk Factors That Contribute to Youth Violence in Savannah." August 27, 2003. City of Savannah, Research Library & Municipal Archives.

Annual Message of the Mayor, 1925.

Annual Message to City Council of Hon. Paul E. Seabrook, Mayor, December 31, 1923.

Annual Message to City Council of Honorable Wallace J Pierpont Mayor, December 31, 1917.

Annual Report of Rufus E. Lester, Mayor of the City of Savannah for the Year Ending December 31, 1886 to which is added the Treasurer's Report, and Reports of the Different Departments. Savannah: Savannah Times Steam Printing House, 1887.

Annual Report of Rufus E. Lester, Mayor of the City of Savannah for the Year Ending December 31, 1888 to which is added the Treasurer's Report, and Reports of the Different Departments. Savannah: Morning News Print, 1889.

Annual Report of the Mayor of Savannah, Georgia to the Board of Aldermen for the Year 1948, 1951, 1953.

Bell, Malcolm, Jr. "Isundiga." Paper presented at Madeira Club, Savannah, November 25, 1975. Madeira Club Files, Georgia Historical Society.

Brewer, Donald D. "Social Welfare Services: Concern, Change and Involvement." Paper presented at Community Leadership Seminar of Savannah, Inc., Savannah, January 9, 1969. Jane A. and Edwin J. Feiler Jr. Collection, Georgia Historical Society.

Burke, John D. "The City and Its Culture." Paper presented at Community Leadership Seminar of Savannah, Inc., Savannah, April 24, 1969. Jane A. and Edwin J. Feiler Jr. Collection, Georgia Historical Society.

"Citizens' Report." March 2008. City of Savannah, Research Library & Municipal Archives.

"CNT Drug Enforcement Plan." By Dan Flynn, Chief, SCMPD, February 3, 2004. City of Savannah, Research Library & Municipal Archives.

"A Communication from His Honor, The Mayor [Robert M. Hitch], submitting a report of his term of office." Proceedings of Council, January 18, 1939. *Minutes of City Council, April 29, 1936-May 24, 1939.* Clerk of Council Chambers,City Hall, City of Savannah.

"Crime Control Collaborative: Recommendations to Control Crime in the Community, July 1993." City of Savannah, Research Library & Municipal Archives.

Deutschberger, Paul. "Social Problems and Services in the Metropolis." Paper presented at Community Leadership Seminar of Savannah, Inc., Savannah, January 6, 1966. Jane A. and Edwin J. Feiler Jr. Collection, Georgia Historical Society.

———. "Social Welfare Services: Present Realities and Future Prospects." Paper presented at Community Leadership Seminar of Savannah, Inc., Savannah, January 6, 1966. Jane A. and Edwin J. Feiler Jr. Collection, Georgia Historical Society.

———. "Social Welfare Services: Toward the 'Good Life' in Savannah." Paper presented at Community Leadership Seminar of Savannah, Inc., Savannah, January 5, 1967. Jane A. and Edwin J. Feiler Jr. Collection, Georgia Historical Society.

Dobereiner, David A. "Planning: Why, How, How Much?" Paper presented at Community Leadership Seminar of Savannah, Inc., Savannah, January 11, 1962. Jane A. and Edwin J. Feiler Jr. Collection, Georgia Historical Society.

Drewry, Aubrey L., Jr. "Savannah's Economic Health." Paper presented at Community Leadership Seminar of Savannah, Inc., Savannah, December 12, 1963. Jane A. and Edwin J. Feiler Jr. Collection, Georgia Historical Society.

Federal Reserve Bank of Minneapolis, Consumer Price Index (estimate) 1800. https://www.minneapolisfed.org/community/teaching-aids/cpi-calculator-information/consumer-price-index-1800 (accessed January 21, 2017).

From Vision to Action: Savannah's Poverty Reduction Initiative. April 2005. City of Savannah, Research Library & Municipal Archives.

Gadsden, [?]. "The Negro's Political and Civic Life." Public lecture. Savannah, January 13, 1867. Georgia Historical Society.

Gadsden, Robert W. "The Education of the Negro." NAACP lecture, January 20, 1967, Savannah Public Library Auditorium. Bull Street Library, Kaye Kole Genealogy and Local History Room, Savannah.

Gamble, Thomas. "Changing Currents in Savannah's Commerce." Address, Atlantic Deeper Waterways Association Convention, Miami, November, 1941. Gamble Collection, Bull Street Library, Kaye Kole Genealogy and Local History Room, Savannah.

Gibson, Frank K. "The Growing Metropolis." Paper presented at Community Leadership Seminar of Savannah, Inc., Savannah, November 14, 1963. Jane A. and Edwin J. Feiler Jr. Collection, Georgia Historical Society.

———. "Savannah: An Overview." Paper presented at Community Leadership Seminar of Savannah, Inc., Savannah, November 14, 1963. Jane A. and Edwin J. Feiler Jr. Collection, Georgia Historical Society.

———. "Whither Savannah?" Paper presented at Community Leadership Seminar of Savannah, Inc. Savannah, May 22, 1969. Jane A. and Edward J. Feiler Jr. Collection, Georgia Historical Society.

Green, James L. "Economic Signs in Savannah." Paper presented at Community Leadership Seminar of Savannah, Inc., Savannah, n.d. Jane A. and Edwin J. Feiler Jr. Collection, Georgia Historical Society.

[Mayor Gamble]. *Message to City Council.* February 21, 1945.

Mayor's [Mayors] Annual Report. Savannah, 1867–1952.

"Minutes of Savannah City Council." 1865–1939.

"Minutes of Savannah City Council, August 23, 1865." Clerk of Council Chambers, City Hall, City of Savannah.

Municipal Report of Edward C. Anderson, Mayor, December 31, 1874. Savannah: Savannah Morning News Printing House, 1875.

Municipal Report, 6th Annual Report of the Honorable George W. Tiedeman, Mayor Together with the Reports of the City Officers of the city of Savannah, Georgia, for the year ending December 31, 1912. Savannah, n.d.

Operation: Clean Sweep, A Blight Eradication Plan" (Savannah, November 2004), City of Savannah, Research Library & Municipal Archives.

Ott, J. Roy, Jr. "Savannah's Economic Health: Good, Bad or Indifferent." Paper presented at Community Leadership Seminar of Savannah, Inc., Savannah, February 8, 1962. Jane A. and Edwin J. Feiler Jr. Collection, Georgia Historical Society.

———. "Savannah's Economic Health: Good, Bad or Indifferent." Paper presented at Community Leadership Seminar of Savannah, Inc., Savannah, December 11, 1962. Jane A. and Edwin J. Feiler Jr. Collection, Georgia Historical Society.

Pierpont, Wallace J. "Practical Effects of Prohibition in the City of Savannah, Ga." Address by Hon. Wallace J. Pierpont, Mayor of Savannah, at Celebration of Prohibition Victory, the Auditorium, Atlanta, March 19, 1917. Georgia Historical Society.

Pikl, James I. "Savannah's Economic Health: Good, Bad or Indifferent." Paper presented at Community Leadership Seminar of Savannah, Inc., Savannah, December 11, 1962. Jane A. and Edwin J. Feiler Jr. Collection, Georgia Historical Society.

"Proceedings of City Council." 1919–52. Savannah.

Report of Edward C. Anderson, Mayor of the City of Savannah for the Year Ending December 31, 1873 to which is added the Treasurer's Report, and Reports of the Different Departments. Savannah: Morning News Steam Printing House, 1874.

Report of John Screven, Mayor of the City of Savannah for the Year Ending September 30, 1871.

Report of Mayor Thomas Gamble to the Board of Aldermen, City of Savannah, Georgia, Departmental Operations and Financial Operations, 1935.

"Restoring the Land Use and Transportation Connection After the I-16 Ramp Removal." Presentation at Spring Conference, American Planning Association, Georgia Chapter, Peachtree City, May 12–13, 2011.

"Safe Streets–Safe Kids: Improved Community Safety through Aggressive Enforcement and Youth Control." Savannah, June 7, 2005. City of Savannah, Research Library & Municipal Archives.

"Savannah's Public Safety Task Force Final Report, May 15, 2005." City of Savannah, Research Library & Municipal Archives.

Silverman, [?]. "The Growing Metropolis." Paper presented at Community Leadership Seminar of Savannah, Inc., Savannah, n.d. Jane A. and Edwin J. Feiler Jr. Collection, Georgia Historical Society.

"Summary Report of the Issues Group Task Force of Mayor Susan Weiner, June 1, 1992." City of Savannah, Research Library & Municipal Archives.

"Violence Reduction Plan: A Cooperative Effort to Combat Violence in Savannah, Draft: Dated March 9, 2000." City of Savannah, Research Library & Municipal Archives.

Wood, Robert C. "The Metropolis: An Overview." Paper presented at Community Leadership Seminar of Savannah, Inc., Savannah, November 9, 1961. Jane A. and Edwin J. Feiler Jr. Collection, Georgia Historical Society.

Other Sources

Adderton, Donald, "Adams is steering Savannah to new era." *The Sun Herald,* [n.d.]. Vertical File, Bull Street Library, Kaye Kole Genealogy and Local History Room, Savannah, Georgia.

Annual Reports of the Superintendent of Public Schools for the City of Savannah and County of Chatham for the Years 1866–7 and 1867–8. Bull Street Library, Kay Kole Genealogy and Local History Room, Local History Room, Savannah.

Bret Bell, "In With the New." [*SMN*], [n.d.]. Vertical File, Bull Street Library, Kaye Kole Genealogy and Local History Room, Savannah, Georgia.

Bryan, E. F. *Savannah: A Brief Sketch of Savannah's Commerce, Industries and Advantages Lines of Rail & Water Transportation.* Savannah: Press of G. N. Nichols, 1884.

———. *Savannah: Georgia's Chief Seaport: First Seaport of the South Atlantic: First Atlantic Second American Cotton Port: First Navel Stores Port of the World.* Savannah: G. N. Nichols, 1884. Georgia Historical Society.

By-laws, Community Leadership Seminar of Savannah, Inc. Community Leadership Seminar of Savannah References and Speeches for First–Seventh Seminar, Jane A. and Edwin J. Feiler Jr. Collection, Georgia Historical Society.

[Confederate Veterans Association of Savannah]. *Addresses Delivered Before the Confederate Veterans Associations of Savannah To Which Is Added the President's Annual Report.* Savannah: George N. Nichols, 1898.

"Floyd Adams Jr., Mayor City of Savannah Biography." Vertical File, Bull Street Library, Kaye Kole Genealogy and Local History Room, Savannah, Georgia.

Fulford, Edward, "Farewell to the Chief." Vertical File, Bull Street Library, Kaye Kole Genealogy and Local History Room, Savannah, Georgia.

Hopkins, June. "Harry Hopkins and Work Relief During the Great Depression." 2011. http://socialwelfare.library.vcu.edu/eras/great-depression/harry-hopkins-and-work-relief-during-the-great-depression/ (accessed November 7, 2016).

Hubert, Benjamin Franklin. "Savannah Present and Future." [Sigo Myers Prize essay], 1929. Special Collections, University of Georgia.

Johnson, Charles J. "History of the Savannah Public Library." December 16, 2003. Seven-page paper in possession of the author.

Land, Jonathan E. *Savannah: Her Trade, Commerce and Industries.* Savannah: Jon. E. Land, 1884.

Le Hardy, J. C. *Yellow Fever: Its History, Causes, Nature, Pathology and Treatment: Considering Exclusively the Epidemic of 1876 in Savannah.* Atlanta: James P. Harrison and Co., 1878.

No. 1. General Rules Savannah, Florida and Western and Charleston and Savannah Railway Companies, with Extracts From The Railway Laws Of The States Of South Carolina, Georgia and Florida, In Effect July 1st, 1883. Charleston: Walker, Evans & Cogswell, Printers, 1883.

An Ordinance to Assess and Levy Taxes and Raise Revenue for the City of Savannah for 1870. Savannah: Morning News Steam-Power Press, 1870.

"Otis S. Johnson, PhD, Mayor City of Savannah Biography." Vertical File, Bull Street Library, Kaye Kole Genealogy and Local History Room, Savannah.

Otto, Albert S. "The Public School System of Savannah and Chatham County. Vols. 1 and 2. Bull Street Library, Kaye Kole Genealogy and Local History Room, Savannah.

Otto, Ely. *Yellow Fever Record: Year 1876.* Savannah: Ely Otto Publisher, 1876.

Parker, Evelyn. "The Doctors McKane." Paper for Historical Research Class, Dr. Roger Warlick, Professor, November 1, 1993, Armstrong State College. Georgia Historical Society.

Port of Savannah Waterfront Pass, 1918. Georgia Historical Society.

Rules, Regulations and Ordinances, For The Government Of The City Police of Savannah. Edw. C. Anderson, Mayor. Savannah, March 7, 1866. Savannah: Daily Advertiser, 1866.

"A Sidelight on Georgia: Prohibition in Savannah." [1914.] Leaflet, Special Collections, University of Virginia.

Spracher, Luciana M. "History & Highlights of the City of Savannah's Council-Manager Form of Government, 1954–2004." City of Savannah, Research Library & Municipal Archives.

The Thunderbolt, 1966, 1969 pamphlets. David M. Rubenstein Rare Book & Manuscript Library, Special Collections, Duke University.

"The Trouble with Al." Vertical File, Bull Street Library, Kaye Kole Genealogy and Local History Room, Savannah.

Waring, James J. *The Epidemic at Savannah, 1876: Its Causes, the Measures of Prevention Adopted by the Municipality During the Administration of J. S. Wheaton, Mayor.* Savannah: Morning News Steam Printing House, 1879.

———. *A Communication to the City Council on the Privy System of Savannah.* Savannah: Savannah Morning News, 1877.

What makes a mayor?" Vertical File, Bull Street Library, Kaye Kole Genealogy and Local History Room, Savannah, Georgia.

Yearly Health Records. Vol. 8, no. 12A. Bassett Papers, Georgia Historical Society.

Index